INSIDE
THE
MEDIA

INSIDE THE MEDIA

Conrad C. Fink

University of Georgia

Longman
New York & London

Inside the Media

Copyright © 1990 by Longman.
All rights reserved.
No part of this publication may be reproduced,
stored in a retrieval system, or transmitted
in any form or by any means, electronic, mechanical,
photocopying, recording, or otherwise,
without the prior permission of the publisher.

Longman, 95 Church Street, White Plains, N.Y. 10601

Associated companies:
Longman Group Ltd., London
Longman Cheshire Pty., Melbourne
Longman Paul Pty., Auckland
Copp Clark Pitman, Toronto

Executive editor: Gordon T. R. Anderson
Development editor: Elsa van Bergen, assisted by Jeffrey L. Campbell
Production editor: Halley Gatenby
Text design: Joe Gillians/Renée Kilbride-Edelman
Cover design: Kevin C. Kall
Production supervisor: Priscilla Taguer

LC: 90-5470

ISBN 0-8013-0257-9

ABCDEFGHIJ-DO-99 98 97 96 95 94 93 92 91 90

This book is for my parents, Mary Ruth and Donald Fink, Sr., and for my aunt, Olive Fox, a pathfinder who pointed my way to those distant horizons.

Contents

CHAPTER 7 INSIDE THE AMERICAN MAGAZINE

CHAPTER 7   INSIDE THE AMERICAN MAGAZINE   157

▶ Part III America's Electronic Communicators   189

Insider Views

▶ Personality Profiles

▶ Career Hints Written By . . .

▶ **Case Studies**

Preface

Think you might like a career as a reporter or an editor? Want to talk that over with a leading newspaper publisher or editor? Or would you like to get *inside* a magazine to see what careers that offers?

Fancy yourself on TV or radio, perhaps as a news anchor or disk jockey? Or do you see yourself behind the scenes, directing others, running things? Wouldn't it be helpful to see, *from the inside*, how that's done?

Perhaps persuasive communications—advertising and public relations—attract you. Would you like to talk with men and women who run some of the world's most famous advertising and PR agencies?

Well, this book can't make it possible for you to talk with those folks, of course. But it is written to do the next best thing—take you with them on a fact-filled, insider's tour of newspapers, magazines, TV stations, radio stations, ad and PR agencies, and other media that make up the powerful American free enterprise communications system.

Perhaps you have other things in mind—scholarly study of mass communications and critical assessment of the media. Maybe you simply want to learn how the media operate and why they have such an enormous impact on our daily lives. For you, this book places both communications theory and media operations in a global and societal context that I hope will provide a broad base of understanding and simultaneously open areas worthy of deeper study.

Whatever your career or study interests, I have written *Inside the Media* to help you wrestle with two compelling realities. First, the media are changing rapidly, evolving into new forms as new technology opens opportunities unimaginable just a few years ago. To ensure that the very latest information is available to you, I've obtained contributions from men and women inside the media, written specially for this book, on the media today and future shapes they might take.

Second, the important American mass media are part of a profit-oriented, free enterprise, highly competitive communications system. That forces them to respond to their marketplace (advertisers) and to media "consumers" (you, me, other readers, viewers, listeners). The media must also respond to society's broader expectations, as reflected in the law, regulatory practices, and so forth. Throughout, this book is designed in "reader-friendly" fashion to illustrate the reality that the media must operate with great sensitivity to their wider societal and marketplace environments.

Inside the Media generally is upbeat about the media. Even after nearly 25 years as a foreign correspondent and print and broadcast executive plus experience since 1982 as a teacher, I am excited and challenged in writing about the media. For you, my student readers, I see the media opening career opportunities that are immensely attractive—offering personal fulfillment and reward and also helping you contribute to a better, more just society. That doubles my excitement in taking you behind the scenes in the pages that follow.

This book is not a cheerleader's manual, however. Much is right about the media, much is also wrong. I attempt to highlight all dimensions, and I urge you to take a discerning and, when necessary, constructively critical view as you move ahead with me.

I hope that when you finish this book, you will possess a firm understanding of the mainline print, broadcast, advertising, and public relations industries and that your understanding will be suitably seated in the broader sweep of global communications and media history. From this I hope you can draw sound career guidance, perhaps deciding on a combination of coursework and hands-on media experience that you can start putting together now in preparation for a lifetime's work.

STRUCTURE OF THIS BOOK

For students of the media, one of the most significant trends today is the accelerating move toward bigness and global operations. Huge media conglomerates are getting larger, and they are expanding internationally to exploit the growing globalization of business. To put you on the tip of that developmental spear, I open this book with a three-chapter Part I titled "The Global Context." In Chapter 1, we'll look at the broad international picture as a backdrop for examining, in Chapter 2, the historical mainstreams of American media development. These two chapters will position us for a study, in Chapter 3, of America's media conglomerates today.

In Part II, "America's Print Communicators," I begin a format followed throughout the book: for each mainline medium or industry, a chapter giving overview, historical perspective, special concepts, terms, industry data, and the like precedes one giving you an insider's on-the-job view of a specific paper, station, or whatever. Thus Chapter 4 is a survey of the American newspaper industry, followed in Chapter 5 by an inside look at a community newspaper similar to one that might provide you with your first job: the *Columbus* (Ga.) *Ledger-Enquirer*. Similarly, Chapter 6 is a broad overview of the magazine industry, Chapter 7 an inside look at one organization in the important newsmagazine field, *U.S. News & World Report*.

Another of the newest trends, development of media forms that combine print and electronic technologies, is covered in Chapter 8.

America's broadcast communicators are examined in Part III. Chapter 9 surveys the industry, Chapter 10 takes you inside a local TV station, and Chapter 11 inside a local radio station.

American media must adapt to the diversity in our society, and we explore this in Part IV. Chapter 12 examines minority media and women in the media. For those of you interested in research careers, Chapter 13 discusses the vital research efforts under way in all forms of media.

In Part V, I turn to an examination of advertising. Chapter 14 describes the industry and many of the big players in it. In Chapter 15, we take an inside look at how one of the world's most famous agencies, N. W. Ayer, operates.

Public relations is the subject of Part VI, again in a two-part approach: Chapter 16 surveys the industry, and Chapter 17 goes inside a PR agency.

Film and music industries, essential to understanding mass communication, are covered in Part VII's Chapter 18.

Part VIII, "Getting There Yourself," is my effort to help those of you by now interested in media careers to pick potential employers and start your career climb. This part's single chapter, 19, spells out how to write a résumé, make job contacts, and handle yourself in an interview.

Like most books, this one has been planned for front-to-back reading. I've structured it to introduce you, early on, to principal strategic considerations that drive the media. Then, gently, I hope, I escalate the dialogue so that you should arrive in the final chapters with a sophisticated understanding of the media, their ownership and structure, their function, and their effect on society. However, each part and chapter is written as a stand-alone "window" on a specific sector of the industry and can be read out of sequence.

A final point on structure: I've used devices to highlight certain important information and provide lively background material on certain topics. These include historical highpoints and insider's lingo, career hints by practitioners in their own words, personality profiles, data selected and presented to give you insights into each of the media, case studies, photos especially chosen to bring you into the industry, and much else that I think might surprise, amuse, inform, or help. All these elements are integral to the overall thrust of the book. Look for a numbered sidebar whenever you see this symbol followed by a number in the text: ▶ .

ACKNOWLEDGMENTS

This book had its beginnings in the moments following my lectures to sessions of the Introduction to Mass Communication course at the Henry W. Grady College of Journalism and Mass Communication at the University of Georgia. Students would come forward in the huge auditorium to ask questions: How does a newspaper operate? Who runs a TV station, and how? What careers are available in public relations? Advertising? How about magazines?

Most of those students were freshmen or sophomores getting ready to declare a major and wondering if a sector of the mass media might offer careers they could prepare for while at the university.

From their questions came the idea for this book, and to those students go the thanks of this professor, who on some days learns more from students than he teaches them.

Special thanks, too, to Gordon T. R. Anderson, executive editor of the College and Professional Book Division of Longman, for seeing the book in all this. Elsa van Bergen, Longman developmental editing supervisor, was instrumental in the final shape of the book. No author could ask for stronger backup than Elsa provides.

At the Grady College, Ellen Bennett was most helpful, reading the entire draft manuscript and making sound suggestions based on her teaching of our Introduction to Mass Communication course. Segments were read by my Grady colleagues Al Hester, George Hough, and Tom Russell. My thanks to them for their suggestions, and to Tom for being a most supportive dean.

My gratitude goes to colleagues elsewhere in academia who reviewed portions of the manuscript and acted as sounding boards: Sandra Vander Gaag, County College of Morris; Vance Kepley, University of Wisconsin; Robert Finney, California State University, Long Beach; Jean Ward, University of Minnesota; James Hoyt, University of Wisconsin; and Robert Bohle, Virginia Commonwealth University.

A great many of my media colleagues contributed to this book, often taking time out from the "daily miracle"—getting the paper or magazine on the streets, the newscast on the air—to write especially for you, the student reader. These men and women are among major reasons why any student who seeks a career of excitement, involvement, and satisfaction should think seriously about the media. They are truly great professionals, and I tip my hat to them.

THE GLOBAL CONTEXT

I t happened while much of America slept, in the predawn hours. With incredible impact—for bad as well as good—a global communications network that had been generations in the building snapped together. The world would never be quite the same again.

It was October 19, 1987, "Black Monday" on financial markets in the United States and around the globe. By television, newspaper, telephone, newsletter, radio—but above all through computer-generated, high-speed transmissions via satellite—spread news and gossip, information and misinformation. Financial panic raged in the Far East, and as the trading day opened in America, word of that panic bombarded New York City markets with such speed that no human mind could possibly collate and analyze it. Well, computers were programmed to handle that, weren't they? Indeed, computers in New York "talked" to computers in Chicago, then onward to others on the West Coast and back around the world to more computers in the Far East. Automatically programmed sell orders flooded trading floors. That forced share prices down, in turn triggering other computers to sell.

A worldwide nightmare exploded as investor psychology shifted wildly toward fear and doubt. Eventually, even the elaborate, expensive electronic information systems fell far behind. The Dow Jones Industrial Average, a closely watched price indicator, fell 508 points, a record-breaking 22.6%. Shares lost $500 billion or more in value. Investors dropped fortunes, and financial institutions were shaken to their foundations.

It was an information-fed, computerized near meltdown of the trading system, and it demonstrated with stunning force the pivotal role communicators play in minute-by-minute life around the world today. It laid bare the web of interrelationships linking national economic, political, and social systems and the computerized electronic systems built to move news and information between them. It illustrated the difficulty people have in handling efficiently and reasonably the massive amounts of information generated by today's communications systems. It revealed that today's communicators have a responsibility far greater than simply getting the story and displaying it on front pages or on the evening news. Black Monday made clear that news and information must be placed in the correct context and adequately analyzed and explained, or true meaning is lost.

Indeed, it showed that new communications technology, with its speed and complexity, introduces not only benefits but great dangers, that it not only transmits news and information but also changes their meaning by moving them instantaneously. Robert Brusca, an American serving as chief economist in New York for Nikko Securities, a major Japanese brokerage house (note the internationalism there!), told *New York Times* reporter David E. Sanger: ''We are learning that when we compress the time in which things happen, they happen differently.''

Clearly, whether you are seeking media career information or simply preparing to be a media ''consumer,'' our discussion must go beyond the techniques of print and broadcast journalism, or advertising and public relations, and into the *impact* those techniques and their technologies have when tied into global communications systems. Black Monday demonstrated the need for a global backdrop for our study of American media and mass communications.

Although this book will peel back layers of media operations and influence until we reach small-town American newspapers and broadcast stations, let us first gain the requisite background by examining global mass communications, in Chapter 1, then the historical and theoretical development of the media in Chapter 2. In Chapter 3, we'll start our in-depth study, from the inside, of the American media.

The Shifting International Scene

I t's not mere happenstance that modern media systems and the information they provide have an enormous—and nearly simultaneous—impact in world political and financial centers. After all, if stocks and bonds are your business, you can breakfast in Hong Kong over the *Wall Street Journal* or in New York City over the *Financial Times* of London, and both will carry share prices from Zurich, commodities quotes from Singapore, and corporate news from boardrooms on all continents. If it's general news you seek, you can flick on the TV in your Copenhagen hotel room and catch Bernard Shaw of Cable News Network (CNN) anchoring the news in Washington, or in nearly any major city of the world, you can pick up *Time* or *Newsweek*. If it's entertainment you want, you can while away an evening in Omaha by watching the British Broadcasting Corporation (BBC) creation "Masterpiece Theater" or in Jakarta laugh away an hour or two with an old Laurel and Hardy movie distributed in Southeast Asia by an American company. If you have a product to sell or an image or idea to promote, you can contact almost any major advertising or public relations firm, wherever you are, and it will have foreign subsidiaries or contacts that will handle the job.

All that is possible because some very big players in global communications are shifting strategies to meet new needs in the changing world they serve. Once content to strive for journalistic influence and profit primarily in their own countries, these big players are now using new managerial concepts and technologies to establish truly global media empires. They are following—exploiting—the expanding and increasingly complex web of interrelationships between national economies and political systems.

The stakes, in profits and influence, are huge in this global race. The implications are enormous for consumers of information and for the societies in which they live.

THE NEW MEDIA STRATEGIES

To this day, in what used to be the British Empire in Asia and Africa, you see evidence that a superbly developed communications network was key to London's influence. Britain's BBC still targets areas with broadcasts, British cable and telephone companies serve them, and British newspapers and magazines circulate there—all reminders that in the heyday of imperialism, extension of political and economic influence depended in part on ability to collect, analyze, and distribute information quickly *and control its use.* It was the same with the Germans, French, Belgians, and other colonial powers, who also possessed sophisticated communications networks for their day.

Later, when the cold war divided East from West following World War II, governments extended their official information—and propaganda—systems with vigor. The United States and its allies bombarded the Soviet bloc with information and misinformation, designed to win hearts and minds; Moscow fired back with broadcast and pamphlet, film and book. Governments still abuse each other. But official voices are considerably muted, and the tone of the East-West struggle has softened.

Today, extension of influence throughout the world is taking new forms. First, under pressure of increasing globalization of business, industry, and finance, old geopolitical boundaries are blurring. Many formerly inward-looking national economies are expanding outward, blending into a global economy. For example, in Europe, 12 Common Market nations, representing 320 million persons, targeted the mid-1990s for elimination of commercial, financial, and customs barriers. Elsewhere, new economic relationships are developing. Soviet tractors are sold in the United States, American wheat in Moscow; Japanese autos and TV sets are everywhere. Investors trade all day on American stock exchanges, then at nightfall use telephone and computer terminals to move with the sun to Tokyo and other Far East trading centers, finally buying and selling the *very same stocks* on Eu-

It's more than just a job.

Caterpillar dealer servicemen in Southeast Asia are something special. They take pride in putting your machines back into production fast and right.

Those men who work on Caterpillar machines enjoy unusual satisfaction because they get training . . . custom tools . . . and parts back up to do the job the way they know it must be done.

Caterpillar gives dealers the best support worldwide because we, too, think the work you do with your machines is of utmost importance. You can depend on it.

Every day.

CATERPILLAR

Caterpillar Far East Ltd.
G.P.O. Box 3069
Hong Kong

American firms are expanding rapidly overseas—and American media and advertising agencies are going international, too, to help them sell goods and services. Here, Caterpillar Inc., of Peoria, Illinois, advertises for sales in Asia.

ropean exchanges before starting all over the next day in New York. Not all political, cultural, or language barriers are down, of course. Truly free international exchange of ideas and media services is far off. But those business deals, those stock exchanges are linked in 24-hour electronic communications webs that pierce many barriers and, via satellites, jump many national frontiers.

Second, media firms are expanding behind that internationalization of business. Indeed, they speed the process. The tractors, wheat, Japanese autos, and, certainly, the stocks—all are bought and sold in response to news and advertising of prices, market conditions, and other factors. Those transactions in turn create new

As part of its global strategy, Gannett Co. sells its *USA Today* in Rome. *Courtesy Gannett Co.*

All this concentrates in a relatively few global media conglomerates enormous wealth and power. By merging with other firms or taking them over, conglomerates create layers of international holdings that are widely diversified in many countries—in newspapers, magazines, television, films, book publishing, and more. Their annual revenue can be in the billions of dollars, their impact on public thinking and dialogue huge.

All this is done mostly for business, not ideological, purpose. Important global media firms are products of free, noncommunist, nontotalitarian societies. Profit, not proselytizing, is their motive. This yields corporate structure and mentality that revolve around certain procedural steps:

waves of news and advertising that ripple around the world, often independent of governments or ideological boundaries, stirring yet more transactions. In pursuing profit and influence that come from serving international business, global media firms target much of the world as their market. And that is the essential distinction between yesteryear and today: global, free enterprise media giants, once content with only limited international presence outside their own countries, now map truly worldwide strategies.

DOW JONES STRATEGY

> ❝ Our international strategy is based on the simple premise that business news and information needs are truly global. . . . The *Wall Street Journal* became a truly national newspaper after World War II by establishing printing sites across the country, linking Wall Street with Main Street. Dow Jones is going through the same type of transformation now—taking our business news and information to all the world's major business centers by wire service, database publishing, and in print publications. . . . What we report—business, financial, and economic news and information—knows no national boundaries.[1] ❞

> *Ray Shaw, then president of*
> *New York–based Dow Jones & Company, Inc.*

1 They *identify markets* they can serve profitably with news or media services—a city, five counties, a country, a continent. Or markets can be special constituencies within an area—say, certain types of newspaper readers or television viewers with common attributes that advertisers want to reach. Thus the *Wall Street Journal* serves up to advertisers well-to-do subscribers who buy computers, Cadillacs, and other expensive products; CNN reaches out for viewers who may not be so upscale financially but who number many millions and live in countries where advertisers do business.

2 They *identify and analyze media competitors* who might resist their entry into selected markets.

3 They *create a news product* or *offer a media service* that meets the needs of the selected market and is strong and unique enough to meet the challenge of competition. Thus, having studied foreign competition, the *Wall Street Journal*, the *New York Times*, and other American publications found market niches in Europe and Asia; *Miami Vice* is a top-rated TV program in Spain because local programming doesn't offer that type of entertainment.

4 They *sell the product or service* with promotional and marketing expertise. Launch promotion by Gannett Co. in each market where it distributes *USA Today* is as hard-hitting as sales promotion by any company for any product.

5 Through research and user feedback, they *adjust their product or service* on a continuing basis, responding to marketplace influences.

Throughout this book, you will encounter companies displaying those five characteristics as they move toward profit and influence.

Note that the global effort is aimed at delivering audiences—readers, viewers, listeners—attractive to advertisers. It is mostly advertising revenue that supports the newspaper, magazine, television, and radio empires we will study. That adds another characteristic for identifying big players in media globalization:

6 They follow *advertiser-driven strategies* in determining where to operate and what news or media services to offer. They must deliver to advertisers who pay the bills the type audiences the advertisers want.[2] (See Figure 1.1.) To attract important advertisers, global conglomerates estab-

lish efficient operations capable of taking a single advertising order in, say, New York or London, then arranging publication or broadcast of the ad around the world. The concept of one "buy"— a single negotiation for an advertising contract— is enormously attractive to advertisers, who must otherwise negotiate independently with scores of media worldwide to achieve the desired impact for their ad campaigns.

Most successful global conglomerates operate in English, the international language of business and, even in Asian capitals, a second language of millions.

THE BIG PLAYERS IN PRINT

Huge capital investments—and managerial genius of the first order—are required in the race for global media profits and presence. That inevitably limits the number of big players.

Small companies are gobbled up. A wave of acquisitions and mergers in the five years ended 1989 created seven global giants with more than $4 billion in annual revenue from publishing magazines, newspapers, and books, plus broadcasting, cable, music, and film or TV programming. One each had headquarters in West Germany, Australia, France, and Japan, and three were American.

Let us look quickly at some of the leading American companies involved in global expansion.

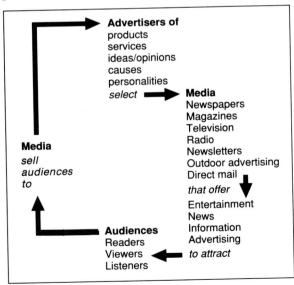

FIGURE 1.1. Primary Goal of a Media Conglomerate: Collecting an Audience Attractive to Advertisers.

Time Warner Time Inc. began 1989 with annual revenues over $3 billion, primarily from U.S. magazines and huge cable TV and video holdings. Later that year, through merger with Warner Communications, it became the world's largest media conglomerate with assets of $18 billion and annual revenues over $10 billion plus new subsidiary companies active in movies and TV, music publishing, and books. The flagship *Time* magazine has printing plants in the United States, Canada, the Netherlands, Singapore, and Hong Kong and sells nearly 1 million copies weekly outside the United States.

Gannett Co. A $3 billion corporation diversified in newspapers (90 in 1989), television, outdoor (billboard) advertising that now is using its enormous financial, journalistic, and managerial resources to push overseas with *USA Today*. The colorful paper is printed in Singapore, Hong Kong, and Switzerland.

Dun & Bradstreet Corp. This company concentrates on high-quality financial news services for private subscribers—credit-rating services for businesses, petroleum news, technical data of many kinds. Its market research includes Nielsen audience-measuring services for television in 30 countries. D&B's revenues exceed $3 billion annually.

Knight-Ridder, Inc. This $2 billion corporation for years drew 90 percent of its revenue from American newspapers and the rest mostly from U.S. TV and cable operations. Now, the company, which calculates that its products already reach nearly 100 million persons daily, is expanding worldwide with electronically delivered news services for bankers, brokers, and other private subscribers. Knight-Ridder has offices in 24 countries.

Washington Post Co. This diversified company has an overseas presence with *Newsweek* magazine and a one-third ownership (in partnership with New York Times Co. and Wil-

liam S. Paley, chairman of CBS, Inc.,) of the *International Herald Tribune*, a newspaper with headquarters in Paris and circulation worldwide. Of *Newsweek*'s 4 million circulation, large portions are in Europe, Latin America, Asia.

McGraw-Hill From New York, this company operates a global magazine, book, and information service empire. It publishes more than 60 magazines. Most are highly specialized—*Aviation Week & Space Technology*, *Chemical Engineering*, *Coal Age*, *Textile World*. *Business Week*, largest at nearly 1 million circulation, has substantial international sales.

Dow Jones & Co. After establishing a strong U.S. base with its *Wall Street Journal*

Three architects of the pioneering strategy that created a true global media conglomerate out of New York–based Dow Jones & Co.: (*left to right*) Ray Shaw, retired president, early innovator in international business news; Peter Kann, Pulitzer prizewinning foreign correspondent, now president; Warren Phillips, who joined the *Journal* as a copyeditor in 1947, then rose to become chairman and chief executive officer.

(nearly 2 million circulation and America's largest daily newspaper), Dow Jones acquired community newspapers (now 23) and expanded private subscriber news services for business people. In the mid-1960s, Dow Jones executives began pioneering expansion internationally. For decades, American news firms had covered the world, and news services—the Associated Press and United Press International—had distributed news overseas. But Dow Jones led in creation of truly diversified global media operations. Today, the *Journal* is printed in six countries and is expanding rapidly in Europe and Asia. Electronically delivered economic, business, and financial news speeds to more than 50 countries. Dow Jones is synonymous with authoritative, reliable news.

Reader's Digest Association   This $1.5 billion company operates in recorded music, book publishing, and direct mail advertising services. Its *Reader's Digest* launched an international edition in 1948, one of the first U.S. magazines to do so, and today reaches nearly 29 million subscribers, about 10 million overseas.

Other major U.S.-based players on the global scene include the Associated Press and, to a lesser degree, United Press International. We will discuss these later.

Some global media powers are non-American:

International Thomson Organization   From headquarters in Toronto, Canada, this $5 billion company operates newspapers and

---

1 ▶ Global Media Moguls

Rupert Murdoch   Robert Maxwell

Two of the biggest players in global communications began empire building outside the United States. But the rich U.S. market attracts their attention today.

The two are from vastly different backgrounds but are very alike in their unceasing efforts to expand their international news and entertainment holdings.

Rupert Murdoch is a native Australian who became a naturalized U.S. citizen to meet legal requirements that only U.S. citizens may control broadcast stations in this country. Murdoch inherited a small media company in Australia, became that country's wealthiest citizen, moved

to London and established one of Britain's most important media companies, then jumped the Atlantic to America. Because of his often sensationalistic journalistic style, he is one of the most controversial as well as most successful global media entrepreneurs. His companies have revenues in the billions of dollars and employ more than 25,000 persons. In 1988, he astounded the media world by paying $3 billion for Triangle Publications, Inc., owner of *TV Guide*, *Seventeen* and *Good Food* magazines, and the *Daily Racing Form*, the "horse player's bible." It was the largest price ever in a media deal.

Robert Maxwell was born Labji Hoch in 1923, son of an unemployed Czechoslovakian farm laborer. The Germans killed most of his family during World War II, but he escaped and joined the resistance forces. He later fought with the British army and was decorated for bravery, commissioned an officer—and renamed by a senior army officer. From those unlikely beginnings, Maxwell built an international empire around his British Printing and Communications Corporation PLC, worth in excess of $3.5 billion with annual revenues of over $1.6 billion.

Both Murdoch and Maxwell have uncanny instincts for what consumers of news and

magazines in many countries. Its Thomson Newspapers Ltd. owns 116 U.S. daily newspapers and 24 weeklies, more than any other company. Thomson is notorious among journalists for buying small papers without head-on competition from other papers, then squeezing them for all possible profit—to the detriment of news quality.

News Corp. Ltd.

Headquarters are in Sydney, Australia, but management is in New York City with principal owner Rupert Murdoch, a roving native Australian who became a U.S. citizen to facilitate expansion of his global empire in the richest media market of all, the United States. Murdoch has a voracious appetite for buying companies throughout the world. ▶ 1

Maxwell Communications Corp.

Chairman Robert Maxwell says the media future belongs to companies big enough—and smart enough—to integrate space-age communications technology with news and information into truly global strategies. His London-based companies own book publishers, newspapers, nearly 400 mostly specialized magazines and journals (including the *Journal of Insect Physiology*), and British cable systems. Maxwell established U.S. headquarters in Greenwich, Connecticut, hired American-trained executives, and invested more than $550 million in commercial printing firms and other companies throughout the country. In 1988, he paid $2.7 billion for the American book publisher Macmillan Inc. and said he would turn it into a global giant. ▶ 1

---

66 Does Murdoch . . . want to own the world? Well, maybe. **99**

James W. Michaels,
editor of Forbes magazine[4]

---

entertainment want. For Murdoch, that includes what will amuse and titillate the customers.
  Says Murdoch:

> As communicators we need, more than anything else, an audience. And as businessmen, we need customers—little matter if we call them viewers or readers. We must define and understand our markets and our job, know whom we want to reach and how to keep them turned on and tuned in.[5]

  On that philosophy, Murdoch operates serious newspapers such as the *Australian* and the *Times* of London, both national papers, and some that pander to base instincts with sensationalistic news and photos of bare bosoms. Murdoch is pushing into Asia and, with satellite-delivered TV entertainment, into Europe. But the U.S. market is the big one, and he has acquired American TV stations, Fox Broadcasting Co., 20th Century-Fox Film Corp., and others.

  Maxwell, intensely competitive and hardworking, once fired his own son for being late for an appointment (but later rehired him). He publishes relatively high-cost specialized publications and services that deliver information crucial to readers. He says:

> It's no use trying to compete with me because I publish the authoritative journal in each field. I'm dealing in high-penalty information. If you're building a chemical plant and you don't know about the latest development in that area, the mistake could cost you 10 million pounds [about $18.3 million]. So people will pay 1,000 pounds [$1,830].[6]

  In the United States, Maxwell owns Pergamon Press, publisher of books and journals, and firms dealing in computerized databases, software, and compact disks. His companies provide satellite communication services and print magazines, catalogs, and directories.
  In 1989, Murdoch and Maxwell, longtime rivals for preeminence in global communications, reached an accommodation. They signed a five-year, multimillion-dollar deal under which Murdoch's satellite TV entertainment will be delivered via Maxwell Cable Television, the largest cable TV system in Britain.

Because English is an increasingly international language and the United States is the most lucrative and stable market, most of the media world's big players are those with publications and information services based in Britain or the United States. In book publishing, however, a German firm, Bertelsmann A.G., is the world's largest. An American company, Simon & Schuster, an arm of the giant Gulf & Western conglomerate, is second largest. Third largest is Hachette S.A. of France, a $3 billion company founded in 1826 and strong in book publishing and magazines. *Elle*, a 1 million–circulation Hachette magazine, is published in many languages, including English. Although American publishers are not the world's largest, they exported $925.2 million worth of books to foreign countries in 1988.

Print is the oldest true mass communications medium. Widespread need for printed news and information first sparked media globalization. But television and an international desire for more and better entertainment are luring important new players into the global media game.

THE BIG PLAYERS IN TELEVISION

Many countries have developed strong domestic television industries since the 1950s, when TV first appeared as a commercially viable medium. But only two, the United States and Britain, export more television programming than they import. As in print, one reason is language. Programs in English have a wide foreign audience, particularly in Europe. But the primary force behind U.S. and British international TV companies is the economic strength they draw from their domestic operations.

British Broadcasting Corp., thanks to government financing, can export many highly regarded entertainment, news, and documentary shows, especially to the United States.

However, it is U.S. television that is having a dramatic and truly global impact in both TV news and entertainment programming because the enormously rich domestic market gives American business and programming experts the financial muscle to back up their strategic vision. In 1988 alone, advertisers poured more than $26 billion into U.S. network and local television (and $7.7 billion more into radio).

One of the earliest and today most important global TV players is Ted Turner, an Atlanta-based entrepreneur who, though sometimes perilously close to financial disaster, built his Turner Broadcasting System into a conglomerate with more than $500 million in annual sales. His company owns WTBS-TV Atlanta, Cable News Network, CNN Headline News, the MGM film library (and even the Atlanta Braves baseball and Atlanta Hawks basketball teams). ▶ 2

The CNN Broadcasting System and film library give Turner international strength. He delivers news and information globally through television; his old movies (including such greats as *Gone With the Wind*) play well in any language. In just three years, 1985–1988, after deciding to go global, Turner extended CNN into 58 countries. Note the distinction: CNN not only *covers* news of the world, as do all major networks, it *delivers* news via satellite and cable to countries where English is not the primary language.

Other major U.S. networks are pushing abroad, although more tentatively. As in global print strategy, the goal is to reach an audience with demographics—income, education, and other attributes—attractive to advertisers. Richard C. Wald, senior vice president for news of ABC, says that audience "is a broad cut of English-speaking population in the business and professional world outside the United States." He describes it as not large but "demographically desirable."[7] ABC's "World News Tonight," anchored by Peter Jennings, is telecast on Japan's government-supported NHK network. CBS programming, including "CBS Evening News" with Dan Rather, is aired in Japan, France, Switzerland, Monaco, and much of Italy. NBC and Public Broadcasting Service (PBS) are making similar moves overseas.

2 ▶ Ted Turner: Global Broadcaster Extraordinary

Ted Turner

Some people say he is egotistical, the showoff "Mouth of the South." The *Wall Street Journal* calls him "iconoclastic." But no one ever accuses him of being dull or lacking vision.

Indeed, Robert Edward (Ted) Turner III may be the pioneering visionary of global broadcasting in our time. From his Atlanta base (not New York? cynics asked), Turner, with dash and flamboyant showmanship, created in his Turner Broadcasting System one of the world's most important broadcasting and entertainment conglomerates.

Since 1979, Turner's Cable News Network (CNN) has done what ABC, NBC, and CBS either could not do or lacked the vision to do: It created a popular all-news format and is now expanding into places such as the Soviet Union and China never before reached by free enterprise global broadcasting. And CNN's brand of journalism has been applauded by critics.

What drives the energetic Turner is unclear even to close friends. But he has been aggressively expanding since age 24. His father left him a small billboard advertising company near financial disaster; he turned it around and in

1970 swapped $3 million of its stock for a failing TV station in Atlanta, Channel 17. "I was 30 and I was bored," he later told a *Venture* magazine reporter. The reporter noted that since the station was losing $600,000 annually, some people in Atlanta decided he also was crazy.

But the station was profitable within 18 months—and Turner then spotted the broadcasting potential in satellites. Channel 17, dubbed the "superstation," soon began bounding across America via burgeoning cable TV systems, into millions of homes. Turner's subsequent acquisitions included the Atlanta Braves baseball and Atlanta Hawks basketball teams (which provide programming for the superstation) and MGM/UA Entertainment Co. (for its treasure trove of films—more programming). He tried to buy CBS and looked longingly at NBC.

"Global communications, properly done, can be a force for good," he says. "That's my plan." He often speaks of his broadcasting opening understanding between the United States and other countries. It's expensive to be an international ambassador of TV goodwill. In 1988, Turner's costs hit $8 million annually to serve Europe alone, and his overseas ventures were money losers.

Turner is a multimillionaire (with several homes, farms, and plantations), even though at times his company is in difficult financial water. "I owe more money than anybody in the world," he once said.

Danger—and deep water—are nothing new to Turner. He is a world-class yachtsman who, among other things, survived a terrible storm in 1979 that drowned 15 sailors off Britain's coast. Turner also won the race.

ENTERTAINMENT'S GLOBAL IMPACT

By some estimates, more than $700 million in television programming is sold abroad by American firms each year. That's about 80 percent of worldwide television exports by all nations. The largest single purchaser of American shows is Silvio Berlusconi, who buys about 15 percent of all U.S. exports for his stations in Italy.[8] (American *film* exports hit $1.1 billion in 1988.)

Many American TV programs are top hits

internationally: ''The Cosby Show'' (Australia), ''Santa Barbara,'' a soap (France, South Africa), ''Starsky and Hutch'' (France), ''Dallas'' (Italy, Sweden, West Germany), ''St. Elsewhere'' (South Africa), ''ALF'' (Australia), ''Miami Vice'' (Spain), ''Falcon Crest'' (Sweden), and ''Dynasty'' (West Germany) are representative.[9]

Two developments spur sale of American programming abroad. First, many governments, particularly in Europe, are relinquishing control of television to private companies or, as in Britain, permitting privately owned stations to operate alongside government networks. This at least doubles the number of stations needing programming. The investment opportunities attract media moguls who spurn the educational programming favored by government TV and instead seek lively entertainment programming likely to attract large audiences, which in turn attract advertiser support. TV owners abroad are well aware that it can cost $500,000 or more to create an hour-long drama while one can be purchased from an American company for $50,000 or less.

Second, production costs in America are so high that studios cannot cover their expenses through fees charged American networks or stations for first-run use. For some expensive shows such as *Miami Vice*, losses on U.S. sales are as much as $200,000 to $500,000 *per episode*. Increasingly, production companies such as Lorimar Telepictures Corp., 20th Century-Fox Film Corp., and MCA Inc. must sell rerun rights outside the United States to make a profit (although comedy shows don't do well overseas; American humor is uniquely American, it seems).

DR. RUTH TAKES SEX INTERNATIONAL

66 FRANKFURT—Achtung, young lovers, wherever you are. Dr. Ruth is talking to you—in German, French or English, on television or radio, daytime, nighttime, anytime's the right time. So pull up a chair and pay attention as America's celebrated sex therapist offers advice on how to spice up your love life. 99

*International Herald Tribune,
published in Paris.*[10]

All this leads to international coproduction agreements. NBC produces travel shows in collaboration with television interests in Italy, France, and Australia. ESPN, a cable company owned principally by Capital Cities/ABC, agreed with Arab interests to produce 1,000 hours of sports programming annually in Arabic, French, and English. French and West German companies cooperate in distributing American programming. Sometimes American companies find it cheaper to produce programs abroad. Disney produces animated cartoons in Japan for about half the cost of U.S. production.

If newspapers, magazines, and TV companies expand globally in search of readers and viewers attractive to advertisers, can advertising agencies—and their first cousins, public relations agencies—be far behind?

THE BIG PLAYERS IN ADVERTISING

Globalization of advertising is explosive, and international public relations activity is increasing, too, as part of a new concept in marketing (the packaging, advertising, and selling of products) that holds the world to be potentially one huge market. It's a controversial concept, but the idea is to get as many people as possible around the world drinking Coca-Cola, driving Toyotas, eating Mars candy bars, and using other products once limited to consumers in their countries of manufacture.

Of the ten biggest spenders in advertising, ranked by ad spending outside the United States, seven in 1986 were non-American, led by Unilever of Rotterdam and London (with $598.6 million non-U.S. and $517.7 million U.S. spending; Procter & Gamble was second by a considerable margin). Interestingly, however, most top advertising agencies are American. ▶ 3

Several factors are behind the ad agency expansion overseas:

◆ The creation of privately owned television systems permits broadcasters to sell commercial time. Government-run TV systems normally bar

3 World's Largest Ad Agencies

Eight of the top ten worldwide advertising agencies are American; the others, Dentsu (ranked 2) and Hakuhodo (10), are Japanese. Agencies are ranked by "billings"—the amount spent through them by their customers. Each agency keeps a percentage of the total, usually 15 percent.

Agency	Billings
1. Omnicom Group	$6.2 billion
2. Dentsu	5.9
3. The Ogilvy Group	5.0
4. Young & Rubicam	4.9
5. Saatchi & Saatchi	4.2
6. BBD&O	3.6
7. McCann-Erickson	3.4
8. Backer Spielvogel Bates	3.2
9. J. Walter Thompson Co.	3.1
10. Hakuhodo	2.9

Standard Directory of Advertising Agencies, June-Sept. 1988.

The international reach of advertising is illustrated by this photo taken outside a store overlooking Tiananmen Square in Beijing, China, not long before the political turbulence of 1989. *Wide World Photos.*

commercials, subsidizing operations with taxpayer funds; privately owned systems carry advertising to survive.

◆ The technology that permits media globalization serves advertising, too. Advertising rides along on communications circuits and satellites with newspapers, magazines, and television programming. And even in some countries where governments control broadcast television, privately owned cable TV systems take programming and commercials via satellite.

◆ Language barriers are crumbling, permitting multinational ad campaigns in a single language, particularly English. Even where language and cultural differences are severe, multinational ads can be effective. A Coca-Cola jingle can sell Coke regardless of language barriers. (Pepsi-Cola, the first advertiser to buy TV time in the Soviet Union, used commercials featuring pop star Michael Jackson to appeal to Russian taste buds. Although, as we will see later in this chapter, some cultural barriers are impenetrable.) ▶ 4

The globalization of advertising includes the export of creative talent. For example, Joe Sedelmaier, one of America's top producers of TV commercials (Wendy's "Where's the beef?") uses his unique sense of what sells to create winning commercials in France, Britain, and other countries. Nancy S. Giges, international editor of *Advertising Age*, puts it this way:

Advertising is certainly not the same in all countries around the world; needs, desires and lifestyles certainly vary. But . . . the world is becoming much smaller and the marketplace is becoming much more global. Some large media groups dream of a day not too far in the future of a truly global TV network via satellite [when] a product as universal, say, as Coca-Cola could be adver-

A key to successful international advertising is the use of symbols that will sell a product in any language. The Coca-Cola bottle continues to beckon the thirsty in many lands; the photo was shot in Shanghai in the 1930s. *Courtesy of the Coca-Cola Company.*

American agency Ogilvy Group, a merger designed to create a mammoth international company with over $13.5 billion in annual billings.

Most international ad activity is centered in New York and London. American advertising techniques have proved extremely successful. Why is no mystery to Denys Henderson, chairman of Britain's largest manufacturing company, Imperial Chemical Industries PLC. ''The States,'' he says, ''is a big hype country,'' adding that his and other international companies must learn how to advertise and sell their products better.[12]

Some agencies operate in countries where consumer spending doesn't warrant major advertising efforts but growth potential is great. One is China, whose billion people are viewed as a huge market. China, however, is an example of how tricky it is for American agencies to operate in distant lands whose customs differ dramatically from those in the West. Language and cultural barriers are many, and the complexities of working with Chinese media are deep.

Japan is another country tough for American agencies to crack. Japan's business and governmental culture is structured to protect Japanese firms and exclude foreign companies. Also, the strong performance by Dentsu and Hakuhodo restricts opportunities for American agencies in Japan.

Public relations agencies lag behind ad agencies in expanding globally. Formally structured ad agencies have been active much longer than PR agencies, in general, and PR agencies have been busy developing business in their domestic markets. However, many large American ad agencies have PR subsidiaries operating overseas, and Burson-Marsteller, the world's largest PR agency, is American. A British PR practitioner, Peter Gummer, is creating in his Shandwick Group a network serving clients in the United States, Australia, Japan, Singapore, and Hong Kong, in addition to Britain. He built the company, now among the world's largest, by acquiring smaller firms. Gummer's U.S. acquisitions positioned him as a public relations firm

tised at the same time all around the world. In Europe, companies are becoming increasingly aware of the importance of standardizing their brands in order to make pan-European appeals. So while I'm sure nations want to retain a certain sense of tradition, there is growing commonality.[11]

Serving burgeoning advertiser needs creates mammoth ad agencies. Omnicom Group, with headquarters in New York, employs more than 10,000 persons worldwide. The second largest agency, Dentsu, employs more than 6,000 from its Tokyo headquarters. In 1989, Martin Sorrell, 42-year-old chairman of a British agency, WPP Group PLC, agreed to pay $864 million for the

▶4 Pan-European Humor

There is universal appeal in certain themes used in successful TV commercials. Humor, children, rugged men with beautiful horses, and, particularly, cute animals—all seem to sell products. That became clear in the First Annual European Creative Advertising Awards in 1987. Among work submitted by 192 agencies throughout Europe, winners included these: A canary eats the advertiser's birdseed and with newfound courage energetically stalks a cat (Spain); a huge hippopotamus lolls on a mattress, proving beyond doubt its durability (Britain); a man in a mouthwash commercial breathes on a dog,

and the dog faints (Sweden); dogs kick a man out of his car and drive off in a commercial on plight of abandoned pets (Italy).

A French ad agency, Jungle, attempts to rise above the advertising clamor by driving a truck around Paris carrying a mock guillotine with the slogan "Jungle, the agency that takes your head!" *Wide World Photos.*

---

with expertise in government information, entertainment, high technology, and autos.

Clearly, developments in international public relations, advertising, and the print and broadcast media underline fundamental changes of attitude by media consumers, who today look beyond national frontiers for news, information, and entertainment. For the global media, meeting consumers needs and fulfilling advertiser demands can be accomplished only through use of startling new technologies developed only recently.

THE NEW TECHNOLOGY

It's the stuff of science fiction. Print and broadcast media, the ad and PR agencies, are expanding internationally astride the marvels of communications satellites, powerful computers, high-speed transmission circuits, and the genius of a

worldwide scientific community that is concentrating as never before on improving modes of communication.

The new technology is virtually redefining mass communications by offering a variety of important characteristics.

Speed It's possible to communicate internationally with instantaneous transmission via computer-generated data circuits, not just voice circuits such as telephones. Particularly in private subscriber news services, whose broker and banker clients need instant data, the speed of the new information technology is transforming how business is conducted. The mass media are always under deadline pressure, and they, too, use speed to great advantage to reach millions throughout the world.

Volume The new technology transmits enormous volumes of information with speed. The

Associated Press transmits 9,000 words per minute to newspapers. An international newspaper, such as the *Wall Street Journal* or *USA Today*, can lay out its front page, then transmit a photo of it via satellite to distant presses—transmitting thousands of words plus graphs and illustrations in mere seconds. Dow Jones reported that by 1989, its computerized databases offered subscribers news and information at any given moment totaling more than 90 billion characters—"the equivalent of more than three times as much information as was contained in all the articles published in the *Wall Street Journal* since its founding in 1889." [13]

Analysis Computers permit mass communicators to analyze quickly and thus use more efficiently and intelligently masses of information pouring in quickly. Newspaper and broadcast editors, for example, program computers to scan thousands of stories flowing across news service wires and alert them when desired information arrives. Dow Jones programs computers to analyze millions of stock trades and business transactions, then advise broker clients when a stock price reaches a certain level or produce charts that display the trading trends.

Access As never before, information consumers have direct, instantaneous access to huge reservoirs of information. Think about it: You can sit before a relatively inexpensive terminal, enter a few commands, and access libraries of information that would have been beyond the wildest dreams of the most powerful kings and their counsellors in ancient times. And you can access other consumers directly, participating in an entirely new worldwide flow of information outside the traditional mass media. The electronic billboard—the computerized, person-to-person exchange of information via telephone hookup—is just one example of how information no longer has to go from a news source (say, a scientist) to print or TV editors for their relay to you. Even strangers on the other side of the world can exchange news directly through electronic means.

Flexibility The new technology is amazingly adaptive. For example, the computer's ability to store information can be married to its ability to manipulate and "massage" it, then spew it out in virtually any desired form—as electronic impulses for transmission to, say, a distant book-publishing firm or to a low-cost but high-quality printer in your own home. That second scenario—storing, manipulating, and printing information at low cost—is called *desktop publishing*. It permits private individuals with very little financial capital to produce inexpensive but high-quality books and publications even at home. The new technology raises the very real question of whether traditional mass communicators—say, book-publishing firms and magazines—will be reshaped in the future. And think of the nightmares it gives authorities in communist and totalitarian countries, who visualize unauthorized, underground publications and electronic billboards cropping up on kitchen tables everywhere! This already is happening in the Soviet Union. Lev M. Timofeyev, a Soviet dissident, told a *New York Times* reporter he produces an "alternative" newspaper in his Moscow apartment, employing a used Japanese-made computer and a small American desktop printer. Said Timofeyev, "Modern technology will spread and come into its own. The authorities already are losing control over the spread of information." [14] Recognition of that may be one reason Premier Mikhail Gorbachev began loosening Soviet control over free speech in the late 1980s.

Traditional media also gain enormous strength from the new technology's adaptability. For example, new editing devices and computerized presses open the possibility of newspapers producing not a single, broad-based edition of, say, 100,000 circulation but many separate editions of 10,000 circulation or so, each tailored in news content for the narrow needs of smaller audiences of readers, such as sports fans or arts and entertainment buffs.

Mobility and Portability You've seen them, perhaps outside a football stadium: a van the size of a furniture moving truck with a small

New technology at work: Japanese cameramen used lightweight, mobile cameras to cover arrivals at the Imperial Palace in Tokyo where Emperor Hirohito lay dying. Transmissions via satellites sped news, still photos, and video around the world. *Wide World Photos.*

Highly mobile vans, such as this one owned by WTKR-TV, Norfolk, Virginia, can be used to transmit the story from the dish on the roof to a satellite 22,300 miles high in orbit, then back to the home TV station. *Knight-Ridder photo.*

antenna on top, or a satellite dish on a rooftop. Well, that's a TV production and transmission unit that not many years ago could be housed only in a huge building. It can transmit signals from a shoulder-held camera on the sidelines to living rooms all over a state, country, continent—or throughout the world. More than 100 U.S. TV companies have such mobile vans out covering the news. Foreign correspondents will soon cover a war with a hand-carried camera, then send their story home via a backpack transmitter. Just as surely as laptop, computerized writing and editing devices pop out of briefcases on airplanes, so shall portable backpack transmission units take the electronic eye everywhere. Such mobility and equipment help mass communicators conquer the barriers of time and space.

Cost Efficiency New technology can be awesomely expensive. It can easily cost $50 mil-

lion to $100 million for a metropolitan newspaper to construct a new production facility; simply renting space on a General Electric communications satellite can cost $44,000 to $80,000 per month. But those investments can offset the even greater costs of doing things the old-fashioned way. For example, the per-unit cost of storing information in a computer and then transmitting it electronically via satellite is dropping rapidly. Meanwhile, the cost of printing information on paper—in a newspaper or magazine—and then transmitting it via car, truck, train, and plane is rising rapidly. Will it always make economic sense to put news on paper and let a 14-year-old on a bike distribute it? Or will future mass communicators and information consumers find it cheaper, easier, and cleaner to do it via satellite into a desktop video receiver in the home? Electronic delivery of specialized news to bankers, brokers, and other private subscribers is being welcomed as both cost-efficient and crucial to effective business management. However, consumers of general news such as sports and weather have not taken to the new technology. As tests by Knight-Ridder and Times Mirror Corp. show, general news consumers prefer standard television programming and newspapers (of which, in America alone, they buy 63 million copies daily, 48 million weekly).

Other technological innovations promise radical change.

Fiber Optics This already proven technology uses transmission circuits of hair-thin glass. Information encoded in electrical impulses is translated into impulses of light, is transmitted, and is then retranslated at the receiving end. A single circuit carries enormous quantities of information at extremely high speeds. For example, a fiber-optic cable that began service between the United States and Japan in 1989 is capable of carrying 40,000 telephone conversations simultaneously. Picture a single fiber-optic circuit into your home carrying telephone service, 100 or more cable TV channels, a burglar and fire alarm system, and home shopping and banking services. Telephone companies could eventually get into home delivery of news and advertising in a big way, a fear of many newspaper and magazine publishers that was heightened in 1989 when U.S. courts cleared the way for American Telephone and Telegraph Company to enter electronic publishing.

Superconductors Ceramics and other nontraditional materials have been found capable of transmitting electricity without the resistance that copper and other metals offer. This opens the possibility of data transmissions perhaps 100 times faster than possible via today's fiber-optic networks. It is estimated a single circuit could carry 15 million simultaneous telephone conversations or send the entire contents of the Library of Congress in two minutes. One huge problem, however, is that currently known superconducting materials must be cooled to several hundred degrees below zero or they don't work.

High-Definition TV (HDTV) HDTV involves transmitting more information into the picture tube, thus producing images perhaps five times sharper than those of today's TV sets. "It is like looking through a window," one technician says. "The clarity is exceptional." Japanese firms plan to produce sets, which initially would sell for several thousand dollars each. Converting to HDTV would cost hundreds of billions of dollars worldwide eventually. In 1988, however, the U.S. Federal Communications Commission (FCC) ruled that the so-called advanced TV transmissions must be compatible with conventional American TV sets so that all sets need not be replaced immediately.

Telecomputers Proponents say that this system could combine several technologies with fiber optics to create two-way ("interactive") communications networks and let viewers actually participate in programs and control what they see. Viewers could "interview" speakers or "fly" airplanes on large screens with life-size images. Some futurists say that U.S. investment in high-definition TV would be a waste and that the nation should leapfrog directly to telecomputers.

Parallel Processing This requires revolutionary designs to create computers 100 times or more faster than current computers. The technology involves splitting a problem into many pieces, which then are assigned to numerous parallel data processors (not just one, as currently) in a computer. Bits and pieces of each processor's solutions then are reassembled by the computer. The concept is highly controversial because billions of dollars are needed to develop it. However, IBM announced in 1987 that it would pursue parallel processing, and the concept is gaining acceptance.

Videocassettes Their technology is well developed, of course. The excitement is in new ways of using them. Americans spent an estimated $8.1 billion buying or renting home videos in 1988, for instruction as well as entertainment.

Famous athletes such as Jack Nicklaus sell videocassette instructions, as do chefs, master gardeners, hobbyists, fitness experts, career training specialists, and others. *Wide World Photos.*

Worldwide use is having a dramatic impact on movie theater attendance; fewer people go out to the movies now. Some advertisers use videocassettes to get into consumers' homes, bypassing traditional print or broadcast media. The German car manufacturer Porsche sells (for $24.95, at 1988 prices) 30-minute videocassette documentaries on its cars.

Compact Disk Read-Only Memory (CD-ROM)

This involves using laser optics to code information on 4.72-inch disks, which then are read on devices similar to compact disk players. CD-ROMs store huge amounts of information that is easily retrieved and read. Grolier Electronic Publishing, Inc., put the entire 20-volume Academic America Encyclopedia, with its more than 30,000 articles, on a *single* disk selling (in 1988) for $299.

Direct Broadcasting from Satellite to Home (DBS)

Television visionaries—especially Rupert Murdoch—are planning on broadcasting to large areas via a single "uplink" transmission to a satellite and then down simultaneously to millions of homes equipped with rooftop antennas. This would eliminate costly landlines now used by TV and cable companies to distribute channels and would cross national frontiers with news, entertainment, and advertising.

Other breakthroughs include linking distant computers in a network with access to electronic libraries, or "morgues"—information storage and retrieval systems for, say, investigative reports in search of stories. Knight-Ridder's VU/Text system links computers holding the full text of 32 newspapers and six news services from 1983 to present, 12 business databases, four magazines, and other resources. All-electronic cameras that use a 2-inch-diameter reusable magnetic disk instead of film will revolutionize still photography. Electronic darkrooms, pioneered by the Associated Press, permit computerized developing and editing of photos. And devices already in general use, such as cellular phones and fax machines, of course do much to facilitate mass communication.

Clearly, consumers worldwide are creating unprecedented demand for more and better information and entertainment programming delivered more quickly at lower cost, and global media conglomerates are rushing to serve them. So barriers to the free flow of information must be tumbling, right? Not really.

BARRIERS TO GLOBAL COMMUNICATION

It's true: Coke advertising *is* almost everywhere. American TV, the *Wall Street Journal*, and *Time* magazine are available in many major cities. But the world is still a very diverse place, and in that diversity lie many barriers to the free flow of international communication and the true globalization of modern media. We shall discuss six aspects of that issue: cultural barriers, economic disparity and instability, economic turmoil, developmental incompatibilities, war and civil unrest, and governmental control and censorship.

Cultural Barriers   Many media strategists believe that newspapers, magazines, TV, and radio create a sense of community, a commonality of news needs and advertising interests. Newspapers and TV, for example, stake out a city, cover its news to attract readers, and then declare to advertisers that a market exists. That strategy works only if the newspaper or TV station appeals to a community that is, in a cultural sense, essentially homogeneous. Its residents must speak the same language, come from similar backgrounds, live just about the same lifestyles, and thus find the same news and entertainment acceptable.

Will that strategy work internationally, across widespread areas that are culturally diverse? Will Rupert Murdoch, successful with national strategies in the United States, Britain, and Australia, succeed in quite the same way across, say, Asia or Europe?

No, according to Cathleen Black, publisher of *USA Today*, which is opening its own global strategy.

There's been a shift in thinking about global media among media people themselves. For a long time, the prevailing belief was that the media could create a global community. The idea was that whoever received the news shared something with everyone else who received it, and in that way, a community was formed.

That has not turned out to be true. Millions of people see the same pictures and read the same articles, but they still have nothing in common.

Media decision makers are now defining the community first, then working to make the media more relevant to the people [they] serve . . . , both news consumers . . . and advertisers.[15]

Note Black's distinction: Forcing worldwide acceptance of the same media product—a newspaper or TV programming—will not work; rather, media conglomerates must study local needs, then finely tune different news and information products for those different needs.

ADDRESSING CHINESE IN ENGLISH

66   Bilingual ads on the sides of buses and elsewhere indicate that English is the unofficial second language of the new China.   99

Paul Theroux, reporting from Shanghai for the **New York Times.**[16]

CORN FLAKES BOMB IN BRAZIL

66   Corn flakes have been a tough sell in Brazil. When Kellogg Co. first entered the market in 1962, cereal was for Brazilians a dry snack, like potato chips are to Americans. Many Brazilians did not eat breakfast at all. . . .

Global marketing proponents say modern communications and travel have so shrunk the globe, consumer wants have been homogenized and cultural differences rendered insignificant.

Obviously, the theory doesn't hold with corn flakes in Brazil. Nor has it worked in a seemingly growing number of other instances. . . .

These cases suggest that the much-heralded age of global marketing is not yet at hand.   99

Advertising Age *reporters Julie Skur Hill and Joseph M. Winski.*[17]

WATCH YOUR TONGUE!

66   Imagine General Motors' dismay when they found out that their Nova model, when translated into Spanish, meant "it doesn't go," or when "body by Fisher" became "corpse by Fisher" in Japan. (Or when Kentucky Fried Chicken described its legs-and-breasts container with a word used only to define a pail for slopping hogs.)   99

Lee B. Hall, senior vice president/ international, Playboy Enterprises.[18]

Some countries, eager to protect national cultural diversity, resist media globalization. Canada, for example, fears a sort of cultural imperialism if its newspapers, TV, and other media are swamped by huge, vigorous U.S. media. Canada's minister of communications, Marcel Masse, told the *Wall Street Journal* in 1989 that Canada "is dominated by U.S. cultural products" and that his job is to protect Canada from that. Canadian law prohibits foreign (read "American") control of Canadian media (foreigners are limited to 25 percent ownership of Canadian publications and 20 percent of broadcast stations—ironic in that two Canadian companies alone, Thomson Newspapers Ltd. and Hollinger, Inc., own well over 200 U.S. newspapers). Canadian tax law makes it nearly impossible for American media to solicit advertising aimed exclusively at Canadian readers. *Playboy* had to discard advertising supplements before the magazine could be shipped into Canada. The number of American feature films that can be shown in Canada is limited to guarantee a market for Canadian-produced films (still, U.S. studios produce about 80 percent of the films shown to Canadian audiences).

A French law prohibits investors from outside the European Community from owning more than 20 percent of a French publication. U.S. law prohibits ownership control of radio or TV stations by noncitizens, a prohibition considered outmoded by some, particularly because there are about 1,000 commercial TV stations in the United States, more than 9,400 commercial radio stations, 11,000 magazines, 1,600 daily and 7,600 weekly newspapers—a media diversity that prevents any single owner, American or foreign, from controlling the flow of news and information.[19]

The European Community parliament voted in 1989 to limit American TV programming shown in Europe. The goal is to ensure that European programming comprises at least 50.1 percent of all programming aired in the EC by 1993 and to limit advertising to 15 percent of airtime. Britain's Robert Maxwell, whose U.S. operations are hugely profitable, said of the decision, "If my American friends don't like this, then they had better lump it."[20]

Cultural barriers are thrown up not only to protect infant domestic media industries but also to keep out films, TV programming, and publications deemed offensive or immoral. Richard Reeves, an American columnist, covered a London conference in which Prime Minister Margaret Thatcher and her ministers discussed the future of TV in Britain. He quoted one TV executive as saying, "The government wants as much [media] competition as possible against a background of maintaining standards." Commented Reeves, "Translated into American, that means: 'We accept the inevitability of uncontrolled satellite and cable broadcasting but we will do whatever we can to stop the game shows, the fictional history of docudramas, the toy advertising, the violence, the pornography that are allowed in the United States.'"[21] In the Economic Community, cross-border television encounters strong laws in individual nations against advertising aimed at children, alcohol and tobacco ads, and material considered indecent.

LEGAL PICKET FENCES

66 The big barrier [to cross-border satellite television] isn't money; it isn't programming, and it isn't technology. . . . The big question mark is really one of law and policy. . . . [They] stand like a picket fence from one nation to another and inhibit the free flow of information.

If we want to see something accomplished in our time, advertisers all over the world and those companies looking to develop media must have an alliance for world communications.

Mega-marketers are going to have to employ the tools of power, public relations and politics to fight these barriers. 99

John M. Eger, New York attorney and adviser to U.S. presidents.[22]

Economic Disparity and Instability

Economic factors greatly influence media strategies and capabilities and thus worldwide flow of news and TV entertainment. Like any other company, a media firm seeking expansion internationally must carefully choose a market—again, a city, country, or continent—offering economic rewards. Whether the firm's principal ownership is an individual—a Murdoch, a Maxwell—or a group of shareholders, the first requirement is to return a profit. But it's not just a little profit that's sought by major players in media globalization. Free enterprise companies are driven by "the rising tide of shareholder expectation."[23] It's an inexorable demand by investors, whatever the company, for more profits.

The bottom line, inevitably, is heavy media investment in countries or cities with wealthy, stable economies and avoidance of huge areas of the world offering slim chances for economic reward. Vital centers of international business such as Tokyo, Hong Kong, London, Zurich, and New York attract enormous media investment. Every international news company needs strong news coverage in those cities; all want to sell to them. Conversely, wide areas of less developed and less wealthy Africa, Asia, and Latin America often draw only passing interest from itinerant foreign correspondents looking for a story.

For any news organization, covering the world is enormously expensive. The *Los Angeles Times* calculates that $250,000 to $300,000 is the cost of maintaining a single correspondent overseas for one year. The paper had 25 correspondents abroad in 1988; the *New York Times*, 40; the *Washington Post*, 22. At those rates, the *Los Angeles Times* is spending annually between $6.3 million and $7.5 million to maintain correspondents overseas. For the *New York Times*, the bill runs between $10 million and $12 million. Not even the largest news-gathering organizations station American correspondents in every nation. Rather, they shift correspondents around as news breaks. For example, deepening economic and political deterioration in Mexico led American news organizations to increase the number of correspondents based in Mexico City to 92 in 1987 from 26 in 1975. If the Mexico story quiets down, some will be shifted to other hotspots.

Economic Turmoil Unrest jeopardizes media investment in some countries that otherwise might draw attention from global conglomerates. Business expansion in, say, Argentina is

Two correspondents in London's financial district, one of the world's trading centers heavily covered by global media.

thrown into sad disarray by price inflation of 500 percent or more annually. Fluctuations in currency rates can suddenly increase the costs of an American company doing business overseas. (Volatile rates led *Advertising Age* magazine to comment, "Advertising in Latin America requires courage, flexibility and a spirit of adventure.")[24] Conversely, currency fluctuations can aid global media expansion. For example, the U.S. dollar weakened against some foreign currencies in early 1988—and that made it cheaper for the French company Hachette S.A. to buy American book and magazine publishing companies: Hachette needed fewer francs to buy the dollars needed to buy the companies.

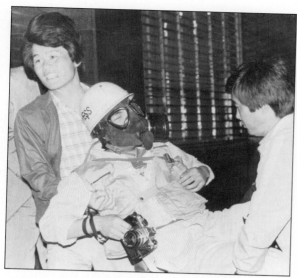

Reporters are frequently killed or injured in pursuit of news. This photographer was injured by a firebomb during a student riot in Seoul, South Korea. *Wide World Photos.*

Roving correspondent Sam Dillon of the *Miami Herald*, an expert on Latin America, interviewing a Nicaraguan in Managua. *Knight-Ridder photo.*

Developmental Incompatibilities

Gaps in technology, education, and personal wealth give media companies further reason to be extremely selective in where they do business. What appeal does a computer-generated economic news service, spewing out millions of stock market statistics, have in poor villages of Africa or Asia? Where in those villages is there money to buy *USA Today* or *Time* magazine? Where, indeed, is the educational development, the language capability, needed to use those periodicals or American TV? For those villagers, the satellites, the computers, the high-speed transmission circuits could be on the moon.

If we combine these economic and developmental disparities with the fact that most major international media conglomerates originate in the West—primarily the United States and Britain—we can see the danger of a worldwide information flow that is generated, transmitted, and sold with a decided Western tilt. That is the heart of one of the most crucial issues in international communications today.

A ''new world information order'' is often demanded by Third World countries in the United Nations Educational, Scientific and Cultural Organization (UNESCO). There is no consensus on what exactly this should be, except that it should end Western domination of the primary international news flow generated by AP, UPI, Reuters, and other Western news services, plus the major international newspaper and broadcast operations. Many studies have been done in both the West and Third World on the content and tone of this news flow. Depending on which you read, the Third World is or isn't adequately covered, and it is or isn't covered with prejudice by Western reporters serving primarily their more lucrative clients in the West. The Soviet Union and Eastern Bloc allies in the United Nations seized this issue for a vigorous international campaign aimed at restricting, not opening, global information channels and at licensing journalists. For decades, the issue was fought in UNESCO. The Soviets gained little ground, large Western companies still dominate the free enterprise global media scene, and many Third World countries are still unhappy with how they are covered and portrayed.

War and Civil Unrest

Political turmoil throws up serious barriers to the free flow of information. Freedom House, a New York–based study group, counts 25 journalists killed worldwide in both 1987 and 1988 while trying to cover the news (it was 18 in 1986, 31 in 1985); 14 disappeared or were kidnapped in 1988, and 225 were arrested. Harassment of journalists is almost fashionable with some police and military forces. In 1986, the American Newspaper Publishers Association counted 227 U.S. journalists who died covering wars or other conflicts since World War I.

For foreign correspondents, terrorism and "low-intensity" guerrilla conflicts present dangers that surpass those of covering major wars. Around the next corner, in a seemingly peaceful village, ambush may await; along the next path, land mines may be planted.

Governmental Control and Censorship
Government interference is the most dramatic barrier to global communications. It can take obvious or subtle, almost imperceptible form.[25]

At worst—in communist or authoritarian countries—government owns all media and, to the extent possible, controls news flow into and out of the country. Indeed, media are considered a vital *tool* of government, to be employed along with the police, military, and other official forces to support the regime's policy. In many communist and authoritarian countries, foreign media are considered dangerous because they transmit news that could cause unrest, even destabilize a regime. Thus foreign media are restricted, manipulated when that will work, lied to, and subverted if the opportunity arises.

Over the long run, that can be self-defeating. It creates a closed society without the exchange of information or freedom of thought necessary for technological and economic progress. Besides, no society can be completely closed. Underground media crop up, private information systems and rumor networks mushroom, and foreign governments reach across ostensibly closed borders with shortwave broadcasts or clandestine news. It may be that in the new information age, no government can either afford or accomplish complete censorship or control of news.

Consider this: If economic progress requires, as it does, millions of computers throughout the country, linked by high-speed transmission lines, can the Kremlin unleash "thought control" police as in days gone by? Whatever the motivation for *glasnost* ("openness") or however deeply it will penetrate Soviet society, Moscow in 1988 began permitting unprecedented access to the media, both Soviet and foreign. For correspondents who reported from the "old" Soviet Union, the most amazing sight was American TV anchors broadcasting, free of censorship, directly from Red Square.

In 1989, new mass communications systems established by China's Communist regime as part of economic reforms served to spread word throughout the world of political turbulence sweeping that nation. Indeed, from the regime's viewpoint, the media became part of the political problem. News of student unrest in Beijing was transmitted live via satellite by CNN and CBS to the United States, then back into even remote areas of China by the Voice of America and the BBC. Thus alerted, students from throughout China flocked to the capital to join the demonstrations.

Still, any government can restrict much of what its citizens read, hear, and view. Chinese authorities shut down live transmissions by foreign correspondents. In some countries, journalists are arrested, even assassinated; privately owned newspapers are shut down or denied newsprint supplies; advertisers are forced to withhold support from offending media.

Any country can strongly influence what the rest of the world thinks about it. Foreign journalists can be denied entry; those admitted can be restricted as to travel and whom they see. Restricting access to news is "censorship at the source." Correspondents who probe too deeply are often expelled from authoritarian or communist countries.

Of course, every government has military, political, and economic secrets. In Britain, a nation of democratic openness envied by much of the world, the government not infrequently wields the Official Secrets Act to suppress publication of stories deemed dangerous to national security. In the United States, the screen of national security is used, arguably overused at times, to restrict information. Even in democratic countries, real or imagined threats to national security lead to clampdowns dangerous in themselves to democracy.

PLAY BALL—OR ELSE!

66 The reason [intimidation of the press] works great in some places is because in some places they can kill you, or torture you, or jail you, or throw you out if you don't play ball. 99

Dana R. Bullen, executive director,
World Press Freedom Committee.[26]

So government intimidation, censorship, and self-censorship generated by pressure in some nations are additional complexities in an already complex global media picture. What does all this mean for the next generation of media communicators?

ISSUES AND CHALLENGES OF THE INFORMATION AGE

Peering too far ahead in a rapidly changing world is risky. But already we can identify major issues and challenges likely to confront global mass media communicators in the 21st century.

Worsening Imbalance in the International News Flow
Information represents power, and as in international economics and politics, there are "have" nations in communications media and "have-nots."

The existing imbalance between the West and the poorer Third World is likely to worsen, for sophisticated research and hugely expensive technology are needed to create new information systems. Perhaps, however, the new technology—national policies permitting—will help close the gap. One possibility is the sharing of communications resources. The United States

and other Western nations, for example, help Third World nations rocket communications satellites into orbit. Even the Soviet Union offers (for the very capitalistic price of $24 million to $30 million) to launch satellites for other countries.

But the international news flow—and the power it represents—will remain essentially in Western hands. The alternative, distasteful to any believer in a free press, is what the Soviet Union has pursued for years: a "new information order" of government-controlled information systems, a thinly disguised move toward government licensing and thus control of journalists to ensure that only "official" news is published.

YES, TECHNOLOGY CHANGES THE MEDIA . . .

66 But whether these changes enrich or impoverish, provide more access to information or limit our choices is not clear. One school of thought posits that technological change brings new options and opportunities for those who can benefit from its richness and its reach. Another view emphatically argues that it will bring a new form of social and economic deprivation, wherein less-advantaged segments of society—if not of the world—will be dispossessed, cut off even more from the mainstream of growth and change. 99

Everett E. Dennis, executive director,
Gannett Center for Media Studies,
New York City.[27]

Growth of Privately Controlled Global Media Giants
Is big in global communications automatically bad? Is it wrong for a media conglomerate to pursue profit? Well, the alternative to free enterprise media is government-supported (and thus controlled) media. And not many major government-controlled media perform with objectivity and dedication to facts on an international scale. Some of the best, most probing news work is done by the *New York Times*, the *Washington Post*, CBS, ABC, NBC, the *Times* of London, and other free enterprise, profit-oriented companies around the world.

Yet there is great unease—and not just in Third World nations—over powerful billion-dollar companies extending their ownership and control into every media nook and cranny around the world. It's an unease born of seeing International Thomson of Toronto sweep up hundreds of newspapers around the world and similar conglomerates moving with equal force into global television, magazines, book publishing, and other forms of communication. It's unsettling for many to see international business information flow, in the main, through four companies—Dow Jones, Knight-Ridder, and the Associated Press of the United States, plus London-based Reuters.

On balance—although this argument doesn't play well in the Third World—the best bet for the future lies with free enterprise media. To flourish, they must survive in a competitive marketplace, responding alertly to reader, viewer, and listener. And if there is better insurance against misuse of media power, I don't know what it is.

Rising Elitism in the Media

Because of their advertiser-driven marketing strategies, free enterprise media focus on audiences most attractive to advertisers. Particularly among newspapers and magazines, that means information consumers "upscale" in education and income—in the United States, for example, people with college educations and $50,000 or more in annual income. By definition, many newspapers are "elitist," constructed of news and information attractive to such upscale readers. They are less attractive—if at all—to persons of less education and income. The *Los Angeles Times* reaches fewer than 25 percent of households in Los Angeles County, but the readers it does reach are upscale and very attractive to advertisers. National editions of the *New York Times*, the *Wall Street Journal*, and the *Times* of London are edited to reach just the uppermost fringe of readers, in demographic terms. Across the media world, mass-circulation magazines are nearly a thing of the past. Magazine publishing strategy today revolves around finding and addressing a narrow market niche highly attractive to advertisers. Thus we in the United States have many small magazines for aviation buffs, car owners, skiers, and so forth. Even in broadcasting, normally considered a mass medium, there are efforts to "narrowcast" with, say, a certain type of music ("golden oldies" for older audiences) and reach small segments of the market desired by advertisers.

All this raises a question of whether free enterprise media in the 21st century, preoccupied with profit-oriented marketing strategies, will put aside any sense of societal obligation to serve as vehicles of education and uplift for the less fortunate. Will there be serious, high-quality U.S. newspapers for persons earning less than $20,000 annually? Will global media conglomerates select as markets only countries and population segments that promise profit?

Meshing the Volume of Information with Consumer Processing

In the 21st century, millions now herded behind censorship barriers will inevitably see the world via satellite-delivered TV and international computer hook-ups. Cheap transistor radios and shortwave broadcasts—possibly even satellite TV—will break the poverty barrier and reach many poor, isolated villages in Asia and Africa. The media will reach societies starved for the news and information that can lead to economic progress and a better life. But in many nations, particularly in the wealthier West, the media already inundate readers, viewers, and listeners. A sort of Gresham's law of communications is at work—a flood of often frivolous news and information, advertising and entertainment threatens to drive out information that is truly essential to meaningful life and to submerge high-quality entertainment that can make life more uplifting. In the United States, the media clamor is rising through 1,600 daily newspapers, 7,600 weeklies, 11,000 magazines, thousands of TV and radio stations, numerous billboards, and countless matchbook covers. It never stops. The enormous volume of information and the speed of its delivery place on readers and viewers a burden for which few have the time, inclination, or professional training to sift and sort through the torrent in search of what they find important and meaningful. For communicators, the challenge is not simply to publish bulkier newspapers or more magazines or to feed 150 cable TV channels into homes instead of 30. For advertisers, the challenge is not simply to turn up the volume with more and louder commercials. For all communicators, the challenge is to gauge the needs of information consumers more precisely, then deliver the information needed in understandable, manageable form.

Integrating the New Communications Technology
Communications technology is leaping ahead. At times, it outstrips the needs of information consumers and their abilities to handle it properly. Videotex proved extremely effective for Knight-Ridder and Times Mirror Corp., which launched separate home delivery services in the early 1980s. But householders didn't need access to all that information (nor did they want to pay $30 to $50 monthly fees for it). Both companies shut down their operations (Knight-Ridder at a $50 million loss).

In 1988, IBM, the world's largest computer manufacturer, and Sears, America's largest retailer, launched Trintex—now called Prodigy—which not only delivers news but also enables users to shop and order goods from home via personal computers hooked into telephone lines. By 1989, IBM and Sears had spent more than $500 million developing the service, and if anybody can make the concept work, those two companies can. But we now know that more and faster information is not perceived by consumers as necessarily better. IBM, Sears, and others who try must ensure that new home delivery technology is matched more carefully with consumer needs and consumer perceptions of those needs.

Sometimes, new technology creates a generational gap and takes longer to get established in general use than its inventors imagine. The U.S. Census Bureau found in 1984, for example, that just 53.5 percent of adults in computer-equipped households reported using them; nearly three-quarters of children in those homes were using the computers. Obviously, when this generation of child users reaches maturity, the personal computer will be a household tool. But it's clear that unless computers become less expensive, any new information system based primarily on them will be elitist in an economic sense. The Census Bureau found computers in 22.9 percent of homes with $50,000 or more in annual income but in just 1.7 percent of households with less than $10,000 income.[28]

Obviously, mass media communicators cannot plunge forward with unthinking exploitation of the new technology or new managerial and marketing concepts available to them. Keen attention must be paid to the historical context of mass communications and the societal and philosophical ramifications of the media in the 21st century. To those considerations we turn in Chapter 2.

☆ SUMMARY

Following—and exploiting—an increasing globalization of business, private-enterprise media firms are expanding with truly international strategies. Firms once content with publishing or broadcasting in smaller markets now see much of the world as offering profit and influence.

For these global conglomerates, most of them originating in the United States, Britain, and other prosperous Western nations, the goal is profit, not proselytizing, so they concentrate on prosperous countries and wealthy trading centers. Sometimes less developed cities and nations are neither well covered by correspondents seeking news nor well served by media companies selling media services.

Perhaps as few as 10 companies will dominate global news and information. Today, two countries—the United States and Britain—export more television programming than they import. The big players in global advertising and public relations are mostly American, although Japanese and British firms are expanding rapidly.

New technology permits transmission of enormous volumes of information at high speed. Powerful computers give individuals unprecedented access to information and permit its quick analysis. And the cost of electronic transmission of information is dropping, while cost of more traditional forms of communication, such as newspapers and magazines, is rising rapidly.

Many barriers to the free flow of information exist: cultural and language differences, economic instability, war and civil unrest, and government restrictions such as censorship.

Issues facing mass media communicators include imbalance in the international news flow. Some Third World nations complain that local news—and national image—is reflected primarily through Western news organizations. There is unease, not restricted to the Third World, over the power of huge free enterprise media conglomerates that buy newspapers, magazines, broadcast stations, and other forms of communications in many countries.

A severe problem is the rising elitism of mass media that cater to well-educated, high-income audiences desired by advertisers. Who will publish newspapers or magazines for the less advantaged?

Already, new communications technology has capabilities far beyond the average news consumer's needs. Matching the information flow with the consumer's ability to handle it is a challenge for mass communicators.

☆ RECOMMENDED READING

Staying abreast of fast-moving developments in global communications is a challenge. Fortunately, there are excellent sources.

Topical sources include regular and high-quality coverage in the *Wall Street Journal*, the *New York Times*, the *Los Angeles Times*, the *Washington Post*, and *Newsday*. Important periodicals include *presstime*, *Washington Journalism Review*, *Columbia Journalism Review*, *Editor & Publisher*, *Broadcasting*, *Electronic Media*, *Advertising Age*, *Adweek*, *Public Relations Journal*, *PR News*, *Communication World*, and *IABC News*. See *Film Critic* and *Film Quarterly* for ongoing coverage of the motion picture industry. For book-publishing news, see *Publishers Weekly* and *BP Report*. *Folio* covers the magazine industry.

Scholarly sources include *Journalism Quarterly*, *Public Opinion Quarterly*, the *Journal of Communication*, and the *Gannett Center Journal* for a general overview of communications research. *IPI Report*, *World Press Report*, *FIEJ Bulletin*, and *IAPA News* are more topical. Also see the *Journal of Broadcasting & Electronic Media* and *Television Quarterly*. In advertising and public relations, note the *Journal of Marketing*, the *Journal of Advertising Research*, the *Journal of Advertising*, and *Public Relations Review*.

Mainstreams of American Media Development

In a presidential campaign, thousands of reporters, TV cameramen and producers, technicians, and other media support troops trail around the country watching a handful of politicians court the voters. In 1988, as many as 2,500 crowded into Iowa as politicians went after the state's 1.5 million registered voters. Media competition was fierce, and the coverage was sometimes breathless and often repetitive. Reporters outnumbered voters at some functions, and as one wag put it, scarcely was there a farmer not interviewed at least twice on how he would vote. Then the parade moved on.

That media scenario is approximated thousands of times by newspaper, magazine, and broadcast reporters covering politics, murders, economics, or whatever across America. To outsiders, mysterious chemistry works at such times: Certain events, in particular places at certain times, are "news," and reporters pile on the selected stories. They pick some individuals as "newsworthy" and bypass others; they develop some "angles" or approaches to stories and reject others. Reporters feel not only that they have a right to be on such stories but that they are compelled to be there on behalf of a concept that they might describe, if pressed, as "the people's right to know." And often to the astonishment (or disgust) of the general public, that can embolden a reporter to ask a presidential aspirant not only for his views on Afghanistan but also whether he is, say, having a secret extramarital affair with a young model.

Who decides what is news? Why is news covered as it is? What organizations do this, and for what real purposes?

It's all part of an amazingly complex national media system of telecommunications and print publications that has evolved in America over the years. It is designed to get the news as quickly and accurately as possible to news consumers—readers, viewers, listeners. And the object of that is to collect sufficiently attractive audiences who can be "sold" to advertisers in return for their economic support, which is vital to our free enterprise media system. Some news-gathering organizations involved in this are large, some small; all are driven by their own distinct journalistic and business personalities plus the imperatives of their own corporate self-interest.

If we are to proceed toward understanding the mainline American media industries as they are today and might be in the future, we must first examine mainstreams of development in the media. We will concentrate on five:

The historical mainstream. Events and social history shape the American media and, as with any institution, determine how the media fit into our society. We'll look at shaping forces, such as law and ethics, but won't attempt a detailed historical review (that's a full book in itself). Our discussion will be predominantly print-oriented, of course, because radio did not join the historical mainstream as a major player until the 1920s and TV not until the 1950s.

The ownership and business motivation mainstream. Whether government, special-interest groups, or private investors own the media has an enormous impact on how they operate. We will study how the American media are operated today—for journalistic principle, to serve a cause, to make a profit.

The technological mainstream. The efficiency of mass communication through history has depended in large measure on the marriage of media and technology; certainly, technology will play an enormously important role in how the media evolve in future years.

The journalistic mainstream. News, information, and commentary are all products of the American media today. We shall explore how the media define, collect, and distribute these products.

The entertainment mainstream. TV and radio today dominate mass media entertainment. We'll investigate how the early media, newspapers and magazines, developed entertainment coverage, then later gave way in that arena to the electronic media. Because the entertainment function of the media is so important, we will leave full exploration to later chapters on TV, cable, radio, and film.

We will put all this into a theoretical context, discussing theories of communications as foundation for our examination, in Chapter 3, of the major American diversified media conglomerates.

THE NATURE OF THE INSTITUTION

Let's say you decide that come the next presidential election, you will be a reporter among the 2,500 trooping around Iowa with candidates. Or let's say your goal is simply a better understanding, as a news consumer, of what all those reporters are up to, how news-gathering companies are structured, and how they plan news coverage.

If you seek guidance by listening in on reporters gathered for a big story, you will likely be disappointed. Mostly, they talk about such mundane things as where to get a good meal before the fast-moving political campaign moves on or how to get laundry done quickly.

If talk turns to the reporter's craft, it may be talk about a "beat" or a "scoop"—how one reporter got into print or on the air with a major news development ahead of rivals. Newspaper reporters might talk about how they "fronted"— got a story important enough to make page 1; TV reporters might say, with pride, that their stories "led at 6"—were so newsworthy and professionally done, they were used in the number one spot on the 6 P.M. newscast.

Mostly, reporters of leading print and broadcast organizations try to cover the news with dispassionate objectivity, striving to keep personal feelings out of their writing. True objectivity may be an unattainable goal. But reporters talk a lot about striving for it.

Those are the dynamics of news coverage— a competitiveness born of a strong personal, at times almost egocentric need to succeed; a high degree of professionalism as defined by media colleagues (and not outsiders); a sense, though sometimes ill-defined, of ethical and social obligation; and an overwhelming desire to find something fresh and topical—something "newsy"— to report.

Seldom do reporters talk about the philosophical rationale for what they do. They don't refer to themselves as the "Fourth Estate" or "media watchdogs." Questions to politicians aren't prefaced with, "On behalf of the people's right to know, Senator, . . ." Such terms simply don't figure in the everyday language of reporters. Indeed, nowhere in the U.S. Constitution, the very fountainhead of our legal system, can you find "Fourth Estate" after delineation of the three others—legislative, judicial, executive. The "media watchdog" label lacks any direct constitutional legitimacy and can in fact be worn by just about anyone who decides to be a reporter. And "people's right to know"? That isn't in the Constitution either. Yet it's in the fiber of American journalism, and reporters use it every

Atlanta Journal and Constitution cartoonist Dale Dodson spoofs reporters who practice "pack journalism."

day to push through closed doors in search of that prize of all prizes, a good news story.

But how can American media, ever present, loudly vocal, enormously influential, assume such important roles in our lives on such thin constitutional precedent? It all comes down to a few words in the First Amendment to our Constitution, which guarantees freedom of the press,

THE FOUNTAINHEAD

66 Congress shall make no law respecting an establishment of religion, or prohibiting the free exercise thereof; or abridging the freedom of speech, or the press; or the right of the people peaceably to assemble, and to petition the Government for a redress of grievances. 99

First Amendment to the U.S. Constitution.

a complex mosaic of subsequent legal interpretations, and historical and societal forces quite outside the written law that today define the media's niche in our society. Both role and niche are ever changing; relationships between the media and other institutions in our society are constantly shifting.

Let's trace how this came about.

SOME EARLY BATTLES

American broadcast and print media today enjoy a freedom from official control almost unique in the world. They are independently adversarial—probing and questioning—toward government and other institutions. They are instrumental in delivering the news and information so crucial to informed decision making in our democracy. All that is true because of vigorous battles fought, sometimes at enormous personal cost, by supporters of a free press almost since invention of the printing press, the dawn of mass communications as we practice it. ▶ 1

The Chinese used movable type by A.D. 1100 or so, but in the West it wasn't until the 1400s that Johann Gutenberg, a German, popularized movable type and hand presses in book production. Officialdom quickly recognized the printing press for what it was—and remains: a communications technology that permits the free flow of information outside official sources and enables, indeed encourages, independent thought and a questioning by the governed of how they are governed. Today's modern broadcast and print technologies, like those early presses, permit widespread sharing of information, and that means, importantly, a sharing of power that comes from possessing information. That is today, as in times bygone, the crux of the battle between the people who would restrict the free flow of information and those who labor to keep it flowing.

Much of American law and democratic tradition has roots in Britain, where one of the earliest, most important battles over the printing press occurred. England's first printing shop was established in 1476 by William Claxton. Autocratic rulers realized that unrestricted use of the printing process by their critics threatened their power and prestige, and in 1529, King Henry VIII issued a list of prohibited books. In 1534, he required printers to be licensed—thus establishing the shape of the battle to come.

Clearly, bureaucratic overuse today of the "top secret" stamp in Washington and other manipulation by the governors of what the governed shall view, read, and hear flow directly from Henry's book ban and similar restrictive efforts down through history. Many people in our government and out would permit only officially approved journalists to cover the news. Such would-be censors chip away at the First Amendment and want to establish standards or "guidelines" that in the end would accomplish Henry's goal, control of the press. Today, strong, well-financed special-interest pressure groups outside government are among the forces that try to influence how the American broadcast and print media operate.

The battle over a free press arrived on American shores with the colonists. They were seeking political and religious freedom, of course, plus economic opportunity. But like those whose rule they fled, the colonists had strong opinions on how things should be run. In the New World, it was very much a toss-up whether a free press would flourish. The Puritans, for example, established the first print shop in America, in 1638, not to create news coverage and commentary as we know it today but much more narrowly to provide printed materials for their strictly run church schools and Harvard College.

Across the Atlantic came the Old World requirement of official approval before publication. Today, the right to publish without prior restraint is a cherished freedom of any democracy; it is jeopardized anytime any organization or individual—president, mayor, advocate, or critic—demands the power to decide, in advance, what news will be published or aired.

In an early conflict, the king's governor in Massachusetts closed down America's first newspaper, *Publick Occurrences, Both Foreign and Domestick*, after a single issue. That was in 1690, and the unfortunate publisher was Benjamin Harris. His mistake was not obtaining prior approval. Others who later obtained official approval stayed in business. A weekly, the *Boston News-Letter*, which first appeared in 1704, carried the notice "Published by authority." Note the "*by* authority." Journalists today attempt to write stories *with* authority—stories authoritatively based in factual information from expert sources. At times, this takes reporters close to officialdom and, if the reporters aren't careful,

1 ▶ Communications History High Points

c. 1100 The Chinese use movable type.

c. 1400 Gutenberg popularizes movable type in Germany; by 1450, hand presses are producing multiple copies of books.

1476 William Claxton establishes England's first printing shop.

1529 Recognizing the power of the press in challenging authority, England's King Henry VIII issues a list of prohibited books; in 1534, he requires printers to be licensed.

1638 Puritans establish America's first print shop.

1690 *Publick Occurrences, Both Foreign and Domestick*, America's first newspaper, is shut down by the king's officials after one issue.

1721 James Franklin publishes *New England Courant*, the first newspaper to succeed without government approval.

1735 John Peter Zenger's acquittal on a seditious libel charge establishes truth as defense in libel cases.

1741 The first magazines appear in America and quickly fail financially.

1791 The Bill of Rights is ratified; the First Amendment protects freedom of the press.

1821 The *Saturday Evening Post* launched.

1833 The "penny press" era opens as Benjamin Day publishes the *New York Sun*.

1839 Louis Daguerre of France develops still photography.

1844 Samuel F. B. Morse's invention, the telegraph, goes into operation.

1848 The Associated Press is founded.

1888 Thomas Edison and William Dickson develop a workable motion picture camera.

1897 Guglielmo Marconi patents the wireless telegraph.

1903 The film *The Great Train Robbery* is released.

1912 Congress licenses radio.

1920 KDKA broadcasts in Pittsburgh.

1922 *Reader's Digest* is founded; *Time* follows the next year.

1923 The American Society of Newspaper Editors issues its Canons of Journalism, the first widely accepted ethics code.

1927 NBC and CBS begin network broadcasting.

1936 TV broadcasts begin in Britain. *Life* magazine is founded.

1951 CBS achieves the first coast-to-coast TV link.

1965 The Early Bird communications satellite is put in orbit.

1967 Gannett goes public and begins its climb toward becoming the nation's largest newspaper owner.

1969 Moon landing is telecast live.

1972 *Life* halts weekly publication.

1981 The federal government reduces regulation of radio.

1986 Capital Cities Communications acquires ABC, becoming a $4.1 billion conglomerate.

---

leads to reflecting, not challenging, the official line.

The first notable success in America in publishing in defiance of authority came in 1721 when James Franklin (Ben's big brother) launched the *New England Courant*. In the five years his paper lasted, Franklin established a style of writing and reporting that profoundly influenced the devel-opment of American journalism. First, he stood in true opposition to ruling circles. He probably wouldn't have used the term, but Franklin practiced adversarial journalism, today recognizable in the sharp, probing attitude many journalists take toward government and other institutions in society. Second, Franklin displayed a knack for reporting from the reader's point of view rather than the government's. He sensed what readers wanted and developed stories with high appeal on topical subjects. Today, the *New York Times* or the *Wall Street Journal* accomplishes the same thing—but by spending millions of dollars to research reader news needs and desires scientifically, then producing newspapers that fulfill them.

In 1735 occurred a development that reverberates even today in American newsrooms and courtrooms. A German immigrant printer, John Peter Zenger, was tried on a charge of seditious libel because the New York paper he edited for a group opposed to the governor reported on a controversy involving illegal land deals and incompetent administration. In a brilliantly argued defense, Andrew Hamilton won Zenger's acquittal on the grounds that his stories were true. For decades, the case had little direct effect on journalism or law. But the principle it established—that truth is a defense against a libel charge—eventually resurfaced and is a foundation of our media law today. As never before, the media today are subject to attacks from critics who use libel law as a club. In this legal climate, the Zenger verdict lives every time a print or TV editor says to a young reporter, "Are you sure? We'll go with the story if it is true. Do you have the facts pinned down?"

Efforts by so many journalists today to produce balanced, "objective" reporting would be unrecognizable to journalists active in the years leading up to the American Revolution. Many regarded themselves as political activists—propagandists, really—and wielded their pens as political weapons. Writers such as Samuel Adams and Tom Paine and papers like the *Boston Gazette* and the *Pennsylvania Gazette* bitterly attacked the British crown. They practiced "attack journalism" that was openly and frankly seditious, as that term was then understood. Groups loyal to the crown had their newspapers, too. The newspapers, of course, had very limited circulation—hundreds or a few thousand copies turned out on the creaky, hand-operated presses of the day. They were poorly printed and not very pleasant to the eye. But there was an incredible

thirst for the message, and leading writers could be certain that what they wrote would eventually spread far. Today, news agencies and syndicates pick up articles and editorials from newspapers and transmit them in an instant throughout the world. In Samual Adams's day, travelers or a few postal couriers carried newspapers throughout the colonies, mostly along the eastern seaboard, and in weeks, perhaps months, the word spread. And for many, the word was *revolt*.

Congress declared independence on July 2, 1776. Congress ordered printing of the Declaration started on July 4; the full text wasn't published until July 6. Not until August 17 did London papers report the story. And although the news didn't penetrate the consciousness of some authoritarian nations, such as Russia, for many years, the Declaration of Independence and its stirring words of hope and freedom entered the mainstream of political thought. Today, we have almost daily examples of cause-and-effect relationships linking journalism directly to what happens in politics and economics, peace and war. News reports of a Palestinian leader's assassination stir immediate protest riots in Arab territories; news from Washington of rising interest rates causes bankers in your hometown quickly to raise the interest rate for a home or auto loan. For responsible journalists, this cause-and-effect relationship is a sobering reality.

For early American journalists, the partisanship of revolutionary journalism—using the pen to persuade rather than objectively to inform—was not put aside after victory. The newly independent nation coalesced along differing political and economic lines, and so did journalists and newspapers line up in support of different causes. This identification of some newspapers with specific economic and political policies is an earmark of American journalism that lasted well into modern times.

In our young nation, an early major division was between the Republicans, with Thomas Jefferson at their head, and Alexander Hamilton's Federalists. Hamilton believed in an aristocracy and a strong central government directed by special-interest groups, not the American public.

Newspapers popular among the wealthy and commercial classes frequently lined up behind him. Jefferson believed in a farm-based economy and a social structure founded in agrarian life. An intensely emotional issue of the day, the French Revolution, further divided the two camps. It was an age of Federalist and anti-Federalist newspapers featuring a brawling, opinionated journalism designed not to inform but to ridicule. It is unusual in American journalism today for the media to divide along such sharp partisan lines and also unusual for one newspaper to attack another. Perhaps American media that today delight in closely scrutinizing other institutions in society—government, business, the church—would do well to stop treating themselves with kid gloves.

In 1798, the Federalists offered one of the most serious challenges, before or since, to the right to publish without prior restraint. They sponsored the Alien and Sedition Acts of 1798, aimed in part at permitting the government to deport undesirable aliens and, more important, to move against critics of the government. The acts provided for a fine of up to $2,000 (big money in those days) and up to two years in prison for anyone who "shall write, print, utter, or publish . . . any false, scandalous and malicious writing . . . against the government of the United States, or either house of Congress . . . or the said President . . . or to excite against them the hatred of the good people of the United States."

Some historians say the acts weren't all that bad, that because of the John Peter Zenger case, only *false* criticism of the government could be punished. However, the intent of the acts was clearly to permit the government to punish anti-Federalist critics by squelching free speech. Even in Federalist circles, there was great unease over the acts. Revulsion grew, and just two years later, in 1800, the acts were allowed to expire. Such second thought—a sort of societal self-correcting mechanism—has come into play several times in American history when press freedom was threatened. For example, the Reagan administration in 1983 barred reporters from accompanying troops on a secret invasion to overthrow the leftist government of the Caribbean island of Grenada. There was immediate public support for the White House's position that the media (which for generations had accompanied American troops in the field) had to be excluded to protect secrecy. But when the real meaning of such a secret invasion began to sink in, public mood shifted to support the media's position that reporters should be present on battlefields as surrogates of the people as long as nothing printed or broadcast would jeopardize military missions or lives.[1]

NEWSPAPERS OR GOVERNMENT?

66 The basis of our government being the opinion of the people, the very first object should be to keep that right; and were it left to me to decide whether we should have a government without newspapers, or newspapers without a government, I should not hesitate a moment to prefer the latter. 99

Thomas Jefferson, 1787.[2]

In the election of 1800, Jefferson took into office a strong record of support for a free, independent press. During his years in office, however, aggressive, partisan, and very hard-hitting journalism continued. Like many of his successors, Jefferson wearied of the constant attacks but nevertheless said he would continue to protect his enemies "in the right of lying and calumniating." But some of his followers did try to suppress more vocal Federalist critics, and Jefferson complained bitterly to friends that the American experiment in encouraging free speech and criticism of government was subjecting him to unfair attacks. Today, we repeatedly see public officials support—and court—a free press during their climb to power. All are aware, of course, that a favorable image in newspapers and on television is a prerequisite to political success. Yet once office is attained, some political figures tire of media scrutiny. Then often comes withdrawal from frequent contact with reporters (denial of access, a very real form of censorship) and erection of barriers to the free flow of information. Sometimes there is outright distortion or lying. The mainstream of information flow we are tracing has powerful origins in our Constitution and national traditions. But it is a fragile thing, demanding constant nurturing by those committed to free press and free speech.

LIBERTARIANISM VERSUS AUTHORITARIANISM

TRUTH IN THE MARKETPLACE

66 Let all with something to say be free to express themselves. The true and sound will survive, the false and unsound will be vanquished. 99

John Milton, British writer, 1644.[3]

Passing down to us a concept of press freedom that today is central to our democratic society, Jefferson actually relayed philosophical reasoning that originated much earlier. It included the idea that truth, if unleashed, would triumph in the marketplace competition of ideas, a belief firmly held by philosophers in the early 1600s. But not until well into the 1700s was there significant acceptance of the idea that we should be free to criticize the government. The birth of that right ended the earliest era of our press development, the era of authoritarianism, when the relatively small ruling elite decided what would be openly discussed and written. That gave way to libertarianism, a theory that the people can recognize truth and that the press, if free to feed news and information into the contest of ideas, can assist the people in arriving at informed decisions that will dictate public policy. (Later we'll discuss two other theories that scholars use to describe media systems—communism and social responsibility.)

Around 1800, our young nation's press began a period of explosive growth concurrent with—indeed, dependent on—the economic and population growth of that time. Publishers until then really made their livings as printers, not newspapermen. But as economic activity expanded dramatically in the original colonies and as settlers moved west, newspapers followed. It was an early example of a truism that exists in the American media today: When population and economic expansion occur, media expansion and prosperity follow.

Historians Michael and Edwin Emery report that Philadelphia, a center of early commerce, had six dailies by 1800; New York had five; Baltimore, three; Charleston, two. By 1804, publishing was established as far west as Indiana—the *Indiana Gazette* opened for business in Vincennes. Detroit had a paper, the *Gazette*, by 1817.[4]

Still, the flow of information was but a trickle. Frontier conditions were rough, printing facilities were inadequate, and there was little advertising to provide the economic support so vital to an active, independent press. In many cities, the primary economic support was official advertising—today we call it legal or public notice advertising—along with government printing contracts. And when official dollars feed the press, enormous economic pressure can be exerted on publishers to moderate their views. American newspapers did not achieve independence from official control until they developed alternative sources of revenue—initially from readers and later principally from advertisers (by 1887, advertisers provided about half of newspaper revenue; by 1909, about two-thirds; today, 80 percent or more.)

Compounding economic and technical difficulties, those early publishers operated without governmental or societal acceptance of a concept we today consider vital to a free press: that not only does the press have a right to publish and criticize but also the right of access to official information and the right to report it. At the time, little legal precedent existed for the people's right to know or the press's right to find and tell. After all, the founders of the nation drew up the Constitution (and the Bill of Rights) behind closed doors; not until the 1830s did the federal government publish information on its doings fully and with dispatch.

As the American media and their role in our society evolved, characteristics that distinguish our print and broadcast media today gradually appeared:

Societal support for the concept that freedom to publish is virtually meaningless unless accompanied by freedom of access to information and the right, on behalf of the people, to report

Economic support from advertisers that eliminates reliance on special-interest groups and is essential to keeping the press free of official control

Redefinition of the journalistic mission toward today's middle-of-the-road, evenhanded reporting of all political and economic sectors, not simply assuming partisan positions

Technical capability in print (and today, of course, in broadcast as well) to collect, analyze, and transmit information speedily and in manageable form to people who need it for informed decisions in their daily lives

An ethical framework within which the media are expected to discharge professional and social responsibilities inherent in their power and position in our society

Last to emerge was the massive effort to entertain as well as inform, a characteristic so evident in today's TV and radio media.

AN AGE OF GROWTH

The journalistic character of American media, as we know it today, began to take definite shape by the mid-1800s. Newspapers assigned reporters to go out and gather news, instead of relying solely on comment and interpretation. Their writing style was flowery, often convoluted. Nevertheless, reporters were out searching for news, an important development in American journalism.

Also, a vigorous press began seriously serving business communities. Correspondents rowed out to meet sailing ships arriving from Europe, then rowed furiously back to shore with news certain to have an impact on trade in America. Delivering business-related news from Washington to newspapers elsewhere became extremely important. Sometimes fast horses were used in a sort of pony express system. The right news, delivered at the right time, could create enormous profit in those days—just as it does today in the banks, commodities-trading houses, and brokerage firms of the world.

Still, there was no true mass communication as we know it. Relatively few Americans were literate or wealthy enough to be consistent newspaper readers. Today's newspaper marketing experts—charged with identifying the market and then adjusting the newspaper's content to serve it—would recognize the problem immediately. The social structure of the day virtually ruled out vast sectors of the population as newspaper consumers. Many people lacked not only the education but also the political involvement that made avid newspaper readers; many were farmers with a limited need to stay abreast of the news. Newspapers structured content and tone to serve the educated and wealthy elite. The same elitism is at work in American journalism today, particularly among such upscale newspapers as the *New York Times*, the *Los Angeles Times*, and the *Wall Street Journal*. It is a still-developing turn in American journalism that will have an enormous effect on the shape of things to come. We will return to it later in this book.

Socioeconomic change caused one truly revolutionary turn in early American publishing. As so many times subsequently, revolution in publishing followed revolution in society.

In 1828, Andrew Jackson and his Democrats won the White House. The "Jacksonian revolution" created widespread interest in politics and government. Education became available to more people than ever before. An industrial revolution created new wealth and, to an unprecedented degree, gave millions a piece of it, turning those millions into mass consumers of goods and services. An advertising industry began. But for publishers, developing new mass markets required two additional breakthroughs: First, there had to be a mechanical means of producing large numbers of newspapers quickly and efficiently; second, the per-unit cost of producing them had to be lowered. It was an early, classic example of the interdependence of mass communications and technology. Today, computers and satellites make possible new marvels of mass communications; in the 1820s and 1830s, the revolution was steam-driven presses. Concurrent breakthroughs in manufacturing produced cheaper newsprint and ink.

Strengthened by new technology, lured by the potential profits of serving millions of newly aware readers, American publishers developed newspapers for the masses.

THE *SUN* OPENS A NEW ERA

Benjamin Day first figured out how to publish a true mass-circulation newspaper. His formula combined new technology, keen insight into what people want to read (lots of crime, excerpts from the police blotter), and an entertaining, racy, readable journalistic style. His product was the *New York Sun* and, importantly, he sold it for one penny, *one-sixth* the price of competing papers.

The *Sun*, launched in 1833, was an immediate success and opened the "penny press" era of popular journalism. Day's strategy—find what readers want, then given it to them—built media fortunes in America then and is still building them today.

Day's form of newspapering had these enduring characteristics:

◆ *Cheap prices* put newspapers within reach of, eventually, millions.
◆ *Mass circulation* made newspapers (then magazines and later television) attractive to advertisers, who could reach many consumers of goods and services. Thus began the shift toward relying mostly on advertisers, not readers, for principal economic support. Today, advertisers provide 80 cents or more of every dollar received by most newspapers; readers, 20 cents or less. In magazines, readers provide about 51 cents of every dollar received. In broadcast, of course, advertisers pay the entire dollar.

◆ *Journalistic independence* arose from the *economic independence* inherent in selling large numbers of papers and, in turn, "selling" readers to advertisers. Newspapers were no longer forced to pander to narrow political or economic interests.
◆ *Great, dominant personalities* emerged—strong-willed, brilliant publishers and editors with flair and charisma. For the next century, newspapers featured strong, highly individualistic management styles.
◆ *Sensationalism* became a fixture. Crime in the streets, war overseas—mayhem sold newspapers. Cause journalism and crusading gave newspapers zest. For many readers, newspapers became an addiction: They were needed every day, were crucial to getting along in life—and that is a relationship with readers that editors strive for to this day. And, of course, sensationalism *was* entertaining. As we will discuss later in this book, television today is charged with sensationalizing entertainment through "trash TV" and "reality" programming of gruesome crime stories. Those early penny press editors would surely recognize TV's tactic of building large audiences through such programs.

Benjamin Day exhibited another quality that today marks print and broadcast journalism: competitiveness. He installed high-speed presses at the *Sun*, jumping within months to 8,000 daily circulation and, by 1837, to about 30,000—more than his 11 daily competitors in New York City combined. Soon other great names emerged.

James Gordon Bennett launched the *New York Herald* in 1835, plunging into sensationalistic coverage that built a huge circulation for its time and attracted advertisers. Bennett was an extraordinary innovator of journalistic content, much of it still characteristic of papers today. He developed sports coverage and society columns, opened his pages to letters from readers, and built

In the James Gordon Bennett tradition, *Los Angeles Times* editors present a wide variety of news. Note that a human interest story ("Mother, Jailed Since '87, . . .") balances other front-page stories. The boxed index shows readers where to find, among other things, "Dear Abby," horoscopes, and the comics!

The penny press era spread to other cities, but publishing success was elusive. Scores of newspapers appeared briefly, then died. Modern media strategists would call it a shakeout. Publishers tried new ideas against stiff competition; some gained a foothold, some didn't. The media have gone through many such periods. Since the 1960s, for example, some newspapers have been under severe financial pressure because their cities are suffering socioeconomic deterioration. Scores of new magazines are launched each year into highly competitive markets; some make it, some don't. Television is in extraordinary flux, with future relationships among networks, local stations, and cable TV entirely unclear.

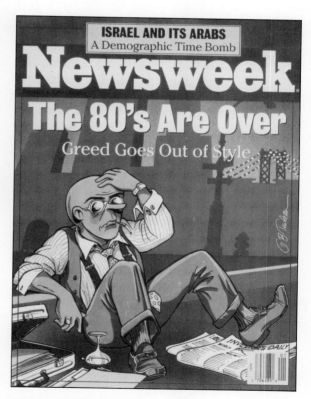

Newsweek editors, though severely limited in front-cover space, strive for a mix, too. Here they use a "Doonesbury" cartoon character as a lighthearted teaser to draw readers inside to in-depth reporting on a serious subject, greed in America. The box at top signals another important story inside.

a strong business news section. And seldom was it dull. His reporters delved deeply into (some say wallowed in) sensational trials, prostitution, crime—all part of Bennett's news "mix." Look at tonight's TV news or this morning's front page. Don't you find a mix of serious news with stories that are entertaining as well as informative? Even the most serious, mission-oriented editors try, as Bennett did, for that balance.

GREELEY, NEW TECHNOLOGY, AND WAR

By 1840, compelling political, economic, and social issues loomed. From our perspective today, we see them leading to civil war. In response to the heated national dialogue of the day, American newspapers turned toward thoughtful coverage of the issues. Editorial commentary, hard-hitting and penetrating, was a feature of this turn.

Horace Greeley personified all this with his *New York Tribune*, launched in 1841. Greeley was a champion of poor workers and farmers. He fought for social reform and was a major player in American life well into the 1870s. His *Tribune* became one of the nation's outstanding papers. In 1966, then known as the *Herald Tribune*, it died, a victim of changed economic and competitive circumstances, mourned by journalists throughout the nation.

The *New York Times* (a competitor that eventually helped do in the *Herald Tribune*) was first published in 1851 by Henry J. Raymond. He too was a serious journalist who, with managing editor Charles A. Dana, began building news coverage and editorials and commentary. Raymond and Dana looked to the *Times* of London for their model, and to this day the New York and London papers often are mentioned in the same breath in discussions of authoritative, high-quality journalism that has enormous impact on political, economic, and social issues.

It became important to receive quickly the latest news from Europe, Washington, and elsewhere. As would happen so many times subsequently in the evolution of American mass communication, new technology appeared to make it possible. Railroads expanded their track networks and developed faster locomotives, reducing the time needed for news to cover vast distances. Fast ships delivered news across the Atlantic.

Then, on May 24, 1844, came the big technological breakthrough. Samuel F. B. Morse, in Washington, tapped out a coded message via his invention, the telegraph, to an assistant in the next room (''What hath God wrought?''), and a new age opened for news distribution. In 1848, New York publishers set up a news service using the telegraph. A descendant is today's Associated Press, the world's largest general news agency. The telegraph and AP began linking news event to newspaper and thus to reader with an immediacy that became one of the enduring characteristics of American media. Fresh news, particularly if ahead of a competitor's, sells newspapers; on TV, it boosts ratings. In boardrooms, news received by private wire service ahead of a competitor is ''news to profit by.'' Being ahead of the other fellow was part of journalism before Morse's invention. But the telegraph put new meaning into ''scoop.'' Today, speed is ingrained in the journalistic fiber.

Coverage of the Mexican War (1846–1848) and extension of the telegraph west (it reached the Pacific in 1861) were warm-ups for the coming national trauma, the Civil War. North and South, newspapers and the still-young magazine industry (the *Saturday Evening Post* was founded in 1821, *Harper's Weekly* in 1857) took sides. In the North, antislavery editors thundered at the South. As always when passions are unleashed, there were victims—a lesson valid today for all journalists covering volatile situations. One antislavery editor, Elijah Lovejoy, was lynched by a mob in Alton, Illinois, in 1837. He is remembered today as an editor who paid the ultimate price to publish what he believed.[5] In the South, secessionist editors known as ''fire eaters'' urged breaking away from the North. One, Robert Barnwell Rhett of the *Charleston* (S.C.) *Mercury*, became known as the ''father of secession.''

Far-reaching change in American journalism was crammed into the four years of the Civil War. News collection systems and reporting and writing styles set journalistic standards followed in war correspondency even today.

Huge numbers of soldiers fought a bloody, total war that involved civilian populations. Demands were heavy for comprehensive coverage, and that sent hundreds of correspondents roaming over battlefields. Eyewitness coverage was given major display in newspapers, as it is today on front pages and in broadcasts.

Well into the 1930s, Associated Press telegraphers such as these pounded out news dispatches in Morse code. At each man's ear was a sounding box that magnified the incoming signal. *Wide World Photos.*

For the first time, correspondents—"specials"—became near folk heroes. William Howard Russell, a transplanted Briton who had covered the Crimean War, became famous. So, in the North, did Raymond of the *New York Times* and B. S. Osborn of the *New York World* and

The modern foreign correspondent is a direct journalistic descendant of newspaper "specials" who roamed Civil War battlefields. Here, Morley Safer, now a "60 Minutes" correspondent, covers the Vietnam War for CBS. *Courtesy CBS News.*

later the *Herald. Frank Leslie's Illustrated Newspaper, Harper's Weekly*, and other magazines sent artists into the fray, and their woodcut illustrations, combined with detailed reporting, sent circulations soaring. Newspapers and magazines flourished in the North, where there was a nearly insatiable demand for news of the war.

Southern newspapers, lacking newsprint and other supplies, fared worse. But important journalism was produced by the *Richmond Dispatch*, the *Charleston Courier*, the *Mobile Advertiser*, the *New Orleans Picayune*, and others. A *Courier* "special," Felix Gregory de Fontine, built a reputation for brilliant reporting second to none, North or South.[6] The "star system" of developing skilled war correspondents, then advertising them to build circulation (and later TV ratings), was born.

The cost of coverage was so high that papers shared resources, and that gave a huge boost to the Associated Press, a cooperative whose member newspapers jointly underwrite costs. In the South, papers collaborated through the Confederate Press Association. (AP came out of the war a strong news agency; PA vanished.) Correspondents filed copy to the home office by telegraph, and this had a strong influence on writing

Like the magazine artist of Civil War days, today's news photographer goes where the action is. Horst Faas (*right*) of the Associated Press, shown in Vietnam, won two Pulitzer prizes for combat photography. *Wide World Photos.*

style. A premium was on brief spurts of information with important details summarized in a "lead" or first paragraph. Telegraph rates were based on word count, so importance was attached to what journalists call "writing short." From that came, for the news services, a "bulletin" form of filing—a short but publishable item, perhaps only a single paragraph of highlights. On the night of April 14, 1865, Lawrence A. Gobright of the New York Associated Press filed this bulletin: "The President was shot in a theater tonight and perhaps mortally wounded." To this day, a news service bulletin will tell you who won, who lost, and at what cost. Details follow. By war's end, Civil War correspondents were filing copy that was tight and to the point. It is not considered necessary today to jam "who, what, where, when, why, and how" into every first paragraph. But most editors want that information in at least the first four or five paragraphs. Some Civil War writing could be published today.

The Civil War created a tension between the press and officialdom that any war correspondent today would recognize. Army commanders were quick to bar reporters or censor inaccurate or negative copy. Some commanders suspended newspapers for fear they were printing information valuable to the enemy. The government issued accreditation papers to correspondents— a practice continued today.

Nevertheless, American journalism emerged from the Civil War energized by high circulations and newfound prosperity.

GROWTH, CITIES, AND CHANGE

The United States grew and changed dramatically after the Civil War. And the American press grew and changed right along with it.

For the nation, 1865–1900 was an era of tidal waves of immigrants doubling the population. Cities grew huge, factories boomed, wealth multiplied. Public schools and universities expanded. Interest in literature, cultural events, and the sciences increased.

For the press, one effect was concentration in large cities of masses of literate, well-to-do potential readers. Unlike rural Americans, these Americans were mass consumers of manufactured goods and services and thus targets for advertisers. They presented the "critical mass"— sufficient numbers of readers with attractive income and education—needed to support profitable newspapers. Finding such a critical mass and establishing a franchise by serving it is the target of all media strategists today.

As the character of America changed, so did the definition of news and how it should be covered. Social turmoil arose from those crowded cities and smoky factories. Crime and corruption and government scandals surfaced and were fodder for the vigorous, never more powerful press. Out of this period came public perception of the press as a watchdog of society. The *New York Times* and *Harper's Weekly*, for example, helped break the Tweed Ring, corrupt politicians who siphoned off millions in New York City public funds in the 1870s. Newspapers criticized scan-

This first front page of the *Los Angeles Daily Times*, published on December 4, 1881, is typical of the appearance of the large-city newspapers that grew rapidly following the Civil War.

(there are more than 11,000 today).[7] Some of the important papers around the turn of the 20th century are still read today: the *Los Angeles Times*, the *San Francisco Chronicle*, the *Portland Oregonian*, the *Dallas News*, the *Atlanta Constitution*, and the *Louisville Courier-Journal*, to name a few.

Above all, this was an era of emerging great names: Charles Dana of the *New York Sun*, Edwin Godkin of the *New York Post*, William Randolph Hearst, Edward W. Scripps, and, of course, the great Joseph Pulitzer.

Dana first achieved journalistic distinction as Horace Greeley's managing editor at the *New York Tribune*. He is believed to be the first to carry that title, which today identifies the person in charge of day-to-day direction of a newspaper's news coverage (some in television, including Dan Rather of CBS's *Evening News*, use that title, too). Later Dana bought the *Sun* and became identified with what is today called "people-oriented" journalism. The *Sun* concentrated on covering New York City and "translating" issues in easily understood language.

Journalism with a conscience was Edwin Godkin's trademark. Godkin launched *The Nation*, a magazine of thoughtful opinion that, despite limited circulation, helped establish a national agenda of issues. Thoughtful journalists down through American history have poked the national conscience with similar magazines, perhaps never achieving financial success but "trending" public dialogue through sheer force of intellect and keen insight into crucial social, political, and economic issues.

The years leading up to 1900 were marked by the rise of influential newspaper families. Many current big players in the media are heirs to old newspaper-owning families that established managerial and journalistic approaches still evident today.

For example, two half brothers, James E. and Edward W. Scripps, saw lucrative markets waiting among working-class people in rapidly growing industrial cities in America's economic heartland. They moved into Cincinnati, St. Louis, Buffalo, Cleveland, and Detroit with

dals in President Grant's administration and campaigned against social and economic injustice. "News" took on a much broader meaning; newspapers went after it with an increasing sense of responsibility. It is a direct line from that early type of aggressive investigative news coverage to, say, the Watergate scandal of the early 1970s and the role played by the *Washington Post* and other newspapers in reporting illegal activities in the Nixon administration and forcing the president's resignation.

By 1900, there were more than 1,900 dailies with 15 million circulation (in 1988, there were over 1,600 dailies with 62.8 million circulation). Weeklies numbered over 12,000 (down to fewer than 8,000 in 1988, with 51.6 million circulation). Magazines mushroomed to more than 3,500

newspapers championing the working class. Workers arose before dawn in those days and hurried to plants and mills with little time for reading morning papers; so the Scrippses developed afternoon papers, inexpensively priced. One, the *Cleveland Press*, became known as the greatest blue-collar afternoon paper in the country until it, like many other metropolitan afternoon dailies, fell victim to changing times and folded in 1982.[8]

The names Pulitzer and Hearst stand above all others in the mainstream of American press development in the late 1800s. Pulitzer, a penniless immigrant from Hungary, served in the Union army during the Civil War, gained experience as a newspaper reporter, and in 1878 bought for bargain prices two St. Louis dailies, the *Post* and the *Dispatch*. In a few years, his combined *Post-Dispatch* was a journalistic and business success. Pulitzer was a hard-driving owner, never content with his staff's performance. That led him into what, for the day, was impressively detailed, hands-on management. He built an executive staff and administrative structure capable of producing results. He favored investigative stories that dug deep beneath the news. But not all *Post-Dispatch* content was high-toned, selfless, community service journalism. Pulitzer knew how to appeal to readers with sensationalistic, frothy coverage, too. A little sex here, a little sin there—that was part of the Pulitzer formula. With the *Post-Dispatch* on the way to greatness (it is one of America's top papers today), Pulitzer bought the *New York World* in 1883. This was to be his ultimate triumph. With his keen sense of what big-city readers wanted (many were immigrants like himself, so he understood them), Pulitzer supported liberal political candidates, crusaded for popular causes, jerked tears with human interest stories, and wrapped it all up in intensive promotion campaigns such as the newspaper industry never had seen. Within months, *World* circulation and profits mushroomed. It made Pulitzer a multimillionaire, but his many years of intense labors broke his health. He died in 1911. The *World* survived as an independent paper until 1931. After a succession of mergers and consolidations, Pulitzer's gift to journalism, then known as the *New York World Journal Tribune*, folded in 1967.

William Randolph Hearst expanded Pulitzer's strategies into his own highly personal—and controversial—formula for newspapering. It delighted his fans, infuriated his critics, and built a media company that is among America's largest today.

Hearst's empire had unlikely beginnings. Hearst was born in 1863 to a rich and prominent Californian. Academically, he was a failure at Harvard (expelled for practical jokes in his second year). Little in his background indicated that Hearst either needed to succeed in journalism or possessed the character to do so. But friend and foe alike agreed that the man had a certain flair. And Hearst had a sense of the enormous power that goes with publishing major newspapers.

In 1887, at age 24, Hearst started editing the *San Francisco Examiner*, which his father owned. Young Hearst showed a striking ability to attract extremely talented editors and managers. He often raided competitors for staffers who could produce his style journalism. But the style, the tone of Hearst's newspapers came from him alone. He practiced a crusading, sensationalistic brand of journalism, invading New York, buying the *Journal*, and touching off a circulation war with Pulitzer's *World* marked by daily front-page sensations. The competition extended even to cartoons. Both papers ran a cartoon featuring the Yellow Kid, an amusing character dressed in a yellow shirt. "Yellow journalism" came to identify an entire era of newspaper publishing during which press lords pulled out all stops to catch the public fancy.

Hearst showed uncanny ability to capture the public fancy. He titillated with sensational crime coverage, amused and entertained as a "champion of the people." Sensing the public mood, Hearst promoted expansion of U.S. power abroad with ringing jingoism. If it was war they wanted—and many Americans did—Hearst would promote one. All wars have many rabble rousers, and the Spanish-American War of 1898 was no exception. Prominent among the fanners

Because of his controversial views on many subjects, William Randolph Hearst (*right, being interviewed*) was a news story as well as a newspaper publisher. *Wide World Photos.*

of flames was William Randolph Hearst, who saw great circulation gains in exploiting public emotion with reporting marked by passion more than accuracy, editing and layout that incensed readers, and editorials that beat the drums of war. So it was with many crusades that Hearst ran while building his media empire.

At his zenith, about 1935, Hearst published papers in 19 cities. Circulation soared into the millions. Although his company at times had serious economic difficulties, Hearst made a fortune—and spent much of it on lavish living, complete with a castlelike home, San Simeon, in California, as fully dramatic as that of the idle rich his papers loved to report on for working-class readers. Hearst died in 1951.

THE LEGACY OF GIANTS

One great concern today about the broadcast and print media is that communications companies, including Hearst's and others with roots in the late 1800s, are collecting too much power. Some

critics fear political and social manipulation through influence over public opinion by executives who direct scores of newspapers, magazines, and broadcast stations, employ thousands of persons, and count their annual corporate revenues in the billions of dollars. Particularly in the 1950s and 1960s, there was a "conspiracy theory" that somewhere, somehow a small group of media executives was directing how the news would be covered.

Actually, there is not much evidence that media empires are very interested in manipulating public opinion for some secret, Machiavellian purpose. That would be counterproductive to the primary mission of producing profit. To sit today in some mountaintop San Simeon (or New York City skyscraper) and order editors across the country to slant the news would draw immediate public—and probably governmental—attack, and today's media giants know that. But the memory of Hearst's doing it is enough to alert media critics to the danger of its happening again.

One Hearstian legacy is copied today, however: the concept of group management. Hearst built a corporate staff of expert editors, business managers, technicians, and production executives, then, like a general at war, he shifted them between circulation battles, to wherever action was hottest. Tough and intensely competitive, they expanded Hearst's operations to new cities, attacking competitor newspapers with news and business techniques proved elsewhere. Some competitors they drove out of business. Today, every media conglomerate of consequence has "flying squads" of executives capable of moving on short notice to new danger spots and new opportunities.

Another crucial lesson drawn today from that earlier era is that a publishing strategy that works brilliantly can prove disastrous if not adapted to changing conditions. A newspaper must have a critical mass of readers attractive to advertisers, who provide the main economic support. When Hearst entered publishing, that critical mass was found mostly among working-class readers bunched in large cities. Those cities were prosperous business centers, and newspapers

William Randolph Hearst helped build the management concept in American newspapers, but he wouldn't recognize this staff conference at *USA Today*. Hearst's staffs were all male. *Courtesy Gannett Co.*

had shown the way to enormous profit and influence. They built administrative structures to run newspapers efficiently as businesses. A new class of newspaper executives—business managers—rose to prominence to wrestle with unions, rising costs, new production techniques, and the difficulties of mass distribution. In short order, business managers assumed an influence that today can overshadow the role of editors in some newspapers. Broadcast media are similarly in the grip of profit-oriented managers, as we shall see later.

In small-town America, newspapers were part of the local power structure, as important as church, business community, and political organizations. A publisher or editor was (and is) influential indeed.

In newsrooms, great change was under way. Roving correspondents expanded internationally the role of star reporters that began in the Civil War. Famous bylines appeared regularly over dispatches from far-off places. At home, reporters developed specialities—sports, law, the arts—to meet the increasingly sophisticated news needs of their audiences. Dispassionate, "objective" reporting grew more popular. Its goal was to present facts and keep reporters' views out of the story. This move away from partisan reporting became necessary as newspapers sought readers in ever-widening circles of society, appealing simultaneously to the rich and the lower-middle class, to liberals and conservatives. The move gained further impetus from the increasingly influential Associated Press. Because it served newspapers of all persuasions, in all sections of the country, AP had to play the news "straight."

Demonstrating again the tight relationship between journalistic progress and technical innovation, the industry bounded ahead with the telephone and the wireless (patented in 1897). Invention of the Linotype, a typesetting device, on larger papers supplanted old-fashioned printers, who hand-set type, and speeded newspaper production. Use of photos spread throughout the industry. High-speed presses and cheaper newsprint permitted greater mass circulation.

didn't face today's array of broadcast and other competitors. So Hearst and other publishers shared the rewards, and for decades, competing newspapers flourished in the same cities. However, starting in the 1950s, new competitors (primarily TV) appeared, and socioeconomic deterioration began riddling many large cities. Many businesses and affluent readers moved to the suburbs, where newly developing suburban newspapers waited to serve them. Newspapers anchored downtown, as Hearst papers were, suffered often extraordinary economic decline.

Today, media conglomerates avoid head-on competition with other newspapers of like size and characteristics. They acquire small-town newspapers, broadcast stations, and other businesses to balance the uncertainties of big-city publishing. Hearst Corp. itself now is widely diversified, more active in magazines than in newspapers. It has closed some big-city newspapers and purchased small-town papers William Randolph Hearst wouldn't have dreamed of owning. Across America, only a handful of cities have independently owned newspapers competing with each other.

The big-city ills were not evident as the 20th century approached, and the newspaper industry was strong. Pulitzer, Hearst, Scripps, and others

In the early 1900s, technology in use in the Associated Press stock market service included an old-fashioned ticker, a telephone, and pencils. Today, huge computers and high-speed transmission circuits do the job at more than 9,000 words per minute. *Wide World Photos.*

Confronted by common problems, enticed by common opportunities, newspapers organized into state associations that lobbied for the industry. Newspapers in 1887 created the American Newspaper Publishers Association (ANPA); it now is one of the nation's most powerful trade groups, with a primary goal of enhancing the newspaper as an advertising medium.

New and significant competition for advertising appeared. Magazines developed rapidly thanks to the expansion of railroads and low postal rates, which permitted widespread distribution. Magazine owners kept their cover prices low to encourage mass circulation nationwide— a great attraction to advertisers. New magazines included *Ladies' Home Journal*, launched in 1883; *Cosmopolitan*, 1886; *Collier's*, 1888; *Munsey's*, 1889; and *McClure's*, 1893. Among magazine publishers, a new force appeared: Cyrus H. K. Curtis, who launched *Collier's* and in 1897 bought the *Saturday Evening Post* as the flagship of what was to become a media powerhouse, Curtis Publishing Co.

Magazines became important influences in the American media mix in the early 1900s and remain so today, even though television has sup-

planted them as primary sources of entertainment in millions of American living rooms.

THE CENTURY OF CHALLENGES

The American media's sense of journalistic mission and social responsibility has been refined by unprecedented challenges in the 20th century. Never has so much change affected so many people so quickly as in the years since 1900: world war, economic depression and complex social upheaval, world war again, then cold war. Ahead is a new century that promises change fully as profound. Consider what this means for print and broadcast media today.

◆ Journalistically, they must report and interpret extremely complex economic, political, social, and scientific change worldwide. And journalists must report with precision and sophistication to meet the news needs of increasingly discerning, better-educated audiences.[9]

◆ Among themselves, the media face the challenge of realigning competitive boundaries as new contestants arrive in the mass communication of news, entertainment, and advertising. Early in the century, new magazines rushed into the marketplace. Newspapers moved over to accommodate the magazines. Then radio arrived, then TV, and more shifts occurred. Ahead are new forms of electronic technology, not yet precisely shaped but certain to advance the revolution in communications.

◆ Shifts in American lifestyles change the socioeconomic context within which the media operate. Soaring costs and new attitudes among readers, viewers, listeners, and advertisers force change in the industry.

◆ As never before, media ethics and law—the role of the media—are on the agenda for public discussion. Public ownership, under which companies offer stock for sale to investors, creates a new constituency—thousands of shareholders— to which the media must respond. The resultant "rising tide of shareholder expectation"—investor demand for ever-increasing dividends—

pushes media companies into diversification in search of new revenue sources, including distinctly nonmedia businesses. Tribune Co. owns the Chicago Cubs baseball team, for example. Are such firms true media companies under the First Amendment tent? Or will society consider them just another form of business and rethink the special status granted media companies since colonial days? Profit-oriented professional managers, taking over from family owners, raise new questions, too: Who are these men and women running these influential media companies? What are their personal and corporate philosophies? Should they, like politicians, be asked to reveal all?

Looking back, we can see how these questions developed. Early in the century, for example, newspapers (still the dominant medium, of course) were increasingly recognized as profit-oriented and economically powerful entities. Nevertheless, many were distancing themselves from "big business." For underpaid, overworked masses of Americans, it was a time of social injustice, of economic ills—and that was the point of journalistic attack for Scripps, Pulitzer, and Hearst. Though splendidly comfortable themselves, those wealthy publishers took as their mission comforting the afflicted and afflicting the comfortable. That certainly showed good business sense, and it boosted circulation. But journalistic conscience and social responsibility also began to stir. Thus the feeling among many journalists today that of course the media, like any business, must make a profit but that they have a very important watchdog mission, too.

In the early 1900s, mainstream newspapers and magazines so identified with the people that they preempted alternative publications espousing radical political or economic ideologies from gaining more than a foothold. So active were some in digging up social wrong that President Theodore Roosevelt labeled them "muckrakers." Socialists particularly tried to establish an alternative press but had only limited success in attracting reader and advertiser support. That is still the case today. The mainline broadcast and print media successfully serve America's huge middle class, and publications with extremist views, either left or right, have little success.

American journalism early in the century took many forms, from sober, thoughtful, responsible coverage of truly important global issues to light, frivolous, and often sensationalistic 1920s "jazz age" journalism.

The *New York Times* took an early position as the leading "serious" newspaper in 1896, when Adolph S. Ochs bought the *Times*, then a moribund near-failure. Ochs was a business genius who willingly plowed profits back into building a great newspaper. He thus established one of America's most important journalistic traditions, for today his descendants run it the same way. His grandson, the current publisher, Arthur Ochs Sulzberger, is lauded for willingly spending money to improve journalistic quality. A. M. Rosenthal, executive editor in the 1970s–1980s, said, "When in trouble, [a paper] can either put more water in the soup or more tomatoes. The *Times*'s publishing tradition has been to add tomatoes."[10]

Many newspapers recognized entertainment as a goal, too. Some frankly pandered to base instincts with titillating sex, crime, and gossip. Some of these were *tabloids* ("tabs"), with page sizes smaller than full-size or *broadsheet* papers.[11] (To this day, the term *tabloid* stands more for sensational journalism than for handy size.) Today, few daily papers intentionally seek demographically downscale readers with news selected to titillate and entertain to the exclusion of news that informs, educates, and uplifts. Conversely, television, needing huge audiences to satisfy national advertisers, emphasizes programming that entertains (and sometimes titillates).

Modern practitioners of American journalism use another media strategy developed in the early 1900s: exploitation of the amazing ability of some newspapers, magazines, and broadcast stations to produce profits unparalleled in other businesses. Achieving such profits requires avoiding the high cost of delivering high-quality news and information. One publisher who raised that strategy to an art was Frank A. Munsey, who at his death in 1925 owned many newspapers and magazines. Although he has rivals today, Munsey is regarded as a classic example of the profit-hungry owner who ignores social responsibilities. William Allen White, renowned publisher of the weekly *Emporia* (Kan.) *Gazette*, marked his passing in this way:

> Frank A. Munsey contributed to the journalism of his day the talent of a meatpacker, the morals of a money-changer and the manners of an undertaker. He and his kind have about succeeded in transforming a once-noble profession into an eight per cent security. May he rest in trust![12]

Weekly newspapers—then as now splendid barometers of rural and small-town life—flourished in the first half of the 20th century. Some achieved national significance through the insightful reporting and writing of their editors.

For magazines, the 1920s and 1930s witnessed exciting journalistic pioneering. Magazine entrepreneurs exploited reader interest in the great economic and political tumult of those years. *Time* was launched in 1923, *The New Yorker* in 1925, and *Newsweek* in 1933. *Life*, launched in 1936, took advantage of widening interest in photography and became a virtual national institution, with millions of readers snapping up copies every week.

Radio arrived in the 1920s, changing forever the media scene. For the first time—but not the last—an electronic medium challenged existing competitive arrangements in the battle for the public's time and the advertiser's dollar.

Radio's first offering was news—election results broadcast by KDKA, Pittsburgh, in 1920. Some newspapers, recognizing the threat, refused to publish radio program listings. The newspaper-dominated Associated Press for years declined to serve radio newsrooms.

However, radio station owners soon recognized the limitations of their medium in competing in news against newspapers and magazines. Quickly, radio shifted to entertainment as a principal mission. Comedy programs, soap operas, and adventure stories were packaged neatly with commercials in 30-minute segments (a format recognizable today in television). Sports programming and eyewitness broadcasting brought unprecedented drama to mass communication.

The impact on newspapers and magazines was enormous. First, radio attracted millions of dollars in advertising revenue the print media had previously enjoyed exclusively. Second, radio announcers skilled in live-event broadcasting and play-by-play coverage of sports events—base-

Edward R. Murrow of CBS broadcast live from London rooftops during World War II bombing raids and gave radio a unique eyewitness role in war reporting. Murrow later became a CBS TV star correspondent. *Wide World Photos.*

ball, football, boxing—forced the print media to change their news coverage methods. Sports-writers could no longer emphasize merely who won; that was broadcast yesterday. Rather, print reporters had to emphasize why and how a team won. Radio forced print to turn toward interpretive, analytical coverage, not simply spot news reporting.

It took years, but newspapers and magazines adjusted to the new competitor. They "moved over" in the marketplace and accepted the reality that radio was here to stay. This adaptability of the media to new competitors, new technology, and new ideas is a major characteristic of the American free enterprise system.

Radio enjoyed its role as the nation's principal form of mass entertainment for a very short time—only until television arrived in the 1950s as a commercially viable medium. That caused another shift in the marketplace. All media, including radio, had to move over to accommodate the newcomer.

Television was an immediate success. We'll discuss it in greater detail in subsequent chapters, but three factors are important to our survey of mainstreams in media development.

First, TV's sight-and-sound combination proved irresistible to millions—and to advertisers seeking to reach those millions. In just a few years, TV became the leading challenger to newspaper dominance in advertising. In 1988, some 22.0 percent of all ad dollars spent in the United States went to TV. Daily newspapers received 26.3 percent, radio, 6.5 percent.

Second, despite strong efforts in news in the 1960s and 1970s, TV, like radio, was lured by huge profits in offering entertainment and missed its chance to become dominant in news coverage. It left to print media the in-depth, interpretive coverage so necessary for understanding current events. Today, network news operations, including CBS News, once broadcast's best, are being cut back severely. Nevertheless, TV news is perceived by millions as being adequate.

Third, television had an enormous impact on the American way of life. To a degree not yet

Milton Berle—"Uncle Miltie" to millions—was an early star in television. This shot was taken during a 1951 TV show. *Wide World Photos.*

fully understood, television changed the nation. TV quickly won applause from supporters for its unrivaled ability to communicate visually and to reach millions of living rooms simultaneously. Critics accused it of causing everything from increased street violence to falling reading scores among "couch potato" children. Never in the history of mass communications has a medium had such an immediate and far-reaching impact.

For other communications industries, the 20th century has been a period of growth, too. Advertising became firmly established as a large, profitable, and influential industry. Public relations took its place in the communications mix. Some media assumed entirely new and powerful social and economic positions in our society: book publishing, movies, the direct mail (or direct response) industry, newsletters, alternative city and regional publications, and electronic home delivery have all become important.

Within each industry, enormous change mirrored fundamental changes in our society. Unions fought to prominence in the media, reflecting society's determination that working men and women deserved a better deal. Ensuring that women and minorities get a fair shake in hiring and promotions has since the 1970s been one of the media's most urgent challenges. But of all change, perhaps none is more striking than the rising debate over media ethics.

MEDIA ETHICS
IN THE 20TH CENTURY

Heated and widespread public debate over media ethics is a major characteristic of American journalism unique to the 20th century.

Early on, there was an ethical awakening among journalists. By the 1940s and 1950s, academics and others outside the media were discussing the media's role in society. Today, what journalists do and how they do it are matters of public debate. Everyone, it seems, has strong opinions on whether newspapers should investigate the sex lives of politicians or whether TV correspondents should shout questions at the president of the United States, the leader of the free Western world!

Two points here are essential. First, ethical debate is not new. Nearly 2,500 years ago, in Greece, Socrates discussed "good" and "justice" before he died in 399 B.C. A journalist today can find in the teachings of Socrates' student Plato, who died in 347 B.C., a sense of responsibility for adopting personal ethical principles and holding to them despite what other people may think. Ethics has been argued for centuries; only the form of the argument is different today.

Second, widening public concern over journalism ethics is recognition of the media's enormous influence in our society. The media are powerful, able to set agendas for national debate, able to change things. By entering the ethics debate, many Americans are in effect demanding that such power be used wisely and responsibly.

THE CRITICAL SERVICE

66 The critical service that the electronic and print media perform in focusing discussion is neither accidental nor the result of a grab for power. In a society as complex, diverse and divided as ours there must be some mechanism for sorting out issues and placing them in an order of priority so that citizens will be able to exercise properly their responsibility for choosing among competing political alternatives. The press has become our great sorting mechanism, bringing some order to the chaos of demands by special interests and the varied challenges to public decision at home and abroad. 99

Michael A. Weinstein,
Purdue University political scientist.[13]

Ethics is a code of conduct, a morality, a system of principles, values and rules of life that give guidance on what is right or wrong, good or bad.

Journalists who believe that their craft should be directed toward creating the greatest happiness for the greatest number of people—for promoting general well-being—subscribe, whether they realize it or not, to what ethicists call *utilitarianism*. That concept traces back to two Britons, David Hume (1711–1776) and John Stuart Mill (1806–1873). A sense of duty, of social responsibility, began developing in the early 1900s. At that stage, it was more a feeling of professionalism, from which grew the thought that press freedom carried with it responsibility to society. That gave birth, in 1922, to the American Society of Newspaper Editors (ASNE), still the premier organization for editors. Significantly, ASNE the very next year adopted the Canons of Journalism, an expression of newspaper ideals—public service, truthfulness, independence, accuracy.

The canons (supplanted in 1975 by ASNE's Statement of Principles) were an ethical breakthrough. They led to ethical statements by other journalistic organizations and development of ethics codes by many media companies.

THE JOURNALIST AND RESPONSIBILITY

❝ The right of a newspaper to attract and hold readers is restricted by nothing but considerations of public welfare. The use a newspaper makes of the share of public attention it gains serves to determine its sense of responsibility, which it shares with every member of its staff. A journalist who uses his power for any selfish or otherwise unworthy purpose is faithless to a high trust. ❞

American Society of Newspaper Editors' Canons of Journalism, 1923.

Ethics codes adopted by journalism organizations were idealistic and sweeping. None required adherence or mandated expulsion for infractions. This is the case today. Many journalists believe that codes could lead to the licensing of journalists. Professions such as medicine and law have mandatory codes, with expulsion from practice among punishments for infractions. In part because journalism has no mandatory codes, social commentators generally deny journalism the label "profession."

Changes in media economics and public attitudes had a major influence on ethical thought between 1920 and 1950. Radio and TV, along with thousands of magazines and newspapers, gave Americans alternative sources of information and entertainment and offered advertisers other means of reaching consumers. To hold what had become a better-educated, more discerning public, journalists had to meet more critical standards. Narrow, partisan journalism would not do. With costs rising, wider economic support was needed from advertisers. Thus it made good business sense to practice ethical, socially responsible journalism.

Then ethical ferment entered the public mainstream. In 1947, a call for a responsible press was issued by the Hutchins Commission, a panel of 10 university scholars and others chaired by Chancellor Robert W. Hutchins of the University of Chicago and financed principally by Henry R. Luce of Time Inc. The commission warned that press freedom was endangered. First, the com-

mission said, the "machinery of the press" (including newspapers, radio, movies, magazines, and books) was developing in a manner that decreased the number of persons who could express their views through the press. (Large media conglomerates were developing, and huge capital investments were necessary to get into daily newspaper ownership.) Second, the press stereotyped some groups in society and were not providing service "adequate to the needs of the society." Third, the press sometimes engaged in practices condemned by society that, if continued, would lead to regulation of the press.

A journalism professor, Theodore Peterson, wrote in 1956 of need for social responsibility in the press. Many editors and publishers objected, but the concept that responsibility is attached to press rights and freedoms became part of the journalistic credo in America.[14]

It wasn't until the 1950s that "people's right to know" became popularly accepted. General Manager Kent Cooper of the Associated Press, a leading crusader against barriers to free flow of information, helped popularize the concept. This boosted the idea that the media Fourth Estate is instrumental in determining how the country is governed.[15] (Some broadcasters prefer to call the electronic media the Fifth Estate.)

In its early years, radio was preoccupied with meeting federal regulations governing content and conduct of broadcasting. Radio formed the National Association of Broadcasters (NAB), a voluntary-membership trade organization, in 1923. In 1929 NAB established its first code, which dealt more with advertising and programming standards than news ethics. Not until 1958 did NAB strongly urge members to pledge code adherence (of stations then on the air, 14 percent signed the pledge). NAB adopted a TV code in 1952, but it was virtually meaningless until 1961, when NAB established a code authority. By 1974, just 57 percent of stations were NAB members; only 41 percent subscribed to the codes.

Many radio and TV executives believed that federal regulation was sufficient, that there was no need to develop a consensus within the industry or in individual stations on questions of ethics. Thus federal regulation (along with broadcast's entertainment and profit orientation) may have blunted independent development of ethical thinking by some broadcasters. In 1982, a federal court held that NAB's code dealing with length and number of commercials violated the Sherman Anti-Trust Act; NAB suspended the entire code. No industrywide codes on conduct of stations or networks are currently in place. However, some organizations, such as the Radio and Television News Directors Association, have codes for individual broadcast journalists.

For all media, the early 1980s brought a new concern: the "credibility gap." Public disenchantment with what the media were doing and how they did it was growing. Surveys showed falling confidence in the media, suspicion that the news was biased. Readers and viewers said that too much bad news was hitting front pages and TV screens (although surveys also showed that bad news was read and viewed closely). A. M. Rosenthal, by then retired as executive editor, wrote in a 1988 *New York Times* column:

> Most of the important news stories journalists deal with are sad or dreary. People are killed, hijacked, swindled. Nations go to war, or spend their energies and fortunes preparing for it. Earthquakes, explosions, plagues. Everybody is always saying something nasty about somebody else. That's the way things are in the world—or that is how it comes out by the time we are finished slicing it up into words or pictures.[16]

Three areas of ethics are of major concern:

Ethics in News For individual journalists, the challenge is to develop a personal code of ethics—a professional conscience—covering, simply, what they will and will not do in pursuit of news. Reporting is a tough business. It can lead to harshly adversarial attitudes among reporters and invasion of the privacy of people in the news. For media companies, a basic question is whether to lay down strict corporate codes of ethics governing staff conduct as just another management guideline for employees. Opponents say that put-

ting such a complex subject on paper is impossible to do with any precision—and, further, that codes could lead to self-censorship or government licensing of journalists.

Ethics in Business Do corporations have social responsibility? Some commentators say no, that a corporation's responsibility is to make a profit, offer products or services that meet public needs, treat employees fairly, and play by the rules governing business in America. Others say that corporations do have social responsibility to readers, viewers, listeners, community, and society, as well as shareholders. Luckily, our media history is filled with examples of media companies proceeding in the public interest even to their own disadvantage. But there also are cases of the media caving in to advertiser or government pressure or otherwise defaulting on their responsibility for accurate and, insofar as possible, objective reporting.

Ethics in the Media and Other Institutions in Society The media claim—and have been given—special status as watchdogs of other institutions in society. But who watches the watchdog? Obviously, forcing the media to meet standards established by outside groups, government or private, would end a free press. But many media critics are uneasy at the press's wielding its enormous power largely without cross-checks or controls from any other balancing institution in society. Many media executives respond that if the media wander astray, people can stop buying newspapers and magazines or watching TV.

Still, critics continually seek safeguards in the law. Thus the evolution of media law in America is crucially important to the role newspapers, magazines, radio, and TV play in our society.

THE MEDIA AND THE LAW

Serious legal threats to First Amendment guarantees and the right to publish without prior restraint reared up in World War I during a "red scare" over socialism, at the time menacing capitalism in Europe. The Espionage Act of 1917 and the Sedition Act of 1918 were used to close some socialist and German-language publications espousing unpopular causes. A censorship board was given power over news transmissions out of the United States, and the Committee on Public Information (called the Creel Committee) handled war information (and propaganda) and created voluntary censorship codes. The American press, caught up in overwhelming public support of the war, cooperated.

After the war, the U.S. Supreme Court injected into the legal mainstream two important tenets: only in extreme national emergency ("clear and present danger") should prior restraint be allowed, and First Amendment protection should be applied at the state level. The latter came in a Court ruling in 1931, in *Near* v. *Minnesota*, that a state "gag law" was unconstitutional. The publication involved, *Saturday Press*, was a scandal sheet that few ethical journalists would support today, but its challenge of prior restraint is of fundamental importance in our media law.

A number of other legal sectors similarly crucial:

Defamation This is communication that subjects a person to contempt, ridicule, or hatred; it is falsehood, printed ("libel") or spoken ("slander"), that harms the reputation of an individual or corporation, lowers persons in the esteem of their fellows, causes them to be shunned, or injures them in business or their calling. Enormously expensive libel suits and judgments running into millions of dollars have a chilling effect on aggressive investigative reporting. No editor can proceed on a sensitive story without wondering if it will lead to a bankrupting libel case. Provable truth is the primary defense in a libel case.

Freedom of Information Not until 1967, when President Lyndon B. Johnson signed the Freedom of Information Act, did U.S. citizens gain the right to see, within limits, what is in the files of federal agencies. The act adds a substantial right of access to the First Amendment rights of free speech and free press. Each year, federal agencies receive 250,000 to 300,000 requests for release of information under FOI. Many government officials attempt to withhold information for national security or other reasons. The act gives reporters leverage in prying it loose.

Free Press versus Fair Trial The First Amendment guarantees a free press; the Sixth guarantees that a criminal defendant will receive a speedy, public trial by impartial juries; the Fourteenth guarantees due process under the law for every citizen. Do they conflict? Does media coverage prejudice juries and make a fair trial impossible? When judges close trials to the press, the U.S. Supreme Court tends to strike down such restraints and give preferred status to the First Amendment. But principled editors and jurists are careful to balance the public's right to know against a defendant's right to a fair trial.

Regulatory Law Because they use limited public resources (the airwaves), radio and television are regulated by the Federal Communications Commission. A fundamental question is whether the FCC should be limited to ensuring orderly use of the airwaves or should also control news, entertainment, and advertising content in the "public interest." Many critics argue for control of obscenity. But trends are toward deregulation of federal control over both ownership and management of broadcasting. Many broadcasters argue that only marketplace forces should regulate the electronic media and that electronic news, entertainment, and advertising should have the full First Amendment freedoms now extended to the print press.

Other legal activity includes the Equal Employment Opportunity Commission, established in 1964 to end discrimination in hiring and employment. The media are generally far behind society's expectations in employing women and minorities. Under the Occupational Safety and Health Act of 1970, federal inspectors check the

The trial of Marine Lieutenant Colonel Oliver North in the Nicaraguan *contras* scandal was one of the most heavily covered in recent media history. Do the media's rights under the First Amendment conflict with a defendant's right to a fair trial? *Wide World Photos.*

safety of working conditions in newspapers and broadcast stations. Antitrust laws, designed to protect free competition in business, are important in this age of expanding media conglomerates. The Federal Trade Commission, established in 1914, monitors, among other things, deceptive advertising and business practices violating consumer interests.

LOOKING AHEAD: THE THEORETICAL CONTEXT

Little is certain about the American mass communications system of the future except that what you see today is not what you will get tomorrow. Great change is under way. Nevertheless, some definable directions and forms are taking shape.

The theory of social responsibility, for example, will surely take on new and, for the media, perhaps threatening edges. Societal attitudes toward the media are increasingly negative and questioning. Some journalists say that public dis-

trust is at an all-time high. Others argue that the credibility gap is nothing new, that the media have had an up-and-down love affair with the public for generations, and that things will improve if journalists just get on with their job of reporting the news.

Throughout the 1980s, pollsters revealed warning signs:

◆ One-fifth of the adults polled deeply distrust the media, and three-fourths have "problems" with media credibility. Three-fourths say that reporters only want a good story and don't care if they hurt people to get one. One-sixth say the media are biased, invade people's privacy, sensationalize news, and emphasize bad news too often.

◆ Among U.S. adults, 79 percent approve of investigative reporting, but many disapprove of how some journalists go about it (65 percent disapprove of reporters' disguising their identity, 58 percent disapprove of using hidden cameras and microphones, 56 percent disapprove of paying informers, and 52 percent disapprove of quoting unnamed sources).

◆ Among institutions in which Americans have confidence, media ranked low. ▶ 2

For media companies, public distrust could threaten future profits. If readers distrust newspapers and viewers doubt TV's credibility, they will turn away. So most major media organizations are sensitive to what news, entertainment, and advertising the public wants. Rare is the publishers' conference without seminars on how to establish better links with readers; television goes to elaborate, expensive lengths to find out who watches which programs and why.

For individual journalists, a major challenge is to produce high-quality and responsible news coverage on issues crucial to readers and viewers. A news medium that is considered nice to have but not crucial to daily life will not survive. Thoughtful interpretation and commentary are needed on editorial pages; TV journalists must balance silly game shows and phony "docudramas" with solid, reliable news reports on compelling issues of our day.

Some challenges journalists face can be clarified if we relate them to separate elements in the communications process. Scholars generally agree that there are eight such elements.

1 A *source* initiates transmission of a thought to others. In interpersonal communication, such as a chat with a friend, you (the source) often have the advantage of knowing what thought will be relevant to your friend. In mass communication, however, your thought must be relevant to millions of readers or viewers who are unknown to you. That means a reporter (the source) must make great effort to understand as well as possible the audience's news needs and wants, or communication will fail. In mass communication, the source is an organization involving many people, so there is an institutional need to understand the receivers (the audiences). Thus millions of dollars are spent for research that helps reporters and editors to tune in on audience thinking.

2 Next, the source *encodes* the thought,

2 ▶ The Media's Image Problem[17]

Confidence in Institutions

Church, organized religion	62%
Military	53
Banks, banking	51
U.S. Supreme Court	42
Public schools	39
Newspapers	**38**
Congress	28
Big business	28
Organized labor	26
TV	**25**

Gallup has found substantial differences in public attitudes toward the various media:

Most Believable News Medium

Television	51%
Newspapers	22
Magazines	9
Radio	8
Undecided	10

Most Believable Advertising Medium

Newspapers	42%
TV	26
Magazines	11
Radio	11
Direct mail	5
All about equal	2
No opinion	3

which in print journalism means writing and editing and in TV means combining sight and sound to shape a newscast. The challenge is to ensure that reporters encode with precision and clarity and that editors and others involved in encoding eliminate sloppy writing that inhibits communication. TV news encoded in irrelevant video coverage simply to show motion won't meet standards of precision and clarity. So journalists must place news in a context of clear, understandable commentary and background. That includes not only reporting who, what, where, when, and how but also explaining why it is important. Those involved in the encoding chain often are called "gatekeepers" because they decide how—or if—a news story will reach the public. Their professionalism and sense of ethical responsibility are crucial to effective, truthful mass communication.

3, 4 Newspapers, magazines, and TV programs are *messages*; sight and sound *channels* carry messages to your eyes and ears (those perfumed advertising inserts in magazines are attempts to reach another channel, your nose). In print media parlance, message and channel involve "packaging"—creating newspapers and magazines in "reader-friendly" formats that assist the communication process. For print journalists, this is an exciting stage in the communication process. Color photos and easy-to-understand charts (of the *USA Today* type) are transforming many newspapers and magazines. For TV journalists, the challenge is to ensure that coverage of news crucial to viewers' daily lives doesn't get lost in the obsession with the medium's enormous video and graphic strengths.

Contrasted with one-on-one interpersonal communication, mass communication is of course very public. It's a sobering thought: When a writer at CBS goofs, Dan Rather can mislead millions of viewers coast to coast. A mistake at the *New York Times* can be front-paged for an international audience.

5, 6 The fifth and sixth elements in the process are *receiver* and *decoding*—in mass communication, readers and viewers who interpret messages and "translate" them into their own terms. Herein lie huge problems and frustrations for journalists. Receivers can number in the millions, often sharing little in common. They are separated from the source (the reporter) in both space and time. They are on the other side of town—or the world. A TV reporter who does a

4 P.M. "standup" on the White House lawn might not reach viewers until an 11 P.M. newscast; a Washington newspaper correspondent who files an afternoon dispatch doesn't gain access to morning readers until 6 to 8 A.M. the next day. In the interim, a great deal can change in the news environment. Also, readers and viewers are self-selecting. They, not journalists, decide when (or if) they will begin the decoding process by reading or watching the news. Enticing them into the process regularly is a major problem for the media. When decoding does begin, readers and viewers do so in accordance with their own attitudes, cultural backgrounds, and prejudices. Responding to charges that the press is biased, Warren Phillips, publisher of the *Wall Street Journal*, commented, "Could it be that bias sometimes is in the eye of the beholder? Do we sometimes have slanted readers?"[18] The answer, of course, is yes. Dealing with that reality is a major challenge for journalists.

7, 8 The final elements in the communication process are *noise* (everything interfering with the process) and *feedback* (negative or positive signals from the receiver on whether the message is understood). To control noise while talking to a friend, you ask the friend to turn off the radio or put down a book and concentrate on decoding your message. Then you ask, "Understand?" A quick nod or shake of the head gives you immediate feedback. But pity the journalist who fights constant "noise" bombarding receivers from all sides, distracting them from the message. And, of course, feedback doesn't arrive for days or weeks—until letters to the editor arrive or, perhaps, until circulation figures or program ratings come in. Accurate, timely feedback is almost never available in journalism. In the extreme, a foreign correspondent can be out of direct touch with readers for months. Feedback is limited to cables from an editor or newspaper clippings weeks late in arriving from the United States—and they indicate only whether editors, not readers, are getting the message. Feedback informs the reporter of decoding problems read-

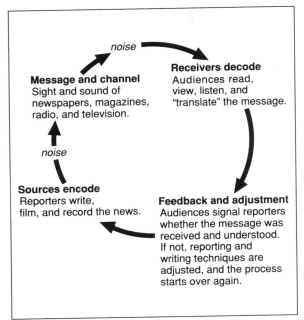

Figure 2.1. Journalism and the Communication Process.

ers and viewers have. Responsible journalists adjust their reporting and writing accordingly.

In Figure 2.1, theory is applied to the daily task of a reporter trying to fight through noise (interference) to reach viewers, listeners, or readers with a message (the news) that will be understood.

However, effective communication often is impaired by many other factors. Authoritarian regimes sometimes use thugs or mobs to intimidate journalists. Formal censorship restrains what is published or transmitted abroad. In many communist countries, restricted access to news sources or travel limitations hamstring reporters. Governments sometimes exert economic pressure by manipulating newsprint supplies and prices. Advertisers attempt to influence coverage or editorial policies by threatening to withdraw their ads. Special-interest groups often attempt to influence news coverage by arranging boycotts by readers, viewers, or advertisers. Society itself exerts pressure on the media by setting legal, eth-

ical, and moral standards. And sometimes the media exercise self-censorship by pulling their punches for reasons as varied as patriotism or economic self-interest.

☆ SUMMARY

The U.S. Constitution does not confer Fourth Estate or watchdog status on the media and never mentions ''people's right to know.'' Media influence flows from the First Amendment's guarantee of a free press and subsequent court rulings plus historical and societal forces outside of the law.

Battles for a free press arrived in America with early colonists. They continue to this day.

Early American journalists were printers and political activists, not reporters. After the Revolution, society divided along economic and political lines, and so did newspapers. ''Objective'' reporting didn't develop until much later.

Late in the 1700s came freedom to criticize government. That marked the end of authoritarianism, and launched libertarianism, the concept that the people can recognize truth if the press can disseminate news freely.

In the 1800s, the press began gaining the right of access to official information. Economic support from advertisers lessened reliance on special-interest financing.

New technology produced high-speed presses and low-cost newsprint, permitting mass distribution of newspapers priced at a penny. Sensationalistic news aimed at entertaining more than informing characterized some papers of the period.

Invention of the telegraph in 1844 opened new horizons to reporters. Hundreds followed Civil War armies, developing reporting and writing styles recognizably in use today.

By 1900, more than 1,900 dailies with 15 million circulation were published. Weeklies numbered over 12,000; magazines, more than 3,500.

New competitors, first radio, then TV, changed the media mix forever. Advertising blossomed in the 20th century into a profitable, influential industry, as did public relations. Of all developments in the new century, none was more striking than the awakening of professionalism and ethical thought among journalists. Today, media ethics is a matter of full public debate.

The next generation of journalists will have to deal with the so-called credibility gap and rising public distrust of some things reporters do.

☆ RECOMMENDED READING

A superb history of the American media is Michael Emery and Edwin Emery, *The Press and America: An Interpretive History of the Mass Media* (Englewood Cliffs, N.J.: Prentice Hall, 1988). An insightful view of magazine development appears in Theodore Peterson's *Magazines in the Twentieth Century* (Urbana: University of Illinois Press, 1964). For broadcast history, note Lawrence Lichty and Malachi Topping, *American Broadcasting: A Sourcebook on the History of Radio and Television* (New York: Hastings House, 1975).

On ethics, expanded views appear in Conrad Fink, *Media Ethics: In the Newsroom and Beyond* (New York: McGraw-Hill, 1988). Also note H. Eugene Goodwin, *Groping for Ethics in Journalism* (Ames: Iowa State University Press, 1983). Media law is covered superbly in Kent Middleton and William Chamberlain, *Law of Public Communication* (White Plains, N.Y.: Longman, 1987).

Media business strategies are explored in Conrad Fink, *Strategic Newspaper Management* (New York: Random House, 1988). Also note John M. Lavine and Daniel B. Wackman, *Managing Media Organizations* (White Plains, N.Y.: Longman, 1988) and Barry L. Sherman, *Telecommunications Management: The Broadcast and Cable Industries* (New York: McGraw-Hill, 1987).

Communications theory is handled well by Ray Eldon Hiebert, Donald F. Ungurait, and Thomas W. Bohn in *Mass Media IV* (White Plains, N.Y.: Longman, 1985) and Joseph R. Dominick in *The Dynamics of Mass Communication* (New York: Random House, 1987).

The American Media Today

T he American media approach the 21st century with economic strength and societal influence that would have stunned Hearst, Pulitzer, and other press moguls of yesteryear. In the forefront are giant communications conglomerates that in only the past decade or two have expanded nationwide in both print and broadcast under the driving empire building of a new, wealthy American elite—professional media managers.

How strong and how influential are they?

◆ America's leading 100 media companies today enjoy total sales in excess of $58 billion annually; their parent firms take in $47 billion more from other businesses.[1]

◆ Of media revenue, $36.9 billion is collected by just the 20 leading conglomerates; 17 have annual revenue over $1 billion each.

◆ The media leaders are expanding into all information, advertising, and entertainment industries. About 36 percent of their revenue comes from newspapers, 14 percent from magazines, 25 percent from broadcast, 14 percent from cable, and the rest from other media sources, including book publishing, films, and private subscriber information services.

◆ In both print and broadcast, conglomerates are sweeping up privately owned companies. Those colorful editors and publishers who worked— *lived*—in community journalism are mostly memories. Groups with headquarters in New York, Miami, Chicago, Los Angeles, and other cities own 76 percent of all daily papers (plus many weeklies) and account for 83 percent of all daily circulation (see Figure 3.1).

And it all is happening very quickly:

◆ Not until the 1950s did television become a commercially viable medium. Yet its annual advertising revenues today exceed $22 billion, and its influence on American lifestyles is pervasive. Two TV-oriented companies, Capital Cities/ABC and CBS, are among America's largest media conglomerates.

◆ As recently as 1946, total newspaper advertising for an entire year was $1.1 billion. Today, the *Los Angeles Times alone* takes in $1 billion

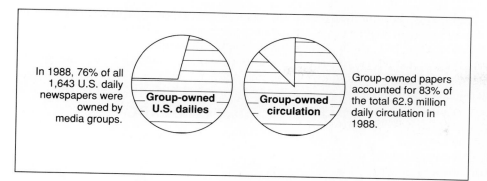

In 1988, 76% of all 1,643 U.S. daily newspapers were owned by media groups.

Group-owned U.S. dailies

Group-owned circulation

Group-owned papers accounted for 83% of the total 62.9 million daily circulation in 1988.

Figure 3.1. GROUP DOMINATION OF NEWSPAPER OWNERSHIP. *Sources: American Newspaper Publishers Association; John Morton, Lynch, Jones & Ryan, Washington, D.C.*

annually. Total newspaper advertising is over $31 billion; all-media advertising, $118 billion.

◆ Only in 1967 did Gannett Co. go public, mapping the growth route for other conglomerates by demonstrating that a media company can sell shares to raise capital for use in acquiring newspapers. Today, Gannett is a $3.3 billion corporation that owns nearly 90 newspapers.

These huge conglomerates have an enormous impact on society with their multiple influences in news, opinion, entertainment, and advertising. Clearly, we have compelling reasons to look, here in Chapter 3, at conglomerates and the men and women who run them.

THE BIG PLAYERS: AMERICA'S MEDIA CONGLOMERATES

No matter where you live in America or what are your reading, viewing, or listening habits, you need not go far to see a media conglomerate in action. One probably operates in or near your hometown.

America is a rich market for media companies—a solid launching pad for international expansion—and conglomerates are searching throughout the country for profitable newspapers and magazines, radio and TV operations, and other communications businesses. They search in small towns and large cities alike.

Giant $4.1 billion Capital Cities/ABC publishes the 43,000-circulation *News-Democrat* in little Belleville, Illinois, and the huge *Star* and *Times*, 494,000 combined circulation, in Kansas City, Missouri. If you watch KGO-TV in San

Francisco or listen to KQRS-AM/FM in Minneapolis, you are tuned to Capital Cities/ABC.

CBS is much more than Dan Rather each evening and "60 Minutes" on Sundays. It also owns many local broadcast stations—among them, WBBM-TV in Chicago, WCAU-TV in Philadelphia, and, in radio, KTXQ-FM in Dallas–Fort Worth and WYNF-FM in Tampa–St. Petersburg.

Time Inc. for years reached readers and cable viewers in widespread areas with *Time, Life, People, Sports Illustrated, Progressive Farmer, Southern Living*, and many other magazines. It owned Book-of-the-Month Club, huge cable TV systems, and, among others, the Cinemax and Home Box Office cable services. In 1989, Time moved strongly into filmmaking and other entertainment by merging with Warner Communications.

John Morton, a leading newspaper analyst,

calculates that of 143 newspaper groups he tracks, 62 have a total daily circulation of 50,000 or less (out of nearly 63 million total U.S. daily circulation). An additional 29 have just 50,000 to 150,000. Thus many "groups" are really small-town companies that own just two or three papers.[2] In broadcast, many groups are Mom and Pop operations, run by husband and wife teams that own just a couple of radio stations.[3]

But the largest conglomerates have the most impact on American journalism. Let's look for clues to their management style and the career opportunities they offer. If a conglomerate draws most of its revenue from newspapers, the company will have newspaper-oriented executives in top positions. A company that draws most from television probably won't be a heavy print player in the near future. Draw conclusions about the companies and careers they offer in our review of the industry's 15 leaders. (Revenue is for 1988, in millions of dollars, and before the merger of Time and Warner.) ▶ 1

1. Capital Cities/ABC

Media Revenue

Broadcast	3,508.5
Newspapers	468.9
Magazines	370.0

This company became the nation's largest media firm overnight in 1986 when Capital Cities acquired ABC. Cap Cities over the years had built holdings in radio, television, magazines, and

---

◢1▶ The Basic Documents

Companies that sell shares to the public must, by law, publish specific information about their operations. For students of the media, two documents offer particularly valuable information: the annual report and Form 10-K.

Annual Report

Most companies produce annual reports to state corporate goals, describe their business, and list operating centers and subsidiaries. Most feature highly detailed financial results for the past year and over a period of perhaps 10 years. Senior executives and directors are often profiled. The Securities and Exchange Commission (SEC), the federal agency charged with ensuring that publicly owned companies are fair in revealing information about their affairs to investors, insists that annual reports cite bad as well as good news to give investors a true picture of the company's position. But some reports emphasize successes more than failures. To obtain an annual report, contact the corporate secretary of any publicly owned company (companies also issue quarterly reports that are more timely, of course, but contain less information).

Form 10-K

Form 10-K is issued through the SEC. It must describe ownership, financial matters, competitive situation, and other factors that might affect the company's fortunes—and its share price. For copies, contact the Securities and Exchange Commission, Washington, DC 20549.

Other Documents

Another document that can be revealing about a publicly owned company is the notice of the annual meeting of shareholders. It is mailed to stockholders before the annual meeting and discusses issues to be voted on. If you want to find out how much media moguls are paid and how much stock they hold, obtain a copy of this document!

For nonaccountants who want to analyze financial figures in annual reports and on 10-K forms, the brokerage firm Merrill Lynch, Pierce, Fenner & Smith Inc. offers excellent guidance in *How to Read a Financial Report*, 5th ed., available through its headquarters, P.O. Box 520, Church Street Station, New York, NY 10008.

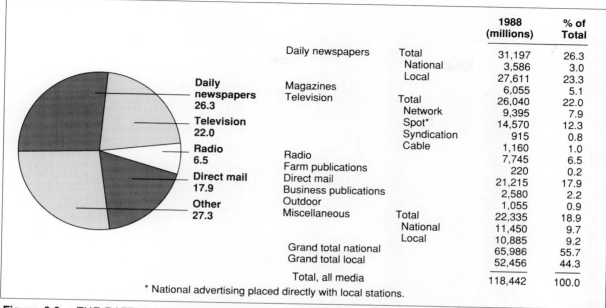

		1988 (millions)	% of Total
Daily newspapers	Total	31,197	26.3
	National	3,586	3.0
	Local	27,611	23.3
Magazines		6,055	5.1
Television	Total	26,040	22.0
	Network	9,395	7.9
	Spot*	14,570	12.3
	Syndication	915	0.8
	Cable	1,160	1.0
Radio		7,745	6.5
Farm publications		220	0.2
Direct mail		21,215	17.9
Business publications		2,580	2.2
Outdoor		1,055	0.9
Miscellaneous	Total	22,335	18.9
	National	11,450	9.7
	Local	10,885	9.2
Grand total national		65,986	55.7
Grand total local		52,456	44.3
Total, all media		118,442	100.0

Pie chart labels: Daily newspapers 26.3; Television 22.0; Radio 6.5; Direct mail 17.9; Other 27.3

* National advertising placed directly with local stations.

Figure 3.2. THE BATTLE FOR AD DOLLARS: MEDIA SHARES OF ADVERTISING EXPENDITURES, 1988. *Sources: McCann-Erickson; Newspaper Advertising Bureau; American Newspaper Publishers Association.*

newspapers as a highly profitable, if not journalistically distinguished, company. Acquiring ABC offered the opportunity to become number one, and Cap Cities executives leaped at it. Today, ABC generates nearly half of the company's revenues.

But Cap Cities also acquired problems with ABC. Cable television is eroding prime-time network viewing, and advertisers are following viewers to other media (see Figure 3.2). Network costs are soaring, and profits are down.

Capital Cities/ABC performs strongly with diversified interests around the country that give it corporate "balance"—revenue in various media sectors outside ABC. They include radio, TV, many specialized magazines (*Modern Photography, High Fidelity, Skin & Allergy News*), and newspapers in 11 states. Like many media firms, Capital Cities/ABC is strongly invested in cable. It owns or has major holdings in ESPN, the cable sports network, and the Arts & Entertainment network.

2. Time Inc.

Media Revenue

Cable	1,934.0
Magazines	1,752.0

As those 1988 revenue figures illustrate, media conglomerates diversify into different news and entertainment fields to reduce risk from a downturn in any single sector. Time's merger with Warner Communications in 1989 created the world's largest media firm.

In the early days, Time's basic strengths were *Time* and *Life* magazines. But the cost of distributing millions of copies of national magazines became extremely high. Publishers had to raise ad rates to heights unacceptable to advertisers. And starting in the 1950s, television could deliver larger national audiences to advertisers at lower costs per viewer. In 1972, that forced Time Inc. to kill *Life* as a weekly (it now appears monthly), and it currently threatens *Time* (and

Like many American conglomerates, Time Warner is diversifying globally, producing magazines in Japanese, or in English for areas of Asia where that is the language of international business. *Courtesy Time Warner.*

other national newsmagazines, such as *Newsweek*).

Responding to new cost and competitive realities, Time Warner is now following two courses:

1 It is diversifying into nonmagazine areas. In cable and video, it is a major player with millions of subscribers.

2 In magazines, Time Warner is experimenting with new types of publications and killing off those that don't do well. One, *Picture Week*, folded in 1986 after just 15 months. Time Warner is moving away from broad-based national magazines and toward publications narrowly focused on special news interests—*Money, Sports Illustrated, Fortune*, and the like.

The price tag on diversifying and staying in the media big leagues is high. In 1986, Time wanted Scott Foresman Co., an educational book publisher, and had to pay $520 million for it.

3. General Electric Co.

Media Revenue

Broadcast   3,638.0

As the media became more influential, a question often discussed was what would happen if a major mass communications company fell into the hands of, say, a manufacturing firm with little experience in international news or high-quality entertainment. GE will answer that question in the next few years.

Overnight, in June 1986, GE—maker of aircraft engines and kitchen appliances, minor player in broadcast—became one of the nation's largest media conglomerates. In a $6.4 billion deal, GE acquired RCA, parent of the National Broadcasting Co.

GE's first move at NBC was predictable. It sent in a GE executive, Robert Wright, as president to make NBC more "efficient." Within months, Wright announced personnel reductions to cut costs. In 1987, profits soared.

NBC's television network, with 207 affiliated stations, is strongly competitive in news ("Nightly News with Tom Brokaw" has been a winner) and entertainment ("The Cosby Show" and "Today" are two national favorites). But GE's long-term plans for network operations are unclear.

4. Gannett Co.

Media Revenue

Newspapers	2,549.3
Broadcast	390.5
Outdoor, other	226.5

Among critics and admirers alike, no media conglomerate is more discussed than Gannett. Since the late 1960s, it has been a leader in profitable media diversification.

Explosive growth began in 1967, when Gannett went public, offering 500,000 shares of stock to investors. The company then owned 28 small newspapers with annual revenue of $186 million. It used that relatively small base to acquire small papers in cities without direct daily newspaper competition. It was a formula for huge profits that pushed the company to its giant size today.

Gannett crossed many media frontiers in the 1980s. It diversified for the first time into big-city papers (*Des Moines Register, Detroit News, Louisville Courier-Journal*) and into broadcasting, entertainment programming, and outdoor advertising. Its *USA Today*, launched in 1982, entered the national newspaper competition and revolutionized the use of color and graphics. (It also introduced a short, snappy writing style criticized by some as shallow.)

Gannett led the media in hiring and promoting women and minorities. Many Gannett executives are women and minorities.

For the current chief executive officer, John Curley, major problems are ahead. *USA Today*, from day one a hit with millions of readers, never gained sufficient advertiser support. It has lost hundreds of millions of dollars. Advertisers want demographically attractive readers with high incomes and educational levels, and *USA Today* readers are less attractive than those of the *New York Times* and the *Wall Street Journal*. *USA Today* also delivers fewer readers than the many millions of viewers delivered by national television.

Gannett rewarded its stockholders with new gains every year after going public. Rapid acquisition of new properties and consistently increased profits and dividends boosted the market value of the stockholders' investment. But the company still feels pressure from the "rising tide of shareholder expectations" of bigger rewards. Executives of top media firms are under great pressure to perform well or lose their jobs. (But rewards for living with that pressure can be tremendous.) ▶ 2

5. CBS Inc.

Media Revenue

Broadcast	2,776.8

CBS has been the victim of two major developments certain to influence other American media in the years ahead: takeover mania and the fundamental readjustment of competition in the broadcast industry.

Takeover mania—the often frenetic efforts by some companies to acquire others—hit CBS in the mid-1980s. Firms unwelcomed by CBS management ("hostile" raiders, in Wall Street parlance) tried to gain control by buying stock and winning over CBS directors and managers. Enormous costs of defending against takeover, plus a turndown in business, left CBS $1 billion in debt.

At the same time, new competition confronted CBS (and other networks) with declining audiences and increasing costs—a recipe for plummeting profits. Cable TV, home videos, and other electronic entertainment ate into CBS's financial foundations.

All this gave Laurence A. Tisch, chairman

2 ▶ The Big Players and Their Compensation, 1987

In an analysis of "corporate America's most powerful people" in 1987, *Forbes* magazine listed 15 executives of print and broadcast conglomerates. Each executive's total compensation for the year includes salary, bonus, stock gains, other fees, and commissions.

Company	Sales (millions of dollars)	Chief Executive Education (Professional Background)	Compensation
Affiliated Publications	490	William O. Taylor Harvard '54 (finance)	2,230,000
Capital Cities/ABC	4,400	Thomas Murphy Cornell '45 Harvard MBA '49 (administration)	801,000
CBS	2,762	Laurence Tisch NYU '42 Penn MA '43 (finance)	1,181,000
Dow Jones	1,314	Warren Phillips CUNY Queens '47 (journalism)	1,101,000
Gannett	3,079	John Curley Dickinson '60 Columbia MS '63 (journalism)	1,345,000
Knight-Ridder	2,073	James Batten Davidson '57 Princeton MPA '62 (journalism)	1,059,000

of Loews Corp., a firm with holdings in insurance, tobacco, and other businesses, an opening to gain control of CBS. He sold off a CBS TV station and all publishing operations and then slashed costs at CBS itself. Hundreds of employees were cut from the company's famed news division.

Another problem is that many television stations across the country are expanding their own local news operations and lessening dependence on network coverage. The long-term implications of that will almost certainly be a severe weakening, perhaps even the disappearance, of the high-quality international news coverage that CBS and other networks began building during radio's heyday prior to World War II.

All major publicly owned media firms are erecting defenses (often at high cost) against hostile takeovers. And those heavily invested in network-affiliated broadcasting are diversifying into media activities less vulnerable to competition and changing economics.

Company	Sales (millions of dollars)	Chief Executive Education (Professional Background)	Compensation
Lin Broadcasting	237	Donald Pels Penn '48 NYU JD '53 (administration)	17,400,000
McGraw-Hill	1,751	Joseph Dionne Hofstra '55 Columbia EdD '65 (operations)	888,000
Media General	715	James Evans Purdue '42 (administration)	510,000
New York Times Co.	1,690	A. O. Sulzberger Columbia '51 (journalism)	1,240,000
News Corp. Ltd.	3,529	Rupert Murdoch Oxford MA '53 (journalism)	1,538,000
Time Inc.	4,193	J. Richard Munro Colgate '57 (operations)	7,413,000
Times Mirror Corp.	3,080	Robert Erburu USC '52 Harvard JD '55 (legal)	1,302,000
Tribune Co.	2,160	Stanton Cook Northwestern '49 (engineering)	3,459,000
Washington Post Co.	1,315	Katharine Graham Chicago '38 (administration)	1,176,000

6. Times Mirror Co.

Media Revenue

Newspapers	1,997.7
Magazines	298.5
Cable	282.7
Broadcast	99.0

Times Mirror, a communications empire that grew out of the *Los Angeles Times*, is remarkable on several counts. First, company executives publicly commit to excellence in both the journalistic and business sectors (the *Times* and the company's *Newsday* on Long Island are among the nation's best papers). Times Mirror executives say that a communications company will prosper financially only if it delivers journalism and service to readers or viewers, advertisers, and the communities where it operates "with the highest standards of accuracy, fairness, quality and timeliness."[4] This corporate approach is not universally accepted by media conglomerates.

Second, the company shows uncommon willingness to restructure itself, shedding newspapers and other properties that don't produce journalistic and business excellence. Times Mirror sold its *Dallas Times Herald* and *Denver Post* because it could not overcome two strong competitors, the *Dallas Morning News* and, in Denver, the *Rocky Mountain News*.[5] Altogether, Times Mirror sold off $1 billion in assets in a three-year restructuring, then acquired nearly that much in new properties, including the *Baltimore Sun* and several television stations and cable systems. The company is also strong in magazine and specialized publishing.

7. Advance Publications

Media Revenue

Newspapers	1,681.1
Magazines	745.0
Cable	229.4

Family-owned private media companies sell shares to outside investors usually for two reasons: (1) to raise money for estate taxes levied by the Internal Revenue Service when the company passes to surviving heirs or (2) to raise capital for owners or improve the company and acquire new properties. The Newhouse family has had to pay whopping estate taxes, and it raises money all the time, but their Advance Publications, the nation's seventh-largest media firm, remains very private.

Two brothers, Donald and S. I. Newhouse, Jr., sons of founder Samuel I. Newhouse, control the company and its estimated $2.2 billion in annual revenue (financial records are not published like those of publicly owned companies).

The Newhouses are masterful in diversifying outside their roots–newspapers (*Cleveland Plain Dealer, Newark* [N.J.] *Star-Ledger, Portland Oregonian*, and others). The company's Conde Nast Publications publishes some of the nation's most successful magazines—*New Yorker, Bride's, Glamour, House & Garden, Mademoiselle, Self, Vanity Fair*, and *Vogue* among them.

In the early 1980s, the Newhouses thought that network-affiliated television stations had seen their better days. They sold a major group of stations and reinvested in cable, network TV's primary electronic competitor. The company also owns major book publishers: Random House, Alfred A. Knopf, Ballantine Books, Vintage Books, and Modern Library.

8. Knight-Ridder, Inc.

Media Revenue

Newspapers	1,917.4
Other	159.7

This company united two great names in American publishing through merger, in 1974, of Knight Newspapers, launched in 1903, and the Ridder group, started in 1892 with Herman Ridder's purchase of the German-language *Staats-Zeitung* in New York City. It produces high-quality journalism (53 Pulitzer prizes for company newspapers by 1989) and is rapidly diversifying into international financial news services. We will discuss Knight-Ridder in an in-depth case study.

9. Hearst Corp.

Media Revenue

Magazines	919.0
Newspapers	689.0
Broadcast	263.0
Cable	15.0
Other	100.0

Overall, Hearst Corp. is far improved over the company William Randolph Hearst built with such flair. But the chain of metropolitan newspapers that was his pride has shrunk, and today the magazine division is the largest single contributor of revenue.[6]

Of all major groups, Hearst was hit hardest by big-city changes that in the 1960s and 1970s made metropolitan publishing so tricky. Hearst closed newspapers (in Cleveland and Baltimore), sold some (in Milwaukee and Boston), and suffered as others slid to distant number 2 positions against competition (in Los Angeles, Seattle, and San Francisco). A new generation of managers, led by company president Frank Bennack, steered the company into journalistically sound—and immensely profitable—magazines (*Colonial Homes, Cosmopolitan, Esquire, Harper's Bazaar, Redbook*, and others). Bennack also acquired television and radio stations, cable and video services, and book publishers (Arbor House, Avon, Beech Tree).

The company is still private, as its founder intended. Analysts agree that the company is enormously profitable and perhaps one of the richest private firms in the country.

One change from the old days is that although some Hearsts are still in the company, none is in the top corporate leadership!

10. Tribune Co.

Media Revenue

Newspapers	1,561.7
Broadcast	423.8

Of the 15 largest U.S. media conglomerates, 12 have roots in newspapers or magazines. But all are diversifying to avoid putting all their corporate eggs in one basket.

For Tribune Co., diversification was crucial because its principal "basket" was in two older, large cities—Chicago and New York—where newspapers faced difficulties. Socioeconomic deterioration spread in many core cities, and dailies anchored downtown suffered as affluent readers fled to the suburbs. Competition developed from city magazines, TV, and daily and weekly papers around the cities.

In New York, the company's *Daily News*, once the nation's largest-circulation daily and hugely profitable, wilted as the environment changed. Today, its circulation trails that of the *Wall Street Journal* and *USA Today* and continues to drop. In Chicago, the company's *Tribune*

was forced to shed an old-fashioned, right-wing image and become a more middle-of-the road, forward-looking paper. Today, it is regarded among the best, journalistically, in the nation.

The experience showed management the danger of pegging the company's fortunes on two newspapers, no matter how prestigious and successful in the past, in two cities where business and competitive patterns can shift so quickly.

Huge investments were made in broadcast (the company paid a record $510 million in 1985 for KTLA-TV in Los Angeles) and in other newspapers. Tribune Co. is now a media owner in nine states and also owns the Chicago Cubs (a profitable operation that provides programming for its WGN-TV in Chicago), newsprint production facilities, a highly regarded news and feature syndicate, and entertainment production companies.

11. TCI

Media Revenue

Cable	1,750.1

Testimony to the growth of cable TV in the United States is the rapid expansion of Denver-based TCI, the nation's largest operator of cable systems. In just one year, 1987–1988, TCI leaped from 17th-largest media company in the country to the number 11 spot.

TCI has more than 3.6 million subscribers and holds major interests in such cable companies as United Artists Communications, Heritage Communications, WestMarc, and others.

12. New York Times Co.

Media Revenue

Newspapers	1,380.1
Magazines	249.1
Broadcast	62.5
Cable	8.4

No major media company has undergone more startling and successful transformation than New York Times Co. In the 1960s, the company was essentially one newspaper, the *Times*. Though perhaps the world's most prestigious journalistically, it was financially desperate. New York City was changing rapidly, its competitive media environment worsening. The *New York Times* was not doing much to position itself for a successful future—until Arthur Ochs ("Punch") Sulzberger became chairman. ▶ 3

Sulzberger assembled expert managers and editors who turned the *Times* around and simul-

3 ▶ Sulzberger of the *Times*

By virtue of birth, Arthur Ochs Sulzberger could have lived on New York City's social circuit, flitting with the idle rich between a Manhattan apartment and a Connecticut estate. He was, after all, the wealthy heir to a *New York Times* fortune with enormous status in New York society.

Yet Sulzberger has devoted his working lifetime to the *Times*, building it into a diversified international media conglomerate that surely would surprise his grandfather, Arthur S. Ochs, a media empire builder in his own right.

Ochs, who bought the *Times* in 1896, is credited with creating in the paper's quality one of the world's most splendid journalistic traditions; Sulzberger must be credited not only with maintaining it against huge odds but also with carrying it across new horizons.

Few of Sulzberger's colleagues thought he would succeed when he was appointed *Times* publisher in 1963. The *Times*'s marketing base, New York City, was in socioeconomic deterioration, and the paper's editors and business executives didn't have a strategy for setting things right.

Little in Sulzberger's background indicated he had answers. Born in 1926 to Arthur Hays and Iphigene Ochs Sulzberger, he lived a rich youth. Twice his education and career were interrupted by war: he was a marine in World War II and Korea (emerging as a captain). Not until 1951 did he graduate from college (Columbia, BA). Then the usual jobs most publishing families arrange to season a son and heir: reporter and foreign correspondent for the *Times*, 1951–1955 (except for one year at the *Milwaukee Journal*); assistant to the publisher, treasurer, general manager, 1955–1963.

"Punch" Sulzberger (so nicknamed because his sister is named Judy) wasn't first in line to succeed his father as publisher. The job went to Orvil E. Dryfoos, Sulzberger's brother-in-law, and to "Punch" only when Dryfoos died unexpectedly two years later.

So at age 37, Sulzberger took over the *Times* at a critical moment in its history. The financial picture was threatening; bitter quarrels divided executive ranks. Editors (who regard working for the *Times* as a religion, not a job) were struggling for power; feuds between the high-powered Washington bureau and the news desk in New York City assumed huge—and very public—proportions. (Watching power struggles at the *Times* is a favorite indoor sport for newspaper men and women everywhere.)

Within a few years, some powerful executives were retired or shunted aside. Sulzberger showed keen ability to select executives capable of taking the *Times* ahead. Naming A. M. Rosenthal, a Pulitzer-winning foreign correspondent, as executive editor (1977–1986) was a masterstroke that won admiration from journalists everywhere. Sulzberger became chairman of New York Times Co. in 1973 and in 1979 appointed Walter Mattson president and chief operating officer. Sulzberger graciously maintains that "the team" of executives turned the New York Times Co. into a $1.7 billion media goliath by 1988. Rosenthal in turn lauds Sulzberger for giving his editors the resources needed to produce outstanding journalism.

Though publicly owned, the company is controlled by family members in the Ochs-Sulzberger tradition. Sulzberger's son, Arthur, is in training as assistant to the publisher.

taneously built the dynamic, nationwide media conglomerate that is New York Times Co. today. Some business managers had poor journalism backgrounds, but they knew how to make a profit. The presence of such men and women in corporate management is a major characteristic of media conglomerates today. Many companies turn to expert accountants and general managers to run operations once directed less efficiently by journalists ill-trained for business.

For New York Times Co. shareholders, the Sulzberger direction was rewarding. Their holdings in a financially moribund newspaper were converted into a piece of one of the nation's most successful media companies. In diversifying, the Sulzberger team bought medium-size dailies and weeklies in the Southeast and TV stations. The company also owns newsprint production facilities and one-third of the *International Herald Tribune*, published in Paris.

The success formula for the *Times* itself influenced newspapers nationwide and was truly a major turn in American journalism. A. M. ("Abe") Rosenthal, then executive editor, devised highly authoritative special coverage for each day (sports and business on Mondays, science on Tuesdays, and so forth). The improvements enhanced the *Times*'s already strong appeal for affluent readers so desired by advertisers. Testimony to its success is the fact that the *Times* has won 61 Pulitzer prizes, far more than any other newspaper. The Sulzberger-Rosenthal approach broadened the newspaper's appeal to readers far from New York City and its socioeconomic problems. With the advent of satellite technology, which permitted transmitting the paper to printing plants throughout the country, the *Times* became a true national newspaper.

13. News Corp. Ltd.

Media Revenue

Broadcast	620.0
Magazines	509.6
Newspapers	195.7
Other	358.0

This is the American arm of Rupert Murdoch's international media conglomerate discussed in Chapter 1. Though initially interested in American newspapers, the Australian-born Murdoch is now expanding rapidly in magazines, television, book publishing, and films.

Murdoch astounded the media world in 1988 by paying $3 billion for Triangle Publications, which publishes *TV Guide* and other magazines. It was the largest price ever paid in any media deal.

Murdoch's American newspapers include the *Boston Herald* and the *San Antonio Express-News*. Magazines include *New York*, the *Star*, and many others.

14. Cox Enterprises

Media Revenue

Newspapers	739.0
Cable	471.8
Broadcast	367.4

Cox is unique among major media conglomerates: For years, it operated its newspaper half as a private company, its broadcast half as a public company. Then, in 1985, its principal owners, descendants of the original Cox founding family, purchased the outstanding shares of publicly owned Cox Communications and took the entire operation private once more.

Today, the family owns 97 percent of the stock and has one of its own, James Cox Kennedy, installed as chairman. Profits are thought to be high from the company's 21 dailies (1.3 million combined circulation) and diversified holdings in television, radio, cable, video, magazines, and nonmedia businesses.

The company's flagship papers, the *Atlanta Journal* and *Constitution*, are being challenged in one of the richest markets, suburban Gwinnett County (for years the fastest-growing county in the country). The challenger is the New York Times Co., which in 1987 paid one of the highest prices ever for the suburban 27,500-circulation *Gwinnett Daily News*: $88.2 million, or $3,207.27 *per subscriber*. The price illustrated how willingly media companies would pay high prices in a market with growth potential. The ensuing circulation and advertising war has been enormously costly to both companies.[7]

15. Washington Post Co.

Media Revenue

Newspapers	682.7
Magazines	327.5
Broadcast	180.2
Cable	115.2

Three things are striking about this company. It is headed by the most powerful woman executive in the United States, Katharine Graham. Its flagship *Washington Post* is one of the nation's most successful newspapers, financially and journalistically. And the company has a major problem with its *Newsweek* magazine, which contributes fully 28 percent of its corporate revenue.

The Katharine Graham story reads like fiction. Her father, a wealthy banker, bought the *Post* in 1933 and eventually turned it over to her husband, Phil. Graham, by her own account shy and lacking self-confidence, settled into suburban life as wife and mother. Then, in 1963, Graham's husband committed suicide, and Graham took over the newspaper. Lacking experience, she hired editors and managers who helped build the company into today's diversified media giant.

The *Post* sets Washington's news agenda. *Newsweek*, though slipping financially, is of course an important national newsmagazine. The two publications give Graham a voice in the highest circles of government. In the news industry, she built influence on her own. She worked doggedly to learn the business and became a tough, discerning manager. She was the first (and so far the only) woman chairman of the American Newspaper Publishers Association, the industry's leading lobby group, and first woman elected director of the Associated Press.

Graham and a son, Donald, now *Post* publisher, decided that the newspaper would concentrate on the District of Columbia and surrounding suburbs and not try for national circulation like the *New York Times* and the *Wall Street Journal*. That game plan has been hugely successful. The *Post* reaches (or, in newspaper parlance, "penetrates") 58 percent of all homes in the district with its daily editions, 76 percent on Sundays. (Many metropolitan papers can claim only 25 percent.)

In sum, the 15 largest American media conglomerates are widely diversified, highly energized, and profitable. Their influence is expanding; the big will get bigger.

Other Important Media Companies

◆ *Dow Jones & Co.* In impact on public policy and government thinking, this company's flagship *Wall Street Journal* is second to none. In influence on business, the company is a leader with electronic news services. The company is widely admired for its journalistic quality and sharp, professional managers.

◆ *McGraw-Hill.* In magazine and book publishing and private information services, this company spreads across vast sectors of American business. Scarcely is there a specialized news niche that escapes McGraw-Hill. The company's flagship is *Business Week*, a highly regarded magazine of more than 900,000 circulation. The company publishes more than 60 others with extremely narrow journalistic and authoritative focus (for example, *Textile World, Coal Age, Electronic Wholesaling*).

◆ *Scripps Howard.* This $1.2 billion company diversified from its Midwest origins into nationwide broadcast, cable and video, book publishing, and news syndicate operations. It was privately held after E. W. Scripps started with newspapers until it emerged in 1988 as a publicly owned corporation. Two-thirds of its revenue and 80 percent of its profits come from 20 daily newspapers in 12 states and Puerto Rico.

◆ *Viacom International.* Broadcast and entertainment are this company's mainstays. It produces and syndicates the highly successful "Cosby Show." Viacom exemplifies companies that are expanding rapidly to meet America's voracious appetite for entertainment.

◆ *Westinghouse Electric Corp.* This company's Westinghouse Broadcasting Co. (Group W) is a major player in television. It owns stations across the nation in major cities.

Those are some of the biggest media conglomerates as measured by revenue. But what are these huge companies like on the inside? Let's examine one, Knight-Ridder.

INSIDE KNIGHT-RIDDER: A CASE STUDY

It's an international "communications conglomerate," but in Akron, Ohio, it is the *Beacon Journal*; in Lexington, Kentucky, the *Herald Leader*.

This is Knight-Ridder, Inc., a $2 billion company with headquarters in Miami that employs 24,000 and is owned by 11,300 shareholders in all 50 states. It is renowned for excellence, the winner of 53 Pulitzer prizes.

Knight-Ridder, in sum, meets the free enterprise system's imperative of delivering profit to shareholders and simultaneously creates high-quality journalism. For some media conglomerates, the only goal is profit. But even among companies that try for both, Knight-Ridder's accomplishments stand out.

Like most conglomerates, Knight-Ridder offers career opportunities in many subsidiaries, divisions, and separate operating units, all managed under the same corporate roof (see Figure 3.3).[8]

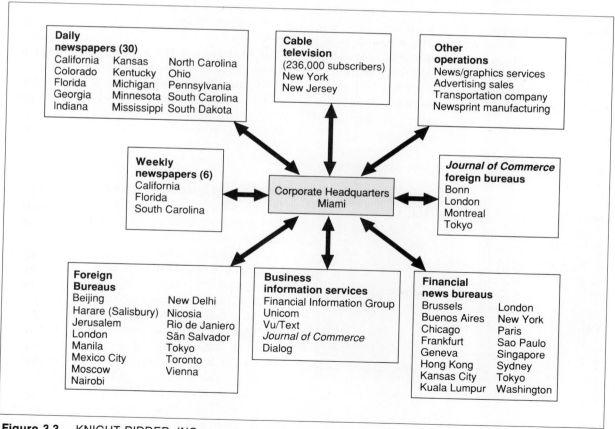

Figure 3.3.   KNIGHT-RIDDER, INC.

Newspaper Division This is Knight-Ridder's financial heart and professional soul. Top executives grew up in newspapers; the company itself was created, in 1974, from merger of two family-run newspaper companies, Knight and Ridder. Today, newspapers contribute over 90 percent of total revenue and, through their prize-winning journalism, most of the company's very considerable prestige.

Knight-Ridder's 31 daily newspapers, published in 15 states, in 1988 had 3.9 million circulation weekdays, 4.8 million on Sundays. Five are the core of this division: the *Philadelphia Inquirer*, the *San Jose Mercury News*, the *Miami Herald*, the *Charlotte* (N.C.) *Observer*, and the *Detroit Free Press*. For years, the *Herald* was the group's big moneymaker, a prizewinning paper that seemed to have unlimited expansion potential. But the *Herald* hit hard times, suffering from socioeconomic deterioration in Miami, alienation from the city's expanding Hispanic population, and vigorous suburban competitors. The company also has trouble in Detroit, where its *Free Press* hemorrhaged losses for years ($18 million in 1987 alone, the company says) because of similar city deterioration and strong competition from a cross-town rival, Gannett's *News*.

The *Inquirer* won 13 Pulitzers in 16 years under Gene Roberts, one of the nation's best editors. The *Herald* continually breaks big stories, including, in 1987, Senator Gary Hart's weekend meeting with a young woman—a story that forced him out of the race for the Democratic presidential nomination. That same year, Knight-Ridder's *Charlotte Observer* won a Pulitzer for breaking news of financial scandals in the religious organization PTL.

In cooperation with Tribune Co., Knight-Ridder sells news and features to more than 200 U.S. and Canadian newspapers plus nearly 40 overseas, with 30 million total circulation.

Knight-Ridder's newspaper division is strong, but having over 90 percent of its eggs in one newspaper basket is unsound, so the company is diversifying.

Television/Cable Division Knight-Ridder was late in entering broadcast. It bought eight television stations that brought in well over $100 million annually, then launched a joint venture with Tele-Communications, Inc., that reaches about 300,000 homes through cable services. In 1988, the company decided to sell off all broadcast TV stations and cable.

Business Information Services Each day, rivers of information flow through the business world—gold prices in Zurich, corn prices in Chicago, stock prices in Tokyo. Knight-Ridder is an important supplier of such specialized information (along with Dow Jones, Reuters, and the Associated Press). Knight-Ridder business news activities include electronic delivery of information via satellite and video display screens, plus one of the oldest commercial newspapers in America, the *Journal of Commerce*. In 1988, Knight-Ridder paid $353 million for Dialog Information Services Inc., which operates more than 320 databases for 91,000 subscribers in 86 countries. Dialog offers information for business and the sciences.

Through its Vu/Text electronic information

Knight-Ridder sells news, photos, and illustrations to other media. Here, artists in the Washington, D.C., bureau discuss how to illustrate the day's news with charts for transmission electronically. *Knight-Ridder photo.*

Knight-Ridder's financial services maintain bureaus in 16 cities throughout the world. Here, Paul Lowe, Asia editor, and a Japanese coworker plan coverage in Tokyo. *Knight-Ridder photo.*

retrieval service, Knight-Ridder sells access to what it describes as the world's largest newspaper databank—the full text of 37 newspapers, 150 regional business journals, and articles from hundreds of trade publications. In the databank are the *Los Angeles Times* and *Newsday* and magazines such as *Money, Fortune,* and *Sports Illustrated.* In the mid-1980s, Knight-Ridder attempted to sell a computer-based retrieval system to general news consumers. The service, though a technical success, failed to lure people away from newspapers and television news. The experiment cost Knight-Ridder about $50 million.

That is how Knight-Ridder is structured. But who runs the company? A look inside the company will serve as a case study of how conglomerates are managed.

Inside the Councils of War In any organization, from a small student group to the world's largest corporation, there generally are two ways of looking at how things get done. One is to examine the formal "table of organization," normally a vertical chart showing the flow of authority (see Figure 3.4). The other is to look deeper for informal but important currents of managerial direction, which may not follow the table of organization.

In theory, at least, policy direction flows from the company's shareholders. Every year, shareholders elect a board of directors under the "one share, one vote" principle. Directors are selected to represent a cross section of shareholder interests, set corporate policy, and bring outside expertise to company management.

Knight-Ridder's directors in 1988 were 16 men and one woman. Eleven were present or former employees of the company. These inside directors included members of the Knight and Ridder families. The six outside directors were Clark Clifford, former U.S. defense secretary and a lawyer; Barbara Barnes Hauptfuhrer, also director of a life insurance company and Raytheon Co.; Jesse Hill, Jr., life insurance company executive; C. Peter McColough, former chairman of Xerox Corp. and director of several other companies; Thomas L. Phillips, chairman of Raytheon Co.; and John L. Weinberg, investment banker with Goldman, Sachs & Co. The personal backgrounds, professional experience, and age of directors are certain to have an impact on corporate policy.[9]

Directors meet regularly with management executives, who report on company activities, and set policy, often by formal vote. The chief executive officer implements policy through his subordinates, the president of the company, division chiefs, vice presidents, and so forth.

That is how it works, according to the table of organization. But that's not the full story.

First, some directors carry more weight than others. At Knight-Ridder, the big hitter is James L. Knight, who with his late brother, Jack, formed the company out of newspapers inherited from their father. James Knight votes 8,235,372 shares—14.14 percent of the total.[10]

Second, the chairman of the policy-setting board, James K. Batten, is also chief executive officer—an employee charged with carrying out policy. Further, Batten is a significant stockholder, owning 258,466 shares in 1989. Wearing those three hats, Batten concentrates enormous power that doesn't show up on the table of or-

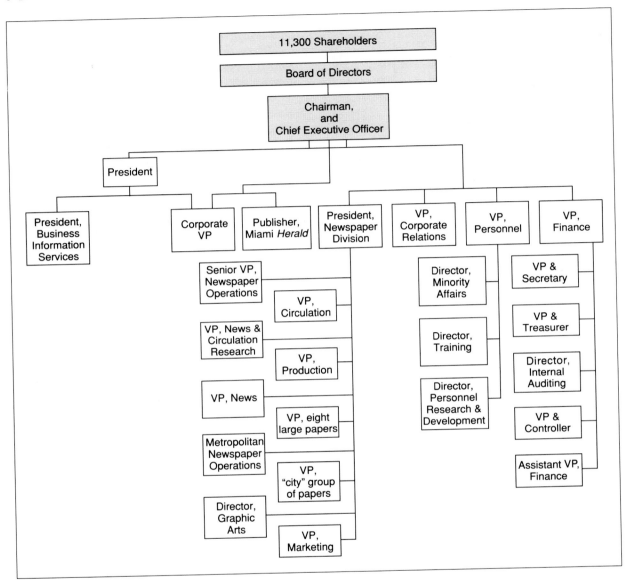

Figure 3.4. KNIGHT-RIDDER'S TABLE OF ORGANIZATION.

ganization. In many publicly owned media con-glomerates, similar power is held by a single in-dividual.

Third, important strategic decisions are for-mulated by a group not even shown on the table of organization: the nine-member executive com-mittee. Here, cross-pollination occurs between board and executive staff in a blend of long-range policy considerations and short-term manage-ment moves. Seven members of the committee are members of the board; the other two are top executives in operations and finance.

But who are the professional managers, who join in the executive committee's creation of corporate strategy and who then guide daily operations?

The people who run America's multibillion-dollar media conglomerates are among the nation's most influential. Their decisions at corporate headquarters in Miami, New York, Chicago, Los Angeles, and other cities shape tomorrow morning's headlines.

These corporate chieftains don't mimic Hearstian excesses of yesteryear by pulling strings to decide precisely which story will dominate tomorrow's headlines or network news. Even critics of "big media" find little evidence of widespread news manipulation. To the contrary, a criticism of conglomerate journalism is that top managers *ignore* the quality of news produced by their far-flung outposts and are preoccupied with expanding their companies and courting shareholders.

Nevertheless, corporate executives do have a large influence on local news coverage in small towns and cities where their newspapers, broadcast stations, and information services operate.

First, through statements of corporate mission and contacts with employees, top executives set company tone or style. Knight-Ridder's executives link talk of higher profits with calls for better journalism. Every annual report or employee publication stresses prizewinning journalism. Not all conglomerates act similarly.

Second, top executives influence group journalism through hiring, training, and promotion of employees. Knight-Ridder's publisher in Detroit, its Washington correspondents, the bureau chief in Tokyo—all were selected in accordance with standards laid down at the Miami headquarters. These people hold their prestigious, well-paying jobs at Miami's pleasure—and the corporate discipline that results from that fact is well defined. Simply put, Knight-Ridder local managers produce profits and journalism at expected levels—or else. (In some companies, it works the other way, of course. Local managers produce profit, or else, and if journalistic quality suffers, so be it.)

Third, group executives exert influence through business plans and budgets that local managers must submit for approval. Obviously, local managers, no matter how well intentioned, cannot produce high-quality journalism if corporate headquarters denies them sufficient funds for reporters and editors. This is how notoriously profit-oriented groups answer public criticism of their low-quality journalism. They state that they don't interfere in local news coverage, but they deny managers the wherewithal to improve coverage.

Who these top executives are is easy to answer. Most are white, male, well educated, and willing to sacrifice much of their private lives to hard work. Knight-Ridder says that in searching for effective leaders, it identified these characteristics essential to success: general intelligence, verbal reasoning strengths, quantitative reasoning, analytical thinking, supervisory knowledge, practical judgment, energy, seriousness, social aggressiveness (willingness to stand for what is right), sociability, emotional stability, objectivity, friendliness, and thoughtfulness.[11]

What the top corporate executives are, in background, is also easy to answer. They come from all sectors of society; some are educated in the liberal arts, others in journalism, law, public affairs, or even engineering. Whatever their origins, those at the top managed to get varied media experience. ▶ **4**

Advertising, for example, is crucial to a media firm's financial success—so the people at the top (and all who want to follow them) must have advertising experience. That doesn't mean total dedication to the business side. Batten is a journalist by background. But no one can run a media conglomerate without knowing where the dollars come from and how to dispense them with care!

The media's prosperity and influence in our political and social life have created a powerful, wealthy managerial elite.[12] Let's turn to another powerful media institution—news agencies and syndicates—to see how its members and the executives who run them tie in with media conglomerates.

4 ▶ Paths to the Top

There is no guaranteed route to the top of any media corporation (unless your father or mother owns one, or course). Certainly, Knight-Ridder executives in important corporate jobs followed different career paths.

Alvah Chapman, board chairman until 1989, graduated from the Citadel and served as a bomber pilot during World War II. He started on the business side with the *Columbus* (Ga.) *Ledger-Enquirer*, then joined the *St. Petersburg* (Fla.) *Times* as vice president and general manager. Three years followed as president and part owner of the *Savannah* (Ga.) *Morning News and Evening Press* before he joined Knight-Ridder and became vice president, general manager, and president of the *Miami Herald*. He became president of Knight-Ridder in 1973, chairman in 1982. Chapman's route was up through the business side of newspapering.

James Batten, Chapman's successor, followed a different route, the news side. After Davidson College (he also has a master's in public affairs from Princeton), Batten joined Knight-Ridder's *Charlotte* (N.C.) *Observer* in 1957. He was a Washington correspondent, then assistant city editor of the *Detroit Free Press*, then moved back to the *Observer* as executive editor. He became a corporate vice president in 1975, senior vice president in 1980, and president in 1982. His promotion to the company's number 1 job confirmed Knight-Ridder's determination to continue emphasizing journalistic quality.

P. Anthony Ridder, president of Knight-Ridder's newspaper division, held news and administrative jobs at company papers in Aberdeen, South Dakota; Duluth, Minnesota; Pasadena, California; and St. Paul, Minnesota and then joined the *San Jose Mercury News* in 1964, where he became general manager (a post that ordinarily involves business, not news, functions). He became *Mercury News* publisher in 1977 and newspaper division president in 1986. Although he is from a founding family and has substantial stock holdings, Ridder is known as a first-rate executive who rose on merit. He is a University of Michigan graduate.

Richard G. Capen, Jr., former publisher of the company's flagship *Miami Herald*, now is vice chairman and a member of the corporate board of directors. He is a Columbia University graduate whose background is both newspapers (the Copley group, San Diego, California) and government (three years in the U.S. Defense Department in legislative and public affairs). He joined Knight-Ridder's corporate staff in 1979.[13]

These top executives are handsomely rewarded for their business and journalistic successes. Cash compensation in 1988 (not including bonuses or other perquisites): Alvah H. Chapman, Jr., as board chairman and chief executive officer, $866,200; James Batten, as president, $743,333; P. Anthony Ridder, president of the newspaper division and director of the company, $451,704; Richard C. Capen, Jr. (as publisher of the *Miami Herald*), $400,558.[14]

THE HIDDEN FORCE: NEWS WHOLESALERS

Travel across the United States and you'll notice that if your morning paper fronts an important story from, say, New Delhi, afternoon papers along your route will carry follow-ups.

And if you're wondering whether Snoopy of *Peanuts* fame will return from a bombing mission over France or how prices are moving on Wall Street, newspapers in Los Angeles, New York City, and everywhere in between will keep you up to date.

If you're a TV viewer, news footage you see on the *Today* show or other morning news reports may be repeated on the noon news hundreds of miles away, where you stop for lunch. And you'll probably be able to watch follow-up reports on the 6 P.M. or 11 P.M. news in your hotel that night.

All that is the work of news and feature "wholesalers," a global web of agencies and syndicates that, although little known to the general public, are among the most influential forces in the media world.

For the print or broadcast media, wholesalers cover the globe and deliver an incredible diversity of news, features, photos, comics, video reports, and entertainment programming—all at a fraction of what it would cost if developed separately by an individual newspaper or television station. This network gives the smallest country daily, in effect, its own reporter in New Delhi and access to a worldwide network of correspondents it could never afford on its own. The smallest broadcast station, a Mom and Pop radio station operating over a shoe store just off Main Street, can give its listeners live reports ("actualities," in radio parlance) from New Delhi, too.

For readers, listeners, and viewers, the global web ensures high-quality news and entertainment almost everywhere, at reasonable cost. At a per-copy price of 25 or 35 cents, that small country daily provides decent coverage of Washington and foreign capitals and throws in "Dear Abby" (and "Peanuts"), plus stock prices and other news. Johnny Carson, Bill Cosby, and other internationally known entertainers are available on the smallest television station.

Problems arise in all this, of course. One is an awful sameness in news content that settles at times over the American media. Combined with fads in layout and the use of color, this sameness creates newspapers that appear strikingly similar. For certain, television news—or Johnny Carson and Bill Cosby—appear in one town as in another.

A second problem is that overuse of material from a news service or syndicate can stunt local journalistic and entertainment initiative. Many editors fill columns or airtime with relatively inexpensive news service copy (much of it irrelevant, albeit of high quality) rather than go to the trouble and expense of reporting local stories crucial to local readers. Local entertainment programming by television stations is almost unheard of; it's simpler and cheaper merely to plug into a network "feed" or buy a syndicated show.

News and feature wholesalers, then, have an enormous influence on the media.

Lucille Ball (*left*) made millions laugh in "I Love Lucy." The show is still popular in TV syndication, nearly 40 years after this scene was shot in 1952. *Wide World Photos.*

THE BASIC NEWS SERVICES

Beyond doubt, the single most important force in the American mass media—and the least known to the general public—are the basic news services that link the world to newspapers and broadcast stations by satellite and wire. Among them, the Associated Press is dominant in general news. Consider these facts:

◆ AP serves 1,458 daily U.S. newspapers, or 88.5 percent of all papers in the country (1989 figures). Member papers (AP is a cooperative with members, not clients) represent 94 percent of all daily newspaper circulation. AP also serves 230 college, nondaily, and non-English-language papers.

◆ More than 6,000 television and radio stations and networks receive AP. More than 1,000 radio stations receive AP audio service, making AP the largest single U.S. radio network.

◆ Worldwide, more than 8,500 foreign subscribers receive AP service. Many are news agencies serving national customers, and AP calculates that it thus serves more than 15,000 newspapers and broadcasters worldwide—and they in turn place AP news before more than 1 billion readers, viewers, and listeners daily.[15]

AP is also influential in developing new media technology. It pioneered electronic editing on computer-controlled VDTs, filmless cameras, portable photo transmitters, and electronic darkrooms and is a major carrier of other news services on its satellite circuits and landlines.

In the United States, AP's principal challenger, United Press International, is a distant number 2 and slipping rapidly. After decades of vigorous competition, UPI in the 1970s began encountering marketplace changes that eroded its financial support: AP expanded into every conceivable niche of news service activity, denying UPI any exclusive strength; other competitors entered the field; and cost controls at many papers forced editors to chop expenses—and many chopped UPI. Today, UPI is a mere shadow of the fiesty old United Press, created by E. W. Scripps in 1907, and International News Service, launched by Hearst in 1909 (the two merged in 1958). In 1987, under new ownership, UPI lost $24 million on shrinking sales of $72.6 million; AP's budget approaches $300 million.

Internationally, AP faces vigorous competitors, principally Reuters, a $1.8 billion (in 1988) London-based news service among the best-managed in the world. Reuters concentrates on financial news services to private subscribers (more than 90 percent of its revenue) and has only about 70 U.S. newspaper subscribers.[16] Paris-based Agence France-Presse is the only other significant international news service competitor to AP. AFP, founded in 1835, is smaller than AP and dogged by a perception among journalists that it is controlled by the French government (about 56 percent of its $90 million budget in 1985 came from news sold to government offices). Nevertheless, AFP is strong in places, particularly Latin America.

Many countries have strong national news services, among them Kyodo of Japan, Press Trust of India and United News of India, Deutsche Presse Agentur of West Germany, EFE of Spain, and ANSA of Italy. But they do not compete globally and in fact get much of their international news from AP, UPI, or Reuters. In the communist world, TASS, the Soviet agency, is dominant. In the West, TASS is significant only as a news collection (not distribution) agency. It funnels huge amounts of economic and industrial news back to Moscow; in addition, TASS covers general news for Soviet newspapers and television. The Xinhua News Agency distributes news internally from Beijing to Chinese newspapers but is not a significant supplier for media outside China.

AP's primary strength is its cooperative structure. This adds the news-gathering resources of thousands of member newspapers and broadcast stations to AP's own 3,000 employees in 308 bureaus in 71 countries worldwide (187 bureaus are located throughout the United States). The result is an unrivaled news web covering much of the world, daily transmitting millions of words and thousands of photos. Let's look at how it works.

U.S. newspaper and broadcast members are obligated by contract and, more important, bound by a century of cooperative tradition to contribute their news to other AP members. For example, say a plane crashes outside Chicago. The *Chicago Tribune*, the *Sun-Times*, and many of the city's radio and TV stations, all AP members, will throw scores of reporters and photographers on the story. Their reports and photos will be quickly available to AP's bureau in Chicago, which will transmit coverage to AP members throughout Illinois. A significant story will be moved also on national circuits to AP members elsewhere in the United States and to clients overseas.

Abroad, many AP newspapers and broadcasters also have contracts obligating them to cover for AP. So the AP web pulls in news collection resources of thousands of foreign clients (foreign newspapers and broadcasters are "clients" without the voting rights U.S. members have in the cooperative's affairs).

AP is a two-way, 24-hour exchange system that never shuts down as it scouts the world for news. ▶ 5

5 ▶ AP's Woman in Nairobi

Didrikke Schanche

Out of sight of the general public, and often at great risks to themselves, correspondents roam the world for newspapers and broadcast stations back home. Here are excerpts from AP correspondent Didrikke Schanche's report of how wrong things can go on the news beat in Africa.

With a strong shove from behind, I went flying into a cell filled with 17 Nairobi prostitutes who laughed and clapped at my soaring entrance. They weren't used to getting "wazungu" (Swahili for whites) as cellmates.

I was one of three Western journalists tossed into the fetid jail at Nairobi's Central Police Station after paramilitary police beat and arrested us Sunday, Nov. 15 [1987] during rioting at the University of Nairobi.

We were picked up while watching scores of screaming riot troops go after students protesting the arrests of some of their leaders.

From atop a dormitory roof, I could see several officers repeatedly slam their batons over the back of a BBC correspondent they found on the campus interviewing students.

A few minutes later, however, the batons fell on me as two other foreign correspondents and I were thrown into the back of a police vehicle even though we kept identifying ourself as members of the press. . . .

At the station . . . under a hail of blows and kicks, I was shoved inside . . . into a tiny area on the floor already jammed with students and the other reporters.

Any attempt at speech was met with a blow.

The beatings stopped after we were led into a bare, cold room. An officer . . . ordered us to remove our shoes, socks, belts and watches before we were questioned.

It was the first of five interrogations during which I had to repeat my name, passport number, organization and reason for being at the riot scene.

I then was led . . . into a corridor lined with cells and joined the women who said they were prostitutes. . . .

The air reeked of excrement and urine. A small slit in the middle of the approximately 8 foot by 12 foot cell served as the latrine. . . .

I left the cell once for questioning and eventually was removed from it and returned with the other Western journalists to the bare hall.

We remained there for another hour before being taken upstairs to give statements. The officer questioning me had to leave the room and ask permission from a higher authority before allowing me to include the police beatings in my statement. . . .

Before we were allowed to leave, an officer, who refused to identify himself but said he spoke for the provincial administrator, told us we were wrong to have gone onto the campus without permission from the university vice chancellor, who he said had decided not to file trespass charges.

The riot troops who directed us to view the rioting from the dormitory must have been "overworked," the officer said.[17]

AP's influence on American media is not limited, however, to "spot" news coverage, and its presence goes far beyond those familiar (but easily overlooked) front-page signposts: "From the Associated Press" or "(AP)." Feature stories, sports statistics, stock market prices, illustrative charts and graphs for both newspapers and television—all flow in a never-ending stream through the cooperative's headquarters at 50 Rockefeller Plaza in New York City. And much is of high quality. Only the *New York Times* has won more Pulitzer prizes than AP.

AP's single greatest contribution to American journalism is its long tradition, vigorously protected by generations of reporters and editors, of covering the news "straight"—as objectively as possible. Opinion, whether a reporter's or AP's, has no place in AP coverage, and AP consequently has a worldwide reputation for accuracy and reliability.

AP has a major, hidden influence in "trending" the news. With other major news organizations (*New York Times, Wall Street Journal, Washington Post*, and a few others), AP establishes the nation's news agenda. For hundreds of print and broadcast editors, news is what AP says is news. Front-page story priorities and newscast schedules are constructed in many cities around AP's reports. AP men and women, mostly anonymous even at newspapers and broadcast stations, make minute-by-minute decisions on which stories to transmit, at which length, in which form. They are "gatekeepers" of the world's most important flow of general news. (*Regardie* magazine included one AP editor, William Sautter, among the most influential 100 private persons in Washington, D.C., simply because he compiles AP's "Daybook," a wire list of events scheduled daily in the capital. The magazine said Sautter had "enormous influence" because "an event's inclusion in the daybook lends it the imprimatur of newsworthiness; its exclusion, more often than not, amounts to the kiss of death.")[18]

Obviously, no individual can manipulate a news flow emanating from hundreds of AP bureaus throughout the world, plus thousands of newspapers and broadcast stations. The news flow is so huge that it sometimes defies efficient handling, let alone manipulation. Still, questions arise about how the organization is managed.

Policy is set by a 22-person board of directors, 18 elected by newspaper members nationwide (four from broadcast are appointed by the board). AP's bylaws ensure that directors represent all geographic sections and sizes of newspapers. Board policy is passed to the president, a full-time employee who directs daily management. Almost every top executive, including the current president, Lou Boccardi, came up through the news ranks. All corporations have secrets, of course, and AP is no exception. But the organization is remarkably open to outside scrutiny. Finances are audited by newspaper members independent of the board.

By its very nature, AP tends to magnify the influence of important media conglomerates studied earlier in this chapter. AP is run for and by the U.S. media, and AP directors tend to represent the largest companies because they have the most votes in AP elections.

AP and other basic news services are not the only major behind-the-scenes influence on American media.

SUPPLEMENTALS, SYNDICATES, AND OTHERS

Listen to the news and read the newspapers just a little more carefully and you'll notice repeated reference to the *New York Times* reporting this, CBS or the *Washington Post* revealing that. Wherever you go, 10 or 15 metropolitan newspapers and the TV networks have enormous influence on the shape of the news and thus public opinion.

In part, this is because these newspapers and networks have many reporters stationed in major news centers who "break" important stories, which are quoted widely.

But there is another reason. Since the early 1970s, leading newspapers have become major players in the international news service business. For profit and prestige, they sell news, features, and photos to newspapers and broadcasters around the world. Their sales activity isn't really new; their emergence as highly successful "supplemental news services" reaching thousands of clients is.

The *New York Times* made the first significant venture into the field and today serves 550 clients worldwide, 350 in North America alone. Two journalistic powerhouses, the *Washington Post* and the *Los Angeles Times*, jointly operate a news service for 629 clients worldwide (1989). A third important "supplemental" (an agency that supplements but doesn't supplant AP) is Knight-Ridder/Tribune News Information Services, originally formed by Knight-Ridder and the *Chicago Tribune*. Today, KNT sells news from about 40 contributing newspapers. Smaller services are operated by Scripps-Howard, Newhouse, Copley Newspapers, and others. Some, such as Gannett News Service, are available only to newspapers and broadcast stations owned by the corporate parent.

The supplementals are strongly competitive in the news agency world because they offer high-quality coverage from prestigious papers and, because their costs are relatively low, their services are inexpensive compared to AP's. This helped put UPI on the downward slide. Many editors opt for AP basic service, then drop UPI to save money and add one of the available supplementals for a prestigious yet inexpensive different view of the news.

Other influential suppliers of the media are syndicates, which sell thousands of features, columns, photos, comics, crossword puzzles—if it's published in a newspaper or magazine, they sell it.

As in supplemental news services, the names of huge media conglomerates—New York Times Co., Washington Post Co., Hearst—crop up in the syndicate world.

It's a $100 million-a-year business ("Peanuts" alone can cost a large newspaper $1,000 weekly). Charles H. Schulz, creator of "Peanuts," had earnings in 1987 alone estimated by *Forbes* magazine at $30 million. Much of that came in royalties from firms using Snoopy and other Schulz characters on products.[19] One syndicate, United Media, a Scripps Howard company, earns millions annually by licensing Garfield, Snoopy, and other cartoon characters for use on over $1 billion worth of products such as coffee cups and T-shirts!

Writing advice columns earns millions for twin sisters "Ann Landers" and "Abigail Van Buren." The Landers column, distributed by Creators Syndicate, appears in 1,100 newspapers worldwide and is seen by an estimated 85 million readers. "Dear Abby" is distributed by Universal Press Syndicate, which claims that it reaches 90 million readers (of whom about 10,000 write "Dear Abby" each week for advice.)[20]

For cartoonists and writers, syndication can bring not only wealth but also a chance to be creative before international audiences.

COWPOKE WITH PEN

66 As a child, I wanted to grow up to be a cowpoke. Instead, I became a poker of sacred cows. **99**

Doug Marlette, Pulitzer-winning editorial cartoonist for Newsday *and author of the nationally syndicated comic strip "Kudzu."*

Syndicates provide even small papers with high-quality features they otherwise could not afford. "Op-ed" pages (those facing the editorial pages) blossomed across the nation in recent years with in-depth, analytical writing by syndicated famous journalists. In total, syndicates add important journalistic dimensions to the nation's newspapers.

Some syndicate activity is directed at television. United Media produces award-winning specials on CBS ("A Charlie Brown Christmas," "Here Comes Garfield") and develops programming for both broadcast and home video from some of its features ("Miss Manners" and food shows with Barbara Gibbons). United also creates TV Data television listings for more than 3,000 publications, publishes the weekly *TV Update* magazine, and produces cable services.

Tribune Media Services is a major producer of TV listings and services.

Meanwhile, another major news service war is raging in America.

THE HIDDEN WAR IN BUSINESS NEWS

Beneath the surface of American business, hidden from the general public and most newspaper and television editors as well, runs a river of news created by some of the most important news agencies. It involves specialized economic, business, financial, and commodity news sold to banks, brokers, commodities dealers, and industrial firms. This news has a phenomenal impact on how life is lived, for it is a minute-by-minute commentary on the state of the world (particularly its economic condition) on which traders and executives make decisions that move many billions of dollars every day.

Economic and business news is an international commodity of high value. But it is in America, richest trading center of all, that the principal battle between private subscriber news service giants is being fought. For the victors, the prizes are multimillion-dollar contracts to supply news.

Until the 1960s, the American market was dominated by Dow Jones. The company's *Wall Street Journal* was must reading in business; its teletype wires reached all trading centers of significance. Then Dow Jones decided to follow American business in its international expansion and with Associated Press launched AP–Dow Jones services that now reach 50 countries. London-based Reuters, until then operating primarily outside the United States, headed for the riches of Wall Street. It ended a cartel system established decades earlier, under which international news agencies carved out exclusive spheres throughout the world.[21]

Today, Dow Jones business publications bring in nearly $1 billion annually; private subscriber services, well over $250 million.[22] The most famous DJ service is the Broadtape, a teletype wire into 39,900 terminals in private subscribers' offices. Subscribers receive news on a printer or on video display terminals that at the press of a button "pull up" from computers the news of how stocks are trading, whether interest rates are rising or falling, which companies are merging, and so forth.

This wire news has none of the "color" or

featurish writing found in your daily newspaper or on the evening newscast. Dow Jones emphasizes abbreviated, tightly edited writing that gets quickly to the "news to profit by."[23] Dow Jones reporters are not all experts in business or finance when first hired. Dow Jones prefers to hire general newspaper reporters with proven records for accuracy and speed. Dow Jones then teaches new reporters the special skills of handling economic, business, and financial stories.

WHY BUSINESS NEWS MUST BE ACCURATE

66 The number flashes first, just the number. Boom. You react. You start taking positions. Is the number big? You sell dollars. Small? You buy. **99**

Alfred Driever, vice president, Salomon Brothers, Inc., telling how billions of dollars are traded in minutes after news services flash monthly U.S. trade deficit figures from Washington.[24]

News agencies are amazingly inventive in creating services valuable to the business community. For example, one DJ service, Professional Investor Report, tracks 5,400 common stocks traded on U.S. exchanges, alerting subscribers to unusual movements in the price or volume of shares traded. DJ computers monitor

each trade (millions of shares are bought and sold daily), and DJ reporters then file explanatory stories on important developments. DJ has computerized databanks containing, among other things, profiles and financial records of more than 750,000 companies and the full text of business articles appearing in 140 regional newspapers and magazines.

DJ produces business news briefs for cable TV's USA Network and audio reports for AM and FM radio stations (DJ estimates that its FM subscribers reach 76 percent of the nation's FM listening audience).

Other big competitors in business news include Knight-Ridder (particularly strong in commodities news), Dun & Bradstreet, and McGraw-Hill.

But media giants aren't always competing with each other.

THE AMERICAN MEDIA LOBBY

Despite their hot infighting in the marketplace, the American media are banded together in powerful industry lobbying groups that wield enormous political, social, and economic clout.

Their motive is self-interest, the protection of the benefits and social position and especially

News of developments that will affect stock market prices stirs immediate and frenetic action on the floor of the New York Stock Exchange. *Wide World Photos.*

the profits that newpapers, magazines, radio, and television enjoy. The effect is a magnified institutional influence for the media among other institutions in our society.

Lobbying is multitiered, starting with city press clubs that, although they appear fraternal and social, have considerable influence. Reporters and photographers in cities such as Chicago and New York, for example, command all sorts of favors from local officials (including, in many cases, immunity from traffic citations while pursuing the news). The powerful Washington Press Club commands the presence of politicians and presidents who dutifully show up for an annual roasting at the club's sometimes bawdy Gridiron Banquet. Correspondents are organized to pressure officialdom on press passes, access to news sources, and similar issues.

Lobbying gets especially serious at the state level, where newspapers and broadcast stations are organized in frequently powerful associations. Generally, the media's business and financial interests are the tie that binds. Most state associations have full-time directors who lobby for such things as repeal (as in Florida in 1987) of taxes on advertising or (in many states) passage of "sunshine laws" that force admittance of reporters to government meetings. It's not unusual to see media executives who are bitter competitors back home cooperate warmly as fellow officers of state associations.

Some media industries are organized on a regional basis. The Southern Newspaper Publishers Association has respectful listeners among politicians south of the Mason-Dixon line when it speaks from its Atlanta headquarters. The Inland Daily Press Association (Chicago) and the New England Press Association are strong.

At the national level, the media often roll out very heavy artillery in their own self-interest. The most powerful lobby group is the American Newspaper Publishers Association. It represents newspapers publishing 90 percent of all U.S. daily circulation, and its officials are the media giants of our time—Sulzberger of the *New York Times* (1988 chairman), Graham of the *Washington Post*, Phillips of Dow Jones, Chapman of Knight-Ridder, Curley of Gannett, Bennack of Hearst.[25] Imagine the influence those names carry in Congress and in the Oval Office! On occasion, ANPA officials go to both, carrying the newspaper industry's self-interest to government, right along with farmers, unions, and other special-interest groups. One powerful group is the Newspaper Advertising Bureau. The American Society of Newspaper Editors, made up of the top news executives of each member paper, can seize the attention of any politician in the United States. The Associated Press Managing Editors Association, made up of editors in charge of daily news operations at AP member papers, is another strong group. Sometimes these groups lobby in the public interest, as when pressing for open meeting laws. But much lobbying is in naked self-interest—as when ANPA lobbies against telephone company entry into the news business or against local ordinances restricting placement of newspaper sales racks (such restrictions infringe on the First Amendment, ANPA says).

The Magazine Publishers Association actively lobbies against postal rate increases that would hurt magazines distributed through the U.S. postal system.

Broadcasters have an influential voice in the National Association of Broadcasters, representing the networks, 900 television stations (90 percent of the total), and 5,000 radio stations (about half of all on the air.) Two smaller but powerful groups are the Television Information Bureau and the Radio Advertising Bureau. All three deal with the industry's business interests. News matters are a primary concern of the Radio-TV News Directors Association. In broadcast, as in print, lobbying groups often are led by executives from huge media conglomerates. Among their primary efforts are lessening federal regulation of broadcasting and winning the same First Amendment guarantees enjoyed by the print press.

These lobbying groups are not cabals of media executives who secretly determine, for some nefarious purpose, the news and opinion to be printed and broadcast in the United States. Any serious student of the media can only marvel at the clamorous diversity of competing journalistic voices in this country. But two things are clear. First, although associations and societies are ostensibly organized by media professionals to improve standards of their industry and produce better, more responsible, and ethical journalism, they often lobby government in naked self-interest and fight unions. Any industry has that right (some would call it a duty) in a free enterprise system, of course, and there is nothing wrong with the media's striving to protect their economic interests. A student of the media, however, should be aware that a lobbying effort put forward as a defense of the First Amendment or the "people's right to know" can sometimes have more commercial aims.

Second, the media institution—represented by groups whose members are 90 percent of all TV stations or whose members publish 90 percent of all daily newspaper circulation—can throw around more weight than, say, an association of gas station operators or antique dealers.

A DEFENSE OF FREE ENTERPRISE JOURNALISM

66 The press in the United States is able to exercise its freedom because of our capitalist, free enterprise system. Capitalism permits financial independence. And financial independence liberates the press to do its job with all the vigor and aggressiveness it can muster. A financially dependent press cannot be truly free.

Watergate is a prime example. When the *Washington Post* was reporting the Watergate story, the Nixon administration attempted to intimidate us by, among other things, bringing about challenges to our television station licenses. That caused our stock to plummet, and it cost over a million dollars to defend. An organization with limited financial resources could not have paid this price. An organization that depended on government subsidies in one form or another would have been under severe pressure to abandon the story.

In addition—and perhaps even more important—you have to be financially solvent to edit quality publications, to attract the best writers and editors, and to do the stories that take time to develop. **99**

Kay Graham, chairman,
Washington Post Co.[26]

The media power in all that is a major issue for our society in the decade ahead.

☆ SUMMARY

American media have economic strength and social influence that would have stunned yesteryear's media moguls. The leading 100 media companies have $58 billion in annual sales and influence all sectors of mass communications.

Capital Cities/ABC, CBS, Time Warner, Gannett, and others search for broadcast stations, magazines, and newspapers to acquire. The people who manage these companies are among America's most influential—and wealthiest. Some earn millions of dollars annually.

Knight-Ridder Inc. is a powerful media conglomerate, a $2 billion company with 24,000 employees and 11,300 shareholders in all 50 states. Knight-Ridder emphasizes journalistic quality as well as profit; it has won 53 Pulitzer prizes.

A hidden force in the American media are the news wholesalers—news services and syndicates that sell news, photos, and thousands of features, columns, cartoons, and comics. They introduce sameness in American journalism but do give even the smallest newspapers and radio stations high-quality international coverage they couldn't otherwise afford.

Among basic news services, the Associated Press is dominant. Its member newspapers represent 88.5 percent of all U.S. dailies and 94 percent of all daily circulation. In broadcast, AP serves 6,000 networks and TV and radio stations.

Hidden not only from the general public but from many newspaper and broadcast editors as well, a war rages among Dow Jones, Reuters, Knight-Ridder, and others specializing in economic, business, and financial coverage for private subscribers.

Throughout "big media," there is managerial cross-pollination. Executives of media conglomerates help set policy for the Associated Press; many operate supplemental news agencies and syndicates. And they unite in industry groups that lobby in media self-interest.

☆ RECOMMENDED READING

Excellent daily coverage of corporate activity among leading media conglomerates is available in the *New York Times* (its business section's "Media Business" page) and the *Wall Street Journal* (Section 2's "Media and Marketing" page). Excellent periodicals include *presstime* and *Editor & Publisher* (newspapers), *Broadcast* and *Electronic Media* (TV and radio). *Advertising Age*, particularly in its summary of 100 leading media firms each June, is excellent. Superb analysis is available through *Newspaper Newsletter*, issued periodically by John Morton of Lynch, Jones & Ryan, 1037 Thirtieth Street NW, Washington, DC 20007. For magazine developments, see *Folio: The Magazine for Magazine Management*.

Questions of ethics and social responsibility are covered regularly and well in the *ASNE Bulletin*, the *Washington Journalism Review*, the *Columbia Journalism Review*, and, to a lesser extent, *Broadcast*. The Associated Press Managing Editors Association and the Society of Professional Journalists often issue excellent, in-depth treatments of challenges journalists face. Full texts of major codes of ethics appear in Conrad Fink, *Media Ethics: In the Newsroom and Beyond* (New York: McGraw-Hill, 1988), pp. 287ff.

Ben H. Bagdikian is thoughtful in commentaries on Big Media, especially in *The Information Machines: Their Impact on Men and the Media* (New York: Harper & Row, 1971). Also see Benjamin M. Compaine, *Who Owns the Media? Concentration of Ownership in the Mass Communications Industry* (New York: Harmony Books, 1979) and Michael Schudson, *Discovering the News: A Social History of American Newspapers* (New York: Basic Books, 1978).

AMERICA'S PRINT COMMUNICATORS

Talk about scrappy competitors! In an era of communications satellites, of ever-present television and radio, and of high-speed computer communications—in a time of unprecedented change in America's national mass media system—newspapers, magazines, and other forms of print communications are flourishing.

That's right. A form of mass communication dating back in Western culture to Johann Gutenberg's movable type in the early 1400s is prospering in the electronic age, despite fears that America is becoming visually oriented, too busy to read, or, in certain sectors, functionally illiterate. Despite all that (and the fact that ink still rubs off on your fingers), the print media are popular with millions of readers, are considered crucial by many advertisers, and are extremely important in setting the national news agenda that determines what we think and talk about and argue over.

However, life isn't problem-free for the print media. Recall the shifting conditions revealed in our Chapter 1 survey of expanding global information systems. Reflect on the review in Chapter 2 of how each medium faces new challenges. And remember from Chapter 3 how even the most prosperous newspaper and magazine companies are diversifying to prepare for future unknowns. No, nothing is certain for any form of mass communications.

To gain an inside look at how all this affects the American media, we must start, here in Part II, peeling back the layers of each media sector.

We turn first to the newspaper industry, not to assign it any priority or out of respect for age (broadcast and other electronic marvels are just youngsters, compared to newspapers) but rather because newspapers dominate our mass communications system in news and information (though not entertainment, of course) and are the medium around which other communicators create their competitive strategies. We'll survey the industry in Chapter 4, looking at various types of newspapers, their opportunities and challenges. In Chapter 5, we'll go inside Knight-Ridder's *Columbus* (Ga.) *Ledger-Enquirer's* internal organization and see where the jobs are.

In Chapter 6, we'll survey the magazine industry (it's booming). In Chapter 7, we'll look inside *U.S. News & World Report*. And other print communicators—newsletters, books, direct mail, desktop publishing—will be covered in Chapter 8.

The American Newspaper Industry

"Dollar Mixed Despite Selling by Europeans," the *Wall Street Journal* headlines for its international readers.

"U.S. to Set Limits on Airliners' Use," the *New York Times*'s national edition informs its audience.

"State Colleges May Lose Bargaining Powers," the *Boston Globe* warns its New England regional readers.

"Koch Kitchen Rocked by Cheese Caper," says the *New York Post,* alerting city readers that Mayer Ed Koch's personal chef is "suspected of swiping tubs of city-owned cream cheese."

"Commissioner to Farmers: Some Milk Reforms in Effect," the weekly *Cobleskill Time-Journal* tells its upstate New York village and farm audience.

That diversity of headlines aimed at different audiences illustrates how American newspapers are positioning themselves against competition from electronic and other media in the 21st century. Newspapers are carving out exclusive market niches. Some are filling an international or national market niche (*Wall Street Journal, New York Times*); others are speaking to regional, city, or village audiences; and each is trying to serve reader, advertiser, and community as no other medium can.

The *Journal* and *Times*, for example, concentrate on truly meaningful subjects—the state of the dollar, airline safety—and assign them to highly professional reporters for in-depth, analytical coverage that radio and television, with their severe time limitations, cannot equal. The *Boston Globe* relies on decades of areawide news expertise to produce a daily information menu that is both irresistible to thousands of New Englanders and beyond the news collection capabilities of any competitor. And which competitor, in broadcast or in print, can match the street-smart, wisecracking *New York Post*'s investigation of the mayor's kitchen? Who challenges the *Cobleskill Times-Journal*'s coverage of news important to farmers in its surrounding Schoharie County? Do Dan Rather and CBS keep watch over Cobleskill? Do ABC and NBC cover city councils and schools in thousands of villages and neighborhoods where weekly newspapers flourish? Do *Time* and *Newsweek* drop in regularly? No, and that's why "target marketing"—focusing on special-interest audiences—is bringing unprecedented prosperity to the American newspaper industry as it shifts strategies to meet changes in its environment. Three particularly important sectors of change influence newspapers: how America lives, media competition, and new technology and management skills.

NEWSPAPERS REACT TO HOW WE LIVE

The American newspaper industry is in an evolutionary stage that started with post–World War II changes in the nation's lifestyle. ▶ 1

Older large cities, particularly in the Northeast and the Midwest, continue to lose affluent residents in a migration to the suburbs that started in the 1950s. One result is the accelerated withering of some core-city metropolitan papers ("metros"). Smaller but vigorous suburban papers spring up. Since the Second World War, the number of U.S. dailies has declined; in 1988, there were 525 morning and 1,150 evening papers, plus 834 on Sunday.[1] The loss since 1950 was 129 papers, or 7.2 percent. Some papers that went down—*Washington Star* (died in 1981), *Philadelphia Bulletin* (1982), *Cleveland Press* (1982), and others—were among the nation's most famous. This was the most traumatic shakeout in the industry's history.[2]

America's work force, increasingly better educated, is shifting from blue-collar factory and farming jobs to white-collar office employment. Workers who once rose before dawn for a 6 A.M. or 7 A.M. shift and thus preferred to read afternoon newspapers after work now have time for a morning read over breakfast before going to the office at 9 A.M. or so. And daytime traffic builds to such snarled dimensions around cities that delivery trucks cannot get afternoon newspapers out at the optimum time of 4 P.M. For morning papers, predawn delivery over empty streets is easy. As a result, afternoon papers, though still numerous (mostly in smaller cities), are increasingly shifting to morning publication. Morning circulation outstripped afternoon circulation for the first time in 1982. (Some of that morning circulation, it should be noted, is accounted for by three large national newspapers: the *Wall Street Journal,* the *New York Times,* and *USA Today.*) Sunday papers increased from 549 in 1950 to 834 in 1988 for similar reasons. ▶ 2

Since the 1950s, television—and now cable—has been a competitor perceived by millions of viewers as a source of not only entertainment but also news and by advertisers as a great way to sell soap, razor blades, and beer. Communications scholars will strive decades hence to determine TV's precise impact on America. But this much is clear: TV is responsible in considerable measure for changes in American lifestyles and the competitive media environment that has affected newspapers so seriously.

Consider, for example, this afternoon lifestyle: home from the office at 5:30 P.M. or so, dinner at 6:00 or 7:00 P.M., followed by an evening of TV viewing. Little time for an afternoon newspaper in that schedule! Consider also how America's newsmakers structure their lifestyle for TV. To get their 20-second "sound bite" on TV and directly before the public, politicians and

▶ 1 High Points in American Newspaper History

1783	*Pennsylvania Evening Post and Daily Advertiser* becomes America's first daily.
1810	Steam-powered press is invented.
1833	*New York Sun* is launched, opening the "penny press" era of cheap, popular newspapers.
1835	James Gordon Bennett launches the *New York Herald* with aggressive news coverage techniques.
1841	Horace Greeley starts the *New York Tribune,* featuring strong editorial opinion.
1844	Morse's telegraph permits rapid transmission of news across vast distances.
1848	Associated Press is founded.
1878	Joseph Pulitzer founds the *St. Louis Post-Dispatch* with a news formula that is informative, lively, and entertaining.
1883	Pulitzer buys the *New York World*; feud with Hearst's *Journal* opens the "yellow journalism" era.
1884	Mergenthaler invents the Linotype, revolutionizing newspaper production.
1894	AP reorganizes into its modern form, which makes it the world's largest general news service in the 1900s.
1896	Adolph Ochs takes over the *New York Times* and launches it toward international distinction.
1917	The press accepts voluntary censorship in World War I.
1923	American Society of Newspaper Editors formulates Canons of Journalism, precursor of codes of ethics.
1933	American Newspaper Guild, a journalists' union, is formed.
1941	Bernard Kilgore takes over the *Wall Street Journal* and launches it toward today's leadership in business news.
1942	The press again cooperates with military censorship in World War II.
1947	Hutchins Commission states the need for a socially responsible press.
1950	Photo offset proves a cheaper, faster alternative to "hot metal" production.
1963	Katharine Graham takes over the *Washington Post*, becomes nation's most powerful woman executive.
1965	Early Bird satellite opens the era of national newspapers.
1970	AP begins the industry's first large-scale use of computer-based electronic editing terminals.
1972	*Washington Post*'s Watergate exposé topples President Nixon.
1978	Research reveals a "credibility gap" between the public and the media.
1981	The *Washington Star* folds, followed within a year by the *Philadelphia Bulletin*, revealing the jeopardy of metropolitan afternoon dailies.
1982	*USA Today* is launched, featuring a new approach to color and graphics in "research-driven" newspapers.
1987	Gannett, the nation's largest newspaper owner, records $2.7 billion media revenue.
1988	Total U.S. daily newspaper ad revenue reaches a record $31.1 billion.

officials schedule important statements for mid-afternoon. That's just in time for evening television news—and too late for afternoon papers, which go to press around noon. A midafternoon news story won't get into print until the next morning. One study indicates that 90 percent of news in America breaks in morning papers. Con-sequently, morning papers are increasingly filled with hard news and information; afternoon papers often are featurish, warmed-over "soft" versions of morning papers. This gives even more impetus to the spurt in morning circulation nationwide.[3]

Amid all this comes change in advertiser at-

2 ▶ Morning Papers on the Rise: Circulation, 1950–1988

Year	Morning	Evening	Total Morning & Evening	Sunday
1950	21,266,126	32,562,946	53,829,072	46,582,348
1955	22,183,408	33,963,951	56,147,359	46,447,658
1960	24,028,788	34,852,958	58,881,746	47,698,651
1965	24,106,776	36,250,787	60,357,563	48,600,090
1970	25,933,783	36,173,744	62,107,527	49,216,602
1975	25,490,186	36,165,245	60,655,431	51,096,393
1980	29,414,036	32,787,804	62,201,840	54,671,755
1985	36,361,561	26,404,671	62,766,232	58,825,978
1986	37,441,125	25,060,911	62,502,036	58,924,518
1987	39,127,409	23,698,864	62,826,273	60,111,863
1988	40,132,107	22,823,395	62,955,502	62,939,574

*Source: Editor & Publisher/*American Newspaper Publishers Association.

titudes, with an enormous impact on newspapers (which draw 80 percent or more of their revenue from advertising).

First, advertisers selling mass consumption products—soap, razor blades, beer—see TV as a marvelous way to reach many millions of consumers nationwide. In the late 1980s, 50 million persons settled back Thursdays at 8 P.M. to watch "The Cosby Show" on NBC—and, advertisers hoped, the commercials interspersed throughout. Even at $400,000 or more per 30-second commercial, many advertisers regard "The Cosby Show" and others like it as a cost-effective way to sell to mass audiences.

Second, research shows that newspaper readers as a group are more affluent and better educated than TV watchers. These "big spenders" are attractive to advertisers selling pricey items such as fur coats and Cadillacs, so they turn to newspapers. That serves to create elitist newspapers driving upscale in search of readers with high earnings. Newspapers accomplish that with news and information carefully selected for upscale appeal—reviews of opera, not country music; travel tips on the Caribbean, not Coney Island; and so forth.

In sum, two important things are happening. First, despite TV, newspapers are more prosperous than ever and advertising growth continues in an unbroken upward curve, as it has since the 1950s. Newspaper ad revenue now exceeds $30 billion annually, the largest single slice of the national advertising pie. (Circulation revenue from readers was $8.4 billion in 1988.) In fact, newspaper advertising growth often exceeded the growth rate for the gross national product (all goods and services produced in the United States) from 1946 to 1988. ▶ **3**

Second, because of TV, newspapers are changing how they cover news. TV is strong in the picture story, weak in analytical, in-depth coverage. Newspaper editors, remarkably successful in meeting competitive challenges in news, create in-depth daily reporting. They also

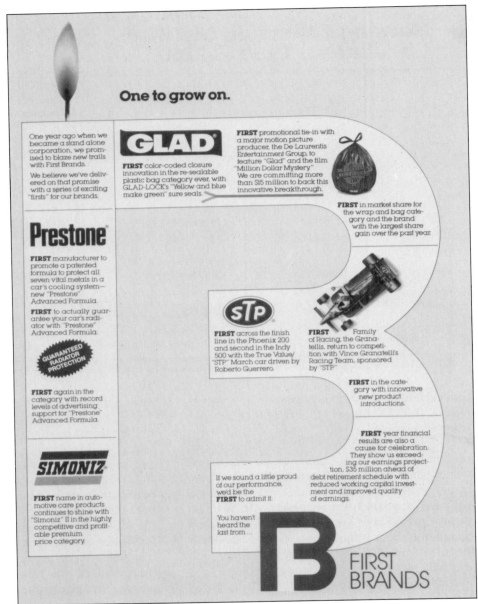

In their competition against television for advertiser dollars, newspapers boast that their ads can carry more product information than TV commercials. Note the number of First Brands Corp. products described in this newspaper ad. *Courtesy Burson-Marsteller Inc.*

fashion newspapers of record—births, graduations, job promotions, weddings, obituaries; for millions of Americans, only newspapers cover such important events. Newspapers also offer virtual cafeterias of subjects—sports, science, art, entertainment, stock market coverage. If it interests significant numbers of people, it is probably in the daily newspaper. And newspapers can package it all in handy form, aiding readers by "anchoring" daily fixtures—putting comics on

3 ▶ How the Ad Dollars Grow!

Year	Newspaper Advertising (millions of dollars)				Gross National Product (millions of dollars)	
	National	**Local**	**Total**	**Index**		**Index**
1946	238	917	1,155	100.0	212.4	100.0
1950	518	1,552	2,070	179.2	288.3	135.7
1955	712	2,365	3,077	266.4	405.9	191.1
1960	778	2,903	3,681	318.7	515.3	242.6
1965	784	3,642	4,426	383.2	705.1	332.0
1970	891	4,813	5,704	493.9	1,015.5	479.1
1975	1,109	7,125	8,234	712.9	1,598.4	752.5
1980	1,963	12,831	14,794	1,280.8	2,732.0	1,286.3
1985	3,352	21,818	25,170	2,179.2	3,998.1	1,882.3
1986	3,376	23,614	26,990	2,336.7	4,206.1	1,980.3
1987	3,494	25,918	29,412	2,546.5	4,487.7	2,112.9
1988	3,586	27,611	31,197	2,701.0	4,863.1	2,289.6

Sources: U.S. Department of Commerce; Newspaper Advertising Bureau; American Newspaper Publishers Association.

the same page every day, stocks in the same section, and so forth. For years, many journalists didn't believe it, but most do today: Newspapers are stronger because editors shifted to meet TV's challenge. ▶ 4

BROADCAST'S FAVOR TO NEWSPAPERS

66 Radio and television did newspapers a great favor. We had to find a new role. We decided that we had to think about the causes of human tragedy and of human suffering, not just the big bang in the night or the actual event, but what caused the event. 99

James Reston,
Pulitizer-winning
New York Times *columnist.*[4]

NEW TECHNOLOGY AND NEW STRATEGIES

Improvements in newspaper content would not be possible without breakthroughs in new technology and newspaper marketing strategy.

In technology, three developments help editors produce more attractive, colorful newspapers and do so quickly, at acceptable cost. First, a *cold type and offset printing* process reduces tremendously the time and money spent on production. We won't get deeply into mechanics. Suffice it to say that the old hot metal process (used until the mid-1960s) locked editors into a costly, time-consuming procedure around which the entire newspaper revolved. Today, editors are fairly free of that "tyranny of production."

4 ▶ The Language of Print

Newspapers, magazines, and other forms of print publishing have a vocabulary all their own. This glossary defines a number of common "insider's" terms.

Adversarial journalism—aggressive, sometimes combative investigative reporting.

Agenda setting—media influence over public perception of issues and their importance; some media (e.g., *New York Times, Washington Post*) are agenda setters for other media.

Alternative press—nontraditional publications such as "underground" newspapers, radical magazines.

A.M. newspaper—paper edited in late evening or early morning for optimum delivery around 6 A.M.

Audit Bureau of Circulations (ABC)—nonprofit organization established in 1914 by newspapers, magazines, and advertisers to verify circulation data.

Bulk sales—quantity sales of publications or subscriptions to one purchaser such as a hotel or an airline at a reduced rate; whether these should be counted as valid paid circulation is controversial.

Business press—publications dealing in specialized information covering business, finance, economics, or a specific industry.

Carrier—individual or organization distributing newspapers or magazines.

Churn—the effect of subscribers who take, then drop, a publication; a major problem for newspapers and magazines that must continually replace a high percentage of their subscribers.

Circulation—total number of copies sold through home delivery and on newsstands.

Cold type—process for pasting news and advertising copy on page layouts, which then are photographed to create plates for printing press.

Combination ("combo") sale—selling subscriptions to, or advertising in, two different publications at special reduced price.

Commercial speech—expression of views through advertising; does not have full First Amendment protection.

Controlled circulation—free distribution to every household in an area ("total market coverage") or to a selected audience ("selective market coverage").

Cross-media ownership—individual or company owning both print and broadcast media in the same city; limited by law.

Cycle—for newspapers, either the A.M. (morning) or P.M. (afternoon) publication period.

Database—information storage system, usually computerized.

Desktop publishing—using personal computers to design and print documents of a quality normally requiring a much more expensive process.

Electronic carbon—news copy transmitted from one computer to another.

Electronic darkroom—computerized, nonchemical processing and, often, transmission of photographs.

Electronic mail—computer-to-computer exchange of messages, often via telephone circuits.

Electronic publishing—computerized production of news content for display on a computer monitor or TV screen.

Flexographic printing—cheaper, less complicated process than several in use (see *offset*).

Franchise—in publishing, a strong position in serving readers or advertisers in a given territory.

Freedom of Information Act (FOI)—a 1966 law giving the public the right of access to many government files; frequently used by investigative reporters.

Gatekeeper—individual, such as an editor, in position to select or influence information that reaches the public.

Household penetration—ratio of circulation to number of households in a given area; an extremely significant measurement of a publication's success with readers.

Interpretive reporting—analytical (rather than straight news) coverage of complex subjects.

Investigative reporting—method of reporting that emphasizes long-term, deep digging for information (as contrasted with ''spot'' news, written quickly).

Jazz journalism—sensational, lively reporting or writing style associated mostly with racy tabloid newspapers of the 1920s.

Linotype—now generally obsolete typecasting that uses hot lead and is manually operated.

Marketing—in publishing, producing a journalistic product that responds to consumer needs and wants as revealed through research.

Market segmentation—creating publications for narrowly focused audiences (magazines for joggers or business people, for example) rather than mass or unsegmented audiences.

Marriage mail—several advertising pieces distributed in a single cover via third-class mail.

Motor route—delivery of publications via car or truck by adult carriers.

Muckrakers—President Theodore Roosevelt's term for crusading journalists.

Newshole—portion of total newspaper or magazine space dedicated to news and not advertising.

News pool—usually small group of reporters designated to cover an event for the entire press corps.

Offset—printing process of transferring images from photosensitive plates to rubberized ''blankets,'' then to paper; used by most newspapers.

Ombudsperson—publication employee assigned to represent the public's interests with reporters and editors and to critique journalistic performance.

Op-ed page—page facing the editorial page normally dedicated to guest columnists and opinion pieces.

Pagination—computerized layout of pages on a video screen; extremely important breakthrough in publishing technology.

Paid circulation—copies of a publication purchased through a single-copy vendor or by subscription; an important yardstick of a publication's success with readers.

Pass-along audience—individuals who read a publication they didn't purchase; important measurement of a publication's reader attraction.

Penetration—see *household penetration*.

Penny press—inexpensive popular newspapers of the 1830s and 1840s.

P.M. newspaper—newspaper produced in the late morning or early afternoon for delivery around 4 P.M.

Positioning—in journalism, creating a product for a special market and differentiating it from competing publications.

Precision journalism—use of scientific research, often computerized, in reporting complex, technical stories.

Shopper—free newspaper carrying mostly advertising and little or no news copy.

Split run—breaking total circulation into limited editions (or press runs), often with news and advertising focused on special audiences.

Teletext—transmitting information to TV screens and equipping the viewer with the capability of holding or ''freezing'' portions for perusal.

Video display terminal (VDT)—writing and editing device that permits computerized writing and editing on a viewing screen.

Videotex—interactive or two-way communications system that permits users to recall information from a distant computerized database.

Yellow journalism—in the 19th century, sensationalized reporting, mostly in big-city newspapers, that was designed to maximize circulation.

Despite automation, newspaper production is cumbersome and expensive: The pasting up of page layouts is labor-intensive and expensive presses spew out newsprint that costs more than $650 per ton. *Courtesy Gannett Co., Inc. Photos used with permission.*

They have more time for creating strong news packages, although production is still cumbersome and costly and still disadvantages newspapers competitively.

Second, *computerized writing and editing* on video display terminals (VDTs) increases the efficiency of preparing news copy and lowers its cost. This system's importance is that it captures the keystrokes of reporters and editors. A reporter writes a story on a VDT; it's edited by another person on a VDT—and the reporter's (and editor's) original keystrokes go directly into electronic typesetting machines. Before this process (AP pioneered its large-scale use in news in 1970), Linotype operators "rekeystroked" the

reporter's copy to set it in type. The huge expense and delay of that is now gone.

Third, *pagination* is arriving on the scene. This is computerized layout, on VDT screens, of entire pages. Pagination is expensive and technically complex, so it's being implemented gradually. But it eliminates many steps in the production process—again, at enormous savings in cost and time.[5]

Nevertheless, newspapers compete successfully with TV and other media only because newspaper staffs—reporters, editors, technicians, salespersons—are cooperating internally as never before under new marketing and management strategies.

Faced with reader habits that are changing and new demands from advertisers, newspapers are getting much more businesslike. There was a time when editors watched the news stream by, plucking out an item here, an item there, that they thought would attract readers. Marketing executives—advertising persons and others who price and sell the newspaper—then offered space to advertisers. They could tell advertisers how many papers were being sold but not precisely who was buying them—particularly not in demographic terms (income, age, education, and so forth).

Today, newspapers spend millions to re-

USA Today editors daily discuss top stories for the front page. Note the previous day's pages hung on wall for ready reference so that today's layout won't be the same as yesterday's! *Courtesy Gannett Co. Inc. Photo used with permission.*

search readers' desires (we will explore this further in Chapter 13). Editors then fashion news and information content precisely for those readers. Promotion experts devise advertising to get the newspaper's strengths before prospective readers. Skilled circulation executives sell and distribute the paper through vast networks that reach households (*Newsday* has more than 10,000 teenage carriers) or single-copy points such as newsstands and coin boxes. Then more research determines precisely who is buying the

newspaper and when and how they are "consuming" it—right down to which pages readers open and how deeply into selected stories they go. Advertisers want to know because they buy "adjacency," space next to news and editorial content, so that their ads will be seen by interested readers. Researchers for leading newspapers can tell advertisers the ages, education, incomes, and buying habits of their readers and much more. (In Denver, the *Rocky Mountain News* researched, among other things, how many widows live in the city and how many read the *News* rather than the rival *Denver Post*!)

This cooperative effort by all departments is the *marketing concept*. It treats the newspaper as a product to be fashioned and sold in response to market and competitive factors. In other industries, everything from soap to sailboats has been marketed for generations. But the concept is new to newspapers, and not everybody is happy about it.

Opponents of such integrated management argue that newspapers have social responsibilities that other businesses don't—to cover the news even if it offends advertisers, for example—and that they should be edited by professional journalists responding to their training and instincts on what is news, not what research reports say readers may want in news at the moment. Opponents also argue that the marketing concept cheapens journalism and tends to push newspapers toward a centrist, "safe," and very bland sameness—toward trying to please everyone instead of taking firm, principled stands on the news and compelling issues of the day.

.Advertisers seek "adjacency" of their ad with relevant news copy. Financial ads and one from a hotel catering to businessmen are placed next to stock market news in the *Los Angeles Times* in hopes of attracting potential customers.

NEWSPAPERS WITH LESS BITE

❝ Fewer newspapers have to battle a daily competitor for a story, let alone for survival. We have less of the bite and idiosyncrasy that once gave every reader the feeling that the paper was something that he had selected personally from among a number of contenders. ❞

*Leo Bogart, researcher
and former executive vice president
of Newspaper Advertising Bureau.*[6]

The marketing concept's supporters argue that competitive and cost realities simply force newspapers to be more scientific in both news and business. Certainly, transfusion of business expertise into newspaper management is taking the industry to new profit heights. Whether it is strengthening them journalistically is another story, although many people maintain that more good journalism is being produced in America today than ever before (even if some does lack the bite or distinctiveness of yesteryear). Certainly, the marketing concept and professional management techniques save some newspapers that otherwise would fail financially—and a newspaper failing financially will fail journalistically.

Anyway, even in the marketing era, smart editors need not give up their professional prerogatives or journalistic ethics and principles. They can achieve distinct tone and appearance for their newspapers.

One competitive strength newspapers gain from the marketing concept is the ability to create "zoned" editions. Editors can create not simply one large-circulation paper per day but several, each of smaller circulation, with news tailored for different audiences. Newspapers can offer a zoned edition with, say, news focused on a northwest suburb and circulated only there. This lowers the advertiser's cost but increases efficiency for it reaches just those households of interest (a hardware store owner in the northwest suburb knows that householders on the southeast side aren't going to drive 25 miles across the city to buy a screwdriver—and the owner doesn't want to pay for newspaper circulation down there). This is called *selective market coverage*. Broadcast TV, which throws its signal over a wide area, cannot match it. Cable TV may be able to develop some zoning capability in the future. Often advertisers ask to reach all households in a market. Newspapers reach some with the paid daily and the rest with free-circulation shoppers (filled with ads, not news) that are dropped at nonsubscribers' households. That is called *total market coverage*. With some advertisers demanding blanket coverage and others selective distribution, *direct mail* is a severe threat to newspapers (and magazines). Billions of pieces of low-cost advertising matter flood American homes each year, and although much is thrown away unread, some advertisers feel that direct mail lets them reach precisely delineated markets—all dentists in a county, for example, or all credit card users or auto owners.

For newspapers, one danger in the market-

USA Today's photos and glitzy illustrations reinforce its fast-paced, modern stance. *Wall Street Journal* editors stick with a sober, serious appearance for its traditional investor and business readers. USA Today *photo reprinted with permission.* Journal *photo Copyright 1987 Dow Jones & Company, Inc. All Rights Reserved. Reprinted by permission.*

Editors lay out front pages for the special news needs of their own readers. This led to three distinctly different front pages on the same day in New York, Dallas, and Los Angeles. Such tailoring for local readers creates wide diversity in American newspapers. *Reproduced with permission.*

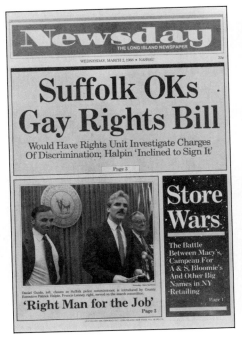

Zoned editions: *Newsday* produced one front page for readers in Suffolk County, on Long Island, and a different one for its readers in New York City. *Reproduced with permission.*

ing concept—and the attendant preoccupation with profit—is that it tempts managers to sacrifice newshole (the space available for news) and jam in too much advertising. Editors traditionally regarded a 60–40 ad-to-news ratio about right if both advertisers and readers are to be well served, and this ratio has been maintained in daily papers. However, by 1986, ads took up nearly 70 percent of total space on Sundays.[7] That can produce huge short-term profits. Over the long haul, however, it can mean disaffected readers who no longer find sufficient news to hold their interest. When that happens—when readers no longer find a newspaper crucial to daily life— the newspaper will fail.

So the picture for the newspaper industry is generally rosy. But future editors and managers will not have smooth sailing.

FOR NEXT-GENERATION JOURNALISTS: CHALLENGES

Major problems lie ahead for newspapers. First, although circulation increases every year and now is nearly 63 million on weekdays and Sundays, it is not keeping pace with growth in population and households. This is a crisis, for it demonstrates that advertisers—on whose shoulders the industry stands—cannot rely on the paid-circulation daily newspaper to get their sales message into all households where buying decisions are made (primarily by women 18 to 40 years old). In 1950, some 124 newspapers were sold per 100 U.S. households; today the rate is fewer than 68. In part, this is because surviving dailies offer stronger news coverage, so few households need more than one. Newspapers are also bulkier—351 pages on an average Sunday, 91 for weekday morning editions, and 77 in the evening, according to an American Newspaper Publishers Association 1986 survey. Whatever the reason, newspaper "household penetration" is too shallow for many advertisers. The fabled *Los Angeles Times,* for example, has less than 25 percent penetration in its home county, and some advertisers are turning elsewhere.[8] Editors tend to judge success by the percentage of household penetration because newspaper strategy, responding to advertiser desires, is to get the paper—and its ads—into homes. But success can be measured another way, in copies sold per capita. That statistic is dismal, too. In 1970, 46 papers were sold per 100 adults; in 1980, 38; 1986, 37, and in 1987, 35.[9] ▶ **5**

Second, many editors fail, despite their market research and scientific approaches, to construct sufficiently compelling news packages. Shallow penetration demonstrates conclusively that not enough Americans regard newspapers as crucial to their daily lives. ▶ **6** Millions believe that they need only 24 or 25 minutes of an evening broadcast (30 minutes minus commercial time) to stay abreast of world and national news. Yet when he anchored for CBS, Walter Cronkite complained a single front-page column of the *New York Times* contained more words than he could get on an entire evening newscast. Much local TV news is a mere shadow of the detail offered by local newspapers. Nevertheless, millions of Americans accept TV's glancing blow at the news as sufficient.

Third, many newspapers have a terrible image as being dull and stodgy and containing little of compelling interest. This complaint comes particularly from the young, who, as the next generation of readers, must be top-priority targets for newspaper strategists. (The growth of alternative publications covering current music and other youth-oriented subjects proves that newspapers aren't covering those subjects sufficiently well and that young people will read what interests them.) Many Americans regard newspapers as distant and arrogant. Getting the daily newspaper warmly received as an invited guest in more American households will be tough (particularly when TV viewers seem to identify personally with TV anchors and invite them into the living room each evening!). Part of the image problem is the reader perception we noted in Part I that newspapers carry too much bad news.

Fourth, newspapers in the future will have more difficulty meeting competitors than in the past. The electronic marvels described in Chap-

5 ▶ Newspaper Circulation, Home and Abroad

	Number of Dailies	Circulation (thousands)	Circulation per 1,000 People
1. Japan	125	57,380	562
2. East Germany	39	9,199	550
3. Liechtenstein	2	15	536
4. Finland	67	2,599	535
5. Sweden	99	4,340	521
6. Norway	82	2,071	501
7. Soviet Union	724	116,096	422
8. Iceland	4	113	469
9. United Kingdom	108	23,206	414
10. Monaco	2	11	408
. . .			
19. United States	1,687	63,263	268

Sources: UNESCO *Statistical Yearbook*; American Newspaper Publishers Association.

6 ▶ **Where They Get Their News**

Leo Bogart, a leading newspaper researcher, warns editors and publishers that the public's news preferences are shifting to TV.[10] Bogart uses these statistics from surveys on where Americans go for news on big stories:

	1982	1987
Get enough details from TV	30%	42%
Want added details in newspaper	53	26
Both valuable; want both	16	25

Bogart says the public depends most heavily on newspapers for local news but most heavily on TV for international and other types of news. Here are survey responses on which medium the public relies on:

	Newspapers	TV
Local events	61%	17%
The economy	41	45
Sports results	40	46
International affairs	35	53
Entertainment	34	46
Fashion, lifestyle	32	27
Health, science	31	35
Politics, elections	31	54

ter 1 are giving both readers and advertisers new alternatives that will increasingly disadvantage newspapers. The cost of electronically storing and transmitting information is dropping rapidly. The costs of newsprint and newspaper production are soaring.

Frank Hawkins, Jr., Knight-Ridder vice president for planning, sees "megatrends" in U.S. society posing huge problems for newspapers. For one, the growth of Asian and Hispanic communities and other widening divisions in U.S. society make it difficult for newspapers to serve all sectors as a traditional mass medium. A growing gap between haves and have-nots in income, education, and interests creates further diversity difficult for a mass medium to serve. Changes in the middle class, long the foundation for newspaper circulation, portend a weakening of the traditional family, which newspapers are structured to serve, and the growth of nontraditional households (with a single parent or working parents), which newspapers cannot easily serve. Illiteracy and rising school dropout rates are creating a class of citizens unable to use newspapers.

Who is winning or losing against those challenges?

THE PLAYERS, BIG AND SMALL

Ownership of American newspapers is increasingly being divided into two classes: huge nationwide conglomerates that are snapping up large and medium-sized dailies, and minor-league groups that can profitably operate dailies and weeklies too small for conglomerates. ▶ **7**

There isn't much of an "in-between"—not many individuals or families independently operate a single large daily or even weekly newspaper. Of the top 15 newspapers in circulation, just one is not group-owned. That's the *New York Post,* which Rupert Murdoch sold in 1988 under pressure from a Federal Communications Commission ruling that he otherwise had to sell a TV station he owns in the city (FCC rules prohibit such cross-ownership.) ▶ **8**

The huge circulations of leading newspapers create for some critics the specter of enormous influence being concentrated in a few hands. Their concern is heightened because most large newspapers have no direct competition of like size and characteristics. In 1989, just 25 U.S. cities had dailies fully and profitably competitive.

However, competing media of other types seriously erode reader time and advertiser dollars, which prevents newspapers in general from establishing true monopolies.

"Natural" (and legal) monopolies arise if newspapers win a competitive fight fairly, and our society takes a rather liberal view of so many

7 Largest U.S. Newspaper Companies

(in circulation)

	Daily Circulation	Number of Daily Papers	Sunday Circulation	Number of Sunday Papers
1. Gannett Co.	6,104,578	89	5,594,668	65
2. Knight-Ridder Newspapers	3,910,996	30	4,736,245	25
3. Newhouse Newspapers	2,939,984	25	3,463,321	22
4. Tribune Co.	2,761,217	9	3,638,972	7
5. Times Mirror	2,610,097	8	3,140,834	7
6. Dow Jones & Co.	2,587,646	24	429,046	12
7. New York Times Co.	1,950,578	27	2,508,438	17
8. Thomson Newspapers	1,907,184	109	1,287,002	56
9. Scripps Howard Newspapers	1,676,623	23	1,732,472	10
10. Hearst Newspapers	1,445,343	15	2,529,617	11
11. Cox Enterprises	1,336,618	29	1,657,556	16
12. News America Publishing (Murdoch)	1,087,198	3	517,354	2
13. Ingersoll Newspapers	1,066,753	37	952,353	23
14. MediaNews Group	1,043,149	22	1,109,234	15
15. Freedom Newspapers (Hoiles)	959,448	29	972,449	20

Source: John Morton of Lynch, Jones & Ryan, Washington, D.C. Circulations as of March 31, 1988.

8 ▶ Largest-Circulation Newspapers

	Daily			Sunday	
1.	*Wall Street Journal* (nat. ed.)	1,931,410	1.	*New York Times*	1,663,530
2.	*USA Today* (nat. ed.)	1,341,811	2.	*New York Daily News*	1,526,413
3.	*New York Daily News*	1,230,186	3.	*Los Angeles Times*	1,423,310
4.	*Los Angeles Times*	1,119,840	4.	*Chicago Tribune*	1,137,447
5.	*New York Times* (nat. ed.)	1,117,376	5.	*Washington Post*	1,149,856
6.	*Washington Post*	812,419	6.	*Philadelphia Inquirer*	1,010,530
7.	*Chicago Tribune*	740,154	7.	*Detroit News*	820,655
8.	*Newsday*	697,509	8.	*Boston Globe*	787,385
9.	*Detroit News*	676,025	9.	*Newsday*	707,787
10.	*Detroit Free Press*	629,275	10.	*San Francisco Chronicle & Examiner*	700,989
11.	*San Francisco Chronicle*	556,196	11.	*Detroit Free Press*	693,943
12.	*Chicago Sun-Times*	554,670	12.	*Newark Star-Ledger*	675,980
13.	*New York Post*	535,407	13.	*Atlanta Journal & Constitution*	665,186
14.	*Boston Globe*	509,573	14.	*Minneapolis Star Tribune*	650,317
15.	*Philadelphia Inquirer*	500,136	15.	*Chicago Sun-Times*	595,311

Source: Audit Bureau of Circulations, as of March 31, 1989. All are morning papers except *Detroit News, Newsday* (published on Long Island), and *New York Post*, which are "all-day" papers, publishing both morning and evening editions.

cities being left with a single dominant daily. And in 18 cities, newspapers, though journalistically competitive, legally share business and production facilities under so-called joint operating agreements (JOAs). Congress decided back in the 1930s it was so important to maintain separate journalistic voices in cities that it would permit JOAs if one newspaper partner would fail otherwise. JOAs have operated since 1970 under the Newspaper Preservation Act.

ARE NEWSPAPERS MONOPOLIES?

66 Newspapers are a marvelous business. It's one of the few businesses that tend toward a natural, limited monopoly. Obviously it competes with other advertising forms, but not with anything exactly like itself. Show me another business like that—there isn't one. 99

Warren Buffet,
who built a billion-dollar fortune
largely on media company stocks.[11]

66 The concept of the daily newspaper monopoly is now practically a myth. The newspaper phenomenon of slippage in newspaper household penetration rates is the most telling evidence of the real competition that so-called monopoly newspapers face in today's exacting marketplace. Television, movies, radio, national newspapers, home computers, video games, and cable television all compete with our metropolitan and community newspapers for our readers' time and attention. Only with the highest-quality product can we compete effectively. 99

Alvah H. Chapman, Jr.,
Knight-Ridder, Inc.[12]

66 I won't say that most of the nation's 1,700 daily newspapers are monopolies, but I will say that from a competitive standpoint, the local newspaper publisher has less to worry about than, say, the local acupuncturist. 99

Michael Gartner,
former Wall Street Journal *editor*
and Gannett Co. executive,
now head of CBS News.[13]

Bigness doesn't characterize the entire newspaper industry. And not all newspapering involves the glamour of being a foreign correspondent or roaming the halls of Congress. Most jobs in daily journalism are in cities such as Bloomington, Illinois; McAlester, Oklahoma; and Lakeland, Florida, which are served by medium-sized newspapers.

Despite the impact of large metropolitan newspapers on American thinking and way of life, most daily papers are still small. Of the 1,645 dailies operating in 1987, 1,394, or 84.7 percent, had under 50,000 circulation.[14]

Below small dailies is yet another layer of print journalism—weekly newspapers. Many are thriving; total circulation between 1960 and 1989 leaped a whopping 152 percent. ▶ 9

Weeklies do several things better than just about any other form of mass communication. For readers, they offer detailed local news no other medium touches. Few are concerned with Afghanistan; what the Japanese are doing can be covered by somebody else. But if you want to know the local school lunch menu for tomorrow—and many mothers do—check the local weekly. If you want to know chain saw prices these days—news on farms outside small-town America—check the local weekly.

For local retail advertisers, weeklies offer loyal readers who devour each issue (research shows that many read the classified ads even when they don't want to buy anything!) and a long "shelf life." That is, weeklies are normally kept around the house for five or six days as shopping tools, and thus ads are read carefully (dailies are often thrown out each day). Weeklies also offer advertisers "efficient" rates that are bargains compared to what dailies or TV charge because weeklies reach potential buyers who live near advertisers' stores.

Although many remain "folksy" in local news orientation, weeklies are changing in structure and management just like dailies. The old country editor of the past is largely just that—

9 ▷ The Exploding Weekly Newspaper Industry

Figures from prior to 1985 include only paid circulation; from that year on, both paid and free circulation are included.

Year	Total Weekly Newspapers	Average Circulation	Total Weekly Circulation
1960	8,174	2,566	20,974,338
1965	8,061	3,106	25,036,031
1970	7,612	3,660	27,857,332
1975	7,612	4,715	35,892,409
1980	7,954	5,324	42,347,512
1985	7,704	6,359	48,988,801
1986	7,711	6,497	50,098,000
1987	7,600	6,262	47,593,000
1988	7,498	6,894	51,691,451
1989	7,606	6,959	52,919,846

Sources: National Newspaper Association; American Newspaper Publishers Association.

past. Today's weekly is most likely owned by an experienced manager who groups several weeklies in a single administrative and news structure. The *Cobleskill* (N.Y.) *Times-Journal,* for example, is one of four weeklies owned by the same publisher. His aim is to produce all in a single building, thus reducing the cost of having separate staffs and printing presses scattered around upstate New York. That is a nationwide pattern developing in weekly newspapers.

The daily and weekly newspaper industries are prosperous and offer careers of involvement in public affairs, sports, business, and many other news sectors—and, yes, often the adventure of being on a big story. But the modern newspaper offers much more—careers in advertising and circulation sales, research, accounting, technical, and other areas. Newspapers are one of the nation's largest employers, with 462,200 on their payrolls in 1987.[15]

That's the American newspaper industry. Let's look at the *individual newspaper.*

THE NEWSPAPER'S ROLE

For an institution that's been around as long as the newspaper, people have amazing difficulty agreeing on just what the newspaper's role is.

There is general agreement that a newspaper should deliver news and information on which informed decisions are made in our democracy. It should serve as a watchdog on behalf of the citizenry, monitoring the conduct of other institutions in society. And it should assist, through its advertising, the sale of goods and services. Broadly, a newspaper should facilitate an orderly, progressive, prosperous, and just society while treating its employees fairly, living within the rules (and laws) society establishes, and, of course, fairly rewarding its owners for their investments and risks.

Note the absence of world news from this front page of the weekly *Cobleskill* (N.Y.) *Times-Journal. Reprinted with permission.*

A NEWSPAPER'S ROLE: TWO VIEWS

66 If you could find the truth and share that truth with readers, then they would be better informed, and a better-informed world is a better world. So I think the impact a newspaper has is to leave it a little bit better than it was. 99

Ben Bradlee, executive editor,
Washington Post.[16]

66 I think that in some ways our main functions are to try to take the news that appears daily in this news junkie town and put it in some perspective through the point of view of our values, then to holler up a storm when outrageous things happen. 99

Meg Greenfield, editorial page editor, **Washington Post,**
and **Newsweek** *columnist.*[17]

How is all that translated into what the newspaper does day in and day out? We'll look inside several newspapers for clues. Note, however, that this inquiry makes several assumptions. One is that there is no definitive list of which newspapers perform "best," and journalists agree only generally on what a newspaper's societal role is and how that should be discharged. One can only come up with a "maybe best" list of the 10 or so newspapers mentioned often by authorities (we'll discuss them in the order chosen by journalists, academics, and others who selected them for *AdWeek* magazine in 1987).[18]

1 *New York Times,* a perennial choice for consistently strong reporting of international and national affairs plus pioneering high-quality coverage of specialty news such as science, art, and entertainment.

2 *Los Angeles Times,* reputedly the world's most profitable newspaper—and one not afraid to spend for high-quality news and editorial content. The *Times* has a strong corps of foreign and Washington correspondents.

3 *Washington Post,* famed for its hard-hitting, high-quality coverage of national affairs. The *Post* sets the political news agenda in America and dominates coverage of the capital and the surrounding suburbs.

4 *Wall Street Journal,* by far the leader in the world for what it does. It is arguably the best-written and best-edited paper in the nation; strong editorials and analysis help set the tone of debate in our society over current issues.

5 *Philadelphia Inquirer,* led by one of our day's great editors, Gene Roberts, moved in 10 years from second-rate status to one of the greatest investigative newspapers ever. It consistently wins Pulitzer prizes for national stories but also covers its city and suburbs like a blanket.

6 *Newsday,* a suburban paper that grew to international prominence in 20 years. It originally staked out the rich Long Island market, then used top-flight news and photo coverage to beat out all competitors (including the mighty *New York Times*) and is now invading Manhattan.

7 *Christian Science Monitor,* a paper of limited dimensions, able to stay in business only through Christian Science church subsidies, but its international news coverage and analysis (free of religious bias, incidentally) are top-flight, and the paper doesn't attempt broad-based national or local coverage.

8 *Chicago Tribune,* a strong, highly profitable paper that covers the Midwest and pushes token national circulation but without competing against true national papers (*Wall Street Journal, New York Times, USA Today*). Under editor Jim Squires, the *Tribune* moved from dull and stodgy to lively and colorful yet substantive coverage.

9 *Boston Globe*, admired for New England regional and Washington coverage plus sports; a paper that learned how to prosper against fierce suburban and broadcast competition.

10 (tie) *Miami Herald* and *San Jose Mercury News,* two Knight-Ridder papers, the *Herald* admired for maintaining high quality despite socioeconomic deterioration in its city and the *Mercury News* for forging ahead to huge profits and international recognition for journalistic quality.

Because such lists are highly subjective, other leading papers should be mentioned: *USA Today* (for pioneering in color and graphics); *Dallas Morning News* (new hot contender in the Sunbelt); *St. Petersburg Times* (aggressive, high-quality paper that spends heavily on news); *Baltimore Sun* (traditional leader in international news, now building strong local coverage); *Seattle Post-Intelligencer* (cited by *AdWeek*'s judges for strong Northwest coverage).

Another assumption we must make is that in measuring a newspaper's success, the only reasonable yardstick is whether it meets its own stated goals by properly serving the readers and advertisers it chooses to serve in its own marketplace.

Kay Fanning, former editor of the *Christian Science Monitor* and president of the prestigious American Society of Newspaper Editors, describes what journalistic excellence means to her:

Subordinating the newspaper owner's private agends to the public needs of the community

An obsession with accuracy

Greater investments in newsrooms: sufficient newshole, adequate staff, better trained, and better pay

Willingness to admit and correct error

Integrity, ethical behavior, and humanity that inspire trust

Feedback, for readers to talk back to the paper through letters and guest columns and for staff members hungry to know if they are on target

Vitality expressed in fine writing, lively graphics, pictures, and layouts

Attention to topics readers care about, such as ethics, religion, and morality

> It also means expanding the reader's horizons with a world view. The excellent newspaper must excel in covering its own community, but it needn't be parochial. Advancing technology and increased international travel bring the world to everyone's doorstep—even in the most isolated village.

Fanning adds:

> Excellence means the courage to print all the important news; the wisdom to know what *is* important; the discernment to know what to leave out; the sensitivity to consider the impact; the perseverance to get the whole story and offer it in context; the knowledge to present the historical background; the fairness to print the other side; the tenacity to probe to the bottom of the story; and the vision to help the reader look ahead.[19]

THE *WALL STREET JOURNAL* AND *USA TODAY*

Both these newspapers aggressively stalk circulation, advertising, and journalistic influence coast to coast. Both are flagships of enormously important international media conglomerates, and both employ space age technology. But there the similarity ends, which is the fascination of comparing them as we look at the national newspaper in America. No newspaper beats the *Wall Street Journal* on the *Journal*'s own playing field. There is, however, some doubt that *USA Today* knows quite where its playing field is. Six years after launch, *USA Today* was still losing money.

For the *Journal,* the game is unashamedly to drive upscale with high-quality "news to profit by" aimed at the most affluent Americans. And it succeeds. The *Journal* boasts nearly 2 million subscribers and newsstand buyers, with an average household income of $146,300 annually. Journalistically, the *Journal* is a powerhouse. Its 500 reporters and editors produce global news coverage that "moves markets." Stock prices rise or drop and money changes hands on investors' interpretations of those stories. But *Journal* excellence extends far beyond business news. Its in-depth coverage of foreign affairs, politics, even sports and the arts is admired by journalists everywhere. The *Journal* is one of the "Big Three" (along with the *New York Times* and the *Washington Post*) in ability to sway public policy with editorials. *Journal* editorials are must reading in Washington and many world capitals. Although increased competition and rising costs have eaten into the paper's profits in recent years, it is a money machine, contributing most of the $757 million revenue produced in 1988 by the parent Dow Jones & Co.'s business publication division (total corporate revenues exceeded $1.6 billion).[20]

USA Today (produced by a news staff of 370) circulates nationwide, just like the *Journal,* but at a different demographic level. *USA Today*'s parent, Gannett Co., and the paper's creator, Al Neuharth, made a strategic decision at launch in 1982 not to compete head-to-head against the *Journal* (or the *New York Times*'s national edition) in either style of news coverage or type of reader sought. Neuharth & Co. decided to slip *USA Today* into a demographic niche just below that of the *Journal* and the *Times* but still high enough to attract important national advertisers. In those days, Gannett was awash with talk of serving rising young (dare we say "yuppie") corporate executives, the vice presidents striving to make $75,000 to $100,000 a year, dashing about—New York yesterday, Chicago today, Los Angeles tomorrow, and at every airport, in every hotel, the familiar, friendly, upbeat *USA Today* would await them. For busy young executives on the run, long and involved articles like the *Journal*'s simply wouldn't do. Short, snappy, crisp, to the point, yet global in outlook—everything—briefly—that executives need. That was the reporting and writing style Gannett decided was needed; that was what *USA Today* produced. And what happened?

First, *USA Today* achieved faster circulation success than any newspaper in U.S. history. Within just a few years, it hit 1.6 million circulation Monday through Friday and is now right behind the *Journal*.

"McPAPER" OR PIONEER?

66 No editor or reporter I know has a good word to say, at least publicly, about *USA Today*. It is McPaper, McNuggets, television news masquerading as print, etc. Yet no single paper has had as much influence on the American press, at least in my lifetime, as *USA Today*. **99**

**Julius Duscha, director of
the Washington Journalism Center.**[21]

Second, however, *USA Today*'s audience came in, demographically, much lower than expected. The most popular of the paper's five sections turned out to be sports, which for every newspaper delivers readers who, though extremely loyal to their newspaper, drink more beer than champagne and drive more pickup trucks than Cadillacs. Thus they are less attractive to upscale national advertisers. In 1987, *USA Today* reported that 26 percent of its readers have household incomes of $50,000 plus—impressive in some newspaper leagues but virtual paupers compared to *Journal* readers.[22] And with much of its circulation through single-copy sales, *USA Today* really cannot prove to advertisers' satis-

faction who reads the paper on a consistent basis. Consequently, *USA Today* has been a financial disaster. By its fifth year, the paper had lost nearly $600 million.[23]

Third, because of its zippy writing and its brief yet panoramic coverage ("a mile wide and an inch deep," say some critics), *USA Today* is one of the most controversial newspapers ever published in the United States. Its detractors are many. Yet its color printing—the best ever in American newspapering—and its graphs and illustrations have had an enormous effect on other newspapers' layout and style. Aspects of the paper have been copied by hundreds of editors.

Clearly, *USA Today* would have foundered but for several factors: Gannett's highly profitable other operations subsidizing the new paper and the dynamic Neuharth combining his driving personality with managerial courage, determination, and satellite communications technology, putting *USA Today* (and the *Journal*) into the space age and for the first time permitting a truly national newspaper. ▶ **10**

USA Today is edited at Gannett's headquarters in Rosslyn, Virginia, then transmitted via satellite to 33 U.S. printing sites and three overseas (Hong Kong, Singapore, and Switzerland). The *Wall Street Journal*, edited in Manhattan's financial district, is printed at 18 U.S. sites and in the Netherlands, Switzerland, Japan, Hong Kong, and Singapore. Readers thus have overnight news at breakfast—important whether you're a *Journal* reader heading for Wall Street and wondering what happened last night on world markets or a *USA Today* reader wondering whether your favorite basketball team won.

National dailies follow strategies of creating "upper layer" circulation atop the metropolitan and smaller papers serving individual communities. National papers assume that they are "second buys"—that their readers also buy a local paper.

These national dailies face major challenges. For the *Journal,* most important is fending off multiplying competitors—national, regional, and city business magazines; local papers with im-

10 ▶ Al Neuharth: What Makes Him Run?

Al Neuharth. *Courtesy Gannett Co. Inc. Photo used with permission.*

For two years after school (University of South Dakota, 1950, *cum laude*, Phi Beta Kappa), Al Neuharth worked as an Associated Press reporter in the lonely outpost of Sioux Falls, South Dakota. Then a bright idea hit: With a buddy, he raised $50,000 from friends and relatives to launch, of all things, a statewide weekly sports tabloid named *SoDak Sports*.

Quickly, the paper failed, the dream vanished—along with the $50,000—and Neuharth was broke and in debt. But as he would many times subsequently, Neuharth bounced back from that failure, landing a reporting job at the *Miami Herald*, a Knight-Ridder paper. Within just six years, in 1960, he was named assistant executive editor of Knight-Ridder's *Detroit Free Press*.

From then on, the newspaper industry watched Al run—right up the ladder of professional success. In 1963, he became general manager (a business job, not a news job) of Gannett's Rochester, New York, papers. By 1966, he was executive vice president of the entire company; in 1970, its president and chief operating officer. In 1979, exactly 25 years after going bust in South Dakota, things really boomed for Neuharth: He became Gannett chairman, president, and chief executive.

Neuharth displayed genius for predicting where population and wealth (and thus newspapers) would grow. He launched *Today* in Cocoa–Cape Canaveral, Florida; it is now a profitable, 70,000-circulation daily. He learned how to parlay Gannett assets into acquisitions that make the company today the second-largest owner (behind Thomson) of U.S. daily newspapers and (at more than 6 million) unchallenged leader in circulation. Neuharth diversified Gannett into outdoor advertising, television and radio station ownership, and entertainment programming—thereby developing a company with $3 billion in annual sales.

In 1986, Neuharth turned over company operations to President John Curley and traveled the United States (in a plush custom-fitted bus) and the world (by corporate jet), writing articles on life and how he saw it.

Throughout, Neuharth maintains a sense of humor (presumably, parlaying his early $50,000 failure into his later multimillion-dollar personal fortune helps that!). In a speech poking fun at *USA Today*, Neuharth imagined headline writers at four distinctly unalike newspapers handling the same "ultimate story," the end of the world:[24]

"World Ends, Third World Countries Hardest Hit"—*New York Times*

"World Ends, Stock Exchange Halts Trading Early"—*Wall Street Journal*

"World Ends; White House Ignored Early Warnings, Unnamed Sources Say"—*Washington Post*

"World Ends. State-by-State Demise on Page 8A. Final Final Sports Results on Page 8C."—*USA Today*

proved business news sections; the *Financial Times* of London, and *Investor's Daily,* a new U.S. publication. *Journal* executives must also decide whether to increase circulation by broadening the paper's appeal to audiences wider than its core business audience. That could dilute reader demographics that are especially attractive to *Journal* advertisers and is therefore unlikely.

For *USA Today* editors, the primary challenge is simple to define, difficult to solve: Their newspaper lost money long after Neuharth promised Gannett shareholders it would be profitable. The paper's losses make investors nervous. Gannett's president, John Curley, announced on April 10, 1988, that *USA Today* would not generate a profit that year, as promised; the next day, Gannett shares dropped 1⅛ points each, a substantial 3.2 percent.[25]

Now let's take an inside look at another type of newspaper and its role.

THE *LOS ANGELES TIMES*

Journalism that is among the best ever produced in the United States—and among the most profitable—pours out of some big dailies across the land. Survivors of newspaper battles dating back to the 1930s, no class of newspapers is as strong and dominant as the American metropolitan dailies. And no American metro quite matches the *Los Angeles Times* in what it does.

The *Times* is huge (1.1 million circulation, fourth largest in the country), and for its parent Times Mirror Co., it is a gold mine (more than $1 billion revenue in 1988). Journalistically (16 Pulitzers by 1988), the *Times* is extremely strong, and in news, production, and marketing it is highly innovative in devising strategies against a surrounding multitude of print and broadcast competitors.[26]

As in so many things journalistic, the *Times*'s strength in both news and countinghouse flows primarily from the basic economic power of its market, which is second only to New York

City and northern New Jersey in population and advertising dollars available to the media.

The *Los Angeles Times*'s vital statistics are impressive. For readers, a news and editorial staff of 850 in the home office and 36 bureaus (22 overseas) produces daily and Sunday papers of tremendous journalistic variety. The daily paper has seven sections: main (worldwide) news, metro (local, regional, editorials, analysis), sports, business, View (social, cultural, person-

Successful newspapers pay close attention to the special news needs of their readers. The *Los Angeles Times,* which serves a large West Coast audience, covers news important in the Pacific Basin. *Courtesy Los Angeles Times.*

alities, lifestyle), Calendar (entertainment, arts, TV), classified (world's largest), and, on Thursdays, food. The Sunday *Times* has all that and more: the *Los Angeles Times Magazine* (full-color, general-interest), *Television Times* (TV, pay TV, and cable listings), Opinion (including guest contributors), separate real estate, travel, and book review sections, and comics.

For advertisers, the *Times* penetrates fewer than 25 percent of households in Los Angeles County (some smaller dailies get 80 percent in their home counties). But those reached are for the most part very affluent. For example, the *Times* calculates an advertiser using four consecutive issues of the Sunday paper will reach 68.7 percent of all households in Los Angeles County and neighboring Orange County with annual incomes over $50,000. That ad schedule would reach 72.2 percent of adults in affluent occupations (professionals, managers, technicians, etc.) and 79.1 percent with a college education or more. Such audiences buy goods and services, and advertisers crowd into the *Times* to make it the world leader in ad volume each year (7,105,000 column inches in 1988).

Underscoring the *Times*'s (and other newspapers') reliance on advertising revenue, newsprint and ink in the average daily paper in 1987 cost 38 cents. Subscribers paid 35 cents; thus the *Times* would have lost 3 cents on every copy sold if it weren't for ad revenue. (This loss on reader sales is an accepted industrywide strategy to keep prices low to attract large reader audiences and thus keep the "mass" in newspaper mass communications.)

Despite the fact that the *Times* and other metros are mammoth, profitable enterprises, not all is rosy. Serious problems lie ahead for America's metros. First, the shallow household penetration worries advertisers. Many metros, particularly in old, deteriorating cities, can't deliver either deep penetration or high *Times*-like demographics.

Second, metros are trapped by high costs. Each ton of newsprint costs the *Times* $650—and the *Times* uses 450,000 tons annually. Wages are high, either because unions force them up or, as at the *Times,* management pays more to keep unions out.

Third, metros are being attacked by scores of competitors. The *Times* for years fought the crosstown *Herald Examiner,* a Hearst metro that had one-fifth the *Times*'s circulation but nevertheless stayed in the fight until it folded in 1989. More important, the *Times* must battle strong suburban papers (the competing *Orange County Register* has the nation's second-largest advertising volume). And 15 television and 80 radio stations plus 19 cable systems compete for reader time and advertiser dollar in the *Times*'s two-county market.

THE BOTTOM LINE FOR NEWSPAPERS

66 These days, everything favors newspapers. The economic atmosphere favors newspapers. The competitive atmosphere favors newspapers. The government atmosphere favors newspapers. The social atmosphere favors newspapers. The technological atmosphere favors newspapers. There is only one cloud, and that is this: Newspapers are proving to be such good businesses that people are bidding up the prices so high that they need tremendous profits to pay the debt incurred in buying the paper. That profit is readily available, but to get it, some buyers are cutting into the quality of the paper. It's easy to do, and there's really no one—not the reader, not a competitor, not an advertiser, not a government, not an employee, not a union—with the power or inclination to stop this mugging.

I take that back. There is a second cloud, too. And that is this: Some newspapers, blinded by the increasing revenue and the handsome profits, are losing their markets, and they don't realize it. . . . These papers could be in trouble in the long run. But they're the minority, I think, and their problems are simply problems of bad management, not of an industry gone awry.

I might as well mention a third cloud, too. And that is illiteracy: By one estimate, there are as many functionally illiterate persons in this country as there are newspaper buyers—roughly 60 million. That's frightening. 99

Michael Gartner,
former Wall Street Journal *editor*
and Gannett Co. publisher,
now head of CBS News.[27]

Some American metros stand a distant number 2 behind the market leader and lose millions of dollars annually. In metro newspapering today, being number 2 is, with few exceptions, a recipe for disaster.

For future journalists, some of the best jobs will be on either side of hot competition pitting large metros against vigorous suburban dailies and weeklies. The *Times,* for example, publishes not only a metropolitan daily edition but also three others for nearby areas. Once weekly, it creates nine for even more circulation areas. That zoning creates many suburban news bureaus and hundreds of jobs for reporters, advertising salespersons, and managers.

We turn next to medium-sized dailies—by far the most numerous and by far the largest source of entry-level jobs. Chapter 5 is devoted to the subject.

☆ SUMMARY

Newspapers carve out market niches with journalistic and advertising content for different audiences: international or national; regional, city, or village and rural. For national audiences, the *Wall Street Journal,* the *New York Times,* and others concentrate on serious issues (state of the dollar, state of the world); regional papers such as the *Boston Globe* emphasize area coverage; metropolitan papers such as the *New York Post* cover city and suburbs; rural weeklies concentrate on Main Street.

Newspaper operations are affected by American lifestyles. Lifestyle changes give morning papers competitive advantages. Television forced major changes by newspapers, but new journalistic and business strategies make newspapers more prosperous than ever.

New technology—offset printing, VDT writing and editing, pagination—gives newspapers a competitive boost. So does the controversial marketing concept that treats the newspaper as a product to be fashioned in response to market demand.

But severe problems exist: Circulation growth isn't keeping pace with population growth; editors often fail to demonstrate that newspapers are needed, and millions of Americans perceive TV news as adequate or superior; newspapers have an image of being dull and stodgy; and new competitors, especially electronic media, loom ahead.

Global conglomerates—Gannett, Knight-Ridder, and others—dominate daily and Sunday newspaper circulation. Gannett leads with more than 6 million papers sold daily. The *Wall Street Journal* is the single largest-circulation paper, at nearly 2 million a day. Nevertheless, most newspapers—1,391 of a total 1,643 in 1988—have under 50,000 circulation. Weeklies are enjoying explosive growth—to nearly 53 million circulation in 1989 from 20.9 million in 1960.

The *Wall Street Journal* and *USA Today* are national papers. The *Journal* is enormously successful journalistically and financially. *USA Today,* though a hit with readers, has lost nearly $600 million.

Many big-city newspapers are delivering some of the best journalism ever produced in the United States and huge profits. Their challenges are to keep costs down, keep journalistic quality high, and fight off multitudes of competitors, print and electronic, that surround them.

☆ RECOMMENDED READING

For newspaper industry information, request *Facts about Newspapers* and other background from the American Newspaper Publishers Association, The Newspaper Center, P.O. Box 17407, Dulles International Airport, Washington, DC 20041. Research in advertising, readership habits, and newspaper competition against television is available from the Newspaper Advertising Bureau, 1180 Avenue of the Americas, New York, NY 10017. Circulation studies can be obtained from the Audit Bureau of Circulations, 900 N. Meacham Road, Schaumburg, IL 60195.

For background on individual newspapers,

contact their advertising departments for "promotion" or "marketing" kits. Many will also provide research done by outside survey firms.

The following works are all excellent: Edwin Emery and Michael Emery, *The Press and America,* 6th ed. (Englewood Cliffs, N.J.: Prentice Hall, 1988); Anthony Smith, *Goodbye Gutenberg: The Newspaper Revolution of the 1980s* (New York: Oxford University Press, 1980), a study of technology's impact; Loren Ghiglione, ed., *The Buying and Selling of America's Newspapers* (Indianapolis: Berg, 1984); Robert Gottlieb and Irene Wolt, *Thinking Big: The Story of the* Los Angeles Times, *Its Publishers and Their Influence on Southern California* (New York: Putnam, 1977); Jerry Martin Rosenberg, *Inside the* Wall Street Journal (New York: Macmillan, 1982); Harrison E. Salisbury, *Without Fear or Favor* (New York: Time Books, 1980); and Peter Pritchard, *The Making of McPaper: The Inside Story of* USA Today (New York: Andrews, McMell & Parker, 1987).

Inside a Community Newspaper

I t doesn't have the global influence of the *Wall Street Journal*, the *New York Times*, or other American national dailies. It doesn't have the huge staff or regional impact of the *Los Angeles Times* or other metropolitan dailies. But in "middle America," it is deeply involved in how life is lived and is one of the most journalistically vital (and profitable) sectors of our national communications system.

This is the medium-sized or small community newspaper, by far most numerous of all types of newspapers (84.6 percent of all dailies in 1988 had less than 50,000 circulation). This type of newspaper is close to its community and offers the most entry-level jobs for new graduates.

Examining the "hometown newspaper" will complete our survey of the American newspaper industry. We'll go inside the *Columbus* (Ga.) *Ledger-Enquirer*, exploring its structure and personalities and the kinds of new employees the paper seeks. Along the way, we'll comment on other newspapers to flesh out the picture for those of you planning media careers and also for you "media consumers" who simply want to know more about what you are getting for your 35 cents!

THE *COLUMBUS LEDGER-ENQUIRER*: A CASE STUDY

Down along the Chattahoochee River, on Georgia's western border with Alabama, sits Columbus, Georgia, the hub of a three-county trading area with about 500,000 residents. Columbus is a lot like other American cities that size. About 200 manufacturing firms operate in and around the city. The U.S. Army's Fort Benning is nearby, and Columbus has a couple of small colleges, a medical center, and the usual convention and cultural centers. It also has a first-rate newspaper, the *Ledger-Enquirer*.

The *Ledger-Enquirer*, which traces its origins back to 1828, is now part of the Knight-Ridder group. It has 56,000 daily circulation, 68,500 on Sundays, and (in 1988) revenues of

$25.9 million. Of that, 71.8 percent came from advertising, 23.3 percent from circulation, 4.2 percent from commercial printing, and 1.7 percent from other sources.[1] That's fairly standard for newspapers this size (see Figure 5.1). Knight-Ridder (and most other owners) won't reveal profits for individual papers. But many groups shoot for 30 to 35 percent operating profit margins—that is, of every dollar in advertising and circulation revenue, these groups want 30 to 35 cents left over after they pay operating expenses such as wages, newsprint, and electricity (but not taxes, interest on loans, or the like).[2] Many businesses are not nearly as profitable. (Whatever its precise profit levels, the *Ledger-Enquirer* was able to finance a $21.1 million building and press renovation in 1988.)

The *Ledger-Enquirer*'s market contains about 80,000 households. So you can see that with 56,000 daily and 68,500 Sunday circulation, *Ledger-Enquirer* editors do a good job of fashioning news and editorial offerings attractive to their local audiences. The median age in the Russell, Muscogee, and Chattahoochee county area is 28, so editors must "think young." Apparently they are succeeding: On commission from the *Ledger-Enquirer*, an outside research firm, Belden Associates, Inc., surveyed the metropolitan area composed of Columbus and Phenix City, just across the Alabama border, and found that 51 percent of adults 25 to 34 years old (a very important group to advertisers) read the daily *Ledger-Enquirer* and 76 percent read the Sunday paper.[3] Like most newspapers, the *Ledger-Enquirer* is better read by older folks: The survey found that 67 percent of those 50 to 64 years old read the daily paper, and 84 percent of those 35 to 49 read the Sunday paper. Advertisers love to reach audiences in those age ranges also.

Importantly, the *Ledger-Enquirer* reaches the educational and work force elite: 82 percent of area residents with a college education or more read the Sunday paper; so do 84 percent of those described as "white collar." But the *Ledger-Enquirer* (and other medium-sized or small papers) cannot be elitist in journalistic content, like the *New York Times* or the *Los Angeles Times*. Many residents in the *Ledger-Enquirer* market have only high school degrees (the newspaper figures it reaches 57 percent of them with its weekday editions and 80 percent on Sundays).[4] Certainly, the *Ledger-Enquirer* cannot stretch thinly across its market, picking up only millionaire readers (the *Wall Street Journal* claims that almost a half million of its readers are millionaires). In Columbus, Georgia, there aren't enough mil-

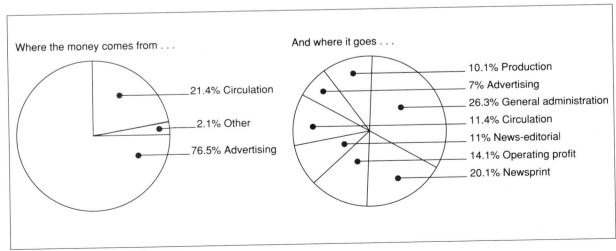

Figure 5.1. THE "TYPICAL" 50,000-CIRCULATION DAILY. *Adapted from a 1982 study by Inland Daily Press Assn.*

lionaires—and anyway, unlike the *Journal*'s national advertisers (computer firms, banks, brokerage firms), the *Ledger-Enquirer*'s local advertisers (food stores, discount houses, hardware stores) want to reach deeper into the market for a more demographically diverse audience, including medium-income readers.

So the journalistic character of the *Ledger-Enquirer* and hundreds of other medium-sized newspapers across the country must be quite different from the tone of national and metropolitan newspapers. Of course the *Ledger-Enquirer* must report, at least briefly, international and national news, generally by depending on Knight-Ridder's Washington bureau and roving correspondents plus the "news wholesalers"—news services and syndicates. *Ledger-Enquirer* editors will use their own resources—staff, money, time, newshole—primarily to cover Columbus-area politics, education, business. A good feature on vacations might concentrate on how to have a cheap family outing near the city, maybe a picnic in a free park along the Chattahoochee River. Such differences in content are an important distinction between community and metro journalism. Foreign news, for example, will fill 30 to 40 percent of the newshole in many issues of the *Washington Post, New York Times*, and *Los Angeles Times* but only 15 to 20 percent of a paper such as the *Ledger-Enquirer*.[5] Compare the front-page character of the *Ledger-Enquirer* with the national and metro front pages reproduced in Chapter 4.

The business strategy of the *Ledger-Enquirer* must be to position the paper solidly as a local enterprise, interested in local residents, and, through its advertising and community involvement, as a major player in local industry and commerce.

How is this newspaper structured to accomplish all that? First, look at Figure 5.2, a simplified organizational chart showing how the *Ledger-Enquirer* (and other medium-sized community newspapers) operates internally. Like most medium-sized dailies, the *Ledger-Enquirer* has a lean organizational structure. Just six departments report directly to the president, but the president knows everybody on the staff.

A medium-sized community newspaper often keeps international stories to under 20 percent of its newshole, devoting most to thorough coverage of local events. *Reprinted with permission.*

Billy Watson, Georgia native and longtime Knight-Ridder employee, is president, publisher, and chief executive officer, responsible for overall *Ledger-Enquirer* journalistic and financial performance. He reports to Knight-Ridder headquarters in Miami. The *Ledger-Enquirer* must meet performance standards Miami sets—or Watson must have good answers as to why he fell short. His performance bonus, a substantial portion of a publisher's annual compensation, depends on it. So does Watson's long-term career with Knight-Ridder.

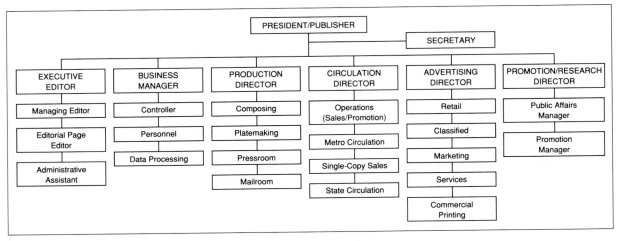

Figure 5.2. ORGANIZATION OF THE *COLUMBUS* (GA.) *LEDGER-ENQUIRER*. *Courtesy* Columbus Ledger-Enquirer.

WHAT IT TAKES TO BE A PUBLISHER

by Billy Watson, Publisher, *Columbus Ledger-Enquirer*

The abilities required to be a publisher are similar in many ways to those required of the chief executive officer of other businesses, but they are also different.

They are similar in that sound judgment and good decision-making are critically important. They are different in that a newspaper is a different sort of business from almost any other. This is largely because of the unique role played by the news-editorial division in fulfilling its First Amendment responsibilities, but it goes beyond that. Different departments of a newspaper often seem to tug against one another—news-editorial versus advertising on content, production versus news-editorial and advertising on copy flow and deadlines—instead of working hand in hand in pursuit of a single objective.

A key responsibility of the publisher, then, is to make sure that any tension is of the creative and productive sort and to balance the differing goals and objectives so that both a good and a profitable newspaper are possible. This requires an intimate knowledge of the news and editorial operation and how it fits into the big scheme of things.

I have found the 20 years I spent in the news and editorial area to be extremely valuable since becoming publisher. I have always thought that the job of editor was the most difficult of any in newspapering. That's because there are no firm guidelines to follow, no absolute rights and wrongs. Most news and editorial decisions are subjective, based in part on experience, in part on a sense of what the newspaper's role in the community ought to be, in part on common sense. A publisher has to make or defend many of those same kinds of judgments. The reputation and community standing of the paper and its image among other newspaper professionals depend heavily on those day-to-day decisions. I would feel far less comfortable with our news and editorial decisions if I did not have the experience to participate in them in what I think is a positive way.

Of course, knowledge of how each department and function of the paper operates is essential, but that knowledge does not have to be deep and wide if the publisher has good managers and can find out what he needs to know in a particular instance.

I guess the publisher mainly needs to be able to perform a daily and ongoing balancing act, protecting the integrity and quality of the news-editorial product while producing a reasonable amount of profit.

Heads of six major departments report directly to Watson:

Executive Editor and Vice President Jack Swift's title reflects the expanded view of what editors must do in American journalism these days—help formulate overall strategy and share responsibility for the paper's total performance, in addition to taking direct responsibility for news content. Reporting to the executive editor is a managing editor, in charge of day-to-day news coverage. ▶ 1

On most newspapers, the circulation director also has expanded duties these days. He helps design overall marketing strategy, as well as supervise distribution to subscribers and single-copy purchasers. This expanding field is wide open for college graduates who want to enter newspaper marketing. The *Ledger-Enquirer*'s circulation director is Bud Windham.

Advertising Director Richard M. Stone, with direct responsibility for most *Ledger-Enquirer* revenue, is a key player on Publisher Watson's management team. Stone's main concern is retail (or local) advertising, which can make up 70 to 80 percent of all advertising in a paper this size. But classified and national ads (those placed by, say, General Motors or IBM, not a local retail store) are important, too. In many newspaper companies, advertising is a route to top management.

The business manager supervises accounting, personnel, data processing, and building maintenance and acts as a business consultant to the publisher. Normally, the business manager has no direct influence on news content.

The production director is in charge of composing (page layout), platemaking (preparing pages for the presses), the pressroom, and the mailroom (where printed papers are prepared for distribution). At the *Ledger-Enquirer*, this ex-

Publisher Billy Watson (*left*) and one of his key department heads, Executive Editor Jack Swift, look at a now obsolete Linotype machine. *Reprinted with permission.*

ecutive supervises 61 full-time and 22 part-time employees and needs people management skills plus expert mechanical knowledge.

The promotion/research director supervises market research (for the advertising, circulation, and news departments, plus advertisers) and conducts community relations and promotional campaigns. This executive is assisted by a public affairs manager, who handles public service programs and public relations, and a promotion operations manager, who designs promotion ads run in the *Ledger-Enquirer* and edits a company house organ. For public relations students, this area of newspaper operations presents rapidly expanding career opportunities.

Three departments—news, advertising, and circulation—are key in newspaper strategy and offer most entry-level jobs.

See the World on the Way to the Top

When Jack Swift took his first journalism course in college, he had already been a reporter for three daily newspapers, leader of an Air Force combat news team in Vietnam, a professional karate fighter, and a welder.

And that, says the executive editor of the *Columbus Ledger-Enquirer*, should tell two things to anyone aspiring to a newsroom executive career: First, get hands-on experience in reporting anywhere and anytime you can. Second, and more important, get varied experience and see a bit of the world on the way to the top.

"My concern with fresh journalism graduates is that they lack a sense of the real world," Swift says. He should know. Many are among the 73 men and women he manages in the *Ledger-Enquirer* newsroom.

Swift began sensing the real world early, taking knockabout jobs and enlisting in the Air Force (where his assignment included leading photographers and writers into action to record the Air Force's view of the war). He became a serious student of the martial arts (the first story he ever sold was for *Black Belt* magazine). His academic background is equally varied: junior college in St. Petersburg, Florida; William and Mary; and, finally, the University of South Florida (double major in English and journalism, 1971; two years of graduate study in linguistics).

While in school, Swift worked for the *Newport News–Hampton* (Va.) *Daily Press*, the *St. Petersburg* (Fla.) *Independent* (as a sports reporter), and the *Tampa* (Fla.) *Times* (as general assignment reporter and assistant city editor). Swift also worked as a contract writer for *Newsweek*, the *New York Times*, and other publications.

"I did it backwards," he says. "I got all that experience before I started formal training in journalism."

Just two years after graduation from South Florida, and already a seasoned newsman with supervisory experience, he was hired in 1973 by the *Ledger-Enquirer* as city editor. That began another round of varied experiences: Swift was a daily columnist, associate editor, assistant executive editor, managing editor, then executive editor.

At the *Ledger-Enquirer*, Swift's ability to perform in different circumstances, under changing conditions, is crucial to his success. He helped convert the paper to computerized electronic editing, was instrumental in its transformation from separate morning and afternoon papers to a single morning paper, and serves on Publisher Billy Watson's top management team—all in addition to carrying overall responsibility for newsroom staff hiring and training, quality of the news product, and getting the paper out on time each day!

Small wonder that the one thing he never found time for is marriage. "I'm married to the newspaper business," he says.

INSIDE THE NEWSROOM

Advertising and circulation are a newspaper's pocketbook; the news and editorial department is its heart and soul.

Whatever the size of a newspaper, whatever its business goals, nothing works unless news-editorial gets on the correct wavelength and produces news, information, and reading entertainment that readers find crucial to their lives. That means that *Ledger-Enquirer* editors must pro-duce panoramic, high-quality local news. But balanced content—some international news, a little national, a few entertaining features—is necessary. And bringing all that together each day to get out the paper is complex. It's known as the daily ordeal or the daily miracle.

Typical newsroom jobs are shown in Figure 5.3. The executive editor is in overall charge of news and editorial functions. This employee sets the newspaper's tone and oversees the daily and long-range operations of about 70 full-time and

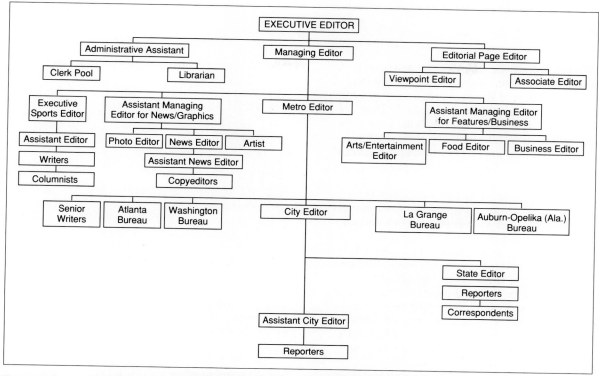

Figure 5.3. *COLUMBUS LEDGER-ENQUIRER* NEWSROOM ORGANIZATION (SIMPLIFIED).

15 other staffers. The executive editor reports to the publisher and is corporate vice president for news.

In day-to-day charge of news operations, the managing editor helps direct longer-range coverage plans. In charge of about 60 professionals, 10 part-time paraprofessionals, this staffer reports to the executive editor. The ME supervises the daily production of the newspaper through five major departments: sports, news/graphics, metro desk, feature/business, and city desk. Swift says that those departments must be run by editors with "superior news judgment, a good knowledge of the community and its people, and a working knowledge of newsroom sections other than their own—and of other departments of the newspaper." ▶ 2

The assistant managing editor for news/graphics is in day-to-day charge of the copy desk, the photography section, and the newsroom art-

ist. This is the person responsible for the paper's overall appearance and the accuracy of much of its content. The assistant managing editor supervises 17 professionals and reports to the managing editor.

The assistant managing editor for features/business directs a staff of 11 professionals and 2 paraprofessionals and edits much of their material. This employee reports to the managing editor.

The metro editor provides overall guidance to the city, state, and bureau reporting staffs and senior reporters. This staffer plans reporting projects and edits and oversees the editing of local stories. At this paper, the metro editor also supervises the editor of "Viewpoint," a Sunday opinion section of letters and articles by Columbus-area residents.

The executive sports editor directs eight sports writers and editors in producing the sports

2 ▶ Women Newsroom Managers

Women are making their mark in newsroom management—but slowly. A 1987 survey showed that 13 percent of all newsroom managers were women—up from 5.2 percent in 1977. That, critics say, isn't fast enough growth. They point out that since 1977, a majority of students in communications have been women (59.7 percent in 1987). And 35 percent of all newsroom employees were women in 1987.

In becoming directing editors, women have most success as managing editors of newspapers of less than 10,000 circulation. Women accounted for 21 percent of all MEs in 1987. (*Directing editor* is defined by the American Society of Newspaper Editors as a top newsroom manager with the title of editor, executive editor, managing editor, editorial page editor or the like.)

Of 114 U.S. newspapers with more than 100,000 circulation, only 5 had women directing editors. Barbara Henry was editor of Gannett's *Rochester* (N.Y.) *Times-Union and Democrat and Chronicle*; Deborah Howell, senior vice president and executive editor of Knight-Ridder's *St. Paul* (Minn.) *Pioneer Press Dispatch*; Janet Chusmir, executive editor of Knight-Ridder's *Miami Herald*; Kay Fanning, editor of the *Christian Science Monitor*; and Sandra Rowe, vice president and executive editor of the *Norfolk* (Va.) *Virginian-Pilot and Ledger-Star*.

Women are playing increasingly important roles in newsrooms but progressing into management only slowly. *Courtesy Gannett Co.*

In the 10,000-plus circulation category, 113 women were directing editors, or 12.5 percent.

Women have less success becoming the top business executive—publisher or general manager. Of 1,454 newspapers surveyed, only 79 (5.2 percent) were headed by women. Gannett, with 20 women publishers, accounted for about one-fourth of the total.[6]

section and also does some writing, reporting, and editing. This employee reports to the managing editor.

The editorial page editor is in overall charge of the editorial page, the op-ed page, and the Sunday "Viewpoint" (local opinion) section. This is the person responsible for the paper's day-to-day editorial voice. He or she writes editorials, edits, and directs two professionals and reports to the executive editor.

The photo chief directs five professionals in planning and carrying out photographic cover-

age. This staffer reports to the assistant managing editor for news/graphics and must be thoroughly familiar with taking and processing photographs.

The city editor gives day-to-day direction to 15 professionals and 13 correspondents on city, state, and zoned supplement staffs. This employee, who reports to the metro editor, assigns and edits stories and must have an excellent knowledge of the community.

The news editor selects wire service stories for inside pages and potential page 1 use. He or she directs seven copyeditors in the production of most news pages and reports to the assistant managing editor for news/graphics. This employee must be highly skilled in copy editing, layout, headline writing, and must understand production requirements.

For reporters and editors, the modern newsroom offers many career specialties—sports, features, business, national affairs (Washington bureau), state affairs (Atlanta bureau; Publisher Watson reported from there early in his career), and many others. On metro and city desks, reporters specialize in crime, education, city politics, science—a host of interesting news sectors. And every newsroom has an editor called something like systems editor, responsible for providing reporters with computer backup plus, often, computerized news "morgues," or libraries. Another growing specialty is graphic and illustrative art, inspired in part by *USA Today*'s success in that field.

For entry-level reporters, newspapers the size of the *Ledger-Enquirer* and owned by quality-conscious companies are great places to start. They are large enough to afford tough, demanding professional editors (the likes of Jack Swift are what every young reporter needs), yet small enough to give beginners well-rounded experience in many reporting and writing areas.

WHAT IT TAKES TO BE A REPORTER

by Jack Swift, Executive Editor, *Columbus Ledger-Enquirer*

In selecting entry-level reporters, assuming the given qualifications of intelligence and basic skills, we look first for energy, curiosity, and commitment.

A candidate for reporter at the *Ledger-Enquirer* will be, above all, willing. To do what it takes, whatever that is. Nights, weekends. Making the extra three telephone calls. Grinding to the sweat level, eager to get his or her shoes muddy. Getting it fully and getting it right.

It's assumed that the candidate will have some experience. Aggressiveness and motivation will show in how many and what kind of opportunities the candidate pursued before applying with us—internships, work on the school paper, free-lancing, summer newspaper jobs, apprenticing for free with a pro, whatever.

We want people who, without becoming parochial, are willing to make a conscious loyalty transplant to the community they will serve. Our prime directive here is, we do what we do for readers, not principally for ourselves. The attractive entry-level candidate will possess a vigorous idealism but will have an equally strong sense of humility toward reflecting the many lifestyles and belief systems of the people whose stories he or she will tell.

Capable entry-level reporters understand that the sophisticated professional is a product of experience, that excellence in journalism comes from having been there. Novices will therefore welcome any assignment as a challenge. They will write obituaries and scouting briefs with the same enthusiasm and attention to detail with which they tackle big investigations.

We prefer reporters with college degrees, including either majors or minors in journalism. We especially prefer people who have studied liberal arts in the classic sense. Journalism training is important but secondary. And we like candidates who have some experience in living. Someone who has kicked around the planet or spent some summers welding or slinging hash will understand the needs and loves and sorrows of our readers significantly better than someone who has only sat in a classroom.

We like reporting candidates who write poetry or short fiction in their free time, people with a passion for the written word—but who have the maturity to accept tough criticism from good editors. However, if we have to choose between hiring a writer or hiring a reporter, the reporter wins every time. The *New York Times* op-ed page editor once said that all it takes to make a good reporter is a pair of strong legs, quick ears, alert eyes, and a knack for beating hell out of a VDT. Or something like that.

We take as a given that entry-level reporters will be able to spell and to use a dictionary and stylebook, to type, to take accurate notes, to know that everything between quotation marks must be an exact, unhedged quote. They need a working knowledge of laws and libel and privacy. Familiarity with state sunshine legislation helps. They must understand and have an unflagging commitment to ethics in journalism.

The best job for the new reporter is without a doubt the police beat. The police beat encompasses the community. The police reporter actually does the things you see in the old movies: racing to a crime scene; interviewing criminals and blasé detectives; interrogating witnesses who may or may not be lying. The police reporter learns about human nature, about records, about scrupulous accuracy, about deadlines and hurried rewrites between editions. About juggling three small stories and one medium-sized one for the next day's paper while also making progress on an investigative piece for the weekend. And about what an editor is and how to forge a working relationship with one.

Most important, the police beat is where new reporters learn whether this is the life and the profession for them.

Experience on a paper such as the *Ledger-Enquirer* can be a steppingstone to a larger metro or national paper. Young talent trained by Knight-Ridder, known for journalistic quality, is often recruited by the *New York Times*, the *Wall Street Journal*, the *Los Angeles Times*, and others. But for many journalists, the medium-sized newspaper offers satisfying careers. For them, community journalism is where the action is.

Community journalism is not "bush league" just because papers of the *Ledger-Enquirer*'s size concentrate on high school sports as much as the pros or because they write more editorials about the mayor than about the president of the United States. Community journalism gets right down to people—their taxes, the education of their children, crime in their streets. At no other level of journalism can reporters feel quite the same daily involvement in their readers' lives. But personal does not imply pedestrian. Important stories that win national recognition often break first in com-

As sports reporter Rick Hudson knows, school sports are a big part of community journalism. *Reprinted with permission.*

munity journalism. The *Ledger-Enquirer* has won many journalism awards, including two Pulitzers—in 1926 for editorials taking on the Ku Klux Klan and in 1955 for revealing political corruption in Phenix City, Alabama. ▶ **3**

INSIDE THE CIRCULATION DEPARTMENT

If the newsroom does its job and creates alluring news and editorial content, the circulation department must bring in readers by promoting, selling, and distributing the paper—and then collecting for it. That puts circulation careers on the cutting edge of newspaper strategy. The *Ledger-Enquirer*'s circulation director, Bud Windham, describes his department as "a great place to start a newspaper career." He explains:

The demands on today's circulation manager go far beyond distribution of the paper to customer's doorstep. A circulation manager must now manage a sales organization. The primary objective is to "grow" circulation, and providing excellent delivery service is only part of that.

Circulation managers must be well-edu-

3 ▶ Small Papers Win Big

Not only national or metropolitan newspapers produce award-winning journalism. Numerous smaller papers were awarded Pulitzer prizes in 1988. The *Montgomery* (Ala.) *Journal* (20,000 circulation) won for a series on infant mortality. The *Lawrence* (Mass.) *Eagle-Tribune* (56,000) won for revealing that furloughed prison inmates were committing crimes. The *Odessa* (Tex.) *American* (29,000) won for spot news photography of a child caught in a well.

Other winners were national and metropolitan papers: the *Chicago Tribune*, the *Philadelphia Inquirer*, the *New York Times*, the *St. Paul Pioneer Press Dispatch*, the *Washington Post*, the *Orlando Sentinel*, the *Atlanta Constitution*, and the *Charlotte Observer*. The *Wall Street Journal* and the *Miami Herald* each won two.

cated, self-motivated, and enthusiastic and must possess good communication skills. They must be creative and resourceful. But most of all, they must be willing to work hard.

Perhaps no position within the company will test one's desire and sense of commitment quite as much as the job of district manager, directly supervising the carriers who deliver the paper. It will quickly develop supervisory skills and will teach a person how to sell a new subscription and how to service a new customer.

Even in community journalism, circulation is a big and complex business. Subscribers and single-copy purchasers paid $5.6 million for the *Ledger-Enquirer* in 1988 (nationwide, newspaper circulation revenue was $8.7 billion).[7]

For readers, the *Ledger-Enquirer* circulation department must handle not only daily and Sun-

day distribution but also four once-weekly "Friends" sections. These present readers in each of the four zones with highly detailed local coverage. Newspapers use this technique to offer grass-roots journalism that national newspapers, TV, and many other media cannot. Ensuring that each zoned edition reaches the right readers is a challenge for the circulation department.

For advertisers, the circulators handle an equally challenging task: distribution of free-circulation "preprints." The *Ledger-Enquirer* distributes preprints in 17 zones, offering advertisers the opportunity to buy as much as 80,000 circulation or as little as 2,633. Even small neighborhood stores can afford to advertise in the *Ledger-Enquirer* if they buy only a few thousand in circulation. That gives the newspaper a distinct competitive advantage over TV.

For circulators, the primary challenge is to increase circulation by selling the paper to the right people in the right areas. Advertisers don't want just more circulation; they want household penetration in areas near their stores and among people willing and able to purchase their goods and services.

The circulation director is responsible for all aspects of distribution (city, state, and single-copy sales), newspaper-in-education, promotion, customer service, sales, and marketing. This manager, who reports to the publisher, must increase household penetration and maintain acceptable service levels.

The metro circulation manager manages the city home delivery department's service policies, sales programs, and collection procedures and oversees the daily and long-term operations of 15 full-time managers and 149 part-time employees. This employee reports to the circulation director.

The zone manager is responsible for the delivery force within a designated area, its customer service, sales, and collection, and maximizing circulation penetration. This staffer, in charge of 2 full-time managers and 28 to 30 part-time employees, reports to the metro circulation manager.

The single-copy manager is responsible for the maintenance and stocking of vending machines and providing good service to all retail sales locations and expansion of the dealer network.

The state circulation manager is responsible for circulation outside the metro area. He or she supervises six district managers covering counties outside Columbus and reports to the circulation director.

The newspaper-in-education coordinator develops programs for area schools using the newspaper in classrooms as part of an effort to capture young readers.

INSIDE THE ADVERTISING DEPARTMENT

If the newsroom creates attractive news content and if circulation exploits the reader appeal in that and sells the newspaper in the right households—only then can the advertising department successfully woo advertisers. If the advertising department fails in that, the entire newspaper effort fails, for, as we have learned, newspapers can't get by with just circulation revenue.

The advertising department staff is among the most able (and highly paid), and its director is a top aide to the publisher. Luckily, for Richard M. Stone and his *Ledger-Enquirer* ad staff, the news and circulation departments have done their jobs. The newspaper reaches readers desired by advertisers. However, as any community newspaper must, the *Ledger-Enquirer* reaches more deeply into its market than national or metro newspapers do theirs. The *Ledger-Enquirer* reaches the lower-income not-so-well-educated in addition to the affluent. ▶ 4

Clearly, the *Ledger-Enquirer* has strong reader loyalty; converting that to advertiser support is crucial.

Broadly, work responsibilities and career opportunities in the advertising department fall into three areas: managerial and administrative, sales and customer contact, and creative and support.

Department chief Stone and his managers have a major voice in Publisher Watson's management group when overall newspaper strategy

Melanie Reuter (*standing, foreground*), *Ledger-Enquirer* coordinator of newspaper-in-education programs, shows students how to use the paper as a study tool as part of an effort to attract young readers. *Reprinted with permission.*

is discussed. They must also organize the department and hire, train, motivate, and sometimes fire employees. Methodical attention to detail is needed.

Regardless of the *Ledger-Enquirer*'s other efforts, from beat reporter to circulation strategist, nothing happens to keep the newspaper prosperously in business until an ad salesperson sells a customer. The entire ad department is driven by that realization, and selling—how to do it, when, and to whom—is what staffers here talk about.

It is also extremely important to create attractive advertising layouts that will catch readers' eyes—and sell goods and services. Fine careers are open in newspapers to people who can write ad copy that sells or who can design winning layouts. Every ad department also contains support staffs that handle research, advertisements, sales, and promotional materials and billings.

Key positions have been established in the advertising department to achieve all that. The advertising director is in overall charge of retail, classified, national, marketing, and commercial printing plus the day-to-day operations of the ad-

4 ▶ Who Reads a Community Newspaper?

Based on a 1982 survey by Belden Associates, Inc., the *Columbus Ledger-Enquirer* tells advertisers that placing ads in five issues of the paper will reach these readers in the city's three-county trading area.

Demographic Group	Total Population	Reached with Five Issues (%)
Education		
Part high school or less	73,000	73.3
High school graduates	55,900	81.5
Part college	32,100	78.7
College graduates	19,100	89.9
Graduate study	7,900	91.1
Annual Household Income		
Under $10,000	32,200	65.7
$10,000–$14,999	26,700	72.8
$15,000–$19,999	31,900	90.4
$20,000–$24,999	15,700	74.7
$25,000–$29,999	22,100	85.0
$30,000–$34,999	7,300	78.0
$35,000–$49,999	11,100	98.4
$50,000 or more	7,000	86.7
Sex		
Male	73,400	81.1
Female	80,600	80.0
Occupation		
Professional/manager	32,800	82.1
Clerical/sales	19,700	84.4
Craftsman/foreman	16,300	83.0
Military	19,500	76.0
All other employed	32,100	82.9
Retired	20,600	80.3
Others other employed	13,000	67.7
Age		
18–24	35,100	67.0
25–34	37,400	80.3
35–44	26,500	89.3
45–54	19,400	91.0
55–64	16,600	82.0
65 and older	18,300	83.4

The *Ledger-Enquirer*'s art services director, Carol Bunn, works on an ad layout for a client. *Reprinted with permission.*

vertising division. He or she plans marketing strategies for the current year and the long-range future of the division, oversees 54 full-time and 5 part-time employees, and reports directly to the publisher.

The retail advertising manager is in charge of day-to-day operations of retail (local) advertising sales, support, current-year direction, and long-range planning. This manager directs 11 full-time sales people and 3 part-time sales assistants and reports to the advertising director.

The classified advertising manager directs day-to-day telephone sales, outside sales, and telemarketing. This employee is directly responsible for three full-time outside sales employees, nine full-time phone salespeople, two part-time telemarketing salespeople, and a secretary. He or she reports to the advertising director.

The advertising marketing manager is responsible for preprint distribution, creative art services, and national advertising, oversees six full-time and two part-time employees, and reports to the advertising director.

The advertising services manager is charged with the day-to-day layout of the newspaper. This staffer, who reports to the advertising director, supervises incoming copy, outgoing proofs, and tearsheets for advertisers.

The commercial printing manager is responsible for the sale and production of outside commercial printing and printing support for the advertising division. This manager supervises seven production-related personnel and reports to the advertising director.

HOW TO GET STARTED IN ADVERTISING

by Richard M. Stone, Advertising Director, *Columbus Ledger-Enquirer*

Entry-level applicants for advertising jobs should have a friendly, outgoing personality; sales skills; a positive, almost tenacious attitude toward goal accomplishments; and a strong sense of responsibility.

Most of these traits must be exhibited during at least three separate interviews with three different managers. We also administer tests that measure intellectual aptitude, both verbal and numerical; sales abilities; and traits proven successful in sales.

An applicant must have a valid driver's license, access to an automobile, and the ability to type. We prefer a college degree or some college background, but that is not a requirement.

The most desirable entry position in advertising for career preparation is telephone sales. Training and experience gained from telephone sales best prepares an individual for any type of sales. Skills are sharpened for appointments, "closes," and timesaving information gathering that prove essential for successful sales. The entry-level individual also learns the very valuable lesson of service to both readers and advertisers, which again is essential for a successful sales career.

Well, that's some of what is happening at the *Ledger-Enquirer* as editors and managers look to the challenges of the 1990s. Costly improvements being made at the paper led to a promotional slogan: "The *Columbus Ledger-Enquirer*. Now more than ever." In the decade ahead, it will indeed take "more than ever" for community newspapers, one of the most important journalistic institutions in America, to hold their competitive position. ▶ 5 New competitors—and reinvigorated old ones—are scrambling for their readers' time and their advertisers' dollars. In Chapter 6, we turn to one of the old yet new competitors, the magazine.

☆ SUMMARY

The medium-sized community newspaper doesn't have the global or regional impact of national and metro newspapers, but it is deeply involved in life in Middle America and is among the most vital and profitable of media.

The *Columbus* (Ga.) *Ledger-Enquirer* typifies the class: 56,000 daily circulation, 68,500 on Sundays, with revenues of $25.9 million in 1988. Of that, 71.8 percent came from advertising and 22.3 percent from circulation. Its market is a three-county area with about 80,000 households, and the paper succeeds in reaching readers attractive to advertisers: 51 percent of adults aged 25 to 34 read the daily paper (76 percent on Sundays), and so do 84 percent of white-collar adults.

That means that this community paper goes much more deeply into its market than national newspapers, which hunt across America for an audience of virtual millionaires. Columbus doesn't have enough millionaires to make up a newspaper audience, and anyway, local advertisers want a more demographically diverse audience than do national advertisers who use the *Wall Street Journal* and the *New York Times*.

So like community papers everywhere, the *Ledger-Enquirer* fashions news content that is primarily local. Its business strategy ties in tightly with local readers and businesses.

The paper's publisher is responsible for both

| 5 | **Best by a Dam Site?** |

Believing that newspapers say something about themselves in picking their slogans, Mal Mallette of the American Press Institute put together a collection:[8]

"All the News That's Fit to Print"—*New York Times*

"Published in the Apple Capital of the World and in the Buckle of the Power Belt of the Great Northwest"—*Wenatchee* (Wash.) *World*, published near Grand Coulee Dam

"Florida's Best Newspaper"—*St. Petersburg Times*

"The Best Newspaper in Florida"—*Orlando Sentinel*

"Covers Dixie Like the Dew"—*Atlanta Journal*

"Where the spirit of the Lord is, there is liberty"—*Indianapolis News* (quoting II Corinthians)

"The Only Newspaper in the World That Cares Anything about Itawamba County"—*Itawamba County* (Miss.) *Times*

"Best newspaper by a dam site"—*Bent County* (Colo.) *Democrat*, published near John Martin Dam

---

news and financial success. His top aides are the executive editor (also a company vice president), the directors of circulation and advertising, the business manager, the production director, and the promotion/research director.

In the newsroom, community reporting has top priority. Many young reporters seek training at a paper such as the *Ledger-Enquirer* and then move on. But love of community involvement leads many to choose careers in places like Columbus.

In the circulation department, the mission is to exploit the newsroom's presentation of news that is attractive to readers. That is done by promoting, selling, and distributing the paper—and collecting for it. Many career opportunities are open in circulation.

In the advertising department, the goal is to exploit accomplishments of both the newsroom and circulation by selling advertisers on using the *Ledger-Enquirer* to reach consumers of goods and services. This department is the route to top management jobs for many.

☆ RECOMMENDED READING

Six industry groups periodically issue strong studies of newspaper organization and operations:

American Newspaper Publishers Association, The Newspaper Center, 11600 Sunrise Valley Drive, Reston, VA 22091

Inland Daily Press Association, Suite 802 West, 840 N. Lake Shore Drive, Chicago, IL 60611

Southern Newspaper Publishers' Association, 6065 Barfield Road, Suite 222, Atlanta, GA 30328

American Press Institute, 11690 Sunrise Valley Drive, Reston, VA 22091

National Newspaper Association (primarily weeklies, small dailies), 1627 K St. NW, Suite 400, Washington, DC 20006

Suburban Newspapers of America (primarily free-circulation publications), 111 E. Wacker Drive, Chicago, IL 60601

Also see Jon Udell, *The Economics of the American Newspaper* (New York: Hastings House, 1978); Herbert L. Williams, *Newspaper Organization and Management* (Ames: Iowa State University Press, 1978); D. Earl Newsom, ed., *The Newspaper* (Englewood Cliffs, N.J.: Prentice-Hall, 1986); and Conrad Fink, *Strategic Newspaper Management* (New York: Random House, 1988).

The American Magazine Industry

F orbes, Entrepreneur, Harper's, and Muscle & Fitness are magazines. So are Plastics World and Indiana Prairie Farmer, U.S. News & World Report and Foreign Affairs, Rolling Stone and Modern Bride.

Welcome to the American magazine industry. It's incredibly diverse, energetic, creative, and—long after television declared print dead or dying—profitable.

We will look in this chapter at what is happening to one of the oldest types of mass media, examining the magazine industry's structure, economics, and big players. We'll get into the special role magazines play in our society, and how they compete with other media, and challenges they face in the 1990s. And we'll describe job opportunities for those of you with magazine careers in mind.

Note as we proceed how magazines, newspapers, and other media are similar and dissimilar. One primary thrust of this book is the interplay among the media, the competitive adjustments under way as new media forms and technologies burst on the mass communications scene, changing it forever. The shape of media strategies against each other should start to become clear in this chapter.

MAGAZINES MEET CHANGING LIFESTYLES—HEAD-ON

What a fantastic range of reader lifestyles and interests magazines cover! How the venerable magazine industry is changing, just as the social environment in which it flourishes is changing! ▶ 1

Magazines are redefining their roles, looking for unique market niches where they can offer their own special blends of news and information to attract highly specialized readers attractive to advertisers.

And how specialized they get! For example, Forbes, enormously profitable ($128.5 million revenue in 1987), offers discerning, hard-hitting coverage of business news of particular appeal to investors. Forbes calls itself "Capitalist Tool" and unashamedly celebrates wealth and people who have it. The magazine claims to be "read

▶ 1 High Points in American Magazine History

1741	First regularly published magazines in America are Ben Franklin's *General Magazine and Historical Chronicle* and Andrew Bradford's *American Magazine*; both fail financially.
1821	*Saturday Evening Post* is founded, goes on to become an American institution.
1857	Featuring new techniques of engraved illustrations, *Harper's Weekly* launched.
1865	E. L. Godkin launches a journal of news, *The Nation*, precursor of later newsmagazines.
1869	Transcontinental railroad is completed, permitting widespread distribution of magazines.
1879	Postal Act gives magazines relatively cheap second-class postal rates, permitting growth of mass-circulation magazines.
1893	Cheap mass-circulation magazines become a reality as *McClure's* is launched at 15 cents; *Munsey's Magazine* drops its price to 10 cents and builds a large circulation attractive to advertisers.
1907	*Saturday Evening Post*, led since 1897 by Cyrus Curtis, a publishing genius, becomes the first magazine to hit $1 million annual revenue.
1922	DeWitt Wallace launches *Reader's Digest*, an instant success with its reprints of stories from other publications.
1923	*Time*, founded by Henry Luce and Briton Hadden, becomes the flagship of an international media conglomerate, Time Inc.
1925	*The New Yorker* is launched; it is later copied by scores of magazines striving for its upscale sophistication.
1936	*Life* begins publication as a weekly picture magazine; it sets the pace for all photojournalism.
1948	*TV Guide* begins as a New York City magazine, later grows to attain the largest circulation in magazine history on high-quality TV commentary and listings.
1952	*Mad* magazine is launched, followed in the next two years by *Playboy, Sports Illustrated*, and a wave of highly specialized magazines.
1955	In a radical departure, *Reader's Digest* begins accepting advertising.
1956	*Collier's*, founded in 1888, folds, presaging the end of general-interest mass-circulation magazines.
1972	*Life* folds (in 1978, it is reborn as a monthly).
1972	*Ms.* magazine is launched, heralding the emerging women's movement.
1974	*TV Guide* surpasses *Reader's Digest* in circulation.
1977	Reader's average cost for U.S. magazine passes $1 for the first time as the entire industry shifts toward recovering more costs from readers than advertisers.
1980s	Specialty publishing mushrooms.
1985	Number of magazines published surpasses 11,000.

intensely by the richest and most powerful people in America. . . . One out of every 3 of *Forbes'* 735,000 subscribers is a millionaire.''[1] *Entrepreneur*, about 163,000 circulation (1987), cannot brag about millionaire readers, so it is shifting strategy to serve the small business executive still looking for success. Says *Entrepreneur*'s principal strategist: "We're trying to reach the guy who hasn't made it yet. It's the biggest market there is.''[2]

So one important magazine type—the national business magazine—serves the rich and those who aren't so rich but wish they were.

Harper's represents another vital sector—magazines for opinion leaders. *Harper's*, launched in 1857, and similar journals of in-depth analysis and opinion are major influences on American thinking and public policy. In such publications, social issues of great significance are argued and discussed. Few are financial suc-

Examples of the multitude of special-interest magazines. *Courtesy Whittle Communications.*

cesses (*Harper's* at one time lost money for 14 years straight).[3] But such magazines have a journalistic impact far greater than others.

Dramatically different is *Muscle & Fitness*, aimed at the "pant and sweat" crowd, whose obsession with physical fitness spawned an entirely new class of American magazines. There are magazines for joggers, runners, walkers, swimmers—whether they do it for exercise or fun. Advertisers eagerly use such magazines to sell equipment, clothing, vitamins, and other goods. The health fad created new industries, and a new form of mass communication developed to serve them. There is a lesson here: If you can anticipate the next lifestyle fad and get into the market first with a publication designed to serve it, fortune awaits you!

Plastics World and *Indiana Prairie Farmer* illustrate the vast time gulf American magazines straddle. *Plastics World* serves an industry that didn't exist prior to World War II; it exemplifies the publications that spring up immediately when a new industry is recognized. *Computerworld, BYTE, Video & Sound, Electronic Component News,* and *Digital Review* serve the new world of computers. *Indiana Prairie Farmer* and scores of other farm magazines deal with America's origins, the soil, and the people who till it. In the

space age, farm magazines report—as they did 100 years ago—how to raise hogs at a profit and grow tall corn.

And could two magazines differ more than *U.S. News & World Report* and *Foreign Affairs?* *U.S. News* is colorful, abbreviated, fast-paced—a sort of *USA Today* of the magazine world, its largely anonymous editors underlining each week, in as few words as possible, the newsiest events of relevance to the lives of busy readers. *Foreign Affairs*, a quarterly, is ponderous, with long, gray columns of profound thinking under the bylines of foreign relations experts known to opinion leaders everywhere.

Clearly, the magazine is proving, despite its ancient origins, to be one of the most youthful, flexible, and forward-looking of all media institutions in America. Whatever new social turn the nation makes, a new magazine (in fact, often several) is waiting! In their diversity, magazines have mushroomed—especially dramatically after 1950, when television became a viable medium. Like newspapers, magazines counter competition by shifting into new coverage areas.

Not only has the number of magazines increased but their circulation also has leaped forward. Importantly, the industry has succeeded—much more than newspapers—at keeping pace

2 ▶ Magazine Circulation Growth

Year	Number of Magazines or Groups	Single-Copy Sales	Subscription Circulation	Total Circulation	U.S. Adult Population	Circulation per 100 Adults
1950	250	61,998,611	85,270,929	147,269,540	104,596,000	140.8
1960	273	62,295,487	128,136,349	190,431,836	115,461,000	164.9
1970	300	70,701,105	173,462,984	244,164,089	134,118,000	182.1
1980	407	87,854,289	198,592,798	286,447,087	160,179,000	171.7
1985	479	81,613,538	244,754,653	326,368,191	175,834,000	185.6
1986	489	78,696,253	252,870,445	331,566,698	177,672,000	186.6
1987	512	80,768,795	263,717,935	344,486,730	178,325,000	193.2

Source: Magazine Publishers Association. Figures are for the second half of each year and cover magazines whose circulation is verified by the Audit Bureau of Circulations. Comics are excluded. Population figures after 1980 are U.S. Census Bureau estimates.

with population growth. Newspaper circulation is dropping relative to population growth; verified magazine sales are increasing. ▶ 2

Including farm and business publications, magazine ad revenue in 1988 was $8.9 billion, about 7.5 percent of all advertising dollars spent. That's small, compared to daily newspapers' $31.1 billion, or 26.3 percent share, that same year or television's $26 billion, or 26.0 percent.[4] But profits are substantial and attract some of the world's largest media companies into heavy investments in magazines. ▶ 3 They include the newspaper giants discussed earlier—Hearst, Newhouse, Washington Post Co., New York Times Co. Diversification by large media companies sometimes takes them to unexpected places—the prestigious New York Times Co., for example, to supermarket checkout counters, where it sells *Family Circle* magazine. One of the most important new players in U.S. magazines is the French company Hachette S.A., which has about $1.9 billion annual worldwide revenue. In 1988, Hachette agreed to pay $712 million for Diamandis Communications, Inc., an American company that owned *Woman's Day, Car and Driver, Popular Photography*, and 10 other publications, and $448.6 million for Grolier, Inc., an American publisher.

Thousands of magazine titles battle for readers' attention on newsstands throughout America. Note editors' efforts to present attention-getting covers. *Wide World Photos.*

Magazine expansion into narrowly focused specialty areas creates many smaller periodicals. More than 11,000 titles are published in the United States. In this sense, the magazine industry is structured much like the newspaper industry: A relatively few larger magazines are widely known and account for most circulation and ad revenue, but much of the journalistic action and precision targeting of readers and advertisers is with smaller magazines (many of the jobs are there, too, of course).

The magazine industry's diversity is revealed in an analysis of 481 magazines whose circulations are checked by the Audit Bureau of Circulations. Magazines with relatively small circulation are most numerous. A handful of large magazines account for more than half of total circulation.

In 1986, a mere 30 magazines, each with 2 million circulation or more, accounted for 50.9 percent of all circulation; 408, each with less than 500,000 circulation, totaled 20.1 percent of circulation.

Even magazines of larger circulation carve out special markets in serving specific reader needs. Gone are huge general-interest magazines of yesteryear—the weekly *Life, Look, Collier's* and others—with their national circulations based on content that was interesting and nice to have but not crucial. The entertainer today is television. Magazines must find other ways of gaining readers (and thus advertisers.) Each of

3 ▶ The Leading Magazine Companies

(1988 revenue in millions of dollars)

Company	Magazine Revenue	Top Magazine	Revenue
1. Time Inc.	1,752.0	*Time*	349.7
2. Hearst Corp.	919.0	*Good Housekeeping*	129.3
3. Advance Publishing (Newhouse)	745.0	*Parade*	266.5
4. Reader's Digest Association	600.4	*Reader's Digest*	114.0
5. Thomson Corp.	596.0	*Medical Economics*	25.3
6. News Corp. Ltd. (Murdoch)	509.6	*New York; TV Guide*	335.4
7. Cahners Publishing	420.0	*Restaurants & Institutions*	39.7
8. McGraw-Hill	413.7	*Business Week*	227.3
9. Capital Cities/ABC	370.0	*W*	27.1
10. Hachette Group	366.0	*Woman's Day*	115.6
11. Meredith Corp.	365.1	*Better Homes & Gardens*	152.8
12. International Data Group	352.0	*Computerworld*	56.7
13. Washington Post Co.	327.5	*Newsweek*	241.7
14. Times Mirror	298.5	*Field & Stream*	36.9
15. New York Times Co.	249.1	*Family Circle*	134.4

Source: "Media Companies by Estimated Magazine Revenue," *Advertising Age*, June 26, 1989, pp. 5–10.

today's circulation leaders is well known for specialized content. 4

TV Guide, the largest, is needed by serious TV viewers, not so much for listings as for the best TV analysis and commentary published today. Marking its 25th anniversary, in 1978, *TV Guide* put it this way:

> If all viewers want to know is when *Laverne and Shirley* is on, they don't need *TV Guide*. If, however, they also want intelligent, objective coverage of television as an entertainment medium and as what may be the most powerful force for change in our society, they do need *TV Guide*.

Reader's Digest has cult followers worldwide, many of whom are second- and third-generation *Digest* readers. They find in it guidance for daily living, inspirational object lessons, how-to-cope articles. Check this out yourself by analyzing its front-page table of contents. Note that *Digest* editors pick stories almost by formula: a little sex, a little religion, inspiration (dog saves boy, or boy saves dog), a simple-to-understand look behind the scenes of a complicated medical, political, or economic story. And lots of cute stories, jokes, and feel-good-all-over stuff about Mom, the flag, apple pie. There is a highly professional editing strategy in that. In a world dominated by Third World famines, terrorist car bombs, and big-city bag ladies, is there no refuge for the weary reader? Why, yes, there is—in the *Digest*!

Modern Maturity and the *NRTA/AARP News Bulletin* serve a special constituency increasingly courted by politicians (and advertisers): the elderly. Their numbers are increasing, and so is their political clout. They have specialized news needs. They need to know how to cope with medical expenses, loneliness, a rising cost of living—so that is what *Modern Maturity* and the *Bulletin* cover.

What need does *National Geographic* serve? Think about it. That beautifully produced magazine (carefully stored by the millions in attics all over America by its third-generation cult of followers) is beloved—there is no other word for

4 ▶ Largest-Circulation Magazines

(subscriptions and single-copy sales)

		Circulation
1.	*TV Guide*	16,969,260
2.	*Modern Maturity*	16,734,801
3.	*Reader's Digest*	16,566,650
4.	*NRTA/AARP News Bulletin*	16,465,570
5.	*National Geographic*	10,498,594
6.	*Better Homes & Gardens*	8,012,659
7.	*Woman's Day*	6,021,136
8.	*Family Circle*	5,773,484
9.	*McCall's*	5,353,595
10.	*Good Housekeeping*	5,202,526
11.	*Ladies' Home Journal*	5,125,052
12.	*Time*	4,683,348
13.	*National Enquirer*	4,383,227
14.	*Guideposts*	4,290,882
15.	*Redbook*	4,088,739

Source: Audit Bureau of Circulations. Circulation is average paid per issue in the second half of 1987.

it—because it lifts us out of our problems and transports us with excitement and adventure to far-off places we all want to visit some day but never will. Get hassled at the office today? Pick up *Geographic* and go to Nepal. Tired of housework? Take a coffee break and mingle with British aristocracy at Ascot. It's all done with exquisite still photography, a *Geographic* trademark.

A measure of reader loyalty to *National Geographic* is the magazine's phenomenally high 84.2 percent renewal rate among subscribers in

70 countries. In the magazine business, renewal rate is an important indicator of whether a magazine is succeeding journalistically. Many newspapers lose 50 percent or so of their subscribers each year and envy *National Geographic*'s loss of only 15 to 16 percent.[5]

The largest-circulation magazines, then, identify special interest areas and carefully craft alluring content for readers who can be "sold" to advertisers. Note the essential distinction between this strategy and the newspaper strategy discussed earlier: Most magazines (city and regional magazines are among exceptions) seek interest markets nationwide. Most newspapers (the *Wall Street Journal* and other national newspapers excepted) seek more limited geographic markets, then establish journalistic franchises among special readers within those markets. In terms of media careers, the difference is important. An aspiring journalist who, say, wants to write about television for *TV Guide* should develop skills for turning out copy of interest to a national audience. Journalists entering community newspaper reporting should concentrate on communicating with an audience in a city and its environs.

MAGAZINE ECONOMICS: THE CHALLENGE OF THE 1990s

It is terribly expensive to publish magazines—so expensive, in fact, that most of what magazines do today—and will do in decades ahead—must revolve around costs.

The per-copy cost of publishing magazines rose consistently from 1976 to 1986 at a rate two to three times faster than the U.S. consumer price index. Why is there this cost dilemma?

First, a main appeal of most magazines is high-quality color photography and layout. Readers like it and so do advertisers (full-page color photos of new autos and other products really sell). To compete against television, color is an imperative. And that requires slick, high-quality paper much more expensive than the $650-per-ton newsprint used by newspapers.

Young editorial and layout experts who specialize in the use of colors, photographs, and imaginative design produce "target marketing" advertising and publications that catch the eye. *Courtesy Whittle Communications.*

Second, most magazines have national or even international circulation and must use the expensive U.S. Postal Service for delivery to scattered pockets of readers.

Third, except for a few with longtime, near fanatical readers, most magazines have high rates of subscriber churn. Readers take a magazine for a while, then drop it—so the magazine must maintain continuous (and expensive) subscription sales campaigns to replace them. Evidence of this expensive effort is in your mailbox and in TV commercials, offering cut-rate magazine subscriptions and the chance to enter a sweepstakes and "become a millionaire!"

These offers are from direct marketing companies that sell about 2.5 billion subscriptions annually in the United States (of a total 3.5 billion sold). Leading companies are American Family Publishers, Publishers Clearing House, Magazine Marketplace, and Great American Magazines. Larger companies each mail as many as 60 million solicitations annually, offering savings of 80 percent or more below newsstand single-copy and regular subscription prices.

Little—sometimes none—of that revenue goes to the magazines themselves. Their payoff is avoiding the cost and difficulty of selling sub-

"Adjacency" in magazine journalism positions the advertiser's message next to a page of alluring news that is designed to draw in readers and thus expose them to adjacent advertising. *U.S. News & World Report photo.*

scriptions but getting added circulation to offer their advertisers.[6]

There are other high costs—salaries, for example—but those three factors create for magazines a competitive disadvantage in the battle against other media. Subscriber and advertiser rates must be high enough to cover costs and produce a profit. But if rates get too high, subscribers don't renew—and other media with lower rates can slip into the magazine's camp and steal advertisers. Fully 69 percent of magazine costs are in subscription selling, production, and distribution.

The competitive impact of the magazine's cost structure is severe. Of total costs, 31 percent are in circulation sales. A medium-sized newspaper spends about 13 percent on its entire circulation department. (TV, of course, has no directly comparable cost.) Another difference between magazines and their primary print competitor, newspapers, is cost of editorial content: 10 percent of total costs for magazines, about 13 percent for newspapers (see Figure 6.1).

There is in all this a sort of economic catch-22 for magazines. First, general-content magazines cannot attract advertisers even if they de-

liver millions of readers unless they are demographically attractive and exclusive. *Life*, over 14 million circulation and the most popular magazine of its time, was folded as a weekly in 1972 because it delivered just readers, not special kinds of readers particularly attractive to advertisers. To reach *Life*-type readers today, advertisers use television, which can deliver 20 million or 30 million for a single 30-second commercial.

Second, reaching specialized audiences that are attractive to advertisers is enormously costly for magazines. Hiring, say, graduate chemists or MBAs or lawyers as reporters to produce authoritative coverage of chemical news, business, or the law is much more costly than hiring general-assignment reporters. The entire editorial process in specialized magazines—which are reporting for experts—is costly. More important, the main alternatives to general-circulation magazines—zoned editions narrowly focused with news and advertising for targeted audiences—are extremely costly. *Better Homes and Gardens* doesn't produce a single magazine of 8 million-plus circulation; rather, each month it produces 130 to 150 zoned editions. *Newsweek* aims 58 zoned editions at separate geographic and de-

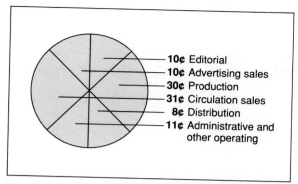

Figure 6.1. WHERE MAGAZINES SPEND THEIR DOLLAR. *Source: Magazine Publishers Association; figures for 1986.*

10¢ Editorial
10¢ Advertising sales
30¢ Production
31¢ Circulation sales
8¢ Distribution
11¢ Administrative and other operating

mographic targets (executives, women, householders). Producing that many zoned editions requires additional employees. Advertising pages are added or deleted, according to the zone being served, but editorial content is often changed, too. Using a process called selective binding, magazines even can address ads within each copy to individual subscribers. Computerized printing facilities eventually could produce, say, 4 million tailored copies of *Time*. But costs will be a factor.

The bottom line, curiously, is that per-copy costs of creating, selling, and distributing magazines is so high that without advertiser support, the more copies a magazine sells, the more money it will lose!

Many publishers therefore have gone over to producing specialized publications with relatively limited circulations. Lower circulation means lower costs—and if all subscribers are attractive to advertisers, profits are much higher!

Given the task of repositioning *House & Garden*, a Newhouse magazine, William F. Bondlow, Jr., cut circulation from 1 million to 500,000. He upgraded editorial content to attract upscale readers and between 1983 and 1986 doubled to $50,000 the median household income of the magazine's readers. That attracted advertisers and permitted Bondlow to charge $23,500 for a four-color advertising page—just about what he charged when the circulation was 1 million.

So costs dropped sharply as half a million circulation was trimmed, revenue increased to $19.5 million in 1986 from $11.1 million in 1983, and profitability skyrocketed.[7]

It has been determined that nearly all Americans (94 percent) read magazines during the average month and that the well-educated and upscale are the best readers of all. Such findings come out of a small but effective organization in New York City that acts as a research center and lobbyist for the magazine industry; its primary task is promoting magazines as an effective medium for national advertising, although it tackles other problems such as escalating postage costs. It is the Magazine Publishers Association (MPA), which says that on average, 11 magazine issues per month are read by 98 percent of all college-educated Americans, 97 percent of persons with $35,000 or more annual household income, and 97 percent of all professional and managerial persons. MPA uses this to convince advertisers that their messages have a greater chance of exposure to more demographically attractive Americans in magazines than in other media.

Magazine publishers acknowledge that among young people, particularly those aged 18 to 34, radio is a popular medium. Much research has been done on the media habits of young people because many are buying cars, getting married, and shopping for houses, furniture, appliances—and that's when advertisers want to get to them. *Bride's* magazine, for example, calculates that the bridal market in 1988 alone generated $24 billion in retail sales.[8] By age 60 or so, most people have already purchased the big-ticket items.

Some magazines get very picky about ensuring that their subscribers are attractive to advertisers. If you request a subscription to McGraw-Hill's *Aviation Week & Space Technology*, for example, the magazine will ask you to complete a card indicating which sector of aviation or space technology employs you. If you are a pilot or involved in manufacturing, buying, or selling airplanes, or defense technology, you will get a lower rate and be added to the magazine's rate base. That's the publisher's guarantee that ads will reach an audience especially interested in an advertiser's products. For example,

5 ▶ Index of Media Exposure

(100 = U.S. average)

Demographics	Magazines	TV	Newspapers	Radio
Age				
18–24	118	94	83	114
25–34	116	85	93	112
35–44	112	87	107	106
45–54	96	103	110	95
55–64	88	112	117	89
65 and older	65	131	100	72
Education				
Attended or graduated college	129	86	123	103
Graduated high school	98	99	100	105
Did not graduate high school	67	121	70	88
Household Income				
$50,000 and over	133	80	133	101
$40,000–$49,999	116	83	127	107
$30,000–$39,999	110	87	113	104
$20,000–$29,999	100	99	100	102
$10,000–$19,999	88	110	87	99
Under $10,000	75	131	63	88
Occupation				
Professional, managerial	129	76	130	102
Technical, clerical, sales	118	84	110	114
Precision, craft	90	85	90	117
Other employed	98	91	90	106
Not employed	84	125	90	86

Source: Magazine Publishers Association.

in one report issued through the Audit Bureau of Circulations, *Aviation Week* reported 20,873 subscribers employed in "avionic/electronic/electrical systems, components, parts & services." It noted 7,049 in U.S. Navy or Marine air arms, and 115,583 living in the United States, 21 in Muscat and Oman, 9 in Qatar—and thousands of others elsewhere in the world. That is typical of the lengths to which magazines will go in assuring advertisers that they can reach specialized audiences. Purity of subscribers is guarded zealously. Why should, say, a farm equipment advertiser use *Indiana Prairie Farmer* if half its subscribers are factory workers or accountants?

6 ▶ Favorite Magazines of Readers 18 to 29 Years Old

Male	Female
1. *Rolling Stone*	1. *Rolling Stone*
2. *Muscle & Fitness*	2. *Mademoiselle*
3. *Gentlemen's Quarterly*	3. *Seventeen*
4. *Skiing*	4. *Self*
5. *Cycle World*	5. *Shape*
6. *Hot Rod*	6. *Glamour*
7. *Audio*	7. *Cosmopolitan*
8. *Popular Hot Rodding*	8. *Omni*
9. *Ski*	9. *Ski*
10. *Cycle*	10. *Vogue*

Source: Simmons Study of Media and Markets, 1987.

Because of the industry's peculiar economics, it is impossible to look at a magazine's total circulation or even its total advertising revenue and tell whether it is profitable. But it's widely known among media analysts that some of the giants are not profitable enough to keep their owners happy. For example, *Newsweek*, with its 3.1 million circulation and $239 million in 1987 ad revenue, has been offered for sale by its owner, Washington Post Co. As a sign of the times, *Newsweek* in 1988 reduced its work force 10 percent to cut costs.

STRATEGIES THAT ARE WORKING

In shifting to meet new cost and competitive challenges, magazine publishers have devised a number of strategies that are working brilliantly.

First, in addition to bringing in those desir-able affluent readers, magazines are persuading them to pay more for the privilege of reading. Most newspapers count on subscribers for only about 20 percent of total revenue. Many magazines get 50 percent or so from subscribers. Magazines are able to increase rates and still hold audiences because readers consider their specialized editorial content important in their lives and worth higher prices. Newspapers stress more general news content and keep cover prices low to encourage mass audiences. Because they charge readers more, magazines can charge advertisers relatively less and thus stay competitive with the ad rates of other media ▶ 7

Second, many magazines shift journalistic signals skillfully to meet changing reader desires.

HOW THEY GUARD SUBSCRIBER PURITY

❝ Only paid subscriptions available. *Aviation Week & Space Technology* is edited for persons with active, professional, functional responsibility in aviation, air transportation, aerospace, advanced and related technologies. Subscriptions solicited and limited to executive, management, engineering and scientific levels in industry, airlines, corporate aviation, government and military. No subscriptions accepted without complete identification, including subscriber name, title, rank or position, company or organization name and primary activity of company or organization. Publisher reserves the right to determine whether qualified or non-qualified price applies. ❞

Statement published in each issue of McGraw-Hill's **Aviation Week & Space Technology.**[9]

The explosive growth of special-interest publications is a direct response to a noticeable shift in reader habits. Magazine Publishers Association studies show that reading is still considered relaxation by millions of Americans but that more and more read for factual, authoritative information on certain subjects: auto buying, operation, and maintenance; beauty and grooming; career selection, preparation, and advancement; clothing and fashion; consumer education (how to be a wiser consumer); cultural interests (arts, literature, religion, science); entertaining; farming, gardening, and landscaping; food planning,

7 ▶ Readers Pay More for Magazines

Figures for the 50 leading magazines according to advertising revenue.

Year	Average Single-Copy Price ($)	Index (1960 = 100)	Average Annual Subscription Price ($)	Index (1960 = 100)
1960	.39	100	4.58	100
1970	.63	162	7.16	156
1980	1.48	379	16.75	366
1985	2.10	538	23.15	504
1986	2.20	564	23.24	507
1987	2.20	564	24.45	534

Source: Magazine Publishers Association.

buying, preparing, and serving; health, both mental and physical; hobbies; home buying, building, and remodeling; home decorating, furnishing, and management; money matters; raising children; raising and caring for pets; self-improvement (psychology, getting along with others, total knowledge helpful in daily living); sports (personal participation, improving skills); and travel.[10]

Editing magazines to catch readers' eyes at newsstands and supermarket checkout counters is an art. Enticing cover layout, catchy headlines, alluring color photos, and varied contents designed for many interests are part of what it takes to induce single-copy sales. So is high-quality content between the covers. Especially important is sales position: A magazine placed up front in a newsrack (so that the full cover can be seen) or near the checkout cash register (where customers wait in line) has the best chance of selling. ▶ 8

Compared to newspapers, magazines give readers more news and information as a percentage of total content. Newspapers traditionally offer 60 percent advertising, 40 percent news. For years, magazines have offered just about a 50–50 ratio.

Magazine covers are designed carefully to catch the eyes of passersby—and it takes a shouted ''buy me'' to catch busy pedestrians on this New York City street corner. *Wide World Photos.*

Of course, many readers consider advertising as informative as news. Ads are, in fact, reader attractions. How many times have you looked with interest at clothing fashions, hair-

8 ▶ Magazines That Catch the Reader's Eye

Next time you pass a newsstand, note whether these magazines catch your eye. They were leaders in single-copy sales in 1987; compare the list with the total circulation figures on page 138.

	Single-Copy Sales			Single-Copy Sales
1. *TV Guide*	8,136,590	9. *Good Housekeeping*		1,680,790
2. *Woman's Day*	5,922,993	10. *Glamour*		1,626,699
3. *Family Circle*	4,626,893	11. *Globe*		1,542,547
4. *National Enquirer*	3,939,661	12. *Woman's World*		1,444,133
5. *Star*	3,309,999	13. *Playboy*		1,317,031
6. *Cosmopolitan*	2,571,753	14. *National Examiner*		1,098,379
7. *Penthouse*	2,023,557	15. *Ladies' Home Journal*		1,038,635
8. *People*	1,892,969			

styles, or new auto designs in ads? That, too, is part of your information-gathering process.

We have looked at how editors select content and how marketing experts position magazines for target audiences. We now must look at how ad salespeople exploit all that by attracting advertisers. ▶ 9 ▶ 10

Successful ad sales strategy involves convincing advertisers of several factors. First, of course, is the magazine's ability to deliver fo-

Note the effort to catch single-copy buyers' eyes with social issues highlighted in these two successive *Newsweek* covers. Also note the boxed "teaser" atop each page, which alerts readers to significant stories inside. *Reproduced with permission.*

9 ▶ Who Uses Magazines to Sell?

When you open a magazine, advertisers try to sell you something. These are the ones you'll meet most frequently in magazines.

Advertiser Classification	Percent of Total Magazine Advertising
Automotive, automotive accessories, equipment	12.6
Business consumer services	9.1
Toiletries, cosmetics	8.4
Mail order	7.6
Food and food products	7.0
Cigarettes, tobacco, accessories	6.2
Apparel, footwear, accessories	6.0
Travel, hotels, resorts	5.1
Computers, office equipment, stationery	4.5
Beer, wine, liquor	3.8
Publishing, media	3.4

Source: Magazine Publishers Association; figures for 1987.

10 ▶ Where the Ads Are: Big Moneymakers

Advertisers so highly value *TV Guide* for reaching millions of consumers that they pay one-third of a billion dollars a year to get into its pages. Other top magazines pull in hundreds of millions of ad dollars annually.

	Advertising Revenue
1. *TV Guide*	$331,188,722
2. *Time*	328,778,875
3. *People*	266,203,908
4. *Sports Illustrated*	263,167,312
5. *Newsweek*	239,252,795
6. *Business Week*	217,483,994
7. *Better Homes & Gardens*	142,170,974
8. *Good Housekeeping*	132,465,976
9. *Forbes*	128,563,495
10. *Family Circle*	123,975,448
11. *Fortune*	122,027,279
12. *Woman's Day*	115,471,862
13. *Cosmopolitan*	111,539,122
14. *Reader's Digest*	107,202,543
15. *U.S. News & World Report*	106,095,938
16. *Glamour*	87,646,810
17. *Vogue*	79,507,690
18. *Money*	78,590,042
19. *Ladies' Home Journal*	76,725,281
20. *McCall's*	67,717,134

Source: Magazine Publishers Association; figures for 1987.

cused specialty audiences. Many media claim target marketing success, but none succeeds like magazines. Cadillac, for example, can hardly do better than advertising to *Forbes*'s one-in-three millionaire readers, and *Rolling Stone* puts an ad for, say, a snappy convertible or a motorcycle right into the hands of a large number of interested potential buyers.

Second is the character of the magazine itself. Slick ads, with bold, high-quality color reproduction, are great sales devices. And the magazine is portable, built for reading in snatches on planes and trains, as well as cover-to-cover in one sitting on the sofa. Importantly, the magazine is available at the time and place of the reader's choosing, and it is not intrusive. A reader who picks up a magazine is actively looking for something. That is the best possible environment for an ad. Contrast it with TV commercials that intrude, against your will, and interrupt your favorite movie or football game! Magazine advocates ask: How many times have you left the room to avoid TV commercials?

A third strong appeal magazines have for advertisers is the way readers use them. The Magazine Publishers Association says the average reader spends 61 minutes on each copy read.[11] That's probably twice the time spent on newspapers, and advertisers know that the longer the reader is in the magazine, the more pages get flipped, and the more ads get exposure. Publishers claim, too, that readers use the magazine as an information-gathering tool. Readers of both magazines and newspapers tend to find print advertising ''appealing,'' ''informative,'' ''believable,'' and ''helpful,'' according to the publishers, while much TV advertising is termed ''annoying or irritating,'' ''exaggerated,'' or downright ''silly/insulting/juvenile.''[12] (Remember, that's what *magazine* publishers say.) Magazines sell advertisers on another reader habit— ''pass-along.'' Magazines are given to relatives or friends, and thus advertisements in them reach far more readers than sales indicate. For example, *Aviation Week* claims an average of 4.16 readers for each copy. Pass-along for newspapers averages 2.2 per copy, 2.5 or 2.7 for some specialized papers such as *USA Today* or the *Wall Street Journal*. Pass-along gives advertisers a bigger bang for their buck and gives magazines (and newspapers) a competitive edge over television. However, readership figures must be regarded cautiously. *Time* asked in one survey about four magazines that were either fictitious or defunct and found millions who claimed to read them!

Let's now narrow our focus to case studies that will reveal challenges and opportunities ahead for magazines.

SUCCESS STORY:
CITY AND REGIONAL MAGAZINES

Did you ever hear of ''professional New Yorkers''? They are people for whom the city is glitter, wealth, excitement. For them, New York is not

bag ladies or subway crime (although there is a certain excitement in that), it's music, theater, fine restaurants, Fifth Avenue shops. Professional New Yorkers love being part of the in crowd. New York is not a place to live, it's a way of life.

And cheering on the professional New Yorker, stroking that sense of mystique, is *New York* magazine. It is one of many around the country that achieve huge success by celebrating a city, state, or region—magazines that identify a way of life as a market niche.

These magazines have been significant since the 1970s in the fight for reader time and advertiser dollars. Some achieve very substantial circulations. ▶ 11

These magazines' success is a competitive triumph over both newspapers and television. Just think: *New York* magazine (owned by Rupert Murdoch) succeeds in a print market dominated by the *New York Times*, the *Daily News*, the *Post* (and throw in, for good measure, a very substantial *Wall Street Journal* and *USA Today* pres-

---

▶11 City and Regional Leaders

		Circulation
1.	*Southern Living*	2,263,922
2.	*Sunset*	1,442,478
3.	*Yankee*	1,018,245
4.	*New York*	428,507
5.	*California*	357,813
6.	*Texas Monthly*	283,340
7.	*Chicago*	201,790
8.	*San Francisco Focus*	197,996
9.	*Los Angeles*	173,651
10.	*Alaska*	170,195

Source: Audit Bureau of Circulations; figures as of January 1, 1987.

ence). In television, New York City offers intense, high-quality competition. *Chicago* magazine isn't published in a media-deprived town, either. The *Tribune* and *Sun-Times* both deliver detailed, high-quality city coverage, and TV is highly professional, too. *Southern Living*, *Yankee*, and *Texas Monthly* serve regions and states also served by strong print and television media. And so it is for other city and regional magazines—they flourish in markets that might appear saturated by media, whose readers already have too much to read, whose advertisers already have other, established means of reaching consumers. So why do they succeed?

First, established media often fail to protect their franchises. They neglect to meet reader or viewer needs with specially focused news and information. This can be due to the character of the mass media. A general-circulation newspaper, trying to appeal to a wide audience, cannot always cover every nook and cranny, and television simply doesn't have time. But newspapers and television at times let down their guard.

Second, that lack of vigilance gives discerning magazine journalists the opportunity to identify a market niche that's not being served and create a specialty publication for it. (Did the *New York Times*, anxious as always about the Third World, overlook its own city, handing *New York* a piece of the market?)

Third, once the niche is identified and the proper journalistic product created, a shrewd magazine publisher can position the publication as offering something exclusive. For example, *New York* clearly offers readers something they think they cannot get elsewhere. That's why 428,000 people buy it every week.

New York uses the device in Figure 6.2 to show advertisers that it delivers 1,008,000 readers who cannot be reached in the city's dominant magazine, the *New York Times Sunday Magazine*. *New York* acknowledges that advertisers who use both magazines will reach 590,000 readers twice with the same message. Obviously, *New York* (or any other magazine) cannot survive if it delivers only readers who also can be reached through other media. So demonstrating exclusiv-

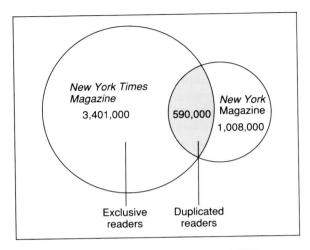

Figure 6.2. *NEW YORK* DEMONSTRATES EXCLUSIVITY. *Source:* New York, *quoting Simmons Market Research Bureau 1987 survey.*

ity with over 1 million readers is very important.

New York must also demonstrate that it delivers *attractive* readers, and it does: $85,200 median household income, $203,400 median residence value, $649,800 median household net worth. To illustrate how refined this marketing approach gets, *New York* goes after alcoholic beverage advertisers by citing these facts:

In an average month, 80.8 percent of *New York*'s subscribers entertain at home.
94.3 percent serve alcohol on such occasions.
In an average month, 97.9 percent dine in a restaurant—73.4 percent five times or more (and, presumably, they drink while doing so).[13]

Clearly, lifestyle magazines conduct the same upscale drive for affluent readers that motivates many major newspapers and other print media. How do *New York*'s editors do that? They stroke ever so gently that mystique we mentioned earlier, that sense of being in with the rich and famous. Throughout city magazine journalism run names—lots of names—of people other people talk about. *New York* announced that it would profile 20 who "profoundly affect our lives" and held a contest to let readers pick them from a list of 50 candidates.

New York's editors have just seconds to snatch single-copy buyers from streams of commuters rushing by newstand displays in train and bus stations. As we've seen, covers have a job to do. However, only 8.8 percent of *New York*'s circulation is single-copy sales, so editors must also build attractive journalistic content that will pull in subscribers week after week.

Analysis of *New York*'s circulation proves it is the New York idea, the way of life, that sells the magazine. Of all subscribers, 26.5 percent don't live in the city—or even the metropolitan region. Many live far away: 1,584 in Missouri, 264 in Utah, 484 in Mississippi, and so forth.[14] Perhaps *New York* transports readers to the city of glitter and excitement as *National Geographic* takes armchair adventurers to Nepal!

When Rupert Murdoch's *New York* ran this cover on the late artist Andy Warhol, everybody in Manhattan was talking about the auction of his personal belongings. *Reproduced with permission.*

Actually, many city and regional magazines play to far-flung audiences. *The New Yorker* (not to be confused with *New York*) has had international appeal since its launch in 1925 because of its high-quality writing and well-known cartoons that poke fun with great sophistication and subtlety. *Yankee* brings out the New Englander in thousands who never lived in New England and sells much of its more than 1 million circulation outside that region. Many magazines spark readers' nostalgia for times they never knew— lifelong apartment dwellers read *Country Living* for a scent of elegant rural life. Again, it's way of life that these magazines sell.

Huge profits are an owner's rewards—if the proper journalistic niche is selected, if both readers and advertisers are served properly, and if competition doesn't get too fierce. Noting *Texas Monthly*'s success, more than 40 similar magazines crowded the Texas market by 1987. Such competition develops in most city markets. In New York, *On the Avenue* was aimed at just 80,000 residents of high-price apartments in specific neighborhoods. Talk about narrow focus! The *Wall Street Journal* remarked: "There are more than 100,000 yuppies in the naked city, and new Manhattan publications are hotly pursuing them."[15]

MONEY, BUSINESS, AND THE "TRADES"

Business news is big business on Main Street as well as Wall Street. And magazines are expanding rapidly in this special niche. While newspapers and television were keeping competitive watch on national business magazines (*Business Week, Forbes, Fortune*), two new classes of business magazines entered the field: city, state, and regional business magazines and publications specializing in personal finance and money management. Newspapers are scrambling to develop business coverage and regain lost ground. But those specialized magazines are solidly entrenched.

A third category of specialty magazine is made up of *trade publications*, hundreds of weeklies and monthlies that serve the news needs of certain industries, often with high-quality coverage, but that are little known to the general public.

In personal finance, the leader is *Money*, a Time Warner monthly that had 1.8 million circulation and $59.8 million in ad revenue in 1987. *Money*, launched in 1972, lost a great deal of money before its editors won reader support and unlocked advertiser spending. The key was the "how to" story—advice for readers on how to budget their spending, how to select financial advisers, how to invest, how to put aside enough for the kids' educations. It's reporting on how to cope in life. *Money*'s readership isn't the millionaire set you'll find in *Forbes*; reader demographics are much less attractive than those enjoyed by the national business magazines. But *Money* nevertheless attracts advertising from brokers and others trying to reach those who are planning their financial future.

City, state, and regional business magazines mushroom in the shadow of top newspapers. In New York, Detroit, Chicago, Los Angeles—the turf of great dailies—city business magazines are flourishing. They also are spreading (with less success) in smaller cities—Jacksonville, Nashville, Phoenix. Their attraction is in-depth local business coverage that many dailies were slow to develop. Some newspapers themselves diversified into business publications. The *St. Petersburg* (Fla.) *Times*, for example, publishes *Trend* magazines dealing principally with local business for Florida, Georgia, and Arizona.

Trade publications are a powerful, if generally hidden, force in magazine journalism. Did you ever hear of *Contemporary OB/GYN*? *Heavy Duty Trucking*? How about *Modern Machine Shop*? All are successful publications in their fields. The trades offer varied and exciting careers in covering specialized news for experts in the field. Authoritative, carefully researched, and accurate reporting and writing are required.

But money and business aren't the only subjects that sell magazines.

SEX AND OTHER THINGS THAT SELL

The headlines *do* catch your eye:

"Losing Your Virginity—Read This Before You Decide"
"Sex for Absolute Beginners"
"How to Be the Best Kisser"

Those are not from *Playboy, Hustler*, or other plastic-wrapped "skin" magazines most newsstands keep hidden from curious children. They are, in fact, headlines from a magazine aimed at American girls 14 to 19 years old. The magazine is *Sassy*, a monthly trying for a piece of the lucrative U.S. teenage market. Its first issue, sold single-copy on newsstands, drew 16,500 subscriptions, which is an unusually strong showing for a new magazine.

Clearly—and students of the media should get used to the thought—there is a powerful desire among editors to sell magazines that push beyond informative, professional journalism into the sensational and salacious.

Of course, a case can be made for informing readers (as *Sassy* did) how to deal with hygiene problems and providing information on AIDS, incest, and "The Sad Story of a 17-Year-Old Stripper" who committed suicide. But media students must ask whether the motive is helping teenage girls through rocky years or simply making a buck by selling magazines. In 1989, the Australian owners of *Sassy* encountered stiff opposition from conservative groups and advertisers over the magazine's daring content. They sold it to an American, Dale Lang, who said the magazine had been "blind-sided by the Moral Majority" but that he would rebuild it. Lang quickly pushed circulation above 500,000.

Insight magazine commented when *Sassy* appeared in March 1988:

The formula is simple: The fresh face that debuted on magazine racks in March promises young females the dope on life's truly important things; the publishers hope to tap the hefty ad budgets of manufacturers that make the products girls cannot live without.[16]

Teenage girls are indeed an attractive market. There are about 14 million of them 14 to 19 years old, and the older girls are calculated to spend an average of $65 weekly on themselves.[17] So many magazines try to catch their attention—*Seventeen*, still young though launched in 1944, had 1.86 million circulation in 1987; *Teen* had 1.2 million, and *YM*, 825,000. But the magazine-reading habit isn't ingrained among teenage girls. Fewer than one-third read any teenage magazine.

Another tough market for publishers is college students of either sex. Newspapers can't reach them consistently, and McGraw-Hill, *Newsweek*, and other publishers shut down campus magazines in 1988. Students say they are too busy to read magazines.[18]

In the adult magazine market, *Playboy*, *Hustler*, and raunchier magazines vie for a public interested in naked flesh. But readers may be tiring of that. *Playboy* suffered huge circulation and financial losses in recent years, in part because the U.S. attorney general's commission on pornography questioned, loudly and publicly, whether retail stores should be selling some magazines. *Playboy*'s single-copy sales in the last half of 1986 dropped 42 percent from the same period in 1985, after retailers heard that message. Christie Hefner, who took over company management from her father, Hugh, says *Playboy* lost 17,000 newsstand vendors in 1986! Readers voted, too: The magazine's 3.7 million circulation in 1987 was roughly half its 1972 peak.[19] *Hustler*'s controversial publisher, Larry Flynt, seems to hear a similar message. He launched four nonsexual magazines in 1987.

A long step back from the sexuality of *Playboy* and *Hustler* are personality or curiosity magazines. They include the enormously popular *National Enquirer* (4.3 million weekly circulation in 1987) and other "supermarket mags" that keep us up to date on what Britain's royal family is doing and plumb such complex topics as "Why Crying Is Good for You." These magazines cover stories that serious journalists wouldn't touch.

But we must wonder whether the drive upscale by so many other magazines is leaving behind a huge sector of readers for whom Princess Di really is important news and UFOs are serious topics. The *Enquirer, People, Us*, Rupert Murdoch's *Star*, and others like them found at supermarket checkout counters do seem to fill a reader niche. (One U.S. publisher, Macfadden Holdings, Inc., demonstrated in 1989 its belief that supermarket mags have a profitable future. It paid $412.5 million to purchase the *National Enquirer*.)

Editors face complex questions of ethics and professionalism when balancing what readers desire (and what sells) with what they need (and might not sell so well). Ray Cave, former managing editor of *Time*, puts it this way: "It is an editor's duty to give readers what they ought to read, not what they want to read. The most difficult task is to make them want to read what they ought to read." Cave spent years studying which magazine content and covers sell and which don't. He says, "There is much less difference between 'what sells' and 'good journalism' than one might think."[20] ▶ **12**

Ellen Levine, vice president and editor in chief of *Woman's Day* (6 million circulation), cites 10 tips from top editors for improving magazine editorial content:

1. Cut story lengths; readers are impatient.
2. When you can't find news, try to create it by conducting surveys.
3. Sex still sells.
4. Give readers information unavailable elsewhere.
5. Strive for exclusive stories.
6. Don't focus on winning [journalism] awards.
7. Lists of information are popular.
8. Don't rely on "proven" formulas for editing magazines.
9. Always be nice to advertisers.
10. Remember your magazine can make readers' lives better or worse with what it publishes.[21]

But magazine competition involves more than one editor trying to outdo other editors.

12 ▶ Ray Cave's Cover Commandments: What Sells

1. Photos sell better than art; cartoons "sell awful."
2. Girls sell better than boys.
3. Cocaine sells better than Coke.
4. "Things that really pain me (my aching back) sell better than things that mentally anguish me (my empty wallet)."
5. "Things common to my experience (marijuana) sell better than things that will affect my experience (genetic engineering)."
6. Politicians sell badly.
7. The economy sells worse.
8. Cities sell terribly.
9. Small towns sell worse.
10. Sports won't sell at all. (Exception: Muhammad Ali will always sell.)
11. Dead popes sell better than wounded popes.
12. When in doubt, run Cheryl Tiegs, the model. (Cave says he did twice, "with gratifying results.")

Cave says these, in order, are the nine best-selling covers in his eight years as *Time* editor:

Dec. 4, 1978	Jonestown Massacre
Dec. 22, 1979	John Lennon's Murder
Mar. 19, 1984	Michael Jackson
Aug. 2, 1982	Herpes
Mar. 6, 1978	Cheryl Tiegs
Dec. 7, 1977	Richard Leakey, Anthropologist
June 2, 1980	Mount St. Helens Eruption
Feb. 27, 1978	Muhammad Ali
Oct. 14, 1980	Aching Backs

Source: Ray Cave, "Musings of a Newsmagazine Editor," *Gannett Center Journal*, Spring 1987, p. 81.

THE COMPETITIVE HEAT IS RISING

Magazines make war on several fronts each day. Internally, they battle the high costs of publishing. Within their industry, they struggle against other magazines. And they battle powerful external foes.

Newspapers are tough competitors because they operate effectively on so many levels: national, regional, city, even (with weeklies) village and neighborhood. Newspapers also attack with specialty coverage. The *Wall Street Journal* competes directly against national business magazines such as *Business Week* and *Forbes*. On the local newspaper level, special-section coverage in business, health, entertainment, and other areas competes with magazines, too. *USA Today* is directly positioned against magazines with its beautiful color, ad rate structured to compete against magazine rates, and *USA Weekend*. This magazine, successor to *Family Weekly*, is inserted in 292 Sunday newspapers with 14.6 million circulation in 1987. It is colorful and zoned into nine geographic sections.

Television is a major competitor, with its sight-and-sound attractions for many millions of viewers and the advertisers who chase them. TV competes somewhat against specialty magazines by offering shows dealing with personal finance, sports events, travel, and the like. But TV viewer demographics are less attractive than those of magazine and newspaper readers, and TV's main competitive weapon must continue to be delivery of mass audiences gathered with entertainment shows. However, the television industry is fractionalizing. Networks are losing audience share rapidly; local stations and cable are grabbing major portions of the audience pie. That will lessen the ability of any single television operation to deliver the gigantic national audiences of the past. This may mark a golden opportunity for magazines (and newspapers) as nationwide reader and advertising media.

NOW, THAT'S CONFIDENCE!

66 In the year 2091, when the travel-weary passenger on the moonshuttle has had his fill of: Dinner on the anti-gravity magnetic tray, three-dimensional TV, intergalactic weather reports and conversational banter with the flight attendants, as they float by—he'll then settle back in his contour couch, and return to that important, private activity each of us does alone. Reading. (It will be, we trust, a magazine.) **99**

Hearst Corp.[22]

Direct mail competes with both national and specialty magazines. Through direct mail, advertisers can reach every household in a market—even tens of millions nationwide—or just a few thousand in a small territory occupied by, say, women who buy cosmetics, men who buy sports cars, and so forth. For all traditional print mass media, direct mail is a formidable competitor.

Whatever the larger competitive picture, magazines offer young entrepreneurs an opportunity to get into media ownership.

Computerized desktop publishing and other new technology reduce the cost of entry. And both readers and advertisers support new magazines if they are expertly edited for a special market niche and are properly promoted and sold. Not every new magazine succeeds, of course. Even huge companies with years of publishing success can fail (Time Inc. lost $47 million on *TV-Cable Week*, launched and quickly folded

in 1983). Nevertheless, many aspiring publishers and editors launch new publications every year. ▶ **13** ▶ **14**

Certainly, major publishing companies show optimism over the future of magazines. In Chapter 7, we'll go inside *U.S. News & World Report* to see how that magazine is structured and where the jobs are.

---

13 ▶ Magazine Launches

Some years, 200 or more new magazines are launched in the United States, many on a shoestring by young entrepreneurs. These are the types launched in 1987.

Category	Number of Titles
City and regional interest	20
Business	16
Travel	14
Sports	12
Health	11
General interest	10
Audio, video, electronics	8
Women's	7
Computers	7
Fashion	6
Home service and home	6
Children's	5
Cultural	4
Music	4
Men's	4
Entertainment, TV guides	4
Outdoor, hunting and fishing	4
Hobbies, collectors	4
Epicurean	3
Boating, sailing	3
Celebrities, movies	3
In-flight	3
Automotive	2
Parents, babies	2
Photography	2
History	2
College campus	2
Other	2
Total	180

Source: Magazine Publishers Association.

14 ▶ Rolling the Stone Upscale

Jann Wenner

At 21, in 1967, Jann S. Wenner was a college dropout (University of California at Berkeley, after one year) with a love of rock music, $7,500 in borrowed funds, and an idea for a new magazine. He called it *Rolling Stone* (from an article he had read about singer Bob Dylan) and aimed it at the world of rock.

Today, the $7,500 has grown into a multimillion-dollar fortune, *Rolling Stone* is hugely successful, and Wenner is proof once more that the magazine industry can offer low-cost entry into ownership if you've got the right idea and strong journalistic and business skills.

It's safe to say that not many bankers would have financed what looked like a counterculture sheet for rock fans in San Francisco, where Wenner launched *Rolling Stone* by, among other things, offering a free roach clip (for holding marijuana cigarette stubs) to new subscribers. So Wenner raised the money from relatives, friends, and even his girlfriend's mother. *Rolling Stone* was launched in November 1967 with 24 pages and a cover story on John Lennon. Optimistically, Wenner printed 40,000 copies. He sold just 5,000.

For years, *Rolling Stone* was the chronicler of the rock music world. But there was journalistic substance in other areas, too. Wenner attracted some of the best writers in America— Truman Capote, Tom Wolfe, William Greider, and the irrepressible, off-the-wall Hunter S. Thompson. Circulation exploded, ad revenues soared. Then everybody got a little older. Wenner did, *Rolling Stone* did, and 1960s readers became bankers and brokers, parents and grandparents. Wenner began rolling the *Stone* upscale.

In 1977, pursued by accusations of selling out, Wenner moved *Rolling Stone* from San Francisco to top-of-the-scale Fifth Avenue in New York City and began repositioning the magazine for both readers and advertisers.

By 1988, *Rolling Stone* had an impressive 1,175,000 circulation. Pass-along readership (high among college students) pushed to more than 7 million the readers of each issue. Today, *Rolling Stone* boasts young, upwardly mobile, college-educated readers whose median age is 25.1 years and median income is $29,893. About 51 percent have attended or graduated from college. It is a magazine about youthful, with-it lifestyles and carries advertising from auto, liquor, and cigarette companies and others anxious to catch the next generation of big spenders. In case

☆ SUMMARY

Magazines are diverse, energetic, creative, and—long after TV sounded a death knell for print—profitable as an industry. The number of magazines is exploding (in 1987, there were more than 11,000). Circulation is climbing rapidly, and advertising revenue accounts for a significant slice of the national ad dollar.

Global media conglomerates are big players in American magazines. Time Warner is largest. Hearst is next. A French company, Hachette, largest magazine publisher in the world, is moving strongly into American magazines.

Rolling Stone used this ad to convince advertisers it had repositioned itself with more affluent, upscale readers. *Reprinted with permission of* Rolling Stone.

advertisers miss the point, Wenner runs ads stressing that *Rolling Stone* readers aren't hippies.

Annual ad revenues passed $55 million in 1988, and *Rolling Stone* is worth probably $150 million or more. Wenner is also 50 percent owner of *Us* magazine, a biweekly with more than 1 million circulation.

Not all Wenner's magazine ideas strike gold. He tried and failed to serve other market niches, including the student market with *College Papers* (later folded into *Rolling Stone*). But that original one idea, back in 1967, carried Wenner to undreamed heights.

Wenner's lifestyle, like the magazine, changed, too. He lives in Manhattan with his wife and two children and is quick to point out that he has stayed married to the same woman whose mother contributed to the original borrowed $7,500.

General-interest magazines with nationwide circulation are nearly a thing of the past. However, smaller specialty publications are expanding rapidly, with focused editorial content for demographically attractive readers.

The challenge is the high cost of publishing. Unless magazines attract upscale audiences, which in turn attract advertising, the more copies they publish, the more money they lose!

Magazines charge readers relatively more and advertisers less than newspapers do, a competitive advantage in the fight for ad dollars. Magazine editors skillfully meet American readers' desire for how-to-cope articles. High readership per copy, a comparatively long period spent reading (61 minutes per copy), and reader use of magazines to seek out information all give the industry competitive strength against television and newspapers.

City and regional magazines are often successful because they celebrate a way of life. Magazines dealing with money, business, and specialized information for specific industries also do well and are influential.

Concerns in the future will include rising internal costs and competition with newspapers, television, and direct mail.

☆ RECOMMENDED READING

Excellent research is published by the Magazine Publishers of America, 575 Lexington Ave., New York, NY 10022. See particularly their 1986 "Study of Media Involvement." *Folio* and *Advertising Age* report on magazines; *Ad Age*'s periodic special sections are particularly strong. The *Gannett Center Journal* often touches on important editorial considerations. The HMS/Ayer *Directory of Publications* contains facts on many magazines.

Also see Theodore Peterson, *Magazines in the Twentieth Century*, 2d ed. (Urbana: University of Illinois Press, 1964); Leonard Mogel, *The Magazine: Everything You Need to Know to Make It in the Magazine Business* (Englewood Cliffs, N.J.: Prentice-Hall, 1979); William Parkman Rankin, *Business Management of General Consumer Magazines* (New York: Praeger, 1980); and William Taft, *American Magazines for the 1980s* (New York: Hastings House, 1982).

Inside the American Magazine

For generations, millions of Americans regarded newsmagazines—*Time, Newsweek, U.S. News & World Report*—as essential to their weekly routine. Since 1923, when *Time* was launched, newsmagazines have added to the national media system a dimension not quite matched by newspapers, radio, or television.

Newsmagazines were a once-weekly stopping point, a place where Americans too busy to follow news daily could catch a summary of the major events of the past week. The newsmagazines also looked ahead into what might happen next week and poked around with special sections on art, the movies, books, lifestyle, and other journalistic sectors that newspapers didn't quite have a grip on. And the newsmagazines, particularly *Time*, wrapped all those bits of news and information in jazzy, "hip" writing that amused and entertained (or, sometimes, angered) as well as informed. It was a journalistic formula of sifting through thousands of news stories each week for the most important ones and then presenting them in a magazine you had to read to be informed, alert, *with it*. For years, that formula was difficult for other media to match, and it worked phenomenally well.

Not anymore. Of all magazine types, none stands at such crossroads of change as the newsmagazines. Americans have new media alternatives. The jazz age is long gone, "hip" is outdated, and more and more Americans are saying, "Just give us straight information, the facts. We'll make up our own minds, and never mind the cute (and opinionated) writing."

That's the way one major newsmagazine, *U.S. News & World Report*, sees it. *U.S. News*, founded in 1933, is changing quickly, convinced that it has the key to the newsmagazine future and that *Time* and *Newsweek* are headed in the wrong direction. It's a fascinating development, and we're going inside *U.S. News* to explore how magazines construct competitive strategies, then implement them. We'll also look at specific magazine jobs and how to get them.

U.S. NEWS & WORLD REPORT: A CASE STUDY

Mortimer B. Zuckerman is a multimillionaire real estate developer, an intellectual who earned four academic degrees, and, it turns out, a big-league gambler. He bet $163.5 million that even though he spent most of his life in real estate, he can outsmart some of the smartest people in the magazine business.

Zuckerman paid the $163.5 million in 1984 for *U.S. News & World Report*, a weekly newsmagazine so distant behind top-ranked *Time* and runner-up *Newsweek* that many journalists had written it off as a confirmed loser. Zuckerman then launched one of the hottest competitive battles raging today in the magazine world.

U.S. News is a perfect case study of sometimes conflicting strategic and economic influences sweeping the American magazine industry.[1] First, remember that having a bigger circulation doesn't necessarily mean that you are in a better financial situation and may in fact mean that you are facing huge cost problems. Second, therefore, being number 3 in circulation may be an advantage, in a business sense, if you can keep your costs down but still deliver for advertisers those desirable affluent, upscale readers. Third, whatever your magazine, it must be different, one that stands out as something special within the highly competitive magazine industry. Those three factors are the core of Zuckerman's strategy against *Time* and *Newsweek*.

Time, the flagship of Time Warner, is by far the leader among newsmagazines. In 1988, its circulation exceeded 4.6 million; its advertising revenue, $283.8 million; its circulation revenue, $328.7 million. For many, *Time* is synonymous with *newsmagazine*. After all, Henry Luce invented the concept and built his publishing empire on it.

Newsweek is not a flagship for its owner, the Washington Post Co.; it is a problem. Circulation, at 3.3 million, trails *Time*'s. So do advertising revenue ($239.2 million in 1987) and circulation revenue ($142.1 million). And *Newsweek* has a serious identity problem. Readers—and advertisers—ask, Is *Newsweek* the same as *Time*? No, it's smaller. What, then, is it? A smaller, me-too version of *Time*? Or something unique? If it is different, in what way?

U.S. News had 2.3 million circulation in 1988 (and thus substantially lower costs), $106 million in ad revenue, $82.7 million in circulation revenue—and it is clearly different from both *Time* and *Newsweek*.[2] It's that difference that Zuckerman is sharpening.

When Zuckerman bought *U.S. News* (it was owned by employees, and many became overnight millionaires), he immediately began an overhaul. Scores of editors and others left. David Gergen, former director of communications for the Reagan administration, came aboard in 1986 as a high-profile editor despite a lack of journalistic experience. Gergen was to lend high visibility to the Zuckerman era at *U.S. News*. After two years, Gergen became editor at large, a sort of roving ambassador. He was succeeded as editor by Roger Rosenblatt, a former *Time* essayist. Zuckerman hired a business colleague, Fred Drasner, to revamp ad sales, circulation, and business operations.

Note the table of organization in Figure 7.1. It is typical of many magazines, except that Zuckerman is chairman and editor in chief. He divides his chief subordinates' responsibilities into three broad sectors. The editor runs the news side. Drasner, as president and chief executive officer, has primary responsibility for implementing business and operations policy. And Publisher Richard C. Thompson takes charge of marketing and sales. (Magazine publishers often concentrate on selling advertising and have little or no influence on news content.)

Lesson: If you want to get to the top in magazines, you must have broad business experience. Major magazines are enormously complicated business concerns, and strong management skills are needed to run them. If you want to edit a big-time magazine, you must know news, be international in your thinking and aware of major public issues, and know how to manage people who report and write. Magazine journalists can

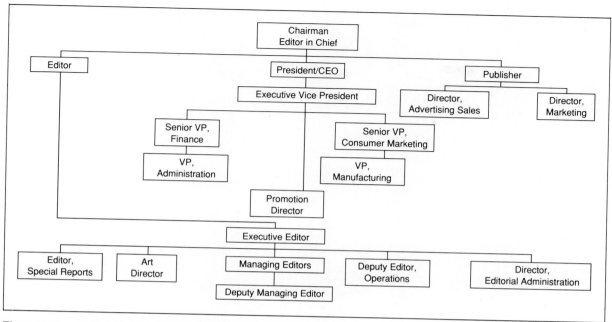

Figure 7.1. *U.S. NEWS & WORLD REPORT* ORGANIZATION.

stay in news work and fashion fine, rewarding careers as reporters, writers, and editors without getting too involved in circulation or advertising. But those journalists often eliminate themselves from consideration for top management jobs.

Because he lacked substantial editing experience, Zuckerman made hiring top-flight editors a priority. The top editor must stay free to concentrate on major newsroom issues—which important stories will be covered, which long-term projects (special issues, investigative efforts) will be emphasized. The editor also decides who will be hired for major newsroom positions. Some were hired from other magazines, including *Newsweek.* For any magazine where "tight" editing is required to cram major stories into limited space, highly skilled editors are essential.

With new leadership in place, Zuckerman turned to creating impact, a splash—a product that would be perceived as different from *Time* and *Newsweek.* This is achieving product differentiation, separating your publication from others and giving both readers and advertisers a choice of something different. *U.S. News* was

redesigned in January 1986 with cleaner, sharper graphics, more color, and a leaner layout. The magazine took on a more businesslike appearance, a "hard-news" orientation. Zuckerman focused on analysis of trends, particularly in business and economics.[3] A section called "News You Can Use" underlined his intention to make *U.S. News* a tool readers use in daily living. It concentrates on subjects such as nutrition, health, and personal finance. Zuckerman insists that *Time* and *Newsweek* devote too much space to rehashing events of the past week and lecture readers too much, telling them not only what happened but also what to think about it (*Time* has a reputation among journalists for getting preachy and for mixing fact and opinion).

U.S. News achieved product differentiation, but it also had to be sure readers and advertisers were aware of the improvements. Zuckerman pumped money into promotion. The self-advertising budget was increased from $1.3 million in 1986 to $1.7 million in 1987. Zuckerman retained a New York ad agency, DFS Dorland, which designed a hard-hitting campaign aimed directly at

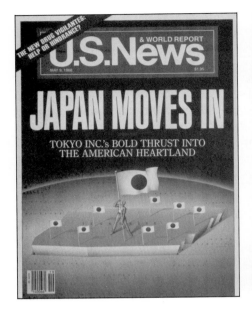

Magazine covers tell a competitive story: *U.S. News & World Report* tries for "harder" news content than *Newsweek*. Note that *U.S. News*'s teaser promotes an inside story on drugs; *Newsweek*'s promotes coverage of men's fashions. *Reproduced with permission.*

Time and *Newsweek*. Those magazines were termed clones of each other in ads published throughout the United States; *U.S. News* was described as being different, as having "clout," a word fashionable in Washington (where the magazine is published) and New York City (where many ad agencies and advertisers have headquarters). For readers, the core message was that *Time* and *Newsweek* are fine for movie reviews and entertainment fluff, but *U.S. News* is the magazine if you're interested in serious, how-to-cope news and information. For advertisers, the theme was that if you want your ads seen by serious readers of serious news, place them in *U.S. News*.

U.S. NEWS AND "HOT MADONNA"

> 66 If you're interested in knowing why Madonna is hot, we're not the magazine for you. 99

Fred Drasner, president,
U.S. News & World Report.[4]

The combined journalistic redesign and promotional campaign was brilliant. First, it did, in the minds of many, draw a distinct line between

U.S. News and its competitors. Second, the combined effort neatly disguised the fact that compared to *Time* or *Newsweek*, *U.S. News* is much weaker in news-gathering resources. *U.S. News* has only a handful of full-time foreign correspondents scattered around the world, backed by "special correspondents"—part-time "stringers," in media parlance. Both its newsmagazine competitors have many more, but *U.S. News* virtually made a strength out of its smaller size by emphasizing its focus on news that *really* counts and by dismissing much *Time* and *Newsweek* coverage as irrelevant fluff.

Third, the Zuckerman effort worked. Just three months after the redesign, *U.S. News* reported that circulation was up 250,000. Furthermore, an outside research firm found that the median age of *U.S. News* readers had dropped to 41.9 from 42.3, and their median household income had risen to $38,096 from $35,057. Such demographic improvement is a primary goal of all magazines that rely heavily on advertisers eager to reach America's younger affluent readers. The Zuckerman team scored a triple bull's-eye: circulation up, reader age down, household income up![5]

Fourth, the campaign held to achievable goals. It didn't set out to convert all advertisers everywhere to using *U.S. News*; rather, it spoke primarily to the almost converted, those already using newsmagazines and thus susceptible to the message. If examined closely, the campaign didn't really take on both *Time* and *Newsweek*. *Time* is hugely influential, highly profitable, solidly entrenched, sure of itself. It was *Newsweek*, for years in turmoil, lagging in revenue, unsure of itself, that *U.S. News* went for. A subtle message for advertisers was not "drop out of *Time*" but rather, "If you need two newsweeklies, *U.S. News* should be the second, not *Newsweek*." The *U.S. News* campaign assumes that *Time* will remain the leader with many advertisers.

Time reacted to *U.S. News*'s moves with keen interest but unshaken confidence. At *Newsweek*, the reaction was panic. Profitability dropped, and Katharine Graham, chairman of the magazine's owner, Washington Post Co., rapidly hired and fired top executives, searching for someone who could solve her basic dilemma: What do you do with a number 2 magazine sandwiched between a dominant and strongly profitable number 1 and a surging number 3? *News-week* had five editors and three presidents in one 10-year period. Some of Graham's picks lasted just months. Some *Newsweek* editors went to *U.S. News*. It's not that *Newsweek* is losing money; it simply isn't producing profit levels generally expected in the media, and conglomerates today often shift resources from marginal operations to ones where more profit can be gained. It's supposed to be a secret, but the Washington Post Co. has talked to prospective buyers about *Newsweek*.

The newsweeklies, then, have been primarily concerned with competition among themselves, with the *real* fight between *Newsweek* and *U.S. News* for rich rewards that may await in a strong number 2 position behind *Time*. However, the fight—indeed the future of all newsmagazines—may be decided by external competitors. They are coming on with a rush.

With satellite technology, the widespread audiences courted by newsweeklies can now be reached by national newspapers such as the *New York Times* seven days a week, the *Wall Street Journal* and *USA Today* five days a week. For daily readers of these papers, there is precious little exclusive news left for the once-weekly

This ad dramatizes that in a week when *Time* and *Newsweek* both covered the same "soft" story (artist Andrew Wyeth), *U.S. News & World Report* covered a middle-class "pocketbook issue." *Copyright U.S. News & World Report, 1987. Reproduced with permission.*

newsmagazines. Sunday newspapers seriously eat into the "week in review" appeal of *Time* and *Newsweek*. The *New York Times* devotes an entire section to "look-back" coverage of the past week. The newsweekly emphasis on analysis and "trend" stories is often preempted by daily newspapers that go in-depth, behind the scenes. *USA Today*, with its graphs, illustrations, and heavy entertainment and sports coverage, puts a serious dent in newsweekly back-of-the-book sections, which once—but no longer—carried exclusive, offbeat coverage of films, personalities, lifestyle, and fashions.

If the widespread, general-interest audience that nurtured newsmagazines is threatened by national newspapers, can't newsmagazines shift focus to narrow market niches that desire specialty news? Yes, but thousands of specialty magazine competitors have mushroomed in recent years. Compounding the newsmagazines' problem, new specialty media are edging into their markets—newsletters, cable television, and other sources of narrowly focused information and, in the case of electronic media, a virtually unending flow of news.

Can *U.S. News* meet these challenges? Let's take a deeper look inside the magazine.

INSIDE THE NEWSROOM

As in all things journalistic, it is in the newsroom that *U.S. News*'s fate will ultimately be decided. Corporate strategy, advertising sales, circulation tactics—all will be to no avail unless reporters, editors, artists, layout specialists, and other staffers produce the type of news and information that will win in a hotly competitive 21st century.

About 94 men and women make up that staff. Within 24 months, Zuckerman replaced 60 percent of them and shifted others to new jobs. He raided the staffs of prestigious news organizations—*New York* magazine, the *Washington Post*, the *Wall Street Journal, Business Week, Newsweek, The Economist* of London. It's fundamental in newsroom management that you can get a quick transfusion of talent by selectively raiding competitors. Says Gergen: "It's a wonderful thing to watch. You bring in another new person and another good story appears in the

Designer Dave Merrill works the old-fashioned way— with his hands—in laying out artwork for *U.S. News & World Report*. Photo: Bill Auth, *U.S. News & World Report*

New technology and journalistic instinct combine to produce *U.S. News & World Report*. Here, Joan Strong, a designer, uses a computer to lay out a page. Photo: Bill Auth, *U.S. News & World Report*

book. It's given us a real sense of momentum."[6] In a departure from tradition, *U.S. News* hires name columnists and gives staffers bylines on important stories. Owner Zuckerman has backed up his editors with money. He doubled *U.S. News*'s newsroom budget in just two years.[7]

Here is how *U.S. News & World Report* describes its newsroom leaders: Owner, Chairman, and Editor in Chief Mortimer B. Zuckerman sets overall positioning and direction in concert with the editor and writes editorials. Editor Roger Rosenblatt is responsible for day-to-day direction of the magazine and oversees weekly decisions on stories, long-term projects, and major hires. Executive Editor Michael Ruby, second in charge, has major responsibilities for editorial quality, runs the magazine in the editor's absence, and oversees the presentation of the magazine on a weekly basis. Managing Editor Peter Bernstein directs the "U.S. News" and "News You Can Use" sections, helps determine the direction of the magazine, and coordinates many special projects. Managing Editor Edwin Taylor, a former art director, is now responsible for design, presentation of special projects and issues, and U.S. News books. Deputy Managing Editor Chris Ma directs the "Business" and "Horizons" sections, helps determine the direction of the magazine, and coordinates many important projects. Deputy Editor for Operations Gerald Parshall edits the "Currents" section and oversees weekly production of the magazine. Art Director Rob Covey supervises the design and the artistic and photographic presentation of the magazine. Editor for Special Reports Mel Elfin is responsible for editing, coordinating special projects, election coverage, and U.S. News books. And Director of Editorial Administration Kathryn Bushkin is responsible for the news department budget, coordination of recruiting, personnel matters, and management issues.[8]

U.S. News has correspondents stationed in major U.S. cities—two in New York, one each in Atlanta, Los Angeles, and San Francisco. Overseas, competing with *Time* and *Newsweek* correspondents in many major capitals, *U.S. News* has only 11 correspondents (and 10 string-

Senior Editor Ken Walsh (*left*) and Associate Editor Peter Ross Range (*right*) interview Marlin M. Fitzwater, press secretary during the Reagan and Bush administrations. *Reproduced with permission.*

ers) placed strategically and given regional news-gathering responsibilities.[9] Each staff correspondent is assigned to cover a wide area of Europe, the Middle East, the Soviet Union, Africa, Asia, or Latin America. Inevitably, this means that *U.S. News* correspondents practice "parachute journalism"—dropping in quickly when trouble erupts, then moving on and never really giving any part of the world regular, comprehensive coverage. This raises complaints by Third World countries that they pop into the news only with war, famine, and pestilence and that world perceptions of them are distorted when thus filtered through understaffed, Western-oriented news organizations.

However, on its revenues ($188.7 million in 1987), *U.S. News* cannot afford much more staff coverage of distant lands. So despite Zuckerman's doubling the newsroom budget and adding field reporters, *U.S. News* remains an editor's magazine. In 1988, when it had 5 field correspondents in the United States and 11 staffers overseas, *U.S. News*'s Washington headquarters housed 10 editors, 18 senior editors, 38 associate editors, 12 contributing editors (mostly experts in fields such as economics and military affairs), 17 researchers, and 14 news desk editors. Separate inside staffs handled layout and production,

Experienced editors are the backbone of any magazine newsroom. Gerson Yalowitz learned his trade with the Associated Press, then became a *U.S. News & World Report* reporter, foreign correspondent, foreign editor and now is an assistant managing editor in Washington. *Reproduced with permission.*

art, photos and other illustrations, and news administration.

This inside crew at *U.S. News* (and other newsmagazines) shapes the weekly product. Most editors labor anonymously, unknown to readers, in a form of "group journalism." They use fact-filled cables from bureaus and news services to write and rewrite the stories that appear in the "book," as those in the business call their magazines. For correspondents, group journalism creates mammoth frustration. They can labor for months on major stories, only to have them shunted aside at the last moment by distant editors marching to different news priorities. Or when stories do appear, they often carry the imprint of those anonymous editors and show little of the distinctive creative personality of the field correspondent. For anyone aspiring to newsmagazine careers, the reality is that the work can be anonymous, and the route to the top is through inside editing jobs.

Newsmagazine editors often use news service copy—particularly AP at *U.S. News*—in writing stories.[10] And always, news services are watched closely up until "close"—the newsroom's deadline as the magazine goes to press. This is a tense time because last-minute news breaks may require throwing out a long-planned and now-finished cover story and quickly writing a completely new one. A major complication is that after it comes off the press, the magazine won't reach most subscribers for three days or so. That forces editors to write, under enormous pressure, from bits and pieces, a story that will "stand"—be journalistically valid—three days later. Editors who can do that are highly valued (and well paid). For example, *U.S. News* was badly beaten by *Time* and *Newsweek* when a major story broke in June 1989. On Friday, June 9, *U.S. News* editors at midnight closed their June 12 edition. Their cover story was on air pollution. *Time* and *Newsweek*, both with later deadlines, were still working on Saturday, putting together their June 12 editions, when Chinese government troops stormed Tiananmen Square in Beijing and killed and wounded thousands of students demonstrating for democratic reforms. It was a major news story, one that grabbed attention around the world and was certain to inspire thousands of Americans to buy newsmagazines. *Time* editors moved their planned cover story (on teenage crime) inside the magazine and displayed on the cover instead a picture of dead students and the headline "Massacre in Beijing." *Newsweek*, which had planned a cover on ethics in the U.S. House of Representatives, used a dramatic photo of a bleeding Chinese student and the headline "Bloodbath." It was a major journalistic defeat for *U.S. News* in the highly competitive newsmagazine world.

As "close," or final deadline approaches, things get tense in the newsroom of *U.S. News & World Report*. Photo: Bill Auth, *U.S. News & World Report*

Despite their anonymity, newsmagazine correspondents involved in such world-shaking stories gain much professional satisfaction. Normally, newsmagazines cover only stories of national and international importance and, unlike reporters on community newspapers, not minor local stories.

THE WASHINGTON NEWSMAGAZINE CORRESPONDENT

by Gerson Yalowitz, Assistant Managing Editor, *U.S. News & World Report*

For a Washington newsmagazine correspondent, the "story" is everywhere around him—and it's usually big news for someone. News sources are numerous and various, from high elected officials making crucial decisions to lowly bureaucrats and clerks with access to the files on $600 toilet seats, upside-down postage stamps, and congressional junkets to Paris.

The journalist—any journalist—who does not find himself or herself "charged up" in this atmosphere should be doing something else.

What particularly drives the newsmagazine correspondent, however, is not just the challenge of reporting such news. More important is the opportunity—the obligation—of the newsmagazine to report, assess, and analyze the repercussions and implications of fast-breaking and often complex events. It is this overriding commitment that sets the magazine correspondent apart from most journalistic peers.

Given such a mandate, the reporters and editors of newsmagazines are generally not journalistic neophytes. There are rare trailblazers who manage to make it from campus correspondent in a single leap, and more and more editors are willing to look at experts, not necessarily trained as journalists, who are able to communicate well. But the most trodden path to a newsmagazine post remains the more familiar one: experience with a wire service or a small daily, then several more years' experience on a large daily, preferably gaining expertise in a particular area such as politics, Congress, international affairs, or business.

Once on the job, opportunities for a correspondent-editor are impressive. The editor portrayed in Calvin Trillin's book *The Floater*—the faceless fellow who piles incoming stories, research material, and reporters' memos on the floor until they reach belt height and then proceeds to write without once looking at them—is a dying breed. Today, the editor or correspondent with initiative can report and write his or her own stories and receive a well-earned byline in the process. Nowadays, for the journalist who has a certain curiosity about the world and the people in it, a sense of responsibility and obligation to report and explain, and a healthy dose of good old-fashioned skepticism, the job of Washington newsmagazine correspondent is hard to match.

For correspondent and editor alike, a challenge is to do all this in in accordance with the marketing concept of the magazine. No newsroom of any kind tries to cover all the news. First, marketing strategists decide how to position the magazine. Second, an overall tone is decided on. Each reporter and editor must select news that appeals to the preselected readers and then write it in language that communicates effectively. At *U.S. News*, that means stressing hard-news content. Gergen explains: "We provide service and information as opposed to entertainment. That's what distinguishes us from the other newsweeklies. We offer 'News You Can Use' on things like personal finance, health, and travel." That achieves product differentiation.

Now, how does the business side at *U.S. News* exploit these news-side tactics?

INSIDE CIRCULATION AND ADVERTISING AT *U.S. NEWS*

Nothing the newsroom does will move *U.S. News* toward success unless the circulation department brings in the right type of readers who can in turn be sold to advertisers by the advertising department.

The circulation strategy is to hammer the theme that *U.S. News* publishes useful news. The advertising strategy is to boast to advertisers that attractive, affluent readers can be reached through the magazine.

U.S. News ads attack *Time* and *Newsweek* directly and by name, telling readers that they can get more coverage of business and personal finance by turning to *U.S. News*. *U.S. News* strategists feel that readers attracted to that type of news are the most attractive, demographically.

Ads directed at advertisers boast that *U.S. News* is either number 1 or number 2 in ability to deliver demographically attractive readers. *U.S. News* also includes among its competitors *Business Week, Forbes, Fortune,* and the *Wall Street Journal*. For *U.S. News*, no competitive boundaries exist between magazines and the business-oriented *Wall Street Journal*.

The tone of *U.S. News* advertisements is aggressive. They hit competitors head-on, speak of "corporate impact" and "power profile," and claim the title "America's fastest-growing newsmagazine." One ad calls *Time* and *Newsweek*

In this ad, *U.S. News* tells readers that the magazine carries essential business news, then tells advertisers that they can use its pages to reach demographically attractive readers. *Reproduced with permission.*

"clone candy" and terms *U.S. News* "brain food." It's *war* in the competitive world of newsmagazines!

Circulation work in magazines is enormously complex. No longer is the job simply mailing several million copies worldwide; today, magazines offer advertisers precision targeting through zoned editions. *U.S. News* breaks its circulation into seven regional zones (see Figure 7.2). Note that the percentage of circulation in each region closely reflects the percentage of the U.S. population there.

Magazines seek a new breed of circulation employee for such complex duties. *U.S. News*

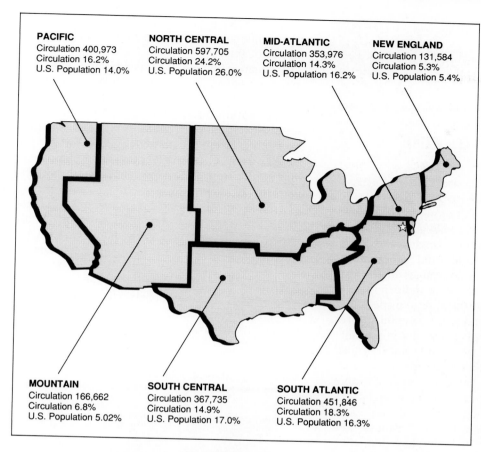

PACIFIC
Circulation 400,973
Circulation 16.2%
U.S. Population 14.0%

NORTH CENTRAL
Circulation 597,705
Circulation 24.2%
U.S. Population 26.0%

MID-ATLANTIC
Circulation 353,976
Circulation 14.3%
U.S. Population 16.2%

NEW ENGLAND
Circulation 131,584
Circulation 5.3%
U.S. Population 5.4%

MOUNTAIN
Circulation 166,662
Circulation 6.8%
U.S. Population 5.02%

SOUTH CENTRAL
Circulation 367,735
Circulation 14.9%
U.S. Population 17.0%

SOUTH ATLANTIC
Circulation 451,846
Circulation 18.3%
U.S. Population 16.3%

Figure 7.2. *U.S. NEWS & WORLD REPORT* CIRCULATION DISTRIBUTION. *Source:* U.S. News & World Report. *Reproduced with permission. Circulations as of June 30, 1987.*

wants circulation staffers with editorial, advertising, and production knowledge. Their policy statement explains:

> Editorial skills are needed to write promotional copy and prioritize key projects. Advertising and marketing skills are needed to develop creative ideas and analyze the effectiveness of these ideas. Production knowledge is needed to typeset, design, print and mail.

A Circulation Director's job is to recognize these talents and *the potential for these talents* in entry-level job applicants. Certainly, not many applicants will have all these skills. What we look for is at least one of them and a ''spark'' that says, ''I am willing to learn and work hard.''

Advertising department employees must complete the job begun by the newsroom (fashioning a magazine attractive to readers) and circulation (pulling in paying subscribers). Accomplishing that marketing effort, the *U.S. News* advertising department brings in about 56.1 percent of the magazine's total revenue.[11]

Heavy advertisers include auto companies, liquor companies, many corporations serving the business world (telecommunications companies, hotels, technology companies, copier manufacturers). Cigarette manufacturers, prohibited from advertising on television, use *U.S. News* extensively.

Because it delivers fewer readers, *U.S. News* cannot charge rates as high as those of *Time* or *Newsweek*. For example, at one time in 1986, *U.S. News* charged $55,000 for a full-color page; *Time* charged $115,000, and *Newsweek*, $84,000.

Magazines offer rewarding careers in advertising—and that department is often a route to top management.

GETTING A JOB IN BIG-LEAGUE MAGAZINE ADVERTISING

by Richard C. Thompson, Publisher, *U.S. News & World Report*

Successful advertising salespeople come from a wide variety of educational backgrounds—business, engineering, education, English literature, communications, marketing, and others. All, however, possess certain disciplines instrumental in pushing them to the top of their field.

One key ingredient is the ability to speak and write well. Being articulate and forceful in presenting ideas and concepts is equally important.

Writing is particularly important because many key decision makers in business are often unavailable or difficult for even the most able salespeople to see and must be contacted by letter or written presentation.

All successful people in this business possess a certain "killer instinct." They don't like to hear "no" and will always come back with alternate plans or proposals even when told the business might be going elsewhere. Simply showing up to visit a client will generally not put pages in a magazine, even one considered a leader in its field.

A high energy level also plays an important role in the successful selling of advertising. You've got to make numerous calls on both advertising agencies and advertisers, talking with advertising managers, marketing managers, product managers, media department personnel, and others.

Attitude is also key. You must believe that you *will* get the business, that it's only a matter of time before decision makers will agree with your proposals. Advertisers are buying an intangible, not a product or service whose benefits they can see. The continuous selling and serv-

icing of advertising accounts even after they've been convinced to use magazines is an important aspect of this.

Because few publishing companies have formal training programs, it is not a bad idea for anyone truly wishing a career in advertising sales to start working for other types of companies with sophisticated sales training programs. Another excellent training experience is to work for smaller trade or industrial publishing companies that don't require the experience major publishing firms demand.

Those of us who are responsible for advertising sales are very impressed with job candidates who have done their homework—who show up for an interview knowing the strengths and weaknesses of the magazine they want to work for. They know who the better advertisers are, which categories of advertising are strongest, which the weakest. But perhaps most important, they bring to the interview a sense of wanting to belong, a strong desire to get the job. My experience is that people able to sell me have been very good at selling advertising.

Magazines not only sell ad space but also offer layout, typesetting, engraving, and other services to advertisers. Here Sherry Lynn Colemen, *U.S. News* administrative supervisor, positions a client's ad page. *Reproduced with permission.*

Of course, much more than selling is involved. *U.S. News* must offer a wide range of services to advertisers, including layout, typesetting, and engraving.

Well, now you know what is happening in one of America's oldest forms of mass communications, magazines. In Chapter 8, we turn to other media—some new, some old.

☆ SUMMARY

Journalistic approaches used by newsmagazines virtually since *Time* was launched in 1923 are no longer valid, and of all magazines, none stands at such crossroads of change as the newsmagazines—*Time*, *Newsweek*, and *U.S. News & World Report*.

U.S. News exemplifies this change. Its owner, Mortimer B. Zuckerman, paid $163.5 million for the magazine in 1984, betting that he could outsmart some of the smartest people in the magazine industry. Zuckerman put together a team to overhaul the magazine, a distant third behind *Time* and *Newsweek*.

The team strives for product differentiation, using a new, colorful layout and a "hard news" orientation. Circulation has risen, and readership demographics have improved.

U.S. News's probable (but unstated) goal is to gain reader and advertiser support by, in part, attacking *Newsweek*, a magazine in managerial turmoil for years, rather than attempting to unseat *Time* as number 1.

For readers, *U.S. News* offers "News You Can Use," such as information on personal finance, health, and education, whereas *Time* and *Newsweek*, it contends, offer irrelevant fluff.

To advertisers, *U.S. News* promises a demographically attractive readership seriously interested in serious news in a serious magazine—and, *U.S. News* asks, what better ad environment could an advertiser desire?

U.S. News is an editor's magazine. It has a limited corps of correspondents throughout the world and relies on inside editors at headquarters in Washington to fashion the news product each week. This results in largely anonymous "group journalism," long a facet of magazine work. But that is changing. Bylines now appear, and working only on top stories, in places like Washington, can be stimulating for journalists.

In circulation and advertising, employees must combine editorial, advertising, and production skills. Both departments compete hard against other magazines. Writing skills are particularly valuable for new employees.

☆ RECOMMENDED READING

U.S. News promotional materials on news content, advertising, and circulation are available from the magazine, at 2400 N Street NW, Washington, DC 20037-1196. *Newsweek* is among magazines examined by William Parkman Rankin in *Business Management of General Consumer Magazines* (New York: Praeger, 1980). Also see Roland Wolseley, *The Changing Magazine* (New York: Hastings House, 1973) and Betsy Graham, *Writing Magazine Articles with Style* (New York: Holt, Rinehart, and Winston, 1980).

Bridging the Gap: New Media and the Old

Neat compartmentalization of print and broadcast media is no longer possible. New technology is freeing mass communications from newsprint and bursting boundaries laid down decades ago by television, giving consumers unprecedented opportunity to construct their own news and information systems and bypass traditional media altogether. New media forms are developing to combine elements of electronic and print media in a sort of "elec-print" approach, using printed word and paper but also video screens, computers, and other electronic marvels to communicate greater volumes of information more quickly and in more manageable form.

Strategists managing America's media conglomerates are anticipating dramatic changes from all this. They are diversifying in search of profit in many types of media. Scarcely does a "newspaper" company survive; most, even those with newspaper roots dug in for a century of more, now own some form of electronic media. Gannett, the nation's largest owner of newspapers, diversified into TV programming, and although it failed with

Coanchors Bill Macatee and Beth Ruyak of "USA Today," a TV show patterned after Gannett's *USA Today* newspaper. *Courtesy Gannett Co.*

"USA Today," an entertainment program based on its national newspaper, the company made major investments in syndicated shows.[1] Large broadcast companies are diversifying, too, often in print.

The final shape of all this is unclear. However, leading American media companies are developing an "information center" concept under which they, as always, collect news and entertainment but, in a radical departure from past practice, distribute it in many forms to different consumer constituencies using a variety of technologies.

Here in Chapter 8, we will look at "elec-print." This may clarify changes in newspapers and magazines we studied in earlier chapters and set the stage for the study ahead of television, cable, and radio.

We will also look at the book publishing industry. Johann Gutenberg wouldn't believe what he started with his hand-operated press back in the 1400s.

INFORMATION CENTER VERSUS BYPASS TECHNOLOGY

When McGraw-Hill's *Aviation Week & Space Technology* covers a major development in its field of specialty, magazine subscribers read about it in next week's issue. The magazine's videocassette subscribers watch on their home VCRs a sight-and-sound presentation by *Aviation Week* experts. This is the *information center* concept at work: a traditional mass medium—a magazine—employs expert editors to sift through the world of news; make informed, professional judgments on what is important; and disseminate their final product—selective information—in a variety of forms. "Magazines" are no longer tied to paper.[2]

Now shift scenarios: Two scientists, one in California, the other in New York, use personal computers linked by telephone circuits to a computer bulletin board in, say, Chicago and exchange technical data. Neither has to wait the many months (sometimes years) it takes for scholarly journals to publish research papers. This is *bypass technology* at work: two information consumers bypassing traditional mass media and dealing directly with each other.

Broadly, those options—information center

versus bypass technology—are being opened for both providers and consumers of news and entertainment. It's unlikely that one will triumph over the other. Traditionally, American media moved over in the marketplace as new forms of communications burst on the scene. Newspapers and magazines made room for radio, then all three shifted onto new ground when television arrived. Today's mass media and bypass technology will also reach an accommodation.

Under the information center concept, the mass media continue their most essential role: a magazine, for example, establishes parameters of its service by defining what it covers and what it doesn't. That attracts some information seekers and repels those looking for something else. A contract is established under which the magazine, for a subscription fee, agrees to deliver certain information (about airplanes but not trucks, for example). Both contractual parties understand that the magazine will undertake the immense task of surveying a world of news and information, selecting only the bits and pieces for which the reader willingly pays. This presumes that the magazine's editors and reporters are experts in their field with resources—time, money, professional skills, and judgment—not possessed by the reader. (A recent statement issued through

Information center concept at work: McGraw-Hill's aviation news specialists create from the same reservoir of news a series of magazines, newsletters, reference books, and videocassettes.

the Audit Bureau of Circulations revealed that 33 leading editors and reporters at *Aviation Week* averaged 12.8 years spent covering aviation for the magazine; all were college graduates, and many had advanced degrees in engineering or management.)

Bypass technology assumes that the information consumer has the time, money, and professional skills to search, as reporters do, the world of news, locate essential bits and pieces, and then pull them together in an understandable, handy, affordable context. Experts such as our scientists linked via Chicago often know what information they want and where and how to get it. In contrast, the mass media serve mass audiences that generally don't have the time, money, resources, or inclination to search far for information. Knight-Ridder, Inc., lost $50 million trying to sell general news consumers the idea of using computer recall devices for information. For them, neither the cost nor the fuss of computer searches was worth it.

In advertising, bypass technology does present a threat to established mainline media. Many advertisers, for example, are using direct mail, telephone sales, and other means of reaching consumers directly, without printing ads in newspapers and magazines or airing commercials on radio and TV.

New technology and information transmission techniques are chipping away at traditional mass media in other ways. Let's look at some examples.

Computer Bulletin Boards   By some counts, 2,000 computer bulletin boards developed in the United States in the decade ended 1987.[3] Some establish computer databanks that offer news and information (SYSLINK in Providence, Rhode Island, specializes in astrology, for example). Most are advertising systems where people with specialized interests buy and sell equipment via computers. In 1987, one in Chicago carrying ads for aviation equipment had

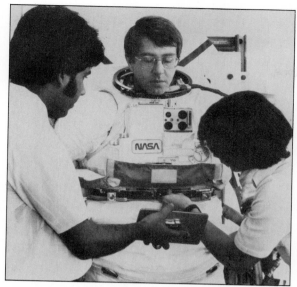

Specialty magazines employ reporters highly skilled in the subjects they cover. Here, Craig Covault, of *Aviation Week & Space Technology* magazine, suits up for a simulation in a pressurized space suit. *Courtesy* Aviation Week & Space Technology.

800 regular users who paid $20 annually and made about 50 calls daily. At that rate, the mass media are hardly threatened.

Electronic Magazines

Electronic magazines make information and advertising available for personal computer use through disks or computer bulletin boards. One Shreveport, Louisiana, firm publishes three monthly software magazines on disks. Some companies provide disks as supplements to magazines. Electronic magazines presume that users are computer-literate and have access to a computer. At this point, they cannot threaten the mass media, either.[4]

Videocassettes

The threat of videocassettes to movie theaters and network television is very real. In 1988, movie theaters sold an all-time high $4.4 billion in tickets; spending on home videos hit $7.2 billion ($4.5 billion in rentals, $3.6 billion for purchases). In 1988, videocassette recorders were in about 53 percent of all American homes; not unexpectedly, in New

York, Los Angeles, Chicago, and San Francisco, the average was 62.5 percent.[5]

Aside from eating deeply into the mass audience for films, videocassettes steal thunder from other mass media. First, they compete with newspapers' reprinting of important speeches when they deal in "near news." Jesse Jackson's widely acclaimed speech to the Democratic convention in Atlanta in 1988 was on tape and in video stores one week later. Politicians ship cassettes directly to voters, bypassing the probing questions and analysis of reporters. When TV evangelist Pat Robertson tried for the Republican presidential nomination in 1988, he sent tapes to 60,000 homes in Iowa and 170,000 in New Hampshire.[6]

Second, videocassettes are becoming a medium of advertising, not simply entertainment or information. Diet Pepsi rode into video homes on the movie hit *Top Gun*; if you rented *Platoon* in 1988, you also got a pitch from Lee Iacocca, chairman of Chrysler Corp. (manufacturer of the

Coverage of political conventions is no longer exclusive to traditional media. One week after Jesse Jackson (*lower left*) spoke to the 1988 Democratic convention, videocassette coverage was on sale in stores. *Wide World Photos.*

Jeep). Ad agencies report that consumer resistance to commercials on videotapes is dropping steadily. Third, sight and sound—and color—are edging videocassettes into the educational market some mass media have enjoyed for decades. You don't have to read what a *Sports Illustrated* writer says is the proper golf swing; world-famous golfers will show you. You need not read a woman's magazine piece on how to bathe your baby; you can rent a cassette that shows you.

Video Shopping and Catalogs These strike directly at the advertiser support that keeps newspapers, magazines, and broadcast television in business. Shopping-by-cable shows demonstrate products, then take telephone orders. One New Jersey firm, Royal Silk, sells 30-minute cassettes ($5.95 in 1987) that feature a fashion show and instructions on how to care for silk products. The company reports customers order about $100 worth of goods for every cassette purchased. But that's just a taste of what IBM and Sears have in mind. They formed a partnership to offer a videotex service, Prodigy, enabling customers to use personal computers for ordering merchandise. The service also offers news, stock quotations, and other information. Other companies failed to interest general-information consumers in such interactive, computer-based services, and some analysts give even industry leaders such as IBM and Sears little chance for success.

Optical and Compact Disks Both types of disks give information and entertainment consumers an unprecedented ability to store and use information. Kodak sells an optical disk the size of a long-playing record that it says holds 100,000 pages of information. It sells a magnetic recording device that crams as much information on a single reel of magnetic tape "as would be in a stack of paper higher than 20 Empire State Buildings."[7]

Private Communications Networks As costs drop for computer storage and high-speed transmission of information, private companies are establishing communications networks to supplant those operated by the mass media. For example, Dow Jones business news wires in times gone by directly served all Merrill Lynch brokerage offices nationwide. Today, the company has its own network serving 600 locations worldwide on a 24-hour, seven-day-a-week basis. Merrill Lynch operates its own news services, with Dow Jones news included for some offices.[8]

In sum, bypass technology in its individual parts has only a minor effect on the mass media; in totality, however, it will force enormous changes. The mass markets painstakingly developed over decades by newspapers, magazines, radio, and television will be increasingly fractionalized. Consumers of news and entertainment will increase their demands for customized service.

Desktop publishing, inexpensive to start up and low-cost to operate, will permit production of information services for small numbers of consumers (no mass medium could profitably operate a service for just 800 customers and charge only $20 annually, as the low-cost Chicago computer bulletin board does).

The Congressional Office of Technology Assessment said in 1988 that the new techniques will so change how information is produced and disseminated that we will have to redefine "who and what is considered 'the press.'" The concept of the press being only established media—newspapers, magazines, television—will give way to a concept of "network," the report said, and "the electronic publisher of the future may act more as a clearinghouse for the exchange of news and information than as a gatherer."[9]

Other analysts fault that interpretation, insisting that most information consumers will still need expert guidance from experienced editors to find the information they seek. And editors, these analysts say, as always, will put together newspapers, magazines, and TV news shows—or control input and output from some huge computer-generated databank, in which case just another mass medium will have been established.

Many traditional media companies are accepting change and using it to their advantage, rather than blindly resisting. Gannett Co. is investing heavily in TV programming. Tribune Co. of Chicago and CBS Entertainment jointly produce TV comedies and dramas. The *Christian Science Monitor* offers TV news, and electronic publishing of some sort is under way at many newspapers.

But writing and printing are not disappearing in the computer age. U.S. consumption of writing and printing paper increased 320 percent between 1959 and 1980, the time when the computer came of age. Reading from computer screens is inefficient, 20 to 30 percent slower than from print, reports Edward Tenner, executive editor of Princeton University Press, and anyway, paper doesn't fall apart for decades, whereas a power surge can wipe out computer memory in an instant![10]

On one thing many analysts agree: All bets are off if telephone companies begin delivering their own news and entertainment services plus advertising to individual homes. In 1989, American Telephone and Telegraph Company was given permission by a federal court in Washington, D.C., to enter the electronic publishing business, raising the possibility that federally regulated telephone companies nationwide could do the same thing. If that happens, the face of the American media will change substantially.

THE TELEPHONE COMPANIES VERSUS THE MEDIA

In 1987, the then largest U.S. media conglomerate, Capital Cities/ABC, had $4.2 billion in revenue. That's peanuts compared to what telephone companies rake in. That same year, two telephone companies (BellSouth and NYNEX) each had revenues of over $12 billion. Ameritech, Bell Atlantic, and Pacific Telesis were in the $10 billion league. "Little" Southwestern Bell was double the size of Capital Cities/ABC.

Media companies that now dominate America's mass communications system fear that the telephone companies will focus their enormous financial and technical resources on turf traditionally occupied by newspapers, magazines, and television. If the "telcos" do so, they could create an entirely new approach to mass media and further blur the distinction between traditional print and new electronic forms of communications.

COLOSSUS ON THE HORIZON

❝ That the times they are a-changin' is evident at every turn these days, and nowhere more than in the revolution of video delivery systems. First there was classic television—free, over the air and ubiquitous. Then came cable—roughhewn at first, stubbornly innovative, unsettling and now ascendant. On the fringes there exists a sort of system of direct broadcast satellites, and high-power DBS may be on the way. But just over the horizon lies a colossus that could dwarf them all: the U.S. telephone industry, now mustering its resources—and its fiber optics potential—for an assault on the telecommunications policy establishment that could position it as a new partner in the Fifth Estate. **❞**

Broadcasting *Magazine*, July 4, 1988.

Telephone companies by law have acted primarily as "common carriers"—that is, they carried services for other companies but haven't created their own news or entertainment services. As recently as the 1984 Cable Act, Congress (heavily lobbied by print and broadcast media) excluded telephone companies from creating household news and entertainment on grounds that their monopoly of local telephone service could create anticompetitive abuses. Cable companies—many owned by newspaper and broadcast companies—were thus sheltered from telephone company competition and became hugely profitable.

However, telephone companies, with their innovative technology, are certain to enter the competition to serve American households. Consumers will demand it. In effect, telephone companies could supplant television and cable systems and offer information, entertainment, and advertising services (thereby threatening newspapers and magazines as well) and provide home banking and shopping services. It's what the telephone companies could do in advertising that has critics upset. Let's examine why.

Advertisers paid telephone companies $7.3 billion for space in the Yellow Pages in 1987. BellSouth alone took in $1 billion—and that's for static advertisements (if a company changes its address, telephone number, or prices, it's locked in by its year-old Yellow Pages ad).

But suppose the Yellow Pages were computerized and available on a real-time basis to any householder through a telephone company bundle of services? Not only could you summon from the Yellow Pages the names and telephone numbers of plumbers but also their current hourly rates as well. Or suppose all food stores in town entered daily prices, permitting shoppers to dial in for, say, the prices of ground beef before setting off on their rounds? An active marketplace could be created, with shopkeepers changing prices frequently each day—raising them if competing stores do, lowering them if the ground beef isn't moving. How would newspaper ads, static and fixed for at least three days, compete with that?

Or suppose that instead of searching page after page of "help wanted" classifieds, you could sit down at the telephone company's console in your home and enter the specifications—field, hours, pay, location—for your dream job and let the telephone company's computer do the walking, in an instant, through thousands of ads and pick out two or three available jobs that meet your specifications?

Those scenarios worry newspaper executives, depending as they do on advertising for 80 percent of their newspapers' revenue.

For television and cable system managers, the nightmares are equally disturbing: telephone companies offering a wide variety of free and pay services that would compete strongly for the bread-and-butter of many newspapers and television stations: weather forecasts, restaurant reviews, entertainment billboards, sports scores, stock market prices, and so forth. The technology is also ready for voice mail message services and electronic mail for facsimile delivery of charts and graphs.

From the consumer's viewpoint, none of the media fighting against telephone company entry into the competitive marketplace can offer such a wide range of services. And that is why pressure—probably irresistible—will eventually build for telephone companies to enter the game. Opponents of the telephone companies argue that once their services were in place, the telcos would have a stranglehold on consumers and be able to dictate terms of service.

Emotions run high in the media world and Congress on this subject, so it would be foolhardy to predict the outcome. But throughout the history of American mass media, superior technology and services have gotten into the competitive marketplace despite efforts to keep them out. Compromise may lie in permitting the federally regulated telephone companies to enter under tightly controlled conditions if other media companies are permitted to use telephone facilities to offer competing services. Established media firms would be wise to start, now, figuring ways to use rather than resist the new technology.[11]

The outcome will be pivotal in the coming decade for our mass communications system. There also is concern over the social impact of envisaged electronic information systems.

IF ELECTRONIC SYSTEMS TAKE OVER

66 The good news here is that you'll have to spend less time hunting for information and less time analyzing it, secure in the knowledge that you can find what you need when you need it.

But there's a catch. What happens if electronic information so focuses your information intake that you read only those articles and ads that you are comfortable with, on subjects you already know, analyze only the information you ask for and try only the products you already know about? How many Republicans would select the editorial pages of the *New York Times* or the *Washington Post*? And how many Democrats would select the *Wall Street Journal*'s editorials? They may not read them now, but at least they are exposed to them.

I have no answer, and I'm worried that technology may enable us to grow mentally lazy just as it has let us grow physically lazy. 99

Ester Dyson, editor and publisher of the newsletter Release 1.0.[12]

NEW VIGOR IN OLD WAYS: NEWSLETTERS

Rumors of what Robert Prechter thinks can unsettle stock markets. What he says can move millions of shares (and dollars) in minutes.

Prechter is not on the influential Federal Reserve Board in Washington. He isn't an economist who speaks for the White House. He doesn't write editorials for the prestigious *New York Times* or market analysis for the *Wall Street Journal*. Robert Prechter is a psychology graduate (Yale, 1971) who wields his influence (and makes a fortune) through one of the oldest forms of communication: He publishes a newsletter in his hometown, Gainesville, Georgia.

On October 6, 1987, rumors spread on Wall Street that Prechter was "bearish" (negative) about the outlook for stocks. The Dow Jones average fell 91.55 points, until then the largest single-day drop in history. The Prechter rumors were only part of what was bothering Wall Street, but such was his newsletter's influence that his thinking was mentioned prominently among the reasons for a $73 billion paper loss investors suffered that day.[13]

The affair illustrated the sometimes enormous influence of newsletter publishers, who in this era of space age communications use one of the oldest communications vehicles, paper, and rely primarily for distribution on the good old U.S. Postal Service. Thousands of newsletters are published, more than 600 with investment advice. There are others for dining out, health, tax matters, education, growing roses—if there is a news need, newsletters are published for it.

For information consumers, the newsletter's appeal is its focus on the exact information desired. For stock market investors, there is none of the general newspaper's coverage of sports, comics, features—just investor news. Many newsletter authors also offer expert treatment of complex subjects. Newsletters often offer computerized research that, say, general-assignment reporters for newspapers, magazines, or television cannot. (The research is not always done with computers. Robert Parker, Jr., for example, personally conducts research for his newsletter,

Wine Advocate, by tasting 70 to 80 bottles daily, three times a week.)[14] Some newsletters offer telephone, wire, or computer-to-computer updates that eliminate delays inherent in mail delivery.

For authors, newsletters can offer low-cost entry into media ownership and, if everything clicks, a chance to make a fortune. When he jolted the stock market, Prechter, then 38, was selling his *Elliott Wave Theorist* newsletter to 18,000 subscribers at a basic fee of $233 annually (to save you the trouble, that works out to $4,194,000 basic revenue annually!). About half paid $377 more for his thrice-weekly taped telephone "hot line" updates.[15] Prechter is notoriously shy about his business, so his costs aren't

---

ROBERT PRECHTER

THE ELLIOTT WAVE THEORIST

New Classics Library   STOCK MARKET   INTEREST RATES   P.O. Box 1618   PRECIOUS METALS   Gainesville, GA 30503

May 1, 1989 ©   **$233 per year** 12 Monthly issues plus Special Reports and Interim Reports

DJIA WAVE STATUS: SUMMARY and OUTLOOK

WAVE DEGREE	DATE BEGAN	WAVE NUMBER	CURRENT DIRECTION	SIGNIFICANCE TO	OPTIMUM STRATEGY	TARGET	ALTERNATE COUNT
GRAND SUPERCYCLE	1987	FOUR or A	DOWN/ SIDEWAYS	U.S. SURVIVAL	PROBLEMS AHEAD	BELOW 400	----
SUPERCYCLE	AUG. 25, 1987	(A)	DOWN	ECONOMIC CONDITIONS	CONTRACTION BEGINNING	BELOW 800	(V)
CYCLE	AUG. 25, 1987	A or I	DOWN	INSTITUTIONAL INVESTOR	HOLD T-BILLS	BELOW 1500	V
PRIMARY	DEC. 4, 1987	②	UP, PEAKING	INSTITUTIONAL TRADER	SEE INSIDE FOR STRATEGY	-----	③
INTERMEDIATE	AUG. 23, 1988	(c)	UP, PEAKING	INDIVIDUAL INVESTOR	SEE INSIDE FOR STRATEGY	-----	-----
MINOR	APR. 6, 1:00	5	UP, PEAKING	INDIVIDUAL TRADER	SEE INSIDE FOR STRATEGY	-----	3
MINUTE	APR. 25, 4:00	v	UP, PEAKING	OPTION/FUTURE TRADER	SEE INSIDE FOR STRATEGY	-----	-----
MINUETTE	----	---	----	SCALPER	SEE INSIDE FOR STRATEGY	-----	-----
SUBMINUETTE	----	---	----	SKIMMER	SEE INSIDE FOR STRATEGY	-----	-----

THE BOTTOM LINE
All three markets are at very exciting junctures. The stock market is as vulnerable technically as it was in the third quarter of 1987. Sentiment indicators have registered extremes, and momentum divergences abound. Once again, a countertrend pattern can be labeled as complete. The bond market is completing _its_ countertrend pattern dating from October 1987 as well, suggesting a sustained decline in both markets into the second half of the year. If gold breaks $365, a downside acceleration is likely.

ITEMS OF NOTE
Now is the _last chance_ to sign up for the 14th Annual Market Technicians' Association Seminar, to be held in Naples, FL, May 18-21. I am very proud to have put together a roster of diverse talent. Topics include futures market indicators, Elliott Wave analysis, global markets and influences, and astronomic correlations with markets. A traders panel features renowned traders Paul Tudor Jones and Martin Schwartz. For details, refer to the brochure mailed last month or call Shelley Lebeck at 212-420-9722.

Dan Ascani will discuss the U.S. Dollar Index for FINEX on May 18 at 4:30 p.m. in Atlanta at the Westin Peachtree Plaza. Admission is only $25. He will also address the MTA Conference on May 19. Dave Allman will address the prestigious Financial Analysts' Federation/Investment Analysts' Society of Chicago conference at the Hyatt O'Hare on June 6. The fee is $425. For info, call 804-977-8156.

Many thanks to those of you who wrote to say you enjoyed the _Haiku Harvest_ gift. It _is_ a gem, isn't it?

The *Elliott Wave Theorist*, one of the most influential stock market newsletters, speaks in a special language to its investor-subscribers throughout the world. Note the "optimum strategy" recommendations made by newsletter author Robert Prechter. *Courtesy New Classics Library.*

known. But the *Wall Street Journal* provides a breakdown of costs sustained by Eric Kobren, publisher of a mutual fund newsletter in Boston. Kobren uses a personal computer and desktop publishing software to write and lay out his newsletter. Printing is done by an outside firm. Total direct production costs are under $200,000 annually. In 1987, when Kobren was 33, about 20,000 persons subscribed at $95 annually (again, to save you the trouble, that's about $1.9 million revenue annually). Kobren started the newsletter just two years earlier with $12,000 savings.[16]

Obviously, not all newsletter authors do so well. Costs are rising for promoting newsletters and mailing them. And subscribers can be fickle. During the 1987–1988 stock market turndown, thousands of subscribers dropped newsletters. But throughout the mid-1980s, newsletters were among the fastest-growing sectors of publishing, and the prospects of large profits attracted many firms into the business.

Some of these operate under the information center concept. PK Services Corp. of Carmel, California, profits handsomely by serving owners and operators of cable television systems and people who invest in them. Such people are often skilled information gatherers themselves. Yet PK Services does well by rounding up bits of cable-

◤1◢ Newsletters Succeed Where Mass Media Fail

Christopher Whittle. *Reprinted with permission.*

It took Christopher Whittle just 18 years after graduation (University of Tennessee, 1969, American studies) to build a communications company (and a fortune) on an idea:

The mass media no longer deliver the impact or audience reach for their advertisers the way they once did. For example, one TV station can carry up to 720 commercial messages every day, and some national magazines contain anywhere from 70 to 100 advertisements. I'd challenge anyone to remember even a few of those. The point is, there are too many of them. It's a great, jumbled, chaotic mass of messages. Little stands out, and little breaks through. There is virtually no impact for the advertiser.[18]

Whittle says target marketing with finely tuned newsletters and other journalistic products is the solution, and his Whittle Communications, with headquarters in Knoxville, is proof that it works. Whittle founded the company with classmates in 1970. The first publication was *Knoxville in a Nutshell*, a "survival guide" for University of Tennessee students. The partnership later broke up, but Whittle retained 22 percent ownership and control of the company, which by 1988 had grown to 35 publications with 850 employees and an estimated $180 million in annual revenue.

When those [mass] media were created, in the late '40s and '50s, America was a very different place. It was largely homogeneous, and we didn't have anywhere near the number of products we currently have. It was a much simpler world.

But it doesn't make sense [for advertisers] to use mass media when you

related information, much of it available through other means, and then issuing it with expert analysis in newsletters that are quick to read. For cable TV alone, PK Services issues 11 newsletters, each focusing on narrow subjects, such as *Cable TV Investor, The Pay TV Newsletters, Cable TV Finance*, and *Cable TV Technology*. PK publishes 12 other newsletters on related broadcast topics, offers seminars in person and on audiocassettes, issues special reports and research publications, and provides services.[17] Specialist entrepreneurs can build a body of expertise and profitably split it many ways to meet focused needs. ▶ 1

DIRECT MAIL'S DIRECT CHALLENGE

In 1988, Advo-Systems, Inc., the largest direct mail company in America, issued a bold challenge to newspapers and magazines. It published an advertisement that said in part:

> Buckle up, you other media. Direct mail has come of age. It's not only a legitimate medium now—it's more cost-effective than newspaper advertising.
>
> And if some joker selling ad space tries to tell you otherwise, don't buy it.
>
> Research shows that only 11% of a news-

Highly imaginative approaches to advertising through wall posters, campus publications, and other target marketing ventures made a multimillion-dollar fortune for University of Tennessee graduate Christopher Whittle. *Courtesy Whittle Communications.*

don't have mass targets anymore. Take Kitten Chow. Less than 4 percent of the homes in America have a kitten.[19]

Whittle takes precise aim with his "products" to serve advertisers. He publishes 17

newsletters, magazines, and "information centers" for health care—of teeth, skin, pets, you name it. Five publications are aimed at colleges (*America Magazine* and *Campus Voice* among them), three are aimed at regions (*Connecticut's Finest, Southern Style, Tennessee Illustrated*), four at business interests, and four at lifestyle sectors. Whittle also conducts product sampling, which, for example, distributes *Campus Voice* in dormitories along with coupons and samples of products manufactured by his advertisers.

Whittle also came up with single-sponsor advertising, giving clients exclusivity in a publication so that their ads don't get lost in the clutter of other advertisements.

Whittle's success and his highly innovative approach to target marketing have won much recognition—and intense scrutiny by media competitors. In 1989, he stirred controversy by suggesting video news services for schools financed by commercials. Whittle stands for new ways of accomplishing old goals, and that stance upsets many more traditional media companies. One competitor, Time Inc. (now Time Warner), saw genius in what Whittle had accomplished and in 1988 paid $185 million for half of his company. Whittle still retained 11 percent, a share worth an estimated $44 million.

paper's readership will ever see the average ad.

So why not get your audience where they look. In the mailbox. That's right. Virtually everybody looks through their mail every day. As a matter of fact, 70% to 90% of third class mail gets either read or looked at. The research types can prove it to you.[20]

The ad (published, incidentally, in a magazine, *Advertising Age*) illustrated the competitive vigor direct mail is bringing to the media marketplace. Direct mail now has the third-largest slice of the U.S. advertising pie ($19 billion in 1987, compared with $29.4 billion for newspapers and $24.3 billion for television). And the industry is growing rapidly.[21]

Detractors term it "junk mail" and deride its effectiveness (the Newspaper Advertising Bureau says that 75 percent is thrown away), but direct mail is finding its own niche. It has certain undeniable strengths. With direct mail, advertisers can reach nearly all households in a given marketplace (total market coverage) or, using selective address lists, get material to recipients with special interests, such as physicians or dentists (selective market coverage). Direct mail companies claim that this eliminates waste. And the Newspaper Advertising Bureau's own research shows that direct mail sometimes provides cheaper delivery than newspapers for inserted supplements (one study showed direct mail costs of $35 to deliver 1,000 advertising tabloids, compared to the $45 to $50 that newspapers were charging).

Direct mail was only a minor player in American advertising until two things happened: in the 1970s, the U.S. Postal Service adjusted postage rates so that third-class mailing, used by direct mail, became economically attractive. Then, in the late 1970s and early 1980s, computers made it possible to compile precise address lists. Commercial firms today sell more than 150,000 lists covering almost all U.S. households, broken down into various categories. Lifestyle Selector of Denver says it lists more than 10 million names and addresses, all cross-indexed for eight demographic characteristics (age, sex, occupation, etc.) plus 52 lifestyle interests (hobbies, sports,

gourmet tastes, travel). Probably the world's largest mailing list is owned by *Reader's Digest*, which uses it not only to mail 28 million magazines monthly in 39 countries but also for selling books, records, and tapes.

Direct mail is the core of a direct marketing effort through which advertisers bypass print and electronic media and go directly to potential consumers. The numbers are stunning. The Direct Marketing Association, based in New York City, says that in 1986 alone, 11.8 billion copies of 8,500 different catalogs moved through the U.S. Postal Service.[22] Other direct marketing techniques include telephone selling, use of coupons, supplements in newspapers and magazines—and even Avon ladies! The *New York Times* in 1987 singled out direct marketing as a growth industry offering new career opportunities.[23]

Now let's look at an older form of mass communication that is showing astonishing new vigor.

BOOK PUBLISHING: STILL GOING STRONG

Computer-generated, electronically transmitted information is where the action is? Generations of TV addicts do nothing but stare at the tube? Videocassettes are replacing the printed word? Somebody forgot to tell the book publishing industry. Books, the oldest printed form of true mass communication, are doing very well, indeed. More than 22,500 book publishers are active in the United States, according to a 1988 survey by the Book Industry Study Group of New York City. About 8,000 publishers started up in the five-year period 1983–1988 (evidence of entrepreneurial opportunity in a media area many thought doomed).[24]

Between 1972 and 1988, the number of American bookstores (not counting college bookstores) more than doubled, to 12,700.

More than 50,000 new titles are published in America each year, and publishers' sales in 1987 totaled $13 billion. Trade books—novels, nonfiction, general-interest books—are the biggest sellers ($3.5 billion in 1987). Textbooks are second (more than $3.3 billion).

Book publishing can be controversial. In 1989, members of the National Writers Union demonstrated in New York City following Iranian threats to kill Salman Rushdie, author of the novel *The Satanic Verses*. Novelist Tom Robbins was among the speakers. *Wide World Photos.*

And book publishing is highly profitable, with industry pretax profits of about 20 percent, substantially higher than those of many nonmedia industries.

How can this be in an era of communications satellites and computers? Well, a great many people read books for hard information. For them, books are splendid "information retrieval systems." And for a great many more, book reading is a pleasurable experience. The Book Industry Study Group's 1988 survey determined that 30 percent of reading-age Americans are heavy readers who account for 90 percent of general book sales. About 20 percent of the reading-age population reads or buys books less regularly. Those figures mean that 50 percent of the reading-age population doesn't read books. That can be seen as a challenge. But it is also an opportunity in that the book industry has a huge potential audience if the right books are published in a form that will pull in new readers (and if, of course, the United States can reverse a trend toward functional illiteracy in some sectors of society).[25]

Some of the shrewdest media moguls see the American book industry poised for new profit potential. The proof is that they are fighting to get into it, as we saw in Part I.

Rupert Murdoch paid $300 million in 1987 for Harper & Row. British entrepreneur Robert Maxwell bid more than $2.3 billion for Macmillan Inc. Bertelsmann A.G. of West Germany bought Doubleday & Co. Hachette S.A. of France spent $1.16 billion in 1988 for publisher Grolier Inc. and other U.S. media companies. Newhouse, Hearst, Time Warner, Thomson, McGraw-Hill, and other diversified American media firms have mammoth holdings in book publishing. Clearly, book companies are regarded by some conglomerates as key parts of their larger empires. As in other forms of mass communications, the trend is toward a handful of big players dominating the industry. A mere 2 percent of the nation's publishers issue 75 percent of all book titles; the top 30 percent issue 99 percent.

Inevitably, the takeover battles between profit-hungry conglomerates raise profound social questions. Is quality in publishing being sacrificed for profit? Is a sense of social responsibility disappearing from publishing? Privately owned publishing houses for generations brought along, often at financial loss, young writers who then went on to add glory to American letters. Will modern publishing executives be willing (or able) to do that and still answer to the "rising tide of shareholder expectations"?

Critics argue that takeovers create such financial burdens that publishing firms concentrate instead on blockbuster books that, though of dubious literary quality, promise strong sales. Takeover executives counter that some firms taken over were in financial jeopardy and that better management and higher profits often come with new ownership. That, they say, permits publishers to gamble on an unknown author or publish a book that is destined to sell poorly but should be published for its literary merit.

CURL UP WITH A VIDEO DISPLAY TERMINAL?

66 I have spent the last couple of weeks using an information-retrieval system that is not one whit short of miraculous. And in its gregariousness and ability to accommodate human whims, it makes the term "user-friendly" seem begrudging by comparison.

Consider these assets: The storage capacity can be awesome, yet the system is portable. It is a rare model that can't be carried in one hand. No electricity is required, not even batteries, so you can use it anywhere—on planes, in waiting rooms, on a picnic for that matter.

The information is set out in logical order—no bouncing around from pillar to post and then trying to collate it all in your head. Indeed, the technology is such that if the information isn't being presented logically, any attentive user will have little alarms go off in his head. You sense discontinuities that encourage a critical questioning.

And if you want to go back and look up a particular item—the Melos massacre, let's say, or the Archons of Athens—you can use an indexing device that will give you what you want within seconds. What is more, unlike most other information systems, this one engages you in a way that lets you almost hear the distinct human voice and sense the mind at work behind it.

And if that doesn't sell you, there's price. Most are under $20.

Small wonder books have not gone out of style. **99**

Tom Teepen, editorial page editor, Atlanta Constitution.[26]

In trade (popular) books, one best seller can reverse a company's fortunes. Harcourt Brace Jovanovich published *For the Record* by Donald T. Regan, President's Reagan's White House chief of staff, in 1988 and within months sold 400,000 copies, recouping several times over its costs and the $1 million advance paid the author. Farrar, Straus & Giroux made millions in 1988 on just two novels, Tom Wolfe's *Bonfire of the Vanities* and Scott Turow's *Presumed Innocent*. In its first 28 weeks on the *New York Times*'s best seller list, Wolfe's book sold 610,574 hardcover copies; the publisher also sold paperback rights to Bantam Books for $1.5 million and movie rights to two producers for an unannounced sum.[27]

In publishing textbooks, publishers can get caught with a loser on their hands—or win very big with major sellers. ▶ 2

Other profitable lines include religious books (which were very active in the 1970s, when an evangelical Christian revival occurred, but less so in the late 1980s after scandals hit several well-known ministries), professional books (medical, legal, scientific, etc.), reference works (encyclopedias, dictionaries, etc.), mass-market paperbacks, and elementary and secondary textbooks.

The basic financial strength of many publishing houses is built around their backlist—books that last for years and are steady moneymakers. Art books, cookbooks, reference works, baby care guides, and some children's books are among perennial favorites. Some have sold 20 million or 30 million copies! The uncertainties of publishing have led many firms to diversify carefully. Note in Figure 8.1, for example, how Simon & Schuster balances its risks by concentrating on four areas of books and information and consumer services. One major publisher, Random House, diversified into games and children's toys.

In trade books, publishers face serious problems trying to anticipate public tastes. It often takes years for a book to move from author's idea to bookseller's shelves, and in the interim public taste can change dramatically. What looked like

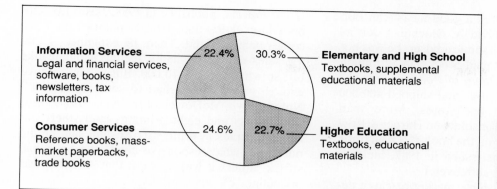

Information Services
Legal and financial services, software, books, newsletters, tax information

Consumer Services
Reference books, mass-market paperbacks, trade books

Elementary and High School
Textbooks, supplemental educational materials

Higher Education
Textbooks, educational materials

Figure 8.1. SIMON & SCHUSTER, INC., SOURCES OF REVENUE. *Source:* Simon & Schuster, Inc., 1987 financial results.

2 ► Classic College Textbooks

If you've read one of the following 19 college textbooks, congratulations—you've read an all-time classic. A *New York Times* survey in 1987 identified them as the biggest sellers ever in college textbooks. All are still in use today, mostly in new editions by current authors who replaced original writers.

Engineering Drawing and Graphic Technology, first published by McGraw-Hill in 1911 and now in its 13th edition.

Otto Kleppner's Advertising Procedure, Prentice-Hall, 1925, nine editions.

Gardner's Art through the Ages has sold more than 1 million copies since first being published in 1926 by Harcourt Brace Jovanovich.

Accounting Principles has sold more than 7 million copies since first published by South-Western Publishing Co. in 1929.

Psychology and Life, published in 1932 by Scott, Foresman, has since sold more than 2 million copies.

A Manual for Writers of Term Papers, Theses, and Dissertations, first issued by the dissertation secretary at the University of Chicago, Kate L. Turabian, as a one-page guide for doctoral candidates, has sold more than 5.3 million paperback copies and is now under the University of Chicago Press imprint.

Harbrace College Handbook, nearly 3 million

copies sold by Harcourt Brace Jovanovich since 1941.

Western Civilization, W. W. Norton, 10 editions since 1941.

Civilization: Past and Present, Scott, Foresman, more than 1 million sold since 1942.

Economics, written by Paul Samuelson in 1948; more than 3 million sold and still selling at the rate of 50,000 annually.

Writing with a Purpose, eight editions since 1950, Houghton Mifflin.

History of the Modern World, 1950, more than 1 million sold by Alfred A. Knopf.

Government by the People, Prentice-Hall, 1952, more than 1 million sold.

History of Art, Prentice-Hall and Harry Abrams, 1962, 3 million copies in 14 languages.

Introduction to Psychology, Harcourt Brace Jovanovich, 1953, more than 3 million sold.

The Enjoyment of Music, W. W. Norton, 1955, almost 2 million sold.

Basic Marketing, Richard D. Irwin Inc., 1960, more than 2.5 million sold.

Economics: Principles, Problems, and Policies, McGraw-Hill, 1963, said to sell 200,000 copies annually.

Biology, written in 1968 by Helena Curtis for Worth Publishers, has sold more than 1 million copies.

a good idea—inded, *was* a good idea—can flop a year later. When David A. Stockman quit as President Reagan's economic adviser, he was hot news. Harper & Row paid Stockman $2 million for his book, *The Triumph of Politics: Why the Reagan Revolution Failed*, and shipped 400,000 hardcover copies to bookstores. More than 100,000 were returned unsold, and Harper & Row reportedly lost money on the book.[28] (Of all trade books or new editions issued in 1987, incidentally, 30 percent were softcover.)

In textbook publishing, market research determines the types of courses being taught, whether existing textbooks meet teacher and student needs, and what market niches might be open for new books. Publishers watch course enrollments to see which subjects are popular. University teachers, some compelled to publish to meet promotion and tenure guidelines, often present publishers with outlines of proposed textbooks. Other teachers comment on outlines and drafts of the text until a final version is ready. The process often takes years and is a gamble by both publishers and authors. A criticism of the process is that it can yield "consensus" books aimed primarily at attracting maximum "adoptions" by school systems and teachers for student use. There have been cases of authors and publishers avoiding, say, religious issues in books aimed at Bible Belt schools or skirting historic controversies (the Civil War, for example).

University presses often handle books deemed important even if they don't promise much profit. Many are nonprofit and operate on small budgets, primarily to publish regional history, poetry and literature, and scholarly monographs for relatively small audiences. The University of Georgia Press, for example, publishes about 80 titles annually on a budget (in 1988) of $1.6 million. But university presses are expanding into wider fields, seeking books that will sell well and make money.

Often it comes down to an editor's instincts for what will sell. But sometimes not even experienced editors know why a book sells. When Paul Kennedy wrote *The Rise and Fall of the Great Powers*, published in 1988, Jason Epstein, his editor at Random House, planned on 7,500 copies being printed. Then, he explains, "I told the sales manager I had a feeling it might take off, so why not print 10,000. But we didn't have enough paper, so we had to settle for 9,000." Noted Edwin McDowell of the *New York Times*: "Six weeks and eight printings later, there are 211,000 copies in print. Mr. Epstein said he did not know what responsive chord the book had struck, unless it was concern that America was in decline."[29]

For decades, the "instant book" was a favorite of publishers who thought they could quickly detect a swing in public reading tastes and, in days, get a book into print. Between 1964, when it published the *Report of the Warren Commission on the Assassination of President Kennedy*, and 1987, Bantam Books published 70 instant books on news events that seized the public imagination. Such publishers move rapidly: Just three days after Lieutenant Colonel Oliver L. North testified in the Iran-*Contra* hearings in 1987, Pocket Books was out with a 753-page transcript of his testimony that sold for $5.95 in paperback. But North's popularity faded quickly, and only half of 775,000 books printed were sold. Pocket Books' profit was small. Television, videocassettes, and rapidly changing public tastes may threaten the future of instant books. As Michael Freitag observed in the *New York Times*, "The American public's appetite for information is growing, but its attention span is dwindling. Today's media sensation is tomorrow's has-been."[30]

One key element in book sales—pricing—is tricky because publishers must accurately judge both their costs in producing a book, which is sometimes difficult, and how essential readers will deem a book and therefore how much they will be willing to pay.

Edwin McDowell, a *New York Times* reporter specializing in covering book publishing, examined the cost of publishing books in 1989 and found the following amounts (in dollars per book copy) typical for a 300-page hardcover novel priced at $19.95 in bookstores, with 10,000 copies printed.

Revenue to publisher from discounted sale to bookstores and wholesalers		10.60
Costs		
Manufacturing	1.75	
Composition, typesetting, jacket design	1.50	
Overhead (rent, salaries, postage, etc.)	2.65	
Advertising, promotion	.60	
Author royalties	2.00	
Total costs		8.50
Profit		2.10

Although $2.10 profit per copy might appear large, McDowell pointed out that typically 45 percent of total hardcover copies printed are not sold but are returned to the publisher for credit. That means publishers are lucky to make $1 profit on a book selling in bookstores for $19.95.

Readers have very different views of what is essential. For example, baseball fans in 1988 paid $45 for Macmillan's *Baseball Encyclopedia* because its 2,875 pages of incredibly detailed statistics (weighing 5 pounds, 11 ounces) are essential to their enjoyment of the game. The book, published in 1969, is updated every few years and by 1988 sold 360,000 copies.[31]

General-interest books perceived as merely nice to have won't sell at high prices. As in any other form of mass communications, publishers look for cruciality—a book that will be deemed crucial to filling reader needs. Paperback publishers encounter severe consumer resistance if prices rise much above $4.95, no matter what the content. In 1987, the average paperback price was $3.60, up from $3.02 in 1984.[32]

Another key element in selling a trade book is getting it accepted by leading bookstores for display. Merely getting a book accepted by two major retail bookstores can help guarantee success. Waldenbooks, a unit of K mart Corp., is the nation's largest book retailer, with 1,248 stores in 1988. B. Dalton/Barnes & Noble is number 2, with 1,000 stores. Publishers believe it is impossible to have a national best seller without being in stores owned by both companies. Book clubs and direct mail companies sell millions of books. Book-of-the-Month Club is largest, with more than 1.5 million members who order books by mail; Literary Guild is second, with about 1 million members. Note the media forms thus combined: book publishing, one of the oldest, with newly invigorated direct mail.

Predictably, "hard sell" has arrived in book publishing, as in other media. Publishers spend millions to "hype" books, advertising widely and arranging appearances for authors on TV talk shows. Testimonials—"blurbs," in publishing parlance—are sought from famous people. One publisher, Contemporary Books Inc., mounted huge advertisements on three billboards near General Motors headquarters in Detroit to announce its exposé of GM, *Call Me Roger: The Story of How Roger Smith, Chairman of General Motors, Transformed the Industry Leader into a Fallen Giant.* If nothing else, the ploy won substantial coverage in the *Wall Street Journal*[33] (it drew no comment from GM). Heavy advertising helped launch a new direction in publishing for teenage girls, the so-called Soap Opera series. Fawcett used the promotional device of issuing a paperback, *Gone to Soldiers*, by feminist writer Marge Piercy, in nine different covers, one aimed at male readers (depicting a haggard prisoner of war), another for "traditional" women (Army nurse), and so forth.[34] Waldenbooks shows videos promoting books on screens throughout stores (leading *Forbes* magazine to ask, "Seen Any Good Books Lately?").[35]

JOBS AND OTHER POSSIBILITIES

Entry-level jobs with major book publishers are among the most competitive in the media world. First, despite their many hundreds of titles and millions of dollars in revenue, many publishing firms have relatively small full-time staffs. Much editing, book design, and layout is done by free-lancers or contract editors who live hundreds of miles from the major cities where many publishers have headquarters (New York, Boston, Philadelphia). Almost all presswork is done under contract by independent commercial printers.

Second, there is a romance about book publishing, the dream of graduating from college one day and the next day wining and dining famous writers in Manhattan's expensive restaurants. For all but a few senior editors, that is an unrealistic dream, but it attracts job applicants eager to start at low pay in what amount to clerical jobs.

For newcomers who do break in, there are three principal career paths: marketing, production, and editorial.

Marketing covers sales and promotion, crucial to the entire publishing process. Marketing experts help decide which authors will be signed, how books will be positioned in the marketplace, at what price, and so forth. In sales, the first job is often as "field rep"—a representative who visits bookstores, university faculties, and other groups targeted as potential buyers. Reps also try to spot potential authors and seek "intelligence" on other publishing firms. Learning that a competitor has a book in the works is important news for publishing strategists. Some marketing jobs involve writing promotional flyers to publicize books. This involves working with authors on which themes to stress. Related to this are publicity (booking author tours, sending out review copies to newspapers, etc.) and subsidiary rights (selling books to clubs, foreign publishers, and others). Marketing combines an affinity for books with a dollars-and-cents approach to bottom-line realities. A business degree and a minor in English (or the other way around) isn't a bad idea.

Many production tasks are "farmed out," so even major publishers often have small in-house staffs. But their tasks are crucial. Much of a book's appeal can be in its appearance—size, type style, cover design, internal layout. Job qualifications for a designer require artistic sense and an ability to use type effectively, plus an instinct for matching a book's content and tone with an appropriate physical appearance; such people usually have special art training. But production includes the manufacturing and business side of things, as well.

Editorial attracts the most job applicants, few of whom realize how many types of editorial roles there are today. The key position is the top editor's job, variously titled editor in chief, executive editor, or the like. This person uses marketing research and personal instinct in key calls on which books to publish and how to attract authors and oversees the writing and editing process. Subordinate editors often are given product lines to supervise. In a textbook division, that might be books in journalism, mass communications, English, and speech. Sometimes, these acquiring or sponsoring editors straddle widely disparate disciplines. Editors "make books," as they say, in areas where they have no personal scholarly expertise. They hire "reviewers" who have. Entry-level jobs are as editorial or administrative assistants, coordinating delivery of manuscripts and handling light editing chores. Pay can be in the $14,000 to $16,000 range. Obviously, a strong background in English and writing is mandatory. But even in editorial, it's necessary to know how to budget the expected costs of a book and to project potential revenue, then produce the book within budget and make a profit. Other categories of editors include production editors, responsible for coordinating projects into finished books; developmental editors, who shape a manuscript and improve its marketability; and line editors or copyeditors, who prepare the manuscripts for typesetting. All of these may be free-lance.

Don't expect job stability. Jobs can be lost through mergers, and publishing is famous for rapid turnover anyway. The trade journal *Publisher's Weekly* reports that promotions and pay raises often come faster for young editors who switch houses.

New technology opens low-cost entry into

book publishing. *Money* magazine examined the economics of desktop publishing in 1987 and found one 36-year-old woman who started publishing in her home with two Apple Macintosh Plus computers. Her total cost was $12,930 for equipment and software that produced $95,000 revenue and $46,000 net profit in one year.[36] Desktop publishers produce company manuals, advertisements, and so forth, but accomplished computer users can turn out beautiful—if inexpensive—books.

New technology is certain to change the book industry in other ways. For example, publishers are working on "multimedia" techniques that will provide audiovisual encyclopedias on compact disks. By touching a button, a "reader" could summon onto a television screen the sights and sounds described in encyclopedias. The effort is to produce more colorful and flashier books for a generation of TV watchers. The encyclopedia industry has the financing for new technology: Encyclopaedia Britannica Inc., the number 2 seller in the United States, hit $590 million in revenue in 1988; World Book Inc., the top seller, doesn't reveal its finances.

In Part III, we turn to another media sector where enormous change is under way—broadcasting.

sumers to exchange information directly and thus bypass traditional media. But the mass media serve mass audiences unlikely to have the resources—time, money, training—to bypass traditional media altogether.

New information transmission techniques include electronic magazines and videocassettes, video shopping and catalogs, and optical and compact disks.

Controversy is building over whether telephone companies will offer news and entertainment services. Most newspaper and television owners argue the "telcos" have such huge financial and technical resources that they could swamp all competitors, creating anticompetitive abuses.

Newsletters are a booming business. Direct mail is challenging traditional media and today enjoys the third-largest slice of the U.S. advertising pie, behind only newspapers and television.

Despite all the computers and video display tubes, American book publishing is highly profitable and expanding. An estimated 22,500 book publishers are active. More than 50,000 new titles are issued annually, and book sales exceed $13 billion a year. Like all media industries, book publishing is attracting global media conglomerates—many from overseas—that want to buy into the action.

☆ SUMMARY

Barriers between traditional media are breaking down and new media are bridging the gap by combining elements of the print and electronic media.

Many media companies practice the information center concept, collecting news and entertainment as always but, in a radical departure from past practice, distributing it in many forms—on paper or electronically—to different consumer constituencies. Their strength is professional editors and reporters who sift the news for readers.

New bypass technology, particularly computer bulletin boards, permits some news con-

☆ RECOMMENDED READING

Students of new forms of mass media—computer bulletin boards, electronic magazines, and so forth—must search for bits of published information to stay current. Some trade publications are helpful, particularly *Advertising Age, presstime,* and *Broadcasting.* Both the *New York Times* and the *Wall Street Journal* are particularly alert to new developments. As traditional media companies—Gannett, Knight-Ridder, Dow Jones, and others—get into combined print and electronic operations, their annual reports and in-house publications become increasingly important sources.

Publishers Weekly is an important source on book publishing, as are *Retail Bookseller* and, for aspiring magazine writers, *Writer* and *Writer's Digest*. On the history of book publishing, see Charles Madison, *Book Publishing in America* (New York: McGraw-Hill, 1967). Also note Ben Compaine, *The Book Industry in Transition: An Economic Analysis of Book Distribution and Marketing* (White Plains, N.Y.: Knowledge Publications, 1978).

AMERICA'S ELECTRONIC COMMUNICATORS

O ur survey so far has revealed evolutionary change under way as newspapers, magazines, and the newer media discussed in Chapter 8 edge toward the yet undefined mass communications future. As we turn now to radio, television, and cable, we stir into that media mix a new ingredient: *revolutionary* change.

The broadcast industry's external competitive relationships with print and other media are changing rapidly. There is more vigorous competition than ever for viewer and listener time and advertiser dollars. In 1988, for the second year in a row, daily TV viewing declined in the United States—to 6 hours and 55 minutes in the average home, from 7 hours and 5 minutes in 1987. The 1988 figure was the lowest since 1982, Nielsen Media Research reported.

Within the broadcast industry, relationships between television— particularly network television—and cable are changing dramatically. Mighty ABC, NBC, and CBS are losing their once-unchallenged viewing leadership. Cable viewing is increasing rapidly (by 1989, the three major networks shared about 67 percent of all TV viewers, down from more than 90 percent a decade earlier).

The network-plus-affiliated-station system that drove television for 40 years is breaking down. New networks are appearing, independent stations proliferating.

As in other media, broadcast ownership and management structures are changing. Increasingly, ownership of any large TV or radio station by an individual or even a family is the exception; in all but small-town operations, Mom and Pop are nearly out, large corporations in.

New technology just over the horizon either promises improvement in broadcasting and cable or threatens their existence. No one is sure which.

Winds of change are blowing in federal regulation of broadcast and in societal concern over what is being broadcast—program quality, decency, and tastefulness.

And all this is happening so quickly! It took hundreds of years for substantive changes in Gutenberg's printing method, and today, newspapers and magazines still put ink on paper, just as he did back in the 1400s. In the electronic world, two years can be a long time; a few decades, an era.

For example, big-time radio got started only in the late 1920s; in the late 1940s, that era was ended by TV. The 1950s opened the era of network TV. That lasted just 30 years until, in the 1980s, cable TV exploded and independent TV stations grew in strength.

Those of you who are planning broadcast careers couldn't be living in more exciting times. And for you media consumers, we don't know precisely what's ahead, but you will have bigger and probably better mass media sources of information and entertainment than anybody in history.

In Chapter 9, we'll broadly survey television, cable, and radio. In Chapter 10, we'll go inside a television station for a feel of how it is run and where the jobs are. In Chapter 11, we'll examine a small-town radio case study that tells how one man, on borrowed money, got into broadcast ownership (yes, small-town radio still offers rags-to-riches ownership possibilities!).

Now, let's look at the American broadcast industry.

The American Broadcast Industry

I f forced to identify the most important developments under way in the American broadcast industry today, we would say two stand out.

First, as became dramatically clear in Chapter 8, viewers and listeners today have more options, thanks to new technology, then ever before when seeking news and entertainment. And they are defecting in droves from network programming to seek choices among the scores of cable channels available in many communities and the syndicated or local programming of nonnetwork stations (the ''independents,'' or ''indies'').

Second, advertisers, who must go where the viewers are, can also go to cable or independent stations. Rather than cast their entire bankroll with nationwide mass audiences offered by networks, advertisers often seek the independents' local *targeted* audiences. And that is extremely significant, for television and radio, like all major mass media in our free enterprise system, are advertiser-driven and, in the final analysis, will answer the advertisers' call—or fail financially.

It's a replay, really, of what we saw happening in newspapers and magazines: media consumers (viewers, listeners, readers) are shifting preferences with respect to what they want and how they want it delivered. And like print, the broadcast industry is changing its ways to meet those shifts.

Unlike the print media, however, broadcast must also meet society's expectations outside the marketplace, as expressed in federal regulation. As regulated media, television and radio must operate ''in the public interest.'' Regulation is one way society expresses its expectations of the electronic media. Another is the way viewer watchdog groups set standards of ethics and social responsibility, then put political and economic pressure on television and radio to conform.

In this chapter, we'll look first at the character of the broadcast industry. We'll note the big players (many are old friends from the chapters on print), and then we'll study major issues facing broadcast in three broad sectors—news, advertising, and entertainment.

TV, CABLE, RADIO: INDUSTRY STRUCTURE AND DYNAMICS

The U.S. broadcast industry enjoys enormous economic strength and wields nearly unfathomable influence on the way we live because of a rather simple proposition: There is a huge reward for enticing you and me—and millions like us—into seeking news and entertainment on television, cable, and radio. ▶ 1

Gaining America's viewing and listening allegiance is the challenge. Winning a huge share of America's advertising expenditures is the reward.

Those, simply put, are the dynamics of broadcasting. That's why those high-powered anchors and series stars try so very hard and are paid so well to capture us. That's why some of the sharpest business and creative minds in America are in the broadcast industry. That's why the industry has a marketplace value of untold billions of dollars and why technological genius is being brought to bear on communications breakthroughs that will make it even more effective and valuable.

The average American home has a TV set turned on nearly seven hours daily. Whether it is being watched all that time, particularly during commercials, is arguable, as is whether all that viewing, in a societal sense, is good or bad. Nevertheless, it's remarkable testimony to how well the industry succeeds in drawing us to the tube. ▶ 2 The rewards are equally remarkable: $26 billion paid for TV commercial time in 1988 alone by advertisers to reach for us with messages about their goods and services. Radio that year won $7.7 billion in advertising support for attracting us with music, talk shows, and "news at the top of the hour."[1]

Radio Radio is a media survivor if there ever was one. Radio enjoyed unchallenged supremacy in electronic news and entertainment, of course, from the late 1920s to the late 1940s. Then TV arrived, and some people thought radio was finished. But the number of stations increased steadily—from 2,819 in 1950, when TV began to gather commercial steam, to more than 10,000 today. Radio found a new marketplace niche for both listeners and advertisers. Its continuing strength rests primarily on two factors: technology and programming.

Although networks are cutting news department budgets, anchors remain famous, familiar faces in American living rooms. Here, interviewing President Reagan in 1987, are (*left to right*) Tom Brokaw, NBC; Bernard Shaw, CNN; Dan Rather, CBS; and Peter Jennings, ABC. *Wide World Photos.*

◤1 High Points in American Broadcast History

1901	Marconi broadcasts a wireless signal across the Atlantic.
1907	First recorded use of the word *television*, by *Scientific American*.
1919	Radio Corporation of America founded; RCA becomes a broadcasting powerhouse.
1920	Westinghouse's KDKA in Pittsburgh is the first radio station to offer continuous, scheduled programs and reports on the presidential election.
1922	WEAF in New York City sells a 10-minute commercial and broadcasts first sponsored show.
1925	Coast-to-coast hookup of 21 stations broadcasts Coolidge's inauguration.
1926	NBC begins programming.
1927	Philo Farnsworth applies for a patent for an "electronic television system." Radio Act of 1927 establishes the Federal Radio Commission, a regulatory body.
1928	*Amos 'n' Andy* is first heard and becomes a nationwide hit.
1930	Edwin Armstrong patents frequency modulation, becoming the "father" of FM radio.
1933	Franklin Delano Roosevelt starts his "fireside chats," enormously successful political use of radio during the Depression.
1934	Communications Act of 1934 establishes the Federal Communications Commission to consolidate the regulation of broadcasting and the telephone system.
1939	RCA demonstrates TV at the New York's World Fair; the first experimental FM station goes on the air in New Jersey.

1940	Edward R. Murrow broadcasts from Europe, gives CBS a wide lead in radio coverage of the war.
1941	WCBS and NBC's WNET, both in New York City, become the first commercially licensed TV stations.
1943	NBC sells its second radio network, which becomes ABC.
1948	FCC freezes issuance of TV licenses; radio has its biggest-revenue year; TV becomes the largest revenue producer thereafter.
1951	NBC airs *Today*; CBS, *See It Now*.
1952	FCC sets UHF TV channels, noncommercial broadcast channels, and color standards.
1954	Army-McCarthy hearings and Murrow's telecast challenge of Senator McCarthy establish TV's role in broadcasting national issues.
1960	John Kennedy beats Richard Nixon in televised debates and goes on to win presidency, inaugurating TV's use as a political tool.
1961	FCC chairman Newton Minow describes TV as a "vast wasteland."
1967	Corporation for Public Broadcasting is created.
1969	Moon landing is televised live; National Public Radio (NPR) network is created.
1970	ABC Radio splits into specialized networks for news, information, and entertainment.
1980	*Dallas* becomes the most watched TV show in history.
1981	FCC deregulates radio.
1989	Due to the growth of cable TV, the three networks' share of viewership drops below 70 percent for the first time.

FM radio can deliver sound quality much superior to AM's, and FM music programming has been radio's success story in recent decades. In 1950, just 733 FM stations were on air; today, well over 5,400 are broadcasting.

Radio proved that shrewd programming attracts listeners and that smart marketing pulls in advertisers. When TV arrived, radio floundered, trying to find its niche. There were fruitless attempts to compete head-on with TV—for ex-

▶2 Broadcasting and Cable: The Numbers

Radio Stations

Commercial AM	4,948
Commercial FM	4,174
Educational FM	1,383
	10,505

TV Stations

Commercial VHF	545
Commercial UHF	517
Educational VHF	121
Educational UHF	217
	1,400
Low-Power TV	624

Cable

Total subscribers	49,538,000
Homes passed by existing systems (and thus potential new subscribers)	73,900,000
Total systems	8,000
Household penetration (of 88.6 million in United States)	54.8%
Pay cable penetration	32.0%

Note: At this point in 1989, Federal Communications Commission construction permits had been issued for an additional 1,201 radio stations, 287 TV stations, and 1,713 low-power TV stations.
Sources: Broadcasting; Federal Communications Commission.

ample, by broadcasting live events better watched on TV. Then radio settled on what it can deliver that other media cannot deliver as well—music, talk, and news formats. ▶ 4 For music lovers, radio has something for everybody, and FM technology delivers it in high-quality sound. Many advertisers use radio because its commercials are relatively inexpensive (radio is inexpensive to operate, compared with TV, and thus can charge less), and narrow radio music formats offer *target marketing*. Advertisers know where to sell pickup trucks—on the 2,421 stations offering country music and the 695 that play classic rock. No other mass communications media offer quite the same opportunities for widespread yet targeted marketing.

Still, radio is the junior player in mass media advertising. Radio had 6.5 percent of the national total in 1988, compared with 26.3 percent for newspapers, 22.0 percent for TV, and 5.3 percent for magazines and farm and business publications.[2]

In radio, as in television, one measurement of market strength is annual advertising revenue. Based on 1987 ad revenue per household, the top 10 U.S. radio markets are San Diego, Miami,

▶3 Radio Terms

Everybody hears radio announcers or disk jockeys talk about AM and FM radio, but not everybody knows what those terms mean.

AM stands for *amplitude modulation*, a means of propagating signals on the radio spectrum reserved for home receivers. On your dial, it's the segment between 535 and 1605 kilohertz (kHz). AM signals travel far, sometimes bouncing off the ionosphere and back to earth. There are 107 AM channels divided into three broad categories. *Dominant clear channels* are reserved for strong stations of 50,000 watts of power that often can be heard broadcasting over large areas of the country with nighttime talk shows, sports, and popular music. *Regional channels* cover large areas, too, but are shared by stations. *Local channels* are often shared by many stations broadcasting to a local community. In 1989, some 47 percent of all stations on the air were AM.

The FM (for *frequency modulation*) range is higher on your dial—88 to 108 megahertz (MHz)—and is hugely popular because it produces superior music quality and is less vulnerable to interference. FM depends on *line-of-sight* transmission from tower to radio receiver, so most stations can be heard no more than 70 miles or so. In 1989, the remaining 53 percent of all stations were FM. Certain technical modifications permit stereo broadcasting (*multiplexing*).

4 ▸ Radio's Favorite Programming

Format	Number of Stations
Country	2,421
Adult contemporary	2,325
Religious, gospel	1,054
Top 40	984
"Middle-of-the-road"	729
Oldies, classic rock	695
Diversified	614
Album-oriented rock	486
Talk	408
"Beautiful music"	403
News	384
Classical	355
Jazz	296
Big band, nostalgia	259
Educational	259

Source: Broadcasting; figures for 1989.

Washington, Atlanta, Phoenix, Dallas–Fort Worth, Houston, San Francisco, San Antonio, and Baltimore, according to *Advertising Age*.

Certainly, radio's social impact—its ability to shape the news agenda or influence lifestyles—is considerably less than that of television, newspapers, and magazines, which have enormous influence over everything from hairstyles to how our democratic society conducts its affairs.

Television Television leaped quickly from newfangled curiosity to national obsession. In 1950, just 9 TV stations were on the air; in 1960, 573; 1970, 872; 1980, 1,013; and today, more than 2,000.

About 99 percent of all American homes, more than 88 million, have radio and TV sets. Of all TV homes, 57 percent have more than one set; 96 percent have at least one color set. The growth pattern paralleled that of the stations, going from 5.9 million homes in 1950 to 45.2 million in 1960. (Let's not overlook radio, though: only in 1986

did the number of TV homes surpass radio homes. In 1988, there were about 505 million radio sets in the nation—72 percent in homes, 28 percent in cars and other places out of homes.[3])

In competitive terms, TV was strong from the start. The novelty of its sight-and-sound pulled in tens of millions of viewers, and its in-home entertainment held them. ▸ **5** TV's first victims were mass-circulation magazines—the weekly *Life, Look,* and others that for decades delivered national audiences to advertisers. Magazine production costs got too high—and thus so did ad rates; and seeing things happen on TV was much more exciting than later looking at even those powerful still photos in *Life*. Television began delivering larger audiences to advertisers at lower costs than magazines could. There were other victims: neighborhood movie theaters closed by the hundreds. Free viewing in one's living room beat going downtown to pay for a "show."

It's important to note television didn't kill competing media industries; rather, it forced change in their form—their delivery method—only. The magazine industry shifted from courting mass audiences with national magazines to searching out narrow, targeted audiences with specialized publications. The film industry is prospering as never before. Television itself became a major market for film producers, of course, and when neighborhood theaters shut down, film distributors shifted to multiscreen theaters in shopping malls and to cable and home videos.

Future mass communicators should avoid being blinded by new technology and surface change in the media. The essentials will remain: Americans will continue to want news and entertainment; mass media that serve those wants—whether through print, electronic, or some other means not yet even dreamed—will succeed.

Early in its expansion, television's principal marketplace thrust came from three networks—CBS, NBC, and ABC—and their "affiliates," local stations that joined networks in a business relationship. The marriage of networks and affiliates profited both highly. Networks produced

5 ▶ TV Terms

To you, the TV viewer, it's just a position on the dial. For the station owners, however, the difference between VHF and UHF is quite extraordinary.

VHF stations broadcast in the *very high frequency* band of the electromagnetic spectrum and occupy channels 2–13. These stations, today 47.5 percent of all full-power stations on the air, were originally owned and operated by networks (and thus known as "O's and O's"). Early TV receivers were manufactured for VHF transmission, and this, combined with network ownership and favorable dial position, gave VHF, particularly network stations and affiliates, a strong early competitive edge.

UHF (*ultra high frequency*) stations went on the air later (starting only in 1952), on channels 14–83. Most were independent of networks and thus known as "indies." UHF signals don't travel as far as those of VHF stations. Other competitive disadvantages: UHF stations didn't have access to network programming and had to run less attractive fare such as old movies, and receiving their transmission often required special tuning. With the advent of cable TV, however, their signals are often available over widespread areas far from the originating stations, and new, attractive programming is available from syndicators and other sources. Today, indies, many of them UHF, are increasing their share of viewer audiences.

LPTV is a *low-power television* station, either VHF or UHF, licensed by the FCC to transmit over a small area, usually only 10 to 15 miles from the transmitter. The FCC originally intended LPTV to encourage local entrepreneurs in neighborhood broadcasting. Print media initially viewed it as potential competition for local community publications or zoned newspaper editions. However, networks and other large broadcast groups submitted most of the initial 30,000 applications, so the FCC began awarding licenses by lottery. Generally, advertisers have not been attracted by LPTV's small viewer audiences, and in 1989, only 624 stations were transmitting.

or bought programs, sold commercial time on them to national advertisers, and piped programs and commercials to affiliates across the country. Networks paid affiliates to carry the programming (thus delivering to advertisers the promised national audiences); the affiliates produced local programming and sold commercial time to local advertisers. The results were fascinating and widespread.

First, some people in TV got very rich. In short order, television became one of the world's most profitable industries. You will recall that newspapers, themselves much more profitable than most industries, may return 25 to 30 percent operating profit (advertiser and subscriber revenue minus operating expense). TV stations quickly zoomed into the 40 to 50 percent bracket. Advertisers "moved" cars, beer, razor blades, and soap as never before. Market strength in television is measured by advertising revenue pulled in annually by all stations in the market. Strong stations—and jobs—are naturally in the strongest markets. Based on 1987 ad revenue per household, the leading 10 U.S. markets, in order, were Los Angeles, Miami, Dallas–Fort Worth, San Francisco, San Diego, Atlanta, Boston, Houston, Phoenix, and Denver.

Second, television's incredible wealth and ubiquitousness translated into influence over the national agenda. Networks and large stations opened new dimensions in mass entertainment tastes and news coverage. TV influenced national awareness. Anyone under, say, 50 years of age probably cannot understand what a thrill ran through the country when, in 1951, network television linked our east and west coasts! CBS put on no less than the famed Edward R. Murrow himself to show, on side-by-side screens, simultaneous live pictures of the Atlantic and Pacific oceans. NBC broadcast its *Today* show *live from New York City*, if you can imagine! It wasn't long before Murrow and other news and entertainment stars were not only helping decide what was news and entertainment but also influencing national lifestyles. Everybody saw how they talk and walk in Los Angeles and New York City and what they wear. New fashions—in food, clothing, language—no longer slowly spread across the nation; they were revealed instantly. (Did you ever notice that news anchors in all parts of the country sound alike? Did you ever realize the impact national TV has had on our disappearing regional accents and customs?) Much programming produced by television's newfound wealth was of high quality. Any journalist is bound to agree, for example, that CBS's news division, coming off a strong history of quality radio, produced outstanding TV journalism. Network television had the money and the professionalism to cover the world as no local television station could (or, to this day, can). Some TV entertainment of that era was classic, bringing to millions of American homes drama, comedy, and dance they would otherwise never have seen.

Third, television got greedy. Lured by advertiser dollars and pushed by shareholder demands for ever-increasing profits, the industry headed for a level and quality of programming promising the largest possible audiences. There was a gradual move toward a lower common denominator. Television proved voracious, devouring programming so rapidly that nobody could possibly feed it continually with high-quality writing and production. And as competition for dollars grew, the unprincipled appeal to base instincts increased: sex grew hotter, violence more bloody, comedy more bawdy. By 1961, the then chairman of the Federal Communications Commission, Newton N. Minow, felt constrained to label much of TV

a vast wasteland . . . [of] game shows, violence, audience participation shows, formula comedies about totally unbelievable families, blood and thunder, mayhem, violence, sadism, murder, western bad men, western good men, private eyes, gangsters, more violence and cartoons. And, endlessly, commercials—many screaming, cajoling and offending. And most of all, boredom. ▶ 6

Gradually, the drive for profits available through entertainment programs strongly squeezed news divisions. Many true news professional were replaced by sound-alike, look-alike anchors who combined happy-talk entertainment with news in an entirely new form of "newscast"

---

6 ▶ What Those Commercials Cost

Next time a 30-second commercial interrupts your favorite TV program, reflect on what it cost the advertiser to buy time for a chance to reach you and millions of other viewers.

The average 30-second commercial on a network show in prime time in 1988 cost more than $120,000. The price was more than $200,000 on a series with top ratings. Spots on low-rated programs averaged more than $80,000.

Advertisers paid $650,000 for a single 30-second commercial during the 1988 Super Bowl. They were paying for access to the estimated 120 million viewers tuned in. NBC charged $369,500 for 30 seconds on "The Cosby Show"!

(In addition, national advertisers in 1987 paid an average of $145,600 to produce each TV commercial.)

In local television, rates for 30-second commercials range from just a few dollars in some markets to $20,000 or more for top-rated series in major markets.

In radio, commercials ("spots") sell for a few dollars in small towns to $1,000 or more in major markets.

(screened each night behind a catchy musical theme or the sirens and flashing red lights of the "action news" format—and did that ever upset news traditionalists!). Lost was the opportunity to take television as a whole to truly great heights in news, public affairs, and entertainment programming. To cut costs, networks reduced news staffs, virtually eliminated lengthy analytical news specials. TV stations, even some owned by networks, began replacing network news in the best time slots with game shows promising more revenue. Even Dan Rather, as "CBS Evening News" anchor the heir to a respected network tradition, took humiliating hits. In 1988, the CBS-owned flagship in New York City, WCBS, shifted Rather from the favored 7 P.M. slot to 6:30 P.M.

to make way for the game show "Win, Lose or Draw." CBS officials explained that the switch would increase revenue by $5 million annually.[4] At many stations, solid, professional newscasts gave way to shallow silliness.

Yet television remains a strong force in American life. Its entertainment programming at times is brilliant; its news still has flashes of greatness, and on some stories, the visual drama and the spectacle of television are unmatched. Even its strongest competitors—newspapers and magazines—acknowledge that television is perceived by millions of Americans as an adequate source of news and information (42 percent in one survey by the Newspaper Advertising Bureau said that TV gave them enough details on big news stories).[5]

The number of viewers continues to increase each year. Advertising revenue increases annually, and the industry's total economic position continues to strengthen. So what's this talk of revolutionary change in the industry? It is a dramatic shifting of forces within the industry: Dollars and viewers enjoyed exclusively for so long by networks and affiliates are going elsewhere, largely to independent stations and cable.

Cable TV Ah cable! *There* is an example of how new technology can put an established media industry through the wringer. ▶ 7

▶7 Cable Terms

Cable has its own language, and if you plan a career in mass communications, you should learn it.

Cable systems operators negotiate *franchises* with local governmental authority, usually a city council or county commission, agreeing to construct a cable *plant* and serve the local community for a specified number of years. Companies that own more than one cable system are called *multiple systems operators* (MSOs). A *receiving antenna* catches programming via microwave circuits or landlines from a distant *earth station*. The local signal is *originated* in a *head-end* or technical facility, then fed into *trunk cables* and onward to subscriber homes, called *drops*, via *feeder cables* underground or on telephone poles (space on which is rented).

Cable began as *community antenna television* (CATV) to provide viewing to remote regions unable to receive adequate over-the-air signals. With the development of true cable service, which imports distant signals or originates local programming, *basic service* was provided on as many as 54 channels by the mid-1970s in some areas. *Pay cable* via *premium* (or *tiered*) channels later developed as systems operators found that they could charge additional fees for Showtime, HBO, the Disney Channel, and other special services.

Pay-per-view (PPV) television involves one-time payment for special events such as boxing matches. A major problem: with current technology it is difficult to use PPV on existing cable systems and identify subscribers who view the events (and thus should be charged extra).

Subscription television (STV) involves equipping subscribers with *decoders* that *descramble* programming *scrambled* at the transmission point to prevent unauthorized (nonpaying) viewers from receiving it. *Satellite master antenna television* uses a single antenna for, say, an apartment building, with programming routed via *private cable* to individual apartments.

Direct broadcast satellite (DBS) could replace existing cable systems if a way is found to make it work economically. Programming is routed—*uplinked*—from an *earth station* to a satellite and then *downlinked* directly to subscriber homes equipped with individual receiver antennas. Formidable costs are involved for equipment, and satellites with stronger signal transmission are needed. DBS technology is limited in that it doesn't promise *interactive* service, with subscribers being able not only to receive but also to order up special programming or interrogate distant computers, as is possible via certain landlines.

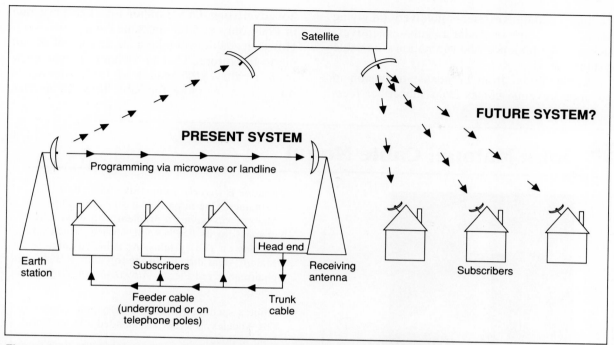

Figure 9.1. CURRENT AND FUTURE CABLE SYSTEMS. Present system involves transmitting via cables to subscribers' homes. Future may feature direct transmission via satellite to a dish at each subscriber's home.

Cable television is soaring to new strengths on basically two developmental streams. First, strong demand is developing among media consumers for individual—virtually customized—services, particularly in entertainment but also in news and information. Consumers want to pick, at times of their own choosing, what they will read, watch, and listen to. Second, in response, cable technology is developing to give viewers a luxury of choice. For the first 30 years of television, viewers mostly had three choices—NBC, CBS, or ABC—for entertainment of any acceptable dimension and quality. Comprehensive news was available only when the networks were ready, normally in limited evening time slots. With cable, 20, 30, or more entertainment options are available; news is available 24 hours daily.

Consumer demand for variety developed first. Marketing disasters can result when communications companies, blinded by new technical capabilities, launch services for which there is no consumer demand. Knight-Ridder lost $50 million because it bet that new videotex technology, offering access to an amazing variety of computerized information services, would create consumer demand. It didn't.

Clearly, cable technology still is evolving. At the left of Figure 9.1 is an artist's rendering of current technology of cable service to individual homes by means of copper wires buried underground or strung on telephone poles. That's so cumbersome and costly (it can run $10,000 per mile in rural areas and $100,000 in urban areas, $300,000 where underground cables are needed) that many homes can't get service. At the right of the figure, the artist depicts direct broadcast satellite (DBS) transmission. But DBS is extremely expensive, too, and the next step may be into fiber optics, which permits transmission of a very large number of services over a single circuit made of fine glass.

Developing cable's potential and managing

the huge capital investments involved are giving rise to a new type of media mogul—executives, such as John Malone, who run nationwide cable systems. ▶ 8

Cable differs from broadcast television in that most revenue comes from subscriber fees, not advertising. Of $13 billion total cable revenue in 1988, only $1.5 billion came from advertisers. However, cable will take a larger slice of the ad pie in the future. That $1.5 billion in 1988 grew from a paltry $100 million in 1980. Americans now spend far more for cable than for movies

---

8 ▸ John Malone: Cable Mogul

John Malone. *TCI photo; reproduced with permission.*

John Malone's track record shows that he's very smart and very tough. In 1973, Malone, at 32, joined a small, almost bankrupt cable company, Tele-Communications, Inc. By 1988, he had built TCI into a giant serving 10 million U.S. homes, more than 20 percent of all those subscribing to cable services. TCI's annual revenue passed $1.7 billion, and the company was enormously profitable. *Forbes* estimated that Malone's stock alone was worth $33.1 million.

Malone's résumé is impressive: Merit scholar at Yale (1963, BS in electrical engineering and economics, magna cum laude). Graduate degrees from Johns Hopkins (1964, MS, industrial management), New York University (1965, MS, electrical engineering), and Johns Hopkins again (1967, PhD, operations research, with special distinction). Jobs with Bell Telephone Laboratories/AT&T (economic planning/research and development), McKinsey & Co. (management consulting), and General Instrument Corp. (group vice president and president of its subsidiary, Jerrold CATV) before joining TCI.

Many stories are told about how John

Malone is fiercely competitive and a hard bargainer. One in particular sums them up. Malone was having a problem with what ABC charged for its ESPN cable service, which was running on TCI systems. As is his custom, Malone went directly to the top man, ABC's then chairman, Fred Pierce. *Advertising Age* tells it neatly:

> While a spectator at the 1984 Olympic Games in Los Angeles, [Pierce] was handed a letter from John Malone.
>
> In it, the president of Tele-Communications, Inc., the nation's largest cable-systems operator, informed Mr. Pierce that TCI would switch off ABC's ESPN on every one of its systems at midnight that day, unless Mr. Malone heard from the ABC boss by 5 p.m. End of message.[6]

Malone got his way.

TCI holds substantial investments in Turner Broadcasting System, the Discovery Channel, Black Entertainment Television, American Movie Classics, the Cable Value Network, and other cable services. Clearly, suppliers of cable programming must get on TCI systems. Some in the cable industry feel no new service can succeed unless run by TCI. That, obviously, gives Malone strong clout in negotiating suppliers' fees (*Ad Age* quotes him as describing—"with gusto"—the confrontation with ABC: "We busted their price schedule").

Industry betting is that Malone wants a vertically integrated TCI—a company involved in program and film production plus movie theaters as well as cable systems. The idea of competing with Malone in everything from script idea through production and distribution to the media consumer has the film industry very upset.

($4.5 billion in 1988) or for buying or renting videocassettes ($7.2 billion).[7]

Once installation costs are paid, cable systems can be extremely profitable. Many are "cash cows" bought and sold for enormous prices. In 1989, Cablevision Systems Corp. paid nearly $3,200 *per subscriber* for a cable system reaching 46,500 homes in suburban Phoenix. (The *Des Moines Register* sold for $688 per subscriber in 1985, the *Louisville Courier* for $1,022 in 1986; both are famous papers.) Reflecting their dramatic loss of viewers, network-affiliated TV stations are being sold at relatively lower prices.

THE BIG PLAYERS

Among broadcasting's big players are familiar names—old friends from our earlier study of global media conglomerates and American newspapers and magazines. Capital Cities, Murdoch, Tribune Co., Gannett—all are here, attracted by the enormous profits available on the broadcasting side of the media fence. ▶ 9

Though cable is relatively new as a major mass communications industry, and although it has its own cast of players, 5 of the top 15 cable operators are big in print—Time Warner,

9 ▶ Broadcasting's Big Players

	Broadcast Revenue (millions of dollars)	% of Total Media Revenue	Top TV Station; Average Households Reached (Rating)	Top Radio Station; Revenue (millions)
1. Capital Cities/ABC	3,213	75.5	WABC (ABC) New York 653,420 (9.5)	KABC-AM, Los Angeles $24.0
2. General Electric	3,165	100.0	WNBC (NBC) New York 481,467 (7:0)	KNBR-AM, San Francisco $11.5
3. CBS	2,762	100.0	WCBS (CBS) New York 440,198 (6.4)	KMOX-AM, St. Louis $18.4
4. Westinghouse	601	100.0	KYW (NBC) Philadelphia 185,712 (7.2)	WINS-AM, New York $23.0
5. News Corp. (Murdoch)	577	46.1	WNYW (Fox) New York 330,149 (4.8)	—
6. Tribune Co.	410	21.7	WPIX (Ind.) New York 226,977 (3.3)	WGN-AM, Chicago $31.0
7. Gannett Co.	357	11.9	WUSA (CBS) Washington 141,823 (8.8)	KIIS-AM/FM, Los Angeles $29.0
8. Gillette	340	100.0	WJBK (CBS) Detroit 134,395 (8.0)	—
9. Cox	328	22.4	WSB (ABC) Atlanta 132,628 (10.5)	KOST-FM, Los Angeles $18.0
10. Opubco (Oklahoma Publishing)	285	61.2	WTVT (CBS) Tampa 102,054 (8.3)	WKY-AM, Oklahoma City $0.9

Notes: Revenue figures for 1987. Ratings show ratio of households watching a station to number of TV households in market, as of February 1988. *Source: Advertising Age*, reproduced with permission.

Cox, Times Mirror, Capital Cities, and New-house. ▶ 10 And among significant owners of movie or special-service cable channels, 5 print companies are important: Time Warner, Capital Cities/ABC, Landmark Communications, Opubco (Oklahoma Publishing), and Hearst. ▶ 11

It's the profit center concept at work, with the big players moving corporate eggs from one basket into several for protection against harsh economic times that might strike one media sector; it's how they maximize profit by using a single corporate structure to operate many properties in different mass communications fields; it's how the publicly owned companies buy properties to add new revenue streams to satisfy shareholder demand for more and more growth.

One result is a complicated web of corporate relationships throughout all media. For example, 32 percent of all cable systems have ties with television or radio companies, about 18 percent with newspapers. And about 20 percent of cable systems have ties with programming producers.[8] Vertical integration can involve a broadcast company in every media activity from collection of news or creation of entertainment to its packaging and delivery plus the sale of advertising to go with it.

Thus Capital Cities/ABC, the nation's largest media firm in 1988 revenue, was number 1 among broadcasting's big players, 15 on the newspaper list, 7 on the magazine list, 13 on the cable list, and among the nine significant owners of movie or special-service channels. Gannett,

10 ▶ Cable's Big Players

	Cable Revenue (millions of dollars	% of Total Media Revenue	Basic Subscribers
1. Time Inc.	1,618	50.0	3,700,000
2. TCI	1,225	100.0	6,244,666
3. Viacom International	806	85.9	1,058,808
4. Home Shopping Network	582	100.0	*
5. Continental Cable	442	100.0	2,112,000
6. Cox	425	29.0	1,438,057
7. SCI (Storer)	420	68.6	1,459,000
8. Warner Communications	387	91.1	1,410,190
9. Cablevision Systems	300	100.0	1,021,426
10. Comcast	287	100.0	1,342,500
11. Times Mirror	240	9.4	933,980
12. United Cable	223	100.0	1,167,355
13. Capital Cities/ABC	221	5.2	*
14. Turner Broadcasting	213	48.8	*
15. Advance (Newhouse)	203	8.5	1,085,478

Note: Revenues for 1987.
* Basic subscribers as of 1988 (Home Shopping, Capital Cities/ABC, and Turner derive revenue from services sold to other cable operators).
Source: Advertising Age, reproduced with permission.

11 ▶ Major Movie or Special-Service Channels

Owner	Service (millions of subscribers)
Time Inc.	HBO (15.9), Cinemax (5.1)
Viacom	Showtime/The Movie Channel (8.4)
	MTV Networks (39.4)
	Nickelodeon (37.9)
Home Shopping	Home Shopping Network (29.6)
Capital Cities/ABC	ESPN (46.1)
Landmark Communications	Weather Channel (31.6)
CVN Cos.	Cable Value Network (18.5)
Turner Broadcasting	CNN (42.9), Headline News (29.2)
	SuperStation WTBS (42.5)
Gulf & Western/MCA	USA Network (41.0)
Opubco (Oklahoma Publishing)	Nashville Network (37.0)
Hearst/Viacom/ABC	Lifetime (35.4)
Non-Profit Cooperative	C-SPAN (33.0)
Playboy Enterprises	Playboy Channel (0.5)
Christian Broadcasting	CBN Cable Network (37.2)

Note: Subscriber numbers for 1988.
Sources: Advertising Age; Wall Street Journal.

largest newspaper company, is a big player in broadcast and second among outdoor (billboard) advertising companies! The FCC estimates that $7.5 billion was spent buying television and radio stations in 1987, more than $6 billion buying cable systems. The stakes are constantly rising.

In financial terms and in impact on society, these large media companies have enormous clout. Capital Cities/ABC, for example, reaches 24.4 percent of all U.S. homes with its eight TV stations.[9] Capital Cities/ABC also sells nearly 1 million copies of its newspapers each day and publishes more than 80 magazines. Clearly, this gives us reason to look closely at how such companies are run. But first we must examine two factors that dictate how the broadcast industry operates: the "ratings game" and federal regulation and social pressures on the industry.

THE RATINGS GAME

Everybody in television and radio plays a multibillion-dollar game in which television executives must answer questions asked by advertisers: Who watches TV? Who listens to radio? Do they watch and listen to commercials as well as programming? With what intensity? Does viewing or listening affect their purchase of goods and services? The answer to all these questions: Nobody really knows for sure.[10]

That very controversial answer unsettles the entire broadcasting industry as well as the ad agencies and advertisers who spend billions of dollars on television and radio to convince millions of us—viewers and listeners—to purchase goods and services. The stakes in the ratings game are enormous because advertiser decisions on which medium to use are based on audience size, viewer and listener demographics (income, age, education, and so forth), and the ability of television and radio commercials to persuade.

For decades, television industry leaders were happy with audience research. More and more Americans each year were reported watching more and more television. That permitted more and more ad rate increases until by 1988 broadcasting ad revenue had become a mountainous $26.0 billion for TV and $7.7 billion for radio.[11] But cable and independent stations began grabbing more ad revenue. Remote-control devices permitted "zapping" (changing channels during commercials) and VCRs allowed "zipping" (speeding through them). And many advertisers, who themselves visited the kitchen or the bathroom during commercials, began wondering if measuring audiences during programs truly reflected audiences during commercials. In advertising circles, disenchantment with all this was growing when, in 1987, the people meter burst on the scene.[12]

People meters are hand-held devices with buttons (similar to remote-control devices) that volunteer viewers punch to indicate when they are watching and what. The leading national audience research company, A. C. Nielsen Co., put people meters in 2,000 TV homes amid much fanfare that definitive audience measuring had arrived at last. For the three major networks, the initial results were devastating. People meters showed a drop in network viewing of 10 percent in just one year. Viewing of some programs was down 25 percent. A second research firm, AGB TV Research of Britain, put its own people meters into U.S. viewer homes and returned audience measurements sometimes 10 to 15 percent off those reported by Nielsen for the very same programs.

The networks charged that people meter results were inaccurate, that viewers tire of punching buttons and that many, particularly children, don't use them faithfully. These complaints were heaped atop long-standing concern that traditional research methodology in television is fundamentally flawed—that viewer samples are too small (even though they are valid statistically), that viewer volunteers are more TV-oriented than nonvolunteers (and thus are not truly representative of national viewing habits), that relatively few volunteers come from low-income, black, and Hispanic homes, and so forth.

Television's print competitors stoked the controversy, of course. Eugene Patterson, at the time chairman and CEO of the *St. Petersburg* (Fla.) *Times*, said not long ago:

> Television holds no business terrors for newspapers. Its commercial challenge is 40 years old, showing there's room for both the paper and the box. Now the numbers are dropping on network viewing as cable multiplies the channels and fragments the TV advertising market. Thus print has a shot at becoming the true mass medium again.[13]

There were charges that television had never delivered to advertisers the audience numbers it boasted and that, anyway, viewers regard commercials as intrusive and to be avoided, whereas readers buy newspapers in part for advertising and are active information seekers when they pick up their papers. One research firm, R. D. Percy Co., reported that its people meters showed that viewing of commercials was on average 17 percent lower than the programs in which they aired. For some commercials, viewing was 40 percent below program viewing. Some ad agency executives asked whether ad rates should be based on program viewing, as always, or switched to commercial viewing.

ARE THEY REALLY WATCHING?

66 We don't know if individuals sitting in front of the set are reading a magazine, [are] playing Scrabble or have muted the sound. 99

Bob Warrens, media research director at J. Walter Thompson USA ad agency.[14]

There were two immediate results to all these doubts as to whether anybody really knows precisely who watches television, when, and with what effect. First, advertisers forced networks to compensate them for audiences promised but, according to the people meters, not delivered. Ad rates are based on promised audience size, and in an "up-front buy," advertisers purchase commercial time as much as a year in advance on a guarantee that the program will deliver a certain size audience. To compensate for failure to deliver, networks had to give up "make good" time—future free airtime. Exactly how much is a secret. But it cost the networks over $100 million.[15]

Second, the entire industry began searching for more reliable measuring methods. Nielsen, which gains far more revenue from advertisers than from networks (each pays about $5 million annually for research), insists that its methodology is accurate. In 1989, the company announced plans to develop a "passive people meter"—a cameralike device that would recognize the faces of family members and record electronically when they begin viewing TV and even note when they avert their eyes to read or hold a conversation. (The *Wall Street Journal* reported, with obvious relief, that the device "can't decipher or record whatever else they're doing, such as necking on the couch.") Arbitron Ratings Co., a major American firm strong in radio and local audience research, announced that it would use people meters but that its research will also show what products TV viewers are buying. Clearly, advertiser demand for that kind of product information will take broadcasting's audience research toward new frontiers. There will be increased emphasis on qualitative as well as quantitative analysis. The mission will be to determine not only how many people are viewing or listening but also precisely who they are (in demographic terms) and whether they are actually motivated by the commercials they see to buy goods and services. ▶ 12 However, current technology and methodology are not yet up to the challenge.

In radio, Arbitron is the leading researcher. It selects listeners at random from telephone books and gives them pocket diaries for listing daily listening, both at home and away from home. In about 175 cities, Arbitron asks 3,000 or so volunteers to list each station listened to and listening time. The largest markets are measured four times annually, smaller markets just once. Results are reproduced in a ratings book sold to stations and advertisers. Two key elements are *rating* and *share*.

◆ A station's rating is the ratio of its listeners to all people in the market (if 10,000 people in a market of 100,000 listened to a certain station, its rating would be 10 for the time period measured).
◆ A station's share of audience is the ratio of its listeners to the total of radio listeners in the market (if 50,000 people are listening to radio and at that time 5,000 are listening to one station, its share is 10).[16]

Asking people to fill out diaries can't guarantee accuracy, of course. Only about half are returned or usable. Some researchers telephone people in a market, asking them to recall what radio they listened to the day before, but that is filled with potential for error, obviously. Neither research method delivers the precise or comprehensive information radio advertisers will demand in the future.

In television, Nielsen is the largest researcher. It measures about 220 markets each year; Arbitron nearly as many. Survey volunteers are selected randomly and given diaries for each TV set in their household. The most important measurements are four annual "sweeps," in February, May, July, and November, when every local TV market in the country is measured. The results, anxiously awaited, are so important that stations try to boost audiences by airing special programming during survey periods (this is called "hyping").

Most public interest in audience measurement comes from Nielsen's ratings of network programming. Viewers learn whether their favorite news anchor or comedy show won or lost against competitors. Nielsen randomly selects 1,700 TV homes across the country. Recording devices attached to TV sets in those homes automatically feed viewing data into Nielsen com-

12 ▶ How Advertisers Target TV Audiences

TV advertisers sift through mounds of statistical data to find the desired audience target. For example, it's known that 88.6 million American homes (98 percent of the total) have TV sets and that the average home has at least one set on for nearly seven hours daily. That's not very helpful for a manufacturer of, say, sports cars trying to reach zesty, with-it males who are potential buyers for something low and fast.

So advertisers and their ad agencies take a second cut at the statistics to find out when those TV sets are on. By far, "prime time" each night—8 P.M. to 11 P.M.—is the most active time slot. Of all TV homes, about 52 percent on average have their sets on at that time. About 30 percent have them on Monday through Friday from 1 P.M. to 4:30 P.M. and about 36.5 percent Monday through Friday from 10 A.M. to 1 P.M.

Advertisers also know that sets turned on during prime time get watched by more people. On average, 1.7 persons per set watch 8 P.M.–11 P.M.; in the 1 P.M.–4:30 P.M. period, 1.44 persons are watching; and 1.41 are watching 10 A.M.–1 P.M. But that doesn't give advertisers enough to go on either. Who is watching? Male sports car nuts? Women? Children? Here, roughly, is how audiences break down:

Percentage of Audience per Average Minute

	Men	Women	Teens	Children
10 A.M.–1 P.M. Monday–Friday	22	48	11	19
1 P.M.–4:30 P.M. Monday–Friday	22	50	11	17
8 P.M.–11 P.M. All nights	37	46	7	10

Sources: Television Advertising Bureau, National Audience Demographics report, July 1987; *Broadcasting/Cablecasting Yearbook* 1988.

Obviously, 10 A.M.–1 P.M. or 1 P.M.–4:30 P.M., Monday–Friday, is not the time to catch men who are potential sports car buyers; the time to go for them is mostly 8 P.M.–11 P.M., Monday–Friday. To catch women, the heaviest TV viewers, the best time is during morning and early afternoon hours.

However, even those statistics don't tell the full tale for advertisers. Who selects programming during prime time? What about weekend viewing?

Audience research must go much deeper to meet advertiser needs. Viewing of each program must be studied, not only for total number of viewers but also for precisely who they are in demographic terms and, increasingly, what their buying habits are.

You can see from this why sports cars (and beer and razors) are often advertised heavily during televised sports events and why soap and other household products fill commercial slots during soap operas and other programs known to have large female followings.

puters (in this research, diaries are not used). There is the potential, of course, for determining whether viewers are switching channels during a program. Could that lead to directors of, say, news programs or talk shows signaling anchors to "hype" things a bit to keep audiences from wandering away? Just how responsive would numbers-driven television executives get?

We'll look at market research from a different perspective in Chapter 13.

1 List your TV channels.

Keep this page open to assist you while filling out your diary.

For all channels this set receives clearly:
- List channel numbers.
- Include call letters/channel identification (WADJ, KABS, etc.) or channel names (HTO, Starvision, etc.).
- Include the city of the TV station or cable company.

Channel Number	Call Letters/ Channel Identification	City	Channel Number	Call Letters/ Channel Identification	City	Channel Number	Call Letters/ Channel Identification	City
33	WADJ	PLAINVILLE						
4	HTO	OAK CITY						
72	KABS	PLAINVILLE						

Begin Here.

2 List all the people who live in your household.

For everyone age 2 or older who lives in this household, write in:
- First Name
- Age
- M (male) or F (female)

If someone who doesn't live in this household watches this set during the week, write in:
- "VISITOR"
- Age (guess if you don't know)
- M (male) or F (female)

When listing visitors, give approximate age if not known.

	Heads of House		Other Household Members and Visitors		
First Name	DANIEL	MARY	PATRICIA	OSCAR	VISITOR
Age	40	38	14	8	12
Sex	M	F	F	M	M

3 Write down what you watch.

Set off or on? Mark an "X" and lines to show how long.

Set is on for five minutes or more, please tell us what you're watching.

Channel number From the dial or button you use. Use lines if channel stays the same.

Call letters/ channel identification Write in the call letters or channel name.

People watching Mark an "X" and draw a line to show how long they watched or listened.

Nobody watching or listening while set was on? Write "O" in first column.

Set off all day? Check (✓) the box at the bottom of the "Evening" page.

IF SET NOT TURNED ON TODAY, CHECK (✓) HERE ▶

Time	TV Set Off	On	Channel Number	Call Letters/ Channel Identification	Name of Program
6:00 6:14		X			
6:00 6:14			72	KABS	NIGHTLY NEWS
7:00 7:14			35	WADJ	GOOD DAYS
8:00 8:14			4	HTO	DISTANT GALAXIES

Much TV research is based on viewer diaries Arbitron places in selected homes. Viewers must list TV watchers by sex and age, among other things. © *Arbitron Company, 1989.*

TO REGULATE OR NOT TO REGULATE

In broadcasting, a rapidly changing industry, one argument that never changes is among broadcasters, lawmakers, and other opinion leaders over the federally regulated status of television and radio. There are two camps. One holds that broadcast must continue to be regulated, as it has been since the Radio Act of 1927, because radio and television stations use, free of charge, a public—and scarce—resource, the broadcast spectrum. This argument holds that broadcast licenses are privileges granted to relatively few citizens—station owners—and that frankly, they are licenses to make money. In return, the argument runs, owners must agree to federal requirements that they serve "the public interest, convenience, and necessity." That means regulation of everything from who gets licenses to the content of children's programs and the fairness of news coverage. And that, obviously, means no free press status for broadcast with the constitutional rights and social benefits enjoyed by newspapers and magazines.

The second broad position is that television and radio must be deregulated, turned loose in a marketplace where viewers and listeners, not the government, decide what is in the "public interest." To some broadcasters, the lure of a deregulated industry joining the free press under the First Amendment umbrella is very strong. So is the dream of shedding onerous and costly federal regulation, with its bureaucratic paperwork and constant danger of serious challenge to a license.

One basic problem, of course, is how to pass out licenses if broadcasters reject linkage between the privilege of getting a license and operating in the public interest. Would broadcasters willingly pay for use of the public spectrum? Hardly. If deregulated TV stations paid the public (the U.S. Treasury) only, say, the 5 percent of gross revenue that many cable television operators pay local municipalities for the privilege of a franchise, huge sums would change hands: 5 percent of television's $26 billion revenue in 1988 works out to a hefty $1.3 billion, give or take a couple of million. For example, if a 5 percent fee were imposed on its 1987 revenue, WGN-AM radio in Chicago would pay more than $1.5 million. License holders are not attracted to that; nor do they like the idea of putting their precious licenses up for distribution by lottery or auction to the highest bidder. Another basic problem in complete deregulation would be maintaining order on the spectrum. Wouldn't a free market-place scramble inevitably result in stations stepping on each other's signals—and wouldn't that be contrary to the public interest? (Such a scramble in the early 1920s, before federal regulation, created chaos on the airwaves.)

One result of all this is a curiously ambivalent stance by many broadcasters. They don't want federal regulation of content, but they don't want to lose their "licenses to make money" either and in fact seek Federal Communications Commission protection against spurious challenge at license renewal time. Some even want the FCC to force cable systems to carry their signals (the "must carry" controversy), which would deny cable operators the First Amendment freedoms that television station owners seek for themselves.

The FCC in recent years has tended toward deregulating broadcasting. Congress, reflecting public pressure, tends toward reinstituting some regulations the FCC put aside. There is particular pressure in Congress for regulation of children's programming to eliminate violence, sex, and commercialization.

FCC regulation is based on the reality that space on the broadcast spectrum is limited and that broadcasting is interstate commerce, which in any form is federally regulated. But other regulation of broadcast occurs, reflecting profound political and social pressures.

Congress passes laws and controls purse strings, both enormous weapons for influencing everything from license allocation to program content. The White House appoints the five commissioners on the FCC; it has other powers of appointment and can also influence congressional and public opinion. Federal courts have enormous clout in their interpretation of federal statutes and adjudication of lawsuits. Many state and local governments pass laws governing the conduct of business and advertising policies.

Public watchdog groups and the industry's own self-regulatory groups are also important. The National Association of Broadcasters has huge powers of persuasion (and an annual budget of over $14 million) and often focuses on business and programming issues.

Broadcasting is pulled and tugged like no other mass medium in America, probably because so many issues attract federal and societal interest.

BROADCASTING ISSUES AT A GLANCE

Antitrafficking Critics complain that speculators buy and sell broadcast licenses for quick profit, ignoring any obligation to operate their stations in the public interest. Church groups, public-interest organizations, and others want trafficking halted, perhaps by a hefty transfer fee on any license bought and sold within three years or so.

Advertising to Children Some TV programming is clearly designed to promote the sale of toys and other goods intended for children. Critics want restrictions on featuring toys in programs and on time that can be devoted to commercials (10½ minutes per hour on weekdays, 12 minutes on weekends are mentioned). The FCC does not regulate individual commercials but in licensing hearings does consider whether overcommercialization by a station is contrary to public interest. Continued commercial exploitation of child viewers by the industry could bring federal intervention.

Comparative Renewals Because they are extraordinarily valuable assets, TV licenses are often fought over when holders seek FCC renewal. Challengers can petition for licenses by comparing past performance with what FCC regulations require. They often claim that current holders are not serving their communities properly. Some challengers practice near blackmail, extorting heavy payments from license holders in return for dropping their FCC action. The FCC is seeking ways to change this, perhaps by limiting the size of payments that can be made.

Cross-ownership

Federal law prohibits individuals from acquiring a radio or TV station in the same market where they own a newspaper, on the grounds that that could create a monopoly in news and advertising and grant a dangerously strong impact on public opinion to an individual or company. (Some who do own both are "grandfathered"—permitted to continue because their dual ownership predates the law.) Critics of the law say that media diversity—the thousands of reading, viewing, and listening options open to Americans—precludes monopoly through cross-ownership and that joint operation of, say, a newspaper and TV stations can strengthen service in the public interest. That didn't help Rupert Murdoch. He was forced to sell his *New York Post* to keep WNYW-TV, New York.

Fairness Doctrine

From 1949 until 1987, the FCC required broadcast stations to present all sides of issues of public importance. For example, stations covering one political candidate were required to give all other qualified candidates equal opportunities for coverage and airtime. Newscasts were exempted from that equal-time provision in 1959. But broadcasters still considered the fairness doctrine unworkable and lobbied for its elimination. In 1987, in a wave of deregulation, the FCC did eliminate it. Broadcasters say that that takes their industry a step closer to First Amendment status; in Congress, however, there is strong sentiment for reinstituting the fairness doctrine.

Indecency

One of broadcasting's hottest controversies is over what is indecent and obscene programming, whether limits should be placed on it, and if so, by whom and how? Before 1987, the FCC broadly defined indecency as use of any of seven specific "dirty words" and prohibited indecent programming before 10 P.M. to protect children. In 1987, the FCC broadened its definition to include offensive references to sexual conduct and ruled that such material could be broadcast only between midnight and 6 A.M. A federal appeals panel in Washington struck down that limit in 1988, saying, "Broadcast material that is indecent but not obscene is protected by the First Amendment." The FCC and many public-interest groups continue efforts to restrict material they deem indecent. In 1988, the Planned Parenthood Federation of America released a study by Louis Harris & Associates concluding that 65,000 sexual references are broadcast annually on TV in afternoon and evening prime time (an average, the study said, of 27 references per hour, including 9 kisses, 5 hugs, 10 sexual innuendos, and 1 or 2 references to sexual intercourse or deviant sexual practices). However, the federation said, rarely are the consequences of sex—including pregnancy and sexually transmitted disease—mentioned.[17]

Tastelessness

Says *New York Times* television writer John Corry: "Television is being pulled, inexorably if it doesn't watch out, into a new kind of dumbness: coarse language, shocking pictures and empty thoughts."[18] One term for it is "shock broadcasting." It covers so-called talk show hosts who reach for the shock value of crudity, screaming at guests in gutter language. Also criticized are violence in entertainment and bloody video coverage included in newscasts not so much for news value as for sheer impact on viewers' sensitivities (as when the camera slowly pans across a pool of blood at an accident scene). Citizens' groups, TV critics, and Congress have moved the issue onto the public agenda. Public revulsion reached new heights in 1989 over shock and so-called reality television, often equally violent. Consumer complaints led some firms—Coca-Cola, McDonald's, and Chrysler among them—to cancel commercials on programs that included objectionable material. ABC dropped a special, "Crimes of Passion II," when it failed to attract a single paid commercial.

Many broadcasters resist interference on First Amendment grounds. What they really want to protect, of course, is their ratings. Shock broadcasting does pull in audiences, just as bad news is closely read in newspapers.

"Must Carry"

Many broadcast TV executives want the FCC to force cable operators to carry all local TV signals among services offered subscribers. This, of course, is a request for federal intervention in the business of cable operators and would deny them First Amendment rights. The courts have held such attempts to be unconstitutional. Nevertheless, many television station owners feel that they must get into cable systems or face continued erosion of ratings.

"Syndex" Many television broadcasters, backed by programming producers, want the FCC to force cable systems to black out syndicated programming if it appears on local stations. Producers say they sell syndicated programming exclusivity (thus "syndex") to local stations and that duplicate use by cable systems erodes its value. Cable operators say there is no proof that their "importation" of programming harms local television stations, that the FCC has no jurisdiction in the matter, and that to restrict them would violate their First Amendment rights.

The 12-12-12 Rule To promote diversity of ownership, the FCC limits any individual or corporation to owning 12 AM and 12 FM radio licenses. TV licenses are limited to 12, too, as long as the stations don't reach more than 25 percent of the nation's TV homes. Group owners may hold up to 14 licenses and reach 30 percent of TV households if the stations are more than half owned by minorities and if two stations in each radio and TV category are controlled by minorities. As in the cross-ownership controversy, opponents of the rule argue that media diversity is so great that there need be no limit on broadcast ownership, just as there is none on print media ownership.

Federal regulation of cable, based primarily on the Copyright Act of 1976 and the Cable Act of 1984, involves some important issues of its own.

Monopoly Charges Some independent broadcasters and motion picture executives say that cable is becoming too big too fast and unless tightly regulated will indulge in anticompetitive practices. Those could include refusing to carry signals of local broadcast television stations and otherwise strongly influencing what Americans see on their TV sets. The Motion Picture Association of America argues that cable is an unregulated monopoly that can exert enormous and unfair pressure on filmmakers and distributors. Cable operators argue that anyone selling information or entertainment has many ways to get into the American home, even though local governments do often permit exclusivity in local cable franchises. Citizens' groups charge that cable franchises create monopolies and that once they have a long-term contract in hand, many cable companies raise rates at will and simultaneously let service deteriorate.

Technical Standards Though it argues generally for deregulation, the cable industry sought federal regulation of uniform, nationwide standards to avoid being forced to adhere to a wide variety of local standards. The U.S. Supreme Court in 1988 upheld such federal regulation. Critics argue that that means no regulation because the FCC doesn't adequately supervise cable's technical standards.

Programming Content Some local governments issue cable franchises only on condition that the cable operator provide access channels to interested members of the public. That often means opening channels to extremist political groups, with the system operator having no control over program content. Hate groups such as the Ku Klux Klan fight for access channels. So, often, do individuals with programming generally regarded as indecent. The courts seem to be taking the position that forcing cable operators to offer access channels or universal service is a violation of their First Amendment rights.

GAME PLANS IN BROADCAST NEWS

Major shifts are under way in how the American broadcast industry covers news.

In radio, significant, high-cost international

As radio concentrates on music and talk, this is an increasingly rare sight: a radio reporter doing a "remote" interview from the scene of a story. Many radio reporters like Dawn Feldhaus of WGUS-AM/FM, Augusta, Georgia, shown here, try for jobs with big-city radio stations that do have large news staffs, or aspire to TV news.

and national coverage is fading rapidly. Music and talk shows are cheaper to produce and more rewarding in advertising revenue. Network radio has reduced coverage dramatically; local stations primarily "rip and read" copy from news services for all but local coverage, and many broadcast very little of that.

In cable, due to the Cable News Network's strong position, there is no apparent viewer demand for more than one 24-hour news service. However, there is demand for specialized news services. The Financial News Network is available through cable systems in more than 27 million homes. C-SPAN reaches 33 million homes with gavel-to-gavel broadcasts of congressional hearings and other political events. Cable subscribers want mostly entertainment. But as cable moves increasingly toward specialized programming for narrowly targeted markets, it's likely that there will be more news services covering topics such as health and business.

In broadcast television, enormous change is under way in how news is covered. Two factors are at work. First, the so-called bottom-line syndrome dominates both network and local television. Today, with the trend toward target marketing, advertisers regard local newscasts as highly effective. So it profits local stations to expand their local news. Conversely, the major networks—NBC, CBS, and ABC—are having money troubles, and all have slashed news division budgets to improve profits. ▶ **13**

Second, new technology often permits local stations to do without network news. Mobile vans roam the country for a single station, "uplinking" coverage to satellites, which "downlink" it to the home station; independent stations exchange coverage via satellite; nonnetwork news services transmit tailored coverage to independent stations quickly and cheaply. Many local broadcasters ask, "Who needs a network?"

TV NEWS: END OF AN ERA?

66 We're watching the end of an era. . . . Television news has become a profit center. That's all it is. I think that soon networks will have news divisions hardly a shadow of what they are today. 99

Fred Friendly, former CBS News pioneer.[19]

One effect of all this is strong resistance among network-affiliated stations to expanded network news. Network chiefs years ago had great difficulty expanding nightly newscasts to 30 minutes from 15. Stations wanted to sell that time locally. Later, even Walter Cronkite, the most widely respected TV newsman, couldn't convince CBS affiliates to provide 30 minutes more so that the network's evening news could go to one hour. Conversely, many local stations originate hourlong newscasts; some offer two hours or even more. Advertisers (and station ad sales directors) love it.

So we've seen a shift from newscasts produced by highly professional network news staffs to coverage put together by local newsrooms. Producing two hours or even an hour daily of discerning, intelligent, professional news coverage is a formidable and costly challenge; few local

13 ▶ CBS: Case Study of Network Turmoil

They were bad days at "Black Rock," CBS's tall, modernistic headquarters building in New York, and they sent tremors throughout the television industry. For the first time, CBS—the famed network of William S. Paley, Edward R. Murrow, Walter Cronkite, and other TV greats— was *dead last in the ratings.*

It was 1988, and millions of viewers were fleeing to cable and independent stations. All networks suffered substantial viewer losses; all saw ad dollars they once got being spent elsewhere as advertisers chased the viewers wherever they went.

But it was CBS, for a generation the premier network, that was the focus of attention. Famous CBS executives—some of the biggest names in the business—were fired. Nothing the network tried to regain momentum seemed to work. Entertainment programming strategists who once possessed a golden touch simply couldn't put together a strong schedule of hits. CBS News, once unchallenged, had to struggle mightily against NBC and ABC. And of course there was fear: If the great CBS could falter, was any network—or anyone who worked for one—safe? Indeed, CBS's travails are symptomatic of turmoil throughout network TV.

From its early days in radio, in the 1920s,

CBS grew into a fat, widely diversified conglomerate under the direction of William S. Paley, its first president. But in the 1980s, CBS's profitability began dropping as costs soared. Between 1978 and 1987, spending by CBS News increased to $300 million annually from $89 million. Executives and on-camera talent were paid huge salaries.

CBS shareholders grew restive as profits dropped. Repercussions followed. First, Paley was moved aside, and a succession of management teams tried to put things right. Second—and this is happening repeatedly in the media today—outside takeover artists smelled opportunity at CBS. As CBS's profits dropped, its share price on the stock market dropped, too. Investors won't pay high share prices for companies whose profits are dwindling. Yet CBS's assets—broadcast, record, and publishing companies—were extremely valuable. In such situations, takeover artists see an opportunity to pay low share prices for a company whose fundamental assets are more valuable than those prices indicate.

That motivated Laurence A. Tisch, chairman of Loews Corporation, a $6.7 billion conglomerate with interests in insurance, hotels, and tobacco. He bought 25 percent of CBS's

newsrooms are up to it. Broadcast news consultants—"news doctors," they're called—are frequently called in, and across the land, their touch can be seen each evening on local TV: the "action news" format of flashing red lights and sirens; "happy talk," look-alike, sound-alike anchors; mindless video, lots of it, on animals, on children—on everything, it sometimes seems, but *news.* Larry Grossman, former president of NBC News, uses the term "sleaze journalism"— covering the sensational, the violent, and the bizarre but not the truly important issues that should be covered if a station is to discharge its

social responsibilities. Grossman also complains about "tabloid" or "soft" news, a preoccupation "with personalities and back-of-the-magazine sociological pieces."[20]

Major controversy erupted in 1989 when ABC simulated a news event in coverage of an American diplomat reportedly spying for Moscow. The incident was condemned by many journalists, and ABC News apologized. But the practice of re-creating "news" seemed to be spreading.

In these trends, newspaper journalists recognize a widening need for print's in-depth, ana-

Three key players during CBS's tumultous year: Laurence A. Tisch (*left*), an outside investor who took control of the company; Howard Stringer (*center*), Tisch's choice as president of the broadcast division; and (*right*) Dan Rather, *CBS Evening News* anchor and a CBS "traditionalist" who publicly urged profit-minded executives to avoid pruning the once-great CBS News team.

stock and, as the company's largest single shareholder, was invited to join its board of directors. His business skills inspired the board in 1986 to appoint him president and chief executive officer.

Tisch reappointed Paley as chairman but ran the company his own way—and that included selling the record, magazine, and book divisions. In two years, Tisch reduced CBS's payroll from 16,000 to 6,800. *Business Week* quoted one CBS director as saying, "We've got an accountant running a creative company."

Newsweek spoke of a "Civil War at CBS, . . . [a] struggle for the soul of a legendary network." On one side were the "accountants"; on the other were CBS "traditionalists," particularly journalists and news division executives fearful that the drastic pruning would impair the network's ability to cover the news in a socially responsible manner. (Without doubt, the news division suffered. Its staff and budget were slashed, and, consequently, its effectiveness—and its ratings—dropped.)

It was a classic case of the internal tug and pull in all networks and major television operations in America today. At CBS, the business managers were unquestionably in charge for the 1990s.

lytical coverage of substantive issues. Many believe that TV simply is opting out of comprehensive, serious competition in news.

TV NEWS THREATENS NEWSPAPERS?

66 Television, which threatened to become a mass medium, has fragmented, with special cable channels for each special interest, be it sports or politics or business or weather or what-have-you. Radio, in most markets, has all but given up on news. And newspapers themselves have battled off the local heel-nippers by coming up with their own zoned products or weekly sections or total-market-coverage mailers. So I won't say that most of the nation's 1,700 daily newspapers are monopolies; but I will say that, from a competitive standpoint, the local newspaper publisher has less to worry about than, say, the local acupuncturist. 99

Michael G. Gartner, former editor of Des Moines Register and Louisville Courier-Journal, who in 1988 became president of NBC News.[21]

To fix things at NBC, Michael Gartner, longtime newspaper executive, was hired to head the news division in a move symptomatic of the turmoil in all network news divisions. Like CBS and ABC, NBC for years switched news executives, tinkered with formats, and cut back through the fat of overspending and newsroom waste and into the muscle of substantive news coverage. Ratings jinked wildly. The star system of relying on highly visible, highly paid anchors failed as a substitute for comprehensive world coverage produced by trained reporters of high morale and professionalism. Importation of Gartner, a newspaper journalist, was part of the continuing search to solve the problem of withering interest.

WHOSE BLACK MONDAY WAS IT?

66 When, on October 19, the New York stock market took a 508-point plunge, in the most dramatic breaking news event of 1987, not *one* of the major commercial television networks bothered to interrupt the entertainment schedule that night for a prime-time news special. CBS News did half an hour at 11:30 P.M.; NBC News did 21 minutes, also at 11:30; and ABC, because it was an NFL football night, didn't go on with its usual *Nightline* program until 12:48 A.M.

It was Black Monday, not just for the market but for the network news divisions. 99

Ernest Leiser, for 29 years a CBS News correspondent, producer, and executive.[23]

Part of the networks' problem is that viewers are redefining what is essential news. Many polls of viewers (and of newspaper readers too) show that local news is considered more important than national or international news. Issues that affect people's daily lives—local cost of living, quality of their children's education—attract their attention. And of course, that is what local stations, not networks, mostly offer. People also want entertainment. In 1988, for example, twice as many watched TV movies and reruns as watched opening night at the Democratic National Convention. CBS's "60 Minutes" is the most popular issues-oriented program on network television—yet viewers always rate it well behind "Roseanne," "The Cosby Show," "A Different World," "Cheers," "The Golden Girls," and other, shall we say, less weighty programming. Network at-

titudes toward news have changed, too. NBC's Tom Brokaw says:

> We are now less a daily news diary and more of a daily newsmagazine, offering in addition to a capsule of the breaking news a broader and deeper look at a few of the big stories. We are slowly conceding the breaking news franchise to local stations and to the all-news services.[22]

Many TV news veterans don't like that.

Yet some truly great television news coverage is produced in this country. Earnest, principled TV journalists are on duty around the world. And when it comes to covering a big-picture story—an international skyjacking, a natural disaster—the sight-and-sound combination of television cannot be beaten. The Vietnam War, the *Challenger* disaster, the assassinations of President Kennedy and Martin Luther King, the 1989 San Francisco earthquake—television etches them on our national memory. No written account could match the impact of television's coverage of those events. For millions of viewers, indeed, the events and TV's coverage of them are virtually indistinguishable.

And despite all the talk about "couch potatoes" who simply stare at whatever foolishness TV wants to offer, viewers do turn to TV for important coverage—but only if it is news they personally consider important. The challenge for TV journalists is to cover and interpret truly substantive news in a manner that meets changing viewer expectations.

GAME PLANS IN BROADCAST ENTERTAINMENT

"NBC Wins Prime Time Ratings Race!" "Donahue vs. Winfrey: Clash of Titans." "'Geraldo' Gambles on Talk." "Can It Compete with Johnny?"

Throughout the broadcast industry, TV entertainment programs are hot news. Industry insiders search for signals on who is winning the multibillion-dollar race to entertain all of us.

Advertisers wonder if NBC's ratings lead will hold or whether their dollars should go to CBS or ABC. Is Oprah Winfrey going to win larger talk-show ratings than Phil Donahue? What's Geraldo Rivera up to now? Does *any* entertainer, *any* program, have a chance against NBC's "Tonight Show" host, Johnny Carson?

On such questions rests the fate of many broadcast people and dollars. Never, it seems, has entertainment been so important to so many. Certainly, never has so much money been dedicated to providing it. As in every broadcast operation, the goal is to attract large audiences that can in turn be sold to advertisers.

Radio nearly has given up regularly programmed drama and comedy. Radio built nationwide audiences on such fare in the 1930s and 1940s but broadcasts it today primarily with a "how it used to be" nostalgic note. The last national program for children, the award-winning "Kids America," went off the air in 1988. For both adults and children, drama and comedy are found on TV. After going through an identity crisis, radio decided that its role was offering music, talk (mostly for adults), and some news.

Cable, of course, has enormous strength in entertainment. What's new is made-for-cable programming. The industry once relied on inexpensive old movies or programming already shown on broadcast TV. But in 1988 alone, it spent $750 million for original programs, out of $2 billion total for programming that year. A new made-for-cable film industry is being constructed around cable's voracious appetite. Showtime/The Movie Channel spends as much as $6 million to make a single film.

Syndication companies are exploding in profitable growth as primary sources of programming for cable and independent stations but also for some network affiliates (as in news, some affiliates reject network entertainment programming because it's more profitable to buy syndicated material and sell commercials locally). Syndicators sometimes produce programming themselves, but more often they buy it from independent production houses. Programs are then rented to stations. One syndicator, King World,

takes in more than $200 million annually for "Wheel of Fortune," a game show that costs less than one-tenth that much to produce, prizes and all. Sometimes syndicators operate on a barter basis, renting programs to stations for commercial time, which the syndicators then sell to advertisers. There seems no end to the number of times syndicators can lease reruns. "Barney Miller" and "Star Trek" come around as regularly as the four seasons—some episodes are older than their viewers. Syndication is so lucrative that some programming producers count on losing money in first run but figure on profit from reruns. Producers of "ALF" lost money making it for NBC; they calculated, however, that reruns would bring as much as $2 million per episode.

VCRs are major players in entertainment, and it's been projected that 80 percent of American homes will soon own one.

Radio has its entertainment niche. Cable and independent stations offer entertainment options. Where does that leave the networks? One not-so-flippant answer is, in panic.

The networks originated the early (and now classic) entertainment that established TV-in-the-home as the national pastime. Lucille Ball and Milton Berle (the *New York Times* once called them "icons from television's golden age") were part of that. So were "Rawhide," "Hogan's Heroes," "Gomer Pyle, U.S.M.C.," and other old friends from the 1960s and earlier. But literally hundreds of shows now fight nightly on scores of channels for audiences that those early classics monopolized on just three networks. A blur of situation comedies ("sitcoms") runs across screens where Lucy and Uncle Miltie once pranced virtually alone. Rugged cowboys, tall in the saddle and heroes every one, disappeared before a wave of cop shows, doctor shows, lawyer shows—you name it, there is a show about it. And sports? Major league football and baseball fight for viewers against programs on little-known sports played by teams with hard-to-pronounce names in unheard-of leagues.

The networks try everything—drama, comedy, and a combination called "dramedy" (the hybrid hasn't done well; how do you know when to cry and when to laugh?). "Docudramas" were tried, combining some fact, some fiction in what one critic said resulted primarily in one thing: They "unalterably confused our concept of history."[24] Family shows featuring fathers, mothers, grandfathers, and grandmothers flooded the screens. Miniseries, a movie split into nightly episodes, achieved varying results. In sports, it sometimes appeared that the networks were throwing money at their problem. ABC paid $309 million for rights to televise the 1988 Winter Olympics in Calgary and lost money when advertisers refused to pay commercial rates high enough to cover the network's costs.

Desperate to find programming that clicks, the networks even risk blurring the distinction between entertainment and their news staffs, which were always considered sacrosanct, not to be touched by the hype of entertainment. Distinguished TV journalists became entertainers in programs that combined factual news coverage and "creative" filming and editing that injected drama.

THE NEWS MOVIE: A "NONFICTION NOVEL"?

66 It has been heading there all along; now it has arrived. The news movie is here. CBS News finally gave birth to "48 Hours." What's real is what's real, but properly filmed, edited and scored, it is supposed to reach out and grab us. The news movie is the television equivalent of the nonfictional novel.

It sprang forth unashamedly last week, when "48 Hours," in its debut, visited Parkland Memorial Hospital in Dallas. The first thing we saw was Dan Rather on the front seat of an ambulance, squashed between two paramedics. Pause now and ask why. This is not a frivolous question.

Mr. Rather, in effect, was a prop. The famous anchor was in the ambulance for window dressing. In fact, he did this with grace; it was pleasant to see him, although his presence had nothing to do with the story. Correspondents are superfluous in news movies. Stories unfold visually. Music adds counterpoint. There is a framework, but it has nothing to do with print journalism's who, what, when and where.

The framework arises from theater. **99**

John Corry, **New York Times**[25]

For ABC, NBC, and CBS, February 1987 was a turning point of sorts. In the ratings sweeps that month, they failed for the first time in television history to gain a 50 percent share of the TV audience. For scores of network employees, the shock was great, for in big league television, the rule is produce or else.

PUBLIC BROADCASTING

A significant competitor of the networks for viewer and listener time—and, increasingly, advertiser dollars—is public broadcasting. Public (or "noncommercial") radio and television, however, have their own identity problem. Simply put, noncommercial radio stations and their network, National Public Radio, and noncommercial TV and the Public Broadcasting System find costs rising rapidly for high-quality fare.

So in addition to operating on taxpayer funds and viewer contributions, public broadcasters sell commercials to raise money. Some try to attract commercial support by broadcasting "popular" entertainment in hopes of drawing larger audiences than those drawn to traditional cultural programming.

Does that mean that noncommercial broadcasting is commercial? Is public television moving into the private camp? Will it become captive to its huge corporate "underwriters"? Will public broadcasting be an oasis of culture and high-quality programming or simply offer more of the same fare broadcast by commercial stations?

Two schools of thought argue over the future of noncommercial broadcasting, now a $1 billion-a-year industry. "Traditionalists" hold that noncommercial broadcasting was developed in the early 1900s for educational purposes (educational groups held 171 noncommercial AM radio licenses by 1925) and that "cultural uplift" must be the mission. They argue that public broadcasting must present high-quality news, public-issue programming, and entertainment (such as National Public Radio's "All Things Considered" radio news show and Public Broadcasting System's "Jewel in the Crown," "Nova," "Sesame

Street," "Masterpiece Theater," and the "MacNeil/Lehrer NewsHour") as alternatives to commercial programming that panders to mass viewer tastes in search of all-important ratings. These traditionalists insist that noncommercial broadcasting must seek government financing and private donations but avoid commercialization.

Other people argue that PBS must present popular programming with wider appeal. Says David Othmer, manager of noncommercial WHYY in Philadelphia: "We've grown beyond the point of doing things because they're good for people—castor oil television—and saying, 'You've got to watch this.' We have got to make television that people want to watch."[26] Some say that noncommercial broadcasting must seek wider advertiser support, that because it already accepts support from "underwriting" corporations, it should stop the charade and enter the marketplace fight for money just like any commercial broadcaster. The *New York Times*'s John Corry, among others, questions whether taxpayer dollars should subsidize noncommercial news programming. Corry asks whether that violates separation of government and press and suggests that since tax funds now provide only about 15 percent of public television's annual revenue, perhaps other financing should be found.[27]

The money problem is serious. The Corporation for Public Broadcasting, established in 1967 primarily to funnel federal funds to noncommercial broadcasters, has a limited budget ($228 million for 1989) that in commercial broadcasting is a drop in the financial bucket.

Most of the nation's 317 public TV stations are operated by universities, schools, and community organizations with weak financing. Even the largest are small by commercial standards. WNET in New York, one of the nation's top three or four public TV stations, had just $78.4 million in revenue in 1987. Of that, 27 percent came from viewer contributions. WGBH of Boston, perhaps the most acclaimed public TV station, is seeking support from underwriters such as automobile and oil companies. Most underwriting is short-term, giving public TV little op-portunity to plan long-range. An exception is the largest financial commitment to a program in public broadcasting history—a $57 million, five-year package put together in 1988 by AT&T, Pepsico, and the John D. and Catherine T. Mac-Arthur Foundation for public TV's "MacNeil/Lehrer NewsHour." The Corporation for Public Broadcasting and affiliates committed $62 million to the program over the same period.

Some public broadcasters argue for new federal funding, such as a tax on the sale of commercial stations for the benefit of public broadcasting or a tax on commercial broadcasting's use of the public airwaves for its own promotional purposes.

PBS: CULTURAL OR COMMERCIAL

66 In the same way that a university, a museum or a regional theater serves the people of this country, so does public television. These institutions receive taxpayer support because as citizens we believe that they are important to our development as human beings. In fact, I contend that public television is the most powerful tool for public education, information and general enlightenment freely available to everyone. 99

*William F. Baker, president,
WNET, New York.*[28]

We turn in Chapter 10 to television at the local level.

☆ SUMMARY

Revolutionary change is sweeping the American television, radio, and cable industry. Viewers demand more options than ever before for news and entertainment and are deserting the networks in droves. And advertisers are increasingly supporting cable and independent stations that deliver targeted local audiences.

The broadcast industry has enormous economic strength and social influence. The average American home has a TV set turned on nearly seven hours daily; ad revenue in 1988 was $26.0 billion for TV, $6.5 billion for radio.

Radio found strength in technology, especially frequency modulation (FM), which delivers high-quality music, and in shrewd programming, particularly narrrowly focused music formats that pull in audiences and advertisers.

Television grew from just 9 stations in 1950 to more than 2,000 today. It forced dramatic changes in newspapers, magazines, and the film industry, as well as radio. Television has influence over the national agenda, not only in news and entertainment but also in fashions and lifestyles. But entertainment programming is aimed at a lower common denominator designed to draw huge audiences with programs that are often silly, violent, or tasteless.

Cable is soaring to new strength on two developmental streams: media consumer demand for individual, virtually customized services and cable technology which is providing scores of channels narrowly focused on entertainment, news, and information services.

Radio and television are federally regulated because they use a public resource, the broadcast spectrum.

Complicated issues of ethics and social responsibility confront broadcasting: trafficking in licenses for profit, overcommercialization of children's programming, broadcast licensing challenges that amount to blackmail, and others.

In news, radio has virtually given up comprehensive coverage. Cable is becoming extremely important. In television, networks are cutting back, and local stations are beefing up their news because it can be profitably sold to local advertisers.

In entertainment, cable is eroding network programming; so are videocassettes.

☆ RECOMMENDED READING

Industry news is reported by *Advertising Age, Broadcasting, Electronic Media*, the *Wall Street Journal*, and the *New York Times. Washington Journalism Review* is sound on broadcast journalism.

Broadcasting/Cablecasting Yearbook, published annually, provides a valuable, quick history of American broadcasting, Federal Communications Commission policies, and statistical information.

For the longer view, see Lawrence Lichty and Mal Topping, eds., *American Broadcasting: A Source Book on the History of Radio and Television* (New York: Hastings House, 1975) and Christopher Sterling and John Kittross, *Stay Tuned: A Concise History of American Broadcasting* (Belmont, Calif.: Wadsworth, 1978).

On operations and management, see John Bittner, *Professional Broadcasting* (Englewood Cliffs, N.J.: Prentice-Hall, 1981) and, particularly, Barry L. Sherman, *Telecommunications Management: Radio, TV, Cable* (New York: McGraw-Hill, 1986).

In news, see Carolyn Lewis, *Reporting for Television* (New York: Columbia University press, 1984) and Richard Yoakum and Charles Cremer, *ENG: Television News and the New Technology* (New York: Random House, 1985).

On audience research, see Joseph R. Dominick, *The Dynamics of Mass Communication* (New York: Random House, 1987).

Important journals and publications are *Journalism Quarterly, Telematics and Informatics* (Pergamon Press), *Gannett Center Journal, Journal of Broadcasting & Electronic Media, Television Quarterly*, and *RTNDA* (Radio-Television News Directors Association) *Communicator*. Members of RTNDA (student membership rates are available) receive with the *Communicator* a bimonthly Job Information Service announcement of jobs available nationwide. Write RTNDA, 1717 K Street NW, Suite 615, Washington, DC 20006.

Inside a Local Television Station

Much of the action in American broadcasting is shifting these days to community television, those hundreds of stations throughout the country that pay more attention to city hall than the White House, that worry more about traffic jams on Main Street than what's happening in Afghanistan.

Most of television's jobs—certainly, the entry-level jobs—are in community broadcasting. As we saw, these local stations are wooing advertisers from the networks, further indication that broadcasting's balance of power is shifting.

So our survey of America's mass communicators must go inside a local television station. We're going to Norfolk, Virginia, to look at WTKR-TV, a CBS affiliate.

WTKR-TV, NORFOLK, VIRGINIA: A CASE STUDY

"Year After Year, Viewers Choose WTKR's News 3 at Noon!" For networks and their big-league news teams, that promotional boast doesn't mean much. But in Norfolk, Virginia, it's a call to battle. WTKR is in a fight for the hotly competitive Norfolk television market, and as in many such TV fights across the country, local news is the primary competitive weapon being used to attract viewers and thus advertisers.[1]

The stakes are large: The market—technically, the Norfolk–Portsmouth–Newport News–Hampton market—is medium-sized (ranked 43rd largest in the nation by Arbitron, 45th by Nielsen). Its retail sales annually surpass $8.4 billion.

Television advertising revenue in 1987 was in the $55 million to $65 million range. WTKR's share was $12 million to $18 million. Like most TV stations, WTKR doesn't release the precise amount, but from the figures we do have, we can see that its market share was 21.8 to 27.6 percent.

Competition is fierce. Other TV stations are WAVY (NBC), WVEC (ABC), WHRO (PBS), and two independents, WYAH and WTVZ. In 1987, some 57.8 percent of the market's households received cable TV (slightly above the national average that year of 51 percent.) A total of 40 special channels or services are available through cable. They offer not just national services such as Cable News Network, Home Box Office, and Showtime; they also pipe in programming from three TV stations in Richmond and three in North Carolina, some areas of which are in WTKR's market. Years ago, Ted Turner's WTBS-TV in Atlanta became the first "superstation" by exporting its local programming, particularly sports, to cable systems throughout the country. Today, outsider superstations and their local cable allies are intense competitors for local stations such as WTKR.

There are 22 FM radio competitors in the market, along with 18 AM stations. They offer advertisers narrowly targeted audiences through precision music formats—everything from jazz to gospel to golden oldies. Arbitron figures the Norfolk market is the 33rd largest radio market in the nation, with population of 1,076,100 covered by those 40 stations.

Print competition is very strong. Landmark Communications, a diversified conglomerate with $331 million in revenue in 1987, has its headquarters in Norfolk and publishes its flagship dailies there, the *Virginian-Pilot* and the *Ledger-Star*. There are also strong dailies in Newport News, an important city in WTKR's market. Three major local magazines also scramble for viewer time and advertiser dollars.

WTKR's area of dominant influence (ADI) spreads over 26 counties in Virginia and North Carolina. An ADI consists of counties in which the home market stations receive a preponderance of viewing. Each county in the United States is in one and only one ADI. ADI is an Arbitron term; Nielsen uses designated market area (DMA). For WTKR, there are 544,100 TV households in the ADI to sell to advertisers—if the station can win them away from competitors by airing superior programming. This is complicated for WTKR and other Norfolk stations because the ADI covers many major cities and crowded residential areas. The station's news staff must spread over the entire area, covering affairs in two states, city councils in several cities, and many school systems, police departments, and fire departments.

The market's differing lifestyles and demographics (age, income, education, and so forth) are challenges also. Huge military installations are in the area, so the station must construct news

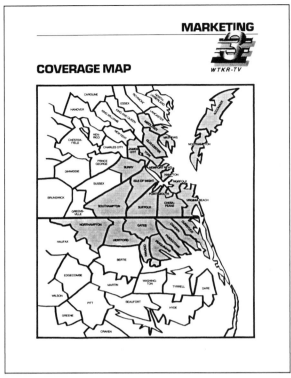

MARKETING

COVERAGE MAP

WTKR-TV

The shaded counties are in WTKR-TV's coverage area.

and entertainment programming that appeals not only to longtime residents but also to transient military families. The military presence means that there are more males than females in the ADI. Reflect on what this tells you about how WTKR must be run. For one thing, much of the viewing audience is male, probably in the 20–40 age bracket, and doesn't have deep local roots. News about the military is important. So is sports coverage, a favorite of men and women in the military. Recall how newspaper and magazine editors research their markets, the lifestyles, demographics, and news interests of people who live there, and then strive to produce news matched to those targeted readers. WTKR executives must similarly ensure a match between their market and their station.

The man in charge of calling the shots at WTKR from 1986 to 1989 was Bill Peterson, an experienced broadcaster who was president and general manager (GM). He had responsibility for primarily two things: first, on a short-term basis, running the station efficiently, improving its ratings, and increasing the profits and second, carefully protecting the owner's long-term investment. WTKR is a VHF station (channel 3), more valuable than a UHF. It went on the air in 1950, the first TV station in the Norfolk region and the second in Virginia. Norfolk is in the Sunbelt, a relatively prosperous area of the country where many media conglomerates seek expansion. Peterson managed an asset with a market value I estimate at $55 million. In 1989, the station's owner, Knight-Ridder, Inc., sold WTKR-TV in a package with another of its stations, WPRI-TV, Providence, Rhode Island. The combined price was a whopping $150 million. Peterson left the station and was replaced by Carol Rueppel, news director, who became acting general manager.

WTKR has 115 full-time employees and 9 part-timers. That's a large staff in a market the size of Norfolk, and it gave Peterson the staff strength to do a first-rate job in all sectors of community broadcasting. The organization of this staff (shown in slightly simplified form in Figure 10.1) is fairly typical of such television stations.

Since the GM's success depends on the performance of the department heads, the GM must select them carefully and spend a great deal of time ensuring that they are performing their jobs efficiently.

General Sales Manager Rufus DeVane supervises local and national sales and "traffic" (scheduling of airtime). DeVane must devise appropriate sales tactics to ensure that WTKR-TV achieves its revenue goals. DeVane takes overall guidance from the GM, then directs subordinates in informal daily meetings and a formal once-weekly sales meeting. It's a key job.

Director of Marketing David Paul Tressel is responsible for programming and promotion. He selects programs from CBS, from syndicators, and from WTKR itself, coordinating this with other departments. "Two of the key considera-

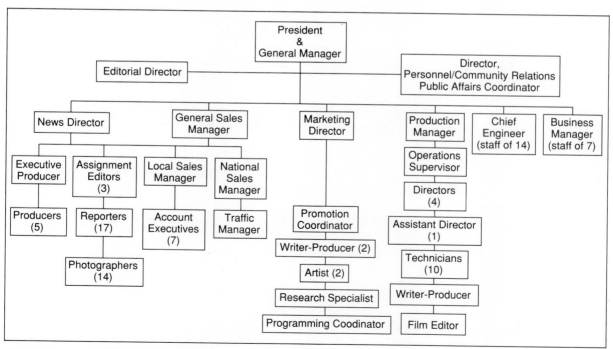

Figure 10.1   ORGANIZATION OF WTKR-TV, NORFOLK, VIRGINIA.

Weekly staff meeting at WTKR.

tions in making a programming selection,'' Tressel explains, ''are how that program can be marketed to potential advertisers and how it can be marketed to potential viewers.'' In devising promotional material, Tressel says he functions ''like an 'in-house' advertising agency.''

Production Manager Philip Armstrong supervises production of programming, promotion, and commercials, both in-house at WTKR and at outside production houses. The job takes strong people skills and an ability to budget time, money, and other resources.

News Director and Acting GM Carol Reuppel is, as she puts it, ''responsible for overall philosophy, policy, and operations of the news department.'' As news director, she oversees production of newscasts, handles personnel (''hiring, firing, evaluation''), and is responsible for the newsroom's spending and any legal matters that might arise.

Editorial Director Dale Gauding writes editorials under supervision of the station's editorial board. However, the GM is ultimately responsible for the station's position on public issues and often reads editorials on the air.

Director of Personnel/Community Relations Julie McCollum coordinates college internships, supervises employee benefits and policies, and makes sure that the station complies with FCC regulations on licensing and community service.

She's active in community organizations and public service.

Business Manager Jack Welsby manages the station's financial affairs, draws up the annual budget, and reports to the GM on whether it is being met.

Chief Engineer Gene Gildow is responsible for the entire technical operation—master control, videotape room, maintenance, transmitter. He must ensure compliance with FCC technical regulations.

Running a major television station with a large staff is something Peterson aimed at for years. Early in his career, he carefully sought experience at a number of stations; that eventually qualified him for leadership at WTKR. If you aspire to lead a TV station, you should (1) settle on an action plan early in your career so that, like Peterson, you can aggressively seek along the way the varied experience needed, and (2) plan on moving a lot.

WHAT IT TAKES TO BECOME A TV STATION MANAGER
by William B. Peterson

The best training for station manager is several successful years as a major department head: general sales manager, news director, program director, or promotion manager. Sales seems the best track to station management, though some general managers come from news.

Just becoming a general sales manager or news director does not put a person on track for general manager. *Quality* of experience is important.

General sales managers must participate in programming, news, and marketing decisions. Participating in industry organizations, such as the Television Bureau of Advertising (TVB) and the National Association of Broadcasters (NAB), helps. Most important, sales managers should become active in civic organizations and community affairs.

The sales manager must be positioned as an executive with wide interests and knowledge rather than just a purveyor of commercials. To their advantage, sales managers become steeped in the *business* of broadcasting, and they are pragmatists. They have to sell the program schedule as it is, warts and all. The general manager, program director, and news director can change the program schedule, but the sales manager must convince advertisers that the schedule, whatever it is, will work.

Once rating services have measured the audience of a program, sales managers know that that is all they can sell. The people who make programming decisions often convince themselves of the quality and value of particular programs, and while the sales manager may personally agree, he or she knows that advertisers are only interested in the audience each delivers. Sales managers become pragmatic quickly.

Sales managers spend most of their careers meeting and talking with the business community. They thus have a good sense of the tastes and interests of the community. They spend a lot of time assessing how the advertising and business community will react to programming changes and station's image—valuable for an aspiring station manager.

The best entry-level position on the way to general sales manager is account executive or local salesperson. In smaller markets, stations hire persons with no broadcasting experience for such positions, although it generally helps to have some sales experience, even if only at the local auto parts store. In larger markets, some broadcasting experience is generally required. These stations often recruit successful TV salespeople from smaller markets or radio salespeople in the same market.

Successful news directors are good candidates for station management because they have been involved in all aspects of station operations except sales and are familiar with equipment and with marketing and promotion techniques. They administer one of the largest budgets in the station, supervise the largest staff, and, like general sales managers, are good with people. They have a strong sense of the community and the important issues. They are generally stronger advocates for local programming, but most are real-

The president and general manager of a station is responsible for its editorial stance on public issues as well as its operations. Here, Bill Peterson reads an editorial on the air.

istic about the high cost of producing such programming. They also tend to be well informed about industry trends.

The decision to pursue promotion into management must be made fairly early in one's career. Unless properly positioned, early promotions can price a reporter out of competition. For example, a young reporter can progress up the ladder and have salary greater than a junior producer's. Moving into a producer position would require a pay cut, yet it is often the faster track to management.

Successful program directors and promotion managers are also good candidates for station management. Ordinarily, they have not managed as many people or as large a budget as a news director does, but they have more exposure to sales. News directors have almost no sales exposure because most stations require that news and sales maintain an arm's-length distance from each other.

In larger markets, entry-level positions in promotion and marketing, such as promotion writer-producer, are becoming the best way to become either program director or promotion manager. Entry-level positions in production, such as studio camera operator-technician, often lead to management in either programming or promotion at smaller stations.

Whatever their specialty or experience, the people who work their way to station management seem to have a common trait: They sought greater responsibility at every level of their career and were willing to be accountable. I believe that people elect themselves to management, knowingly or not. Some who never achieved their management aspirations cast their "votes" when they rejected additional responsibility because it did not bring concurrent increases in pay or prestige.

What Peterson hasn't mentioned is that you must be willing to move many times if you want to rise in television. Take a look at his career:

He started as vacation-relief floor director and news film processor at WSPD-TV, Toledo, between sophomore and junior years at University of Toledo (majoring in electrical and electronic engineering). He was hired full-time in 1964 as night-shift news photographer and film processor.

After a stint in the U.S. Army, 1967–1969, he returned to WSPD as a reporter-photographer; in 1970, he was named news editor ("a title in lieu of a raise," Peterson now says). He was promoted to assistant news director in 1971 and news director in 1973 ("big time!").

In 1975, WSPD's owner, Storer Broadcasting, transferred him to KDST-TV, San Diego, as news director. In 1978, he was hired by NBC's WKYC-TV, Cleveland, as news director. In 1980, he became news director for Washington Post Co.'s WPLG-TV, Miami. Six months later, he was recruited to return to NBC as news director of KNBC in Los Angeles. By 1982, he was back with Storer and KDST as assistant general manager ("an opportunity to learn station management"). In 1986, he was hired as WTKR president and general manager, a post he held until 1989.

Managing a local television station requires being both an inside and an outside executive. Inside the station, the GM draws from department heads their views on future economic trends in the Norfolk market, what the competition (print as well as broadcast) is likely to do, and how the station can improve its position with viewers and advertisers. The GM then draws up both short-range and long-range plans for approval by the station's owners. Many owners give managers considerable latitude in operating their stations. But owners do lay down guidelines on quality of management and profits expected. Rewards—in compensation and promotion—are considerable for successful managers; punishment for maladministration or consistent failure to meet goals can be dismissal. Short-range plans include profit levels expected over the next 12 months. Long-range plans show the owners how the station will be positioned to improve its fortunes over the next several years. This is tricky business, and the GM must meet weekly with department heads on operational matters and planning.

Outside the station, the GM must maintain a high profile in the community, representing WTKR with leading advertisers, civic officials, citizens' groups—the "movers and shakers" so important to the station's business fortunes. One federal condition of holding a television license is that the station be operated "in the public interest," and the GM must demonstrate through community involvement that WTKR is a "good citizen."

INSIDE THE MARKETING DEPARTMENT

For Marketing Director David Tressel, the pressure is always on. What do TV viewers like? What don't they like? What are other stations in Norfolk programming? What's coming down the pipe from CBS that will improve ratings? Do syndicators have anything worth picking up? How about local programming by WTKR? How is news doing? And always, always, always: How are the ratings?

Tressel is responsible, under the GM's direction, for putting together WTKR's programming schedule. With a couple of shrewd moves—

PROGRAMMING

3 WTKR-TV

PROGRAM SCHEDULE
TV SALES (804)446-1310

MONDAY thru FRIDAY

Time	Program	
5:30 AM	Ag Day	
6:00 AM	CBS Morning News	
6:30 AM		
7:00 AM		
7:30 AM	CBS This Morning	
8:00 AM		
8:30 AM		
9:00 AM	Hour Magazine	
9:30 AM		
10:00 AM	Sally Jessy Raphael	
10:30 AM	The New Card Sharks	
11:00 AM	The Price Is Right	
11:30 AM		
12:00 NOON	News 3 At Noon	
12:30 PM	The Young And The Restless	
1:00 PM		
1:30 PM	The Bold & The Beautiful	
2:00 PM	As The World Turns	
2:30 PM		
3:00 PM	Guiding Light	
3:30 PM		
4:00 PM	Donahue	
4:30 PM		
5:00 PM	Live At Five	
5:30 PM	The Judge	
6:00 PM	News 3	
6:30 PM	CBS Evening News With Dan Rather	
7:00 PM	A Current Affair	
7:30 PM	Win, Lose Or Draw	

8:00-10:30 CBS PRIME TIME - SEE PRIME TIME SCHEDULE

11:00 PM	News 3	
11:30 PM	Hill Street Blues	
12:00 MID		
12:30 AM	Lou Grant	Friday The 13th
1:00 AM		
1:30 AM	News 3 Repeat	Music City

SATURDAY & SUNDAY

Saturday	Sunday
	A Better Way
	This Is The Life
Dukes Of Hazzard	Dr. D. James Kennedy
Hello KittyTheater	Day Of Discovery
Jim Henson's Muppet Babies	World Tomorrow
	CBS News Sunday Morning
Pee Wee's Playh.	
Mighty Mouse	Face The Nation
Popeye & Son	Siskel & Ebert
Dennis The Menace	Heroś:Made/USA
Teen Wolf	
Galaxy High	
CBS Sports	CBS Sports
News 3	News 3
CBS Evening News	CBS Evening News
Best/National GeographicSpecials	60 Minutes
News 3	News 3
Friday The 13th	Marblehead
	Top Of The Pops
TV3 Night Screamer Movie	Kolchak: The Night Stalker

WTKR's schedule combines CBS and local programming. Prime time (8 P.M. to 11 P.M.) carries only network entertainment. But local news shows are broadcast six times daily, Monday through Friday.

and a little competitive luck—Tressel can improve ratings and be a hero around WTKR.

Local programming is strong in WTKR's schedule, particularly Monday through Friday. Tressel starts with a locally produced farm program at 5:30 A.M., then goes to network or syndicated programming and back to local news at noon. In a departure from the way the other stations in Norfolk program, Tressel returns to local news at 5 P.M. with ''Live at Five.'' Many per-

sons in the area leave home early each morning for jobs on military bases and in shipyards and other installations. They don't have time for early-morning newscasts or morning newspapers but arrive back home at 4 P.M. or so and are thus prime targets for an early-afternoon news show. Tressel then goes, at 5:30 P.M., to an entertainment show and back to a half hour of local news, at 6 P.M. Like most community television stations, WTKR programs a major newscast at 11

P.M. Tressel repeats that newscast at 1:30 A.M. (for insomniacs, among others).

CBS has had great difficulty staying competitive with NBC and ABC in prime-time programming. A common complaint is that CBS's prime-time shows have been around a long time and have lost viewer interest. Such concerns are very real for Tressel. He must hold audiences for WTKR, so he—along with executives from other CBS affiliates—puts a great deal of pressure on the network to improve prime-time offerings. CBS cannot afford desertions by affiliates and tries hard to keep them happy.

Tressel's schedule weaves in reruns of old standbys—''Hill Street Blues'' and ''Lou Grant'' in late-night and predawn time slots. Early episodes of those shows have been in syndication for years, and Tressel negotiates syndicators' fees for their use. It is an effort to hold down costs and avoid expensive local coverage by using ''canned'' material.

In judging Tressel's schedule, it's important to recall the nature of his market. A station in a stand-alone city—say, Omaha—serves a market relatively homogeneous by comparison, despite its size. WTKR has a split personality, serving both longtime residents and transient military families, and Tressel must thus select programming that straddles their diverse interests, not in just one city but several!

After programming is selected, it must be ''sold'' to viewers through bright and attractive promotion and advertising. WTKR also produces promotional material for use by salespersons and publication in newspapers and other print media.

Because the goal of programming is to increase ratings and thus improve WTKR's ad sales, the marketing director must have an understanding of sales plus varied experience in other departments. Tressel has worked at three stations, in addition to WTKR, and with an advertising agency. His experience includes public relations, advertising, and news and documentary cinematography, as well as programming and promotion.

Assisting Tressel in marketing are two writer-producers, who plan and oversee produc-

David Paul Tressel, WTKR's director of marketing, previews ''promos.''

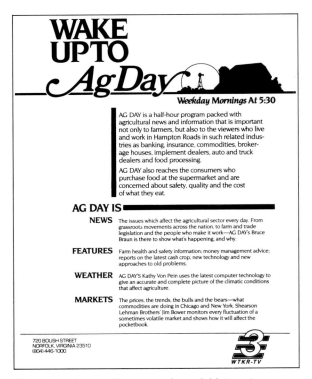

TV stations try to offer targeted special-interest audiences to their advertisers. Here, WTKR tells advertisers they can reach farmers through the station's early-morning ''Ag Day'' show.

tion of individual shows and promotional material; two artists, who prepare graphics and other visuals; a research coordinator, who analyzes the vast amount of audience research necessary for proper programming; and a promotion coordinator, who works at the essential task of attracting viewers to WTKR's offerings.

At many TV stations, local news is both a viewer attraction and a source of advertising profits. So a programming director must understand news, how it's collected, and how it should be broadcast.

INSIDE THE NEWSROOM

As the front page establishes a newspaper's personality, local news coverage sets the tone and image of a community television station.

For most stations, news by far is the most expensive local programming and virtually the only significant local programming that airs day after day, establishing continuity with viewers. At WTKR-TV, the newsroom in 1988 had a $2 million budget and 40 full-time and 3 part-time employees, including 6 producers, 3 assignment editors, 17 reporters, and 14 photographers. The station, among other things, spent half a million dollars for a satellite news truck that can travel anywhere in the country and transmit coverage back to Norfolk. The type and quality of newscasts reflect the professionalism of a station and its identification with its local community. News is a statement on how serious a station is about doing a first-rate job.

In ratings, WTKR's results are mixed.[2] In 1988, its noon news was number one in the market. It's nice to win at any time, but noon isn't the newscast that attracts big advertiser dollars. That comes at 6 P.M. and 11 P.M., Monday–Fri-

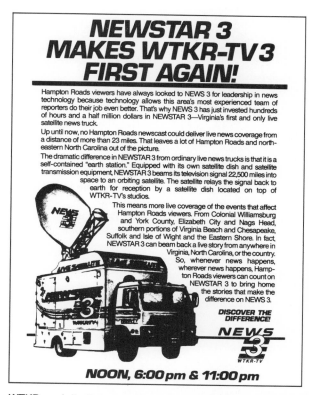

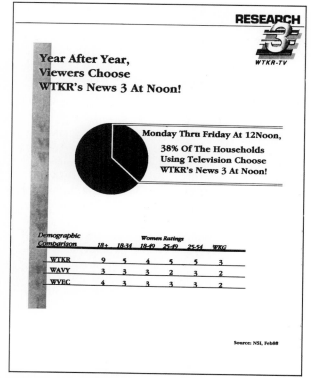

WTKR exploits its news strengths with promotion aimed at both viewers (*left*) and advertisers (*right*).

day. At 6 P.M., WTKR's ratings fluctuate wildly from book to book—that is, it may lead the race in the ratings after one audience measurement sweep but trail in the next book. At 11 P.M., WTKR has been number two.

The 11 P.M. ratings are disconcerting for WTKR. Carol Reuppel, wearing her news director hat, says that WAVY-TV, an NBC affiliate, is consistently number one at 11 P.M. She acknowledges that WAVY is "aggressive and our toughest competitor" but contends that much of WAVY's success is due to the NBC lead-in. It is an article of faith among television executives that whether a news show flourishes or withers depends on popularity of the entertainment programming that precedes it. ▶ 1

Carol Hope Reuppel: Imagination versus Resources

Carol Hope Reuppel expresses the challenge of being news director for WTKR-TV in this way: "Your imagination always outruns your resources. There is always more that you'd like to cover than you have resources for."

That's not an unusual complaint. Most editors, in print or broadcast, feel that they don't have enough people, money, and time. But Carol Reuppel must also somehow improve her station's news show ratings against stiff competition in the Norfolk market. For in television news, as in programming, in sales, and in the station manager's office, it's improve ratings or else.

What's a person like Reuppel doing in a hotspot like that? She didn't start out in that direction. Reuppel majored in English at Ohio University (BA, 1971) and taught for one year. Her duties included supervising the student newspaper, which reawakened her enjoyment of journalism. In 1972, she moved to WSTV-TV in Steubenville, Ohio, as a reporter and news producer.

"I always enjoyed the producing end the most," she says, and newsroom leadership, not reporting, was henceforth her career path.

Leaving Steubenville, she moved to WIIC-TV and then KDKA-TV, both in Pittsburgh. WKYC-TV, an NBC-owned-and-operated station in Cleveland, was next, in 1978. Along the way, she developed skills in creating miniseries, news-talk formats, and news specials. She became WKYC's news manager in 1980 and its executive

For Carol Reuppel (*center*), performing well as news director at WTKR-TV opened a shot at the station's top job. She is acting general manager in charge of all operations.

news producer in 1981 and began pulling in awards—three Best News Emmys and recognition from the Associated Press and United Press International in Ohio for quality coverage. It was on to KMTV in Omaha and, in 1986, to Norfolk as WTKR's news director. She continued her award-winning ways at WTKR, and in 1987, the station won a prestigious National Headliners award for a series titled "Holiday at Sea."

Note in Reuppel's career growth the same mobility we saw earlier in former station manager Bill Peterson's career. Television can really keep you on the move!

As in most media competition anywhere, it's war out there on the streets of Norfolk. Reuppel expresses her situation in combative terms: Her major competitor, WAVY-TV, "meets us on the ground everywhere. . . . Pound for pound, they match our resources." *Tough* and *aggressive* are words that crop up in conversation with her.

Here are job descriptions for WTKR's newsroom executives: The *news director* is responsible for every aspect of the news department and coordinates with other WTKR departments. The *executive producer* is responsible for the content and production of daily newscasts; oversees special projects, series, election coverage, and some advance planning; reads all copy before it airs; oversees graphics used in news; assists in personnel and budget decisions; and works with other departments on a daily basis. The *assignment editor* is responsible for daily news coverage, assigning reporters and photographers; handles many operational details involving camera gear, vehicles, live shots, communications, and travel for daily coverage; and also handles day-to-day planning and some long-term planning. The *chief photographer* oversees the photography and editing staff; offers daily assistance and evaluations to photographers and editors; participates in yearly evaluations of photographers and editors and in hiring and firing decisions; is responsible for the inventory of photographic gear and videotape for the news department; and recommends equipment purchases to the news director.

WTKR's half-million-dollar mobile van is a tremendous asset in news coverage. It can move quickly to the scene of a news story, then "uplink" live coverage to a satellite, which "downlinks" it to the WTKR newsroom. A producer and an engineer are assigned to the vehicle.

WTKR's 17 reporters and 14 photographers are on the go much of the time, of course. And effective use of their time and skills requires tight coordination by the news director and the assignment editors. Capturing the live element of news and illustrating it with high-quality video and graphics is a major part of any TV news job. Strong visual skills are essential.

Producing a local TV news program is a team effort that offers careers behind the camera as well in front of it.

There is, of course, much show biz in television news (and more than a little hype, too). That is simply part of the TV game. Stations promote on-air employees as "talent" and "personalities" as much as reporters and news analysts. Another reality in local and network news is that time constraints severely limit even the most professional efforts to present news of sufficient depth and variety. To work in TV news, you must "write short" and read copy quickly. After time out for commercials in any 30-minute newscast, after all, you have only about 22 minutes to cover your world of news. Split-second timing is essential.

TIPS ON ENTRY-LEVEL NEWS JOBS

by Carol Reuppel, WTKR-TV, Norfolk, Virginia

The best entry-level positions in the news department are associate producer, weekend assignment editor, tape editor, and photographer.

I look for candidates who are intelligent, curious, dedicated, assertive, and articulate. Ide-

Whether in print or broadcast, the news must fit available space and time. Here, Glenn Corey, coanchor and producer of WTKR's noon news, rated number one in the Norfolk market, times copy for a newscast.

ally, candidates should have a college education, although for some part-time positions a partial college education could be acceptable.

For the more technical positions (photographer, editor), candidates should have some exposure to the equipment involved, whether through their school curriculum or an internship.

For associate producer and weekend assignment editor, I look for judgment and decision-making abilities. Candidates must be able to prioritize and analyze and be able to write well.

With so many candidates for broadcast jobs, I look for a strong sense of commitment, evidenced through school internships, part-time jobs, or writing or photography experience for school papers. They should be able to convey their commitment to our business strongly in the job interview.

All candidates should demonstrate an interest in and knowledge of current affairs.

INSIDE THE SALES DEPARTMENT

Everything we've discussed so far that happens at WTKR-TV is warm-up for Rufus K. DeVane and his sales team: The station manager, Trussel and his marketing types, the reporters and editors in the newsroom—all labor jointly to create WTKR-TV's total programming presence in the Norfolk market to attract viewers who can in turn be sold to advertisers. Otherwise, the entire effort fails. For unlike newspapers and magazines, which derive some revenue from readers, and unlike cable television, which gets substantial revenue from viewer fees, WTKR lives entirely on advertiser revenue.

A reality of television in America today is that the sales department is the engine that drives the entire enterprise. People in sales have the loudest voices in a station's inner council of war; people with strong sales experience have the best shot at becoming station managers and network executives.

Many television newsrooms are staffed by serious professionals deeply dedicated to using their medium to cover important news and to serve the people's right to know. Principled marketing and programming executives try hard for program schedules that inform as well as entertain, that uplift as well as titillate. But plainly, in television all of that is second to putting together programming that sells.

Local television is a strongly profit-oriented business. Some diversified media groups that take pride in publishing high-quality newspapers, even at a cost to the bottom line, look primarily for profit in their television stations. Group executives who simply would not countenance second-rank journalistic performance by their newspapers demand less in their broadcast divisions. Television is a different game. And the game is called profits.

As a key player in WTKR's profits game, General Sales Manager DeVane is concerned primarily with selling commercial time to local advertisers and regional and national firms with products or services they want to sell to targeted audiences in the Norfolk market. A third source of revenue is compensation from CBS when WTKR broadcasts network programs that arrive with some commercials paid for by national advertisers (WTKR can also sell local advertisers commercial time left blank in network programming, often between shows).

At many TV stations, the general sales manager is second only to the station manager in experience. That's true at WTKR. DeVane began in Laurel, Maryland, and subsequently became its general sales manager before moving to WTOP radio in Washington as an account executive (salesperson in charge of a list of advertisers, or "accounts"). In 1974, he moved to Hartford, Connecticut, in sales development for WFSB-TV, then to a national sales company in Chicago, and later to WPLG-TV in Miami. In Miami, he became a consultant to Knight-Ridder, Inc., in newspaper sales development. That switch into newspapers is a bit unusual, but some groups are trying to "cross-pollinate" key executives, giving them multimedia experience that eventually should make them strong managers.

DeVane has two principal assistants. National Sales Manager Marjorie Nelowet deals with the station's "national rep," Harrington, Righter & Parsons, Inc., of New York City. WTKR cannot maintain a sales staff in distant cities, so like most stations, it lets the rep do on-scene selling for a percentage of the revenue brought in. The national sales manager also deals directly with the advertising agencies of large national firms that put together a "buy" of a group of stations across the country rather than use network advertising. Nelowet helps DeVane project economic trends and estimate likely demand for commercial time. From such projections come ad rates WTKR will charge.

Local Sales Manager Charlotte Harwood joined WTKR in 1982, after experience in radio sales, and quickly became the station's top salesperson, bringing in 20 percent of its local advertising ("billings," in the trade). She became local sales manager in 1985, a move into the executive ranks often made by top salespersons.

Account executives travel the Norfolk area and report to the local sales manager. The traffic manager keeps track of which commercial time slots have been sold and which are still open. At WTKR, this person reports directly to DeVane.

Television selling can be exciting, financially rewarding, and preparatory to top station and network jobs. In addition to the educational background cited by others, the applicant for sales account executive, according to General Sales Manager Rufus DeVane,

> must demonstrate intelligence, high energy, self-confidence, and personal high standards and must be many things: goal-directed, creative, flexible, achievement-oriented, persistent, organized, warm—and must have a sense of humor as well as the ability to show self-improvement. He or she must demonstrate good listening skills, be curious, competitive, quick-thinking, persuasive, and persistent. I look for evidence of these attributes in casual conversation, body language, and résumé—but also through questions I ask. The type of questions asked by the applicant are important signals, too.

OTHER KEY OPERATIONAL SECTORS

For two very sound reasons, WTKR maintains an active community relations program. First, it's simply good business to be active in the community, to have a "high profile." Second, come license renewal time, the station's owners must demonstrate that they operated WTKR "in the public interest," in part through services and programs responding to the communities it serves. That's required under FCC regulations, and failing could jeopardize license renewal. At best, a challenge from a community group, an individual, or another media company can be extremely expensive; at worst, it can result in losing the license, although that hardly ever happens.

Julie McCollum is in charge of WTKR's community relations. The station describes her as its "emissary to municipal and state governments, nonprofit and service organizations and schools." She gets involved in such things as saving an oceanfront park, raising funds for a food bank, and helping devise a broadcast series on substance abuse. McCollum joined WTKR's sales department, then moved into community relations and a second job she holds simultaneously, director of personnel.

JOBS IN COMMUNITY RELATIONS

by Julie McCollum, Director of Community Relations, WTKR-TV, Norfolk, Virginia

The most favorable initial impressions are created by applicants who have taken the time to find the appropriate person to whom to address a résumé and cover letter. Consideration is given to overall presentation—correct spelling, clarity, format of résumé, and information being up-to-date. Of primary importance in my department is the ability to communicate well, both orally and in writing. During the interview, I also notice the applicant's physical appearance (neatness and hygiene), mannerisms such as eye contact and poise, and enthusiasm.

The applicant's involvement in extracurricular or volunteer activities and participation in an internship program give some indication of energy level and, to a degree, can indicate good skills in working with people. The applicant's assessment of an internship experience can serve as an indication of a strong sense of commitment to the work ethic, also an important characteristic.

Applicants' goals, what they feel they could bring to the position, and what they expect to gain from the position all serve as indications of level of interest. Candidates who ask questions related to specific duties of the position and the company's overall goals and philosophies and those who have taken the time to learn something about the company are the most likely to leave a favorable lasting impression.

Finally, the applicant who takes time to write a thank you letter following a personal interview and follows up on the status of the position indicates courtesy and attention to the importance of following through.

Television stations, media companies that own them, and networks themselves are huge business enterprises that need experts in public relations, promotion, and public affairs. Duties range from writing public service announcements (PSAs) that boost community good works free of charge to designing long-range strategies to improve a company's position in the marketplace.

Another major function in TV—and one of the least visible—is performed by technical employees. Nothing—not programming, commercials, or PSAs—gets on the air unless the engineering department does its technical job.

This department must produce sound and pictures of the best possible quality every minute the station is on the air and do it within strict FCC guidelines that apply to any broadcaster using the public spectrum.

At WTKR, this department is headed by Gene Gildow, who started in radio engineering in Cleveland in the 1950s. In addition to working in both radio and TV station engineering, Gildow has been involved in constructing broadcast facilities. He has a staff of 14 to keep things running at WTKR.

Key jobs in engineering at the network level and in major TV markets require college-level technical training. Gildow trained on the job—as chief engineer of Ohio University's radio station while working toward a BFA degree in radio. For stations the size of WTKR, Gildow says it's preferable that entry-level applicants in engineering have college degrees, but high school graduates can make it with training in the military or in an electronics trade school. He adds that when interviewing,

I look for interests that indicate familiarity with technical matters, such as ham radio, photography, and other technical hobbies. The applicant must be mentally quick to keep up with our fast-paced business. An ap-

Roy Richards, shown here at the master control switcher, is one of 14 staffers supervised by Chief Engineer Gene Gildow.

direction, and pay attention to detail are critical. Flexibility in working schedule is a must.

A strong hands-on background is very important, as are people skills. It is traditionally the spot where an employee can demonstrate desire and knowledge to serve as a springboard for higher-level positions within the department and the station. A considerable number of former entry-level production personnel have moved on to positions in news, marketing, sales, and management. It is a high-profile position where those who want to make a positive or negative impact on our on-air operations have the capability to do so.

So community television offers exciting careers with much opportunity for advancement. Clearly, however, television is becoming a tighter career specialty for beginners. Networks are cutting staff. Smaller stations no longer field three- or four-person crews (reporter, lights, sound, camera). With new shoulder-carried cameras, one person does all jobs. Thus the number of

plicant who has done volunteer or part-time work at a college or public TV station would have a definite advantage.

Another key department is production, where commercials and promotional materials are developed. Production Manager Philip Armstrong supervises directors, technicians, writer-producers, and film editors in this creative process. Working in this department involves combining strong artistic instincts with hands-on skills—set design, camera operations, and so forth.

Many entry-level applicants seek jobs as camera or studio technicians. Armstrong describes what he looks for:

Duties include operation of production equipment for programming, marketing, and commercial functions. A college degree is preferred; one to two years' experience is required. We look for high motivation and a positive attitude. The abilities to learn, take

Using local acting talent, WTKR-TV produces its own commercials for advertisers. Assistant Production Manager Howard Mills (*left*) supervises this production.

openings has been reduced dramatically at many stations, leading to more applicants than jobs. Among other things, that has put downward pressure on beginning salaries.

In Chapter 11, we'll see what's happening inside the American radio station.

☆ SUMMARY

Much of the action in American television is shifting to community stations, where local news and local advertisers are most important.

WTKR-TV, a CBS affiliate in Norfolk, Virginia, illustrates how hotly competitive local TV can get. The station is in a fight with five other TV stations, 40 radio stations, and strong newspaper competitors for the Norfolk–Portsmouth–Newport News–Hampton market. The stakes are well worth fighting over: Television ad revenue alone in 1987 was in the $55 million to $65 million range; WTKR's share was $12 million to $18 million.

WTKR, probably worth about $55 million, has 115 full-time and 9 part-time employees.

Varied experience in broadcasting is necessary for station managers. Most come up through advertising sales.

The marketing department designs the station's total programming stance, combining CBS programs with others from syndicates and some that WTKR itself produces. It's a pressure job, requiring a wide view of which programming is attracting large audiences nationwide, yet also demanding an intimate understanding of what Norfolk-area viewers want. The goal is higher viewer ratings, which attract advertisers.

WTKR's newsroom has a $2 million annual budget and 40 full-time and 3 part-time employees, but the news director says that even greater resources would be required to cover the news authoritatively.

Advertising sales is crucial to commercial television stations, of course, because they must live solely on ad revenue, unlike newspapers and magazines, which derive some revenue from readers. The general sales manager of any TV station is one of the more experienced, higher-paid executives and has an excellent shot at becoming a station manager one day.

☆ RECOMMENDED READING

Additional details on WTKR-TV are available from the station's promotion department, 720 Boush St., Norfolk, VA 23510. *Broadcasting/Cablecasting Yearbook* each year reports on TV markets including Norfolk. *Editor & Publisher International Yearbook* and *Circulation* cover newspaper competitors in the market.

General information on careers in broadcasting is available from the National Association of Broadcasters, 1771 N Street NW, Washington, DC 20036. See particularly the NAB's booklet *Careers in Television*. Anyone aspiring to management in community television should see Barry L. Sherman, *Telecommunications Management* (New York: McGraw-Hill, 1987).

Inside a Local Radio Station

"It's a lovely day to be in Athens." Rain or shine, lovely day or not, that line booms out every morning on WNGC-FM and its sister station, WGAU-AM, in Athens, Georgia. The line is H. Randolph Holder's. The deep voice and show biz flair of its delivery are Holder's too. So, for that matter, are WNGC and WGAU.

This is small-town radio, folks, and H. Randolph Holder is gearing up for another day of doing what small-town radio owners do—a little announcing, prodding salespeople, motivating reporters, courting advertisers, watching profits, and even turning out lights.

The local radio station is an important link in our survey of the American broadcast industry, for three reasons. First, if you are interested in broadcast careers, small-town radio may be your point of entry. Second, if you are interested in eventually owning your own medium of mass communication, small-town radio offers opportunities. Third, if you plan only to be a media "consumer," you'll find it interesting to learn how one of the more than 10,000 radio stations out there is run.

WNGC-FM AND WGAU-AM, ATHENS, GEORGIA: A CASE STUDY

H. Randolph Holder remembers his first opportunity to get into radio station ownership. The memory is vivid because he had to borrow $3,500 to do it.[1] Today, Holder is a millionaire owner of two radio stations in Athens, Georgia, and two in Sonora, California. And in Athens, the pleasant southern town where he lives, everybody knows H. Randolph Holder.

Even today, aspiring entrepreneurs can get into ownership at entry-level cost far below that of most mass communications media. If you're a sound businessperson, if you truly understand radio and where it fits into the competitive media marketplace, and if you've got a little show biz flair, you can make a lot of money at it. But even if you don't, small-town radio can give you community identity—*stature*, if you will—hard to find in other lines of work.

Back in 1956, Holder had been in broadcast 13 years (in Illinois, Iowa, and Kentucky) and was news director of an Athens station when CBS offered a better job in Chicago. To keep him, Holder's employer offered 10 percent owner-

In small-town radio, every staff member—including the owner—performs many duties. Here, H. Randolph Holder, owner of WNGC-FM and WGAU-AM, opens his morning show with a line that has made him well-known in Athens, Georgia: "It's a lovely day to be in Athens."

ship—and that's when Holder borrowed that $3,500. Four years later, Holder decided to leave. But he wanted to stay in Athens, so he and the station's sales manager formed Clarke Broadcasting Corp. (named for Clarke County, where Athens is located) and negotiated to buy WGAU. The owner wanted $105,000, with 29 percent down. To make it, Holder had to borrow once more, this time $15,000. His partner also borrowed $15,000 for his half of the down payment.

There are lessons in this tale. First, if ownership is your goal, learn the radio business on somebody else's payroll before you jump. Holder had 13 years of solid learning experience behind him. Second, recognize that risk taking is part of getting into ownership. Twice Holder had to borrow money to position himself for opportunity.

After they had acquired the station, Holder's partner took over sales management and was also the announcer from 5 A.M. to 9 A.M. Says Holder:

I did all the news, public relations, speeches, and management activities. We both were very active in civic affairs. . . . We also painted the building inside and outside, swept the floors, and carried out the trash. And we tripled the gross revenue that first year.

There are lessons here too: In small-town radio, being the owner doesn't mean letting somebody else do the dirty work; often, it means doing it yourself. And if you're going to succeed, you've got to be visible. There is no eight-hour day for a small-town radio owner.

Holder is succinct: "For the first 10 years, there were no vacations, no time off—just 80-hour weeks. I worked my butt off." Then Holder and his partner decided to expand. They spotted a small station, WLAQ, in Rome, Georgia, and went for it. Again, Holder stuck out his financial neck, borrowing the down payment of $50,000. It was a mistake. The new station was in a hotly competitive market; hired managers ran the station into the ground. Holder and his partner sold out, but the losses "set us back many years in expansion."

Yet another lesson: Setbacks will occur in radio careers; business decisions will, on occasion, go wrong. When they do, all who are determined to succeed take a deep breath and plunge ahead.

A change in competitive circumstance in Athens gave Holder his comeback. He describes it:

In 1969, all our competitors changed their formats to rock, leaving the country music market open. Until then, we had been playing "beautiful music" on WGAU-FM. So we took a chance. We went fully country, the first station to do so in northeastern Georgia, and we were an instantaneous hit.

The lesson this time is that in radio, what's called counterprogramming can be decisive in a competitive fight. Holder's competitors erred in leaving open that country music niche; it was brilliant radio strategy to counterprogram their rock and take his station into country. Radio is an extremely volatile industry. Such programming and counterprogramming can upset competitive relationships and ratings virtually overnight: to win (or lose) 5, 6, even 10 points in market ratings is not unusual. Long experience in broadcasting and understanding his audience helped Holder spot a niche when it opened. His calculated gamble enabled him to fill it; more cautious station managers might have hesitated and missed the opportunity.

Holder's WGAU and WNGC prospered enormously. He bought out his partner and, in 1987, with his son, H. Randolph Holder, Jr., bought KVML-AM and KZSQ-FM in Sonora, California. Let's take a closer look at what that borrowed $3,500 was parlayed into in Athens.

THE MARKET: A GROWTH SITUATION

No medium of mass communication will prosper unless it has an economically strong marketplace. A prizewinning newspaper or magazine will fail unless the economy energizes advertisers and the consumers who support them. It's the same in radio. Fortunately for H. Randolph Holder, Athens is an attractive Sunbelt growth area. The town is on the fringe of the Atlanta metropolitan area, one of the nation's fastest-growing regions. Athens has its own economic strength: The University of Georgia, with 26,000 students and 5,000 faculty and staff, gives it a solid economic base.

With his 100,000-watt FM station, WNGC, Holder calculates he serves a 15-county area in Georgia, South Carolina, and North Carolina. That includes more than 650,000 population, 321,000 households, and an economy with about $2.2 billion retail sales annually.[2]

WGAU-AM covers a much smaller, 6-county trade area tightly surrounding Athens with a population of 174,000 in 61,800 households, and retail sales of $837 million annually. Holder's major investments (in, among other things, a 1,189-foot transmission tower) are in the FM station. So are his best prospects for success.

Holder is not the only media owner to see the economic potential of Athens. There are seven radio stations in Athens, plus one in nearby Jefferson that really is a competitor in Athens. Two of the eight are noncommercial PBS or listener-supported stations. For its size, Athens is overrun by radio stations. Morning and afternoon daily newspapers, a vigorous weekly, and student newspapers are in the competitive mix, too. Atlanta newspapers and TV stations compete

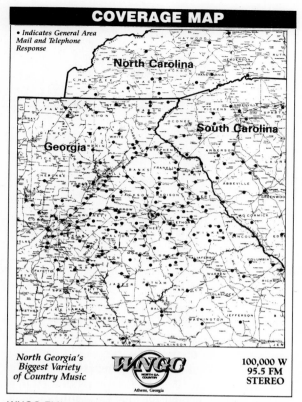

WNGC-FM's signal reaches parts of three states. Each dot represents a town where listeners have responded by mail or telephone, indicating that they receive the station.

strongly in Athens. Cable television includes one channel that carries local news, entertainment, and advertising.

In sum, Holder is in an economically strong market—essential for success in radio. But he has to fight for it and thus has to manage his station carefully. He does so in a manner typical of many local radio stations across the country.

STATION ORGANIZATION: AN INSIDE LOOK

WGAU-AM and WNGC-FM may be small-town radio, but they can't be run with minor-league management tactics. The stations' operations are complex, and there is less margin for error than

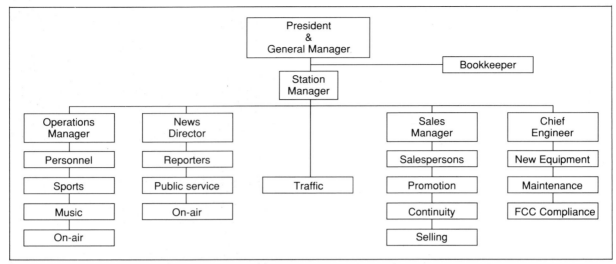

Figure 11.1 ORGANIZATION OF WNGC-FM AND WGAU-AM, ATHENS, GEORGIA.

in a rich major-market TV station. So Holder talks about tables of organization and efficient management, just like his colleagues in major-market stations or the networks.

The modified table of organization in Figure 11.1 illustrates not only the station's descending line of authority but also the varied tasks each person must undertake in a medium-sized radio station. Note, for example, that the operations manager is in charge of personnel, is the station's leading sports commentator, oversees music programming, and serves as an on-air personality! There simply aren't enough employees for a one-person, one-job setup. (That's not all bad for career beginners, incidentally. Joining a small station is one way to pile up a great deal of valuable experience in many sectors of broadcasting.)

Holder's staff totals 22 full-time employees and 9 part-time. He serves as president and general manager and has 6 key subordinates reporting directly to him (although he knows everybody on the staff and the tasks each is performing).

Holder and his department heads have written descriptions of the key jobs.

General Manager The first concern of the GM is for profit. Without profit, the station

ceases to be of value to its owner or community.

The GM must have broadcasting experience, business knowledge, and the ability to supervise people effectively. The required people skills include being able to listen to employees and understand their problems. Coordination with key supervisors, particularly the station manager and sales manager, is extremely important. The GM must be intimately familiar with goals programs under which each employee knows what is expected of him or her over the next year or so.

At WNGC-FM and WGAU-AM, of course, Holder establishes overall station policy with the aid of his board of directors. GMs who are not owners take policy guidance from owners and are responsible for day-to-day operations.

The GM must ensure that the station complies with FCC regulations and federal laws on equal opportunity and nondiscrimination in employment practices. The GM must also be active in civic groups, ensuring that the station is service-oriented and close to the community it serves.

Station Manager This executive has day-to-day responsibility for supervising major departments: operations, news, engineering, traffic, bookkeeping, copy, and public service.

Key tasks include making sure that the station's sound is the best possible, both in programming and technical quality, and managing station personnel—reviewing each person's performance annually and planning promotions and pay increases. Working with the sales manager is a major function and includes helping to design sales campaigns and promotions.

Motivating employees is a major goal. Station Manager Mary Betts explains:

> I feel it is my responsibility to teach and train and help our people reach their potential abilities, and if they need to be promoted out of the station, it's our responsibility to help them get where they want to go. Our success includes staff success.

Operations Manager In a market the size of Athens, this job includes a lot of things. For Larry England, it involves hiring and maintaining staff for both stations. Good people are hard to find for a medium-sized market, harder to keep. He strives for staff harmony and insists that any criticism be constructive.

Larry England is a small-town radio switch-hitter: Inside the station, he's operations manager, with planning and supervisory duties. Outside, to the listening audience, he's known as a leading radio sports commentator.

▶ 1 The Payola Scandals

The multibillion-dollar record industry depends heavily on programming decisions at local radio stations—and occasionally that's the stuff of scandal.

If a new record is played enough on radio, listeners will buy it in huge quantities. So record companies try to convince disk jockeys to schedule their offerings. Periodically, this creates a "payola" scandal, with companies accused of bribing disk jockeys to play their records—a violation of FCC regulations and federal law. The term *payola* was coined during the 1950s when a series of secret payments to disk jockeys was uncovered. Maximum penalties upon conviction can be many years in prison and hundreds of thousands of dollars in fines.

He also auditions all music to be aired on FM and makes sure that it suits the station's image. He maintains contact with record companies and plans locally originated special shows. ▶ 1

Larry England also does air work. To keep a feel for the audience, he works the early-morning drive, striving for a bright, upbeat show; he selects all music and information carefully and delivers it with a responsible, factual tone. He also does six sportscasts daily, with actualities and local flavor.

News Director The news director is responsible for all news operations and, with station management, determines news policy. Supervising the news staff, training, assignments, and performance is important. Good writing must be emphasized constantly.

In a medium-sized market, the news director is also a reporter, a newscaster, and a public affairs director, responsible for arranging political and community programming, debates, interviews, and other special events.

Says Holder:

> The news director should believe wholeheartedly in the importance of news as a broadcast product, must be dispassionate, even-handed and fair, eschewing "advocacy reporting." The news director should believe in the importance of immediacy in radio news—"Hear it now! See it tonight! Read it tomorrow!"

Sales Manager As in any media corporation, generating the advertising revenue that keeps the station going is a crucial job.

With the general manager, the sales manager establishes sales policies and rate cards and supervises daily sales. This manager also assigns account lists to the salespeople and develops promotional campaigns and literature. Weekly meetings are held to train, encourage, and assist the sales staff. The sales manager also supervises continuity (copywriting).

Traffic Manager This person puts together the daily program log, using a computer system that combines local, regional, and national commercials, plus local and network programming. The log becomes the bible that all on-air talent follow and serves as a permanent record of station programming.

Chief Engineer A love of electronics is essential for this job. So is the ability to stay abreast of fast change in equipment and procedures. Electronics is developing so quickly that new equipment can be obsolete the day it's delivered. In a medium-size market, the chief engineer purchases equipment, installs, and maintains it— and must be able to repair anything in the building.

In addition to those department head positions are four other important jobs of particular interest to those of you considering entry-level employment.

News Reporter The primary duty is collecting local news and selecting stories from the Associated Press wire and CBS audio network, then editing and rewriting for the local audience. A reporter must cover town meetings, elections, car wrecks, fires, and the like, making extensive use of taped actualities (on-scene voice reports). Regularly covered meetings include city council, county commission, board of education, planning and development commission and, sometimes, local civic clubs such as Rotary and Kiwanis.

Reporters also serve as anchors, airing newscasts that combine international, national, state, and local news, plus area weather.

The job requires aggressive, enthusiastic investigative skills and a news sense of what is important and what makes a good feature story. An excellent command of English is mandatory.

RADIO NEWS WRITING AS A CAREER

Ted Whitcomb is a longtime professional newsman who chose a career in radio after graduation (Middlebury College, BA, English/Drama, 1956). He is a senior editor of ABC News in New York City and has written for Peter Jennings, John Cameron Swayze, Ron Cochran, and other notable anchors. In the following question-and-answer session, Whitcomb explains radio's attraction and what he thinks its future will be.[3]

Question: *What's the biggest challenge radio news faces?*

Answer: To remain highly competitive with the other media such as TV and newspapers. Radio has the advantage of being highly mobile and with fewer restrictions than television. If a big story breaks, we can air the report immediately rather than wait for a soap opera to end, and do it without going through a cumbersome routine to get a bulletin on the air. . . . Radio's challenge is to continue doing this and continue being first with the news.

Question: *What ethical issue troubles you the most?*

Answer: First and foremost is to present the news in a fair and balanced way in the short amount of time allowed. In handling complex issues, social or political, radio must do it quickly and concisely without wasted words or thoughts. . . . We don't have the luxury of space that the news-magazines and newspapers have.

Question: *Don't radio writers long for the glamour of being on the air?*

Answer: Certainly, there is a drive to be on-air talent in radio and television. The money is perhaps the biggest attraction, and exposure and career advancement are certainly applicable. But there is much satisfaction with writing for yourself or another person. You have control of the words and what the correspondent for whom you're writing will say. The important person is not always the one behind the microphone or the camera.

Question: *Speaking of money . . .*

Answer: The material rewards for writers are not bad. . . . Our people start at $22,000 a year with upgrades every year. . . . You can make up to $45,000 to $50,000 a year . . . plus you have up to seven weeks' vacation after 25 years and many health and pension benefits.

Question: *What makes a good radio writer?*

Answer: One who can read wire copy and quickly distill the basic information and write the story in a brief and concise manner—a manner that will attract the ear of the listener. We have the listener's ear for only a few short minutes, and we have to make contact by being brief, clear, sometimes repetitive, and interesting. Brevity is the key word in radio; you have to grab the audience and hold it.

Question: *How difficult is it writing for someone else's delivery?*

Answer: When writing for other people, you learn their particular habits and char-acteristics and favorite words and phrases. If you work long enough with this person, you know how they write and talk, and you write accordingly. . . . Some are easier to work with than others.

Question: *So you write for a variety of services?*

Answer: Beginning in 1968, ABC split into four networks or program services, and now there are six: Information, FM, Contemporary, Rock, Entertainment, and Direction. These aim at certain demographic groups. . . . The so-called youth nets are Rock, FM, and Contemporary. We try to pick stories and tape that interests a younger audience. . . . Information spends more time on politics. . . . Direction is our consumer-oriented network. . . . There are also sports programs, features, and interview shows that are geared to a special audience or age group.

Question: *What is radio's future?*

Answer: Very bright. The latest surveys show that more people are listening to radio and radio news. The ABC networks have some 2,200 affiliates across the country. Radio is still a highly mobile medium, and when breaking news happens, radio is right there to get the story on the air first. . . . The listener *hears what's happening*, the sound of the news, like gunfire in the Gulf or the anguish of a little girl trapped in a well. Radio can take the listener quickly to where the story is happening.

Question: *What's the best preparation for a career in radio news writing?*

Answer: Certainly English courses, writing, and public speaking will help form a good broadcast news writer. But I firmly believe that experience in a small market, in a radio or TV outlet or a small newspaper, will go a long way in forming a good broadcast writer.

Announcer-Producer An announcer-producer must have good diction and be able to use correct English with ease and must be able to read aloud with expression. Technical skills are required for operating studio controls, turntables, tape machines, and other equipment. The announcer-producer must also keep a station programming log accurately, noting the broadcast times of all programs, commercials, and public service announcements.

The announcer may read commercials live but will generally produce them on tape, then play the tape in its proper time slot. The mechanization of electronic equipment today makes the announcer truly a producer. Announcers are not simply "DJs" or "jocks." They concentrate on producing informative and entertaining programs, selecting music (much is preprogrammed on tape) that is "mood-sequenced" for listener enjoyment.

The announcer-producer must use a "one on one" approach, not talk to "all you folks out there in radioland." Radio listening is by one person, not a group. Showmanship is required to create a pleasant program that will make an audience feel part of the family. The announcer-producer must deliver news authoritatively, produce a "happy," quality sound, and use time management to get it all done at the right time—while sounding relaxed and having fun!

Copywriter The copywriter must write commercials that sell advertisers' products or services. That involves taking sometimes sketchy information from the salesperson, then putting ideas into creative form in a script announcers can read smoothly and effectively. The copywriter's language skills must be impeccable. A creative personality, broad interests, and, above all, a vivid imagination are required.

The copywriter must produce different approaches in commercials—hard or soft sell, an institutional approach that entertains or informs. But the goal is to sell, and that requires writing to create listener desire to purchase. The ability to write under pressure is required.

A career in small-town radio is attractive for some announcer-producers who spurn the fast pace and competitiveness of major markets. Joel Shiver has been an on-air personality in Athens for over a decade.

Salesperson To be effective, a salesperson should be outgoing, have a pleasant personality and a determined outlook, be able to make friends easily, and want to make money. All that equals the ability to sell.

A salesperson must be strong in verbal communication, enthusiastic, imaginative, competitive, and a strong believer in radio.

The job requires being familiar with the station's program schedules and its audience demographics so that sound suggestions can be made to advertisers on advertising that will help increase their business. Each salesperson has an account list and must provide complete service to advertisers on it. Their problems are the salesperson's problems.

The salesperson passes information from advertisers to copywriters in continuity, along with ideas on how commercials should be written.

Collections are part of the job in small-town radio because salespersons are paid a percentage of the revenue they bring in. If the advertiser doesn't pay, the salesperson isn't paid.

Well, that's how Holder organizes his station and staff. It's typical of the inner workings of many local radio stations. Now let's see how Holder attracts audiences.

INSIDE RADIO PROGRAMMING STRATEGY

The community newspaper is immune from direct competition from national newspapers, and so is the local radio station free of direct competition from networks—provided that both remember precisely what they are (and aren't) and what they can offer that no other medium can.

H. Randolph Holder cannot cover the world

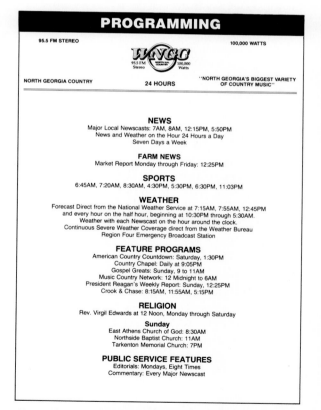

PROGRAMMING

95.5 FM STEREO   100,000 WATTS

WNGC
95.5 FM Stereo   NORTH GA COUNTRY   100,000 Watts

NORTH GEORGIA COUNTRY   24 HOURS   "NORTH GEORGIA'S BIGGEST VARIETY OF COUNTRY MUSIC"

NEWS
Major Local Newscasts: 7AM, 8AM, 12:15PM, 5:50PM
News and Weather on the Hour 24 Hours a Day
Seven Days a Week

FARM NEWS
Market Report Monday through Friday: 12:25PM

SPORTS
6:45AM, 7:20AM, 8:30AM, 4:30PM, 5:30PM, 6:30PM, 11:03PM

WEATHER
Forecast Direct from the National Weather Service at 7:15AM, 7:55AM, 12:45PM
and every hour on the half hour, beginning at 10:30PM through 5:30AM.
Weather with each Newscast on the hour around the clock.
Continuous Severe Weather Coverage direct from the Weather Bureau
Region Four Emergency Broadcast Station

FEATURE PROGRAMS
American Country Countdown: Saturday, 1:30PM
Country Chapel: Daily at 9:05PM
Gospel Greats: Sunday, 9 to 11AM
Music Country Network: 12 Midnight to 6AM
President Reagan's Weekly Report: Sunday, 12:25PM
Crook & Chase: 8:15AM, 11:55AM, 5:15PM

RELIGION
Rev. Virgil Edwards at 12 Noon, Monday through Saturday
Sunday
East Athens Church of God: 8:30AM
Northside Baptist Church: 11AM
Tarkenton Memorial Church: 7PM

PUBLIC SERVICE FEATURES
Editorials: Mondays, Eight Times
Commentary: Every Major Newscast

WNGC-TV, like any successful local radio station, must cover its local community like a blanket. Note the emphasis on local events in this schedule.

or the nation as well as a network; nor can he match Atlanta's major radio stations on regional or state coverage. So Holder sticks to his home market—and so must all local radio station owners who want to succeed.

Like print editors and programmers in television, radio station managers must ensure that their music and information offerings are tailored for the maximum number of listeners. WNGC-FM's country music format (Holder describes it as "modern country with lots of oldies") is a big hit in northern Georgia. Let's discuss for a moment his other programming elements.

◆ *News.* Although many radio stations cut back on news, Holder airs four major *local* newscasts daily, seven days weekly. Think of the competitive edge that gives him: His print competitors cannot be on the streets with local news until predawn with the morning paper or about 4 P.M. with the afternoon paper. Delay in the cumbersome production process of newspapers gives radio an advantage in being fast. Television won't cover Athens until 6 P.M. or 11 P.M.—and Atlanta stations cannot present much detail on Athens stories. They've got wider responsibilities. So Holder wisely makes WNGC-FM the place for quick news updates.

THE VALUE OF RADIO NEWS

  66   Radio news is something like pure water in the taps: You may forget you have it, but you would be very uncomfortable without it. **99**

Richard C. Wald, senior vice president, ABC News.[4]

◆ *Farm news.* In rural northern Georgia, farm news is big news. That 12:25 P.M. daily market report is a fixture with farmers (and advertisers who use WNGC to reach them).

◆ *Sports.* To journalists, it appears at times as if America is sports-crazy. Double that for Georgia; *triple* it for Athens, home of the University of Georgia Bulldogs. Seven sports reports on WNGC aren't too many.

◆ *Weather.* Weather is extremely important information. The immediacy of radio makes it crucial to anyone interested in weather (and that's just about everyone).

◆ *Feature programs.* Religion is big in northern Georgia, and Holder has "Country Chapel" and "Gospel Greats" among feature offerings. A local minister is on the air each noon, and on Sundays, the station carries services from three local churches.

◆ *Public services features.* Holder more than fulfills his FCC requirement to broadcast "in the public interest." He has strong opinions and gets many into editorials and commentaries. Many radio stations don't analyze local news or provide community leadership. This one does.

Now let's look at Holder's programming strategy for his AM station, WGAU, a CBS affiliate.

First, the station doesn't serve the farflung *rural* audiences of its FM sister. Rather, it covers a six-county area hubbed on Athens, home of the University of Georgia and expanding center of retail commerce and small industry. That means that the type of audience is different. It's much better educated relative to the north Georgia audience, more cosmopolitan, and better paid.

Second, WGAU is an AM station, technically incapable of the high-quality music of FM. Everywhere, audiences perceive AM stations as inferior to FMs in listening quality. (Nationwide, FM captured about 75 percent of all radio listening in 1988.)[5] And even though WGAU broadcasts in stereo, a technical upgrading of its sound quality, the FM band is where Athens residents seek quality music.

WGAU blends various programming inputs. Its "soft adult contemporary" music contrasts with the country format of its FM sister. Also, WGAU broadcasts the Metropolitan Opera. That plays well with university faculty and city residents; it doesn't do so well among north Georgia farmers. "Soft adult contemporary," incidentally, comes packaged from a music syndicator, Bonneville International Corp., of Chicago. WGAU's announcers simply plug in a tape cassette for hours of preprogrammed music. ▶ 2

2 ▷ Syndication and the Automated Station

How do you run a radio station with two employees? You call Transtar Radio Network or Satellite Music Network, two programming syndicates that provide 24-hour programming, either on tape cassettes that are plugged in and aired or in live broadcasts transmitted via satellite to affiliated stations across the country.

Other companies sell individual programs. Westwood One Companies, a Denver-based firm that absorbed both the Mutual Broadcasting System and NBC radio networks, provides programming for more than 5,000 affiliated stations. It offers more than 50 "hit" programs of music, news, sports, or talk.

Satellite Music offers seven music formats. The fee is $1,150 monthly (1988 rates)—inexpensive compared to the salaries of on-air talent and other station costs.[6] And many stations don't pay that. Satellite Music sells commercials to national advertisers and gains revenue for having them aired on its affiliated stations.

Local listeners are often not aware that disk jockeys and talk show hosts they hear are actually broadcasting from distant studios owned by programming distributors. A Georgia station reports getting telephone calls from listeners who wanted to talk to the disk jockey—who was broadcasting from Chicago![7]

If FM stations corner much of the music market, what can AM stations emphasize? News and information. WGAU, a CBS affiliate, uses extensive network news and information programming. Seven days weekly, WGAU airs CBS on-the-hour news updates. The famous "CBS World News Roundup" is broadcast each morning. Local sports are emphasized on WGAU, along with local weather and religious programming.

WGAU's programming is aimed at university and city, not rural, audiences: city politics

WGAU-AM relies heavily on CBS programming and syndicated music. But it still manages substantial coverage of local news and special events.

("Inside Athens"), classical (not country) music, programs on the arts. That is how radio programmers aim at a narrow market niche, just as newspaper or magazine editors carefully select news aimed at target audiences.

What's the result of all this?

THE PAYOFF: LOCAL RADIO'S BOTTOM LINE

Let's evaluate WNGC and WGAU in terms of the four constituencies they (or any media) serve—consumers (listeners in this case, of course), advertisers, community, and owner.

Listeners get quality and variety not always found in small-town radio. Some stations are au-

tomated, employing a few technicians and tape cassettes to produce canned programming 24 hours a day. Not so at the Athens stations. Both pay close attention to local audience needs. Listeners give WNGC and WGAU high marks.

Advertisers are happy if listeners are happy—and WNGC and WGAU are the most popular radio stations in the Athens area. So in serving advertisers, the stations meet the first test: They deliver audience. Also, advertisers get a complete range of services not always available in small-town radio. Seven account executives help advertisers plan tailor-made sales campaigns. They recommend ways in which retail merchants can budget advertising dollars, how and when to place ads, how to strike responsive chords with consumers—and the stations write the ad copy. Rates are affordable for local merchants. In 1989, for example, the FM station's *top* rate was $36.50 for a 60-second commercial during the "best" times available—5:30 A.M. to 10 A.M. and 3 P.M. to 7 P.M., when radio achieves top listenership. That rate descended to $18.85 per 60 seconds for commercials repeated a number of times. The AM's top rate was $16.50, descending with usage to $10. An advertiser who used both stations in combination got even lower rates (contrast that with $1,000 per minute at WBBM radio, Chicago, or the hundreds of thousands of dollars TV networks charge national advertisers for just 30 seconds on a prime-time hit show). The dominant advertising medium in Athens is definitely the local daily newspaper. But WNGC and WGAU are popular with many advertisers because low rates permit frequent use of commercials.

Regarding the community, national newspapers and TV networks, in news coverage and editorial analysis, contribute to the democratic dialogue in our country. The *Wall Street Journal* serves its "community," the world of business. Daily and weekly newspapers cover local government. Judging the impact of radio stations on all this is difficult, if not impossible. WNGC and WGAU devote much time and energy to covering local government and local public affairs; not all small-town stations do.

WNGC and WGAU reward their owner handsomely. Holder calculates that in 1989, radio advertising in the Athens market totaled about $3 million for all stations.[8] His share was 50 percent, a tidy $1.5 million that year alone.[9] Holder doesn't provide details beyond that. But radio can be enormously profitable business, and 35 to 40 percent of that $1.5 million could head for the bottom line. ▶ 3

Now how about employees? What's their bottom line?

Holder operates in a way that sets him apart from many small-town radio owners. In 1989, he paid a beginning reporter just out of college $275 to $300 weekly (that assumes radio work or internships during college). That was above the national average (even though the cost of living in Athens was below the national average). Aside from top executives, salespersons earned the most. Outstanding salespersons could earn $45,000 or so annually. They were paid no salary but received a $200 weekly "draw" (advance) against sales commissions, which are a straight 15 percent on all ad revenue collected.

SMALL-TOWN RADIO: TIPS ON GETTING STARTED

by H. Randolph Holder, owner, WNGC-FM and WGAU-AM

There are nearly 11,000 radio stations in the United States, and job opportunities are numerous. How can you take advantage of these opportunities?

The sooner you get started the better. If you didn't hang around your local radio station when in high school, start now. If you're in college, apply to the college station immediately to do any job it needs done. If your school has no station, apply to all the small stations nearby. Demonstrate your interest to the program director. Offer to work nights and weekends. Keep bugging them in person (not on the telephone or by letter). Try to write and produce commercials, and get them critiqued.

Ask the program director for old news copy and old commercial copy, and practice reading

---

3 ▶ Station Prices Soar

The profit potential of radio is drawing investor attention and pushing station prices skyward. In 1988, Command Communications, Inc., of New York City paid the highest prices ever for radio stations: $79 million for KJOI-FM, Los Angeles, and $40 million for KRLD-AM, Dallas.

Three factors push station prices higher. Deregulation expanded to 12 AM and 12 FM (from 7 and 7) the number of stations a single company can own, creating buyer demand; rising advertising revenues signal a prosperous future for the industry; and the demand for stations outruns the supply of those for sale, which boosts prices.

Buying and selling stations has been big business for years. In 1988, stations worth $1.8 billion changed hands; in 1987, the figure was $1.2 billion (for TV stations, the figures were $1.7 billion and $1.6 billion, respectively).[10]

---

aloud for interpretation and style. Owners and managers like enthusiasm. If you are turned down or kicked out, go to another station. Keep trying. Keep practicing, and when a job opens you'll be ready for it.

If you tend toward electronics, find an engineer to talk to and help. Most technical people love to meet others with interests in their field.

If your interest is in sales, it's still better to do programming first, so that you know about broadcasting. Learn the business from the inside. Most stations like to promote from within, so if you're already on the job but see another in the station you want, prepare for it. If you are an announcer, for example, and you want to move into sales, ask the sales manager for sales information you can study. Be ready when a sales job opens.

Often, you must move to another station in your career development. So be prepared to travel a bit.

Whatever your job, remember not to worry about working extra hard. Put in extra hours to get the job done. That will get you noticed—and promoted.

If you want to move up to station ownership, you must be thoroughly competent in all facets of radio broadcasting. That will take you at least 5 to 10 years. If you know the business, banks will lend you the money to get started. If you are able to stand the pressures of taking risks, go for it. Then let the banks do the worrying. You do the work!

☆ SUMMARY

Small-town radio offers aspiring entrepreneurs ownership at a cost far below that of most mass communications media.

WNGC-FM and WGAU-AM of Athens, Georgia, owned by H. Randolph Holder, illustrate that if you're a sound businessperson who truly understands broadcasting and has a little show biz flair, you can make a lot of money in small-town radio. And it gives an owner community stature hard to match in other work.

Tracing Holder's growth from a borrowed $3,500 to millionaire owner of four stations, it's clear that learning broadcasting on somebody else's payroll is the first step toward ownership. Learning to take risks is another, because there are plenty in operating a station.

Effectively programming music, news, and information—and counterprogramming against competitors—can spell success in radio; mistakes can mean failure.

An economically strong market is the first requirement for success in radio. Strong organization and precision management are mandatory. Key jobs are general manager, station manager, operations manager, news director, sales manager, traffic manager, and chief engineer. In small-town radio, however, all hands must perform many duties.

Radio executives must understand clearly what their listeners want on a broadcast schedule. Broadcasting classical music to a rural north Georgia audience won't work; neither will an unchanging diet of country music hold a city or university audience.

News and information are important in radio, particularly on AM stations, which are perceived by the listening public as technically incapable of delivering FM's high-quality sound.

Well-run radio stations can reward listeners with high-quality varieties of listening; advertisers can get loyal audiences at low ad rates; a community can be well-served by a station that conscientiously covers local government; and owners can be rewarded with handsome profits. Testimony to all this is in the increased interest investors have in buying radio stations. Prices for stations are at all-time highs.

☆ RECOMMENDED READING

Further information on WGAU and WNGC is available from H. Randolph Holder, president, 850 Bobbin Mill Road, Athens, GA 30610. For details on the market and the Atlanta Area of Dominant Influence, see *Broadcasting/Telecasting Yearbook. Editor & Publisher International Yearbook* and *Circulation* provide details of newspaper competition.

The National Association of Broadcasters, 1771 N Street NW, Washington, DC 10036, can provide information on the broadcast industry and, in its booklet, *Careers in Radio*, helpful guidance on entry-level jobs in radio.

For continuing coverage of the radio industry, see *Broadcasting, Advertising Age, Electronic Media*, and the media news pages of the *Wall Street Journal* and the *New York Times*.

AMERICAN DIVERSITY AND THE MASS MEDIA

We turn now to two areas extremely important to our continuing study of the media in the United States.

Chapter 12 looks at the role of ethnic groups, minorities, and women in the media. We'll look first at ethnic and minority media. Some are expanding, others withering. Then we will examine minorities and women in the media workplace. Despite improved hiring and promotion practices, the media are generally far behind society's expectations in building work forces that mirror the ethnic, racial, and gender makeup of our population.

Then, before turning to advertising and public relations, we will in Chapter 13 survey media research. We will first look at methods modern media managers use to understand and address their audiences and the changes taking place. We will look at innovation in research from the news gatherers' standpoint, too, and discuss how computer-assisted research is producing Pulitzer prizewinning journalism.

Subcurrents in the Mainstream

O f all mass media in America, none is quite so distinctively diverse—or so awash in change—as ethnic newspapers, magazines, and broadcasting.

We look first in this chapter at how ethnic media developed special marketplace niches, a sense of mission, and their own journalistic flavor over years (and sometimes generations) of serving the special economic, political, and cultural interests of Italian-Americans, German-Americans, Hispanics, and others.

Then we look at the black media. Profound changes are under way.

The chapter concludes with a survey of the struggle of minorities and women to gain equal treatment in media hiring and promotion practices. The media have far to go in ensuring full equality.

These subjects are not merely fascinating bits of media Americana; they are essential to the wider media survey pursued in this book.

THE ETHNIC MEDIA SUBCURRENT

Ethnic media are one of the strongest subcurrents in the American media mainstream. Four factors are at work and sometimes at odds with one another.

First, "mainstream" general-circulation media have great difficulty serving the highly specialized news and advertising needs of some ethnic and minority groups. Since the early 1800s, when waves of immigrants began arriving on our shores, it has been so. By definition, *general-circulation* media must aim for the widest possible audiences, providing consensus news and advertising content designed to cross social, economic, and cultural boundaries and scoop up

broad, homogeneous followings. In America, that means publishing in English. Many immigrants arrive neither speaking nor reading English and initially, at least, retain strong cultural ties to "old country" ways. For them, foreign-language newspapers, magazines, and broadcasting sprout up, particularly in large cities where immigrants tend to gather. ▶ 1

Second, however, many new citizens quickly learn English to help them find good jobs and move into the economic, political, and cultural mainstream. Old-country ties weaken. Many children of immigrants spurn the language of their heritage and learn only English. As a result, newspapers published in certain languages wither. Just one Italian-language daily is pub-

1 Foreign-Language Press Peaks

Statistics on the foreign-language media in America have always been somewhat unreliable. Small publications come and go, and most are privately owned and don't publish audited financial or circulation figures. However, it's clearly been downhill since the early 1900s for foreign-language newspapers, both in numbers and influence.

Foreign-language papers have been around a long time. One bilingual paper, *El Misisipi*, was launched in New Orleans in 1808. In their authoritative history, *The Press and America*, Michael and Edwin Emery say foreign-language dailies peaked at 160 in 1914, foreign-language publications of all kinds at 1,323 in 1917. Dailies totaled 2.6 million circulation in 1914. German-language papers were most numerous, with 823,000 circulation; Yiddish papers were second, with 762,000. Other languages strongly represented were Swedish, Norwegian, Danish, Italian, Spanish, Polish, French, Chinese, and Japanese.

In 1988, there were perhaps 200 foreign-language newspapers, of which 40 or fewer were dailies. Publications in Spanish were expanding most rapidly.[1]

lished, for example—*Il Progresso Italo Americano*—and it's sinking fast. The paper, over 100 years old and once a fixture in America's Italian community, has less than 50,000 circulation. Ad revenue is so low that the paper negotiated grant support from the Italian government.[2] The Yiddish press, once strong, has almost vanished. There are no Yiddish dailies, and one leader, *The Forward*, is down to once-weekly circulation of 20,000 (from 238,000) and is losing money.[3]

No such doom and gloom grips Asian or Hispanic publishers. Newspapers and magazines in Spanish, Korean, Vietnamese, and other Asian languages are increasing to meet new waves of immigrants. In New York alone, 11 Chinese-language dailies fight for readers among the city's 250,000 or so Chinese-Americans. In San Jose, California, a half dozen newspapers and magazines in the Vietnamese language compete for 60,000 to 80,000 Vietnamese of reading age in the city. Filipino-Americans in Los Angeles have a twice-weekly, the *Philippine-American News*; Japanese and Koreans have their own well-established media service, including importation of newspapers from "home."

Asian-Americans, numbering about 6 million in 1988, are increasingly affluent and thus attractive to advertisers. In response, national magazines—*AsiAm* is one—attempt to cross old-country political boundaries and appeal to all Asian-Americans as a group. The attempt is hampered by divisive politics such as quarrels between Taiwan and the People's Republic of China. It remains to be seen what the current changes in political ideologies and economic systems will mean for the media trying to reach various national interests.

Strong political orientation marks the Native American media. Most of the approximately 350 Indian publications (one publishes daily, the others weekly or less regularly) are owned by tribes. Political, economic, and cultural issues on Indian reservations are standard fare for Indian journalists. In 1988, just one Indian paper of substance was independently owned—the *Lakota* (S.D.) *Times*, a weekly with about 8,000 circulation on eight reservations in South Dakota, North Dakota, and Nebraska. Tribal-oriented radio stations also are strong political voices.

If ethnic and minority media appear, it is because mainstream media don't serve their communities' interests sufficiently well. One reason they don't is that advertisers have not demanded anything else. Basically, all new ethnic media face the same crucial question: Will they, like so many of their predecessors, be of only interim generational interest, or will they last longer?[4]

END OF AN ERA

❝ We kindly ask that you do not renew the subscription to the paper. Father died last week. There is no one here anymore who can read the paper. ❞

Letter to the Danish-language Pioneer.[5]

A third factor influencing the evolution of ethnic media is the fundamental change many have undergone in their sense of mission. Traditionally, foreign-language newspapers not only covered news of interest to their special communities but felt driven to protect Old World culture in the New World and the economic and political interests of their readers. Today, many ethnic media are shifting to profit-driven strategies at work on behalf of advertisers, as elsewhere in America's free enterprise media. These strategies are not designed to defend old ways but rather to unlock for advertisers the growing affluence of ethnic communities. This is particularly true with newspapers and broadcasters serving the Hispanic community, which numbered 18.8 million persons in 1988 and is projected to grow to about 55 million by the year 2020. And it is affluent: Hispanic Americans in 1988 had an estimated $134 billion in buying power.[6] To advertisers, that's an attractive target in any language. Increasingly, the language isn't Spanish; English is used in many newspapers aimed at Hispanics. And non-Hispanic firms are entering the competition to reach them. Particularly in television, "mainstream" communications companies are big players for the Hispanic market.

A fourth factor crucial to the evolution of ethnic media is that mainstream media haven't integrated sufficient numbers of minorities into their staffs, particularly in upper management. Most mass communications companies do not have minority representation on their staffs anywhere near the minority presence in their marketplaces. Can the media adequately cover their minority communities if few or no members of those communities are on the staff? Whatever the reality, the perception is widespread in black and other minority communities that many metropolitan newspapers and TV stations do not cover minority news properly. This creates among minority journalists a desire to "fill the gap" with publications and broadcasting produced by staff drawn from ethnic communities. Yet with very few exceptions, ethnic communities across America don't provide sufficient economic support for truly high-quality, financially successful minority media. The dilemma: As ethnic Americans prosper economically, they shift to mainstream media. Their interest is no longer old neighborhood or old country; rather, it's IBM, the stock market, national politics, general economic trends—how to get a piece of the American action. And that requires reading the *Wall Street Journal*, not a neighborhood Hungarian-language weekly; it leads to interest in what CNN, ABC, NBC, and CBS offer, not only Spanish-language soap operas on a local cable channel. Advertisers follow this shift, using the *Journal*. CNN. and the others to reach second-generation Americans and minorities who progress economically and become attractive as consumers. Most ethnic and minority media are thus left with fewer readers and viewers—and those they do retain are demographically less attractive to advertisers.

For ethnic media, then, the American experience has been one of ups and downs, but one sector is growing rapidly.

HISPANIC MEDIA: ON A ROLL

Projections that Hispanics will be America's largest ethnic group in the mid-21st century attract much entrepreneurial interest in the profit-minded media. Hispanics are being targeted less as an immigrant group to be served by narrowly focused, culturally defensive media and more as an important special-interest group—and an increasingly affluent one at that—that can be pulled in with tailored news and entertainment.

In 1988, Standard Rate and Data Service, a research firm, identified more than 400 media serving Hispanic markets across the country—radio, TV, daily and community newspapers, business publications, consumer magazines, direct mail, and outdoor advertising. Many are aimed at major Hispanic groups—Mexican-Americans, Puerto Ricans, and Cuban-Americans—in New York City, Los Angeles, Chicago, Miami, Houston, and San Antonio.

Because many Hispanics only recently ar-

Arturo Villar publishes *Vista*, distributed to more than 1.2 million households as an insert in metropolitan newspapers across the nation.

THE HISPANIC UNCERTAINTY

66 What remains uncertain is whether the various sub-groups of an increasingly English-oriented Hispanic population will be interested in publications that separate them ethnically from the rest of the population.

For instance, would a Hispanic teenage girl who likes reading English want to read a magazine about Hispanic teenage girls, or go straight to *Seventeen* or *Mademoiselle*? 99

New York Times *media analyst*
Alex S. Jones.[7]

Some mainstream media giants are betting huge sums that whatever their language of choice, Hispanics will be attractive to advertisers. In 1988, Hallmark Cards, Inc., paid $585 million for Univision, the nation's leading Spanish-language TV network and 10 Hispanic TV stations. Another non-Hispanic company is the number two player in Spanish-language television, Reliance Capital Corp., controlled by a New York financier, Saul P. Steinberg. Reliance owns the Telemundo Group of five Spanish-language stations and, like Hallmark, provides Hispanic programming to affiliated stations.

Both companies regard Hispanic TV as one of the fastest-growing sectors of television, and both are in it for profit, not cultural altruism. Principal national advertising support comes from Philip Morris Co., Procter and Gamble, Pepsi-Cola, Ford, and Bartles & Jaymes (which broadcasts commercials with its famous character, Frank Bartles, pitching wine coolers in Spanish). The Hispanic market is still relatively small: Total 1987 ad revenue accounted for less than 1 percent of all TV advertising.[8] But it will grow. By 1988, fully 24 of the top 25 advertisers on network television were buying commercial time on Univision.[9]

Some Hispanic leaders express concern over non-Hispanic companies' dominating Spanish-language TV and radio. They question, for example, whether Hallmark, a Kansas City, Missouri, greeting card company, can properly serve Hispanic audiences. The answer, of course, is

rived in America, Spanish was the language of their media well into the late 1980s. *Advertising Age* research in 1987 indicated that 66.5 percent of all Hispanics felt most comfortable speaking Spanish, 15.4 percent chose English, and 18.1 percent were comfortable in both languages. However, that same research showed younger Hispanics tending toward English. The U.S. Census Bureau estimated in 1988 that 75 percent of growth in the Hispanic population came from children born in America. They, of course, will be targets for English-language media. Says Arturo Villar, publisher of *Vista*, an English-language newspaper supplement aimed at Hispanics: "All those Hispanics born in this country may want to make love in Spanish, but when it comes to reading and writing, if they learned that in English, they probably don't read or write as well in Spanish."

that in America's free enterprise media system, Hallmark (or any other company) will serve Hispanic viewers properly or fail. The decision of what is the "right" news or entertainment for Hispanics will be made in the marketplace by Hispanic viewers who tune in or tune out.

Ted Turner's Cable News Network bets it has the "right" formula. It produces Spanish-language news programming for Telemundo (broadcast as "Noticiero Telemundo–CNN").[10] MTV produces music video shows ("MTV Internacional") for Telemundo.

In print, similarly aggressive moves are under way to penetrate the Hispanic market. But in this mass communications sector, the ethnic picture is much more complicated. At least four distinctly separate categories of competitors are involved:

◆ *Small "mom and pop" publications owned by individual Hispanics or families.* These come and go—mostly go—because few are well financed or managed. The National Association of Hispanic Publishers says that in the United States in 1985, there were 10 Hispanic dailies, 140 weeklies, 76 "less than weeklies," 114 magazines (of which only 20 to 25 were published regularly), and 91 journals and other publications.

◆ *Large Hispanic companies that publish dailies, weeklies, or magazines.* Well-financed and professionally managed firms publish two of the five most important Spanish-language dailies. The Lozano family of Los Angeles publishes *La Opinion*, with more than 62,000 circulation. Founded in 1926, it is the oldest continuously published Hispanic daily. In Miami, Horatio Aguirre publishes *Diario las Americas*, with 67,000 circulation. Aguirre, a Nicaraguan exile, founded the paper in 1953.

◆ *Mainstream print companies that compete in the Hispanic market purely for profit.* These include Knight-Ridder, whose *Miami Herald* publishes for its large Hispanic community a Spanish-language paper, *El Nuevo Herald*, with 94,600 daily and 102,000 Sunday circulation; News World Communications, a company controlled by followers of a Korean evangelist, the Reverend Sun Myung Moon, and his Unification

Church, which publishes *Noticias del Mundo*, founded in 1980. Gannett Co., the nation's largest newspaper owner, published *El Diario-La Prensa*, a New York City daily, from 1981 to 1989, when it sold out (for a reported $20 million) to local investors because the paper's 54,800 circulation was failing to keep pace with growth of the city's Hispanic population.

◆ *Hispanic-owned media firms that distribute their products to Hispanic homes by piggybacking as inserts in mainstream English-language newspapers.* Piggyback distribution is achieved notably by *Vista*, a magazine inserted as of 1988 in 27 English-language mainstream dailies in nine states. The tabloid-sized weekly claims 1.2 million total circulation—137,000 of it as an insert in the *New York Daily News*. Another large carrier is the *San Antonio Express News* (100,000). *Vista* was launched in 1983 by Arturo Villar, who was born in Spain, reared in Cuba, and educated in the United States. News content is selected at *Vista*'s Miami headquarters for appeal to Hispanics but written in English. Villar says readers by a small margin prefer English—and anyway, publishing in English ensures that the magazine will reach a higher demographic audience (the theory being that low-income Hispanics read only Spanish). Advertising (about $2.7 million worth in 1987) is often in Spanish.[11] Clearly, the reach upscale for more demographically appealing readers affects all publishing, regardless of language.

It's easy to oversimplify who qualify as "Hispanic" and their news and advertising needs. *El Diario–La Prensa* calculates that it serves Spanish-speaking readers from 21 nations. Many have distinctly different views on main news issues (U.S.-Cuba relations, for example).

The main Hispanic magazines—*Hispanic* and *Hispanic Business*—attempt to serve three major Hispanic groups with roots in Mexico, Cuba, and Puerto Rico. Both publish in English.

The complexity of Hispanic affairs lured Knight-Ridder into an enormously costly strategic error. As refugees from Fidel Castro's Cuba poured into Miami, Knight-Ridder decided that its flagship *Miami Herald* would wait until these new Americans learned English and turned to the

Herald as an information tool for making it in the New World. But Miami's Cubans built a "Little Havana" in Miami, retained Spanish in business, and not only spurned the *Herald* but labeled it unfriendly to Cuban-Americans. The *Herald*, its circulation dropping, began in 1976 publishing a Spanish-language section called *El Miami Herald* and in other ways tried to reach the Cuban-American community. But the *Herald*'s own research showed that 6 out of 10 Hispanics still believed that the paper was not involved in their community. Roberto Suarez, a Cuban-born Knight-Ridder executive brought in to set things right, explains:

> In retrospect, it's clear that the *Herald* did not respond as sensitively as it should have to the changes in its marketplace. . . . Like much of old Miami, the *Herald* was slow to comprehend fully the depth of the pain endured by our new Cuban-American neighbors, uprooted from their country by a brutal Communist dictatorship. Too often, the Cubans were seen, wrongly and simplistically, as conventional immigrants to America, when the reality was much more complicated than that.[12]

Now Knight-Ridder also distributes a free-circulation advertising weekly, *El Anunciador*, to 162,000 Hispanic homes that don't take *El Nuevo Herald*.

The complexity of serving Hispanic audiences is illustrated by the fact that 11 nations contributed to the Hispanic population of Dade County, the Herald's home. Cubans, numbering 650,000, dominate the Hispanic community; Nicaraguans are second, at 79,000; Colombians third, at 75,000. Obviously, no single news and editorial policy will satisfy the needs of such multinational Hispanic audiences.

Los Angeles Times editors decided their Hispanic market was so complex that it needed a bilingual publication. In 1989, the *Times* launched *Nuestro Tiempo*, a monthly section offering English- and Spanish-language news stories side by side. Most ads are in Spanish. The section is distributed to about 420,000 households in areas of Los Angeles and Orange counties with large Hispanic populations.

Nationwide, advertising and marketing firms are moving strongly into Hispanic markets. The *Standard Directory of Advertising Agencies* counts 41 ad agencies, some owned by non-Hispanics, specializing in print ads and TV commercials aimed at Hispanics. Many major ad agencies operate in-house divisions specializing in Hispanic advertising, at the insistence of major clients. *Advertising Age*, the influential trade publication, frequently publishes special sections on marketing to Hispanics.

In the entertainment world, Hispanics are important targets. Galavision, a Spanish-language cable network based in Los Angeles, supplies 24-hour service to more than 2 million Hispanic households through 300 cable systems in 12 states and the District of Columbia. Galavision offers 18 hours of news and entertainment and 6 hours of variety shows in each 24-hour segment for a primarily Mexican-American audience (Mexican-Americans constitute 64 percent of the nation's 18.8 million Hispanic population).

Hollywood sometimes runs separate Hispanic marketing campaigns for films produced primarily for English-speaking audiences. Robert Redford's *Milagro Beanfield War* was promoted with general audiences in 1988 as a quaint and pleasant story; for Hispanics, Universal Pictures promoted it as a confrontation between rich *gringos* and a poor Hispanic farmer.[13]

BLACK MEDIA: AT THE CROSSROADS

A fundamental irony is at work in the black media. Racial integration, for which many black newspapers and magazines campaigned so long, may threaten their existence.

For decades, many black newspapers lived off advertising from separate, identifiable black business communities in many cities. *Freedom's Journal* (New York City) appeared in 1827, *The North Star* (Rochester, N.Y.) in 1847. Many others followed: *Tribune* (Philadelphia, 1884), *Afro-*

American (Baltimore, 1892), *Defender* (Chicago, 1905), *Amsterdam News* (New York, 1909), *Courier* (Pittsburgh, 1910).

However, after the 1950s, when integration got under way, many small black-owned businesses failed as black consumers shifted to—and were welcomed by—white-owned businesses. Demographically, more blacks became attractive targets for advertisers outside black communities, and that created an economic need for mainstream media to expand coverage of black community news and court advertisers seeking black audiences. There was also considerable societal pressure on mainstream media to deal more fairly with blacks and other ethnic groups. The National Advisory Commission on Civil Disorders, appointed by President Lyndon B. Johnson and headed by Governor Otto Kerner of Illinois, issued a stinging indictment in 1968 of media coverage of black affairs. The Kerner Report said that because so few members of minorities were employed in the media, coverage was shallow, unfair, and often inaccurate.

But it was mostly in response to business pressures that mainstream media attitudes began changing, most dramatically in large cities. Examining black media in New York City, the *New York Times*'s Pulitzer-winning media analyst, Alex S. Jones, put it this way:

Many black publishers say with a bitter irony that it was integration in the mid-1950s that ended the golden age of black papers.

Blacks flocked to white businesses that had spurned them, and many of the small black businesses of Harlem and Brooklyn that had been advertising mainstays went broke. Some famous black papers, such as *The New York Age*, followed suit.

Of the black papers at that time, only *The Amsterdam* survived. It has prospered despite periods of financial difficulty and a circulation that is about 40,000 compared to 90,000 in the early 50s.[14]

Clearly, more New York City blacks read mainstream newspapers—particularly the *Daily News* and the *New York Post*—than any black newspaper. Only one black paper is a daily, the *New York Daily Challenge*. (Though the most prosperous, *Amsterdam News* is a weekly.) Only one other black newspaper is a daily, the *Chicago Defender*.

Black-oriented radio is strong and erodes the position of black newspapers. Discussion of social and race-related issues, long a mainstay of black newspapers, has shifted largely to "talk" radio. So has some black-oriented advertising.

The black media's future may revolve around two issues: First is whether the trend toward marketing segmentation will give new life to the black press. Perhaps, some black media executives say, this trend will attract advertisers who want to focus on black consumers. Second, and this harks back to why a black press was necessary in the first place, some black executives say that a black press will have a receptive audience as long as social injustice exists and as long as blacks need vigorous journalistic defense of their interests.

It's doubtful that the trend toward marketing segmentation will bring new advertising support to black media. The *Wall Street Journal* surveyed black advertising agencies in 1988 and concluded that advertisers were cutting back the $350 million they had targeted for black consumers (compared to $490 million for Hispanic advertising):

While advertisers commonly cite budget cuts as one reason for the slowdown, many also feel that the $200 billion black consumer market can be reached as easily through general marketing. Specialized advertising to Hispanics—a $134 billion market—is easier to justify, they argue, because of language and cultural differences.

The *Journal* quoted one major advertiser, General Foods Corp., as saying:

The fact is that black people and white people watch the same TV programs, and we can reach them the same way. But Hispanics have a different culture and speak a different language. You have to consider them a different market.[15]

Some black media executives argue there is racism in that thinking, that advertisers don't want their products identified as "black" products. Others, however, argue from a purely economic viewpoint that advertisers must approach the black consumer differently to sell goods and services. Tom Burrell, owner of Burrell Advertising, Inc., the nation's largest black-owned ad agency, argues: "A black face in an ad doesn't make it a black ad. There are cultural, historical, sociological differences. Black people are not just dark-skinned white people."[16] He adds, "We have different preferences and customs, and we require a special effort" by advertisers.[17] The *Standard Directory of Advertising Agencies* in 1988 counted 17 ad agencies making that special effort by concentrating on clients trying to target black consumers.

Historically, the black press was mission-oriented, defending black social, political, and economic rights. That spirit lives. One of the most respected black publishers, C. A. Scott of the *Atlanta World*, puts it this way:

> There will always be a need for a black newspaper in communities where there are a substantial number of black Americans. The general [white] papers cannot afford the expense to publish news of particular interest to blacks. . . . When the black reaches middle-class status, the white media do not meet his needs, especially from a political point of view. Blacks had to use what is considered racial or bloc voting to gain [their] present status . . . due to racial barriers. . . . Particularly in the South, where the one-party system has existed over a century, there is a need for sound-thinking black newspapers to pioneer in encouraging an intelligent electorate which would support the best candidate over any particular label.[18]

At that writing, Scott (whose grandfather was a slave) was 80 years old and had been *World* publisher since 1934. Like many older black journalists, he is preoccupied with the mission of black journalism. But the *World*, which became a daily in 1932, is not a huge economic success.

It now publishes only four days weekly and operates on a shoestring: Circulation ranges between 14,000 and 16,000, Scott says, and total revenue in 1986 was $583,790. Many mainstream *weeklies* have more revenue.

Competition often is strong among local black publications in cities with large black populations, reducing the advertising support any single publication can expect. That in turn makes it difficult for any black publication to afford the large staffs and modern production facilities required for high-quality journalism. In Atlanta, four black publications compete for readers and ad dollars—and all must fight the dominant *Atlanta Journal and Constitution*, with 550,000 daily circulation and well over 620,000 on Sundays. Like many general-circulation metro dailies, the *Journal and Constitution* has increased enormously its coverage of black affairs. Aside from minor neighborhood and social news, not much exclusive content is left for black newspapers.

A NEWSPAPER FOR ALL

❝ We want to publish a newspaper that oozes diversity, that gives something to the rich or the poor, the black or the white, the old or the young. ❞

Publisher Jay Smith,
Atlanta Journal and Constitution.[19]

Attempts to publish black national newspapers have failed, but that is not true for magazines. Johnson Publishing Co., with headquarters in Chicago, is highly successful, with *Ebony* and *Jet* and other black-oriented businesses, including radio. In 1989, the company had revenues of $216.5 million and was the second-largest black-owned business in the nation (No. 1 was TLC Group of New York City, a diversified general business conglomerate with $1.96 billion in sales that year).

Although Johnson Publishing magazines editorially represent a black view in public affairs (and gain much reader loyalty for doing so), the company is run primarily as a profit-oriented business, not a political instrument. *Ebony*'s circulation tops 1.7 million, and *Jet*'s is near 1 million. Demographically upscale black readers are the company's primary target. One company magazine, *Ebony Man*, is aimed at upwardly mobile black men and covers fashions, personal finance, and fitness. This is a direct assault on mainstream publications such as *Esquire* (which in 1985 estimated that 22 percent of its readers were black) and *Gentlemen's Quarterly* (which says that 17 percent of its readers are black).[20] An *Ebony* ad directed at national advertisers read:

> *Ebony* reaches and sells more Black consumers with money to spend than any other magazine. In fact, *Ebony* reaches over 55% of all U.S. Blacks earning $30,000.00 a year or more.
>
> With a readership of over 8 million monthly, *Ebony* reaches 50.2% of all Black adults, giving you a special edge in marketing your product to Blacks.

For certain, Johnson Publishing has taken its owner, John Johnson, upscale. He won't discuss personal finances, but *Forbes* magazine back in 1984 estimated his net worth at $160 million. (Johnson began his publishing company in 1942 with a $500 loan—another media success story!)

Upscale drive characterizes another successful black monthly, *Black Enterprise*. The magazine, published in New York City by Earl G. Graves Publishing Co., Inc., subtitles itself "Black America's Guidebook for Success." Articles on personal finance, business strategies, and entrepreneurship are designed for middle- and upper-income blacks—and that can conflict with what some readers feel should be the mission of a black magazine. One reader wrote *Black Enterprise*:

> Although I read your magazine and find it very interesting, there is one thing that disturbs me. As is the case with all black publications, it seems to be geared toward the black upper-middle class, that is, those people with good jobs, successful careers and, especially since *Black Enterprise* is a business magazine, money to throw around.

Magazines and newspapers aimed at black audiences compete on newsstands with publications of all sorts. *Wide World Photos.*

> I'm sure *BE* is aware that there is a very large portion of blacks who are working for minimum wage and barely making ends meet. When are black publications going to concentrate less on catering to affluent readers and start focusing on those who are not as fortunate?[21]

The dilemma for black publications is just that: Should they respond to marketplace realities and strive for upscale readers attractive to advertisers, like most media, black or white? Or should they retain the mission-oriented approach to black affairs that characterized black journalism in the beginning?

In television, mainstream networks and stations all but preempt any special market niche black-oriented stations might carve out. Almost no TV stations are exclusively black-formatted. As in print, advertisers prefer to use mainstream media and programming to reach both black and white consumers simultaneously. Bozell Inc., a consulting firm, in 1989 released a study based on A. C. Nielsen data showing that blacks watch an average of 44 percent more TV than white audiences and that standard network (not cable) programming was most popular. CBS estimated that blacks made up 18 percent of TV's total prime-time audience in 1986—not a large enough segment to entice programmers into producing exclusively black-oriented entertainment. CBS says it's "foolhardy" to broadcast programming for any audience segment that represents less than 30 percent of total viewers. Consequently, only 10 percent of all ad dollars spent to reach black audiences goes to TV, according to one estimate.[22]

TV entertainment featuring black stars— NBC's "Cosby Show" and CBS's "Frank's Place," for example—are neither written to address black-oriented issues nor aired primarily for black audiences. From every perspective— program content, appeal to advertisers—those hit shows are designed for wide audiences, regardless of race. However, some TV analysts do detect special efforts to woo black audiences through programming that features black actors and social issues of particular interest to blacks— sitcoms with all-black casts that deal with racial themes, for example. Clearly, the motive is profit.

THE COLOR IS GREEN

66 In an average week, black viewers watch nearly 50 percent more television than the rest of the population. What's more, black households tend to be slower to purchase VCRs and be wired for cable, the two technologies that most threaten the networks' franchise. No wonder the TV industry is finally wooing black audiences. They've come to embody its favorite color, which is, of course, green. 99

Newsweek, in 1988.[23]

In radio, there is more black-oriented programming. But again, mainstream stations design formats often successful at crossing racial lines and preempting much of the audience black stations might otherwise pick up. Of 10,038 radio stations on the air in 1988, only 211 had "black" formats. One network, National Black Network, links nearly 100 AM and FM affiliates in 26 states and the District of Columbia, providing programming and national advertising.

What about the racial, ethnic, and gender makeup of management teams and newsroom staffs that run mainstream media? How does that affect policymaking in general-circulation newspapers, magazines, and broadcasting?

MINORITIES AND WOMEN AT WORK IN THE MAINSTREAM MEDIA

If numbers tell a tale, the story of minority and female employment in mainstream media is dismal. Minorities, who make up 21 percent of the total U.S. work force, held 16 percent of all newspaper jobs in 1988—and only 7.54 percent of newsroom professional jobs (reporters, editors, etc.). Women, 47 percent of the work force, had 43 percent of newspaper jobs—but only 13.8 percent of jobs as directing editors (who make newsroom policy). ▶ 2 Just 79 of 1,645 U.S. daily newspapers had female publishers.

2 Newspaper Employment
(in thousands)

Year	Total Employment	Men	Women
1960	325.2	260.0	65.2
1965	345.4	269.5	75.9
1970	373.0	275.3	97.7
1975	376.8	257.3	119.5
1980	419.9	262.3	157.6
1985	450.5	266.5	184.0
1986	457.5	266.8	190.7
1987	462.2	265.2	197.0
1988	477.8	272.5	205.3

Source: U.S. Bureau of Labor Statistics.

In television, just 13 percent of the newsroom force was black. News directors at network-affiliated stations were 9 percent female; at independent stations, 41 percent. In radio, 27 percent of news directors were female.[24]

A five-year study by the University of Missouri, funded by the Gannett Foundation and released in 1989, stated the position of women this way: They account for 53 percent of the nation's population but hold only 6 percent of top management jobs in the media and earn only 92 cents for each dollar earned by male counterparts in the same top jobs. The report said, "Women begin their climb up the ladder in sufficient numbers, but many forces combine to knock them off." The report pointed to biases in salaries and promotions and a tendency of employers to assign women to dead-end jobs, as support staffers and not decision makers.

Trends for blacks are especially discouraging. Black representation in TV news was *down* to 13 percent from 15 percent in 1979, and although blacks win good jobs as on-camera talent, their total numbers in TV—particularly in management—are not near their representation in the U.S. population or the work force.

In 1988, two decades after the Kerner Commission condemned minority hiring practices, the American Newspaper Publishers Association found that only 38 percent of 546 newspapers responding in a survey had an "active voluntary affirmative action program." More than 55 percent of all newspapers have *no* minority journalists.

IT'S NOT A NEW PROBLEM

66 Along with the country as a whole, the press has too long basked in a white world, looking out of it, if at all, with white men's eyes and a white perspective. That is no longer good enough. 99

National Advisory Commission on Civil Disorders (the Kerner Commission), 1968.

And if schools of journalism and mass communication constitute a "pipeline" of future media employees, the picture for minorities isn't going to brighten soon. In 1987, just 10 percent of journalism and mass communications graduates were minorities—a percentage unchanged for three years. A little over 5 percent of journalism faculty members were minorities. For women, the picture is somewhat brighter. In some schools, 50 percent or more of enrollments in the late 1980s were females. About 20 percent of full-time faculty members were women in 1987, double the figure of a decade earlier.

Two issues come out of these numbers. First, they testify to great social inequity. An industry that considers itself the watchdog of society does not meet society's expectations in hiring and promoting minorities and women. Second, how do ethnic and gender makeup of the media work force affect news coverage and the media's social responsibility to serve all sectors of our society? Despite best efforts, can white male news strategists truly anticipate news trends important to women, blacks, Hispanics, American Indians? Al Neuharth, then chairman of Gannett Co. and a principal architect of its growth to a $3 billion communications conglomerate, stated bluntly: "Promoting and practicing equal opportunity is not only the right thing to do, . . . it's the smart thing to do. . . . No newspaper can cover all the community unless it employs all of the community."[25]

At Gannett, Neuharth engineered the industry's most successful program of hiring women and minorities and promoting them to well-paid positions of responsibility. In 1988, fully 24.5 percent of all Gannett publishers were women; 8 percent were minorities. Both figures were far above industry averages.[26]

In news coverage, Gannett pursues nondiscrimination policies with a practice called "mainstreaming." This requires reporters to seek comments from minorities on major news stories—and not just those dealing with minority issues.

The business sense in Gannett's policy is clear. Nancy Woodhull, president of the company's research and development unit, says, "The biggest growth potential of newspapers isn't in expanding their circulation area. It's in reaching more groups of people, including women."[27]

For example, Gannett sees a growth oppor-

Left: It's not a "man's world" at Gannett's *USA Today*—39 percent of the readers and many of its editors are women. Cathleen Black is publisher. *Gannett Co. Inc. Used with permission.*

Right: Within three years of graduation from college, Durmeriss Cruver-Smith was married, became a mother, and won promotion to assistant features editor of Gannett's *Cincinnati Enquirer*, 200,000 daily circulation, 300,000 on Sundays.

tunity in the fact that just 39 percent of *USA Today*'s readers are women. Gannett's top executives, mostly male when the paper was launched in 1982, created content heavily skewed toward male interests. By a wide margin, the sports section—traditionally aimed at males—was *USA Today*'s most popular feature. Later, when more women were promoted to executive positions, *USA Today* took on a tone more attractive to women. Obviously, however, with a 61 percent male readership, Gannett hasn't yet exploited potential female readers.

Social equity aside, such compelling business reasons will probably be most effective in persuading the American mass media to build staffs more representative of the communities they serve and to direct more resources toward pulling in ethnic and minority readers and viewers. Because Gannett's top managers are convinced of the business need for strong steps, the entire company is energized. Executives scout minority and female recruits from universities and smaller newspapers and TV stations. Recruiting of minorities is so intense that black publishers complain they cannot pay competitive salaries and thus lose promising reporters and

editors to mainstream media. Gannett also makes affirmative action in hiring and promotion one standard by which publishers and other executives are judged. Failing to succeed can cost a Gannett publisher heavily at bonus time. Clearly, however, affirmative action got under way in the media, as in much of American society, only because of direct social pressure. The 1964 Civil Rights Act, under Title 7, created a federal body, the Equal Employment Opportunity Commission (EEOC), to investigate charges of discrimination based on color, race, sex, religion, national origin, or age. It requires all businesses to avoid discrimination and to take affirmative action to ensure that terms and conditions of employment are nondiscriminatory. In broadcasting, the FCC encourages female and minority ownership, but with limited results. In 1988, just 3 percent of all broadcast stations were owned by women or minorities (up from 1 percent in 1978, when legislation granted tax breaks and other concessions to station owners who sold to women and minorities).

Women and minorities themselves exert enormous pressure on the media. Sex and race discrimination suits have been filed against some of the nation's largest media companies—*New York Times*, Associated Press, *Washington Post, Newsday, Detroit News, Atlanta Journal and Constitution*, among others. The National Association of Black Journalists has for years been a vocal pressure group. In broadcast, the National Black Media Coalition has threatened challenges against licenses of broadcast stations at renewal time. In general, however, achieving fairness for minorities and women remains a major challenge facing the media in the next decade.

Let's now turn our survey of the American mass communications system in another direction and look at the research industry.

☆ SUMMARY

Ethnic media are both distinctive in their marketplace niche and awash in change. Mainstream general-circulation media must serve broadly homogeneous audiences, which traditionally has given ethnic media the opportunity to serve immigrants who don't read English. However, most immigrants are quickly assimilated into the American mainstream, limiting the life span of ethnic publications.

Many ethnic media are changing their sense of mission from defending immigrant rights and old-country ways to seeking the economic reward of delivering special-interest readers to advertisers.

Hispanic media attract advertiser interest because of projections that Hispanics will be America's largest ethnic group in the 21st century. Because many Hispanics only recently arrived in America, Spanish is the language of many publications and broadcast stations directed at them.

Integration, for which many campaigned so long, threatens the existence of black media. Since the 1950s, many black consumers have stopped shopping exclusively in black-owned stores, and this has destroyed much of the advertising base that supported black newspapers and magazines for generations. Many advertisers now prefer to use mainstream media that will catch both black and white consumers.

New ethnic voices are being heard in Chinese, Korean, Vietnamese, and other languages of Asian nations now contributing waves of immigrants. Many publications aimed at earlier European immigrants are withering as their audiences are assimilated into the English-speaking mainstream.

A crucial challenge for mainstream media is to hire and promote more minorities and women. Minorities account for 21 percent of the total U.S. work force but have just 16 percent of all newspaper jobs. The picture in broadcast is equally dismal. Women, 47 percent of the work force, had 43 percent of newspaper jobs but few top policymaking positions.

☆ RECOMMENDED READING

For the history of ethnic media, see Michael Emery and Edwin Emery, *The Press and America*, 6th ed. (Englewood Cliffs, N.J.: Prentice-Hall, 1988). Also note Roland Wolseley, *The Black Press, USA* (Ames: Iowa State University Press, 1971) and Jonas Backlund, *A Century of the Swedish-American Press* (Chicago: Swedish-American Newspaper Co., 1952). Carl Wittke looks at once-vigorous German-language newspapers in *The Germany-Language Press in America* (Lexington: University of Kentucky Press, 1957).

Current research in minority and female hiring is available in the American Society of Newspaper Editors' *ASNE Bulletin* and the American Newspaper Publishers Association's monthly *presstime*. As a leader in minority hiring, Gannett Co. publishes much valuable research in *The Gannetter*, its in-house magazine. Substantial research on the hiring of women, conducted by Dorothy Jurney and Jean Gaddy Wilson, is available through the National Federation of Press Women and the *ASNE Bulletin*.

Understanding and Addressing Media Audiences

Diversity is a two-edged sword for the media. As we have seen, the media themselves are incredibly diverse. And the audiences they serve are also diverse and equally complex.

Without precise and scientific research, understanding the media or their role in our society is impossible. So in this chapter, we will look first at how media companies use research internally to guide day-to-day operations and long-term planning and how they use it in the marketplaces they serve. Without research, the media would be unable to locate, understand, and address with any precision the audiences they seek.

We'll also look at scholarly research being conducted into media impact on society. In just a few decades, this area of research has exploded in importance.

Note as we proceed that rewarding media careers await men and women skilled in research techniques. More than ever, leading media companies are using highly scientific research in charting future operations.

BROAD GOALS OF MEDIA RESEARCH

Many communications companies reach across the nation—even around the world—with enormous power. Their handling of information, entertainment, and advertising helps decide what is news and what isn't, what the next clothing fad or hairstyle will be, who gets elected and who doesn't, which stock prices rise and which fall. Billions of dollars pass through the hands of influential men and women who run those companies.

Indeed, the entire American free enterprise mass communications structure depends on one proposition: Day in and day out, the mass media must please two constituencies, information and entertainment *consumers* (you, me, and millions like us) and *advertisers* who provide economic support for the media (in return for access to you, me, and those millions of others).

In simpler times, media managers learned

quickly and directly whether they were pleasing their constituencies. A small-town editor could stroll Main Street and by counting frowns and smiles learn whether that week's editorials were well received. (Some even were horsewhipped or challenged to duels—proof that the paper was being read, if not wholly appreciated.) Advertisers signaled their feelings by either buying or not buying ads.

Today, however, media managers don't know everyone in their audiences. They deal anonymously and from a distance with huge, sometimes global audiences whose moods shift rapidly. The stakes for accurately judging those shifts have risen dramatically. Billions of dollars are in the balance as editors and media managers try to gauge what people are thinking "out there." The rising number of competitors in every media sector increases pressure on editors and managers to understand public opinion.

Enter the media researcher, a relatively new but important member of the management team in mass communications. For many, research is an exciting career.

THE THRILL OF RESEARCH

66 I found that research was much like the highest type of investigative reporting: Define a problem or question, then dissect it, get as many facts as possible, and then draw conclusions based on who would be affected by the problem and its possible solutions. . . .

You become a bloodhound. You scent the blood and go for the jugular. It's the same in marketing research. I think that's why I really get excited by it.

The thought of researching and investigating the problems of an important industry, such as newspapers, and finding solutions is exhilarating. . . . You can affect society by affecting how well the newspaper does its job of informing the public. 99

Laura Wilkinson,
research director for Knight-Ridder's
Macon (Ga.) Telegraph and News.[1]

The researcher's job is to judge scientifically the desires of media consumers and advertisers, to remove as much guesswork as possible from publishing and broadcasting. Researchers with many specialties are hired by the media but, broadly, their effort has two main goals. One is to assist internal adjustments by editors and marketing experts in constructing newspaper and magazine content and radio and TV programming that will draw readers, viewers, and listeners. Filmmakers, book publishers, and others in mass communications also seek to ascertain public desires and then construct "products" that meet those desires.

The second goal is to develop research that can be used externally. Research is used to persuade advertisers, for example, that one medium is superior to another for distribution of a commercial message. Research is also used to convince readers, viewers, or listeners that one medium, not another, best meets their needs and desires. In this research, media examine themselves and their ability to perform. The results are then formatted in sales brochures or self-advertising promotion.

HOW MANAGERS USE RESEARCH

by Edmund Olson, President and Publisher, *Macon (Ga.) Telegraph and News*

As publisher of the *Macon Telegraph and News*, I depend on research data to help me make informed decisions. This data is also made available to our editors and managers.

In the newsroom, research plays a substantial role in the decision-making process, particularly in terms of evaluating the interests and preferences of readers.

We always have to remember that reporting the news involves a good deal more than printing what the reader is interested in. Many stories that the reader needs to know about would not fit into the high-interest category. Still, as we allocate our resources, we would be shortsighted if we did not pay attention to the way our readers spend their time, what they like to know about, and what they spend their free time doing. We also need to know who our readers are and who we want our readers to be. This kind of information can come from well-planned and well-executed research.

Our advertising division uses data to sell our newspaper against the multitude of competitive choices available to an advertiser. We provide to our advertisers not only readership data but also demographics, shopping patterns, consumer preferences, and other information they can use to make strategic plans as well as media choices.

Our circulation division uses research to track customer satisfaction and to determine target areas for solicitation.

Recently, our marketing committee and various interdivisional task forces have used research data to develop new products and search for new ways to meet our customers' needs. Because of these successes, I see an even greater emphasis on research in the future.

Research into public and consumer attitudes is a major industry. In-person interviews are one widely used method. *Courtesy Burson-Marsteller.*

Some feedback editors and managers receive is audience-generated and qualitative. That includes, for example, a viewer telephoning a station with complaints about a program. Though important, audience-generated feedback is random and nonscientific and doesn't provide reliable statistical evidence. People who write letters to editors or telephone TV stations are rarely representative of the larger audience and are generally expressing personal opinions.

Most media companies therefore rely on quantitative research that they or outside research companies initiate. This involves scientific selection of a representative sample of the relevant population to be measured. This could be 1,000 of a newspaper's local readers (or nonreaders), for example, or a selection of TV watchers nationwide to be surveyed on, say reader or viewer recall of commercial messages.

The question of advertising recall is controversial. Newspaper executives argue that TV commercials drop quickly from viewers' consciousness. TV executives argue that the sight-and-sound combination of television ensures commercials are remembered better than print ads.

A link does seem to exist between ad aware-

ness and sales of products advertised. SRI Research Center, Lincoln, Nebraska, reported that with one exception, the 10 advertisers with the "highest cumulative unaided recall" for their ads in 1987 also were market leaders in product sales. SRI asked 1,000 persons, of all the advertising they had encountered in the previous 30 days, which came to mind first. First-mentioned were Coca-Cola, McDonald's, California raisins, Budweiser/Bud Light, Miller/Miller Lite, Ford, Chevrolet, Chrysler, and Bartles & Jaymes. All but Bartles & Jaymes were number one sellers in their product category.[2]

Research is conflicting on whether people remember more or fewer advertisements than in past years. Video Story Board Tests Inc. says that people find it increasingly difficult to remember TV commercials they consider special. In 1982, the research firm says, people on average singled out 1.7 commercials they liked; in 1987, the average dropped to 1.2 (says Video President David Vadehra, "People believe more and more that all brands are basically the same, so they figure, 'Why watch commercials?'").[3] SRI Research reported that in 1987, fully 32.3 percent of those polled were unable to name a specific ad when asked to recall the first that came to mind—an improvement over the 49.8 percent who drew a blank a year earlier.[4]

STEPS IN THE RESEARCH PROCESS

Major media companies carefully plan and execute their research. Let's examine the steps involved in market research by a metropolitan newspaper (remembering that the process is ap-

plicable to other forms of mass communications research; see Figure 13.1).

First, management decides that research must be initiated for short-range or long-range planning. That could involve, for example, looking into what journalistic changes readers desire over, say, the next 12 months or how the newspaper should be positioned to meet expected reader desires five years ahead. Or management could call for research on, say, the basic economic strength of the newspaper's market plus the age, income, education, and other demographic characteristics of readers. This data is used to convince advertisers that they should use the newspaper to reach potential customers. Many mass media regularly conduct such research every few years, often through outside firms under the guidance of an employee who is a research specialist.

Second, management decides which data to seek, which questions to ask, and, generally,

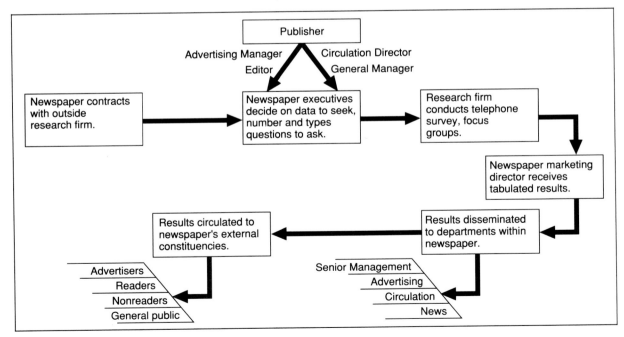

Figure 13.1. MARKET RESEARCH PROCESS AT A METROPOLITAN NEWSPAPER. Note that each key department participates in formulating research plans and shares in feedback. *Source:* Adapted from *Macon* (Ga.) *Telegraph and News.*

what the research must accomplish. At a metropolitan paper, the publisher, the advertising and circulation directors, and the editor and general manager are often involved in this.

Third, research is conducted through telephone surveys, one-on-one interviews (slow and expensive), or mail surveys (less reliable). Sometimes, focus groups are used. Persons drawn from the relevant population meet for in-depth discussions of, for example, the newspaper's news coverage or its editorial page. Focus groups sometimes meet with editors or other executives, but best results are obtained by trained interviewers skilled in drawing out discussion and representative responses to questions. Obviously, key in research is to draw truly representative samples and to construct questionnaires or employ interview techniques that provide reliable feedback. Researchers often strive for triangulation, which means using more than one measurement on the same subject to obtain more valid results. For example, a focus group might be employed to refine the direction of research and questions to be asked. Then mail questionnaires, telephone surveys, or in-depth personal interviews could be used as well.

Fourth, research results are received by the newspaper's marketing director and prepared for distribution.

Fifth, private or proprietary results go to departments where operational decisions are made. These include advertising, circulation, and news. Each must respond appropriately to the research data. For example, editors must improve coverage if a survey reports, say, reader discontent with sports coverage or business news.

Sixth, results also are circulated publicly to the newspaper's external constituencies—advertisers, readers, nonreaders, and the general public. Next time you see a newspaper use a billboard, or a "house ad" in its own pages, to announce, "We're Number One!" you will be looking at research data formatted for promotional purposes. And when you hear your favorite station announce, "Our News at Eleven is tops in our town," you will be hearing research used by the station's promotion department.

An entire research industry has grown up to meet needs of the media and other industries. *Advertising Age* magazine counts more than 130 marketing, advertising, and public opinion research companies in the United States alone. The top 50 had total revenues exceeding $2.6 billion in 1988. The largest is A. C. Nielsen Co. (important in TV audience measurement). Its revenue in 1988 exceeded $880 million. The second-largest, Arbitron/SAMI/Burke (radio and TV audience measurement plus other research), had $320 million revenue.[5]

Internationally, research has become a mammoth industry. Worldwide revenue exceeds $5 billion—and as in other media-related industries, a handful of companies dominate the field. *Advertising Age* estimates that 25 of the world's largest have a 55 percent share of the research market. The reach of these research giants is wide: Gallup International of London has subsidiaries or affiliates in 46 countries; Research International of London, 20.

Much research is directed at new product testing (whether more Americans would buy toothpaste with red or green stripes) and public opinion polling, used for political and other purposes. Most research initiated by the media is designed for external use in sales.

RESEARCH DESIGNED TO BOOST SALES

The media use sales-oriented research to reach advertisers with four basic themes. The first is that a market exists for the advertisers' products or services. Newspapers and TV stations use research to delineate their geographic markets and the demographic characteristics of readers or viewers, such as income, education, and age. Sophisticated research reports on reader and viewer psychographic characteristics—the values and attitudes by which they live and, presumably, make decisions on which media to use and which products to buy.

Second, extensive research is conducted to highlight market attractiveness. This involves data on retail sales, household incomes, general economic activity—all of interest to advertisers seeking lucrative markets.

Third, the media use research to show they deliver the market—their circulation or broadcasts reach sufficient households or they reach enough demographically attractive residents to meet advertiser needs.

Fourth, research is used to demonstrate that the media generate response. Newspapers give advertisers research proving that consumers are much more likely to make a purchase based on reading an ad than seeing a commercial. TV research aims at proving that television reaches more potential purchasers and is the preferred advertising medium.

Newspaper researchers concentrate on circulation patterns in a newspaper's market—in this case, the "primary market area" of the hypothetical Anytown, Illinois, and the "retail trading zone" of White, Green, Red, and Blue counties surrounding the city. *Courtesy Audit Bureau of Circulations.*

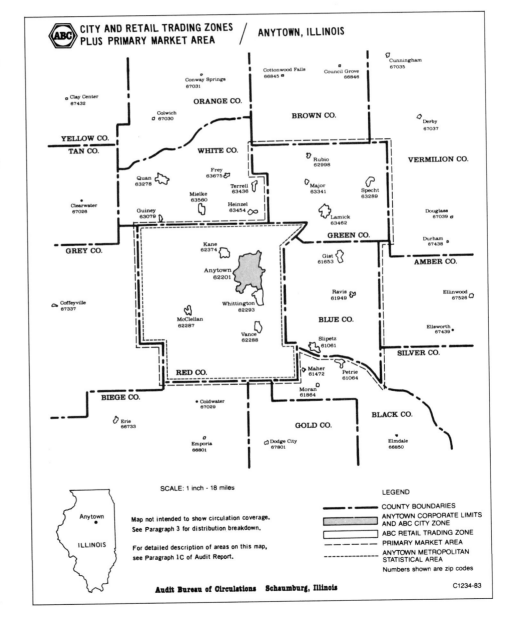

The *St. Petersburg* (Fla.) *Times and Independent* issued a 116-page research report titled "Suncoast '86: Golden Marketing Opportunities on Florida's Gulf Coast." It describes the market in attractive terms ("Florida's most prosperous, most populous marketplace") to entice business to the area and boost the *Times* as the mass medium most capable of serving advertisers ("Suc-

cessful advertisers found the *Times* . . . their best investment ever").

Magazine Publishers Association research demonstrates the "pull" of magazines; television and radio research shows the enormous importance of broadcast to advertisers.[6]

Some communications companies purchase research firms. Dow Jones, Inc., publisher of the

AUDIT REPORT:

Audit Bureau of Circulations

THE TRIBUNE (Evening)
Anytown (Red County), Illinois

TOTAL AVERAGE PAID CIRCULATION FOR 12 MONTHS ENDED SEPTEMBER 30, 19--:

1A. TOTAL AVERAGE PAID CIRCULATION (BY INDIVIDUALS AND FOR DESIGNATED RECIPIENTS):		Evening 41,315

1B. TOTAL AVERAGE PAID CIRCULATION (BY INDIVIDUALS AND FOR DESIGNATED RECIPIENTS) BY ZONES:
(See Par. 1E for description of area)

CITY ZONE

	Population	Occupied Households
1980 Census:	80,109	29,143
#12-31-87 Estimate:	80,500	30,000

Carrier Delivery office collect system, See Pars. 11(b) & (c).....	1,875
Carriers not filing lists with publisher......................	18,649
Single Copy Sales......................................	2,168
Mail Subscriptions.....................................	47
School-Single Copy/Subscriptions, See Par. 11(d)	50
Employee Copies, See Par. 11(e)	100
Group (Subscriptions by Businesses for Designated Employees), See Par. 11(f)	50
TOTAL CITY ZONE	22,939

RETAIL TRADING ZONE

	Population	Occupied Households
1980 Census:	268,491	75,140
#12-31-87 Estimate	272,000	79,000

Carriers not filing lists with publisher	15,138
Single Copy Sales......................................	1,549
Mail Subscriptions	908
School-Single Copy/Subscriptions, See Par. 11(d)	25
Employee Copies, See Par. 11(e)	25
Group (Subscriptions by Businesses for Designated Employees), See Par. 11(f)	50
TOTAL RETAIL TRADING ZONE	17,695
TOTAL CITY & RETAIL TRADING ZONES	40,634

	Population	Occupied Households
1980 Census:	348,600	104,283
#12-31-87 Estimate:	352,500	109,000

ALL OTHER

Single Copy Sales & Carriers not filing lists with publisher	256
Mail Subscriptions	375
School-Single Copy/Subscriptions, See Par. 11(d)	20
Employee Copies, See Par. 11(e)	20
Group (Subscriptions by Businesses for Designated Employees), See Par. 11(f)	10
TOTAL ALL OTHER	681
TOTAL PAID CIRCULATION (BY INDIVIDUALS AND FOR DESIGNATED RECIPIENTS)	41,315

1C. THIRD PARTY (BULK) SALES:

Airlines — Available for passengers	1,000
Hotels, Motels — Available for guests	500
Restaurants — Available for patrons	500
Businesses — Available for employees...................	50
Other	600
TOTAL THIRD PARTY (BULK) SALES.....................	2,650

#S&MM Estimate. See Par. 11(a).

At a glance, advertisers can tell how much circulation the *Anytown* (Ill.) *Tribune* offers. Such research illustrates the efficiency of using a newspaper to reach consumers. *Courtesy Audit Bureau of Circulations.*

Wall Street Journal, owns a leading marketing research journal, *American Demographics*.

Research firms often specialize in data aimed at customers of the media. Standard Rate & Data Service, Inc., for example, researches publications, circulations, ad rates, and so forth and sells the results to advertising agencies that deal with newspapers. Audit Bureau of Circulations data on newspapers and Nielsen and Arbitron research in broadcast are sold to advertisers.

In the music industry, *Billboard* magazine surveys radio stations weekly on which records are being played the most. Each week, *Variety* and Standard Data Corp. research which films are tops at the box office.

Television and filmmaking research what is likely to please the public. This is called concept testing when surveys gauge audience reaction to brief sketches of proposed programs. Respondents are asked whether they would like to see a TV series on, say, two female cops doing undercover work or a couple of construction workers in a large city. In pilot testing, samples of viewers are shown a program already produced and are asked to indicate whether they would like a TV series along similar lines. Paramount tailored the conclusion of its hit film *Fatal Attraction* in response to similar research.

Another media sector where research activity is booming is the newsroom.

RESEARCH AND THE REPORTER

It was a journalistic exposé that delighted investigative reporters: The *Atlanta Journal and Constitution* revealed a pattern of discrimination against blacks applying for home mortgages from Atlanta banks. The public outcry was enormous. Banks changed policies. Things improved overnight for black homeowners. The story won a Pulitzer prize in 1989. And it all resulted from a new strategy in the *Journal and Constitution* newsroom: employing experts in statistical research to provide computerized data searches and analysis for reporters.

Dwight L. Morris, assistant managing editor for special projects, ran records from more than 100,000 home loans through computers and provided facts for articles that never would have been possible in precomputer days.

In a similar manner, *Seattle Times* reporters used computers to reveal patterns in police searches for a vicious killer. The *Providence (R.I.) Journal-Bulletin* used computers to search prison release records and found that dangerous criminals had been set free illegally. Other reporters use computers to hunt down patterns in plane crashes, to search Internal Revenue Service records, and to build a research base for hard-hitting, factual stories.

Research specialists provide reporters with a wealth of background detail that would have been prohibitively time-consuming and costly just a few years ago.[7] This new breed of researcher often enters news work from a nonjournalistic background. The *Journal and Constitution*'s Morris, for example, is a political science graduate who has a master's degree in political science. He worked as a researcher for the *New York Times* and Opinion Research Corp. before moving to Atlanta.

"Computer-assisted journalism is the new future of this business," says Morris. "We must use the powers of computers to tap into the myriad databases that are out there and, when they aren't there, build them."[8] Elliot G. Jaspin, who built the *Providence Journal-Bulletin*'s database, says, "I can do in a slow morning what it would take a small army of reporters to do in a year."[9]

Computerized databanks are big business for some organizations. Mead Data Central of Dayton, Ohio, sells a Nexis service of full texts or abstracts from 15 newspapers, including the *New York Times* and the *Washington Post*, and more than 30 specialty magazines plus major news services and many newsletters. Knight-Ridder offers the resources of more than 35 newspapers, the Associated Press, an encyclopedia, and other databases through its Vu/Text Information Services Inc. Dow Jones offers the *Wall Street Journal* and other news resources through a retrieval system.

Knight-Ridder QuickPolls involve preselected groups of readers who agree to be surveyed four or five times annually, giving editors regular and fast feedback on issues in the news.

Much public opinion polling, done by firms such as the Gallup Organization, quickly finds its way into news reporting. In election years, many newspapers and TV networks conduct their own opinion polls.

But serious questions are raised by the media's increasing ability to conduct precision research.

ISSUES AND CHALLENGES

Should newspaper and magazine editors run stories on what surveys show readers *want* or stories on what experienced editors think they *need* to know? Should TV newsrooms cater to popular fancy and run warm, comfortable stories to build ratings or dig deeply into important but disturbing and less popular stories, even if ratings suffer?

Such questions arise, interestingly, because the media have become so sophisticated in using computers to research reader and viewer wants and then construct news products to satisfy them. It is an example of new technology and advanced methods raising new ethical questions. It divides some journalists into two camps.

One camp says that journalists experienced in news and watchful of what is important should decide what is news and serve it straight, without fancy dressing or attempts to cater to current public tastes. The other camp says that the media, as businesses, must serve the public what it wants and that new research techniques and computers can assist in that.

A more reasonable position is between those extremes: Yes, news media are businesses that must keep customers happy, but responsible editors must at times serve up unpalatable news because it is important.

Other issues crop up. Exit polling during elections is criticized as an invasion of voting privacy and interference in the democratic process.

In the 1988 presidential election, voters were interviewed after leaving polls in the East, and TV networks used computerized projections to name George Bush the winner long before West Coast voters finished balloting. Despite demands that such projections be withheld, the media will use even faster research methods in the future.

Some editors feel that public opinion research is often fed to the media in misleading fashion. Political pollsters, for example, sometimes put a special spin on research to further the cause of candidates employing them. This tactic led John Seigenthaler, publisher of the *Nashville Tennessean* and editorial director of *USA Today*, to comment:

> Every one of those consultants is looking for some unsuspecting reporter who can be sold a bill of polling goods that will make the pollster's candidate look better than he or she really is. . . . Polls, to coin a phrase, don't lie but liars poll.[10]

Obviously, the media must employ editors wise in the ways of computers, research—and pollsters.

Another problem is wildly inconsistent results research sometimes delivers. In 1987, for example, two nationally known research companies reported adult readership of *TV Guide* at 43.2 million and 46.8 million; *Reader's Digest*'s numbers were 37.5 million and 50.9 million. Wide disparities appear in broadcast research too—and the effect is to erode confidence in all research.[11]

Crucial research on the media as businesses comes from Wall Street analysts who monitor the financial fortunes of publicly owned companies. Brokerage and investment firms employ experienced analysts (usually MBAs with a media background) to spot developments important to investors. Analysts, for example, monitor advertising trends, then issue buy or sell recommendations for a media company's stock based on a projection of its business prospects. Brokerage firms issue highly detailed studies of companies that are valuable sources of information for students of the media.

ACADEMIC RESEARCH IN MASS COMMUNICATIONS

For decades, there has been nagging concern that the media are too powerful in their influence on daily life. They are sometimes feared as negative influences. Distorted use of the media, as in wartime propaganda, heightens the concern.

Responding to such concerns, American academics in the 1930s began serious media research. By the 1950s, a new area of scientific investigation was established for researchers from various scholarly disciplines, including sociology, psychology, and the other behavioral sciences. Today, much of this research is in schools of journalism and mass communications.

Researchers often concentrate on specific questions:

◆ What people and institutions initiate mass communications? What are their backgrounds, values, beliefs, motives? Those who decide what news will be printed or broadcast often are called "gatekeepers."
◆ How does information spread, and how effective are the various media in spreading it? A big quarrel between the print and broadcast media, of course, is which method of "information diffusion" is more effective at communicating news and advertising.
◆ What is the effect on the audience of what is printed and broadcast? A great body of research is being built on TV and the impact of its graphic scenes of violence and sex.

Researchers analyze media content, survey listener and reader opinions, conduct field studies (observing gatekeepers as they decide which stories to use, for example), and conduct experiments in such things as audience perceptions of news. The goal is empirical evidence drawn scientifically and objectively from observable fact rather than subjective opinion. The process usually starts with a hypothesis—say, that lurid rock lyrics cause sexual promiscuity among teenagers. Research is then designed; surveys and questionnaires are planned and implemented. Through careful analysis of results, the researcher arrives at conclusions. Perhaps there is a null hypothesis, or no relationship between the elements in question (rock does not cause sexual promiscuity). Perhaps causality is determined (rock music does cause promiscuity).

Unfortunately, many media companies have limited ties with journalism schools and their research. Most companies conduct their own research or join in supporting industry research. The American Society of Newspaper Editors, for example, financed excellent readership studies and didn't involve university scholars. Important research in ethics, technology, and management is done off-campus by the Gannett Center for Media Studies in New York City and the Poynter Institute in St. Petersburg, Florida. Everette E. Dennis, executive director of the Gannett Center and a former journalism dean, explains that most journalism schools

are so busy educating students that they have little time to be media critics or analysts. Also, through the years, the research coming out of the journalism schools has been quite uneven and has rarely bridged the gap between the academy and the profession. We are trying to do just that: Our work here is neither the self-serving kind of research that an industry organization would do, nor is it the more abstract work of the ivory-tower scholar.[12]

On campus or off, research opens exciting careers. Compared to other research in, say, medicine or science, research in mass communications is still a young, wide-open field.

☆ SUMMARY

The American free enterprise mass communications structure rests on the ability of editors and media managers to please consumers of news and entertainment, and advertisers who provide crucial economic support. In bygone times, editors could stroll Main Street and determine whether they were pleasing those two important constituencies. Today, media managers deal anonymously with huge, sometimes global audiences whose moods shift rapidly.

Thus research has become a primary tool in analyzing public desires. Internal use permits editors, filmmakers, and book publishers to construct products that meet those desires. Research is used externally in media sales to convince advertisers to use one medium over another.

Audience-generated and qualitative feedback, such as letters to the editor, is valuable. But it is unscientific, rarely representative of public opinion. So media managers prefer quantitative research based on objective methodology in their planning.

Research techniques—and computers—assist investigative reporters. Many newsrooms employ research specialists.

At issue is whether the media should respond to public likes and dislikes, as revealed in research, rather than exercising professional judgment on what is important news and what isn't. The media are businesses that must please customers. But they must also offer important news, even if it is unpalatable to the public.

Academic research in mass communications combines many scholarly disciplines, including sociology, psychology, and the other behavioral sciences. Much research concentrates on communicators (who initiate mass communication in our society), the message (how to communicate effectively and what is being communicated), the channel (the media themselves, particularly TV), and the audience (who receives a message and its effect on them).

☆ RECOMMENDED READING

Scholarly research into media subjects is available in *Journalism Monographs, Journalism Quarterly, Journal of Communication, Communication Research, Critical Studies in Mass Communication, Communication*, and *Communication Quarterly*.

Trade journals such as *presstime, Advertising Age*, and *Broadcasting* often have first word of new research conducted by trade associations, such as the American Newspaper Publishers Association, the American Society of Newspaper Editors, the Magazine Publishers Association, and the Radio-TV News Directors Association.

For an introduction to research methods, see Roger D. Wimmer and Joseph R. Dominick, *Mass Media Research* (Belmont, Calif.: Wadsworth, 1987) and Frederick Williams, *The New Communications* (Belmont, Calif.: Wadsworth, 1983).

THE ADVERTISING COMMUNICATORS

Archaeologists tell us that as far back as 3000 B.C. or so, an ointment dealer in Babylonia used clay tablets to advertise his wares.

Well, as they say in advertising, we've moved a lot of ointment since 3000 B.C.—and advertising has been part of the process every step of the way.

Some advertising is for good purpose, some for evil (they advertised rewards for runaway slaves in ancient Egypt). Some is effective, some isn't. Some advertising informs us, some misinforms us, and some irritates us. Some fulfills a useful social function, creating consumer demand that helps turn the wheels of our consumer-oriented economy; some only stirs materialistic graspings for goods and services we really don't need.

Measured in dollars, advertising's impact on our society is enormous. About $118.4 billion was spent on advertising in 1988 alone.[1]

Measured in visibility, the ad industry is all around us—beckoning from nearly every page of our newspapers and magazines, sandwiching commercials between our favorite tunes on the radio, lying in wait for us before and after and throughout our TV programs, waving from the sides of buses, billboards, matchbooks: "Try this . . . buy that . . . you'll like this . . . our product is better than theirs." Man, woman, or child, if you read, listen, or look, you can't escape the American advertising industry.

Yet we've grown so accustomed to being the target of this multibillion-dollar industry that although we daily see and hear its product—ads and commercials—we don't often give much thought to the industry itself. We are being bombarded, but few of us ever think about who is shooting or with what motives. We could go happily through life never knowing, but not if we want to understand how the American mass media system works. Because, as we have seen throughout our survey, advertising is the economic force behind our mass media.

So we turn, here in Part V, Chapter 14, to the American advertising industry, what drives it, who runs it, and where it is headed. In Chapter 15, we'll go inside America's oldest ad agency, N. W. Ayer, for a look at how it is structured and operated.

The American Advertising Industry

Make no mistake, that little old lady who hoarsely shouted "Where's the beef?" in the TV commercial was intended to do a lot more than deliver a memorable line. Behind her performance were highly talented, well-paid writers. A large and expensive production crew carefully rehearsed that commercial before shooting it. A major organization and creative effort was made by the ad agency that put it all together. A significant financial and image commitment was made by Wendy's in deciding on that commercial, at that time, at that cost. For TV networks and stations that ran the commercial, ad revenue poured in. From actress salary to production costs to buying TV time, millions of dollars changed hands. And the entire object was to sell hamburgers. We, the targets of that commercial, were supposed to come away with new hunger for Wendy's hamburgers (and not those of anybody else).

So let's begin with an understanding: Yes, this is an exciting industry responsible for more than $118 billion in annual spending; yes, it is filled with interesting, highly creative people; yes, those commercials and ads truly are a new art form, and some indeed do become part of the American idiom. (Presidential candidate Walter Mondale even used "Where's the beef?" in a 1984 debate with Ronald Reagan over his administration's policies.) But the bottom line is that this is an industry out to persuade, dedicated to selling—to pushing goods, products, services, personalities, ideas, images, policies, and ideologies.

As you survey fascinating careers advertising offers, keep that essential mission—selling—in mind. Not everyone does. Many discussions of advertising avoid direct reference to the "*s* word." For some, advertising is not a commercial enterprise, it's art or presentation or promotion. Note, for example, a widely accepted definition of advertising drawn up by the American Marketing Association: "Advertising is any paid form of nonpersonal presentation and promotion of ideas, goods, or services by an identified sponsor." David Ogilvy, one of the most famous admen of all time, casts his vote for advertising that sells: "Every 10 or 15 years, advertising gets a disease called entertainment. It's very bad, because the people who do it have absolutely no interest in selling anything. They don't think of themselves as salesmen. They think of themselves as entertainers and geniuses."[1]

COMPLEXITIES OF THE ADVERTISING INDUSTRY

The American advertising industry is multifaceted.[2] It is legions of local newspaper, radio, and TV salespersons marching up and down Main Street in small-town America, competing with each other to sell space or airtime to Joe's Shoe Shop and the local pizza restaurant. That's the *local retail* level. The industry is also agency hotshots from the fabled fountainhead of American advertising, New York City, working up a yearlong campaign for an advertiser to use all major media—network TV and radio, national magazines and newspapers—to sell a product in thousands of stores coast to coast. That's the *national* level. ▶ 1

The aim sometimes is to sell directly to consumers (we who buy shoes and pizza) or, in trade and industrial advertising, to reach wholesalers and firms that in turn create or distribute products to consumers. At other times, the goal is to bypass the retail-wholesale structure altogether on behalf of, say, a catalog company or a shop-by-telephone firm. That's direct response advertising. Yet another variation is end product advertising, which attempts to build consumer demand that will force firms to act in a certain way (when unions advertise, "Look for the union label," they are trying to persuade you to tell clothing stores you won't buy anything but union-produced dresses or shirts; the retailer is expected to pass that pressure on to manufacturers).

Advertising, then, is a complex industry, offering careers in small towns or large cities, with local retailers or the nation's largest firms. At all levels, however, a common language is spoken. ▶ 2

Advertising is also a controversial industry. As early as 1614, England's government felt compelled to restrict the size of advertising signs protruding from buildings. Today, controversy continues to dog the industry.

BASIC ISSUES IN ADVERTISING

Advertising is part of the American fabric and is important to how our society functions. Yet Americans still debate whether it is socially useful or wasteful. Let's listen in as advertising critics and supporters discuss that and other basic issues.

Critics: *Advertising is wasteful because consumers ultimately pay for it through higher prices for goods and services they buy. Advertising has no social value.*

Supporters: Advertising provides information consumers need for intelligent choices in the marketplace. Yes, it does create consumer desire. But that stimulates mass consumption, which drives the mass production economy that ensures efficient production and the lowest possible costs under our free enterprise system.

Critics: *But much advertising doesn't deliver information. How does a TV jingle help a consumer make an intelligent decision on which soft drink to buy?*

Supporters: Well, most advertising does supply consumer information and, anyway,

1 High Points in Advertising History

c. 3000 B.C.   Ointment dealer in Babylonia uses clay tablet to advertise wares. (In ancient Egypt, papyrus is used to advertise rewards for returning runaway slaves—an early use of advertising for an evil purpose!)

c. A.D. 79   The city walls of Pompeii, destroyed this year by erupting Mount Vesuvius, carry advertisements for political candidates and eating and drinking establishments.

c. 1480   William Caxton uses Gutenberg's 40-year-old invention, movable type, to print the first known advertisement in English.

1614   In an early restriction on commercial speech, England passes a law limiting the size of signs protruding from buildings.

1625   First advertisement appears in an English newspaper.

1704   A Boston newsletter is the first in America to carry advertisement (seeking capture of a thief and return of stolen clothing).

1840s   Expanding railroads permit the widespread sale and distribution of goods, sparking the need for improved advertising.

1841   First ad agency is organized by Volney B. Palmer, who sells ads on commission for newspapers.

1869   *Rowell's American Newspaper Directory* is the first to list newspapers, ad rates, and estimated circulations for use by advertisers; N. W. Ayer & Son, Inc., is organized to buy newspaper space for ad clients.

1898   At age 18, Albert Lasker enters advertising. He would become an industry giant known for writing catchy ad slogans.

1906   Pure Food and Drug Act, enacted to protect the public health, is the first federal measure to control advertising.

1910   Association of National Advertising Managers (now Association of National Advertisers) is formed to improve the professionalism and the effectiveness of advertising.

1911   States begin adopting truth-in-advertising laws; Associated Advertising Clubs of the World (now American Advertising Federation) launches a campaign for truth in advertising with model language developed by *Printer's Ink*, a leading trade publication.

1914   Federal Trade Commission is established to monitor and regulate advertising, among other things; Audit Bureau of Circulations is set up to give advertisers reliable circulation figures.

1917   American Association of Advertising Agencies is formed; today, members place 75 percent of all national advertising.

1950   Nielsen begins measuring TV audiences, establishing national ratings on which ad rates are based.

1976   U.S. Supreme Court rules that society benefits from the free flow of commercial information as well as political ideas; however, it rules in 1979 that the First Amendment protection for commercial speech is not absolute.

1986   Price for 60 seconds of commercial time on a Super Bowl telecast passes $1 million.

1987   Introduction of controversial viewer-operated "people meters" to measure TV audiences infuriates the networks because it casts doubt on audience sizes and thus ratings-based commercial rates.

1989   Britain's WPP Group pays $864 million for America's Ogilvy Group; this record acquisition makes WPP the world's second-largest ad agency.

without advertising, the consumption-oriented American economy would falter—and with it the richest lifestyle the world has seen.

Critics: *You can't prove that advertising creates demand and mass consumption; perhaps it just shifts existing consumer demand from one product to another.*

Supporters: Something has been driving the enormous expansion of the American economy all these years; clearly, advertising has a major role in that, and we all benefit.

Critics: *Advertising creates a materialistic outlook, a "gimme, gimme" attitude, particularly among vulnerable audiences such as children. And what is the social value of creating desire to be sexually attractive or socially acceptable, as so much advertising does?*

Supporters: Whoa! That's only a fraction of what advertising does. Don't you see the social value in ads that inform mothers how to put nutritious meals on the table? Ads that spell out safety features on new autos? Ads that inform people where to get medical and legal assistance? Besides, our society puts a premium on appearing sexually attractive. Don't blame advertising.

Critics: *Well, advertising is manipulative, playing on our emotions and never really revealing all the facts. It just wants to sell us something.*

Supporters: Yes, advertising is indeed designed to sell. It is a persuasive form of communication. But free choice still remains with consumers; they aren't forced to buy. And don't forget that in ethical advertising (the only kind we support), a company puts its name on the ad and goes openly into the competitive marketplace against other products and services. You, the consumer, still make the final choice.

Critics: *We are swamped by advertising. Everywhere, we see and hear intrusive, repetitious, and sometimes offensive ads. Some are in bad taste, too.*

Supporters: There is a high degree of professionalism in much of the advertising industry, and most ads are not offensive or vulgar. Don't tar an entire industry with that brush. We operate within ethical and legal boundaries, just as reporters do. Admittedly, there is a lot of advertising out there (we call it "clutter"). So we try to make ads enjoyable and humorous—entertaining—as well as informative and persuasive. As for repetition, well, not everybody has heard "Don't leave home without it" or "Have you driven a Ford lately?" We've got to get the message to those who haven't.

Critics: *Two broader issues with enormous implications for our society bother us about advertising. First, advertising permits strong, established firms to dominate their industries because only they can afford the hugely expensive ad campaigns necessary today to be number one. Second, because the media depend on ad revenue, they are susceptible to advertiser influence over their news and editorial decisions.*

Supporters: First, don't you see that advertising makes it possible for new, relatively weak firms to enter the competitive marketplace? How do you suppose Apple was able to challenge IBM? What gave Chrysler renewed vigor against its entrenched competitors, GM and Ford? *Advertising.* Second, there is a need to guard against advertiser pressure on the media. But don't forget that the economic independence the media gain through advertising revenue ensures their journalistic independence from government or special-interest groups on which the media would otherwise have to depend for financial support. Media in totalitarian countries face no advertiser

2 ▶ The Language of Advertising

Certain advertising terms are commonly used not only in the ad industry but in all the media as well.

Account executive—Employee of a newspaper, magazine, broadcast station, or ad agency who works directly with the client and whose primary mission is sales.

Adjacency—In TV, the program or time period immediately preceding or following a program; in print, a space next to news content.

Advertorial—Ad promoting an idea or a political position rather than a product or a service, often designed to look like a news story.

Area of dominant influence (ADI)—All counties in which home market TV stations receive a preponderance of viewing; the market that TV stations offer advertisers.

Audience share—Number or percentage of all TV households tuned to a particular station or program at a given time.

Availability ("avails")—Broadcast time available for advertiser purchase.

Bait (or bait-and-switch) ads—Unethical ads that lure consumers with products or prices that won't really be offered, in the hope of switching them to higher-priced products.

Barter—Exchange of ad space or time for merchandise or other noncash consideration.

Benefit advertising—Emphasizing a product's benefit rather than its physical attributes (showing a dog's glossy coat, for example, rather than the vitamins inserted in dog food).

Billing—Ad agency gross revenue.

Campaign—Special effort by an ad agency, for a specified time, on behalf of a client.

Circulation—audience: in TV, viewers; in outdoor advertising, number of persons with an opportunity to see a display; in print, *prime* circulation is the number of persons who pay for a publication, and *pass-along* circulation includes other, nonpaying persons who see it. Circulation *waste* is the number of persons the advertiser pays for but doesn't want (such as readers distant from a retail store).

Closing—Deadline for copy to meet production schedule.

Clutter—Competing ads or commercials that obscure, distract from, or weaken the impact of an advertising message.

Copy—Text in an ad.

Cost per thousand (CPM)—Cost of reaching 1,000 individuals or homes through a medium.

Cumes—Cumulative audience: unduplicated persons or homes reached by a specified number of ads over a certain period of time.

---

pressure, but you can bet that they print and broadcast what they are told to by the government.

Such issues will not be resolved, of course. Critics will remain convinced that there is no social value in advertising and that it is inherently wasteful. Economist John Kenneth Galbraith, for example, argues that advertising is aimed at creating an expandable desire for social acceptability, sexual attractiveness, or personal beauty because our basic physical needs—food, clothing, shelter—are finite and quickly met. Advertisers,

the reasoning goes, thus must create demand for goods—including fancier food, clothing, and shelter—that will continue to grow even after basic needs are met, or business will not expand.

THE ADVERTISER'S DILEMMA

66 I know that one-half of the money I spend on advertising is wasted. The problem is, I don't know which half. 99

Attributed to Philadelphia retailer John Wanamaker.

Designated market area (DMA)—Precise geographic area in which a station gets most viewing.

Direct marketing—Selling directly to consumers rather than through wholesalers or retailers. Uses mail, TV, and other *direct response advertising* media.

Efficiency—Cost of reaching an audience (usually expressed as cost per 1,000 contacts).

Fixed position—Precise time sold for a TV or radio commercial; in print, the precise place where an ad will be published.

Flight—Period during which an ad campaign runs.

Frequency—Number of times a household or an individual is exposed to a medium over a certain period of time.

Full-service agency—An ad agency that handles all a client's advertising needs, from creation to placement.

Gross rating point (GRP)—One percent of the audience being measured.

House agency—Advertiser's in-house department that handles the entire advertising function.

Layout—Sketch of how an ad will look; also, finished version of an ad or a page.

Local advertising—Local retail advertising, as contrasted with national or classified advertising.

National advertising—Ads by producers and marketers of products through multiple outlets.

Net audience—Total audience minus duplication from, say, subscriber overlap between two magazines.

Out-of-home media—Outdoor boards, buses, etc.

Package—In TV, all the time periods sold at one price for an ad campaign.

Point-of-purchase—Advertising displayed where the product is purchased (in supermarkets, for example).

Position—In print, place where ad will appear; in broadcast, the time when a commercial will be run.

Rate card—List of prices, mechanical specifications, closing dates, and other particulars for newspaper or broadcast advertising.

Rating—In TV, number of TV households in a market capable of receiving a broadcast.

Reach—Total audience of a medium.

Representative (rep)—Person or firm selling space or time to advertisers distant from the newspaper or station.

Retail—Advertising placed by a local advertiser who sells directly to consumers.

Run-of-paper (ROP)—Ad position selected by the newspaper or magazine (contrasts with preferred position).

Run-of-schedule (ROS)—Commercial airtime determined by the station.

Space buyer—Agency employee who selects media for clients.

Traffic department—Department that coordinates the efforts of other ad agency departments to ensure that schedules are met.

IMPORTANT CHALLENGES AHEAD

Advertising, like all forms of mass communication, must adapt to key forces at work in our society. Let's examine some of them.

Proliferation of Media and Messages

In 1956, an advertiser could buy time on television's "I Love Lucy" and once weekly reach 46 percent of all American homes with TV sets. Or the advertiser could use the two other networks and reach a similarly high percentage of homes. Today, with four major networks and a couple of minor ones airing programming, along with scores of cable channels, there is no single spot in televison regularly offering anywhere near a 46 rating. With the wild proliferation of electronic and print media since the 1950s has come an explosion in the number of commercial messages bombarding the American public. *Forbes* magazine estimates that roughly 50 million television commercials were broadcast in 1988 alone.[3] One study showed that the typical American consumer is exposed to 5,000 advertising messages a day.[4] Says Paul Mulcahy, vice president for advertising at Campbell Soup Co.:

Animated raisins strutting their stuff in a TV commercial produced for the California Raisin Growers boosted raisin sales mightily in the late 1980s. Not even the people who produce commercials can always tell why some catch on and others don't. *Wide World Photos.*

"Find me a flat surface, and I'll find you someone selling advertising on it."[5] More commercials will be broadcast as the industry shifts to 15-second commercials from 30-second messages. How many ads will newspapers and magazines publish? How many more pieces of direct mail will you get? How many radio commercials, billboards, and signs on buses will compete for your attention? And where can advertisers go in all that clutter, all that noise, to get a message heard or seen and remembered? How can their ad agencies create messages with a *difference*, with that little extra something to raise them above the clutter and attract attention? Significantly, there are signs that the public is tuning commercials out. ▶ 3

Market Segmentation Sophisticated advertisers demand access to precisely delineated audiences with special interest in their products, and the media respond with special-interest publications and programming to attract them. That in turn demands greater precision in everything the advertising industry does: As we saw in Chapter 13, research must identify the audience more

precisely (exactly who is a prospective purchaser of, say, aircraft engines?). And research must precisely identify media capable of delivering that audience (*Aviation Week & Space Technology* or the science section of the *New York Times*?). The marketing strategy and advertising message must be crafted with great precision. (Aeronautic engineers who read *Aviation Week & Space Technology* will instantly spot—and reject—an ad that contains technical errors or otherwise imprecisely addresses their particular needs.) The future will require more precision research, thinking, and writing and fewer jauntily imprecise slogans ("It's the real thing") cast out broadly at undifferentiated markets.

Demographically "desirable" audiences will be targeted by many advertisers in a crescendo of advertising. Americans who earn $75,000 or more annually, buy fur coats, and vacation in the Caribbean will be pursued by upscale advertisers across the land. That will challenge the creators of advertising to come up with appeals that create awareness.

3 ▶ Advertising Awareness: Test a Friend

A major research challenge in the ad industry is to determine whether an ad or a commercial rises above the clutter and noise of competing messages and is remembered by consumers who will be influenced to buy the advertised products.

Here's an awareness test you can use on a friend: Perhaps 30 minutes or so after you've watched a TV program together, ask your friend to name companies mentioned in commercials, their products, and price or other details of those products.

This is highly unscientific, but it will give you some idea of which ads are getting through. Then ask your friend why some ads are remembered. Is it the music in a commercial, the personality or character that animates the ad?

Social Change One of the biggest challenges ahead for advertising lies in societal unknowns. What will be the future shape of American society? What will be the character of the family? What will be consumer attitudes? Those are enormously important questions because successful advertising depends on anticipating themes and approaches that will strike responsive chords in the targeted audience. Flip through magazines of, say, 30 years ago and you'll see many ads addressed to the then-traditional American family of working husband, stay-at-home housewife, and two children (one boy, one girl, of course)—all seated happily in the kitchen devouring breakfast cereal or out for a Sunday drive in their roomy four-door sedan. Would those advertising themes work today? Not with one-parent families, working mothers, absent fathers. Using foundations of social science and precision research to understand American society and human nature is crucial.

Pressure to Sell In advertising and in the media, advertiser pressure is mounting for results. Few advertisers are satisfied with "enhancing corporate image" as the only payoff for an expensive ad campaign. They want measurable results—improved sales and market share. And if newspapers don't deliver, maybe TV will; if this ad agency can't move ointment, perhaps that one will. Few newspapers or magazines can count on unquestioning loyalty from advertisers; most must sell and resell even clients of long standing. Television is losing advertisers to cable and other media. For ad agencies, client churn is a major problem—advertisers try one, then go elsewhere. To hold business, the media and agencies must strike hard and fast for sales results, and that will create a new shrillness in advertising. In reacting to this pressure, the advertising industry must avoid overselling advertisers on what it can deliver. Advertising cannot solve all marketing problems. Products or services must have intrinsic value that attracts consumers; they must be different or perceived as different from other products or services, and the price must be right. Advertising cannot disguise shortcomings

that undercut consumer appeal—and ad executives must be honest on that, or pressure will mount to try to fix all marketing problems solely with advertising.

Advertiser Cost Resistance Advertising is often hugely expensive, and advertisers are balking. It cost Pepsi between $2 million and $4 million for each of those Michael Jackson spots in 1987, not including his fee (he was paid $15 million for the series). The director of Raisin Bran's commercials starring performer John Denver in 1987 was paid $75,000 per day (that

Carillon Importers Ltd. of Teaneck, New Jersey, exclusive U.S. distributor of Absolut vodka, paid $1 million to produce this ad and run it in three magazines just before Christmas 1988. The effect was achieved with a plastic sheet containing a clear liquid that when pressed against the page sent "snowflakes" floating through the air. *Wide World Photos.*

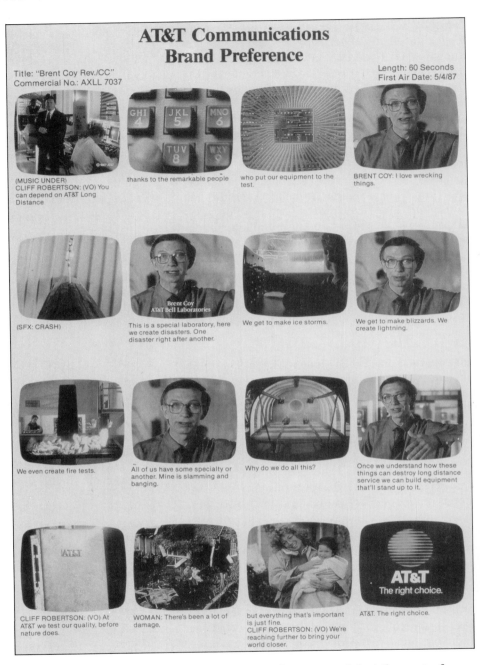

Huge amounts of creative talent—and money—go into producing TV commercials. Note in the ''photoboard,'' which outlines an AT&T commercial, the highly paid actor (Cliff Robertson) and the obviously costly photography involved. *Courtesy N. W. Ayer; used with permission.*

didn't include the producer, actors, cinematographers, or other costs). In addition, advertisers must pay for print space or broadcast time, and ad agency commissions of about 15 percent of total billing. The American Association of Advertising Agencies reported that the cost of producing an average 30-second TV commercial in 1987 was $145,600.[6] Highly creative advertising that sells is costing more—and advertisers are demanding their money's worth.

The New Technology Remote-control devices permit TV viewers to "zap" commercials by flipping channels, and VCRs permit "zipping" by them by speeding up a cassette. Print consumers can choose among thousands of publications. The American consumer has become a moving target; choice of what is viewed, read, or listened to is increasingly in the consumer's hands. How will advertising find and fix that target? And once that is accomplished, how can consumers be held long enough to absorb the message? ▶ 4

4 ▶ The Challenge of Zappers

Next time you "zap" a TV commercial, consider this: Huge amounts of money and creative talent are devoted to holding you, and millions like you, to your TV set during commercials. But remote-control devices and increasing viewer impatience with commercials pose an enormous challenge.

A research firm, R. D. Percy & Co., reports after a study of 1,000 homes in the New York City area in 1988 that the average household zaps once every 3 minutes, 42 seconds.[7] (It's 3 minutes, 26 seconds for households with remote control; 5 minutes and 15 seconds for households with no remote control.) Even worse, in the ad industry's view, highest-income households—the ones advertisers most want to reach—zap most frequently. Households earning $75,000 or more annually zap every 2 minutes and 42 seconds. Those earning under $15,000 annually are more content to stay put: They zap only every 6 minutes and 15 seconds.

Zapping can cut prime-time audiences by 10 percent or more, a devastating loss for advertisers—and for the ad agencies to which they pay hefty sums for commercials that will keep viewers from defecting to the bathroom or refrigerator during programming breaks. If there is significant viewer defection during commercials, ad rates based on viewership of programming actually constitute huge overcharges.

The ad industry tries for creative solutions:

◆ It uses popular entertainers whose presence, even in a commercial, is an attraction (Pepsi commercials featuring singer Michael Jackson lost only 1 to 2 percent of viewers, whereas many commercials were losing 10 percent or more).

◆ It makes commercials a story in themselves. In 1984, Data General aired a computer ad that included a Middle Ages battle scene. (And you've got to admit IBM's version of Charlie Chaplin, trying to catch all those cakes coming off the assembly line, *was* funny.)

◆ It uses short commercials—15 seconds or less—that viewers see whether they want to or not and before they can zap.

◆ It avoids programs that face heavy competition from other channels. During a heavy sports weekend, for example, viewers zap frequently, simply flipping to another basketball or football game when a commercial interrupts the one they are watching. Conversely, zapping is reduced during a major sports event such as the Super Bowl. Sometimes the ad industry catches zappers before they're even aware they are being caught—by placing ads in a background, such as on a stadium fence, sure to be caught by cameras covering an event. Also, in a technique called "product placement," advertisers pay high fees for their product—a beer can, for example—to be shown prominently as a prop in a movie or a TV program.

Of course, zapping can work in an advertiser's favor, too. For example, Percy & Co. found that early in one "CBS Evening News" program, up to 15 percent of viewers zapped out during commercials. Toward the end of the program, however, up to 73 percent more viewers watched commercials. Why? Percy says viewers were zapping in from other channels to get ready for "Wheel of Fortune," a game show that followed the news!

ADVERTISING TOOLS OF THE FUTURE

To compete successfully in the decades ahead, the advertising industry will need to make better use of certain basic tools.

Behavioral Sciences Sociology, anthropology, and psychology are needed because demands for more precision in advertising will not permit guesswork. Everyone involved in advertising will need a firm understanding of the economic and other behavioral systems in which American consumers live (sociology), the influence of cultural background and heritage (anthropology), and, simply, what turns them on to a product (psychology).

We can see the interplay of these behavioral sciences in much of today's advertising effort. We noted earlier, for example, that Knight-Ridder launched a Spanish-language daily in Miami for its Cuban-American audience—once it understood the evolving dynamics of the city's pluralistic society. Anthropological considerations will be crucial to advertisers as ethnic and other subcultures shift across the national scene, some being assimilated, some emerging, others flourishing or withering.

Earlier chapters noted how advertisers use sociological research to understand individuals and groups in their marketplaces. Media executives try to understand readers, viewers, and listeners in terms of income, education, age, and other demographic aspects. The advertising industry needs a sharper understanding of all that. Simply put, it won't work to place ads for $35,000 automobiles in a magazine whose readers earn $16,000 a year.

Psychology, the study of human thought and behavior, was a buzzword in advertising years ago; copywriters considered themselves amateur psychologists who were expert in which key words, illustrations, and layouts would spark responses. Well, in the clutter of today's marketplace, understanding what motivates consumer behavior must be more scientific. To rise above the clamor, ads must address real human needs—which psychologist Abraham Maslow (1908–1970) described as *basic physiological needs* (food, clothing, and shelter), *safety and security needs* (including such things as financial security in old age), *social needs* (companionship, belonging to a group), *esteem needs* (self-confidence, admiration), and *self-actualization needs* (to realize full potential).[8] Next time you read a print ad or watch a TV commercial, consider the copywriter's psychological approach. Is, say, an ad for a mink coat aimed at meeting a woman's basic physiological needs (for clothing) or, more likely, aimed at her esteem (ego) needs?

Marketing Research and Its Supporting Technology This creates a three-way partnership of advertiser, advertising expert, and the media. For example, Anacin in 1988 wanted to quickly exploit a medical report that aspirin helps prevent heart attacks. In the past, it took weeks, even months, to get to widespread newspapers with appropriate advertising. However, a new company, AD/SAT, Inc., of New York City, now delivers ad copy to newspapers nationwide in just minutes, via satellite. It sent the Anacin ad to 25 papers the day after the medical announcement. Increasingly, advertising experts and media get deeply into the advertiser's business, not simply the advertising problem. Media ad executives research retailers' businesses, then map advertising strategies in a comprehensive marketing plan. Beverly Klein, advertising director for the *Milwaukee Journal* and *Sentinel*, says media must become their advertisers' "marketing partner." Let's look at how the jointly owned papers she works for did this.[9]

First, the *Journal/Sentinel*'s audience was diagramed to show advertisers that the papers reach a certain geographic market. Notice that they express that in terms of competition with Milwaukee TV stations: MSA (metropolitan statistical area) is a newspaper market designation; ADI (area of dominant influence) is a TV market designation. The chart at the bottom of the illustration (see p. 287) tells advertiser "partners" the number and percentage of adults reached if five weekday issues or four Sunday issues are used.

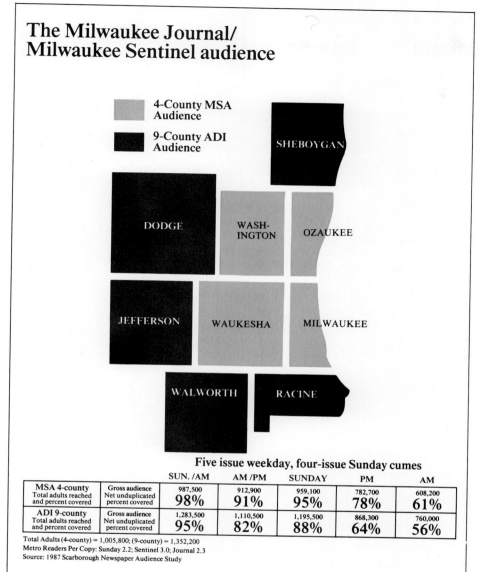

The Milwaukee Journal/ Milwaukee Sentinel audience

4-County MSA Audience

9-County ADI Audience

SHEBOYGAN

DODGE

WASH-INGTON

OZAUKEE

JEFFERSON

WAUKESHA

MILWAUKEE

WALWORTH

RACINE

Five issue weekday, four-issue Sunday cumes

		SUN. /AM	AM /PM	SUNDAY	PM	AM
MSA 4-county Total adults reached and percent covered	Gross audience	987,500	912,900	959,100	782,700	608,200
	Net unduplicated percent covered	**98%**	**91%**	**95%**	**78%**	**61%**
ADI 9-county Total adults reached and percent covered	Gross audience	1,283,500	1,110,500	1,195,500	868,300	760,000
	Net unduplicated percent covered	**95%**	**82%**	**88%**	**64%**	**56%**

Total Adults (4-county) = 1,005,800; (9-county) = 1,352,200
Metro Readers Per Copy: Sunday 2.2; Sentinel 3.0; Journal 2.3
Source: 1987 Scarborough Newspaper Audience Study

Then the newspapers use computer-generated research to inform advertisers of the numbers and percentages of adults they reach. Note that the papers break down population statistics—how many males are in the total 993,000 population, how many females, their demographic characteristics (see p. 288). The papers advise advertisers of the buying habits of Milwaukeeans. For example, the *Journal* and *Sentinel* tell car manufacturers that Milwaukee is a great place to sell used cars—563,200 adults own two or more (and the papers claim to reach 86 percent of them on Sundays!).

Let's move on to the presentation of mar-

The Milwaukee Journal and Milwaukee Sentinel offer advertisers the highest AM/PM newspaper combination reach and the highest Sunday reach of any newspaper buy in the top 30 markets. And the Sentinel has been the fastest-growing morning newspaper in the country for the past five years. In one combination weekday buy, you can reach 76% of the metro audience. Reach 84% of all adult Milwaukee readers any Sunday.

Newspaper advertising can help you reach your target market efficiently and easily. Journal and Sentinel readers are upscale and affluent. They are active consumers who turn to the newspapers for information they need before they buy.

4-County MSA Readership
Adults 18+

	Population	Journal	Sentinel	AM/PM Combination	Sunday	Sunday and Sentinel
Adults	993,000	63%	40%	76%	84%	90%
Male	467,200	63%	46%	77%	85%	92%
Female	525,800	63%	34%	75%	83%	89%
Age						
18-24	157,200	58%	28%	67%	88%	91%
25-34	238,900	56%	38%	70%	84%	90%
35-54	315,500	63%	43%	76%	84%	91%
55+	281,300	71%	45%	85%	80%	89%
Education						
Less than high school	186,700	52%	36%	69%	72%	82%
High school graduate	411,100	62%	36%	74%	86%	91%
Some college	225,500	73%	45%	82%	90%	95%
College graduate	169,700	66%	46%	80%	85%	92%
Occupation						
Managerial/professional	179,800	70%	43%	81%	88%	93%
Technical/administrative/sales	200,300	65%	48%	78%	89%	94%
Production/crafts/repairs	62,900	52%	48%	76%	80%	90%
Operators/laborers	89,900	57%	37%	71%	90%	94%
Service	99,900	54%	36%	66%	77%	85%
Farming/fishing/forestry	8,000	69%	56%	85%	83%	93%
Not employed	352,300	65%	33%	76%	80%	87%
Income						
Less than $15,000	222,500	60%	30%	70%	78%	85%
$15,000-$24,999	235,200	61%	33%	72%	84%	89%
$25,000-$34,999	266,400	63%	44%	77%	87%	93%
$35,000+	268,800	68%	50%	83%	86%	93%

Source: 1985 Simmons-Scarborough Newspaper Ratings Study

Readership by consumption

Adults who...	Number of adults	AM/PM net reach	Sunday reach
Own two or more cars	563,200	76%	86%
Purchased men's suit(s), past 12 months	230,800	74%	89%
Purchased dress(es), past 12 months	4?3,700	76%	85%
Spent over $100 on all clothing purchased, past 12 months	829,200	77%	84%
Purchased new car(s), past 2 years	251,800	79%	91%
Traveled by air abroad, past 3 years	206,900	78%	87%
Traveled by air in US, past 12 months	444,600	77%	88%
Dined in quality restaurant(s), past 30 days	813,000	78%	84%
Went to movie(s), past 3 months	778,300	75%	88%
Purchased small appliance(s), past 12 months	552,200	78%	86%
Own an IRA	273,600	82%	87%
Own securities valued at $10,000 or more	326,700	83%	86%

Source: 1985 Simmons-Scarborough Newspaper Ratings Study

Journal/Sentinel, Inc., used with permission.

keting research and specific information for clothing advertisers (see p. 289). Showing buyer categories in the city helps in drawing up marketing strategies and advertising themes. Look, for example, at the center column ("Women's Clothing"). Most dresses purchased were under $49 each. Are women who pay those relatively low prices motivated by basic physiological needs (clothing) or esteem needs (self-confidence)? If you were an advertising copywriter in

What to wear is never a problem for Milwaukeeans. They are well prepared for every occasion and for whatever the weather may bring. Metro residents shop for the latest fashions, kickiest sports togs, glitziest formal wear. You'll find Milwaukeeans making a fashion statement on the job, too. Receipts from men's and women's suit sales add up to almost $70 million per year.[17] They stay abreast of fashion trends and classic styles in The Milwaukee Journal and Milwaukee Sentinel.

Apparel

37

Men's Clothing Purchased in Metro Milwaukee, Last 12 Months	# Adults Purchasing
Overcoats/topcoats	161,900
Suits, under $174	133,500
Suits, $175 or more	97,300
Sports jackets	17,300
Casual slacks/jeans	542,200
Dress slacks	421,200
Sports shirts	420,100
Dress shirts	314,100
Athletic clothing	289,800
Athletic shoes	393,800
Dress shoes	338,400

Source: 1985 Simmons-Scarborough Newspaper Ratings Study

Women's Clothing Purchased in Metro Milwaukee, Last 12 Months	# Adults Purchasing
Coats	242,600
Raincoats	134,800
Dresses, under $49	192,400
Dresses, $50-$100	123,600
Dresses, over $100	147,700
Blouses/shirts	461,500
Suits	144,900
Jeans	358,900
Athletic clothing	157,700
Dress shoes	402,200
Accessories	333,800

Source: 1985 Simmons-Scarborough Newspaper Ratings Study

Amount Spent on Clothing Purchases Past 12 months	# Adults	% Adults
Less than $100	99,500	16%
$100 - $249	233,700	24%
$250 - $499	261,900	26%
$500 - $749	13,900	14%
$750 - $999	43,800	4%
$1000 - $1249	67,000	7%
$1250 - $1499	27,100	3%
$1500 or more	56,700	6%

Average clothing expenditure per adult = $500 yearly

Source: 1985 Simmons-Scarborough Newspaper Ratings Study

Journal/Sentinel, Inc., used with permission.

Milwaukee, which needs—which themes—would you stress to sell such dresses?

Computerized research, then, improves *addressability*—identifying and reaching the consumers that advertisers want, then delivering them. But even more is needed. The *Journal* and *Sentinel*, in conjunction with the Newspaper Advertising Bureau, also advise advertisers how to write effective ads. They offer a sample ad, pointing out elements such as benefit headline and

Essentials of a good ad

The following suggestions can increase ad readership.

1. Create an identity

Ads with distinctive artwork, layouts and copy enjoy a higher readership.

2. Use a simple layout

Be clever not cryptic. The reader's eye should move in a simple, logical sequence from headline to illustration to explanatory copy to price to your store's name and logo. Too many types and decorative borders can turn attraction to distraction.

3. Have a definite focus

Newspapers are a visual medium. The eye is quickly drawn to a well-chosen photograph or interesting artwork that will lead the reader to read about what you're selling.

4. Feature consumer benefits

Your customer wants to know "What's in it for me?" If price is your calling card, make that your banner statement. If fashion is your focus, make that your eye-grabber.

5. Avoid congestion

Don't overcrowd. The average news page is filled with print and it is your opportunity as an advertiser to clear some of that area with white space giving your copy room to breathe. In ads where a large number of items are featured, as in a storewide sale, an extra effort is required to tell the whole story in the most readable, roomiest way.

6. Tell the whole story

Tell all of the most appealing points there are to know about the product, such as color, size and fashionability. Be enthusiastic to get across the message. A block of copy written in complete sentences is often easier to read than phrases and random words. A boldface lead-in and illustrations accompanying copy are strong aids to readership.

7. Name your price

Readers will often overestimate omitted prices, so you should not be hesitant to list them. If the price is comparably high, justify the higher tag with the item's outstanding features. If the price is low, include the fact that this is a closeout or storewide clearance. Emphasize the savings to the reader and tell him about your credit options and layaway plans as well.

8. Specify branded merchandise

If the item is a known brand, say so. Manufacturers spend large sums to sell their goods, and you can capitalize on their advertising while enhancing the reputation of your store.

9. Include related items

Make two sales instead of one by offering related items along with a featured one. For instance, when a dishwasher is advertised, also show a disposal.

10. Urge your readers to buy now

Ask for the sale. Stimulate prompt action by using such phrases as "limited supply" or "this week only." If mail-order coupons are included in your ads, provide spaces large enough for customers to fill them in easily.

BASIC ELEMENTS OF A GOOD AD

logo (see p. 290). Like ad agencies, the newspapers employ writers, artists, and layout specialists to provide complete service.

Creative Instincts

Creativity is what makes some advertising so successful, some careers so fulfilling and rewarding. Absent creative instincts, advertising—and careers—fail.

The search is always on for the "big idea"—an especially brilliant ad campaign, a catchy slogan, a memorable print ad or TV commercial that will lift a message out of the clutter and sell something. One big idea, well researched and aggressively conducted, can launch a personal career, turn around the financial fortunes of an ad agency, and sell billions of dollars' worth of a client's product.

Sometimes, the big idea turns out to be a little, amusing character. The Lord, Geller, Federico, Einstein ad agency came up with that little tramp who looked like Charlie Chaplin and made IBM's ads memorable. Coca-Cola caught attention with a stuttering, computer-generated Max Headroom. Bartles & Jaymes sold a lot of wine coolers with two amusing yokels who extolled the product on TV.

Why some characters sell products while others don't is unclear even to experienced ad executives. However, David Vadehra, president of Video Storyboard Tests Inc., a research firm, says he does know why children and animals are effective in advertising: "cuteness and honesty." He adds, "Viewers especially love to see talking dogs in ads since they treat their own pets like members of the family." He cites one Denver woman who says her dog watches Kibbles 'n Bits dog food commercials, "hoping the dog in the ad will come and play with him."[10]

No discussion of the mechanics of advertising can neglect the importance of the creative instinct. *Advertising Age*, a widely read trade magazine, warns that advertisers in this age of computer-generated research "must never forget what an inspired agency's creative spark can mean to them and their shareholders."[11] *Ad Age* cites examples:

Philip Morris's Marlboro Man concept, "worth more . . . than all the company's brick and mortar"

"Does she . . . or doesn't she?" (Clairol hair rinses)

"Don't leave home without it." (American Express)

Maura Shea (*center*) is casting assistant and Jim Kruse (*right*) creative director on a TV commercial done by the N. W. Ayer ad agency. Working with cinematographers and actors requires highly creative instincts. *Courtesy N. W. Ayer; used with permission.*

"We try harder." (Avis)

"M&Ms melt in your mouth, not in your hand."

"You deserve a break today." (McDonald's)

Sometimes the instinct fails advertisers, and they drop successful slogans for fear that consumers have grown weary of them or simply to try something new—with disastrous effect. For example, Sara Lee Corp. walked away from "Nobody doesn't like Sara Lee" but returned to it after two new slogans flopped.[12]

Much advertising tends toward one of two extremes: selling on emotion or selling product benefit. For example, is the thrust of an ad to illustrate a unique product strength? (Eat this cereal, not that one, and you'll gain more fiber, a safeguard against cancer.) Or is the ad aimed at creating an image? ("At Ford, quality is Job 1.")

Perhaps the basic motive is comparative advertising, illustrating strengths and advantages of one product against weaknesses of another. (Serve two soft drinks to a panel of blindfolded men and women, and one is sure to fail.)

Sometimes the motive is advocacy of a political idea or philosophical position (an oil company, for example, commenting on energy conservation).

Advertising fads come and go. But an unchanging and fundamental consideration is whether ads should sell emotion or product benefit.

Some car ads don't feature such product benefits as spacious trunks or roomy back seats. Rather, they feature attractive people listening to mellow music and whipping along a glistening mountain road on a rainy night. Such ads don't sell cars; they promise lifestyle and dreams. Tobacco companies don't use product benefit themes to sell cigarettes (which, we are told by no less authority than the U.S. surgeon general, may kill you if used as intended). Rather, cigarette companies sell image (be a rugged cowboy, have lots of friends, look sophisticated).

Product benefit ads appear more in print than on TV because they require more detail. Given a full-page ad, a creative team can present not only a slick, beautiful photo of a car but also its engine specifications, warranty details, prices, and so forth. (Did you ever actually try to read those gas consumption statistics and disclaimers flashed at the bottom of your screen during a car commercial on TV?) Grocery stores and other retailers often use print for product benefit advertising because they can cram a great deal of pricing information into the space available. On TV, they stress general image—we have fresh food, we are friendly.

Sometimes advertisers use emotion verging on fright. Condom manufacturers, traditionally unwelcome on TV, used the spread of AIDS to justify rushing their product into public view, and their theme was as scary as the disease. "I'll do a lot for love," a woman in one ad said, "but I'm not ready to die for it." (Later, condom manufacturers shifted to other themes—humor, discount prices, social acceptability—when scare ads didn't increase sales as expected.)

Emotional response to ads is a key factor for advertisers. Unknowingly, they can produce ads, particularly on TV, that, as *Advertising Age* magazine puts it, may seem innocent but "can clear a room in less than 30 seconds." *Ad Age* financed a survey in 1988 on ads TV viewers most hate. For men, it was ads for feminine hygiene products; for women, ads for beer and alcohol.[13]

Controversy swirls around the use of other emotions in advertising. Does humor really sell? Producers of TV ads love to use it, and each year, funny commercials win Clios (the "Oscars of advertising"). But many experts feel that humor detracts from the sales message. (Not even Isuzu, which created the lovable liar, Joe Isuzu, could be certain that he actually sold autos.) Should death be portrayed in ads? The American Cancer Society decided in 1988 that the answer was yes; it created ads bluntly making the point: Cancer can kill you, so get a checkup. Ads that demonstrably sell goods and services (as contrasted with being merely cute or entertaining) are recognized annually by the Effies, awards made by the New York City Ad Club.

Some experts say that ads have become so slick and unreal that they can't sell anything.

That has given rise to "reality" advertising—TV commercials shakily shot with hand-held cameras, almost like home movies, and "slice of life" ads that look real and show average-looking people (such as a worried executive musing aloud that his job is in jeopardy because he bought the wrong telephone equipment).

ADVERTISING AND ITS REGULATORS

The advertising industry's creative talents are free-spirited in targeting us, the consumers, with print and broadcast ads. But they aren't completely *freewheeling*. Our society places strict restraints on advertising. Covering law, ethics, and morality, they are exercised at four levels:

by individual consumers
by special-interest groups
by government and the law
by the industry itself

As in any form of mass communication in our free enterprise society, the individual consumer ultimately has the greatest say in what is appropriate in advertising and what isn't.

Lawyers, officials, industry critics, and social commentators debate endlessly about what is obscene and isn't, what is ethical and isn't. But none of the debate can equal the impact on advertising practices that occurs when millions of consumers vote no on advertising. They vote no at the cash register, by refusing to buy a product; they vote no by word of mouth, to each other, to store managers—and to poll takers in endless surveys on whether advertising offends or alienates consumers. Reflect, for example, on the virtual disappearance of the dumb housewife from American advertising. She sat around all day in a bathrobe and fuzzy slippers, sipping coffee, aroused only by shame (when a neighbor noticed that her husband's shirt had a dirty ring around the collar) or envy (when the neighbor's kitchen floor was shinier than hers). That image disappeared beneath a tidal wave of objections from women demanding liberation from such degrading nonsense.

In 1989, a Michigan mother created a national stir by calling on advertisers to stop supporting Fox Broadcasting's program "Married . . . with Children" on the grounds that it contained material children shouldn't see. Major advertisers—Procter & Gamble, Kimberly-Clark, Tambrands, McDonald's—promised her they would withdraw their ads. In subsequent months, Chrysler, Sears, Miller Brewing, and others withdrew from TV programming that came under criticism for similar reasons. Commented *Advertising Age*: "The 'New Puritanism,' an attitude of consumers that network TV has gotten too lenient in its treatment of sex and violence, is starting to hit advertiser, agency and network TV executives hard."[14]

Sometimes special groups focus millions of individual objections and thus hurry change. The consumerism movement started by Ralph Nader in the 1960s is an extremely influential lobby for change in advertising. Women's groups demand removal of sexism from advertising; parents' groups work for removal of hidden advertising from children's programming; church groups lobby against indecency. One magazine, *Sassy*, was targeted in 1988 by the Reverend Jerry Falwell's Moral Majority because of its frank articles on sex, abortion, and other topics. Moral Majority published the names of advertisers using *Sassy*, putting enormous public relations pressure on the companies.

In a perfect world, such pull and tug in the marketplace would set social boundaries for advertising and establish the good and bad of it all. But that presumes that buyer and seller possess the same information and equal voice and strength. Of course, in our imperfect world, the consumer cannot possess the same information that the seller has about products or services, and individual consumers' objections, even when raised by a special-interest group, are not always heard.

Enter government and the law. Until well into the 1900s, marketplace forces were expected to determine right and good in advertising. Then, in 1914, Congress passed the Federal Trade Commission Act, which declared unfair competition unlawful. The act established the Federal Trade Commission (FTC) to regulate advertising. Even then, Congress had business-to-business relationships in mind; consumers were left to sort things out for themselves. In 1922, the U.S. Supreme Court made things much more explicit by ruling (in *FTC* v. *Winsted Hosiery*) that false advertising is an unfair trade practice. In 1938, the Wheeler-Lea Amendment broadened the FTC's role in protecting consumers from deceptive advertising in interstate commerce. Under the Robinson-Patman Act, sellers (and their advertising) are required to treat all customers equally. The Food and Drug Administration monitors the labeling of food, drugs, cosmetics, and other products. The Securities and Exchange Commission regulates the advertising of stocks and bonds to ensure that investors get full disclosure of important information. The U.S. Postal Service, which guards against mail fraud, is another federal regulatory agency with influence over advertising.

The courts permitted expansion of FTC powers until today the federal agency has considerable clout over advertising content. Court rulings established several primary considerations: Advertising must not be misleading even to a person of low intelligence, and the key in deciding whether it is misleading (or false or unclear) is in the *overall impression* (not a single word or sentence) the advertising creates. Broadly, the law permits a bit of boasting—"puffery," in the trade—if the advertiser makes clear that it is an *opinion*. Are puffery and opinion misleading to a person of low intelligence? A judge or jury would have to decide. Also, sheer bad taste is not against the law, but obscenity is illegal.

The vigor of enforcement by federal regulators often depends on the spirit of the times and the administration in power in Washington. Some administrations consider themselves "social engineers" whose tools are regulatory agencies and the law, to be used in such matters as advertising. Other administrations tend to keep hands off business and let marketplace forces solve problems.

All this means, of course, that full constitutional protection does not extend to commercial speech, as the U.S. Supreme Court has held repeatedly for most of our nation's history. In the late 1970s, however, the Court ruled that society benefits from the free flow of commercial information (as it does from the free flow of news and the free exchange of political ideas) but that each case must be settled on its own merits and that some restrictions must be allowed (for example, state laws designed to protect consumers from misleading advertising).

Thus the three partners of advertising—advertisers, ad agencies, and media—tightrope-walking between consumer pressure on the one hand and federal regulation on the other. This creates considerable motivation for self-regulation.

CONSUMER PRESSURE AT WORK

66 [Your] article pointed out how willing our Government is to export death and disease for profit by boosting American cigarette sales abroad. Your cigarette ads appearing in the same issue show how shamelessly you want a cut of the action.

It is a curious convention—and one conducive to schizophrenia throughout our culture—that one standard of truth and integrity holds for editorial material and another for space purchased by advertisers. **99**

Letter to the **New York Times.**[15]

Media efforts to create a sense of truth, ethics, and fairness began early. In 1911, *Printer's Ink* magazine campaigned for truth in advertising, which led many media to establish advertising standards. In 1914, newspapers, advertisers and ad agencies established a cooperative, the Audit Bureau of Circulations, to issue reliable circulation figures. Better Business Bureaus grew out of local advertising associations and, with media support, have handled complaints about advertising (and other business matters) since 1916. The National Advertising Review Council was created in 1971 by leading advertising associations to rule on complaints about national advertising. Participation by advertisers and agencies is voluntary.

Guidelines established by individual media

range from general statements of policy to highly detailed standards. Those laid down by the *Milwaukee Journal* and *Sentinel* serve as an example.

ADVERTISING GUIDELINES, JOURNAL/SENTINEL, INC.

The confidence our readers have in the *Milwaukee Journal* and the *Milwaukee Sentinel* extends not just to news and editorial columns but to the advertising columns as well. That confidence is dependent solely on the integrity of the respective columns. Reader confidence is obviously indispensable to the success of Journal/Sentinel, Inc., and of tremendous economic value to our many advertisers.

Our advertising guidelines over many years have helped ensure the integrity of our columns, and although specific guidelines are reviewed as new products and services enter the marketplace, the basic concepts cannot change.

Our policy is to refrain from publishing advertising that is untrue, deceptive, or misleading; that makes unfair competitive statements; that violates law or standards of decency; or that is fraudulent.

Since one of our paramount concerns is reader confidence, we do, based on a combination of past experience, judgment, and general community standards, refuse to accept certain types of advertising. We are always willing to review from the general standpoint of reader protection, not from the standpoint of a particular proposed advertisement.

As a newspaper, it is our belief that we have a duty to our readers to accept responsible opinion-type advertisements without regard to the editorial positions of either paper. Fear of an idea or thought is inherently inconsistent with the First Amendment. However, we shall not knowingly publish a libelous or defamatory statement, nor shall we publish a statement of purported fact that cannot be reasonably verified.

Many newspapers and television operations reject highly lucrative advertisements on grounds they are misleading, indecent, or in poor taste. On several occasions, for example, the *Wall Street Journal*, at considerable cost, rejected advertising from companies that tried to influence its editorial policy.

Throughout many guidelines runs a common theme: A newspaper or TV network must protect the believability of its advertising, just as it protects its news columns. Robert P. Smith, for years head of the *New York Times*'s Advertising Acceptability Department, puts it this way:

> The character of a newspaper is determined not only by its news and editorial content, but also by the advertising it publishes. Those that accept inaccurate, misleading, deceptive, or offensive advertising, or that tolerate slipshod performance by advertisers run the risk of demeaning their most valuable asset—their credibility. That's just plain bad business.[16]

Sometimes pressures from consumers and government plus self-regulation by advertisers and the media come together with enormous impact. Such was the case when, after years of debate, Congress in 1970 banned all cigarette advertising from TV and radio. In 1971, the FTC required health warnings in printed cigarette ads (Congress strengthened the warnings in 1984 and two years later banned broadcast ads for smokeless tobacco products). There is great societal pressure for a ban on all tobacco ads, in print as well as on TV. Opponents of a ban say that would endanger free speech.[17]

Television voluntarily restricts beer and liquor ads (commercials show fun and games over a beer at the local pub—but never does anyone actually *drink* the stuff on camera!) Clearly, greater pressure is building for increased restrictions on alcoholic beverage advertising. In 1989, Surgeon General C. Everett Koop called for eliminating such advertising on college campuses and prohibiting celebrity endorsements of beer and liquor with strong appeal to youth. Alcoholic beverage advertising and promotion "send the message that drinking is a normal and glamorous activity without negative consequences," he said, "and our young people are believing these messages."

Advertising is subject to the law, as is news or editorial content of the media. Libel laws, for example, apply to advertising.

Now let's turn to ad agencies' role in the advertising partnership.

AGENCIES: MAJOR PLAYERS IN ADVERTISING

If you think you'd like a career in advertising, picture two scenarios. You work for a major agency. In scenario 1, you are invited to meet the chairman of a leading manufacturer of autos. The chairman says, "I produce good cars, but they're not selling. Can you fix my problem?" The question is whether you can perform as a *full-service agency*. Can you research the company's marketing problem, its competitors, and its potential customers and devise a strategy—a total plan—to improve sales?

In scenario 2, the owner of a family winery in California summons you. "Look," the owner says, "I'm starting a new marketing push and some of my people and I have some pretty good ideas for ads" (in reference to an *in-house ad agency* run by the company). "We'll do the whole thing, but we want you to do the *media plan*." The winery owner is telling you that your creative instincts or your sales abilities are not needed. The winery simply wants you to sit down with a pile of reference manuals and select newspapers, magazines, and TV stations and prepare a schedule (with costs) for running the winery's ads. Frankly, it's routine, rather dull work—and you didn't have to go to college to learn it.

Can you see yourself in these scenarios? Can you envisage yourself grasping the totality of not only your chosen field of advertising but also in scenario 1, the advertiser's business (autos) as well? Do you have skills in customer relations, sales, research, creativity, budgeting and finance, personnel administration, and pure management that are required in big-league ad agency work? And in scenario 2, can you see yourself submitting on occasion (frequently in your early years) to routine work that is sheer drudgery?

Those scenarios sketch the wide range of activities and talents needed in ad agency work. Of course, you need not do all those things to succeed in an agency career. Major agencies are compartmentalized and offer rewarding careers in just sales or client relations, for example. And there are fine careers outside full-service agencies. Some creative shops ("boutiques") offer only artistic and copywriting services. Others offer only media services, such as buying print space or broadcast time. (Be aware, though, that major full-service agencies are putting great competitive pressure on boutiques and media service firms, causing many small shops to wither.) And of course, you could work for an in-house agency.

At client-agency meetings, agency executives outline advertising and public relations strategies they have devised to further the client's interests. *Courtesy Burson-Marsteller.*

Many advertising careers start with selling to local retail clients. After college, Brad Hagstrom sold for the *Gainesville* (Ga.) *Times*, a small Gannett paper, then moved to Gannett's larger *Pensacola* (Fla.) *News-Journal*, where he is shown using market research in a telephone sales pitch.

5 ▶ The Big Players

Rankings of American ad agencies by size can shift rapidly due to mergers and the gain or loss of large accounts. Here are the standings for 1988 (in millions of dollars).

	Worldwide Billings	Worldwide Gross Income
1. Young & Rubicam	5,390	758
2. Saatchi & Saatchi	5,035	740
3. Backer Spielvogel Bates	4,678	690
4. McCann-Erickson	4,381	657
5. FCG-Publicis	4,358	653
6. Ogilvy & Mather	4,110	635
7. BBDO	4,051	586
8. J. Walter Thompson	3,858	559
9. Lintas	3,586	538
10. Grey	2,886	433

Many local and regional agencies are springing up to serve advertisers seeking narrowly focused, special-interest audiences (and that opens attractive opportunities for young people who want to own an agency but can start only on a shoestring). But for the major players in agency advertising, *big* indeed is the word. ▶ 5

As with other major media activity, the ad agency action tends to be in larger cities. If you're thinking of an agency career, you'll want to think about living near agencies with the largest billings. According to *Advertising Age* figures, agencies in the following cities generated the most billings in 1987 (in millions of dollars):

New York	19,716.9
Chicago	5,145.5
Los Angeles	2,815.6
Detroit	2,619.5
San Francisco	1,307.1
Dallas	897.6
Boston	859.3
Minneapolis	815.4
Philadelphia	743.4
Cleveland	595.3

Agency careers require big-picture thinking. Agencies are "middlemen," of course, contracting their services to advertisers, then coordinat-

ing with the media, where advertising is placed. That requires knowing a great deal about the total American business scene and the large conglomerates that spend most for advertising. Anyone preparing for an agency career must not only learn techniques of advertising but must also study how large advertisers operate, what products they sell, how they fight their competitors, and so forth. According to *Advertising Age* figures, America's biggest national advertisers in 1987 spent the following amounts (in millions of dollars):

Phillip Morris	1,557.8
Proctor & Gamble	1,386.7
General Motors	1,024.9
Sears, Roebuck	886.5
RJR Nabisco	839.6
PepsiCo	704.0
Eastman Kodak	658.2
McDonald's	649.5
Ford	639.5
Anheuser-Busch	635.1

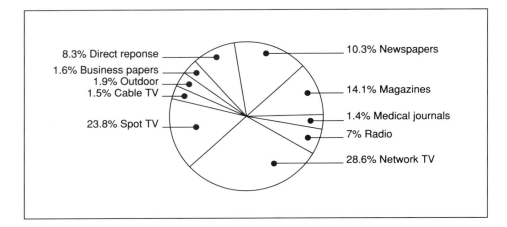

8.3% Direct reponse

1.6% Business papers
1.9% Outdoor
1.5% Cable TV

23.8% Spot TV

10.3% Newspapers

14.1% Magazines

1.4% Medical journals

7% Radio

28.6% Network TV

Figure 14.1. MEDIA BILLINGS BY AGENCIES. *Source: Adapted from Advertising Age; used with permission.*

Working for a major agency can involve you in negotiations with a TV network one day, talks with a newspaper the next—or an outdoor advertising company, a business magazine, or a medical journal! All the more reason that career preparation in advertising should include careful study of the media, how they operate, and how they fit into the "advertising partnership" (see Figure 14.1).

UPS AND DOWNS IN AD AGENCY WORK

If you were managing, say, a shoe company or a clothing manufacturing firm and sales suddenly plummeted, what's the first thing you would do? Shake up the designers? (They may not be styling your products properly.) Investigate quality control? (Shoddy goods may be slipping through.) Realign your prices? (Foreign competitors may be offering cheaper products.) Each is a predictable impulse for correcting a sales slump but, in the real world of business, not always the first impulse. In boardrooms across the country, the first impulse often is to switch ad agencies.

In minutes, millions of dollars can be withdrawn from one agency and shifted to another. The losing firm is often shaken to its financial roots; the winner blossoms with the dollar transfusion. At the loser's shop, careers can be shattered, scores of employees laid off; the winner

promotes madly within and hires quickly from without.

Clearly, an ad agency career can be a fragile thing. If it's ad agency life you seek, be prepared for ups and downs.

In 1988, Hal Riney & Partners, an agency with just $200 million in annual billings, won a $100 million-a-year contract with General Motors for advertising the Saturn automobile. It was a triumph for the inspirational talents of Hal Riney, creator of the Bartles & Jaymes wine cooler commercials and other inventive ad campaigns. (Riney said, "I don't think we'll ever shoot a picture of a car going down a wet, windy road with pylons. We're going to talk to people in different ways than the standard process agencies use.") Suddenly, the ad industry was talking about Riney. He and his small agency were all over the trade journals.

That same year, things broke the other way for Lord, Geller, Federico, Einstein. After a series of executive defections from the agency, IBM withdrew its $120 million computer advertising account. The agency's total billings were only $230 million, so the IBM withdrawal was crippling.

Advertisers are unpredictable in awarding contracts. The *Wall Street Journal* examined GM's Saturn contract award and concluded that the company looked at more than what competing agencies offered in cost and sample campaigns. Noted the *Journal:*

The candidates—Saturn calls them prospective "communications partners"—never proposed any ads. Instead, they were judged on strategic thinking, enthusiasm and compatibility with Saturn. GM officials gauged "personal chemistry" over elegant dinners at which shop talk was discouraged. The eight-person selection committee includes not only advertising and marketing executives but also a GM dealer and a union representative.

Saturn's marketing director, Thomas Shaver, said: ". . . We want to find the Big Idea."[18]

Sometimes the advertiser schedules an "agency review" and in effect says, "You did a great job for us last year. Now how about next year? And by the way, we're inviting other agencies to compete for your contract." Any agency under review on a major contract undergoes enormous tension. Agency image, profits, and many jobs are at stake.

Competition is fierce. In 1988, the *Los Angeles Daily News* had 40 agencies try for its relatively small $1.5 million annual account. (Commented one agency head, "If someone drops a nickel in this town, there are 50 guys bumping heads to get it.")[19]

Two significant trends are developing due to competition:

◆ Battling for business, some agencies use unethical tactics. One is hiring away a competing agency's executives who work on an advertiser's account, then wooing that advertiser's business on the basis of new staff strength. Another is dropping a client—"resigning" the account (clients "fire" agencies)—and then using confidential information gained in working for that client to trade for a contract with one of the client's competitors.

ON THE AGENCY BATTLEFIELD

66 Trying to win an advertising account in a contest with other agencies has to be one of the most intense forms of business competition. Every pitch is a battle of ideas and personalities. I face ethical situations every day that would tempt a saint. And I am unhappy with the level of ethics in the business world in general today, not because I have all the answers, but because I don't see many people even thinking about the questions.

Ethics? In the advertising business? Surely I jest. When I spoke recently at a Center for Communication seminar on 'Ethics in Advertising' the moderator couldn't resist remarking that the discussion might be very brief. 99

Don Peppers,
New York agency executive.[20]

◆ With many agencies clamoring for their business, advertisers are beating down what agencies can charge. Agencies traditionally charged 15 percent of all billings; today, some drop substantially below that or charge negotiated fees based on costs. Advertising lore is filled with shocking stories of some agencies spending client money recklessly and still enjoying huge profits whether the ads sold anything or not. Those days may be over.

☆ SUMMARY

Since ancient times, advertising has served good and evil purposes. It informs and misinforms. Most of all, it sells, and its impact on American society is enormous. More than $118 billion was spent on advertising in 1988 alone, and the ad industry is all around us—in newspapers and magazines, on radio and TV. If you read, listen, or look, you cannot escape its reach.

The ad industry works on the local retail level with hometown merchants and on the national level to sell goods and services nationwide. It targets consumers and, in trade and industrial advertising, wholesalers and others who sell to consumers.

Advertising is controversial. Some critics argue that it is wasteful and forces consumers to pay higher prices. Supporters argue that it helps consumers make intelligent choices and creates mass consumption that drives the U.S. economy.

Challenges for the industry include devising

advertising that will rise above the clutter of commercial messages inundating the American consumer.

Successful advertising requires better use of the behavioral sciences, as a guide to creating more precise advertising; marketing research, to help advertisers solve business problems; and more creative ideas.

Advertising is regulated by individual consumers, who can say no at the cash register; by special-interest groups; by government, particularly the Federal Trade Commission; and through self-regulation.

Full-service ad agencies take over a client's entire marketing problem. Others serve in a more limited capacity, as creative or media services agencies. Some advertisers maintain in-house agencies to do their own ads. At any level, agency work requires understanding the client's business and how the media work.

Competition between agencies is fierce, and some major advertisers shift accounts worth millions as soon as they feel results slipping. This drives some agencies to unethical tactics aimed at holding or gaining new business.

☆ RECOMMENDED READING

The current scene in advertising is covered almost daily by the *New York Times* and the *Wall Street Journal*. *Advertising Age* magazine is essential reading. *Forbes* is strong in reporting cost and strategy trends.

Material on the industry is available from the American Advertising Federation, 1400 K Street NW, Suite 1000, Washington, DC 20005; the American Association of Advertising Agencies, 666 Third Avenue, New York, NY 10017; the Association of National Advertisers, 155 West 44th Street, New York, NY 10017; and the Newspaper Advertising Bureau, 1180 Sixth Avenue, New York, NY 10036.

For the broader view, see Thomas Russell and Glenn Verrill, *Otto Kleppner's Advertising Procedures* (Englewood Cliffs, N.J.: Prentice-Hall, 1988). For copywriting assistance, read David Malicks and John Nason, *Advertising: How to Write the Kind That Works* (New York: Scribner, 1977). A strong look at agency work is Herbert Gardner, Jr., *The Advertising Agency Business* (Chicago: Crain Books, 1983).

Inside an Ad Agency

"A diamond is forever."

"I'd walk a mile for a Camel."

"When it rains, it pours."

"Reach out and touch someone."

"Let your fingers do the walking."

Unless you've spent your life on a desert island, you recognize at least a couple of those advertising slogans. No wonder. They are among the most famous in American advertising history. They have become woven into the fabric of contemporary American life, and for years they have sold a great many diamonds, cigarettes, salt, and telephone services.

Those slogans illustrate the mix of hard sell with creative, at times almost poetic thinking and writing that goes into successful advertising agency work. We turn now to a case study of the agency that developed those slogans, N. W. Ayer.[1]

Our mission is to examine how an agency operates and, particularly, how it pulls together the creative and business strengths necessary to successful advertising today. How does an agency inspire people to write slogans that sparkle with commercial genius? What organizational framework creates campaigns capable of convincing millions of men to give diamonds to express their love? What institutional culture feeds the creativity of copywriters who fix in our minds the image of fingers walking across the Yellow Pages? We will explore such questions and at the same time look at agency jobs that might appeal to those of you thinking about ad agency careers. Matching personal goals and style with those of a prospective employer is essential in career planning. For those of you who intend to be media consumers rather than participants, we'll perhaps clarify how a slogan about diamonds or cigarettes can be imprinted on your memory and be kept bouncing around there until you do something—like buy a diamond or a cigarette!

N. W. AYER: A CASE STUDY

Among intensely competitive American ad agencies, N. W. Ayer is neither largest nor flashiest. In fact, Ayer is only around the 16th largest, with worldwide billings in 1989 running at $1.35 billion annually. But no agency matches Ayer in firsts—breakthroughs in the art of agency advertising—or in solid, long-term accomplishments for major American client companies. Certainly, no other agency matches Ayer's record of being present at the dawn of American agency advertising and competing effectively in good times and bad ever since. Our case study agency was America's first,

formed in 1869, as the agency today says, by "an entrepreneurial 21-year-old Philadelphia schoolteacher," F. Wayland Ayer. (He named the firm after his father, N. W., and added "& Son," thinking that would add maturity and stature to his company.)

Ayer had a revolutionary concept: selling ad space in newspapers, as agent for the newspapers themselves. But he quickly switched to representing advertising clients, another first and one that established the client-oriented thrust of agency business as we know it today. ▶ 1

Ayer's past and present clients are a "Who's Who" of business in America: AT&T, Ford,

▶ 1 N. W. Ayer

High Points in the History of America's Oldest Agency

1869	Founded in Philadelphia by F. W. Ayer.	1922	Arranges first commercial broadcast, for Shur-On Optical Co., over KDKA, Pittsburgh. Coins "I'd Walk a Mile for a Camel" for R. J. Reynolds.
1874	Publishes first issue of *Ayer and Son's Manual for Advertisers*.		
1876	Signs first advertising contract with 15 percent commission on net cost of space bought.	1928	First air travel ad campaign aimed at the general public, for Ford Motor Co. (then producing airplanes).
1880	First issue of *American Newspaper Annual* (later the famous *N. W. Ayer & Sons Directory of Newspapers and Periodicals*).	1929	Opens London office.
		1933	Coins "Snap! Crackle! Pop!" for Kellogg's Rice Krispies.
1887	For client Nichols-Shepard's threshing machine, does first market research study by any ad agency.	1940	Coins "Never Underestimate the Power of a Woman" for *Ladies' Home Journal*.
1892	Hires first full-time copywriter, launches first agency copy department.	1942	Opens a motion-picture bureau.
		1948	Coins "A Diamond Is Forever" for De Beers.
1898	Hires first artist, expands into outdoor advertising.	1967	"If It Doesn't Fit, It Isn't Hanes" coined for P. H. Hanes Knitting Co.
1899	Coins "Uneeda Biscuit" for National Biscuit Co.	1979	Coins "Reach Out and Touch Someone" for AT&T.
1905	Decides against advertising patent medicines (important ethical consideration in those days of unregulated, often shady manufacturing).	1981	Coins "Be All That You Can Be" for the U.S. Army.
		1987	Burger King moves its $200 million account to Ayer in history's biggest agency switch.
1911	Coins "When It Rains It Pours" for Morton salt.	1989	Ayer loses Burger King account, setting a new record for history's biggest agency switch.
1921	Invents "coffee break" for Joint Coffee Trade Publicity Committee.		

Music specially written for commercials is among services offered by N. W. Ayer. Elliott Lawrence, who has won Tony awards for his music, is shown writing music for singer Sarah Vaughan in an AT&T commercial. *Courtesy N. W. Ayer; used with permission.*

General Motors, Citicorp, Honeywell, JC Penney, Pillsbury, Avon, and many others. "Ayer and its clients pioneered the development of modern retailing, name-brand products, the selling of automobiles and the telephone," a company pamphlet explains. "We took part in the take-off of commercial aviation and the establishment of a diamond as the traditional symbol of love, engagement and marriage."

Along the way, Ayer claims to have been the first agency to prepare radio commercials, the first to move into TV, and the first to charge clients a 15 percent commission on all billings as its standard fee.

Ayer is an employee-owned, private company whose "corporate culture" is one of cautious, even slow growth. The agency's client strategy is to fashion durable relationships with major companies of international standing. As of 1989, Ayer had been AT&T's agency for 80 years, De Beers's for 49, Du Pont's for 31, Ya-

maha's for 25, and General Motors' for 17. This conservative stance and the agency's relative smallness in an era of giant global agencies are presented positively in Ayer's self-promotion: "In this era of 'mega-agencies,' we continue to adhere to the simple belief that advertisers still want what they've always wanted from their advertising agencies: personal involvement, service and a superior creative product." However, selling is the agency's basic mission, and that never is far from the surface at Ayer.

AYER'S CORPORATE CREDO

We believe in hard-sell advertising.

However, trying to get the consumers' attention by simply hitting them over the head with facts isn't necessarily going to do this job.

Granted, it might, if we were dealing with a unique product or one-of-a-kind service. But in today's marketplace, even the unique can be "paritied" [equaled by others] inside of 90 days.

That job (our job) is to develop a product's personality in order to differentiate that product in the marketplace. And in the consumer's mind.

Effective advertising recognizes that the consumer's purchase decisions are based on a combination of factors. Some are factual, rational—like product benefits and proven efficacy.

Other factors influencing the purchase decision are strongly held, subjective feelings that go beyond the intellectual and the rational.

Identifying and tapping into these feelings provide a critical added dimension that, when welded to the product benefit, creates an advertising message that is more relevant, more meaningful and much more likely to be acted upon.

At Ayer, we believe it's the balance of the rational and emotional factors built into the communication's strategy and subsequent advertising that begins to differentiate a product and build a loyal relationship between that product and its users.

We call this process making Human Contact.

When advertising makes Human Contact, nothing sells harder.

The tone of Ayer's approach to advertising and the philosophy behind its daily activity are established in large measure by its chairman and chief executive officer, Louis T. Hagopian. Hagopian joined the agency in 1960 and became its chief executive officer in 1976.

VIEWS FROM THE TOP

by Louis T. Hagopian, Chairman, N. W. Ayer, Inc.

The greatness of American business stands on two feet: production and marketing.

Advertising sold hygiene to America: toothpaste, mouthwash, even soap and water. Clothes are cleaner, people smell better, houses are neater, the average American has a healthier life, a better esthetic sense—because of advertising.

We are in the communications business, and our task is to convey information, to persuade, and to sell. I repeat—to sell.

Elected officials are public servants, but the public passes judgment on them just one day every four years. The public says yes or no to our ideas, our performance, our credibility a hundred times a day. It turns us on. It turns us off. It turns the page.

Advertising, like nature, loves variety and nurtures originality, but when nature produces a gray, odorless flower, the bees are not charmed, and the flower dies. Advertising follows such natural laws. Or it dies.

The bad part of advertising in America is that it is so often unnatural, inefficient, ugly. The bad part of advertising is that misspent money, perverse money, greed, avarice, fear can keep inefficiency alive for so long.

I believe that far too often, business is run like a battlefield. Some advertisers don't want to compete for share of market, they want to eliminate the competition. They are hellbent on devastation, . . . destruction. If everybody held that view of business—kill or be killed, destroy, eliminate—if all of us held that view, I believe it would be the end of advertising as an ethical profession and the beginning of the jungle. For I submit that advertising is effective only when it sells products and services—when it builds brand equity—not when it denigrates competition with the idea of eliminating it.

Public hostility toward advertising is shown mainly by the lack of credibility of any and all advertising; a lot of our energy is spent trying to get people to believe the truth. But first, we have to get them to pay attention to our argument that what we are about to say is not a lie; because the public sees too many ads, most of them boring, self-indulgent, or disrespectful, and people have learned to zap advertising with their machines or their minds.

Advertisers and agencies . . . have come to prize the freedom of speech that [newspaper publishers] and editors have protected for us for so long. So believe with me. Act with me. Defend with me, when I say that the freedom of expression belongs to the advocates as well as the observers. Know that any limitation on the freedom to advertise is a direct obstacle to [newspapers'] freedom to cover a trial, write an editorial or publish a political column. . . .

It's in the interest of advertising, as well as safety and health, for the companies and agencies that sell intoxicating drinks to add a heavier dose of social responsibility to their market activities, not only in advertising but in promotions, like those on campuses. It's in their best interests if they apply individual, voluntary and uncodified restraints on advertising that exhorts individuals to take a drink or that equates the consumption of alcohol with achievement in the workplace, on the playing field, or in the bedroom.[2]

What Hagopian thinks and how he directs the agency are important to many people: Ayer employs more than 2,800 persons in 34 offices throughout the world. Its largest U.S. offices, in order of billings, are in New York, Los Angeles, Chicago, Houston, Detroit, and Stamford, Connecticut.

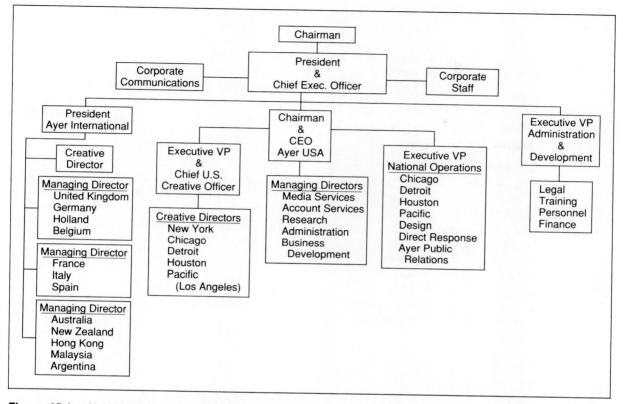

Figure 15.1. N. W. AYER, INC., ORGANIZATION. *Courtesy N. W. Ayer, Inc.*

Ayer deals with all major media, demanding therefore that its employees be familiar with all media operations. In 1987, for example, Ayer placed its clients' advertising in network TV ($292 million total billings), magazines ($142.2 million), spot or local TV ($93.5 million), newspapers ($70.4 million), radio ($37.1 million), direct response or direct mail ($26.4 million), and business publications ($15.3 million). You cannot specialize in one medium in an agency career; you'll need to understand all media if you want to rise at Ayer or any similar agency.

Ayer is organized in two broad efforts: Ayer International and Ayer USA. Hagopian directs the agency through three principal subordinates, one each for international operations, U.S. affairs, and administration and development (see Figure 15.1). Note the company's international scope and the emphasis on creative services in both Ayer International and Ayer USA. Like many ad agencies, Ayer offers public relations services (under "National Operations"), along with design and direct response mail services.

It takes a variety of skills to run a successful ad agency, and a shrewd chief executive officer builds a staff of executives whose experience complements his. Hagopian and three of his top aides represent solid experience in sales, creative and design, client contact, and administration.

AGENCY CAREERS: ROUTE TO THE TOP

The career paths of leading N. W. Ayer executives prove that there are many ways to the top in the ad agency world.

Chairman Louis T. Hagopian graduated

Louis T. Hagopian, N. W. Ayer's sixth chief executive, built the agency into a billion-dollar worldwide advertising and public relations conglomerate. *Courtesy N. W. Ayer; used with permission.*

from Michigan State University (1947, BA, Business Administration, after time out for the U.S. Navy in World War II) and immediately entered the automobile business in his native Michigan. For 13 years, he was in auto sales for Pontiac and Chrysler—good training, as it turned out, for his Ayer career because auto advertising is so important to the agency. Hagopian was assigned to Ayer's Detroit office, where he used his auto industry contacts. He became chief executive officer in 1976.

President Jerry J. Siano graduated from Philadelphia College of Art with a BA in Advertising Design and immediately joined Ayer as an ad designer. Within two years, he was branch office

art director, then took five years out for a job at another agency. He rejoined Ayer in 1964 and moved up on the creative side, becoming senior vice president for creative services in 1970. He took responsibility for all of Ayer's U.S. creative work in 1979. In 1987, he became chief executive officer for all operations in the $1 billion U.S. company and in 1989 was named president of N. W. Ayer, Inc.

Chief Creative Officer Patrick J. Cunningham (University of Wisconsin, BA, Journalism and Advertising, 1965) joined Ayer in 1972 after three years in the U.S. Navy and four years with two other ad agencies. His first job with Ayer was as copywriter in Philadelphia; the title of vice president and creative director of the New York office followed in 1975. Cunningham has worked on a wide variety of accounts, including De Beers (diamonds), AT&T, 7-Up, Avon, Kraft, and the U.S. Army.

Vice President and Account Supervisor Linda Jean Hooper joined Ayer in 1985 after college (C. W. Post College, BA, Fine Arts, 1981) and worked as a media planner (research specialist) and account executive with two other agencies. As account supervisor for Ayer, she coordinates Ayer contacts primarily with Procter & Gamble (Folger's coffee) and Duncan Hines/Canada.

Here are thumbnail sketches of major agency jobs below top executive ranks (note that agencies gather employees with a wide variety of skills and career backgrounds).

General managers of branch offices are senior officers responsible for total performance—sales, creative, research, client relations. Each manager reports to corporate headquarters through the president of Ayer International or the executive vice president of national operations of Ayer USA. Many general managers come from client relations or creative services but must have an overview of all agency functions in order to coordinate departments within an office.

The director of client (account) service is responsible for contact with client executives, selection of agency personnel who work on accounts, and, often, assistance in the design of campaign strategies for top clients. Senior account executives, with five years or so in account service, coordinate day-to-day contacts with clients, sometimes with just one major client but normally with several. Account executives work directly with clients, which requires learning the clients' corporate culture, marketing goals, and operational methods. Assistant account executives are often entry-level employees fresh from school. They work under the direct supervision of account executives.

A corporate chief creative director takes overall responsibility for art and copy. At Ayer USA, this slot is filled by an executive vice president who reports directly to the chairman and chief executive officer. The director sets agency tone in creative matters and supervises creative directors at each of five U.S. offices plus one in Ayer International.

These six individuals are directly responsible for the quality of work done for individuual clients: Creative supervisors direct copywriters and art directors assigned to individual client campaigns. Copywriters create copy for print, television, radio, and other media. Junior copywriters are often newly graduated employees under direct supervision of copywriters. Art directors handle visual material of all media. Art

director-producers are responsible for film and videotape commercials and, often, project budgets and contract bids, as well as shooting and producing finished versions. Junior art directors, often entry-level employees, work on such projects under tight supervision.

Creative services are normally divided between separate print and broadcast teams. Each team represents many skills—experts in type, layout, and graphic arts technology for print; experts in cinematography, music, and talent selection in broadcast. Traffic managers coordinate and expedite the final product for clients.

Media services involve selecting print and broadcast media that will deliver the results desired by a client, within the client's budget. A managing director coordinates such activities throughout Ayer USA and reports directly to the chairman and chief executive officer. Media supervisors direct efforts for a group of clients by supervising research, planning, and buying. Media planners study each client's needs and goals, then select the media to carry the client's ads and get the job done. Buyers normally specialize in ordering either time (broadcast) or space (print). Some experienced buyers may deal in both print and broadcast, or out-of-home advertising (billboards and so forth). Large agencies

Why is Jerry Siano, president of Ayer (*center, facing camera*), surrounded by New York reporters and photographers? Because it's September 29, 1987, and Burger King has just switched its $200 million account to Ayer from J. Walter Thompson. It was the biggest agency switch in American advertising history and made news in the business world. In 1989, in another turn-about, Ayer lost the Burger King account. *Courtesy N. W. Ayer; used with permission.*

George Zuckerman (*with pipe*) is N. W. Ayer's senior vice president and creative director on a major account, Continental Airlines, in the Houston office. Here he discusses advertising themes with his creative team. *Courtesy N. W. Ayer; used with permission.*

have network negotiators for top-level contacts with networks. Research analysts, often after just a year or two of experience, report on media circulations or ratings and other factors that help negotiators, buyers, and planners carry out client wishes.

Research departments at the corporate level in most agencies study consumer attitudes, advertising effectiveness, and other trends affecting agency business. Research account supervisors oversee research for individual clients.

Many agencies have separate departments for direct response marketing (including copywriting, art, and other services for direct mail) and public relations (many agencies offer full PR as well as advertising services). Other separate functions include sales promotion (assisting clients in packaging designs, logos, point-of-purchase displays, etc.) and telephone directory advertising (Yellow Pages).

Regardless of job title, if you work for an ad agency, you are involved in the agency's fundamental mission of helping clients to sell goods and services.

AN AD CAMPAIGN, STEP BY STEP

Way back in 1939, N. W. Ayer convinced De Beers Consolidated Mines, Ltd., that of all ad agencies, it best knew how to create advertising that would sell diamonds. Since then, generations of Ayer executives have labored to deliver the results that De Beers demands. And that, of course, is the first requirement in any agency campaign: Get the business, then hold it.

Getting the business involves convincing the prospective client that the agency is dynamic and creative. It means selling the organization as capable of meeting all client needs. It means selling individual employees as capable of truly understanding how the client firm operates and, just as important, working effectively with client personnel. This is done in head-on competition (''shootouts,'' in industry parlance) with other ad agencies, all trying to persuade the prospective client that they are best suited for the job. Often, lengthy meetings are held between agency and client employees, each side testing the personal ''chemistry'' of the other. Agency executives describe their creative strengths, sketching possible themes and campaigns and attempting simultaneously to build a picture of what the prospective client has in mind for an advertising effort.

When both sides think they've got a good match and a contract is signed, the agency assigns a senior executive to ensure that effective advertising is delivered, that the client stays happy, and that come renewal time in a couple of years, the contract is signed again. At Ayer, Executive Vice President George Eversman is charged with holding the De Beers diamonds account. We can get an inside view of his strategic thinking by examining an outline he and a team of Ayer executives developed for advertising jewelry.[3]

◆ *Situation Analysis.* Agency employees assist in determining where the client's product is positioned currently in the marketplace. Who are competitors, and where are their products positioned? What is the client's image in the eyes of consumers, and what image do competitors have? In sum, before agency and client can proceed, they must decide where the starting point is!

◆ *Goal Setting.* Where does the client want to be positioned? In which market niche, with which product? And what corporate and product image does the client want to achieve? For example, if the initial situation analysis identifies the client's image as, say, a seller of medium-priced jewelry, should the goal of advertising be to reinforce that image and enlarge the client's share of the medium-priced jewelry market? Or should the goal be to move upscale toward a new image as a seller of high-priced jewelry? During this process, agency employees must suggest which goals are atttainable through advertising, how they can be attained, and so forth.

◆ *Establishing Media Objectives.* Having determined where the client wants to go, client and agency executives now consider how to get there. Says the Ayer team: "You need to set a media objective—what you want your ads to do for you. You'll want to reach the largest group of the right

people for the least amount of money."[4] Ayer executives say this involves answering significant questions:

Who is your target audience (in income, education, age, and so forth)?

Where is the audience and the client's trading area? Is it a city, state, five-county area? The nation?

When is the best time to reach the target audience? (Diamond sales are active all year but particularly so before Christmas.)

How much advertising does the client need? Pushing a single campaign for gift rings before Christmas requires a relatively simple message (perhaps advertising a price-reduction sale?). However, creating a whole new image for the client will take more advertising over a longer period.

Now imagine that you are an Ayer executive trying to devise a strategy for De Beers. Do any broad considerations come to mind? Here is how Ayer outlined its strategy for De Beers:

Advertising objective: Sell quality (as contrasted with medium-priced or low-priced jewelry).

Target audience: Adults with household incomes of $50,000 or more annually (who presumably can afford quality diamonds).

Market geography: All of the United States but particularly areas where high-income Americans live. People of similar income and educational levels tend to group together in city neighborhoods or suburbs, and an ad agency must find all areas crucial to its advertiser client. It makes no sense, obviously, to advertise expensive De Beers diamonds in a neighborhood whose residents average $11,000 annual income. Increasingly, U.S. Postal Service zip codes are used to define areas where special advertising emphasis will be placed.

Seasonality: Year round.

Communications: Devise campaigns emphasizing repeated exposure of the sales message.

Now think (and if you were working for an agency, you'd have to think *quickly*), what haven't we pinned down? Cost! A reality of agency work is that cost is never far from the thoughts of everyone involved. The client wants successful advertising that provides results as inexpensively as possible; your agency boss wants you to keep the client happy at the lowest possible cost (for your agency, the difference between what it can charge the client and your expenses in performing the task goes toward profit).

In agency work, you must know the client's business, and that includes spending on advertising. Having been De Beers's agency since 1939, the agency knows that retail jewelers allocate to advertising a little more than 2 percent of total sales. (The Newspaper Advertising Bureau compiles similar figures for all lines of retailing; advertising expenditures range from a low of about 0.8 percent of total sales by gas stations to a high of 5.5 percent or so for movie theaters.)[5]

Obviously, agency employees need both an understanding of every aspect of the advertising business and a knowledge of the client's business and marketing strategy. Now add a third area of required expertise: understanding the media—their operations and their weaknesses and strengths.

For example, the Ayer team has decided that high-priced jewelry will sell best to persons with $50,000 or more in annual income. It must now decide which advertising medium will reach them most efficiently—that is, which will get the sales message across to potential purchasers of jewelry at acceptable cost.

It's axiomatic in advertising that the best way to reach high-income Americans is through selective use of print media. Magazine and newspaper readers, as a group, have higher incomes and better educations than nonreaders or Americans who depend primarily on television for news and entertainment. For example, a magazine focused on expensive overseas travel will attract readers capable of affording such travel—and also capable of affording high-priced jewelry. Newspapers reach upscale consumers, too.

N. W. Ayer advises employees to seek continuing education if they desire promotion within the agency. This not-so-subtle reminder is from an employee magazine, *Ayernews. Courtesy* Ayernews; *used with permission.*

So in evaluating various media for the jewelry campaign, the Ayer team looks first at the composition or purity of audience each delivers. By a substantial factor, the team favors magazines and newspapers. By contrast, Ayer executives assigned to the Burger King account, which the agency handled for several years, looked more closely at TV when considering audience composition. That medium delivers mass audiences—much larger than those delivered by individual print media—and reaches many persons, particularly children, who favor fast foods.

Next the Ayer team considers the coverage (size of audiences) each medium delivers. In its jewelry strategy, Ayer uses this example: In general, 35 percent of the newspaper audience in Chicago has an annual household income of $40,000 or more. The *Chicago Tribune* reaches

300,000 of 900,000 persons in Chicago. That means that an ad in the *Tribune* will reach 105,000 persons with $40,000-plus annually and who are therefore primary targets for high-priced jewelry (that is, 35 percent of the *Tribune*'s total audience of 300,000 are prime targets).

Now the Ayer team must calculate the cost per thousand (CPM) of reaching desirable consumer readers. For our purposes, suffice it to say that this calculation involves closely examining the *Tribune*'s space costs, then informing the jewelry advertisers what their costs will be for each 1,000 persons reached. That CPM is compared with similar figures for other media, and Ayer and client executives then decide where to place ads.

Throughout this process, Ayer executives must consider what they call concepts. They examine the types of media, their tone, the general impression they create in the marketplace. A magazine aimed at, say, corporate purchasing executives might deliver a high-income, demographically attractive audience. But does its news content create an environment conducive to selling jewelry? Probably not. But how about *The New Yorker* magazine? Its topical reporting, sophisticated writing, and page after page of high-quality ads create the type environment Ayer and De Beers seek. As an agency executive, you would next be responsible for obtaining the best possible position for the ad within the print medium (in broadcast, the best possible time). Adjacency is a major factor in advertising. You wouldn't place a diamond advertisement in the sports pages of a medium-sized newspaper. You wouldn't run a diamond commercial during Saturday morning TV cartoons. Rather, you would strive for positioning in *The New Yorker* next to a popular feature or main article sure to draw the maximum number of readers.

The assumption of such panoramic responsibility is a reality of agency work. Another is that there are often wild up-and-down swings in agency work, sudden developments that can bring joy to an agency or plunge it into gloom.

GOOD TIMES, BAD TIMES: BURGERS AND THE ARMY

Despite best efforts, few ad agencies can build into their year-to-year financial performance the predictability enjoyed by many industries.

Most newspapers count on roughly the same circulation and advertising from one year to the next. Magazines hold reader loyalty without fear of devastating defections overnight. However, ad agencies—and employees—live with the reality that just as winning a huge client can create enormous prosperity, so can losing one put an agency into a financial tailspin and destroy jobs. Careers in advertising, as a result, often involve moving to escape the failing fortunes of an agency left behind and to seek financial prosperity with another, luckier agency just ahead.

For Ayer, bad times—clearly the worst in its long history—came in 1986 when it was suspended by the U.S. Army after nearly two decades of handling the army's $100 million advertising account. The Army said that one Ayer executive accepted kickbacks and that there was other wrongdoing in handling the account. The army said that it had evidence of bid rigging and of overbilling by $400,000 in 1979. In 1988, Ayer agreed to pay the army $750,000 without admitting guilt to settle the case.[6]

It was a severe blow to Ayer's image. The agency's recruiting campaign ("Be All That You Can Be") had been extremely successful and helped the army attract enough recruits to build a volunteer force. Ayer always prided itself in long-standing relationships with clients—and suddenly, very publicly, there was a blemish on all that.

Chairman Hagopian characterized the army experience as "entirely alien to the agency's corporate culture." "The loss of the army account was costly," he admitted.[7]

But Hagopian led the agency in bouncing back. Ayer the same year won Burger King's $200 million account. It was the biggest account switch in advertising history. The *New York Times* commented: "While merriment prevailed at Ayer headquarters over the much-needed good news, a pall came over the offices of the loser, the J. Walter Thompson Company.'' There was reason for a pall. About 100 Thompson employees were let go due to loss of the Burger King revenue. The *Wall Street Journal* estimated that Thompson lost $15 million to $20 million in annual revenue.[8]

Thirty agencies competed for the account. In preparing for such a ''shootout,'' an agency can easily spend $250,000. At Ayer, between 50 and 70 employees worked for months on the Burger King presentation. Ayer wouldn't comment on cost, but competitors put the figure at $1 million![9]

Immediately after winning, Ayer executives came under pressure to produce results. Burger King had recently finished a disastrous ad campaign (featuring a fictional character, Herb the Nerd), and sales were flat, while those of its number one competitor, McDonald's, were rising. Ayer's challenge was to create product differentiation in ads that motivated consumers to perceive Burger King hamburgers as different from and better than McDonald's. Achieving differentiation in a marketplace crowded with similar products is an old and very difficult challenge for an ad agency.

The advertising world watched delightedly as the two fast-food chains and their agencies squared off. ''The Burger Wars are back,'' said the *Wall Street Journal*, noting that ''for the past few years, McDonald's has been eating Burger King's lunch.''[10] The stakes were high. McDonald's had 36 percent of the $25 billion fast-food hamburger market; Burger King, 17 percent.

Ayer's principal advertising theme was that Burger King was broiling hamburgers rather than frying them (one TV commercial had a youngster showing a friend grill marks on his hamburger and exclaiming, ''Gee, I can't get those at McDonald's'').

Many members of the advertising community criticized Ayer. *Advertising Age*, the influential weekly trade publication, commented: ''Most anything would be better than what N. W. Ayer has produced in its debut effort following The Biggest Account Change in Advertising History.'' The advertising campaign, *Ad Age* said, was ''sloppy, uneven, confusing and not a little bit bizarre.'' Scarcely a year after Ayer won the account, Burger King's parent, Pillsbury Co., was publicly saying that more effective advertising was needed. Commented *Ad Age*: ''N. W. Ayer's honeymoon on the $200 million Burger

Can you spot the product differentiation N. W. Ayer strived for in this ad for Toshiba's laser printer? (It's the claim that of all printers, Toshiba's is best suited for the high-volume output that can be created by a group of workers.) *Courtesy N. W. Ayer; used with permission.*

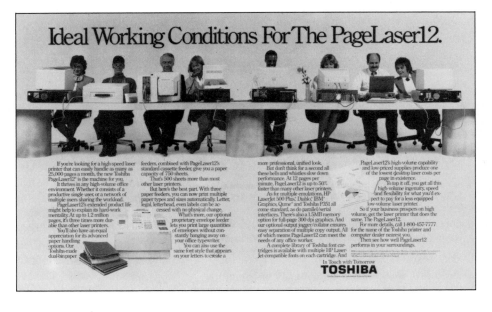

King account, if it ever had one, is over.''[11]

Although many people in advertising felt that Burger King's poor business performance was due to problems within the fast-food chain itself, criticism of Ayer's performance built quickly. In April 1989, just 18 months after awarding it to Ayer, Burger King switched its account (now worth $215 million annually) to two other agencies, Saatchi & Saatchi Advertising and D'Arcy Masius Benton & Bowles. It was a new world's record for the switch of an ad agency account—the second time Ayer was involved in such a record in less than two years!

Four days later, under that cloud, Jerry Siano moved up to president and chief executive officer (Lou Hagopian remained chairman) and faced the task of restoring morale. He quickly landed a couple of new accounts, acquired a 40 percent share of the $202.9 million Canadian agency, Spectrum Group, and thus signaled his intention to expand Ayer internationally.

Life at Ayer, like everywhere else in the ad agency business, is colorful, exciting, often immensely fulfilling and rewarding, and at times completely unpredictable.

☆ SUMMARY

N. W. Ayer, Inc., America's oldest ad agency, is a case study of how an agency can generate campaigns that not only sell products and services but become woven into the fabric of national life. Ayer created slogans such as ''Reach out and touch someone'' and ''Let your fingers do the walking.''

Ayer isn't the largest or flashiest agency. But no other agency matches Ayer in firsts. Ayer was first to represent advertiser clients (as contrasted with newspapers) and first to establish long-term relationships with clients such as Ford, AT&T, and General Motors.

Ayer's corporate credo stresses the agency's mission is to sell clients' goods and services. Louis T. Hagopian, chairman, says that advertising's role is to communicate information, to persuade and sell.

In agency work, some executives rise from creative work, general administration, or client relations. Account services involves working with individual clients; creative services includes copywriting and preparation of TV commercials; in media services, employees select media for client advertising.

In any agency, the first challenge is to get and hold the client's business. That involves selling the agency as capable of meeting client needs and individual employees as capable of working effectively with client executives. When the contract is signed, agency employees analyze the client's product and its marketplace position. Then client and agency set goals on which market niche and image to seek through advertising. That involves identifying the target audience and determining when and how to reach it. The agency then devises a campaign to communicate the sales message to the desired audience for the desired effect, at a cost that is acceptable to the client.

Agency work involves understanding all aspects of advertising, the client's business, and the media.

Winning a large account can bring prosperity; losing one can mean loss of jobs for many employees. Agency careers, therefore, often lack stability.

☆ RECOMMENDED READING

Information on N. W. Ayer is available through Corporate Communications, N. W. Ayer, 1345 Avenue of the Americas, New York, NY 10105. Industry information on agencies is available through the American Association of Advertising Agencies, 666 Third Avenue, New York, NY 10017. Also see Herbert Gardner, Jr., *The Advertising Agency Business* (Chicago: Crain Books, 1977) and Stephen Fox, *The Mirror Makers: A History of American Advertising and Its Creators* (New York: Morrow, 1984). A particularly well done critique of advertising is Michael Schudson's *Advertising: The Uneasy Profession* (New York: Basic Books, 1984).

THE PUBLIC RELATIONS COMMUNICATORS

Public relations is one of the most rapidly expanding—and most controversial—career sectors in the American mass communications system. Although PR techniques have been used to influence public opinion since the dawn of recorded history, the rapid expansion as an organized industry is relatively new. Indeed, the PR industry is still trying to identify itself and its role, and to some extent it is still unsure it can convince outsiders of its legitimacy. Nevertheless, the impact of PR—the highly organized effort to persuade—shapes daily American life on behalf of ideas and causes, both good and bad.

The controversy surrounding public relations is not new. As from the beginning, PR to many means manipulation and distortion—sneaky, hidden efforts to convince and persuade regardless of the truth or merits of the client, personality, cause, idea, product, or service being promoted. However, supporters of the PR function argue that it has legitimacy, that it injects facts and viewpoints into the competitive marketplace of ideas and thus performs a role in our democracy that is not only worthwhile but absolutely essential.

For students of the American mass communications system, this is an opportune time to turn to PR. Great change is afoot in the industry. There is even rethinking of whether PR should exist as a separate discipline or be combined with that other great persuader, advertising, in a new management and marketing tool in business and industry. Many corporate or institutional managers, for example, see the need for a single department handling one all-encompassing effort. Indeed, global business conglomerates are already combining PR and advertising techniques in a single marketing thrust.

In response to the new thinking, major advertising and PR agencies are joining forces through mergers and acquisitions so that they can offer a wide range of services that will help a client, say, package and market a political candidate or position a corporation, product, or cause in the public mind. The corporate structure of all that remains unclear.

One thing is clear: Whatever its organizational form, the PR function will continue to touch you in some way every day, whether used in selling a product or a fund-raising drive for a charity. Like advertising, the persuasive art of PR is part of the American way.

In Chapter 16, we'll look broadly at the industry. In Chapter 17, we'll go inside the world's largest PR agency, Burson-Marsteller, to see how it is structured and where the jobs are.

The Public Relations Industry

T he massive American advertising industry marshals huge sums of money and enormous creative energy to do one thing: to sell. A similar large, energetically creative industry has a closely related basic mission: to persuade.

The distinction between selling and persuading is admittedly thin, and the mindsets of people who sell and persuade for a living and the techniques they use are very similar. Even the bottom-line goal of both advertising and public relations is the same: to spur you, me, and millions like us to take a course of action, to change our minds, to buy something.

The art of persuasion to which we turn in this chapter is not new to our survey of mass communications in America. Every media industry has a persuasive dimension: Advertising sells, newspapers editorialize, and so do magazines and broadcasting. But in PR, we encounter for the first time in our study a communications industry that stands distinctly apart *because* of its persuasive nature. Not all communicators agree with PR practitioners that their form of persuasion, their role as advocates, is as vital or as professional as that of, say, a reporter or an editor. Indeed, relationships between PR and other communications industries are at times adversarial.

PUBLIC AFFAIRS

As press secretary to the governor of Georgia, Barbara Morgan stays in close touch with reporters covering the capitol in Atlanta. Their idle chatter over coffee, as well as what they write and broadcast, is crucial to her job of researching and analyzing opinion in the press corps and, through it, assessing the mood of voters throughout the state.[1] In frequent meetings with the governor, and based on her understanding of reporter thinking, Morgan contributes policy recommendations to help the governor plan his political program and strategy. She recommends themes to stress in speeches, points to make in press conferences, moves to head off problems brewing among reporters and voters or to put to rest ones that have already popped into public view (call it "crisis management"). ▶ 1

At the governor's request, Morgan executes a media program by carrying his message to reporters and, frequently, giving them direct access

Barbara Morgan helps Georgia Governor Joe Frank Harris analyze public opinion and serves as a messenger in delivering his thinking to the media and the public. *Photo used with permission.*

The most important functions in public relations involve researching and analyzing public mood (and the public can be consumers or others, as well as reporters and voters), recommending to management (in this case, the governor) policy moves that respond to the public mood, then executing programs designed to influence the public. All that is followed by monitoring and evaluating results, then more research, analysis, and interpretation—and the entire function starts all over again.

Note the dynamics of that little scenario played out daily in Atlanta:

◆ Morgan must be equally at ease and effective in dealing with an internal constituency (the governor and his close aides) and an external public (reporters and, through them, Georgia voters and power brokers).

◆ She must think in broad strategic terms as counsellor to the governor, then serve in a technical capacity with a deep understanding of how the media operate (even, for example, how much lighting TV cameras need at a press conference).

◆ Finally, Morgan must be able to take the heat that inevitably will come from the media when they can't get to the governor or when he won't answer their questions and from the governor when he's unhappy with how the media are reporting his policies.

to him by setting up press conferences and interviews.

When stories about the governor or Georgia politics hit print or the evening news, Morgan carefully monitors and evaluates the effectiveness of the governor's media relations and his likely impact through the media on voters. Then it's back to coffee and chats with reporters as Morgan begins a new cycle of the circular, never-ending process (see Figure 16.1).

In Barbara Morgan's relationships with the governor and her media and voter public, we see

Figure 16.1. STEPS IN THE PUBLIC RELATIONS PROCESS.

PR is a circular, never-ending process of researching public mood, recommending policy, executing a program, and evaluating results.

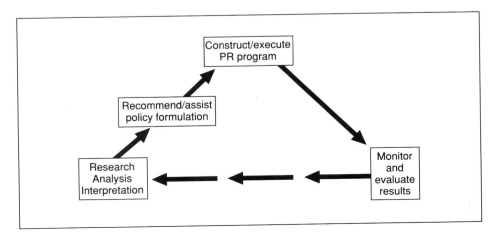

▶ High Points in Public Relations History

c. 100 B.C. — In ancient times, rulers of Babylonia, Greece, and Rome are sensitive to public opinion and strive to influence it ("Vote for Cicero. He is a good man").

1600s — *Propaganda* enters common usage with the Catholic church's *Congregatio de propaganda* (Congregation for propagating the faith).

1620 — Virginia Company campaigns to persuade Britons to settle in the New World.

1641 — Fund-raising in America starts as Harvard sends ministers to Britain to raise money.

1750s — American colonialists campaign aggressively to build public support for independence; Ben Franklin publishes in 1754 a famous cartoon, "Join, or Die," to inspire unity among colonies.

1828 — Andrew Jackson occupies the White House, appoints the first, but unofficial, presidential press secretary, Amos Kendall.

1830s — Railroads and others launch massive campaigns to persuade easterners to resettle in the West.

1888 — Mutual Life Insurance Co. hires Charles J. Smith to handle press releases, improve its image.

1889 — First in-house corporate publicity department created by Westinghouse.

1896 — Political publicity blossoms during the William Jennings Bryan–William McKinley presidential campaign.

1897 — Term *public relations* used by the Association of American Railroads.

1900 — Expansive era opens for PR; a "publicity bureau" is established in Boston, with Harvard and others as clients; Chicago Edison Co., Ford Motor Co., and others begin to assess and campaign to influence public opinion.

1904 — Ivy Lee and George Parker open a pioneering publicity office in New York City.

1906 — Lee becomes the first PR counsel, hired to improve the image of the strike-ridden coal industry; advises substantive steps to inform the public, not a cover-up.

1914 — John D. Rockefeller hires Lee to change his image as a money-grubbing multimillionaire.

1915 — Associated Advertising Clubs of the World establishes the first professional PR groups.

1917 — Committee on Public Information ("Creel Committee") created by President Wilson to influence American attitudes toward World War I.

1923 — Edward L. Bernays publishes *Crystallizing Public Opinion*, defining and popularizing the PR function; earns recognition as a founder of modern PR practices.

1931 — General Motors hires PR chief Paul W. Garrett, assigns him to both ascertain public attitudes and influence them.

1942 — U.S. establishes Voice of America to tell its story abroad during World War II; Office of War Information, under Elmer Davis, handles the overall information effort.

1948 — Public Relations Society of America (PRSA) formed through the merger of smaller predecessor groups.

1953 — President Eisenhower creates the U.S. Information Agency to influence public attitudes worldwide.

1954 — PRSA adopts the Code of Professional Standards for the Practice of Public Relations.

1970 — International Association of Business Communicators is formed (issues code of standards in 1976).

1989 — Foundation for Public Relations Education changes its name to the Institute of Public Relations and heightens its activity on behalf of professionalism in PR.

a PR form defined as *public affairs*. This involves working for government—federal, state, or local—in highly visible capacities. Examples are White House and U.S. State Department spokespersons, who figure in the news daily.

ISSUES IN A PRESS SECRETARY'S LIFE
by Barbara Morgan, Press Secretary to the Governor of Georgia

Question: *In terms of ethical journalism, which issues or controversies create most difficulty for you?*

Answer: Probably the most frustrating experience is being contacted by a writer on deadline for a response by the governor after the writer has spent days, weeks, or even months developing a story. It strikes me as extremely unfair to write a story or put together a broadcast piece that focuses on administration policy or gubernatorial action and only call the governor for a reaction on deadline. He should be afforded the right—and the courtesy—of knowing about the story earlier, when he might have been better able to explain, justify, rationalize, and flesh out a situation that is being critiqued. When this happens, it tells me that the reporter set out with a hidden agenda or a preconceived mission without being fair and objective. Inevitably, the governor and I feel defensive—and respond just that way on occasion.

I cannot say that I have had reporters break an embargo [on release time] set by this office, but frequently leaks occur prior to a scheduled announcement. I do not believe that his personal office staff can be faulted when this happens, but rather individuals elsewhere in the executive or legislative branches.

The governor is unfailingly courteous when "ambushed," and he is adept at not falling into a trap, if that is the intention of the reporter. He won't be led into statements that he is not ready to make. I will credit his always cautious nature for this. I find most reporters with whom we deal regularly to be extremely respectful of the governor and not inclined to ambush interviews.

Question: *In terms of how you operate as a press secretary, do you consider yourself the messenger, a coarchitect of policy, or what?*

Answer: Of course, I function as "messenger" on occasion, including the relaying of information from the media, the public, and elected officials to the governor and conveying information and responses from him to them. I have input on policy development in that I gather information for the governor and help him to analyze situations, facts, and policy options. He will ask my opinion on certain matters, not only those involving press and public relations but also decisions affecting state government. I carry out policy that he sets.

Beyond those functions, I consider myself both a "fireman" and a "forecaster" for him. As a "fireman," I am constantly dousing little fires before they can become full-fledged infernos. As a "forecaster," I remain constantly on watch for issues or developing trends that sometimes can be handled and managed before they become problems or that we need to prepare to handle if there is no way to head them off in advance.

I am aware that, as much or more than any other staffer, the press secretary represents the governor in the eyes of the media and the public, and this responsibility guides me both professionally and in my personal life. It is a privilege and responsibility that I feel very keenly. I am his most ardent defender and attempt to protect him and his views and actions from unfair criticism and misrepresentation. At times and in certain situations, I have more freedom and leeway to explain and analyze his positions than the "politics" of a situation allow him. In that case, we function as a "team" to present his views and statements.

It is critical that I have a close relationship and real rapport with the governor, as any press secretary should. Because I know him well and work at it, I can properly represent him and his views to the media, but I never respond on his behalf to any question if I am not absolutely confident of his views and how he wants his response to be phrased. A press secretary who does otherwise would quickly lose the trust of the governor, would become unable to function effectively, and would in time become less and less relied on by the governor and the media.

Question: *What academic preparation and work experience would you advise for students seeking careers similar to yours?*

Answer: First, because I am a political appointee, [as are most people in] such positions, . . . I could not recommend that one set out to make a career out of the job of press secretary. Having said that, I would stress that one's academic preparation, work experience, and/or natural talent ensure an excellent ability to write. Anyone who can write, naturally or by training and experience, has a great deal of power, essentially, when it is necessary to analyze issues, develop policy options, phrase difficult or technical responses, or sculpt delicate statements. First and foremost, be a writer because writers are thinkers, and thinkers are in great demand in a political office, business, or elsewhere.

I definitely believe that having had journalism experience is a positive advantage to one in my position, but the understanding of deadlines, the necessity of prompt responses, and insight into what the media need can be learned on the job. The disadvantage is the time lost and errors made while learning. I do not believe the media

thought I was any more credible simply because I had been a reporter. Their trust and confidence must be earned; they do not come automatically.

While I tout the advantages of having been a reporter first, I would counsel those making a transition from media to press secretary to understand that one's loyalties must immediately and decisively be switched from the press corps and former fellow reporters to the individual who employs you. You cannot play both sides of the field. Your allegiance is owed to the officeholder, and it is he or she who must be served by your actions, not the media.

In my case, I was fortunate also to have had experience in public relations, another field which complements the duties of a press secretary. This position also involves developing and staging events designed to attract media coverage of the governor's initiatives, and knowing what constitutes good public relations is a real benefit. Several of Governor Harris's public awareness campaigns have received national recognition from the Public Relations Society of America, and he has been cited by the Georgia Chapter of the PRSA for his excellent use and understanding of public relations techniques.

CORPORATE PUBLIC RELATIONS

This is one of the largest, best-financed sectors of public relations. Corporations spend millions to control as best they can the internal and external environments in which they operate. Corporate PR involves managing internal information programs designed to ensure that top management's policies are disseminated throughout the company and are understood by all employees. Newsletters or company magazines are vehicles management uses to "get the word out."

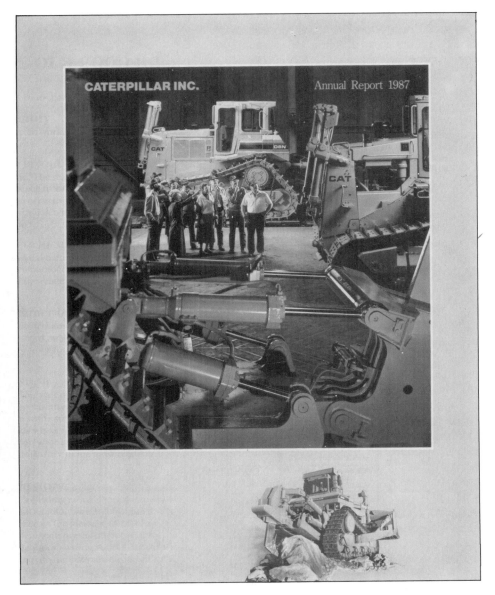

Skills required in corporate communications include the ability to create publications reflecting the company's marketplace image and tone. (Left) Caterpillar's Public Affairs Department produced an annual report cover emphasizing the company's strengths—heavy equipment. (Right) The report also explains company policy on continuing education for employees. In this one document, Public Affairs addresses both external and internal audiences. *Courtesy Caterpillar Inc.; used with permission.*

Externally, corporate PR deals with many constituencies: local community, investors, Wall Street analysts, and so forth. The central thrust is to aid the company in its basic mission of earning a profit. That can involve improving the company's image, publicizing its products and services, helping to recruit new employees—in general, ensuring that the company's environment is conducive to profitable business. Just as they have developed highly professional techniques in production, sales, and general management, so have many American corporate managers developed disciplined and professional approaches to public relations.

Employees attend training session in Caterpillar's Mobile Electronics Training Lab, a classroom and laboratory on wheels.

The work environment is changing, and as it does, Caterpillar's education and training needs are increasing. The company has initiated a variety of new programs to help employees work more effectively in a dynamic workplace. The Mobile Electronics Training Lab, shown above, is equipped with computers, audiovisual equipment, and other technical training aids. It travels to North American facilities where on-site classes are held. The mobile lab eliminates the need to establish duplicate electronics training labs at each facility, giving maximum training coverage at a minimum investment.

In addition to the mobile training concept, Caterpillar has an established training function in most facilities around the world. Classes tailored to the industrial environment are available on topics ranging from math to machining techniques. Many courses are offered on-site during work hours.

The company is also expanding its use of innovative training methods, including education and training via satellite and interactive video instruction.

Employees are continuing their education outside of Caterpillar as well. Tuition reimbursement and educational leave policies have made continuing education more attainable and more affordable. In the United States, the number of college classes completed by employees increased by more than 25% from 1986 to 1987.

The company has expanded its supplier and dealer training efforts as well. Supplier courses are designed to improve quality, lower costs, and move toward just-in-time delivery. Dealer training classes range from selling skills and repair techniques to financial analysis and strategic planning.

19

Career success in PR is guaranteed if you have a bright smile, a pleasant personality, and a people orientation, right? Wrong. Although predicting success in PR is no easier than in any other media sector, it is certain that success won't be automatic just because you're popular on campus. Note the following case study.

Caterpillar Inc. manufactures annually more than $8 billion worth of heavy equipment and engines for earth-moving and construction throughout the world. A Caterpillar executive describes recruitment and training of college graduates for the company's Public Affairs Department at the general office in Peoria, Illinois.

STARTING IN CORPORATE COMMUNICATIONS

**by C. A. Williams, Manager,
College Relations & Recruitment,
Caterpillar Inc.**

Qualifications for Communications Trainee

1. *Good scholastic record*—overall B average or above. Preferably, academic work will have concentrated on communications skills, economics, and political science. Other academic backgrounds will be considered if the other requirements can be met.

2. *Strong communications skills (writing and/or public speaking, with emphasis on writing)*—as demonstrated by high grades in pertinent courses or by experience (college or daily newspaper, magazines, debating, etc.). Writing assignments at Caterpillar include news stories, magazine articles, speeches, governmental affairs bulletins, brochures, public affairs advertising, economic education material, analyses of requests for contributions, audiovisual scripts, and technical writing.

3. *Leadership potential*—as demonstrated by elected office or other positions of responsibility outside the classroom or job.

4. *Analytical skills*—evidenced by an interest in the important issues of the day and the ability to understand and discuss them intelligently. The Public Affairs Department becomes heavily involved in governmental issues at all levels—local (city and county), state, federal, and international (United Nations, European Community).

The Communications Trainee Program

The program covers approximately 12 months during which the trainee becomes acquainted with the manufacturing and marketing of Caterpillar products, the roles of public affairs in a manufacturing plant, and the role of a communicator in marketing and public affairs groups. Upon completion of the program, the trainee is assigned to a job in either Public Affairs or Marketing Support in the general office or in one of the company's facilities.

◆ *College Grad Orientation.* 1 week. Exposure to company products and competitors and company benefits, history, policies, procedures, practices, copyrights, trademarks, antitrust considerations, and handling of confidential material.

◆ *Marketing Training.* 16 weeks. Covers Caterpillar products and parts and service marketing; marketing philosophy and practice. Trainee gets opportunities to tear down Cat components, visit manufacturing and parts distribution facilities, and visit a dealer.

◆ *Graphic Arts Orientation.* 2 weeks. Graphic Arts Department at general office, learning the role of video, film, artwork, slide, and photography production in Caterpillar communications.

◆ *Manufacturing Orientation.* 2 weeks. Trainee learns how to operate various machines: mills, drills, lathes; blueprint reading, standards, and miscellaneous manufacturing processes.

◆ *Foreman Orientation.* 1 week. Time with manufacturing and assembly foreman to get exposure to "life on the shop floor."

◆ *Word Processing Training.* 2 weeks. Trainee learns to operate the word processing equipment in various company communications operations.

◆ *East Peoria Public Affairs Orientation.* 6 weeks. At the Public Affairs division of the East Peoria plant, work includes writing articles and taking photographs for the plant newspaper; helping to write and produce *Tracktalk*, the monthly employee video show; developing a program to improve relations with certain community organizations; and assisting in administering community affairs projects such as the United Way campaign and Junior Achievement.

◆ *Public Affairs General Office Orientation.* 6 weeks. Public Affairs work in Governmental Affairs, Community and Corporate Support, Public Information, and Employee Information. Work includes writing articles for *Folks*, a newspaper; helping to select photos for the annual report; writing copy for a brochure; hosting visitors or assisting at special functions; and updating manuals for Public Information or Governmental Affairs.

◆ *Technical Center Orientation.* 6 weeks. At the Technical Center's Technical Presentations Department, writing and assisting with design of a brochure, writing a script for a videotape, writing articles for *Prototype*, a newspaper, and writing a speech.

◆ *Publications Orientation.* 6 weeks. Writing news service articles for trade press magazines or contributing to *Dealer, Source*, or *Editorial Input*. Trainee will probably visit customers and cover a story.

◆ *Business Orientation.* 2 days. Overview of economics, pricing and scheduling, product control, and product source planning. Trainee will learn about forecasting, scheduling, pricing, and sourcing decisions.

ASSOCIATION AND INSTITUTIONAL PR

Thousands of PR persons are employed by labor unions, trade associations, social, religious, and educational organizations, and other groups that, although they don't sell a product, nevertheless have a cause, idea, viewpoint, or purpose they want represented as best possible in the public mind. Earlier we mentioned the American Newspaper Publishers Association, the National Association of Broadcasters, and the Magazine Publishers Association. All labor unceasingly to improve the external social environment in which their constituent newspapers, TV stations, and magazines do business. That involves efforts to improve the public perception of association members and their activities and lobbying in Washington or state capitals for favorable legislation. The newspaper publishers' association, for example, tries to convince both public and Congress that permitting telephone companies to sell news and information would create huge monopolies, threatening the diversity of media voices now heard in the United States. Next time you see a bumper sticker reading ''Milk Drinkers Are Better Lovers'' or ''Visit Florida Next,'' you'll be looking at evidence the American dairy farmers and the Florida tourism industry are at work through their associations. Internally, working with members, people in association and institutional PR disseminate information, arrange meetings, hold seminars, and so forth, to hold the group together, focus its activities, and make it

An advertising medium advertises: The *Boston Globe* uses outdoor billboards to reach nonsubscribers with the message that they can keep up on politics by reading the newspaper. All major media conduct public relations campaigns of this sort. *Wide World Photos.*

more effective in dealing with external opportunities and challenges. Fund-raising is often an important task in association and institutional PR. Universities, hospitals, and many nonprofit groups depend heavily on their ability to attract donations and grants. Some companies specialize in conducting fund-raising campaigns for a fee.

PUBLICITY

In contrast with advertising, a system of paying to reach the public through the media, publicity is designed to highlight a product, service, cause, idea, or personality as interesting to the public—newsworthy enough to gain free access to the media. In corporate PR, this involves handling press conferences or news releases announcing, say, a technical breakthrough in the manufacture of computers or airplanes, an event reporters gladly cover as news. Reaching the public through news columns or broadcasts lends legitimacy to a product, service, cause, or idea not quite matched in paid advertising. Often, publicity is an activity independent of corporate, association, or institutional PR. For example, publicity specialists undertake the handling of the public image of a singer or an actor. The idea is to force companies or filmmakers to answer newly built public demand by bidding for the entertainer's services. Particularly in Hollywood's early days, but even today, sleazy tactics by some publicists create an aura of tawdry unprofessionalism that to some extent surrounds legitimate publicists and, unfortunately, burdens practitioners of other forms of PR as well.

Other PR careers include working for PR agencies that handle PR for client firms that have no internal PR department or feel they need outside experts. We'll discuss this in the next chapter.

WHAT DOES IT TAKE?

Return to Caterpillar's training program for a moment. Does anything strike you about it? It is a 12-month PR boot camp, Caterpillar's version of basic training. And anyone who joins Caterpillar (or the Marines) hoping to breeze by on a dazzling personality will be sadly disillusioned. Caterpillar first drills trainees in company history, products, and policies, then gets right down to the nitty-gritty: trainees work on equipment, learn to read blueprints, then spend time with foremen to learn "life on the shop floor."

Obviously, Caterpillar wants PR executives who rely on a detailed, substantive understanding of where the company wants to go in its world of business and how it intends to get there. In any PR, it is essential to take a similarly pragmatic approach to the corporate mission. The job in PR is to help the company (university, political leader, cause) to get where it wants to go. What all of this takes is training, dedication, and a global view.

THE GLOBAL VIEW

66 Early on in my years at Notre Dame, I learned that the curriculum I was pursuing—in the Arts and Letters College—was aimed at developing the "whole man" who was able to think about life on a global basis. It was not aimed at developing a technician who was able to churn out numbers or do statistical analyses.

The individual practicing public relations today has got to understand the world. He has got to understand his nation. He has got to understand the social, political, and economic twists and turns of everyday life. He has got to recognize that what works in New York City or Des Moines, Iowa, is not going to play in São Paulo, Brazil, or Paris. He has got to understand trade, economic, and industrial development issues. He has got to understand the flow of money around the globe. And he has got to recognize that political pressures often cause reasonable men to make inadequate decisions. 99

Robert L. Dilenschneider,
president and chief executive officer,
Hill & Knowlton, New York.[2]

ISSUES AND CHALLENGES AHEAD

Public relations practitioners operate in complex, shifting environments of social issues, ethical questions, and legal and organizational problems.

As in other communications sectors, change in the world of public relations is dramatic and fast. And as in the others, success comes only to those capable of adjusting to change.

The social environment for PR careers is marked by three important characteristics. First is the enormous growth of the power of public opinion in America. In everything from the selection of political leaders to the desire for clean air and water, public opinion is paramount. Party bosses don't pick national political candidates in smoke-filled rooms anymore; candidates are selected in the open arena of public opinion. Polluters of skies and streams find it increasingly difficult to continue "business as usual" in defiance of public opinion. In the decision-making process of government and business, at every institutional and managerial level, public opinion must be reckoned with, whether the product is a person, service, idea, or cause. Therefore, the mechanisms of influencing public opinion—and people who make persuasion their career—will be increasingly important to the process in the future.

Second, however, the clamor for public attention is rising. Hugely expensive, tightly orchestrated efforts to persuade are under way on behalf of everything from threatened wildlife species to nuclear power. And advertising clutter—a crescendo of voices with something to sell—is bombarding the American public and, to some extent, turning it off. The PR effort to persuade, to convince, to advocate is just as unceasingly strident—and is meeting increasing resistance. Inevitably, all with something to sell or a position to advocate will raise their voices to be heard above the clamor. How to cut through all that with an important message and reach the right people will surely challenge practitioners in the future.

Third, unrelenting effort to shape public opinion—to lead it, to create it—reinforces lingering doubt in our society about PR's legitimacy. It's only natural for voters, consumers, and other targets to resist the constant tug and pull. Part of the problem is the widespread knowledge that not all PR practitioners are honest, above-board advocates of valid views that deserve consideration in the marketplace of ideas. Society recognizes this by placing legal and regulatory restrictions on PR.

And that means that the legal environment is crucial to anyone planning a PR career. The legal environment for PR—or any other form of communication—is so complex that it deserves a book of its own, but we'll mention three areas of compelling interest to PR practitioners. First, commercial speech, which covers many dimensions of PR communication and advertising, has some protection under the First Amendment to the U.S. Constitution and its guarantee of free speech. However, protection is not as absolute as, say, the free speech guarantee for political expression or for newspaper or magazine journalists. The U.S. Supreme Court, for example, refers to "commonsense" differences between commercial speech and political expression. That permits government regulation of statements made by PR practitioners.

So, second, PR practitioners operate under regulatory laws that often spell out what is permitted and what isn't. For example, the Federal Trade Commission is empowered to guard against unsubstantiated claims in PR news releases and advertising. The Securities and Exchange Commission lays down rigid guidelines for publishing information about publicly owned companies and stock investment news. PR practitioners representing foreign governments must register under the Foreign Agents Registration Act and adhere to guidelines for clearly labeling material they release.

Third, practitioners can be personally liable under the law for what they do, write, and say on behalf of a client, even if participating only as a minor player in a corporate or agency effort. "I was only following orders" is no defense if you violate the law. Areas of the law requiring your personal vigilance include libel, or injury to the reputation of a person (or company); lobbying on behalf of foreign governments, companies, or political groups; labor relations, a sector tightly regulated under the National Labor Relations Act, the Taft-Hartley Act, and other laws; securities and financial PR, or anything involving the release of corporate information to investors; and copyright and trademarks, particularly sensitive because practitioners often use the words and pictures of others in news releases and advertising.[3]

Sometimes practitioners are under enormous pressure to perform successfully against great odds, and that can tempt them to push up to—or over—the edge of the law. For example, a client, agency, or corporate employer will almost always demand that the practitioner gain access to the media. But the practitioner, an advocate and persuader, has no legal right of access to the media. News releases can be accurate, well written, and filled with interesting, legitimate news and still be rejected by editors. Often the practitioner is pressed to "fix" the image of a client company or product when, frankly, neither deserves a better image—and the media know it. In such cases, the practitioner can be tempted to fuzz the facts a bit, overstate the client's case just a little, stretch for an angle that will make the news release irresistible to editors. And in all of that lie dangerous traps for the practitioner, because such fuzzing, overstating, and stretching can be illegal. The Securities and Exchange Commission, for example, is charged by Congress to ensure that that doesn't happen with financial information.

Nonlegal questions create an important ethical environment for PR practitioners. There is ferment at two levels: Significant sectors of the industry are trying to institute ethical guidelines to improve PR's own image in business circles and the public mind, and individual practitioners serious about PR professionalism are developing personal codes of ethics.[4]

Much of the industry effort comes from two organizations, the Public Relations Society of America (PRSA) and the International Association of Business Communicators (IABC).

PRSA, formed in 1948, adopted its Code of Professional Standards in 1954 and has revised it four times to define PR as a profession and to chart ethical guidelines for it. The standards call on members to improve their "individual competence and advance the knowledge and proficiency of the profession" and conduct themselves "with truth, accuracy, fairness and responsibility to the public."[5]

A major problem for many practitioners, of course, is how to serve client and public simultaneously. Not infrequently, the short-term interests of client and public conflict. For example, the public's interest may be the immediate cleansing of rivers polluted by the client; the client's interest may be to "fix" the image problem without the expense of cleaning up the rivers or at least holding off public criticism until a leisurely solution is found. Of course, as any truly professional practitioner will point out to a client, the only real solution to that kind of PR problem is for the client to clean up the rivers—and fast. Without substantive corrective action by the client, PR practitioners have difficulty fixing such problems. Nevertheless, that concept is sometimes difficult to sell to business managers, who feel that the only business of business is business. The sentiment of "public be damned," operative in the robber baron days of earlier America, is no longer acceptable in most U.S. businesses. Still, not all believe that business has social responsibility. Milton Friedman, Nobel laureate in economics, puts it this way: "There is one and only one social responsibility to business—to use its resources and engage in activities designed to increase its profits so long as it stays within the rules of the game." PR practitioners employed by managers who think that way must see business success as priority number one—or lose their jobs.

One PRSA effort toward professionalism is to offer accreditation as "APR" (accredited public relations) to practitioners who have five years' PR experience, have at least two sponsors who testify to their integrity, and pass a full-day written and oral examination. But less than half of PRSA's members bother to become accredited, and, of course, nonmembers are not eligible.

The PR industry has started toward professionalism and industrywide agreement on some questions of ethics and social responsibility. But there is very little self-policing of members and

Shareholder meetings, during which investors question management, are held annually by publicly owned corporations. Burson-Marsteller helps client managers deal with investors and arranges meetings. *Courtesy Burson-Marsteller.*

even less punishment for ethical infractions. So some authorities on PR grant it less than professional status. Scott M. Cutlip, a recognized researcher and writer on PR, terms PR an "organized calling," not a "profession," and calls its operatives "practitioners," not "professionals."

For many practitioners, ethical questions are troubling. John W. Felton, vice president for corporate communications of McCormick & Co., the world's largest spice, flavor, and seasoning company, puts it this way:

> As a profession, public relations needs to earn more respect. I said "earn." Most practitioners expect it to be handed to them. We don't need a license to be considered professional. We need to be professional in the way we do our jobs. We simply have to do the job better than anyone else has ever done it before. We'll get the respect we deserve when more practitioners are willing to roll up their sleeves and earn it by clearly demonstrating the difference public relations can make at their organizations and in their communities. See it, say it, hear it, and act it out. Credibility and respect get earned that way.[6]

Jack Bernstein, frequent writer on PR issues, warns that ethical lapses can kill PR careers but that practitioners can use common sense in avoiding them: "A violation of ethical conduct is a sure way to oblivion, and it doesn't take a high IQ to determine where you're doing something wrong."[7]

So much for the external environment—the social, legal, and ethical context for PR careers. Let's now examine employers' internal environments.

First, despite PR's advances toward professionalism, many corporations don't grant their PR departments the full recognition enjoyed by other departments. For many practitioners, it's a continuing struggle to gain admission to the inner circle of management. Too often, practitioners have no voice in setting corporate policies with huge PR implications. Instead, they are called in after the fact to clean up a PR mess. Of the largest 500 U.S. corporations (by revenue), 60 don't have a PR or communications department. Some use titles, such as "news bureau" or "external affairs," that confirm that PR matters are not among top management's daily considerations.

Second, however, corporations with more enlightened attitudes toward PR often load enormous responsibilities on their practitioners. Ideally, this involves the PR director in every significant management decision so that PR considerations can be anticipated. In corporate PR, this ideal scenario must include the never-ending cycle of contribution Press Secretary Morgan makes to the governor: Research and analyze the corporation's position in the world, monitor and evaluate issues before they erupt to the detriment of the corporation, and educate corporation employees in PR matters and how to handle them.

A third reality of PR's fit in the internal corporate environment is the strong likelihood that it will be considered a competitor by other departments, particularly advertising and marketing. There is often a struggle to gain upper management's ear and the resources—people, money—to represent the corporation externally. Some large companies, including Boeing, FMC, and Sunoco, eliminate competition by combining PR and advertising in one department. Whatever its organizational slot, PR must have strong lines of communication within the company so that it can not only distribute information for top management but also collect it.

THE PR LISTENING POST

66 I remind our Executive Committee that I'm the one who keeps a foot outside the door so I can give them the perspective and feedback they need, not only from employees but from media, shareholders, and the general public. This means that sometimes I tell them what they don't want to hear. Not enough public relations people serve as listening-post advisers to top management. 99

John W. Felton, vice president, corporate communications, McCormick & Co., Inc.[8]

In Chapter 17, we'll look at how all this comes together in one of the most exciting PR activities, agency work. We'll go inside a New York–based PR agency, Burson-Marsteller.

☆ SUMMARY

Public relations is a relatively new but expanding—and somewhat controversial—career sector.

Although the PR function of persuasion has been present from the dawn of recorded history, PR is young as an organized industry. Expansion of PR is a response to the increasingly important role public opinion plays in American life. In government and business, public opinion must be reckoned with; hence the need for experienced PR counsellors. The controversy over PR concerns whether it is a "legitimate" participant in the American marketplace of ideas. Critics argue that PR lacks legitimacy, that it often uses unethical and unprofessional practices in image making. Supporters argue that PR practitioners, by injecting a client's views into the communications mainstream, are essential to the decision-making process in political and commercial life.

The daily routine of Barbara Morgan, press secretary to the governor of Georgia, illustrates the functions of a public affairs advocate: research media and public opinion, contribute policy recommendations to decision makers, execute a media program, evaluate results.

A PR counsellor deals with an internal constituency, such as top management, and with the external public—reporters, voters, and so forth.

Other forms of PR work include corporate public relations, association and institutional PR (universities, labor unions, etc.), fund-raising, and publicity.

All PR requires a solid background in communications skills and liberal arts, writing and speaking strengths, leadership potential, and analytical skills—the ability to understand the environments within which PR operates. Three are crucial. The social environment includes growing recognition of the power of public opinion, a rising clamor of advocates trying to reach the public, and lingering doubt of PR's legitimacy. The legal environment includes regulatory law and other constraints on the PR function. The ethical environment includes strong efforts by the Public

Relations Society of America and the International Association of Business Communicators to establish codes of ethics governing practitioner behavior.

☆ RECOMMENDED READING

Important professional journals and newsletters include *PR News, Communication World* (published by the International Association of Business Communicators), *Public Relations Journal* (Public Relations Society of America), *IABC News*, and *O'Dwyer's PR Services Report*. Both the *New York Times* and the *Wall Street Journal* cover important PR news on their media and marketing pages.

For a broader and more scholarly view, see Scott M. Cutlip, Allen G. Center, and Glen W. Broom, *Effective Public Relations*, 6th ed. (Englewood Cliffs, N.J.: Prentice-Hall, 1985) and Dennis L. Wilcox, Phillip H. Ault, and Warren K. Agee, *Public Relations: Strategies and Tactics* (New York: Harper & Row, 1986).

Inside a Public Relations Agency

G rowing apace with the industries they serve, American public relations agencies are expanding rapidly at home and abroad. Three factors are most important in this agency growth. First, many cost-conscious corporate managers find it cheaper and more efficient to eliminate in-house PR staffs and rely on high-powered and talented outside agencies. Second, many companies never before active in PR now consider it crucial to their success. Service industries, such as hospitals and health associations, are among those newly using PR agencies. Third, globalization of business is giving PR agencies new and lucrative opportunities overseas.

The result of all this is huge PR agencies that employ hundreds of persons, operate on all continents, and count their annual revenues in the tens of millions of dollars. Many PR agencies (including 12 of the largest 20) are associated with ad agencies, usually as subsidiaries. The tendency to blur the distinction between advertising and PR functions is speeding consolidation of many PR firms into worldwide conglomerates.

However, even the largest international PR firms have staffs and profits small in relation to their enormous impact on public thinking. For example, *O'Dwyer's Directory of Public Relations Firms* lists just two firms, Burson-Marsteller and Hill & Knowlton, as having more than $100 million in fee income and more than 1,000 employees in 1987; only eight others are estimated to earn $20 million or more. By contrast, many metropolitan newspapers are much larger in both revenue and number of employees. Worldwide gross income in 1988 for ad agencies was as high as $758 million at Young & Rubicam. Despite their worldwide expansion, then, PR agencies are still small, compared to many other players in American mass communications.

Yet PR agencies offer attractive career opportunities, and that is good reason for us to go inside an agency for a look.

BURSON-MARSTELLER: A CASE STUDY

It's easy to define what Burson-Marsteller is: the world's largest PR agency, with 2,100 employees in 43 offices worldwide; prestigious clients such as Merrill Lynch, Coca-Cola, General Electric; and very comfortable fee income ($148.7 million in 1988).[1] Defining how Burson-Marsteller achieved all that is more difficult. But four identifiable factors mark its growth to international greatness from an unpromising start in 1953 when a New York PR executive, Harold Burson, joined forces with William Marsteller, owner of a Chicago ad agency (they managed only $84,000 in fee income that first year).

First, Burson-Marsteller was lucky. It arrived on the scene as PR activity was increasing nationwide and, in the 1960s and 1970s, benefited greatly from new thinking among American business managers that established effective PR as crucial to corporate success.

Second, Burson-Marsteller greatly ex-panded the definition of PR beyond merely counseling managers and handling press relations. The wider approach made the agency attractive to large corporations with complex PR problems requiring responses far beyond the old-fashioned press release or publicity stunt.

Third, the agency became a leader in exporting American PR techniques, opening offices throughout the world on behalf of foreign as well as U.S. firms.

Fourth, Burson-Marsteller demonstrated great skill in handling some of the hottest PR assignments in recent decades. Clearly, the agency's reputation is built on delivering results for clients.

Burson-Marsteller has headquarters in some of the world's most expensive office space—11 floors of a building at 230 Park Avenue South, New York. Harold Burson is chairman and "senior counsellor," Marsteller having retired in 1979. The company is run by an ex-reporter, James H. Dowling, through an executive staff (see Figure 17.1) located strategically around the

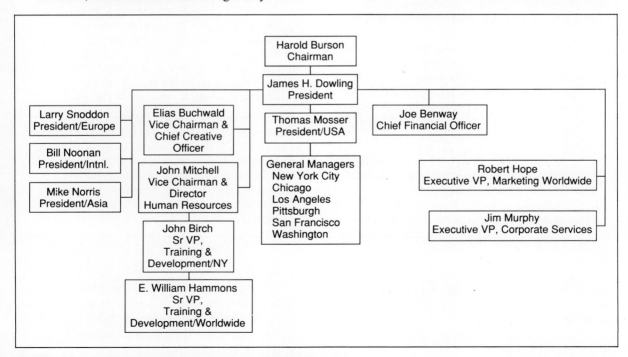

Figure 17.1. ORGANIZATION OF BURSON-MARSTELLER.

Career Focus: James H. Dowling, President and Chief Executive Officer, Burson-Marsteller

James Dowling became chief executive officer of Burson-Marsteller in 1988, succeeding Harold Burson, a co-founder, who continues as "senior counsellor." Note that Dowling, who took the agency into global PR, maintains direct supervision of international activities. *Courtesy Burson-Marsteller.*

For Jim Dowling, the career path to the top in international public relations started at a reporter's typewriter. After college (BA, Journalism, University of Missouri), Dowling reported and wrote for *Newsweek*, United Press, and the Associated Press. A brief tour in public relations at Mobil followed—and Dowling figured he was ready for a PR agency career.

Dowling joined Burson-Marsteller's New York office in 1964, when the agency still was small (just $1.1 million income that year). That was a wise career tactic. Joining a young firm often provides an opportunity to grow with it.

Four years later, Dowling was general manager of the New York office, then took over the Chicago office in 1970, with responsibility for major clients such as Sears, Allstate, Amoco, and Bell & Howell. In 1975, Dowling was named president of all Burson-Marsteller U.S. operations; in 1983, chief operating officer worldwide. By that time, the agency had grown to $63.7 million in annual income.

During those years, Dowling's strategy was to push Burson-Marsteller into truly international activity. Today, the agency's income exceeds $148 million annually, and he spends 40 percent of his time traveling overseas to direct its foreign offices and work with clients on five continents. Dowling explains:

> I am a great believer that public relations is much the same from one country to another; that the differences are merely a matter of timing and maturity and reflect the current market condition in every country in which it is practiced. . . . Europe is our number one priority. . . . We at Burson-Marsteller see virtually unlimited growth for the discipline of public relations in Europe.[2]

In years of PR work, Dowling has become more than a practitioner. He is a leading theorist known for a wide view of PR. In the big leagues, Dowling says, practitioners who succeed know how to communicate but also understand economics and business. Winners "understand the marketplace and what it takes to compete," he says.

world. Since 1979, the agency has been a subsidiary of Young & Rubicam, the largest advertising agency in America.

It was Dowling who built the agency's truly global presence. ▶ 1

Simultaneously, Burson-Marsteller expanded into more than international geography; it pushed into new sectors of business and corporate activity. The agency defines four categories of services to clients.[3]

PUBLIC AFFAIRS

"More than ever," the agency tells clients,

corporations conduct their business amid a whirlwind of political, social and environmental issues. These issues—many now global in scale—originate with governments, the media, customers, competitors, employees, shareholders, communities or activists and can strongly influence the ability of a corporation to achieve its business objectives.

Thus, Burson-Marsteller says, clients must "manage" issues that can damage their business position or corporate reputation. To assist, the agency assigns specialists to these tasks.

Government Relations
Government relations includes helping clients influence the decisions of "elected representatives and government officials at international, national, state and local levels throughout the world." Agency executives lobby officials, work with interest groups "to build their understanding and support

for a client's point of view," and mobilize public support (in one case, by arranging for 5 million postcards to be mailed to members of the U.S. Congress). Burson-Marsteller executives also conduct media campaigns "to raise the visibility and acceptability of a client's point of view on a proposed government action." Sometimes that involves using paid advertising. And sometimes it involves playing political hardball.

Crisis Management
Crisis management involves "assisting clients with crises arising from product tamperings, accidents, scandals, extortion, boycotts, strikes and activist group challenges." Teams of Burson-Marsteller executives are sent quickly "to contain and manage the problem." The teams set up communications programs aimed at a client corporation's constituencies—government, media, customers, competitors, employees, shareholders, communities, activist groups.

Burson-Marsteller says:

Crisis is the corporate world turned upside-down. Rather than a system and an established procedure, chaos takes over in decision making. Rather than well-orchestrated information flow and analysis, there is fragmentary rumor and intuition. Rather than order, there is lack of control. Rather than privacy, there is deliberation in a fishbowl of media scrutiny.

For clients facing corporate crisis, Burson-Marsteller sends in PR counselors who perform three important tasks:

1. *Audit the client's vulnerabilities* to determine where crisis might erupt (or where crisis has already erupted) and what response systems currently exist.
2. *Draw up a crisis plan and a crisis manual* to help the client pull together information and resources to take the correct first steps in dealing with a crisis.
3. *Institute crisis training* for client executives who must learn to deal with crisis. This in-

---

PR, POLITICIANS, AND CLOUT

66 In the battle for the heads and hearts of government officials, companies often overlook the power and potential of going to a politician's source of support—his constituency. When issues are defined solely in policy terms or in terms of a company's or an industry's self-interest, they may not have much political power. But when issues arouse local groups to express their views to politicians, they can generate real clout.

Grass roots support can alter the way in which elected and appointed officials consider and even conceptualize an issue. Public opinion is, for most such officials, measured in what is verbalized opinion, not in what is latent. And what is verbalized by leading vocal constituents shapes an official's view of what is acceptable and desirable policy. 99

James E. Murphy, executive vice president, Burson-Marsteller's Corporate Services Division.[4]

volves teaching them how to develop communications skills under pressure.

Issue Management Issue management deals with long-term challenges some companies face, such as business ties with South Africa that draw criticism in the United States or the potential health impact of products. Burson-Marsteller says it has "gained insight into the key activist groups (religious, consumer, ethnic, environmental) and the tactics and strategies of those who tend to generate and sustain issues." Counteracting such groups is the goal.

Other Actions Issue programming involves helping the client communicate in a way that will stimulate sales or reach special-interest groups with the corporate views. This activity is designed to *stimulate* action, not react to it.

Public affairs counseling helps clients to reorganize their own PR departments and create effective programs.

CORPORATE COMMUNICATIONS

Burson-Marsteller depicts corporate management as "besieged on all sides" as the "market-

place demands the highest-quality, yet most cost-effective, products and services." Society and government also make demands on corporations, the agency says, and "corporate survival is constantly at risk." In corporate communications, Burson-Marsteller aims at helping clients improve relations with such pressure groups. That involves corporate positioning to "present a clear, distinctive identity or image to key audiences."

Burson-Marsteller executives assigned to this sector must understand the client's business and strategy completely, then assist by working with governments (public affairs, government relations), reporters (media relations) and internal communications within the client company. Managers today must communicate effectively with their employees, in both directions. Establishing such two-way communications systems is one service Burson-Marsteller offers.

In wooing corporate clients, Burson-Marsteller depicts itself as a crucial "external adviser," along with a company's bankers, lawyers, and so forth (see Figure 17.2).

CONSUMER MARKETING

In selling its consumer marketing services, Burson-Marsteller addresses a major concern of every firm that enters the marketplace with a

Figure 17.2. How Burson-Marsteller depicts a PR firm's fit with other corporate advisers.

It doesn't look like work, but it is. It's called "brainstorming," and Barbara Smith, Burson-Marsteller creative director in New York (*at easel*), is guiding an account team through the development of a PR program for a client. *Used with permission.*

In this ad, Burson-Marsteller takes its client's corporate viewpoint to the investing public. This is called corporate positioning. *Courtesy Burson-Marsteller.*

product: The world is changing, rapidly, and advertising and sales techniques that work today might not work tomorrow.

Burson-Marsteller tells clients that it can help them deal with change by integrating "communications and promotional tactics for maximum impact" and by providing research on who future customers might be and how they can be reached. The agency emphasizes helping the client build an effective sales and marketing organization. Big-league PR involves much more than writing a fancy handout or holding a press conference. Ideas soundly based in research and staff work are the goal.

INVESTOR RELATIONS

Most large U.S. corporations are publicly owned and thus must be responsive to thousands of shareholders. Those shareholders, through their investment, provide capital for the company's development. In return, they expect suitable rewards—dividends and enhanced value of their stock. If suitable rewards are not forthcoming, shareholders can pressure management, even unseat it. So Burson-Marsteller counsels client corporations on maintaining good relations with shareholders. This involves positioning the client corporation in shareholders' minds. The company says:

> Investors, not surprisingly, shy away from companies that appear complicated, confusing or lacking in growth prospects. They prefer firms that are easily understood and project a clear promise of the future. . . . Positioning, therefore, is more than a catchy buzz-word. It is a distinctive identity that must be carefully constructed. At Burson-Marsteller we follow a proven process of developing the right positioning—and testing it through research to be sure it establishes clearly the "investable idea."

To achieve this, Burson-Marsteller counsels management on strategy, communications, and information systems, then analyzes stock market and investor trends. Its executives also prepare:

Audiovisual presentations and publications, such as annual reports and fact books, that explain the company to investors

Meetings and field trips to company facilities for Wall Street analysts whose opinions are major influences on investor thinking

Speeches and public appearance counseling for client executives whose professionalism in the marketplace is often a crucial part of a corporation's image

Financial advertising and information campaigns aimed at analysts and investors

Press conferences

Internal communications programs to keep employees informed

Burson-Marsteller pioneered PR agency use of satellite communications. Here, Souhei Suzuki (*with headphones*), the agency's account supervisor in Tokyo, moderates a live press conference linking the United States and Japan. *Used with permission.*

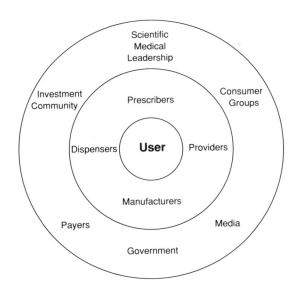

Figure 17.3. One Burson-Marsteller specialty is counseling health care groups. The agency uses this model to show clients how their PR activity must deal with the media, government, and others while reaching the user of health care services. *Used with permission.*

Other Burson-Marsteller specialties include counseling health care corporations such as hospitals and medical associations (see Figure 17.3) and helping clients deal with international financial markets. And in an era of corporate take-overs, the agency also has experts in mergers and acquisitions of companies.

Heart Attack

New therapies are available which may stop a heart attack in progress.

Every year, 1.5 million Americans have a heart attack. Half a million die. Two thirds of those die before reaching a hospital. The incredible news is, many of them die unnecessarily—and for one simple reason.

Denial.

While they're in the midst of the attack, they deny it *is* a heart attack. "Not me," they say. "*Can't* be." "Must be indigestion." "I'm just a little winded … or tired … or nervous."

Most heart attack victims wait three or more hours before seeking medical help, according to the American Heart Association.

solve the clot, restoring blood flow—and saving the heart.

But time is critical, because the earlier the treatment is given, the greater the benefit to the endangered heart muscle.

According to a survey commissioned by Genentech in February, Americans are well aware of the symptoms of heart attack (see chart). But because of fear, they pretend it isn't really happening. They waste precious time denying symptoms, instead of seeking immediate medical attention.

If you or someone you're with experiences any of the symptoms of a heart attack, don't

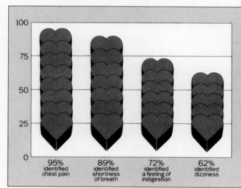

Do you know these symptoms of a heart attack? Most Americans do.

Eighty-one percent of Americans polled by Genentech said they could recognize the symptoms of a heart attack. But in reality, heart attack victims don't act on what they know.

Had they or their friends or relatives sought help immediately, many of them would still be alive.

Because today, *new therapies may actually stop a heart attack in progress.* They can also sharply curtail heart muscle damage if initiated early enough.

The reason: Most heart attacks are caused by a blood clot forming in an abnormally narrowed section of a coronary artery, blocking the flow of blood to the heart. Deprived of oxygen, the heart muscle begins to die. The new therapies can dis-

hope it's just indigestion. Don't be embarrassed. Don't wait to see if it goes away. Act.

Dial your local emergency number or 911.

Get an ambulance. Get to the hospital. Get medical help fast. Be one of the million Americans who lives through a heart attack.

 American Heart Association

Genentech, Inc.

This American Heart Association ad is an "advertorial," designed to look like a news story. *Courtesy Burson-Marsteller.*

CRISIS MANAGEMENT: A BURSON-MARSTELLER SPECIALTY

The crisis hit Johnson & Johnson unexpectedly and with full force. It was September 30, 1982, and a Chicago reporter was telephoning company headquarters in New Brunswick, New Jersey, for comment. Cyanide had been found in a bottle of Extra-Strength Tylenol, a pain reliever marketed by a Johnson & Johnson subsidiary, McNeil Consumer Products. Some people had died from the adulterated Tylenol.[5]

The human tragedy was clear. So was the business crisis. About 100 million Americans used Tylenol. Sales were $400 million annually, and the product was highly profitable.

Alerted by the reporter, Johnson & Johnson swung into action. So did its PR agency, Burson-Marsteller, which saw its mission as helping Johnson & Johnson survive a "murderous intrusion" on Tylenol.

The PR options included "stonewalling"—denying, evading, issuing vague statements that the situation was being investigated, and so forth. But both Johnson & Johnson and Burson-Marsteller felt that complete openness was required.

It wasn't known then how much Tylenol was adulterated. Conceivably, millions of Americans were at risk. So the company decided that the press was key to warning the public of the danger. Burson-Marsteller set up a videoconference between company executives and reporters in 30 cities, using satellite communications. Tylenol production was halted, the product was recalled from store shelves, and a communications center was established at Johnson & Johnson headquarters. Every question from press or public received a fast, direct response.

Johnson & Johnson says that within one week of the videoconference, 90 percent of the public knew of the Tylenol crisis. After the second week, it says, 90 percent knew that Johnson & Johnson was not to blame, that cyanide had been inserted in bottles on store shelves. And Tylenol quickly recaptured 30 percent of the pain reliever market—down just 7 percent from its all-time high of 37 percent before the crisis.

It never was discovered who adulterated the Tylenol, and a second incident involving the pain reliever occurred in 1986. Burson-Marsteller later commented that its mission throughout was to ensure "consistent national media coverage." It added:

> As a result, Johnson & Johnson emerged as a responsible corporate citizen in the view of the media and public. Tylenol made two of the most remarkable comebacks in marketing history, and Burson-Marsteller became known for its crisis communications capabilities.

Since then, Burson-Marsteller has handled similar problems for clients worldwide—the industrial poisoning of thousands in Bhopal, India; food poisoning in Chicago; chemical spills in the Rhine River in Switzerland and Germany.

Moving quickly before crisis erupts is what clients expect of Burson-Marsteller, too. The agency has that capability. Here are some examples.

◆ Ivan Boesky, a well-known New York stock trader, is jailed for insider trading (illegally profiting through use of information not available to the investing public). Burson-Marsteller's Capital Marketing Communications division immediately issues a 17-page advisory for corporate clients on the likely fallout in Washington and in public opinion. The bottom line: "Clearly Congress will attempt to place restrictions on what is seen as irresponsible wheeling-and-dealing" on Wall Street.[6]

◆ Leveraged buyouts (LBOs) become the rage in corporate America as investors gain control of publicly owned companies and take them into private ownership. Public discussion of whether this is best for the national economy reaches new heights. Burson-Marsteller issues detailed guidelines for clients on how to handle public relations aspects of the controversy. Bottom line: Emphasize in your PR the benefits in LBOs for employees, the public, and others.[7]

◆ A sugar company in Spain becomes the target of a "hostile takeover" by Arab oil interests in Kuwait. Burson-Marsteller marshals government and public opinion in the West by escalating the issue "beyond the national boundaries of Spain, focusing on the [Kuwaitis'] sizeable influence and growing investment power in the western world.'' Bottom line: The takeover goes through, but only on terms beneficial to the sugar company's management and shareholders.[8]

"FUN" ASSIGNMENTS AT BURSON-MARSTELLER

They didn't march into the stadium with other teams during the opening ceremonies of the 1988 Seoul Olympics, but Burson-Marsteller PR executives were there. In fact, their team had been ''in training'' for three years awaiting that day.

As official worldwide PR agency for the Seoul Olympic Organizing Committee, Burson-Marsteller was charged with building interest in the Olympics three years in advance, then counseling officials during the games.

Bill Rylance, an executive on the Seoul team, put it this way:

We have helped the Olympic organizers through some sensitive and difficult periods. There has been dynamic economic, social and political development in Korea over the past three years and, in this respect, we had to overcome some major misconceptions about Seoul's suitability as an Olympic host city.[9]

The Burson-Marsteller team contacted editors and sportswriters throughout Asia, Europe, and North America. They arranged TV coverage, helped Olympic executives prepare press material, and published an Olympic newsletter distributed throughout the world. During the games, the team worked with 6,000 journalists covering events.

Burson-Marsteller teams specializing in sports also work with organizers of the America's Cup yacht race, major league baseball, and auto racing. The 82-day, 9,300-mile Olympic torch relay across the United States to open the Los Angeles games in 1984 was a Burson-Marsteller production. The agency says it was seen by more than 30 million spectators and quotes the *New York Times*'s characterization of it as the best-attended sports event in history.

Other Burson-Marsteller executives work in entertainment. In 1986, the agency organized a Frank Sinatra concert in Honolulu's Aloha Bowl and other entertainment events for AT&T. At the time, AT&T was scrambling for long-distance customers in the wake of deregulation of the telephone industry. Burson-Marsteller also works with Sinatra, Dean Martin, Sammy Davis, Jr., and others in American Express promotions.

In all types of PR work, Burson-Marsteller brings enormous technical resources to bear. Its New York headquarters includes a modern au-

Burson-Marsteller's New York City headquarters contains, among other things, complete audiovisual technical facilities. *Used with permission.*

diovisual production facility, three video studios, and a direct satellite transmission link.

But as in any communications work, people make the difference at Burson-Marsteller.

FRONT-LINE TROOPS: THE ACCOUNT EXECUTIVES

At Burson-Marsteller, account executives are responsible for day-to-day work with clients in all sectors. The agency's fortunes rise and fall on their individual skills.

Many account executives are generalists, capable of moving quickly from one client to another, employing standardized public relations skills on a variety of problems. Some, however, are highly experienced specialists.

In corporate services, a Burson-Marsteller specialty, some account executives are former financial analysts, government officials, industrial psychologists, and what the agency calls "political activists." It adds, "Their fluency in the language of a corporate specialty makes them a valued resource at the highest corporate levels." For students seeking entry-level jobs, the meaning is clear: Develop specialty understanding of a business area as well as PR skills.

In consumer marketing, Burson-Marsteller uses account executives skilled in "event marketing"—building educational, musical, or sports programs, for example, that "reach people in new ways, with more impact, in new locations—where they work, where they play, where they relax."

In health care communications, account executives are supported by teams of physicians, health care marketing experts, and other consultants.

Often more than one account executive is assigned full-time to a major client, under the guidance of an account supervisor. The agency demands much more than an eight-hour day from its PR counsellors. It cautions them to "network" in the business community, speaking at seminars, working for charitable organizations, and making friendships among bankers, lawyers, accountants, and others important in a community. "Belong to influential business organizations—not just public relations organizations," it says. "Position yourself as a *businessperson*, not just a public relations person."[10] That's sound advice for anyone launching a public relations career.

Because good recruiting at entry or junior level is difficult, Burson-Marsteller uses a formal program called the Harold Burson Summer Internship in which 16 to 20 college students spend 10 weeks working for the company. They get a firsthand view of public relations by actually working on client businesses as well as by attending weekly luncheon seminars and by participating in teams of interns to develop and present a public relations campaign to Harold Burson himself and other top executives. At the same time, the firm is considering them as future employees. The internship gives juniors the opportunity to demonstrate native intelligence, initiative, creativity, and the ability to work as members of a team. Working on client business shows them the many communication opportunities provided companies by a leading public relations firm. It also exposes them to some of the stress and challenge of a client-oriented business.[11]

THE EXPANDING PR FUNCTION

by James H. Dowling

It seems to me we have moved through three levels of expectation from our clients and our manager.

The first and most basic level was what most of us were originally hired for—our skills in communications. I call it the "how do I say it?" phase. In simpler times, when business was very much a private enterprise, management had very traditional and friendly audiences it had to communicate to. All it needed from us was our assistance in preparing the communication. Management already knew the audience and knew the message. We were needed only to put it into words or pictures or both.

Communicating Effectively About Risk

by James B. Lindheim and Arlene Gordon

The Perceptual Climate

Advances in technology are often seen by the public as a mixed blessing. While people enjoy the benefits of these technologies, they often come to feel that some may threaten disastrous, long-term harm to consumers, workers, communities, or even to mankind. Knowing little about these technologies, people often feel powerless, barely able to comprehend the mechanisms by which these complicated processes are controlled. They see themselves in a world where they have little input or control over events which they believe may be life-threatening. Into this maelstrom activist groups raise the possibility — however remote — that anything could happen. And tragedies such as Bhopal or Chernobyl or thalidomide only add fuel to the fires of concern and uncertainty.

Polls show that the dominant perception of most citizens in the world's industrialized nations is that they face greater risks today than in the past. The real facts are that life spans are longer, that most life-threatening diseases are occurring far less frequently, and that disasters still continue to arise far more often from nature than from man. But these are facts which are ignored, overwhelmed by an underlying unease about a host of modern industrial processes and scientific tools of risk assessment which the public neither understands nor, in reality, wants to understand.

Why? Sociologists, psychologists and anthropologists indicate that the dynamics of risk perception are extremely complex. Several generalizations, however, run consistently through the academic literature.

Rationality and facts do not usually control risk perceptions.

Public perceptions about risk do not follow logical patterns, nor are facts always successful in easing concerns. Studies show, for instance, that the perceived risks from **sensational** causes of death (e.g., AIDS, airplane accidents and disasters) are greatly overestimated by the public while the risks of more commonplace and more prevalent causes of death (e.g., car accidents and heart diseases) are greatly underestimated. When people are shown the statistics which clearly indicate that a plane ride is safer than a car ride, most still won't believe that fact or, more importantly, most will not act on the information.

IMPLICATION: Corporate communicators must not assume that facts — no matter how compelling — will carry the day. The emotional aspects of risk communications are powerful and often overwhelming. To say, for instance, that workers are safer while they are in a company's plant than when they are in their homes may be factually true. But it is not likely to convince a worker's spouse. She has too great an emotional investment in the idea that a home is a safe place, particularly compared to a factory.

Fundamental risk attitudes are hard to change.

Dictated by a complex combination of social and cultural factors and reinforced by

Public relations agencies use newsletters to keep clients informed on developments crucial to their business. Burson-Marsteller's newsletters cover subjects such as consumer news and, as this page shows, how a corporation should communicate effectively with the public.
Courtesy Burson-Marsteller.

But then business became less private. Led by such movements as the environmentalists and the consumerists, a whole host of new and much less friendly audiences started to badger management for information about company policies, procedures, and goals. Unfriendly media, unfriendly governmental bodies, unfriendly communities, all put new demands on these organizations to communicate about issues management never had to answer for before. I call this the "who are these people and what do I say?" phase. In the United States, this brought the corporate public relations function up the corporate ladder in terms of prominence. Chief executives came to depend on the best of the public relations practitioners to analyze these new audiences and help prepare the new dialogues. Senior management made time for these new responsibilities, and public relations at the corporate level flourished. Corporate governance became the new buzzword.

But times and priorities change. Competition became stiff. Profits plunged. Huge companies, once thought immune, became vulnerable to takeovers. Management became less concerned with dialogues; they were wrestling with the very basics of corporate survival. Their own jobs and careers were on the line. Management became less concerned with communications than with action. We had now entered the third and highest level of relationship. No longer was the requirement communications. The need now was action—action that would boost the bottom line, raise the price of stock, boost the productivity of workers, help sell the company's products or services, and, overshadowing all of this, assure company survival. In short, in this phase, management was asking, "what do I do?"

At this, the highest level of relationship with management, the public relations practitioner was now competing for management time, money, and ideas with all the other counsellors who serve management, both inside and outside the company. Competing now with the chief financial officer and his investment banker counsellors, with line management and their management consultant advisers, with the chief legal officer and his outside law firm counsellors. At this level, the public relations practitioner was in the biggest league of his life.[12]

☆ SUMMARY

Public relations agencies are growing rapidly at home and abroad, primarily for three reasons.

Cost-conscious managers find it cheaper to eliminate in-house PR staffs and use outside agencies. Many companies that never used PR as a major managerial tool, such as hospitals and health associations, today regard it as crucial. And globalization of business is giving PR agencies new opportunities overseas.

PR agencies employ hundreds of persons, operate on all continents, and enjoy fee income of tens of millions of dollars annually. Still, PR agencies are small compared to the enormous impact they have on public opinion.

As a case study, Burson-Marsteller illustrates how large and influential PR agencies can become. Burson-Marsteller is the world's largest agency, with 2,100 employees in 43 offices on five continents, prestigious clients, and $148.7 million in annual fee income in 1988. The agency offers major services in these areas:

Public affairs—counseling corporations on how to conduct business in a whirlwind of political, social, and environmental issues

Corporate communications—helping clients improve relations with pressure groups and position themselves to "present a clear, distinctive identity or image to key audiences"

Consumer marketing—advising clients on advertising and sales techniques for products in a changing marketplace

Investor relations—planning how client corporations can maintain good relations with their shareholders, Wall Street analysts, and others

☆ RECOMMENDED READING

Additional details on Burson-Marsteller and its operations are available from the agency, 230 Park Avenue South, New York, NY 10003. *O'Dwyer's Directory of Public Relations Firms*, published by J. R. O'Dwyer Co., Inc., 271 Madison Avenue, New York, NY 10016, is an excellent source of news on agency activity. As in so many sectors of the communications industry, the *Wall Street Journal* and the *New York Times* present regular expert coverage of PR agencies.

THE ENTERTAINERS

Our study of mass communications has concentrated on the mainline media industries—print and broadcast, exchange of news and information in the nation's media marketplace of ideas and in the commercial marketplace where goods and services are sold, and the support industries of advertising and public relations.

But no treatment of American mass communicators is complete without a look at the film and music recording industries, even though career opportunities are more limited in them. Both are integral threads in the national fabric and for millions of Americans are extremely important sources of information as well as entertainment.

What marvels of communication are accomplished in films! What brilliant communicators are directors and actors such as Woody Allen, Steven Spielberg, Eddie Murphy. Is there an American who has been to the movies who doesn't carry a mental image, a message, an emotion communicated by a film? For more than 80 years, development of the film industry has been inseparable from the broader U.S. communications system.

And how music communicates! Among the young particularly, modern music is social commentary fully as meaningful and insightful as, say, the editorial pages of the *New York Times* and the *Wall Street Journal* for other Americans. Music can transmit quickly across the entire nation a generational viewpoint, a collective thought process. The intensity and speed of such communication—and its accuracy—are at times startling to those whose careers are spent in more conventional forms of mass communication.

Our society honors and rewards those who communicate through entertainment much more richly than many who labor diligently but anonymously in other endeavors. *Forbes* magazine, which normally chronicles winners and losers in business, commented with obvious surprise in its October 3, 1988, issue that it had checked what entertainers are paid, and "nowhere else, with the possible exception of Wall Street, are so many making so much.'' *Forbes* calculated 1987–1988 gross income of leading entertainers:

	TWO-YEAR GROSS INCOME (MILLIONS OF DOLLARS)
Michael Jackson, pop singer	97
Bill Cosby, actor-author	91
Steven Spielberg, movie producer-director	64
Sylvester Stallone, actor-writer	63
Eddie Murphy, actor	62
Charles Schulz, cartoonist	62
Bruce Springsteen, rock singer	61
Mike Tyson, boxer	55
Madonna, pop singer	46
Arnold Schwarzenegger, actor	43[1]

Such is the impact of some entertainers that their estates often rake in millions long after they die. *Forbes* projected Elvis Presley's estate would take in $14 million in 1989 from visitors to his home, Graceland, and from selling his music and licensing use of his name in commercial enterprises.

So whether we regard them as forms of communication, commercial enterprises, or pleasureable art forms, films and music must be part of our study of the American mass communications system.

The Film and Music Industries

Significant changes are taking place in the American film industry as it heads for the 21st century.

Hollywood is no longer the unchallenged center of America's film production, as it was for three-quarters of a century. Although about $6 billion was spent making films in California in 1987, $2.3 billion was spent in new York and $219 million in Florida. Even Toronto, Canada, is emerging as a major filmmaking center. American producers seek nonunion labor and lower costs there and in 1987 shelled out $100 million of the $260 million spent making films in the city.[1] ▶ 1

Film industry ownership patterns are shifting rapidly. Most of America's oldest film companies are disappearing into entertainment conglomerates, often controlled by the same moguls emerging in newspapers, TV, and other international mass media. Rupert Murdoch's News Corporation Ltd., a major player in international communications, owns 20th Century-Fox, a leading American studio since 1935. In 1989, Sony Corp. of Japan agreed to pay $3.4 billion for Columbia Pictures. Five major U.S. film companies now are owned by Japanese, Australian, British and Italian interests, and many films produced by Americans are financed by foreign money.

New technology is driving dramatic changes in the film industry. Videocassettes and cable television give film companies new—and profitable—ways to feed the public's voracious appetite for entertainment. This creates new markets for low-cost films (sometimes with quality to match).

In one way, the film industry isn't changing: It has been and remains a very big business. More than 500 feature films were produced in 1987 and were shown on more than 23,000 movie screens, an all-time high. Ticket sales hit a record $4.2 billion; industry revenue from all sources in the United States and abroad reached $7.8 billion.[2] In 1988, ticket sales in America were $4.4 billion and film exports hit a record $1.13 billion, up a dramatic $330 million from 1985.[3]

Costs and risks are high, too. The average studio film in 1987 cost about $20 million to make. Marketing and promotion added $8 million to $10 million. Spending more is not unusual, for film companies know a hit film can rain gold on its owner. ▶ 2 In 1989, *Indiana Jones and the Last Crusade* sold $11 million worth of tickets on a *single day*, breaking the record of $9.7 million set in 1987 by *Beverly Hills Cop II*. In its first six days, *Last Crusade* grossed $46.9 million, breaking the record of $42.2 million set by *Indiana Jones and the Temple of Doom* in 1984. *Last Crusade* was a Hollywood "heavy hitter": George Lucas produced it, Steven Spielberg directed, and Harrison Ford and Sean Connery starred. In 1989, *Batman* beat all their records by selling $100.2 million worth of tickets in 10 days.[4]

The payoff for a hit film can be quick. *Good Morning, Vietnam*, starring Robin Williams, cost about $12 million to produce and in the *first 17 days* pulled in $40.2 million at the box office. *Three Men and a Baby*, which cost $18 million, grossed $120 million in 61 days. In 129 days,

▶ **High Points in Film History**

1839 Still photography is developed by Louis Daguerre in France.

1882 E. J. Marey of France develops a camera that takes 12 still photos per second.

1888 Thomas Edison and William Dickson invent the first successful motion picture camera, called the kinetoscope; it projects still photos in rapid succession.

1895 The motion picture theater is born in France; Auguste and Louis Lumière project films for paying viewers.

1896 Edison stages the first public movie showing in the United States with his new device, the Vitascope.

1900 Three firms—Edison, Biograph, and Vitagraph—compete in the young U.S. film industry.

1903 *The Great Train Robbery*, a classic adventure film, is released.

1906 Kinemacolor, the first color film process, is developed in Britain.

1907 First newsreel, Pathé Journal, is exhibited; newsreels continue to be popular into the 1960s.

1915 Charlie Chaplin develops his beloved film character, The Tramp; *Birth of a Nation*, produced by D. W. Griffith, is the biggest "epic" to date for infant film industry.

1922 Motion Picture Producers and Exhibitors of America formed to police film star conduct and film content; Technicolor is introduced; first important documentary, *Nanook of the North*, is produced by Robert Flaherty.

1927 First "talkie" (movie with sound) is *The Jazz Singer*, starring Al Jolson.

1929 First all-sound color film, *On With the Show*, is released.

1930 Industry for the first time formally structures the Motion Picture Production Code.

1939 One of the all-time greats, *Gone With the Wind*, is released and dominates Oscars.

1941 Orson Welles releases *Citizen Kane*, for some critics even today one of the greatest films ever made.

1946 More than 4 billion movie tickets are sold; with growing strength of TV, movie attendance never again hits these heights.

1953 First wide-screen film, *The Robe*, is released; technique gives directors new artistic freedom, creates new viewer appeal.

1960 Alfred Hitchcock's horror film *Psycho* shocks and delights millions.

1968 Motion Picture Association of America institutes a new rating system, assigning to each film a coded letter (such as "X," meaning no one under 17 admitted).

1975 *Jaws* becomes financially the most successful film ever.

1977 Box office receipts for *Star Wars* surpass those of *Jaws*.

1980 Cost of making average feature film rises to about $16 million; *Superman II* costs $54 million and many other hits cost $40 million to $50 million.

1986 *Variety* counts 515 motion pictures made this year by major U.S. studios and independent producers, up from 174 in 1976.

1987 *E.T., the Extra-Terrestrial*, released in 1982, hits $227.9 million in U.S. and Canada film rentals, becoming biggest revenue producer in American film history.

1989 Globalization of U.S. film industry picks up speed as film exports pass $1.2 billion and an Australian firm acquires United Artists.

1989 *Batman* sells $100.2 million worth of tickets in 10 days, topping *Indiana Jones and the Last Crusade*, which held previous sales record of $100 million in 19 days.

▶ 2 | Box Office Gold

Hit films draw millions in box office revenue. Note the dollars pulled in by these films in *just 12 months* (Jan. 5, 1987 to Jan. 3, 1988).

Film	Studio	Revenue (millions of dollars)
Beverly Hills Cop II	Paramount	153.7
Platoon	Orion	133.2
Fatal Attraction	Paramount	129.4
Three Men and a Baby	Buena Vista	83.9
The Untouchables	Paramount	76.3
The Secret of My Success	Universal	67.0
Stakeout	Buena Vista	65.8
Lethal Weapon	Warner	65.2
The Witches of Eastwick	Warner	63.9
Dragnet	Universal	57.3

Source: Laura Landro, "The Movie Moguls Reel Off One More Tale of Big Bucks," *Wall Street Journal*, Feb. 24, 1988, p. 30.

Fatal Attraction grossed $140.5 million; it cost $13 million to make.[5]

But betting wrong on a film, by misjudging public viewing tastes or spending too much, can ruin a film company. Inevitably, the reward-or-ruin potential gives rise to three characteristics that mark the film industry. First, high costs and risks lead to development of "megastudios" large enough to withstand financial pressures. Large film companies will get larger.

Second, as cable and videocassettes open new profit opportunities, film companies strive for "vertical integration." Under this corporate organizational concept, companies not only produce films but also distribute and screen them in their own theaters, then release the films on cassette. Some companies even own TV stations and cable systems on which the films are shown.

Third, with rewards so great for hits (and risks so high for flops), many film companies handle only "safe" scripts likely to pull in millions of viewers without reaching for artistic heights. That often means silly, superficial story lines, blunt language, violence, and sexually graphic scenes thought to be what the public desires. Much truly creative and artistic use of film is left to small companies and independent producers who turn out low-budget films. More than 40 percent of Academy Award nominations in 1987 were for movies *not* made by major studios.

Bemoaning the attitude of the major studios, Harlan Jacobsen, editor of *Film Comment* magazine, told the *Wall Street Journal* in 1989: "Movies are becoming a product-line business, like Detroit [auto manufacturing] or the cereal business. The products are symptomatic of a social malaise which says we don't want to take risks."[6]

Major studios treat movies as "assets" or "franchises" with massive value at box offices. For example, the first Eddie Murphy movie at Paramount (*48 Hours*), released in 1982, was a hit. In rapid succession, seven more were issued, generating box office revenue of more than $1 billion by 1989. (Frank Mancuso, chairman of Paramount, cracked, "Eddie Murphy is our Kellogg's Corn Flakes.")[7] Paramount also released four *Star Trek* movies between 1979 and 1986 plus *Raiders of the Lost Ark* and two Indiana Jones sequels between 1981 and 1989.

Handling such blockbusters is not for the meek. Who is in charge in the film world?

PLAYERS IN FILM: THE LARGE AND THE SMALL

Once upon a time, Hollywood's major film studios maintained hundreds of acres of sets and shooting locations. Many kept scores of film stars under contract (in 1935, MGM alone had 200 on the books).

Today, the huge studio lots are gone. It's cheaper to lease shooting locations throughout the world for a fraction of what it cost to maintain the old sets. It's also cheaper to negotiate single-picture contracts with actors and actresses so most have no long-term studio affiliation. And no longer are Hollywood's most important people the fabled showmen-producers of yesteryear— flamboyant personalities such as Cecil B. De Mille and David O. Selznick who, surrounded by filmdom's beautiful people, were hot news in newsreels and on front pages in the 1930s. Today's movers and shakers are profit-oriented men and women who run businesses, not film studios. The major film companies have built corporate structures that ensure vertical integration and promise strong bottom-line performance.

◆ *Paramount.* Produced 17 films in 1987 and enjoyed a 19.7 percent share of that year's $4.2 billion box office revenue. Founded in 1912, Paramount is now a subsidiary of Gulf and Western Inc., a conglomerate whose holdings include nearly 500 U.S. movie theaters, others in Canada, plus Madison Square Garden in New York City, the New York Knicks basketball team, and 50 percent of the USA Network. Paramount is building a reputation for "safe" movies, including sure-bet sequels such as *Crocodile Dundee II*, and movies starring box office heroes such as Sean Connery and Eddie Murphy.

◆ *Disney.* Produced 15 films in 1987 and had 18 percent of total box office revenue. Famous for children's features, Disney created Touchstone Films in 1984 to produce films for adults, including *Good Morning, Vietnam, Tin Men*, and *Three Men and a Baby*. Animated films such as *Snow White* and *Cinderella* made the company famous after its founding in 1923. Its parent, Walt Disney Co., owns resorts and theme parks and is deeply involved in merchandising.

◆ *Warner Brothers.* Produced 21 films in 1987 and received a 12.5 percent box office share. This company, founded in 1923, has in recent years produced major films such as *Lethal Weapon, Full Metal Jacket*, and *Empire of the Sun*. Its parent, Warner Communications Inc., owns record and music publishing companies and movie theaters and in 1989 merged with Time Inc.

◆ *Orion.* Though a newcomer (founded in 1978), Orion produced 15 films in 1987 and accounted for 10.4 percent of all box office revenue. Major films include *Platoon, Radio Days, Robocop*, and *House of Games*.

◆ *Fox.* With 15 films in 1987 and 8.7 percent of box office revenue, this company became a centerpiece in Rupert Murdoch's global information and entertainment conglomerate, New Corporation Ltd. Fox productions include *Broadcast News, Wall Street*, and *The Princess Bride*.

Other major companies are Columbia, founded in 1924 and now a subsidiary of Coca-Cola Co.; MGM, founded in 1924; and Universal, founded in 1912 and now owned by MCA Inc., a huge entertainment company. Newer companies that have produced hit films include Cannon (founded in 1979), Lorimar (1987), New World Pictures (1983), and Tri-Star (1982).

Mergers and acquisitions will likely reduce the number of major players in films and entertainment. David Londoner, a New York investment banker and analyst, predicts, "By 1995, it wouldn't surprise me to see three major enterprises embracing 80 percent of the [broadcast and entertainment] business.''[8] One major cause is vertical integration, possible only because the federal government in recent years relaxed regulatory prohibitions against companies amassing such economic power under a single roof.

Because they depend heavily on films and entertainment shows from such increasingly powerful companies, the cable industry and three major TV networks seek to acquire interests in film companies or gain control of films by investing in production. Generally, the Federal Communications Commission, which regulates television, frowns on such moves by the networks on the grounds that they result in unfair competition.

Among the big players edging into the American film industry are foreign companies. Sony Corp., the Japanese electronics manufacturer, has an entire division involved in producing and distributing American-made movies. Films financed by the Japanese include *Bright Lights, Big City*, starring Michael J. Fox; *Betrayed*, with Debra Winger; and *Fatal Beauty*, with Whoopi Goldberg and Ruben Blades. In 1988, a British company, Television South, bought MTM Enterprises, creator of TV's ''Hill Street Blues'' and ''Mary Tyler Moore Show,'' for $320 million.

Financial maneuvering aside, however, the film industry's future depends largely on its ability to assess public viewing tastes correctly.

ARE VIEWER HABITS CHANGING?

Filmmakers interested in profits—and that is most of them—are trying to guess who will go to the movies in years ahead and what type entertainment they want. Such guesswork is difficult, but trends are emerging.

First, although theater revenue in 1987 reached an all-time high of $4.2 billion, the number of tickets sold, 1.1 billion, was lower than in 1982. Since ticket sales are dropping, while population is increasing, in percentages fewer Americans than ever are going to the movies. Clearly, cable television, videocassettes, and other home entertainments are eating into ticket sales.

Filmmakers are laying down whole new strategies to take advantage of the new, highly profitable home market. Some flood rental stores with shoddy films of sex and horror for private viewing. For producers of major films, a key decision is how quickly to release a film for videocassette rental. In 1987, Vestron Pictures released *Dirty Dancing* too quickly. The film could be rented for $2 even as it continued to draw theater crowds at $6 per ticket.

Second, film industry analysts say people over 40 years of age are returning to movie theaters in larger numbers. Jack Valenti, president of the Motion Picture Association of America, says the number of over-40 moviegoers rose 56 percent in 1987 and accounted for 20 percent of all movie viewers, a rise of 5 percent since 1984. Teenage moviegoers dropped from 32 percent of the total in 1984 to 25 percent in 1987.[9]

Third, moviegoers are getting more selective about the films they attend. For example, over the 1987 Thanksgiving weekend, more than 30 major movies were available nationwide, but over 60 percent of all tickets sold were for just four—Disney's *Three Men and a Baby* and reissued *Cinderella* and Paramount's *Planes, Trains and Automobiles* and *Fatal Attraction*. So filmmakers take great risks if they misjudge the public's viewing desires.[10] Some back away altogether. Paramount refused to make *War and Remembrance*, so the American Broadcasting Co. went ahead alone on the most ambitious TV miniseries ever made. It took two years to plan, 21 months to shoot, and a year to edit. Its viewing time is 32 hours, and ABC calculates production costs at $110 million, or $3.4 million *per hour*. At best, ABC expects to *lose* $20 million.[11]

To court older viewers, filmmakers will need appropriate plots and production, not the raunchy, music-oriented movies they ground out for years to draw teenagers. Valenti warns that filmmakers ''no longer can blindly count on growing legions of teenagers to populate the theaters.''[12]

Moviegoers today reject the star system, no longer idolizing actors and actresses as in yesteryear. None of the five greatest moneymaking films of all time— *Jaws, Return of the Jedi, The*

Empire Strikes Back, E.T., and *Star Wars*—revolve around stars. This is an enormous change for an industry that from its earliest days built international celebrity status for stars as a means of selling tickets.

Film companies are increasingly courting Hispanic and black viewers. For Hispanics, Spanish-language soundtracks are used in some general-release films with special promotional campaigns to increase moviegoing. Of 290 prints released of *Stand and Deliver*, a film about an inner-city teacher, 30 were dubbed into Spanish. Columbia Pictures released 77 Spanish-language prints (out of more than 1,000) of *La Bamba*. Box office receipts increase 5 to 10 percent if Spanish-language soundtracks are available.[13]

For producers creating films aimed primarily at black audiences, the problem always has been gaining financial and technical backing. Blacks produced films as early as 1910, and more than 150 independent companies created films between 1910 and 1950 for showing in segregated theaters. But few reached significant size, and by 1988 just 160 blacks were among the more than 7,500 members of the Directors Guild of America. Even *The Color Purple*, a major success whose cast was black, was screenwritten, pro-duced, and directed by whites. By the late 1980s, however, black independent filmmakers still were at work on productions aimed at black audiences.[14]

FILM INDUSTRY ISSUES AND CHALLENGES

Among current challenges confronting the film industry is one that dates back to virtually the first films ever produced: Which subjects are appropriate for treatment in general-release films, and how shall filmmakers—and society—determine which will be shown and which won't?

From the start, the film industry has pushed constantly against conventional standards of acceptability. It would be comforting to suggest that this results from a burgeoning creativity among producers and directors driven to explore filmmaking's enormous potential as an art form. Unfortunately, the increasing brutalization and exploitation of the medium through films of violence and sex are clearly motivated by box office draw. In less than 50 years, the film industry has moved from shocking the nation with the word *damn* (Clark Gable was first to utter it on screen in *Gone With the Wind*, released in 1939) to blasé acceptance of murder, mayhem, foul language, and even what many regard as blasphemy (as in Martin Scorsese's *Last Temptation of Christ*, Universal's 1988 film that suggested that Christ lusted for a woman). The very same film industry that creates truly magnificent art with high-quality films also churns out "exploitation flicks" designed to arouse base human instincts.

In response, church and other social groups have formed to exert pressure on the industry. Confrontations over scenes of violence and sex have been part of filmmaking for decades (thousands demonstrated nationwide against *The Last Temptation of Christ*, which, naturally, created enormous publicity and increased attendance).

As in all such controversies, a basic issue is that what is offensive or blasphemous to one person can to another person be legitimate expression or artistic exploration of a deserving subject.

Oprah Winfrey, a multimedia entertainer, has made millions with her skills in film, TV, radio, and personal appearances. *Wide World Photos.*

Forcing the elimination of "indecent" or "offensive" subject matter, contend some, amounts to censorship.

The solution, far from satisfactory, has been a voluntary movie-rating system under which the Motion Picture Association of America ostensibly guides viewers, especially parents, in selecting appropriate films. A rating system of sorts has existed since the 1930s; the current system was established in 1968, shortly after Jack Valenti became association president. Valenti appoints a chairman and together they select eight persons to review and rate films. Valenti's critics say the system is designed simply to placate the public and preempt any government or social move toward censorship. Valenti argues that the ratings mirror society's values and are helpful in alerting filmgoers to movie content (see Figure 18.1).

The profit motive can lead to manipulation. Filmmakers sometimes add gratuitous violence or sex—maybe a curseword or two—to gain an R or PG-13 rating in the belief that that will attract teenagers or young adults seeking titillation and excitement. Pornographers, of course, don't submit films for ratings. Their self-imposed "triple X" rating is a signal flag for moviegoers seeking raw sex. (In network television, the trend is toward relaxed standards; ABC, NBC and CBS have reduced dramatically the number of employees assigned to eliminating offensive material.)

RAUNCHINESS IS EVERYWHERE

66 When people who now have children were children, there was no Terminator and no Dead Kennedys, no mention of condoms on sitcoms and no videocassettes. On "The Ed Sullivan Show," the Rolling Stones had to change the words of "Let's Spend the Night Together." Roman Catholics over 30 can remember when the Legion of Decency could rate a movie "condemned" for the cut of a neckline.

Now that raunchiness is everywhere, parents are seeking ways to monitor the flow in movies and videotapes, on television and record albums. But aside from the film industry's ratings and gleanings from reviews, they have little guidance. 99

Laura Mansnerus, New York Times[15]

Some critics detect a trend away from gratuitous sex and violence. Michael Medved, a film critic, notes that some hit movies in the late 1980s contained no explicit sex scenes and in fact took stands in support of such traditional institutions as marriage. He cites *Broadcast News, Fatal Attraction, Lethal Weapon,* and *The Untouchables* as a turn "against the freewheeling sexuality that since the 1960s was glorified as a life-affirming alternative to the restrictions of marriage."[16]

Other controversies dog the film industry.

◆ *Artist's Rights.* Broadly, this covers controversy over whether actors and others in filmmaking have a right to protect the product of their labors even if they don't own the films. The argument is heated by the colorizing and editing for TV of famous old black-and-white films. Some are butchered to fit TV's inflexible clock; others are speeded up (in a technique called "time compression"). Turner Broadcasting System purchased libraries of famous Hollywood films

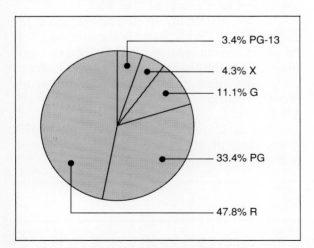

Figure 18.1. TWENTY YEARS OF RATINGS.
In the period 1968–1988, the Motion Picture Association of America's Classification and Rating Administration rated 8,460 feature films: 47.8 percent were rated R (children under 16 must be accompanied by parent or guardian), 33.4 percent PG (parental guidance suggested), 11.1 percent G (general audiences), 4.3 percent X (no one under 17 admitted), and 3.4 percent PG-13 (inappropriate for children under 13). *Source:* Motion Picture Association of America.

and colorized many to meet the perceived demands for color from the TV generation. That artists have "moral rights" in such matters is argued by Woody Allen, Jimmy Stewart, Burt Lancaster, and other actors. Directors agreeing include Steven Spielberg, George Lucas, and Fred Zinnemann. Some call on Congress to declare certain films "culturally, historically, or aesthetically significant" and to prohibit editing. The Motion Picture Association's Valenti argues that it is "desperately wrong for the government to get involved in the motion-picture business."[17]

◆ *Hollywood vs. Cable.* Essentially, this quarrel is over the distribution of films. Filmmakers see cable system operators gaining strong influence over which films are shown and which aren't. The filmmakers want a voice in that. Valenti says, "The public policy issue is this: Is it reasonable and suitable in the long-term interests of the consumer that one person or one entity [cable] controls the flow of television material into the home?"[18] He argues that cable systems are monopolies that must be restrained. Cable operators reply that film companies create their own monopolies (through "vertical integration" ownership of movie theaters) and that over-the-air TV and videocassettes preclude cable systems from monopolizing home entertainment.

◆ *Production Costs.* They are soaring. Film stars demand up-front payments of millions of dollars plus a percentage of box office receipts. Even actors of minor fame demand $50,000 or more for cameo appearances. Unions add enormously to labor costs (hairstylists aren't permitted to touch makeup; truck drivers deliver but refuse to touch equipment). Writers struck for 22 weeks in 1988 for higher wages and residuals—payments each time their work is screened. Shooting costs run $200,000 or more daily on major films; total costs can run $50 million or $60 million for a single film. Promotion of a major studio film alone averages $7 million. The effect is to limit serious film production to companies large enough to afford such expenses. Independent and beginner filmmakers are squeezed out.

THE RECORDING INDUSTRY: UP FROM HUMBLE ORIGINS

It all started with Thomas Edison and his hand-cranked invention into which he dictated "Mary Had a Little Lamb." The invention was the phonograph, and its weak, scratchy playback of the children's rhyme proved that sound could be stored and later retrieved. The year was 1877.

Today, after many ups and downs, music recording in the United States is a multibillion-dollar entertainment industry and an important communications medium as well. In 1987 alone, Americans spent an estimated $5.6 billion on recorded music. Worldwide spending was about $16 billion.[19]

One result is the creation of musical superstars, some of whom become near cult figures and enjoy fabulous wealth. ▶ 3 Another is the

3 ▶ Some All-Time Greats

Some hit albums are phenomenal moneymakers. Leading artists and their best albums at the end of 1988:

Michael Jackson	*Thriller*	$220 million
Bruce Springsteen	*Born in the USA*	$120 million
Prince	*Purple Rain*	$85 million
Madonna	*Madonna*	$55 million
Whitney Houston	*Whitney Houston*	$54 million

creation of huge, extremely profitable recording companies. A few dominate the recording scene. Their financial fortunes rise and fall swiftly, as stars and hits come and go, but let's look at the current leaders.

◆ *CBS Records*. Annual revenue of $1.7 billion attracted the Japanese electronics firm Sony, which bought the company in 1987 for $2 billion. Sony quickly gave a $20 million, multiyear management contract to Walter Yetnikoff, who ran the company for CBS for 13 years. CBS Records had about 24 percent of the top albums in 1987. Its artists include Michael Jackson, Bruce Springsteen, George Michael, Neil Diamond, Billy Joel, and Barbra Streisand. The company sells records under both the Columbia and Epic labels. CBS has interests other than modern music. Research shows that 20 million Americans prefer classical music—and CBS Masterworks serves them with classical titles.

◆ *Warner Communications*. Hit $1.5 billion in records revenue and a 30 percent market share in 1987 with the Atlantic and Electra labels. Artists include Anita Baker, Genesis, Whitesnake, Fleetwood Mac, and U2. Warner merged in 1989 with Time Inc., creating a mammoth news and entertainment conglomerate.

◆ *Polygram*. Had sales of $1.5 billion in 1987 under the Mercury and Deutsche Grammophon labels. The company has large operations outside the United States and is strong in classical music. Artists include Vladimir Horowitz, Def Leppard, Bon Jovi, and Dire Straits.

◆ *Bertelsmann Music Group*. Had revenue of $1.3 billion in 1987, under the RCA and Arista labels. The company is strong in country music. Artists include Bruce Hornsby, the Grateful Dead, the Judds, and Aretha Franklin. Bertelsmann is a West German company.

◆ *Thorn/EMI*. Company labels are EMI Manhattan and Capitol. Music division sales in 1988 were $1.1 billion. Leading artists include Bob Seger, the Pet Shop Boys, David Bowie, and Natalie Cole. Thorn/EMI is a British company.

◆ *MCA*. Labels are MCA and Motown. Motown, acquired in 1988, was one of the nation's leading black enterprises and a vital force in American music for nearly 30 years (with Diana Ross and the Supremes, Stevie Wonder, the Four Tops, and other artists). MCA sales in 1987 were $375 million. Leading artists include Elton John, Tiffany, Belinda Carlisle, and Jody Watley.

Times weren't always flush for the industry. Edison and others (by 1890, three phonograph devices were being sold) initially thought the invention would be used in business. Only after that failed did the phonograph prosper as entertainment. Then radio swept the nation as favored entertainment, and the recording industry was hit badly. It took other severe blows when "talkies"

Country is the single most popular radio format in American music, according to *Broadcasting* magazine. Nashville is its home, and Loretta Lynn and Conway Twitty are two of its biggest stars. *Wide World Photos*.

(sound movies) were invented and when the 1930s economic depression dried up whatever purchasing power many Americans had for entertainment.

Nevertheless, in good times and bad, music fads generated widespread popular enthusiasm for musical art forms and performers. The "jazz age" following World War I boosted the recording industry. So did the "big band era" of the 1930s and 1940s, when Americans became enthralled with the music of Tommy Dorsey, Benny Goodman, Les Brown, and other bandleaders and their singers, such as Frank Sinatra, Doris Day, Dinah Shore, and Peggy Lee.

After World War II, the recording industry prospered. The economy improved dramatically, and Americans again had money for entertainment. Television entered the marketplace as the dominant entertainment medium around 1950. That forced radio to switch from comedy and drama to music. By the 1960s, radio was music, music, music all across the dial—and that whetted the appetites of millions for their own private music collections. Throughout the 1950s and 1960s, enormously popular music forms arrived on the American scene, and sales of recordings soared. Musicologists date the big change around 1955 when the Comets ("Rock Around the Clock") and Elvis Presley burst onto the scene.

The switch from sweet and sentimental big band music to rock and roll launched a distinctive youth culture. Particularly with the 1964 arrival of the Beatles in the United States, an entire lifestyle changed. Clothing and hairstyles, language patterns, a generation's sense of morality—all evolved rapidly along with the new music. Rock and roll changed into new forms—heavy metal, punk, disco, English rock, new wave—and each kicked off its own widening circle of change.

Paralleling changes in music, recording technology improved tremendously. Today, computer-controlled "mixing boards" enable recording studios to weave many tracks into ever-finer sound quality. For consumers, the technology brings not only improved quality but also greater portability.

Technologies are being combined to create new entertainment forms. The Music Television Network (MTV) marries music with video; recording studios produce albums from successful film tracks. Note, for example, what happened to music from the 1987 film *Dirty Dancing*: RCA spent $200,000 to combine a few songs written for the movie with some oldies from the 1960s. The soundtrack album became one of the nation's best sellers. That boosted the film and subsequent videocassette to hit status. A stage show toured the country, featuring some of the original singers. RCA released another album of oldies from the soundtrack, *More Dirty Dancing*. *Business Week* magazine concluded that the various entertainment spinoffs grossed close to $350 million in about a year's time.[20]

The future promises the growth of huge entertainment companies whose music recordings spin off viedocassettes, magnetic tapes, optical disks, and other forms of entertainment. In 1987, Warner Communications, a major filmmaker for decades, had higher sales in records than in movies.

For each recording company, the lure is always the possible discovery of new hit talent. Jerry Moss, co-owner of A&M Records (his partner is trumpeter Herb Alpert), puts it this way: "The next knock on the door could be the next Elvis Presley."[21]

Rock and roll even has its own hall of fame, under construction in Cleveland. Its first inductees were founders of rock—Chuck Berry, Ray Charles, Bo Diddley, Buddy Holly, Elvis Presley, Little Richard. Recent inductees have included the Beatles, Bob Dylan, the Beach Boys, the Supremes, and the Drifters.

Many music stars perform in television commercials—yet another combination of media forms. Michael Jackson, David Bowie, Tina Turner, and others have transformed commercials for Pepsi, Reebok, Coke, and other products into entertainment performances that sell.

So influential is rock music, particularly in music videos, that serious efforts are made to monitor its lyrics and imagery. The American Academy of Pediatrics found that nearly 75 percent of music video story lines contain sexual imagery; more than half contain violence, mostly against women. The academy acknowledges that a single viewing of a music video will not lead teenagers into sex but insists that the cumulative effect of years of watching could be harmful. Tipper Gore, wife of U.S. Senator Albert Gore, Jr., a Tennessee Democrat, has campaigned for years against sexually explicit and violent lyrics. She insists that record companies should label albums that contain offensive material. Others argue, of course, that music, no matter how explicit, is harmless.

Whatever rock's true impact, there is no doubt that it has become one of the important mass communicators of our time.

☆ SUMMARY

The film and music industries are integral parts of the American mass communications system. Movies and music provide social commentary fully as insightful as editorial pages of leading newspapers.

Hollywood is no longer the unchallenged center of the U.S. film industry. New York, Florida, and Toronto, Canada, are major centers for American producers. Global media moguls are building huge empires in filmmaking. Japanese investors finance some American films.

More than 500 major U.S. films are produced each year. In 1987, there were more than 23,000 movie screens, an all-time high. Ticket sales hit a record $4.2 billion. Costs are high, too. The average studio film in 1987 cost about $20 million.

"Megastudios" large enough to withstand financial pressures are dominating the industry. As cable and videocassettes open new profit opportunities, the large companies are striving for "vertical integration," not only producing films but also screening them in their own theaters. Then the megastudios exploit another market by converting the films to videocassettes. Some filmmaking companies own the TV stations and cable systems on which the films are shown.

The huge financial risks tempt many companies to stick with "safe," shallow scripts that include strong language, violence, and sexually explicit scenes thought to be what the public desires.

Paramount, Disney, and Warner Brothers are the largest companies in films produced and box office revenue.

Moviegoer habits seem to be changing. Older Americans are going to movies more. Some experts predict fewer movies aimed at teenagers, a box office staple for years.

The music industry started from humble origins, with Thomas Edison's invention of the phonograph in 1877. In 1987, Americans spent about $5.6 billion on recorded music. Worldwide spending was estimated at about $16 billion.

CBS Records, Warner Communications, and Polygram are the major recording companies.

☆ RECOMMENDED READING

The business of popular entertainment is covered well in *Electronic Media*, *Business Week*, *Forbes*, and, particularly, *Variety* and the *Hollywood Reporter*. *Billboard* is the leading trade publication for the recorded music industry. *Rolling Stone* is an important source. In their media sections, both the *Wall Street Journal* and the *New York Times* cover the film and music industries.

GETTING THERE YOURSELF

We have discussed throughout this book the many career options the mainline media offer. Now let's look at the mechanics of how you can put together a balanced academic and work background to get started in media. Indeed, let's discuss how you can get started toward the top, like the editors, publishers, TV anchors, and others we encountered. Someone will manage Gannett in the decades ahead. Someone will lead Knight-Ridder, manage radio stations, anchor the evening news, publish books like this one. Why not you?

Professionals described the types of entry-level employees they seek in each industry, and we studied the career paths followed by those who succeeded in newspapers and magazines, radio and TV, advertising and public relations. Each industry has its own individual demands, and professionals have different ways of achieving full, rewarding, and successful careers. Yet commonalities do exist in hiring practices throughout the media. We saw a common desire for certain attributes in entry-level employees—including sound academic preparation, hands-on experience, and the ability to communicate.

There is no sure path to success in the media or any other career. Best-laid plans can (and often do) go awry. But it is possible to open options for yourself and improve your odds for success with careful planning, starting now.

The chapter differs somewhat from those in the earlier parts: I write from a personal viewpoint, passing along career hints based on my 25 years as a reporter, editor, foreign correspondent, and media executive, plus a number of years in teaching. As one who has hired (and, unfortunately, fired) media company employees, I strongly feel that if you are a college student, your first concern must be to broaden your intellectual self, to open new paths in life, to learn. Simultaneously planning a career strategy is not inconsistent with that process. In fact, planning can add worthwhile direction to your academic work.

The advice that follows has been well tested and well received by students. I hope it and the career tips from two professionals we have already met serve you well.

Launching Your Career

If you seek a career in the media, you should understand a few things up front. First, some professionals, particularly in newsrooms, argue that your undergraduate major should be in the liberal arts—English, history, economics, political science—and not in one of the nation's 243 schools of journalism and mass communication. The argument is a nonstarter. Most schools seeking approval by the Accrediting Council on Education in Journalism and Mass Communications require majors to take 90 hours of a basic 120-hour graduation requirement *outside* the journalism school, with 65 of those credits in liberal arts. So a "journalism" degree is really a liberal arts degree topped with professional subjects. Also, despite the critics, most new hires in the media come from schools of journalism and mass communication. About 85 percent of entry-level hires in newspapers do. Unquestionably, a degree in journalism or another appropriate area of mass communications can give you a head start.

Second, as was clear throughout this book, competition for media jobs is fierce. Once you get one, performance standards often are high, work pressures sometimes enormous (of 544 newspaper editors surveyed, 39 percent reported health problems they blamed on job stress). And at least initially, pay can be low.

Third, however, professionals demonstrated in this book that careers offer rewarding, fulfilling work that is *important*. Print and broadcast journalism offers involvement, adventure, *a chance to change things*. Advertising and PR take you to the center of the nation's exchange of ideas and commerce. And there are always jobs for the bright, the quick, the committed. Good salaries are available, too, after the first few years of apprenticeship. Some metropolitan papers pay a minimum of $50,000 annually for reporters with four or five years' experience; editors can make $100,000, publishers $150,000 or more. For the successful, broadcast, advertising, and PR offer excellent compensation.

Now let me describe hiring patterns I have seen develop in my international media career of more than a quarter century.

Graduates who rise above each year's crop to land the best entry-level jobs—and who eventually succeed in media careers—generally exhibit three characteristics. First, they sparkle, show excitement about the world around them. They are activist thinkers, men and women interested in what is happening—in Afghanistan, as well as their university; in economics, politics, and government as well as in student affairs. Often this wider curiosity is demonstrated not in grade point average but in reading, travel, unusual jobs.

Second, fast starters construct an educational experience that can best be described as having both horizontal and vertical dimensions. These students dip adventurously and broadly (horizontally) into many different disciplines. They study subjects found on a daily newspaper's front page and on network evening news—foreign affairs, economics, political science—but also get into the arts, literature, and other cultural fields. Job interviewers recognize these people as generalists with broad views built from varied coursework. Simultaneously, fast starters build in-depth (vertical) expertise in a specialty such as science, business, or law. This qualifies them as, for example, beginning reporters who can handle general assignments but who can also dig deeply, with authority, into special areas of news. For those interested in advertising or PR careers, the combination of broad horizontal and deep vertical background adds an attractive dimension recruiters seek.

Third, fast starters build college experience demonstrating commitment to a professional career. Aspiring reporters who get snapped up are experienced in campus journalism, internships, or part-time reporting jobs. Broadcast stations prefer students who obtain hands-on experience outside the classroom, in campus radio and TV stations and internships. PR and ad agencies seek students who juggle their many academic responsibilities to obtain the extra edge of real-life experience. To media recruiters, such extra experience demonstrates that the applicant understands the basics of, say, reporting and editing or handling a TV camera. More important, it demonstrates strong motivation to reach out, to learn. Self-starters are at a premium in the job market. ▶ 1

▶ 1   **Where the Money Is**

Entry-level media jobs traditionally offer relatively low salaries. But many provide good increases after the first few years and excellent long-term compensation. An Ohio State University study found these *median* starting salaries in 1988 for new graduates: PR, $18,356; advertising, $16,380; daily newspapers, $16,120; radio and TV, $15,236. They can increase dramatically with success. The *average* annual salary for an NBC correspondent (excluding star anchors, who are paid millions) was $137,000. For bureau chiefs, it was $106,000. Field producers averaged $79,000; program producers, $50,000 to $136,000. Writers averaged $74,000.

In local TV markets, salaries vary widely. On-air reporters in New York City in 1988 were paid as low as $50,000 and as high as $300,000. The range in Colorado Springs was $16,500 to $18,600, according to a survey by *Electronic Media*. In Eugene, Oregon, it was $15,000 to $34,000. Radio salaries are lower, and full-time news staffs are shrinking.

Newspaper salaries at the top are very attractive. Publishers of major papers often get $150,000 or more annually; editor salaries in the $100,000 range are not unusual. The American Newspaper Publishers Association reported in 1989 the *average* publisher's salary was $105,763; total compensation, including performance bonuses, was $125,461. On average, the top editor was paid $62,998 (with bonuses, $69,976), the top advertising director, $50,388 ($56,691 with bonuses), and the top circulation director, $45,154 ($49,639 with bonuses).

For reporters in 1988, the *New York Times* (after two years' experience) paid a minimum of $1,001 weekly; *Minneapolis Star Tribune* (five years), $822; *Eugene* (Ore.) *Register Guard* (five years), $611; *Lexington* (Ky.) *Herald-Leader* (four years), $460; Associated Press (six years), $695.

In advertising, compensation varies widely. In New York City and other major markets, chief executive officers of ad agencies can earn millions; $700,000 or so annually is not unusual for creative directors. Lower on the executive ladder, and in smaller cities, salaries are naturally lower. In 1988, account coordinators in San Antonio earned $18,000 to $25,000; copywriters, $20,000 to $35,000. In Boston, copywriters earned $30,000 to $75,000; junior copywriters, up to $20,000.

Other findings in Ohio State University studies: Fully 36 percent of new grads hired by newspapers were A or A− students, compared with 30 percent in PR, 27 percent in broadcasting, and 25 percent in advertising. And 10 percent of 1987 graduates from schools of journalism and mass communications were minorities. Of graduates hired by newspapers and news services, 7.8 percent were minorities; by radio and TV, 19.8 percent; PR, 7.3 percent; and advertising, 6.5 percent.

None of this should suggest that students must commit to careers while freshmen or sophomores. Focusing too narrowly too soon erodes the process of discovery important in higher education. Search and poke about. New and exciting worlds may open. If you do decide, tentatively, on a career path, hold open the possibility of taking a new direction at the next fork in the road. Stay flexible as long as possible. Journalism graduates often move into related fields after graduation (see Figure 19.1).

For many students, the first important career decision is selecting a major. In my experience, a major in journalism and mass communications can be enormously valuable to students headed for media careers if appropriate minor study is selected and if the right hands-on experience is obtained outside the classroom. In many schools of journalism and mass communications, four majors are common: *journalism* (sometimes called ''news-editorial''), for those headed into newspaper or magazine news; *broadcasting*, within which radio, TV, or film specializations are often available; *public relations*, which can include corporate or agency work or governmental and association PR; and *advertising*, where, again, many specializations are available. Whichever major is selected, strong writing ability is the core of any media career.

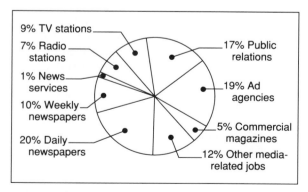

Figure 19.1. WHERE JOURNALISM GRADUATES GO.
Many journalism graduates entered daily newspaper work in 1986, but others competed with advertising and PR graduates or entered broadcasting or other media jobs. *Dow Jones Newspaper Fund.*

Obviously, a liberal arts minor in English, history, political science, or economics adds to your qualifications as a beginning reporter in either print or broadcast. A business minor is excellent if you envisage a media management, advertising, or PR career.

PICKING POTENTIAL EMPLOYERS

Students often are shocked when I say that by their junior year, they should be looking for potential employers. Here is why I advise that. Once you've selected a major and thus a tentative career path, your challenge is to find an employer whose professionalism, corporate success, ethics, and social responsibility most closely match yours. Aspiring reporters, for example, should decide what type journalism they want to practice. Is it to be the serious, highly intense journalism of, say, the *New York Times* or the *Wall Street Journal*? Or will it be the community journalism of smaller papers? Students in broadcast, PR, or advertising should seek potential employers whose structure and method of operation match their own ideals as completely as possible. The happiest of all circumstances is to find a prospective employer who thinks as you do.

Sources of information about prospective employers are numerous. Most important is an employer's own product—the daily newspaper or newscasts, advertising campaigns, PR efforts. Much can be learned about the professionalism, the corporate tone of, say, a newspaper by reading it carefully. For broadcast news majors, a station's newscasts tell the story. Publicly owned corporations issue annual reports loaded with data on operations and management structure. They are available from each firm's corporate secretary, brokerage firms, and most large libraries. Even more informative are 10-K reports, which publicly owned firms must complete annually. They are available from the U.S. Securities and Exchange Commission or a company's corporate secretary. Many media companies, even those privately owned, issue informative booklets describing their operations. Ask for the "marketing kit."

When you identify four or five companies whose operations you admire, make contact with them. Here are some hints on that.

WRITING YOUR RÉSUMÉ

A basic instrument in selling yourself to a prospective employer (and selling is what the process involves) is the résumé. Here are a few pointers.

First, even the best-written résumé will not paper over fundamental gaps in your academic background or professional training. Appropriate coursework and relevant internships or part-time professional experience are mandatory for building a strong résumé.

Second, write the résumé carefully to highlight your strengths. It should be lean and straightforward—forget the tricky, ha-ha approach. When hiring, I once received a résumé on pink paper drenched with perfume. It was designed to "stand out." Instead, it was thrown out.

Third, busy executives have just *seconds* for your résumé. So structure and write it for fast reading. But if you have enough that is significant about yourself, let the résumé run to two pages or more (forget the old rule that everything has to be jammed onto one page).

Let's examine a résumé put together by one of my students (see Figure 19.2).

1. "Employment Objective" specifies the job sought—a reporting position—but goes on to make a statement about the applicant, Alexander Christopher Friedrich. By requesting a job that "exposes me to as many dimensions of the newsroom as possible," Friedrich describes himself as an ambitious person who wants to learn quickly.

2. In "Career Objective," Friedrich shoots for the stars. He announces that he wants to own or manage a daily newspaper. Again, Friedrich says much about the person he is and the professional he wants to be. Further, he creates in the minds of prospective employers a picture of an ambitious career program that will eventually have to be opened for him by any company that wants to keep him.

3. The list of Friedrich's work experience shows how he labored to learn the newspaper business. He worked for four major newspapers and two student publications while at university. Note the detail. A prospective employer can immediately sense the stories he reported and beats he covered. Incidentally, don't feel required to list work experience chronologically. Put your best on top—that's what they do when selling apples! Friedrich lists work on a college radio station. Such relevant experience belongs on a résumé—as does nonmedia experience that demonstrates, say, your ability to handle money or manage the work of others. Unusual experience should be listed. If you were a mountain guide in the Swiss Alps, list it! One editor I know is very proud that he once worked as a welder.

4. The "Education" category should list *relevant courses* taken under your major that support your contention that you deserve the job you seek. This could include courses in reporting, writing, editing, media management, ethics, and communications law. List important courses under your minor, too. And if you pursued an interest in 19th-century British novelists or statistics, list those courses. They set you apart. Let this section give potential employers a wide view of your academic preparation. Should you mention your grade point average? Friedrich's 3.5 GPA on a scale of 4.0 is worth noting; a 1.5 would not be.

5. Don't use a "Miscellaneous" category to dump irrelevant facts. List clubs, honors, scholarships, and activities that say something important about you. And don't wait until the final months of your senior year to join clubs simply to make your résumé look better. That's cheating—and many employers take elaborate steps to check the truthfulness of *everything* on your résumé. Always let a potential employer know if you've worked your way through college or earned a significant share of your expenses. That

Alexander Christopher Friedrich

Home Address
7300 Nantucket Place
Gilroy, CA 95020
(408) 848-6027

Campus Address
677 South Milledge Avenue
Athens, GA 30605
(404) 543-0521

Employment
Objective

To obtain a reporting position, preferably general assignment, that exposes me to as many dimensions of the newsroom as possible.

Career
Objective

The management (and preferably ownership) of a daily newspaper, with complete responsibility for editorial and business operations.

Work
Experience

Management Intern; The Columbus Ledger-Enquirer.
June 1988 - August 1988. Handled several marketing research and promotion projects while cross-training in other departments. Researched demographic makeup of city, helped design ads and organized ''Pages of History'' promotional exhibit at local mall.

Part-time Reporter; The Atlanta Journal-Constitution.
September 1987 - June 1988. Covered three metro-Atlanta communities in a beat for the paper's Gwinnett Extra edition. Covered government meetings/city hall news and wrote features about one of the nation's fastest-growing counties.

Newsroom Intern: The Atlanta Journal-Constitution.
June 1987 - August 1987. Captured an exclusive interview with fallen PTL evangelist Jim Bakker during a two-week PTL assignment in Charlotte, N.C. Also worked downtown Atlanta, covering hard news, spot news, and other general assignments.

Part-time Reporter; The Athens Banner-Herald/Daily News.
January 1987 - June 1987. Covered the Oconee County beat, including county commission, board of education, utility authority and Watkinsville City Council. Also wrote features, special section articles, obituaries and movie reviews.

Part-time Feature Reporter; The Times, Gainesville.
April 1986 - December 1986. Covered general assignments with some hard news and spot news in Gainesville and north Georgia. Made front-page banner headline with story of important Army Corps of Engineers Lake Lanier drought meeting in Atlanta.

Figure 19.2. SAMPLE RÉSUMÉ.

Staff Writer; The Red and Black.
January 1986 – April 1986. Wrote features about various campus activities for this 16,000–circulation UGA student daily.

Editor–in–Chief; The Campus Sentinel.
October 1984 – December 1985. Edited news, assigned stories, recruited staff and laid out this 10,000–circulation UGA student weekly.

Editor–in–Chief; The Trumpeter.
September 1983 – June 1984. Helped start up and edit the student paper of Gainesville High School. By my graduation, The Trumpeter had repaid its start–up loan, added photographs and switched to a better printing process, while still remaining financially secure.

Education

A.B.J., University of Georgia, March 1989
Henry Grady College of Journalism and Mass Communication
News–Editorial major/History minor
GPA: 3.53/4.0

Scholarships and Awards

Spot–News Award, Society of Professional Journalists
Georgia Press Association $1,500 Scholarship
UGA Honors Program Achievement Award
Golden Key National Honor Society
Gamma Beta Phi Honor Society

Organizations

Media Management Club, president
Society of Professional Journalists/Sigma Delta Chi
Phi Kappa Theta social fraternity, Rush chairman

References

Wendell Rawls
Assistant Managing Editor/Local News
The Atlanta Journal–Constitution
72 Marietta Street
Atlanta, GA 30302
(404) 526–5342

Alan Hope
City Editor
The Times
P.O. Box 838
Gainesville, GA 30503
(404) 532–1234

Conrad Fink
Professor
Room 234, Henry Grady College of Journalism
University of Georgia
Athens, GA 30602
(404) 542–1704

says a great deal about you. List computer knowledge, travel, hobbies, or anything else you feel pertinent to understanding you. But don't use "I like people" or "I get along well with others." Such throwaway phrases are jokes to recruiters, who see them on hundreds of résumés.

6. List references, complete with title, address, and telephone number. "References upon request" forces a recruiter to write you, then wait for your response—a process that can take weeks. Busy recruiters want to be able to telephone your references quickly and then decide whether you are worth interviewing. Ask references *in advance* whether they feel able to give you a strong recommendation and, if so, whether you can list them. It's the courteous—and safe—thing to do.

Write a résumé early in your college career. You never know when one can be put to good use. Update it as you add significant academic or work achievements.

MAKING JOB CONTACTS

Actually stepping into the "real world" and making job contacts is difficult, even frightening, for some students. It need not be.

Professionals are generally eager to help young persons entering their field. Sure, you'll get the cold shoulder once in a while. But don't let that stop you from aggressively pushing out to meet professionals. Many visit campuses to lecture, meet with student clubs, or interview prospective employees. Seize every opportunity to introduce yourself. Ask if you can visit the company they represent. *Write a follow-up note and enclose your résumé.* Explain your career goals and seek advice on how to attain them. *Open a dialogue* with professionals. Get them interested in you as a person. And learn from them as you go along.

Attend every professional meeting you can. State press association conventions are great places to meet publishers and editors. Other media have similar meetings. Walk up to professionals, stick out your hand, and say hello. If you

plan travel to a distant city, write ahead for appointments to visit newspapers, broadcast stations, or PR and ad agencies. *Circulate!*

The letter formally applying for an internship or job interview is extremely important. Your résumé will be attached, so the letter can be limited to one page. These elements are essential:

1. Your opening paragraph should state explicitly what it is you seek—a general assignment reporting internship, hands-on summer experience in the creative department of an ad agency, an assistant account executive's position with a PR agency, whatever.

2. The second paragraph should state clearly why you are interested particularly in the job you are applying for. If you're prepared properly, you'll be able to write, for example, that you are interested in the type of investigative reporting newspaper X does or that you want to join an ad agency that does such a splendid job in TV commercials, and so forth. *Demonstrate in this letter your familiarity with the company, its market, its competitive situation.* Show that you know how to do your homework.

3. Conclude by stating that *you* will telephone in a week in the hope that you can confirm an interview date. Don't simply mail your letter and drop the matter in the laps of the gods. *Pursue!*

HANDLING YOURSELF IN AN INTERVIEW

You may think it unfair (and it may be), but after all your hard work in classes, the internships and part-time jobs, you have about 30 minutes in an interview to make the correct impression as you seek the job of your dreams.

How can you win in 30 minutes? First, you practice. During your college years, interview with many recruiters who visit your campus, even if you don't want the jobs they offer. The first interview may be agonizing; the second will be less so, the third a breeze. And come that interview for the postgraduation job you really want, you'll be a pro.

Second, understand what an interview is all about. It is not an occasion for you simply to answer yes and no. Rather, it is an opportunity to make an affirmative statement about yourself. So, third, carefully *prepare a strategy* for those crucial 30 minutes when interviewing for the real thing. Think deeply about yourself. Which *five points* about yourself do you want left in that recruiter's mind when the interview ends? Write each, in a paragraph or two, before the interview and rehearse the delivery. Is it enthusiasm that sets you apart? Your commitment to a professional career? Your writing ability? Whatever makes you uniquely attractive, get it on the table during the interview. It's best if you weave such material into responses to questions. But if the question isn't asked, answer it anyway: "Before I leave, there are just a couple things I want to say about my qualifications for this job. . . ."

Expect questions that make you stretch for an answer. As president of Cox Newspapers, Charles Glover says his favorite questions were these:

"Where do you want to be ten years from now?"

"In your opinion, what are your strengths? What are your weaknesses?"

"If you had to describe your personality, how important would a characteristic like sense of humor be?"

Such questions are designed to elicit introspective responses that signal broader, philosophical dimensions of your personality. Don't panic. They give you perfect opportunity to feed back some or all of the five points you rehearsed as part of your overall strategy. (Incidentally, your primary weakness is lack of professional experience. And that is a weakness you can fix with a job!)

Many interviewers will state the salary offered; others will ask something like "How much money would you need to join us?" The challenge is to lob that question back into the interviewer's court without taking a firm position you might regret later. If you peg your expectations too high, you might price yourself out of the mar-

ket. If your dollar figure is too low, it might be accepted!

I suggest something along these lines: "My primary interest is in joining your company. It is an organization I admire and would like to work for. Of course, money is important, too. But I don't know what the cost of living is in your area. What salary do you have in mind?" If the response is a salary higher than you expected, take it. If it's too low, negotiate.

Here are a few other pointers:

◆ Be self-confident during the interview, but avoid even a hint of boastfulness. Let your résumé do the boasting.
◆ Most recruiters seek candidates who can start producing their first day on the job. Editors want reporters who can cover a school board meeting and write it well. TV recruiters want prospects who can help get the evening news on the air. PR and ad agencies want self-starters. But recruiters always look for prospects willing to take guidance. A know-it-all attitude is the kiss of death.
◆ What really counts in job hunting is substance—your academic performance, internships and part-time jobs. But personal appearance can be crucial. Dress neatly and cleanly in collegiate style (jacket and tie, a conservative dress), and don't overdo it. The graduating senior who shows up in a $500 suit or a long cocktail dress has overdone it. Try for good eye contact and demeanor that is alert and confident, yet relaxed and smiling at times, too. If in doubt, tend toward the serious side. After all, serious business is being discussed: your future and the company's investment in an unknown person.

Let's go now to the other side of the desk.

EVALUATING JOB SEEKERS
by David Paul Tressel, Director of Marketing, WTKR-TV, Norfolk, Virginia

I first look at the applicant's résumé for educational background and whether the applicant has the foundation necessary to do the job. I look at both the major and minor areas of study.

Then I look at past work experience, even

if it is part-time. This will give me some idea of the applicant's willingness to work to achieve goals. Someone who put himself or herself through college by flipping burgers at the student union may be more appealing that someone who worked as a research assistant. Although the research assistant job might be an indication of more training in one's field, the student union job could be evidence of a strong desire to succeed no matter what it takes.

In the same light, I look at the applicant's extracurricular activities. I look at both the quantity and the variety. I feel it is important for any person working in the area of marketing to be multidimensional.

During the job interview, I let applicants talk about themselves: their education, their family, their immediate goals, and their future desires. This gives them a chance to show me how well they can communicate one to one. Any position in the marketing department requires good communication skills, especially in the area of expressing desires and needs to other station personnel. Also during this conversation, I am looking for a special quality—a need, a desire, an urgency, whatever you want to call it, to do great things, to get things done, and to go beyond what is expected. I look for a person who is always thinking and always doing.

LANDING A JOB

by Jack Mitchell, Senior Vice President for Human Resources, Burson-Marsteller

Recruitment at Burson-Marsteller is centrally orchestrated by the human resources department. Referrals from our staff as well as all other sources are channeled to professional human resources recruiters.

Identifying top candidates is most difficult at the entry or junior level because applicants have not had the opportunity to develop good business track records. What the recruiter looks for in the thousands of résumés we receive are signs of potential and signs of success in school endeavors that portend success in business endeavors.

We first look for academic rating, a grade point average (GPA) in relationship to the school. A high GPA in an inferior college may not be as significant as an average to high GPA in a superior college. But grades are only one indicator, albeit extremely important. They indicate the candidate's ability to achieve intellectually, very important to us because Burson-Marsteller has mainly blue-chip clients who usually have hired very bright, highly educated people. To be able to discuss the intricacies of business, goals, strategies, tactics, and the like, we need to hire people on the same intellectual level. The college attended and the GPA give us very clear clues.

Next we look for well-roundedness because highly intelligent individuals with underdeveloped personalities are simply not successful in a client service business. Well-rounded means multifaceted. The person is not a bookworm but is interested in life and has many friends and many interests, on campus and off. Our recruiter looks at whether the applicant participated in extracurricular activities, especially those that involved writing or communication. Did the applicant belong to a fraternity or sorority? Were there evidences of leadership? Did the applicant travel?

What kind of work has the applicant done? We ask this to see if the person worked while in school, getting good grades and maintaining an active social life, which indicate a good potential for the fast-paced public relations industry. If the person did not work at all or perhaps accepted an easy job, this may imply a lack of drive and initiative—definitely not good potential.

Perhaps the three most important aspects in a résumé are intellect, well-roundedness, and initiative. The bottom line, though, is to identify success. Was the applicant successful as a collegian? If the answer is yes, the résumé will be put aside for a possible face-to-face interview. If the answer is maybe or no, chances are there will be no follow-up interview.

The professional recruiter looks for one other quality in a candidate: potential. No set questions or answers clarify whether an applicant has potential. The good recruiter sees something special in the candidate's tone of voice or sparkle in the eyes. The good recruiter has a sense that this candidate, over all other candidates, has that specialness, the hunger, the drive, the energy, the tools for success within our company, that special potential to become a star performer in the organization.

That people already inside the media are on the lookout for "that special potential" is demonstrated by their generous responses to requests for the perspectives included in this book. We have gone behind the scenes and behind the managers' desks, and I hope the result is, for each of you who desire media careers, the feeling of having an added edge. Don't be discouraged if an interview fails to get you the job. Consider it good preparation for the next one!

Notes

CHAPTER 1

1. Ray Shaw, letter to author, Feb. 23, 1987.

2. Conrad Fink, *Strategic Newspaper Management* (New York: Random House, 1988), explores the marketing orientation of modern publishing companies.

3. Robert Maxwell, speech to the International Federation of Newspaper Publishers Management and Marketing Symposium, Madrid, Oct. 23, 1987.

4. James W. Michaels, "Side Lines," *Forbes*, Feb. 22, 1988, p. 6.

5. Mary Anderson, "World Media Moguls," *presstime*, May 1987, p. 6.

6. "Robert Maxwell, Richest Czechoslovakian," *Forbes*, Oct. 5, 1987, p. 140.

7. *Los Angeles Times* dispatch, published as "Networks Realizing Benefits of Beaming Nightly News Overseas," *Atlanta Constitution*, Jan. 5, 1988, p. 7C.

8. Tatiana Pouschine, "I, Berlusconi," *Forbes*, Jan. 25, 1988, p. 59. Also see Richard W. Stevenson, "TV Boom in Europe Aids U.S. Producers," *New York Times*, nat. ed., Dec. 28, 1987, p. D1.

9. "What's Hot in Foreign Countries," *Electronic Media*, Feb. 22, 1988, p. 41.

10. Ferdinand Protzman, "Dr. Ruth Goes International with Sex Therapy for Europe," *International Herald Tribune*, Feb. 15, 1988, p. 1.

11. Nancy S. Giges, letter to author, Jan. 27, 1989.

12. John Marcom, Jr., "Cable and Satellites Are Opening Europe to TV Commercials," *Wall Street Journal*, Dec. 22, 1987, p. 1.

13. Second Quarterly Report, 1988, Dow Jones Inc. (New York: Dow Jones Inc.), p. 1.

14. Bill Keller, "For Soviet Alternate Press, Used Computer Is New Tool," *New York Times*, nat. ed., Oct. 27, 1988, p. 19.

15. Cathleen Black, speech to the Association of National Advertisers, San Diego, Calif., Oct. 21, 1987.

16. Paul Theroux, "Shanghai: The Talk of People's Park," *New York Times Sunday Magazine*, Apr. 3, 1988, p. 30.

17. Julie Skur Hill and Joseph M. Winski, "Goodby Global Ads," *Advertising Age*, Nov. 16, 1987, p. 22.

18. Lee Hall, "'Playboy' Executive Says 'Global' Ads Elude Licensed Editions," *Advertising Age*, Dec. 31, 1984, p. 54.

19. Joe Wax, a Washington attorney, presents a splendid discussion of the American law in "Are the FCC's Foreign Ownership Rules Passé?" *Broadcasting*, Mar. 7, 1988. Ways in which foreign entrepreneurs could get around the law are sketched in "*Parlez-vous* FM?" *Broadcasting*, Feb. 8, 1988, p. 7. For American newspapers' numbers, circulations, and other statistics, see *Facts about Newspapers '88* (Washington, D.C.: American Newspaper Publishers Association, 1988).

20. John Marcom, Jr., "Maxwell Advocates Quotas on Imports of U.S. TV Shows," *Wall Street Journal*, May 2, 1988, p. 24.

21. Richard Reeves in a London dispatch for morning papers, Oct. 3, 1987, published that day in the *Atlanta Journal and Constitution*, p. 27A.

22. John M. Eger, "Plenty of Niches for All Comers," *Advertising Age*, Dec. 14, 1987, p. 60.

23. This is discussed more fully in Conrad Fink, "*Media Ethics: In the Newsroom and Beyond* (New York: McGraw-Hill, 1988), pp. 79–173.

24. Laurel Wentz, "Media Test Advertisers' Spirit of Adventure," *Advertising Age*, July 5, 1987, p. 17.

25. For a concise rundown on various forms of censorship, see "Censorship: What Is It? Where Is It?" a speech by George Theiner, editor of the *Index on Censorship*, London, to the World News Media Action Conference, London, Jan. 16, 1987, available through the American Newspaper Publishers Association. The International Press Institute reports annually on worldwide press restrictions. One recent report is "Worldwide Press Freedom: Some Places Bad, Some Places Better," *Editor & Publisher*, Feb. 13, 1988, p. 16.

26. Dana R. Bullen, speech sponsored by the American Bar Association International Communications Committee, the Annenberg Washington Program, and Northwestern University Communications Policy Studies, Washington, D.C., Feb. 4, 1988.

27. Everett E. Dennis, foreword, ''The Cost of Technology,'' report on a Nov. 9, 1986, conference at the Gannett Center for Media Studies, New York.

28. Washington Associated Press dispatch for morning papers of April 7, 1988, ''Only Half of Adults Who Own Computers Actually Use Them,'' *Atlanta Constitution* of that date, p. B1.

CHAPTER 2

1. A Harris poll two months after the invasion found that the Americans surveyed were convinced, 65 to 32 percent, that the Reagan administration was wrong in not permitting reporters to accompany troops. See ''ANPA, Other Press Groups Decline to Serve on Sidle Committee,'' *presstime*, Feb. 1984, p. 34.

2. Letter to a friend, Carrington, 1787.

3. John Milton, *Areopagitica* (1644).

4. Michael Emery and Edwin Emery, *The Press and America: An Interpretive History of the Mass Media*, 6th ed., (Englewood Cliffs, N.J.: Prentice-Hall, 1988), p. 93.

5. See John Gill, *Tide without Turning: Elijah P. Lovejoy and Freedom of the Press* (Boston: Beacon Press, 1958).

6. For background on Civil War reporting, see J. Cutler Andrews, *The North Reports the Civil War* (Pittsburgh: University of Pittsburgh Press, 1955) and *The South Reports the Civil War* (Princeton, N.J.: Princeton University Press, 1970).

7. Figures for 1900 are from Emery and Emery, *The Press and America*, p. 188; figures for 1988 (rounded) are from *Facts about Newspapers '88* (Washington, D.C.: American Newspaper Publishers Association, 1988).

8. The *Cleveland Press* and other metropolitan papers stricken by socioeconomic change are discussed in Conrad Fink, *Strategic Newspaper Management* (New York: Random House, 1988), esp. p. 210.

9. By the late 1980s, however, illiteracy posed a long-term threat to newspapers and the American Newspaper Publishers Association and other trade associations were urging member publications to start remedial reading programs in local communities. The newspaper industry's Newspaper in Education program is designed to get the reading habit started among schoolchildren.

10. A. M. Rosenthal, letter to author, Mar. 28, 1983.

11. Under a program launched nationwide by the newspaper industry in 1984 to attract national advertisers, standard dimensions for a full-size page were set at six columns, each $2\frac{1}{16}$ inches wide with $\frac{1}{8}$ inch between columns. Columns are 21 to $22\frac{1}{2}$ inches wide, pages 13 inches deep. Tabloid pages are $10\frac{13}{16}$ inches wide and 14 inches deep, with five columns, each $2\frac{1}{16}$ inches wide and $\frac{1}{8}$ inch apart.

12. Edwin and Michael Emery, *The Press and America* (Englewood Cliffs, N.J.: Prentice-Hall, 1978), p. 4322.

13. Michael A. Weinstein, ''Misplaced Sympathy for Media's 'Victims' Could Backfire on Public,'' *Atlanta Constitution*, Feb. 18, 1988, p. 15A.

14. See both Commission of Freedom of the Press, *A Free and Responsible Press* (Chicago: University of Chicago Press, 1947) and Theodore Peterson, Fred S. Siebert, and Wilbur Schramm, *Four Theories of the Press* (Urbana: University of Illinois Press, 1956).

15. See Kent Cooper, *Barriers Down* (New York: Farrar, Straus & Giroux, 1942).

16. A. M. Rosenthal, ''A Poem for Seven Judges,'' *New York Times*, nat. ed., Feb. 5, 1988, p. 27.

17. A major poll by the American Society of Newspaper Editors was published in 1985 as ''Relating to Readers in the '80s''; other polls cited here were published by Gallup in 1983. All are discussed in more detail in Fink, *Strategic Newspaper Management*, pp. 254–261.

18. Conrad Fink, *Media Ethics: In the Newsroom and Beyond*, (New York: McGraw-Hill, 1988), p. 58.

CHAPTER 3

1. For current revenue and profit figures of major conglomerates, plus their media holdings, see the annual reports or 10-K forms for publicly owned companies; *Advertising Age*, which annually publishes surveys of the nation's 100 leading media firms; and *Forbes*, which breaks out financial figures for 500 firms each year. Annual compilations of media ad revenue are available through the American Newspaper Publishers Association.

2. John Morton's most important published research is issued in *Newspaper Newsletter*, from Lynch, Jones & Ryan, 1037 Thirtieth Street NW, Washington, DC 20007. *Editor & Publisher International Yearbook* tracks individual newspapers and newspaper groups.

3. See *Broadcast Yearbook* for annual surveys of radio and television stations and broadcast groups.

4. Times Mirror Co., annual report, 1987.

5. That Times Mirror, so successful elsewhere, could lose in both Denver and Dallas shocked many people, inside the company as well as outside it. Both competitive fights are examined in Conrad Fink, *Strategic Newspaper Management* (New York: Random House, 1988) and *Media Ethics: In The Newsroom and Beyond* (New York: McGraw-Hill, 1988).

6. An excellent detailed examination of Hearst is in William P. Barrett, "Citizen Rich," *Forbes*, Dec. 14, 1987, pp. 141–148. Barrett estimates that Hearst had as much as 14 percent of all U.S. daily circulation in the 1930s and nearly double that on Sundays; he ventures that newspapers contribute a mere 9 percent of the company's cash flow today.

7. Figures on the Gwinnett acquisition are from New York Times Co. Form 10-Q, Sept. 30, 1987, p. 7.

8. Adapted from information supplied by Knight-Ridder, Inc.

9. I discovered in an analysis of annual reports that Knight-Ridder directors in 1986 averaged 65.3 years of age; New York Times Co. directors, 61.4; Gannett directors, 55.9. Is the sprightly, "youthful" *USA Today* one result of Gannett's having younger directors? Further research is warranted into the bearing such factors have on corporate policy.

10. Knight-Ridder notes, in its notice of its 1988 annual meeting of shareholders, that Knight shares voting rights on some of this stock with the Knight Foundation and others. But even so, he votes nearly seven times the shares of any other director or executive.

11. This list of characteristics was provided by Douglas C. Harris, currently vice president and secretary. For a discussion of leadership in a media context, see Fink, *Strategic Newspaper Management*, pp. 11ff.

12. One highly regarded news executive, John Finnegan, vice president of the *St. Paul Pioneer Press and Dispatch*, argues that journalists should publicly divulge their private interests and net worth to avoid any perception of conflict of interest. See Fink, *Media Ethics*, pp. 25–26.

13. Knight-Ridder's 1987 annual report; *Who's Who in America*.

14. Knight-Ridder's annual letter to shareholders, Mar. 6, 1989.

15. AP figures from the Associated Press; U.S. newspaper totals from the American Newspaper Publishers Association.

16. Reuters has never been as open to outside scrutiny as AP, so anyone interested in further study of it will find a treasure trove of detail in a "preliminary prospectus" issued on May 15, 1984, by Merrill Lynch Capital Markets and Morgan Stanley & Co. Inc., when Reuters Holdings PLC offered shares on Wall Street.

17. Didrikke Schanche, "Kenya: Troops Beat Reporters," *AP Log*, Nov. 23, 1987, p. 1.

18. "AP Editor in Washington on Magazine's Power Elite List," *AP Log*, Feb. 22, 1988, p. 4.

19. Allan Dodds Frank and Jason Sweig, "The Fault Is Not in Our Stars," *Forbes*, Sept. 21, 1987, pp. 120–130.

20. Andrew Malcolm, "Dear Ann: About Your Move to the *Trib*," *New York Times*, nat. ed., Mar. 12, 1987, p. 8.

21. I have reason to believe that Reuters was enticed into the U.S. fray by the offer of a rich contract from the world's largest brokerage firm, New York–based Merrill Lynch, Pierce, Fenner & Smith Inc. Merrill Lynch's motive was to introduce competition against Dow Jones and beat down its rates, which cost the brokerage firm millions of dollars annually.

22. In 1987, DJ information services returned 36.8 percent operating income on revenue; the Ottaway community newspaper division returned 22 percent; DJ business publications, 20.6 percent. These profit margins are more than double those achieved by many U.S. businesses.

23. This advertising slogan was made famous by Martin Specter, a New York City adman who handled the Dow Jones account for years.

24. Peter T. Kilborn, "The Monthly Announcement That Makes Wall Street Sweat," *New York Times*, nat. ed., Jan. 15, 1988, p. 1.

25. All were members of ANPA's board of directors in 1988, along with executives of Tribune Co., Scripps Howard, Newhouse, Belo (*Dallas Morning News*), Lee Enterprises, and other high-powered groups.

26. Kay Graham, "Conflict and the Press," speech presented at a conference sponsored by the *Star*, Johannesburg, South Africa, Oct. 1987.

CHAPTER 4

1. *Editor & Publisher*/American Newspaper Publishers Association.

2. See Conrad Fink, *Strategic Newspaper Management* (New York: Random House, 1988).

3. Steven Isaacs, last editor of the *Minneapolis Star* before it folded in 1982. See Ibid., pp. 145–148.

4. James Reston, interview with Poynter Institute.

5. Evolving technical processes are covered in both *presstime* and *Editor & Publishers* magazines.

6. Leo Bogart, Newspaper Advertising Bureau, speech to the American Newspaper Publishers

Association annual convention, Honolulu, Apr. 26, 1988.

7. *Media Records*/American Newspaper Publishers Association.

8. Circulation figures are available in "audit reports" on individual newspapers from the Audit Bureau of Circulations, 900 N. Meacham Rd., Schaumburg, IL 60195. Also see *Editor & Publisher International Yearbook* and *Circulation*, two standard references with detailed figures.

9. Gene Glotz, "Reviving a Romance with Readers Is the Biggest Challenge for Many Newspapers," quoting Executive Vice President Leo Bogart of the Newspaper Advertising Bureau, *presstime*, Feb. 1988, pp. 16–22.

10. Leo Bogart speech, Honolulu, 1988.

11. Patricia E. Bauer, "The Convictions of a Long-Distance Investor," *Channels*, Nov. 22, 1986, pp. 22–29.

12. Alvah H. Chapman, Jr., personal communication, Mar. 16, 1983.

13. Michael Gartner, speech, Gannett Center for Media Studies, New York, Apr. 28, 1987.

14. *Editor & Publisher*/American Newspaper Publishers Association.

15. U.S. Bureau of Labor Statistics, ANPA.

16. Ben Bradlee, interview, Poynter Institute, 1987.

17. Meg Greenfield, interview, Poynter Institute, 1987.

18. "The Best Newspapers," *Adweek*, Apr. 28, 1987, p. 18.

19. Kay Fanning, farewell speech as president of the American Society of Newspaper Editors, *ASNE Bulletin*, May–June 1988, p. 10.

20. Dow Jones doesn't reveal the *Journal*'s precise position. But one analyst estimates that 1987 operating profit margins declined to 25 percent from 30 percent. See Alex S. Jones, "The *Journal* Gets a New Order," *New York Times*, nat. ed., Feb. 1, 1988, p. 21.

21. Julius Duscha, "An Insider's Look at the Human and Financial Toll of Birthing McPaper," review of Peter Pritchard, *The Making of McPaper*, *ASNE Bulletin*, Nov. 1987, p. 38.

22. *USA Today* demographics from Gannett Co. *Journal*'s figures from *Advertising Age*, June 6, 1988, pp. 10–11.

23. Gannett acknowledged after-tax losses of $310 million. The $600 million figure is from a source at Gannett.

24. Al Neuharth, in a speech to the 1988 annual convention of the International Newspaper Association of Marketing Executives, New Orleans, said he was quoting an anonymous editor who penned the headlines (presumably late one night) at the National Press Club in Washington, D.C.

25. "Gannett Shares Drop as Officer Forecasts Loss at *USA Today*," *Wall Street Journal*, Apr. 11, 1988, p. 34.

26. Facts about the *Times* were drawn in part from Times Mirror's 1987 annual report, its annual meeting notice and proxy statement, *Los Angeles Times* marketing research, and "Facts about The *Times*" (Los Angeles: Times Mirror Co.).

27. Michael Gartner, speech, New York, 1987.

CHAPTER 5

1. Publisher Billy Watson, personal communication, Apr. 14, 1988. All details in this case study have been provided by Watson and other *Ledger-Enquirer* executives.

2. For example, Ottaway Newspapers, subsidiary of Dow Jones, shoot for 30 percent. Some papers achieve 40 or even 50 percent. The disastrous impact this has on journalistic quality and community service is discussed in Conrad Fink, *Strategic Newspaper Management* (New York: Random House, 1988).

3. "Columbus, Georgia: Market Characteristics and Newspaper Audience" (*Ledger-Enquirer*, n.d.).

4. Ibid.

5. David Shaw, "America's Overseas Eyes, Ears," *Los Angeles Times*, June 29, 1986, p. 11, quoting a UNESCO study of foreign news content in the three metros.

6. Jean Gaddy Wilson, "Women Make Up 13 Percent of Directing Editors at Dailies," *ASNE Bulletin*, Jan. 1988, pp. 15–18.

7. Watson, personal communication; American Newspaper Publishers Association.

8. Mal Mallette, "Newspaper Slogans," *presstime*, Apr. 1987, pp. 14–15.

CHAPTER 6

1. *Forbes* also claimed in 1987–1988 promotional material that 99 percent of its subscribers maintain investment portfolios averaging $718,000 in value and that 88 percent own corporate stock worth an average of $55,000!

2. Steven P. Galante, "*Entrepreneur* Magazine Changes Its Image to Attract More Small-Business Readers," *Wall Street Journal*, Dec. 22, 1987, p. 21.

3. Patrick Reilly, *Harper's* Turns Profit," *Advertising Age*, Apr. 18, 1988, p. 8.

4. *Facts about Newspapers '89* (Washington, D.C.: American Newspaper Publishers Association, 1989).

5. Based on an Audit Bureau of Circulations report for the six months ended Dec. 31, 1987.

6. Philip H. Dougherty, "Advertising," *New York Times*, July 1, 1988, p. D16.

7. Philip H. Dougherty, "Magazine Finds Less Is More," *New York Times*, nat. ed., Nov. 7, 1986, p. 34.

8. "Everything," *Advertising Age*, June 27, 1988, p. 37. *Bride's* added that its "primary couples"—readers—have a combined annual income of $43,310, some 35 percent above the national average.

9. In 1989, a qualified subscriber paid $64 for a one-year subscription, a nonqualified subscriber, $80, or 25 percent more.

10. Audit Bureau of Circulations, "Study of Media Involvement," 1987; figures for last six months of 1987.

11. James R. Guthrie, letter, *Wall Street Journal*, June 29, 1988, p. 23.

12. Audits & Surveys, Inc., "A Study of Media Involvement," 1986.

13. *New York*, publisher's statement; Audit Bureau of Circulations. Figures for six months ended June 30, 1987.

14. *New York*, publisher's statement.

15. Cynthia Crossen, "In Manhattan, Publishers Aim at Select Niches," *Wall Street Journal*, Jan. 20, 1988, p. 56.

16. "Enter a Totally Awesome Magazine," *Insight*, June 13, 1988, p. 56. Solid reports on *Sassy* are Suzanne Daley, "*Sassy*: Like You Know, for Kids," *New York Times*, nat. ed., Apr. 11, 1988, p. 34; and Cynthia Crossen, "Sexual Candor Marks Magazine for Teen Girls," *Wall Street Journal*, Feb. 17, 1988, p. 31.

17. Geraldine Fabrikant, "Magazine to Pursue Teen-Agers," *New York Times*, nat. ed., Aug. 24, 1987, p. D7.

18. See Johnnie L. Roberts, "Newsweek to Drop 2 Special Editions, for Campus, Health," *Wall Street Journal*, Apr. 8, 1988, p. 24; and Randall Rothenberg, "McGraw-Hill Drops College Publication," *New York Times*, nat. ed., May 3, 1988, p. 52.

19. Gary Levin, "*Playboy* Readies Comeback," *Advertising Age*, Oct. 26, 1987, p. 12; Robert Reed, "*Playboy* Faces Turnaround Fight," *Advertising Age*, Aug. 1, 1983, p. 1.

20. Ray Cave, "Musings of a Newsmagazine Editor," *Gannett Center Journal*, Spring 1987, p. 81.

21. "Editors Air Their Views about Print," *ABC News Bulletin*, Dec. 1987, p. 9.

22. Hearst Corp., "Some Thoughts about a Magazine's Tremendous Audience of One," ad, *New York Times Magazine*, Apr. 10, 1988, pp. 24–25.

CHAPTER 7

1. I made an extensive study of *U.S. News & World Report* and its competitive strategies, particularly against *Time* and *Newsweek*, in 1987–1989. My thanks go to *U.S. News*, particularly Gerson Yalowitz, assistant managing editor, and Kathryn A. Bushkin, director of editorial administration, for their assistance.

2. Financial and other statistical information was drawn from "Leading Media Companies," *Advertising Age*, special issue, June 17, 1988; Magazine Publishers Association; and other sources.

3. Additional information on *U.S. News*'s turnaround is in Alex S. Jones, "New Chiefs at *U.S. News* Stir Anxious Curiosity," *New York Times*, nat. ed., May 4, 1986; Jones, "For New Magazines, Growing Identity Crisis," *New York Times*, June 29, 1988, p. C26; and Noreen O'Leary, "Magazines People to Watch," *AdWeek*, Feb. 16, 1988, p. 11.

4. Janet Meyers, "Drasner Lays It on Line in Spots for *U.S. News*," *Advertising Age*, May 9, 1988, p. 88.

5. Jones, "New Chiefs at *U.S. News*."

6. O'Leary, "Magazine People to Watch."

7. Ibid.

8. Courtesy of *U.S. News & World Report*.

9. Staff figures as of May 9, 1988, for *U.S. News*.

10. For years, *U.S. News* recruited heavily among AP editors experienced in fast, hard-news editing. Many top editors were drawn from AP.

11. Based on 1987 ad and circulation revenues; normally, the magazine says, advertising contributes about 58 percent, circulation, 42 percent.

CHAPTER 8

1. Molly Badgett, "G&G Seeks Jackpot with Television Program Based on *USA Today*," *Gannetteer*, January 1988, p. 13.

2. Moves by McGraw-Hill and others into videocassettes are explored in Ben Dunlap Jr., "Peripheral Areas Offer Room to Expand," *Advertising Age*, June 15, 1987, p. S8.

3. Len Strazewski, "Computer Bulletin," *Advertising Age*, Dec. 14, 1987, p. 82.

4. See L. R. Shannon, "The New Look of Magazines," *New York Times*, nat. ed., Oct. 27, 1987, p. 19; "ABC Prepares to Audit Electronic 'Magazine,'" *presstime*, Nov. 1987, p. 49.

5. Keith Herndon, "Home Videos Had a $7.2 Billion '87 Showing," *Atlanta Journal and Constitution*, Jan. 23, 1988, p. C1.

6. Richard Reeves, "Robertson Bypasses Press by Taking His Program to Voters with 'The Tape,'" syndicated column for morning papers, Feb. 17, 1988.

7. "Memories of a Lifetime Captured by Kodak," ad, *Wall Street Journal*, July 13, 1988, p. 7.

8. Janet Guyon, "Telecommunications Network

Management Heats Up,'' *Wall Street Journal*, Mar. 1, 1988, p. 8.

9. The OTA report is described in detail in "Technology Redefines 'Press,'" *Broadcasting*, Feb. 15, 1988, p. 133.

10. Tenner wrote originally for the Mar.–Apr. 1988 issue of *Harvard Magazine*; his piece then was adapted for use in the *International Herald Tribune*, Mar. 18, 1988, p. 5.

11. For background on the continuing telephone company versus media battle, see Bob Davis, "FCC Proposes Phone Firms Vie in Cable Market," *Wall Street Journal*, July 21, 1988, p. 22.

12. Ester Dyson, *Forbes*, Dec. 28, 1987, p. 107.

13. "Prechter Shines in Stocks, Options," *USA Today*, Oct. 8, 1987, p. 4B.

14. Jerry Adler, "The Merciless Man of Wine," *Newsweek*, Dec. 14, 1987, p. 77.

15. "Prechter Shines."

16. Christopher J. Chipello, "With Few Resources, a Former Marketer Starts His Own Mutual Fund Newsletter," *Wall Street Journal*, Aug. 20, 1987, p. 25.

17. From Paul Kagan Associates, Inc., Carmel, Calif.

18. Sara Fortune, "Whittle Is Right on Target," news release (Knoxville, Tenn.: Whittle Communications, 1989).

19. Ibid.

20. Advo-Systems, Inc., "The Mail Has Arrived and You'd Better Look at It," ad, *Advertising Age*, June 27, 1988, p. 49.

21. *Facts about Newspapers '87* (Washington, D.C.: American Newspaper Publishers Association, 1987).

22. Janice Steinberg, "Cacophony of Catalogs Fill All Niches," *Advertising Age*, Oct. 26, 1987, p. S1.

23. Elizabeth M. Fowler, "Jobs Grow in Direct Marketing," *New York Times*, June 30, 1987, p. D23.

24. The study, "Book Industry Trends 1988," is analyzed in Edwin McDowell, "Optimistic Survey for Book Industry," *New York Times*, July 8, 1988, p. D15.

25. Ibid.

26. Tom Teepen, "Despite Its Marvels, Gadgetry Has a Rival When It Comes to Reading," *Atlanta Constitution*, March 22, 1988, p. 23A.

27. Edwin McDowell, "Farrar, Straus Thrives on Success of 2 Novels," *New York Times*, nat. ed., May 17, 1988, p. 50.

28. William Glaberson, "Will Takeovers Be Bad for Books?" *New York Times*, Apr. 5, 1987, p. C1.

29. Edwin McDowell, "Highbrow Books as Best Sellers," *New York Times*, nat. ed., Mar. 8, 1988, p. 22.

30. Michael Freitag, "On the Endangered List: The 'Instant Book,'" *New York Times*, nat. ed., Nov. 15, 1987, p. F12.

31. Edwin McDowell, "2,875 Pages and Growing: A Publisher's Dilemma," *New York Times*, July 25, 1988, p. D8.

32. Edwin McDowell, "Paperback Industry Fears a Shortage of Paper," *New York Times*, nat. ed., Feb. 9, 1988, p. 29.

33. Jacob M. Schlesinger, "New Book on GM Is Hyped as Exposé by a Publisher Hoping for a Winner," *Wall Street Journal*, Mar. 25, 1988, p. 28.

34. Cynthia Crossen, "Will Nine Different Covers Help Sell a New Paperback?" *Wall Street Journal*, Apr. 5, 1988, p. 39.

35. Kerry Hannon, "Seen Any Good Books Lately?" *Forbes*, Sept. 21, 1987, p. 180.

36. William C. Banks, "Desktop Publishing," *Money*, July 1987, p. 119.

CHAPTER 9

1. *Facts about Newspapers '89* (Washington, D.C.: American Newspaper Publishers Association, 1989).

2. Ibid.

3. Radio Advertising Bureau; A. C. Nielsen Co.; *Broadcasting/Cablecasting Yearbook 1988*.

4. See Peter J. Boyer, "The Shift of Rather," *New York Times*, Aug. 6, 1988, p. 50.

5. Leo Bogart, executive vice president, Newspaper Advertising Bureau, speech to the American Newspaper Publishers Association, Honolulu, Apr. 26, 1988.

6. Verne Gay, "Cable's Power Broker," *Advertising Age*, Nov. 9, 1987, p. 40.

7. *Broadcasting/Cablecasting Yearbook 1989*, p. D-6.

8. *Broadcasting/Cablecasting Yearbook 1988*.

9. Reach calculated by *Broadcasting/Cablecasting Yearbook 1988*, p. A-64, based on Arbitron's 1986–1987 marketing ADI households and percentages.

10. Newspaper and magazine competitors also claim that no reliable measurement exists proving substantial viewer retention of televised information, particularly commercials.

11. *Facts about Newspapers '89*.

12. See Claudia H. Deutsch, "The Battle to Wire the Consumer," *New York Times*, July 26, 1987, sec. 3, p. 1, and Verne Gay, "Nielsen Strikes Back," *Advertising Age*, Nov. 30, 1987, p. 1.

13. Eugene Patterson, "The Newspaper Future," *Washington Journalism Review*, Jan.–Feb. 1988, p. 26.

14. Eleanor Blau, "Now, People-Metering for TV Commercials," *New York Times*, natl. ed., Apr. 25, 1988, p. 19.

15. Peter J. Boyer, "CBS Cites New Meters for $40 Million in Costs," *New York Times*, Jan. 19, 1988, p. 24.

16. Barry L. Sherman puts ratings into an important business context in broadcasting in *Telecommunications Management* (New York: McGraw-Hill, 1987).

17. Eleanor Blau, "A Study Has Found a Barrage of Sex on TV," *New York Times*, natl. ed., Jan. 27, 1988, p. 13; also see John Corry, "A New Age of Television Tastelessness?" *New York Times*, May 29, 1988, sec. 2, p. 1.

18. Corry, "New Age," sec. 2, p. 1.

19. Fred Friendly, interview with the Poynter Institute, St. Petersburg, Fla.

20. Larry Grossman, speech to the Advertising Club of New York, June 22, 1988.

21. Michael G. Gartner, then editor of the *Louisville Courier-Journal*, speech at Gannett Center for Media Studies, New York, Apr. 28, 1987.

22. Tom Brokaw, speech at Gannett Center for Media Studies, New York, Nov. 9, 1986.

23. Ernest Leiser, "Less Style, More TV News, Please," *New York Times*, nat. ed., Jan. 4, 1988, p. 17.

24. Joe Saltzman, "'News' Plugging Docudramas," *Washington Journalism Review*, Jan.–Feb. 1988, p. 54.

25. John Corry, "TV: The News Movie, New Form of Program," *New York Times*, Jan. 26, 1988, p. 24.

26. Peter J. Boyer, "Public TV: That Delicate Balance," *New York Times*, natl. ed., Oct. 25, 1987, sec. 2, p. 1.

27. John Corry, "Why It's Time for Public TV to Go Private," *New York Times*, natl. ed., Nov. 1, 1987, p. H25.

28. William F. Baker, letter, *New York Times*, natl. ed., Nov. 22, 1987, p. H34.

CHAPTER 10

1. This case study was developed in 1988, when Knight-Ridder owned the station, with splendid cooperation from Frank W. Hawkins Jr., Knight-Ridder vice president for corporate relations and planning, Miami; President and General Manager Bill Peterson of WTKR-TV, News Director (and later Acting GM) Carol Rueppel, and members of their staffs. To all, I am indebted. Photos in this chapter are from WTKR, reproduced with permission.

2. However, Knight-Ridder mentioned WTKR in its 1987 annual report as one of three K-R stations that had particular success that year in improving their ratings.

CHAPTER 11

1. This case study was developed with the assistance of H. Randolph Holder in 1988 and 1989.

2. Most of Holder's advertisers are retail merchants in and near Athens not interested in listeners the station reaches hundreds of miles away; it's local listeners that Holder's local advertisers want.

3. Ted Witcomb, personal communication, 1988.

4. Richard C. Wald, "A Ride on the Truth Machine," *Gannett Center Journal*, Spring 1987, p. 15.

5. Crain News Service, "FM Radio Continues to Snare Listeners," *Advertising Age*, June 27, 1988, p. 43.

6. Hortense Leon, "Syndication Boosts Station on a Budget," *Advertising Age*, Aug. 31, 1987, p. S2.

7. Keith Herndon, "Local Radio Not Homespun," *Atlanta Journal and Constitution*, Mar. 21, 1988, p. C1.

8. Holder, personal communication, 1988; Tom Joyner, "FM Radio Aims Signal to Big Cities," *Athens* (Ga.) *Banner-Herald*, Feb. 16, 1987, p. 1.

9. Holder, personal communication, 1988.

10. "34 Years of Station Transactions," *Broadcasting/Cablecasting Yearbook 1988*, p. H-80.

CHAPTER 12

1. Michael Emery and Edwin Emery, *The Press and America*, 6th ed. (Englewood Cliffs, N.J.: Prentice-Hall, 1988). Felix Gutierrez writes of *El Misisipi* in "Marketing the News in Third World America," *Gannett Center Journal*, Spring 1987, p. 89.

2. For background, see Jeremy Gerard in two *New York Times* articles: "*Il Progresso* Printing Again," July 18, 1988, p. D14, and "Dispute Shuts U.S. Paper for Italians," July 4, 1988, p. 33. *Il Progresso* claimed 84,500 unaudited circulation; Gerard quoted a staff member as saying the true figure was closer to 50,000.

3. Joseph Berger has followed the Yiddish press for the *New York Times*. Two important articles of his are "At 90, Yiddish Paper Is Still Vibrant," natl. ed., May 25, 1987, p. 10, and "For Yiddish, a New but Smaller Domain," natl. ed., Oct. 11, 1987, p. 9.

4. A helpful summary of ethnic media activity is Marcia Ruth, "Minority Press," *presstime*, Aug. 1986, p. 22.

5. Marion T. Marzolf quotes this 1919 letter in "A Vital Link: The Ethnic Press in the United

States," *Michigan Alumnus*, July-Aug. 1986, p. 42.

6. Christine Reid Veronis, "Hispanic Coverage," *presstime*, August 1989, p. 12.

7. Alex S. Jones, "Seekers of Hispanic Markets Find a Helpful Tool: English," *New York Times*, June 13, 1988, p. D9.

8. Richard W. Stevenson, "Spanish-Language TV Grows Up," *New York Times*, July 7, 1988, p. D1.

9. "Spanish-Language TV: An Even Better Reception," *New York Times*, June 26, 1988, p. F13.

10. For a rundown on competition in Spanish-Language news, see Roger F. Hernandez, "Univision vs. Telemundo," *Washington Journalism Review*, Dec. 1987, p. 41.

11. Courtesy of *Vista*.

12. Roberto Suarez, speech to Knight-Ridder's annual shareholders meeting, Miami, Apr. 15, 1988.

13. Dual marketing schemes for such films are examined by Jose de Cordoba, "Hollywood Finds Hispanic Audiences Are a Hot Ticket at the Movie Theater," *Wall Street Journal*, Apr. 6, 1988, p. 30.

14. Alex S. Jones, "Black Papers: Businesses with a Mission," *New York Times*, Aug. 17, 1987, p. B1.

15. Laurie P. Cohen, "Slowdown in Advertising to Blacks Strains Black Ad Firms and Media," *Wall Street Journal*, Mar. 23, 1988, p. 29.

16. James Cox, "He's Expanded Black Roles in Ads," *USA Today*, Aug. 19, 1987, p. 8B.

17. Cohen, "Slowdown in Advertising to Blacks," p. 29.

18. C. A. Scott, personal communication, Feb. 26, 1988.

19. Jay Smith, speech at the Minorities Job Fair, Atlanta, Feb. 11, 1988.

20. Jonathan Hicks, "For Black Men on the Way Up," *New York Times*, nat. ed., Nov. 7, 1985, p. 29.

21. "Class Conscience" (letter), *Black Enterprise*, Mar. 1988, p. 15.

22. Issues related to minority media are discussed superbly well in Felix Guttierrez, "Marketing the News in Third World America," *Gannett Center Journal*, Spring 1987, pp. 88–96.

23. "TV's New Racial Hue," *Newsweek*, Jan. 25, 1988, p. 52.

24. Much research has been done in minority and female hiring in the media and journalism education. Important sources are Sheila Gibbons, "Women Newsroom Leaders: Gannett Outranks Most," *The Gannetter*, May 1988, p. 24 (quoting David Weaver of Indiana University on minority and female representation on faculties); "Of 1987 J-graduates Hired by Newspapers, Only 7.8 Percent Were Minorities," *presstime*, June 1988, p. 100 (quoting research by Lee B. Becker of Ohio State University on where graduates were hired); "Blacks Fault the Press for Lack of Recruiting," *New York Times*, nat. ed., Mar. 22, 1988, p. 9 (quoting the National Association of Black Journalists on slippage in TV minority employment); and Arnold Rosenfeld, "Racial Parity Is More than a Head Count," *ASNE Bulletin*, Apr. 1988, p. 10 (on the 1987 ASNE survey of minority employment in newspaper newsrooms). Also see the *ASNE Bulletin* of Jan. 1986, mostly devoted to women in corporate ranks at newspapers.

25. Andrew Radolf, "More Hiring of Women and Minorities Urged," *Editor & Publisher*, July 2, 1983, p. 10.

26. Sheila Gibbons, "Women Newsroom Leaders," p. 24.

27. Ruth Stroud, "Papers Rise to Women's Market Challenge," *Advertising Age*, Mar. 7, 1988, p. S4.

CHAPTER 13

1. Laura Wilkinson, personnel communication, Apr. 14, 1988.

2. Scott Hume, "Market Leaders Also Dominate in Recall of Ads," *Advertising Age*, Feb. 1, 1988, p. 6.

3. Ronald Alsop, "In TV Viewers' Favorite 1987 Ads, Offbeat Characters Were the Stars," *Wall Street Journal*, Mar. 3, 1988, p. 19.

4. Scott Hume, "Ad Awareness on the Upswing," *Advertising Age*, Jan. 4, 1988, p. 3.

5. Jack J. Honomichl, "Research Business 1989," *Advertising Age*, June 5, 1989, p. S-1.

6. Particularly pertinent is *A Study of Media Involvement* (New York: Magazine Publishers Association, n.d.).

7. C. David Rambo, "Database Searches," *presstime*, Mar. 1987, p. 10; Tim Miller, "The Database Revolution," *Columbia Journalism Review*, Sept.-Oct. 1988, p. 35.

8. Miller, "Data-base Revolution," p. 35.

9. Ibid.

10. John Seigenthaler, "Presidential Campaign Season Is a Good Time to Read Up on the Use—and Misuse—of Polls," *ASNE Bulletin*, Dec. 1987, p. 27.

11. Joanne Lipman, "Readership Figures for Periodicals Stir Debate in Publishing Industry," *Wall Street Journal*, Sept. 2, 1987, p. 21; "On Radio," *Broadcasting*, July 11, 1988, p. 71; Adam Buckman, "Study Finds Disparities in Radio Ratings Result," *Electronic Media*, June 17, 1988, p. 30.

12. Everette E. Dennis, personal communication, Jan. 27, 1988.

PART V

1. *Facts about Newspapers '89* (Reston, Va.: American Newspaper Publishers Association, 1989), drawn on a McCann-Erickson annual survey.

CHAPTER 14

1. "A Disease Called Entertainment," *Forbes*, Mar. 7, 1988, p. 150.
2. A superb introductory text is Thomas Russell and Glenn Verrill, *Otto Kleppner's Advertising Procedure*, 8th ed. (Englewood Cliffs, N.J.: Prentice-Hall, 1983).
3. "Disease Called Entertainment," p. 150.
4. Alison Leigh Cowan, "Ad Clutter: Even in Restrooms Now," *New York Times*, natl. ed., Feb. 18, 1988, p. 25.
5. Ibid.
6. Gary Levin, "Cost of TV Spot Pegged at $145,600," *Advertising Age*, Mar. 6, 1989, p. 68.
7. All statistics in this discussion are from Dennis Kneale, "'Zapping' of TV Ads Appears Pervasive," *Wall Street Journal*, Apr. 15, 1988, p. 29.
8. Abraham H. Maslow, *Motivation and Personality* (New York: Harper & Row, 1954).
9. My thanks to Beverly Klein of Journal/Sentinel, Inc., for her assistance.
10. Roger Alsop, "In TV Viewers' Favorite 1987 Ads, Offbeat Characters Were the Stars," *Wall Street Journal*, Mar. 3, 1988, p. 19.
11. "What's a Big Idea Worth?" *Advertising Age*, June 6, 1988, p. 16.
12. Roger Alsop, "Marketers Resurrect Ads from the Past," *Wall Street Journal*, July 18, 1988, p. 21.
13. Scott Hume, "'Most Hated' Ads: Femine Hygiene," *Advertising Age*, July 18, 1988, p. 3.
14. Judith Graham, "'New Puritanism' Colors TV Lineup," *Advertising Age*, May 29, 1989, p. 46.
15. Letter, *New York Times*, commenting on Peter Schmeisser, "Pushing Cigarettes Overseas," *New York Times*, July 10, 1988, p. 1.
16. Robert P. Smith, "Advertising Acceptability Policies Protect Newspaper's Credibility," *INAME News*, June 1984, p. 11.
17. For a discussion of advertising ethics and the tobacco issue, see Conrad Fink, *Media Ethics: In the Newsroom and Beyond* (New York: McGraw-Hill, 1988).
18. Laurie P. Cohen, "Ad-Agency Search," *Wall Street Journal*, Jan. 29, 1988, p. 26.
19. Kathleen A. Hughes, "In Los Angeles, Ad Agencies Expend Great Energy to Win Small Accounts," *Wall Street Journal*, Jan. 29, 1988, p. 26.
20. Don Peppers, "Forum," *New York Times*, July 24, 1988, p. F3.

CHAPTER 15

1. Information on N. W. Ayer was developed in 1987–1989 through the office of Louis T. Hagopian, chairman and chief executive officer. Particularly helpful was Tom Traska of Ayer's Corporate Communications. My thanks to these and other Ayer executives for being so forthcoming with details of their operations.
2. These excerpts are drawn from speeches by Louis T. Hagopian over a number of years. Copies of full speeches are available from N. W. Ayer Inc.
3. Adapted from a presentation to the American Gemological Society and the August 1987 issue of *Jewelers' Circular/Keystone*, among other sources.
4. Ibid.
5. *Newspaper Advertising Planbook* (New York: Newspaper Advertising Bureau), published annually.
6. The army affair is discussed superbly well by Janet Meyers in "No Victors," *Advertising Age*, May 16, 1988, p. 24. Also see Philip H. Dougherty, "Pentagon Faults Army Ad Placing," *New York Times*, July 6, 1988, p. D17.
7. Philip H. Dougherty, "Ayer Wins Burger King Ads," *New York Times*, natl. ed., Sept. 29, 1987, p. 33.
8. For details on the Burger King story, see ibid.; Joanne Lipman, "Burger King Shifts $200 Million Account to N. W. Ayer from J. Walter Thompson," *Wall Street Journal*, Sept. 29, 1987.
9. Ibid.
10. Richard Gibson, "Burger Kings' New Ad Campaign Is a $200 Million Big Mac Attack," *Wall Street Journal*, Feb. 3, 1988, p. 28.
11. Scott Hume, "Pillsbury Puts Heat on Ayer," *Advertising Age*, June 27, 1988, p. 2.

CHAPTER 16

1. I am indebted to Barbara Morgan for information contributed.
2. Robert L. Dilenschneider, personal communication, Feb. 22, 1988.
3. The social and legal context for PR careers is covered well in Scott M. Cutlip, Allen G. Center, and Glen M. Broom, *Effective Public Relations*, 6th ed. (Englewood Cliffs, N.J.: Prentice-Hall, 1985).
4. For more on PR ethics, see Conrad Fink, *Media Ethics: In the Newsroom and Beyond* (New York: McGraw-Hill, 1988).

5. The entire PRSA code appears in Fink, *Media Ethics*.

6. John W. Felton, personal communication, Feb. 2, 1988.

7. Jack Bernstein, personal communication, Jan. 21, 1988.

8. Felton, personal communication, Feb. 2, 1988.

CHAPTER 17

1. James H. Dowling, president and chief executive officer, Burson-Marsteller, and Robert Hope, executive vice president, marketing worldwide, Burson-Marsteller, personal communication, 1988.

2. Dowling, personal communication, 1988.

3. Activity definitions and quotations in this discussion are drawn from position papers Burson-Marsteller sent to its branch offices in 1987 and 1988.

4. James E. Murphy, "Rethinking Grass Roots Mobilization," introduction to a "Corporate Communications Update" in the agency's *Insights* magazine, July 1988.

5. This case is discussed at length from the Johnson & Johnson perspective in Conrad Fink, *Media Ethics: In the Newsroom and Beyond* (New York: McGraw-Hill, 1988).

6. Stan Sauerhaft, executive vice president, and Linda Lichter, "A Changing Merger Game," in a newsletter issued by Burson-Marsteller, May 12, 1987.

7. Harlan R. Teller, senior vice president, "Communications After an LBO," newsletter, Sept. 1987.

8. *Corporate*, an August 1988 newsletter issued by Burson-Marsteller to offices around the world.

9. "Seoul Olympic Games Draw World Attention," Burson-Marsteller's internal newsletter, *Connections*, Sept. 1988, p. 1.

10. James E. Murphy, "Acquiring, Managing, and Building Corporate Business," *Corporate*, Sept. 9, 1988, p. 6.

11. Based on a presentation to corporate recruiters by Jack Mitchell, New York, 1988.

12. Adapted from Dowling, speech, Brinkmann Kommunications Seminar, Copenhagen, Apr. 19, 1988.

PART VII

1. Peter Newcomb, "The New Aristocracy," *Forbes*, Oct. 3, 1988, p. 114.

CHAPTER 18

1. Robert Homan, "Making of Hollywood East," *Electronic Media*, Aug. 1, 1988, p. 1.

2. Laura Landro, "Slowing Royalties for Videocassettes Hurts Movie Firms," *Wall Street Journal*, Feb. 1, 1988, p. 36.

3. Michael Cieply, Los Angeles Times-Washington Post News Service Dispatch, published in *Atlanta Constitution*, as "Behind the Scenes," June 7, 1989, p. C1.

4. Aljean Harmetz, "Batman Sets Sales Record: $100 Million in 10 Days," *New York Times*, nat. ed., July 4, 1989, p. 25.

5. "Market Watch/At the Box Office," *Wall Street Journal*, Feb. 3, 1988, p. 28.

6. Laura Landro, "Sequels and Stars Help Top Movie Studios Avoid Major Risks, *Wall Street Journal*, June 6, 1989, p. 1.

7. Ibid.

8. Michael Cieply and Peter W. Barnes, "Movies and TV Mergers Point to Concentration of Power to Entertain, *Wall Street Journal*, Aug. 21, 1986, p. 1.

9. Laura Landro, "The Movie Moguls Reel Off One More Tale of Big Bucks," *Wall Street Journal*, Feb. 24, 1988, p. 30.

10. Aljean Harmetz, "Now Playing: The New Hollywood," *New York Times*, Jan. 10, 1988, sec. 2, p. 1.

11. A strong analysis of this miniseries is by Dennis Kneale in "How Wouk Epic Became a Sure Loser," *Wall Street Journal*, Nov. 11, 1988, p. B1.

12. Aljean Harmetz, "Hollywood's Audience Gets Older and Pickier," *New York Times*, March 7, 1988, p. 9.

13. Jose de Cordoba, "Hollywood Finds Hispanic Audiences Are a Hot Ticket at the Movie Theater," *Wall Street Journal*, Apr. 6, 1988, p. J1.

14. A valuable look at black filmmaking is Valerie Boyd, "Making Black Movies," *Atlanta Journal and Constitution*, Feb. 21, 1988, p. J1.

15. Laura Mansnerus, "Rating Game: Parents Try to Fill Gap," *New York Times*, nat. ed., Feb. 11, 1988, p. 17.

16. Michael Medved, "Hollywood Gets in the Family Way," *Wall Street Journal*, Feb. 3, 1988, p. 86.

17. Andrew L. Yarnow, "Action But Not Consensus on Film Coloring," *New York Times*, July 11, 1988, p. C13.

18. Ibid.

19. David Lieberman, "Now Playing: The Sound of Money," *Business Week*, Aug. 15, 1988, p. 86.

20. Ibid.

21. Peter Newcomb, "Waiting for the Next Elvis," *Forbes*, Oct. 31, 1988, p. 122.

Name Index

Subject Index

Adversarial journalism, 33, 95
Advertiser-driven media strategies, 6, 10
Advertising
  addressability in, 289
  "adjacency" concepts in, 99, 280
  advocacy in, 292
  agencies, 13–14, 255–257, 278, 283–284, 296–299, 301–313
  awareness of, 282
  behavioral sciences in, 286
  the "big idea" in, 291
  for blacks, 255–259
  broadcast ratings in, 203–206
  bypass technology in, 172
  in cable TV, 200–201
  careers in, 128–131, 296–299, 304–308, 359–369
  clutter in, 279, 281–282, 327
  comparative techniques, 282
  consumerism in, 293
  cost of, 93, 100, 197, 283–284
  cost-per-thousand, 311
  creativity in, 291–293
  deception in, 293–295
  demographics in, 98, 110–111, 140–142, 204
  direct mail, 63, 100, 179–180
  "efficient" rates in, 107
  in electronic magazines, 173
  emotion in, 292
  essentials in, 290
  ethics in, 279, 293, 299, 302
  for ethnic groups, 250–259
  European resistance to, 21
  15-second commercials, 282
  globalization of, 12–15
  guidelines in, 295
  for Hispanics, 252–255
  historic high points, 33, 37, 50, 92, 193, 278, 301, 302
  humor in, 15, 292
  industry characteristics, 276–299
  issues in, 277–280, 281–285
  in magazines, 63, 134, 136, 140–141, 145–147, 158, 166–169
  market segmentation in, 282
  marriage mail, 97
  in media, 6, 37, 63
  mergers and acquisitions in, 278
  "new puritanism" in, 293
  in newspapers, 36, 38, 63, 65, 92–93, 95, 114, 128, 136
  origins, 278
  outdoor, 63, 65
  people meters, impact on, 204
  product benefit in, 292
  professionalism in, 278, 279
  preprints, 127
  product placement in, 285
  racism in, 257
  in radio, 63, 144, 192, 197, 240, 242, 245–246
  reality ads, 293
  recall of, 265
  research in, 263–272, 302
  regulation of, 55, 293–296
  restrictions on, 278
  salaries in, 360–361
  selling function of, 276–277, 283, 292
  sexism in, 293
  "shootouts" in, 308, 312
  social value of, 280
  societal impact of, 275, 283, 293, 304
  spending in, 275
  targeted audiences, 191
  taxes on, 86
  technology in, 285
  in television, 10, 63, 93, 192, 197, 214–216, 230–231
  terms in, 280–281
  truth in, 278
  tobacco, 295
  tools in, 286–293
  videocassettes in, 173–174
  in video shopping, 174
  writing of, 290
  Yellow Pages, 176
  zoning for, 127, 140–141, 166, 220
Advertising agency case study, 301–313
Advertorials, 280
Agenda setting, 51, 72, 82, 91, 95, 109, 195–197
Alien and Sedition Acts of 1798, 35
"All-day" newspapers, 106
Alternative publications, 48, 96, 103
American media
  as agenda setters, 51
  career paths in, 78, 359–369
  characteristics of, 37, 40
  colonial development of, 32–36
  competitive nature of, 46, 47, 66
  conglomerates, 61–73
  credibility of, 92
  discrimination suits in, 261–262
  diversification of, 63, 64, 65, 68, 69, 72, 74, 82–83, 87, 101, 136, 170, 181, 202, 263
  economics of, 60–61, 66, 237, 279
  ethnic diversity of, 249–262
  federal regulation of, 54–55, 62, 105, 351
  as "gatekeepers," 57
  goals of, 45, 48
  group management, 45, 71
  groups in, 61–73
  historic high points, 32, 33, 134, 278
  image problems, 56
  influence of, 60–61, 85–87, 203
  journalistic character, 37
  lifestyles, impact on, 47, 192
  lobby groups, 47, 85–87, 175
  management of, 75–77
  minorities in, 65, 259–262
  minorities, service to, 251
  numbers of, 21, 43
  ownership of, 62–73, 75–76, 104–107, 200

391